OLD MONEY 24; JEWISH
How & WHY JEWS TA
COMPARE TO BOESKY
BETTE MIDLER'S CAREER 79
SCATOLOGICAL 90
III WARREN BEATY PROMISCUOUS, INDECISIVE

Praise for *DisneyWar*

"A compelling and often brilliant tale of how Eisner kept his own—and everyone else's—stress levels churning. . . . *DisneyWar* is a monumental achievement of in-depth reporting—tough and scrupulous. It is also so comprehensive that I suspect no one will ever have to—or even try to—write this story again. . . . Stewart has a cool eye and provides careful balance . . . the larger thrust of this book—and the one that makes it such an important work—is to call into question the system of corporate governance, and the legal and moral responsibility of a board of directors to provide adult supervision of the firm it supposedly oversees. . . . Stewart's painstakingly amassed detail will make readers wonder how he got it all. The answer is hard work and a willingness to go through thousands of original and publicly available documents, and to interview any source. . . . And now, thanks to Stewart, we have the Michael Eisner story—his very own *Sunset Boulevard*."

—Bob Woodward, *The Washington Post*

"A messy, fractious story complete with its own Seven Dwarfs: Sneaky, Screamy, Pushy, Greedy, Grabby, Nasty and Snarky. Snow White is nowhere to be seen. . . . The book is a litany of corporate backstabbings, couched in language that captures the spirit of the organization. . . . It presents this on a Monopoly board of dizzying scope. . . . Stewart aspires to put a Shakespearean spin on such acts of treachery even if Disney is a company that has *Gnomeo and Juliet* in the works."

—Janet Maslin, *The New York Times*

"Burst my notion of 'a magic kingdom' where life is a fairy tale and 'dreams really do come true'. . . [F]amously, by now, the book does offer various details that play a part in current litigation over Disney's management turnstile. But more comes to light than mere courtroom-related squalor. . . . Mr. Stewart's stories are wonderful: the cat fight with Mr. Katzenberg, the overture to Mr. Ovitz, the anger at Mr. Iger, the ruckus with Roy over Disney's direction . . . full of up-to-date details. . . . I kept asking myself: Why am I so hungrily reading this? . . . like Jonathan Franzen's *The Corrections,* it offers up the guilty pleasure of watching this 12-year-old patriarch and his dysfunctional family tear each other to shreds. When Pinocchio is sent to Pleasure

Island, wicked boys turn into donkeys. Now, as Mr. Stewart eloquently tells us, the fairy tale has come true."

—*The Wall Street Journal*

"A sweeping history of the past 20 years of the Disney company's life ... an engrossing story of human foibles running amok in one of the world's most famous workplaces ... thorough. ... Stewart captures the chief executive in rich nuance ... [a] rigorously reported account that pulls no punches."

—*The Boston Globe*

"[The] publishing genre of business scandal narratives is getting a breath of life from James B. Stewart's *DisneyWar.*"

—*Crain's New York Business*

"*DisneyWar* now stands as the best of the fast-growing subgenre of business books about the selfishness and ineptitude that ended the era of the Imperial CEO. ... Stewart is an accomplished storyteller ... [his] story speeds ahead as smoothly as a theme park ride, with a narrative more like a psychodrama than a business book ... a smooth read."

—*USA Today*

"Stewart, who made business exposés hot reading with *Den of Thieves* in 1991, successfully embeds himself in the brutal, often malicious culture of the world's premier family entertainment company. Incredibly, Eisner opened the doors to him not knowing Fort Disney would soon be under siege. ... *DisneyWar* is certainly telling."

—*Daily News* (New York)

"Nobody writes about complex business issues as interestingly and thoroughly as Stewart, but this story is Shakespearean in its proportions. It weaves the creative, corporate, financial and personality streams of the Disney Co.'s fate into one astonishingly complete and gripping real-life drama."

—Alcestis Oberg, *The Houston Chronicle*

"Stewart's fly-on-the-wall access is extraordinary ... tenacious reporting."

—*Entertainment Weekly*

"James B. Stewart's engrossing [*DisneyWar*] will surely be the most talked-about book of the season.... It's an intense, dense piece of work.... *Disney-War* is a plum pudding of a book: It repays the probing or roving finger with many a choice sweetmeat. Obviously, the gossip will attract many readers.... It's one of those books that needs (and deserves) to be read.... In a larger context, it seems to me that *DisneyWar* completes a virtual trilogy—the other volumes being Bryan Burrough and John Helyar's *Barbarians at the Gate* (1990) and Mr. Stewart's own *Den of Thieves*. Together, they vividly capture the whole arc of what, to my thinking, has emerged as the greatest business-finance story of the mega-cycle that began in August 1982, when the stock market broke out. It's the story of the evolving abuse of 'insiderness' in the Greenspan era of (virtually) free money ... elegant prose and exhaustive research."

—*The New York Observer*

"I have read every word of James Stewart's latest bombshell, and I am reeling from this portrait of Hollywood's greatest entertainment entity.... Mr. Stewart won a Pulitzer Prize for his work *Den of Thieves*, and here I think he surpasses that book. The story ... is so readable that you want the world to stop once you open it.... It's the entertainment drama to end all.... Stewart gives us the ultimate story of life and death at the top of entertainment."

—Liz Smith, *New York Post*

JAMES B. STEWART

SIMON & SCHUSTER PAPERBACKS

New York • London • Toronto • Sydney

DISNEY
WAR

SIMON & SCHUSTER PAPERBACKS
Rockefeller Center
1230 Avenue of the Americas
New York, NY 10020

First Simon & Schuster paperback edition 2006

For information about special discounts for bulk purchases,
please contact Simon & Schuster Special Sales:
1-800-456-6798 or business@simonandschuster.com.

Designed by Dana Sloan
Picture Editor: Alexandra Truitt, pictureresearching.com

Manufactured in the United States of America

10   9   8   7   6   5   4   3   2   1

Library of Congress Control Number: 2005297366

ISBN-13: 978-0-684-80993-9
ISBN-10:   0-684-80993-1
ISBN-13: 978-0-7432-6709-0 (Pbk)
ISBN-10:   0-7432-6709-5 (Pbk)

To Benjamin

CONTENTS

CAST MEMBERS

THE DISNEY FAMILY

Walt Disney (1901–1966)
    Lillian, his wife (1899–1997)
    Diane Disney Miller, their older daughter
    Ron Miller, former Disney chief executive, Diane's husband
    Sharon Disney Lund, their younger daughter (1936–1993)
Roy O. Disney (1893–1971)
    Edna, his wife (1890–1984)
    Roy E. Disney, their son

AT TEAM DISNEY HEADQUARTERS, BURBANK, CALIFORNIA*

Michael D. Eisner, chief executive officer (1984–　) and chairman (1984–2004)
Frank Wells, president and chief operating officer (1984–1994)
Michael Ovitz, president (1995–1997)
Robert Iger, president and chief operating officer (2000–　)
Larry Murphy, chief strategic officer (1989–1998)
Peter Murphy (1998–　)
Gary Wilson, chief financial officer (1984–1986)
Richard Nanula (1986–1994, 1996–1998)
Stephen Bollenbach (1995–1996)

---

* Some Disney executives held multiple positions. Generally I have indicated only the most recent or, in a few cases, the position which figures most prominently in the story.

Tom Staggs (1998–   )
Sanford L. Litvack, general counsel and vice chairman (1991–2000)
Alan Braverman, general counsel (2003–   )
Zenia Mucha, senior vice president, corporate communications

ON THE WALT DISNEY CO. BOARD OF DIRECTORS

George Mitchell (2000–   ) and chairman (2004–   )
Michael Eisner
Robert Iger
John Bryson
Judith Estrin
Ignacio Lozano Jr. (1981–2001)
Monica Lozano
Robert Matschullat
Leo O'Donovan
Gary Wilson
Roy E. Disney (1984–2003)
Stanley Gold (1984–2003)
Reveta Bowers (1993–2003)
Thomas Murphy (1995–2004)
Sidney Poitier (1994–2003)
Irwin Russell (1987–2001)
Robert A. M. Stern (1992–2003)
Andrea Van de Kamp (1997–2003)
Ray Watson (1973–2004)

AT THE WALT DISNEY STUDIOS

Jeffrey Katzenberg, chairman (1984–1994)
Joe Roth (1995–2000)
Peter Schneider (2000–2002)
Richard Cook, chairman
David Vogel, president, Buena Vista Motion Pictures Group
   (1998–1999)
Nina Jacobson, president
Stan Kinsey, chief financial officer (1984–1986)

Jeffrey Rochlis, executive vice president, Imagineering (1984–1989)
Rob Moore, executive vice president, operations and finance
(1987–2000)
Bill Mechanic, president, international theatrical and worldwide video
(1984–1993)

AT WALT DISNEY FEATURE ANIMATION

Roy E. Disney, chairman (1984–2004)
Peter Schneider, president (1985–1999)
Thomas Schumacher, president (1999–2003); president, Buena Vista
Theatrical Worldwide
David Stainton, president
John Lasseter, animator (1979–1983)
Ron Clements, animator
John Musker, animator
Howard Ashman, lyricist (1986–1991)
Alan Menken, composer

AT WALT DISNEY PARKS AND RESORTS

Richard Nunis, chairman (1991–1998)
Judson Green, president and chairman (1998–2000)
Paul Pressler, president and chairman (2000–2002)
Jay Rasulo, president
Al Weiss, president, Walt Disney World Resort
Philippe Bourguignon, chairman, Disneyland Paris (1993–1997)

AT WALT DISNEY IMAGINEERING

Martin Sklar, vice chairman and principal creative executive
Peter Rummell, chairman (1985–1997)

AT THE MEDIA NETWORKS GROUP

Anne Sweeney, co-chairman
George Bodenheimer, co-chairman
Angela Shapiro, president, ABC Family (2001–2003)

AT ABC ENTERTAINMENT

Steve Burke, president, ABC Broadcasting (1997–1998)

Steve Bornstein, president, ABC Inc. (1999); ABC-TV Network (2001–2002)

Patricia Fili-Krushel, president, ABC-TV Network (1998–2000)

Alex Wallau, president, ABC-TV Network (2000–2004)

Ted Harbert, president (1993–1996); chairman (1996–1997)

Jamie Tarses, president, ABC Entertainment (1996–1999)

Stu Bloomberg, chairman (1997–2002)

Lloyd Braun, chairman (2002–2004)

Susan Lyne, president (2002–2004)

Steve McPherson, president

AT ESPN, BRISTOL, CONNECTICUT

Steve Bornstein, president and chief executive officer (1990–1999)

George Bodenheimer, president

Mark Shapiro, executive vice president, programming and production

AT CONSUMER PRODUCTS

Steve Burke, executive vice president, Disney Stores (1986–1992)

Andrew Mooney, chairman

AT SHAMROCK HOLDINGS, BURBANK, CALIFORNIA

Roy E. Disney, chairman

Stanley Gold, chief executive

Michael McConnell, managing director

AT CAPITAL CITIES/ABC, NEW YORK CITY

Thomas Murphy, chairman and chief executive (1986–1995)

AT MIRAMAX, NEW YORK CITY

Harvey Weinstein, co-chairman

Bob Weinstein, co-chairman

AT PIXAR, EMERYVILLE, CALIFORNIA

Steve Jobs, chairman and chief executive officer
John Lasseter, executive vice president, creative

AT DREAMWORKS SKG, GLENDALE, CALIFORNIA

Jeffrey Katzenberg, co-founder
David Geffen, co-founder
Steven Spielberg, co-founder

AT INTERACTIVECORP, NEW YORK CITY

Barry Diller, chairman and chief executive

DISNEYWAR

PROLOGUE

Roy E. Disney pulled his red 1999 Ferrari into the parking lot of the Bodega Wine Bar in Pasadena. It was late on a Thursday afternoon, November 20, 2003, just a week before Thanksgiving. Roy loved the Ferrari, one of the few conspicuous indications that the modest, unassuming seventy-three-year-old nephew of Walt Disney was one of America's wealthiest men. The car stood out in the Disney parking lot, where Roy had a space near Michael Eisner, Disney's chairman and chief executive. Because of the car, everybody knew when Roy was at company headquarters.

Roy hated the "Team Disney" building designed by noted architect Michael Graves at Eisner's behest to serve as the Walt Disney Company's corporate headquarters. Though the monumental facade was leavened by bas-reliefs of the Seven Dwarfs in the pediment, Roy felt the building represented everything that was bloated and pretentious in the company that Eisner had created. As he did from time to time, Roy wondered what his uncle Walt would have thought. Walt's office was still there, in the modest old animation building. Eisner had used it as his own office before moving to the new headquarters. Now Roy had moved into it, preferring it to the Team Disney building, so barren and vast that he joked he had to leave a trail of bread crumbs to find his way out.

In recent months Roy's physical separation from Eisner and other top executives had become more than symbolic. Even though he had brought Eisner to the company almost twenty years ago, he now felt deceived and betrayed by him. Eisner had come to Disney after a dazzling career in programming at ABC and in movies at Paramount Pictures. But Roy now attributed Eisner's earlier great successes to his partnerships with others: with

1

Barry Diller at ABC and Paramount; with Frank Wells and Jeffrey Katzen-berg in the early, amazing years at Disney. Since Wells's tragic death in a helicopter crash in 1994, and Katzenberg's acrimonious departure soon after, responsibility for Disney had been Eisner's alone. In Roy's view, the re-sults had been disastrous. As the financial performance and creative energy of the company ebbed, Eisner had clung to power with a King Lear–like in-tensity, convinced that he and he alone had the creative instincts and mana-gerial skills to shepherd Disney into a twenty-first-century world of giant media and entertainment conglomerates. Indeed, Eisner claimed the mantle of Walt himself, appearing each week on TV screens in the nation's living rooms as host of "The Wonderful World of Disney," just as Walt had.

In this respect, Roy felt that Eisner was only the latest in a series of pre-tenders to the throne Walt had occupied. Why was it, he sometimes won-dered, that so many people wanted to embody Walt? Nobody went around Hollywood claiming to be Louis B. Mayer or Cecil B. DeMille. What gave people the illusion that they could fill Walt's shoes? First there had been E. Cardon Walker and Ron Miller, Walt's son-in-law, who, as Disney's chair-man and chief executive, had constantly invoked Walt's memory. Then it was Jeffrey Katzenberg, who claimed Walt's legacy as head of the Disney studio. They had gone too far; Roy had to step in, and they were replaced. Now Eisner was overstepping the bounds.

Roy didn't claim to be Walt, but if anyone was entitled to the legacy, it was he. He was the one paraded before the world as the embodiment of the Dis-ney Company and what it represented, the last company official bearing the Disney name. Just a month earlier, Eisner had publicly praised Roy's efforts on behalf of the company at the grand opening of "Mission: SPACE," the new attraction at Walt Disney World, which had drawn big applause. Crowds al-ways seemed to respond to Roy, perhaps because, at age seventy-three, he bore such a close physical resemblance to Walt. But Eisner's public praise masked a mounting private hostility. When Eisner's wife, Jane, passed Roy and his wife, Patty, shortly before Eisner's speech, they had pointedly ignored each other.

Roy had long ago stopped attending Eisner's weekly meetings with top executives, or the lunches where he had once kept Roy informed of company plans and strategy. Roy had stopped trusting Eisner after he learned that Eis-ner had planted a spy next to him in the animation department to report on everything Roy said or did. They had avoided contact at the recent New York premiere of *Brother Bear,* the Disney studio's latest—and in Roy's view, mediocre—animated feature. Worst of all, when Roy's mother, Edna, and

Walt's widow, Lillian, had been posthumously honored at that year's Disney Legends awards, and Roy accepted on the family's behalf, Eisner hadn't shown up. It was the first time Eisner had failed to attend the event, and soon after, word circulated within Disney that the company's chairman and vice chairman were no longer speaking.

Roy wasn't looking forward to the drink he was about to have with John Bryson, chairman and chief executive of Edison International, the parent of Southern California Edison. Bryson, who'd joined the Disney board in 2000, was chairman of the powerful nominating and governance committee. Roy rarely spoke at board meetings. But his ally, business partner, lawyer, and fellow board member Stanley Gold more than made up for his silence. For years, Gold had been sharply critical of Eisner's management and the financial performance of the company. But his comments at board meetings had fallen on deaf ears. The directors seemed to support Eisner blindly. Those who didn't, such as Andrea Van de Kamp and Reveta Bowers, had been purged, a warning to others of the perils of dissent. Roy was especially suspicious of Bryson, an Eisner loyalist who had first displaced Gold as chairman of the governance committee, and then voted him off the committee altogether.

Beginning the previous September, Gold had issued a series of letters to his fellow board members that were harshly critical of Eisner's performance and compensation. He and Roy thought it would be more difficult to ignore comments in writing, and they wanted to make their views perfectly clear. Most recently, Gold and Roy had opposed Eisner's latest compensation package, which awarded him a $5 million bonus in a year in which the company's operating income declined 25 percent and the company's shares hit a new fifty-two-week low.

Bryson had called Roy a few days before. "I need to talk to you," he said, and insisted they meet somewhere they wouldn't be seen. Roy agreed, though he thought the tone of Bryson's voice had a "mortuary quality" to it. He feared that the Eisner loyalists were going to try to purge Gold. The atmosphere at recent board meetings had been increasingly tense.

"How can I protect him?" Roy wondered about Gold as he walked into the bar. He couldn't understand why the rest of the board would want to cut off the last remaining voice of dissent.

As soon as they ordered their drinks, Bryson dispensed with small talk and got to the point.

"You know, Roy, you're past the mandatory retirement age," he said.

Roy was taken aback by Bryson's directness, and murmured something noncommittal. Yes, technically he was, since the retirement age was seventy-two, and he had turned seventy-three. But it didn't apply to board members who were also part of management, and he was the head of animation. Disney was famous for the longevity of many of its employees.

"The committee has met," Bryson continued, "and Tom Murphy and Ray Watson are going to step down." Murphy, the former chairman of Capital Cities/ABC, had joined the board after Disney acquired ABC in 1995; Watson, Disney's chairman before Eisner's arrival in 1984, was, after Roy, the board's longest-serving member. Both were over seventy-two. Roy wasn't surprised, since they had mentioned to him their plans to retire.

"We've concluded that you shouldn't run for reelection," Bryson said.

Roy looked at him in stunned disbelief. He was speechless. He felt like a knife had been stuck into his heart. It had never crossed his mind that the board would go this far. It wasn't just that he was still one of the company's largest shareholders. He had given fifty years of his life to Disney. He was the only direct link to Walt on the board. Walt had told him stories and fairy tales and read "Pinocchio" to him as a child. Together with Walt, Roy's father had created this company.

There was an awkward silence. Finally Bryson said, "I had to tell Warren Christopher the same thing," referring to Bill Clinton's former secretary of state, who had reached the mandatory retirement age while a member of Edison's board.

"Good for you," Roy said.

"Of course, you can be an honorary director for life," Bryson said. "We'd still like you to show up at the parks, at special events . . ."

Roy cut him off with a laugh. So they still wanted to parade him around like one of the Disney costumed characters. It was insulting.

There was another awkward silence. No doubt they thought he'd go quietly, retreating to his castle in Ireland or his sailboat to sit out his retirement years. But despite his age, he felt a surge of energy and determination. Roy had been underestimated all his life. It had happened before. It was not going to happen again. He had only one thing left to say:

"You're making an awful mistake," he said, looking directly at Bryson. "And you're going to regret doing this."

Then he got up and walked out.

It is late May in central Florida, a brilliant, clear day. Though it's only ten in the morning, the mercury is climbing into the nineties and the humidity is just as high. It doesn't take much imagination to believe that Disney's Animal Kingdom, one of four theme parks that constitute Walt Disney World, is actually located in tropical Africa.

Goofy is standing just outside the park fence, ready to make an appearance. Just as tourists on safari in Africa hope to spot one of the "Big Five" game animals, visitors to the Animal Kingdom look for Disney's "Big Five"— Mickey, Minnie, Donald, Pluto, and Goofy, the biggest celebrities in the Disney pantheon, and the most coveted autographs. Goofy is a dog, of course, with fur, a long snout, floppy ears, a slight potbelly, and big paws. He's also the tallest of the characters, standing over six feet, and on this day he is dressed for the Animal Kingdom. He has on a big safari hat, hiking shoes and socks, lime green shorts in a dinosaur print, a bright red-checked shirt and suspenders, and a khaki neckerchief.

What many people don't realize is that Goofy's eyesight isn't all that good. Those long ears obstruct his peripheral vision, and the oversized nose further limits his view. What he can mostly see is the ground around his feet. Fortunately, Goofy has two human handlers to guide him into the park. They open a door and gently push him forward. He has to duck to get through. Goofy can't really tell where he is, but he hears the murmur of voices in the distance. He's nervous, and he can feel his heart beating. Only seconds have elapsed when he hears: "There's Goofy!"

He hears more children's voices and he sees several running toward him. Goofy waves and demonstrates the "Goofy walk," the silly lope that is one of Goofy's hallmarks. The children love it! More are running over, and their parents are starting to catch up. Suddenly Goofy sees a young girl closing in on him. She looks about five or six, and seems a little apprehensive. As she gets close she shyly extends an autograph book and a pen. Goofy clumsily grips the pen with his paw, and manages to sign the open page, carefully making the backward f that always shows up in Goofy's signature. What a relief, really, that dogs can't talk.

"Hug Goofy!" an adult voice cries out. The young girl looks a little wary, but Goofy extends his arm, and she slips in next to him. He gives her a gentle squeeze. Then, for a moment, Goofy gets a clear look at the little girl's face. The shyness melts away, her eyes widen in delight, and her face glows. She leans in and plants a kiss on Goofy's nose.

Flashbulbs are going off. Goofy wishes he could get his paw over to wipe the tears that have suddenly welled in his eyes. Or maybe it's perspiration.

*   *   *

The moment when a young child's apprehension vanishes, to be replaced by awe and delight, is what most Disney employees are talking about when they use the word *magic* to describe their work. It's why many come to work as high school or college students, and find they're still there twenty years later. Goofy, of course, is real. He was real for that young girl, and in that moment, he was real to me. I was no longer an author and journalist dressed in layers of padding and fake fur. I *was* Goofy.

Although it's a standard part of the orientation for top Disney executives to appear as a character in a theme park, only after I accepted the role of Goofy was I told I wouldn't be able to write about it, at least not in a way that stated or implied that Goofy was an actor inside a costume. People in charge of the theme parks had imposed this condition on the grounds that the illusion the Disney characters are real had never been publicly breached with the company's cooperation. At first I thought this was preposterous. This is about as credible as the existence of Santa Claus, and surely everyone above the age of eight or ten knows there are people inside these costumes. But the people who work in the theme parks insisted, and once I met them, I had a better understanding. Just about everything inside Disney World is illusion: prettier, cleaner, safer, better, more fun than the real world. It was Walt's genius to recognize that it is not only children who want an escape from reality. Like any good magician, you have to believe in the illusion, or it falls apart. It is a secular faith that has been embraced so passionately by so many Americans that the name Disney has become all but synonymous with an idealized American culture in which dreams come true.

Like many aspects of Disney, this changed in the tumultuous year and a half after I made my debut at the Animal Kingdom. After Comcast Corporation, the giant Philadelphia-based cable company, launched a hostile takeover bid for Disney in February 2004, Disney endured a withering barrage of publicity, and an article in *The Wall Street Journal* disclosed that top Disney executives had appeared in the theme parks dressed as Disney characters. With the cover blown to a national readership, Eisner agreed there was no longer any point in my pretending that Goofy was real, and agreed that I could describe my own character experience.

I had first met Michael Eisner many years earlier, before I was a journalist. In 1978 I was a young lawyer at Cravath, Swaine & Moore, a large New York firm, and Eisner was the president of Paramount Pictures. My firm was representing CBS in an antitrust case filed by the Justice Department against the television networks, which argued that they had conspired to drive down the costs of programming produced by the Hollywood studios, who were the instigators of the case and stood to benefit from any remedies. I was assigned to the Paramount aspect of the case and helped take Eisner's deposition.

I remember arriving at his office at the Paramount studios in Hollywood. He had a spacious corner office on the second floor, with an outdoor loggia shaded by a trellis and vines. For someone being questioned by a team of lawyers, Eisner was disarmingly confident and funny, joking about his sometimes contentious relationship with Paramount chairman Barry Diller. He slipped off his shoes and relaxed in his stocking feet—something I'd never seen in a New York law firm. Though we were on opposite sides of the case, Eisner gave me tickets for that night's taping of the "Mork & Mindy" show, then a Paramount hit television series. It was the first time I saw comedian Robin Williams live. In the long stretches when the cameras weren't rolling, Williams continued a frenetic comic monologue that kept the studio audience convulsed with laughter until the early hours of the morning.

This all made more of an impression on me than Eisner; the government ended up dropping the case. When I asked Eisner if he remembered me or the deposition, he drew a blank. Many years had intervened, and he had gone from being the brash young upstart at Paramount to the venerable, successful, and wealthy chairman of Disney. When he arrived at Disney in 1984, the company was faltering, its studio and legendary animation division moribund, its assets coveted by corporate raiders eager to break up the company and sell off the parts. Eisner had not only saved Disney, he had transformed it into the world's leading entertainment company and protected its beloved brand name.

I approached Eisner about writing a book about the company in 2001. Ever since my work on the network antitrust case, I'd been interested in the workings of the entertainment business and Hollywood. Having written books probing the worlds of Wall Street finance and Washington politics, Hollywood seemed like the next major center of power and influence worth exploring. Disney, with its vaunted image, creative success, not to mention a fair amount of corporate intrigue, seemed the obvious choice. Eisner was predictably cool to the idea. John Dreyer, then head of public relations, was polite but discouraging. Even so, as I continued to gather information about the company, Dreyer invited me to meet with him at Disney's headquarters in Burbank.

I hadn't expected to meet Eisner himself, but as Dreyer and I were having lunch in the company dining room, Eisner suddenly appeared and joined our table. He asked a few questions about my proposed book, but then told me how much he had liked a recent article I'd written in *The New Yorker*, titled "Matchmaker," about Erica Feidner, a woman with a seemingly magical ability to find the perfect piano for Steinway customers. I was flattered, but Dreyer looked uncomfortable. "Michael," he said, "I'm not so sure I'd get into that right now," he said, but Eisner persisted. "I see this as another *Mr. Holland's Opus*," Eisner went on, referring to the movie starring Richard Dreyfuss as a beloved high school band director. "I told Nina [Jacobson, president of the Disney studio] to develop this."

I wasn't expecting this twist. I thanked him for his interest, but pointed out that I couldn't very well be involved in a Disney movie while I was writing a book on the company. It didn't dawn on me then that perhaps that was the whole idea, that if Disney bought the movie rights I would drop the book idea. Or maybe it was a combination of the two, since Jacobson later told me that she actually did think the story would have made a good movie. Whatever the truth of the matter, nothing came of it. Several weeks later terrorists attacked the World Trade Center. Disney's theme park business went into a tailspin as tourism collapsed and the Disney parks seemed like obvious potential terrorist targets. Dreyer called to say that cooperation on any book was now out of the question, and I, too, put the project aside to write about the events surrounding September 11, resulting in my last book, *Heart of a Soldier*.

By the time I called again, in early 2003, Zenia Mucha, who brought a new, more aggressive posture to the position, had replaced Dreyer as head of corporate public relations. A former senior policy adviser to New York governor George Pataki, Mucha was elevated to the position after distinguishing herself as head of public relations for the ABC network. Though hardly thrilled by the prospect of a book about Disney, Mucha seemed inclined to offer at least some cooperation. Eisner was going to be in New York in March, and she arranged for the three of us to have dinner.

Eisner chose the restaurant, which was Nobu in Manhattan's Tribeca neighborhood, a favorite of visiting Hollywood celebrities. When he arrived, there was a buzz of recognition in the room, and several people stopped him to say hello and shake hands as he made his way to the table. He was as relaxed and funny as I'd remembered him at the deposition. He seemed willing to discuss any subject I brought up, whether it was ABC's recent unsuccessful courtship of David Letterman, negotiations with the Chinese government to open another theme park, or the looming war with Iraq ("Surely Bush won't do anything so stupid," he told me). Mentioning the near heart attack that almost killed him in 1994, Eisner picked through the menu looking for low-fat options, and urged me to take Lipitor, the cholesterol-lowering medicine that he credits with prolonging his life. Eisner is a good storyteller, a skill that has no doubt guided his selection of countless scripts and treatments that were turned into hit movies over the years.

During that first dinner, I told Eisner my plans for a book: a behind-the-scenes look at the workings of the country's best-known media and entertainment company as it grappled with all kinds of creative and technological challenges. I wanted to see the creative process in action, to show how Disney shaped culture, or was shaped by it, and how executives grappled with both a profit motive and artistic aspirations. To Eisner's credit, Disney had escaped the debacle of a merger like that of America Online and Time Warner, but it was nonetheless still predominantly a company that produced "content," and faced competition from media giants like Viacom, News Corp., and Time Warner that also owned distribution systems such as cable and satellite television. It struck me that Disney was at another turning point in its history, and I proposed to follow it for at least the next year. How the book turned out, I suggested, whether it would be "positive" or "negative" from Eisner's point of view, would in large part depend on what happened. I acknowledged that cooperating with me would be something of a gamble, since there was no way of knowing how the story would unfold. I made no promises; there could be no quid pro quos for any cooperation.

Eisner seemed intrigued. He said business was on an upswing at Disney, and in any event, he was an optimist by nature. He'd written his own book that was published in 1998, called *Work in Progress*, but he was disappointed in the critical reaction, which suggested that he'd glossed over some of the most controversial incidents in his career, especially the departure of Jeffrey Katzenberg in 1994 and Michael Ovitz a few years later. (Eisner later conceded that the book had been heavily edited by lawyers and other Disney executives, who made him cut anything that might have been controversial.)

Eisner said he welcomed scrutiny. "I really don't mind your investigating the company," he said, "because I've got nothing to hide. You may find that we've made some mistakes, but not because we didn't try to do the right thing." By the end of dinner, Eisner seemed to have warmed to the prospect. We got into his chauffeur-driven, black SUV, and he dropped me off near my apartment. Just before I got out, he mentioned that he loved his job. "There's no point in doing something if it's not fun," he said. "So let's have fun with this book."

Of course no one could have anticipated the dramatic events that were about to unfold, sowing turmoil at the company and keeping Disney on the front pages of the nation's newspapers: a boardroom revolt led by Roy Disney and his ally Stanley Gold; Roy's and Gold's abrupt resignations from the board; the collapse of negotiations with Pixar Animation Studios; a management shake-up at ABC; a hostile takeover bid from Comcast; and a shareholder revolt that left Eisner publicly humiliated and stripped of his chairmanship, if not his day-to-day power. I was at a meeting with Eisner in the midst of all this, the day after Pixar and Apple Computer chief executive Steve Jobs abruptly terminated their negotiations to extend the lucrative partnership that had contributed *Toy Story* and *Finding Nemo* to the Disney library.

"I can see your book is turning into *Barbarians at the Gate*," Eisner wryly observed.

Two months after that first dinner with Eisner, on Thursday, May 21, a car picks me up at 6:30 A.M. at the Animal Kingdom Lodge in Walt Disney World. I've been staying at the Lodge, a spectacular interpretation of the thatched-roof safari lodges found in East Africa, for several days while immersing myself in the theme park, revisiting rides like Space Mountain and The Twilight Zone Tower of Terror, roaming through the "backstage" areas reserved for "cast members," and watching preparations for theatrical events like "IllumiNations: Reflections of Earth." I've walked the park with Walt Disney World president Al Weiss, who, in the tradition of Walt, darted over and snatched up any scrap of paper or debris and placed it in a trash receptacle. The habit was contagious; I soon found myself scanning for any wayward trash.

As a child, I'd made two trips to Disneyland with my family, and I remember them as the best family vacations we ever had. My father worked for a small Midwestern television station that carried the syndicated "The Mickey Mouse Club," and we got the red-carpet, VIP treatment (though we did have to wait in lines). I had unlimited tickets for the most popular rides, like my favorites, Fantasyland's Matterhorn Bobsleds and the Tomorrowland Indy Speedway. The Monsanto House of the Future gained a peculiar hold on my imagination, as did the Swiss Family Robinson's fantasy tree house and the aerial view of London from the Peter Pan ride. On our second visit, we visited the Disney studio and ate in the commissary with costumed children appearing in *Mary Poppins*, which was then in production on the lot. I remember the last night of that vacation, waiting for a taxi to the airport outside the Disneyland Hotel. My seven-year-old sister started crying because we had to leave. She was so distraught that she dropped the fleece blanket that she dragged with her wherever we went, and never mentioned it again. Somehow I knew we'd never be back. It was the summer of 1963, just months before the Kennedy assassination. At age eleven, I already felt a nostalgia for a childhood I knew was coming to an end.

Now, four decades later, I arrive at Walt Disney World's entertainment group offices promptly at 7:00 A.M. to begin training for my appearance as a Disney character. Tammy Gutierrez, an ebullient, petite brunette, greets me and explains that the usual five-day orientation is being condensed into a few hours for my benefit. Originally hired to portray Dopey, Gutierrez has spent fourteen years in the more demanding role of Snow White, one of the park's "talking" characters. (Any character with a human face—Cinderella, Snow White, Mary Poppins, Prince Charming—is expected to speak in character to guests.) Gutierrez does in fact bear a remarkable resemblance to my own memory of Snow White. Now she auditions and trains new character actors.

I thought I'd simply be putting on a costume and walking around the park, but Gutierrez quickly disabuses me of that idea. "We look for animation," she tells me. "You have to bring energy and spirit to the role—make it real. We're not people dressed up in costumes," she stresses. "Anyone can do that."

She shows me a video featuring archival footage of Walt talking about his vision of Disneyland, a place that adults could enjoy with their children.

"Photos and autographs will be the bulk of your business," Gutierrez continues once the video is over. "Remember, people have waited a lifetime for the moment they meet you. You may be in a costume, but the photo must look real. You don't speak, but you communicate. You must be animated. There's a lot you can do."

I have to walk like Goofy, bob my head like Goofy, make Goofy's gestures, all of which are quite identifiable and unique to Goofy. Gutierrez gives me a typed sheet that distills Goofy's salient characteristics:

Traits: Frequently uncoordinated, klutzy, ever cheerful, optimistic, heart-of-gold, jolly, likes nearly everybody, bumbling, awkward, devoted, sincere, honest, a dreamer.

Synopsis: Although, in fact, Goofy is a dog in man's clothing, he is quite human. He may strike the passer-by as a typical village half-wit, but in truth he is a kindly, eager soul, a little on the silly side, but always harmless.

Goofy strives to be a gentleman, but when embarrassed, hides his simple, buck-toothed face and utters his favorite expression, "Garsh." Goofy has none of the physical attributes usually associated with a "star." His back is bowed, and his shoulders are narrow, sloping down to seemingly heavy arms and a protruding stomach. As he walks, his head, stomach, and knees seem to take the lead. This, however, has not stopped him from becoming a foremost authority on any type of sport or occupation you can name—each accomplished in his own particularly "goofy" way.

Through his hilarious methods of trial and error, he does everything either wrong or completely backwards. Being the everlasting optimist, he laughs at his mistakes and makes the most of them. Goofy's gangling, homespun charm has proved irresistible. Throughout his career, he has never failed to live up to his name. He is simply himself—Goofy!

After absorbing this, I look at Gutierrez with some dismay. This is more than I bargained for.

Gutierrez takes me into a rehearsal space, which looks like a large dance studio. One entire wall is covered with mirrors. Gutierrez hands me a pair of black shorts and a gray T-shirt and tells me to change. In part this is to get me to shed the identity associated with my street clothes and start becoming Goofy. When I return, Gutierrez has me don the structural aspects of the Goofy costume that require the most adjustment: a padded body suit covered in fake fur that gives me a potbelly and some bulk in my rear; and a pair of huge, flapping, clownlike shoes. Gutierrez demonstrates the Goofy walk and arm motions, and has me imitate her while watching myself in the mirror. It's not as easy as it looks. Goofy uses a slow, loping motion, bending at the knees, as he bends his arms at the elbows and swings them in an exaggerated fashion. I think I'm starting to get the hang of it, but Gutierrez makes me do it over and over. Only then does she strap me into Goofy's headgear, which is something of a shock. It's very heavy, and with the long snout, it's unbalanced, constantly threatening to slip forward on my face. Worse, it's designed so that my eyes look out through the opening of Goofy's mouth. Gutierrez guides me to the mirror. "What do you see?" she asks. I'm not sure what to say. "You're staring upwards into space," she points out. "Goofy is not an easy character, because of the sight lines," she explains. "If you're looking straight ahead through the mouth, then Goofy is tilting his head back. To make it look like Goofy is looking straight ahead, you pretty much have to stare at your feet."

I look again at the typed sheet.

Your role: As Goofy, keep your head down so that your eyes can be seen. When you walk, lope along and let your knees and stomach lead. Try to do something—anything—and when you mix it all up, laugh at yourself and go on to something else. Box with yourself or with an imaginary partner. Play baseball with Donald or tag with Pluto. Pick out a girl, and show her how shy you are. Be extra-polite, dust off chairs for ladies, then bow and chuckle. Be silly, loose, clumsy, and loveable.

Easier said than done. For a nonspeaking character, Goofy certainly seems to be able to make a lot of sounds. After a practice or two, Gutierrez agrees that an authentic "Garsh!" may be beyond my thespian skills. I try walking across the room, watching myself in the mirrors. "Lead with your abdomen," she calls out. "Keep your head down. Splay your feet, put the heel down first and then roll. Keep moving. Nod, turn your head, now wave." All the while I'm staring at my feet. I can't believe how natural all those characters looked in the video; this takes a lot of coordination. Goofy also has a repertoire of gestures I'm expected to master. Since he's tall, Goofy has to get into position for photo opportunities with young children. So he often drops to one knee, arms outstretched, or he makes what Gutierrez calls a "TaDa!" gesture, holding out one arm while he puts the other paw on his knee. Goofy also blows kisses, and can make the sound of a kiss. He laughs by raising his paws to his mouth, but when I try it, Gutierrez says it looks like I'm sneezing.

It's time to move on to autographs, which are avidly collected by adults as well as children. Walt had decreed that each character's signature had to match, wherever it was obtained, to preserve the illusion that each character is unique. The notion that all signatures must match seems to have become something of an obsession, and Gutierrez makes me practice Goofy's distinctive signature over and over until I get it right. This isn't that easy, given that Goofy's gloved paw has just four appendages.

At 10:00 A.M. it's time to leave for the Animal Kingdom, though I definitely could use more practice. This has been too much to absorb in just a few hours. I'm taken to a large cast building just outside the park fences. Inside, other character actors are going through a class of stretching and warm-up exercises. They are trim, limber, and all look like professional dancers. The costume warehouse is vast, with long racks of outfits stretching far into the distance. I pull on a pair of black tights and a tight black spandex shirt. I'm feeling warm even before the padded layer of fur and the colorful safari outfit. Carrying the head, Gutierrez leads me to a van, and she offers encouragement as we drive the short distance to an air-conditioned trailer just outside a door into the park. I feel like an astronaut being taken to the capsule for lift-off. "Remember," she tells me, "to these children, you are a bigger celebrity than anyone you know from the adult world." Inside the trailer, I'm given a cloth cap to keep my hair down, and then the heavy head is placed on my shoulders and fixed to the cap. There's another Goofy in the trailer taking a break between his thirty-minute shifts, and he looks amused as I struggle with the headgear.

Minutes later, I'm in the park. Gutierrez is hovering nearby in case of emergency. After my first successful encounter with the young girl, I'm feeling exhilarated. My adrenaline is kicking in. People surround me. Children are lining up to get my autograph; shy faces, glowing with excitement. I frantically try to remember everything Gutierrez taught me: nod, laugh, wave, blow a kiss, gesture, get down on one knee. Act "silly."

With my impaired vision, I fail to notice a young boy has come alongside, and when I turn my head, I bump him with my nose. Moments later, I hear a shrill voice: "Mommy, Mommy, Goofy hit me on the head." Oh my God, a lawsuit, I'm thinking. But Gutierrez doesn't seem to be reacting, and in any event, there are too many other autograph and photo seekers competing for my attention. Plenty of adults want their pictures taken, too, which gives me a welcome opportunity to stand up. "It must be hot in there," murmurs one man as the flash goes off.

"You'd better believe it," I'm thinking, even though I maintain a strict silence. In all the excitement I'd barely noticed how hot it was, but I'm now so drenched in sweat that the cloth cap to which the Goofy head is attached is starting to creep down my forehead. Soon it's past my eyebrows, and my already limited vision is further obscured. Locked inside my costume, there's nothing I can do to stop it. At this rate, Goofy is going to go blind in a matter of minutes.

Out of the increasingly narrow slit through which I can still see, a young boy has approached. He has blond hair and looks like he might be three years old. "Give Goofy a hug," someone says. He stands frozen in place, and looks like he's about to cry. Gutierrez has warned me that the characters frighten some children, and when that happens, not to make any sudden gestures. I hear her voice now: "Give Goofy a high-five," she says. I slowly hold up my cloth paw, and the boy reaches out and touches it. Then he quickly pulls back. He circles me warily, then comes closer and holds up his palm. I give him the high-five. His face lights up in a huge smile, and people around us start to applaud.

Just as my ability to see disappears, I hear Gutierrez say, "Goofy is going to have to go. Say good-bye to Goofy." I hear a chorus of young voices calling out to me as Gutierrez steers us to the exit, which is mercifully close by. I feel like I've only been "onstage" for a few minutes, but in fact I've completed a standard thirty-minute shift. It's a relief to get the heavy head off and recover my vision. Still, I can see why people like Tammy Gutierrez would keep at it for fourteen years. Once you've seen those children's faces, nothing else seems quite the same.

Part One

THE WONDERFUL WORLD OF DISNEY

ONE

On Monday morning, September 24, 1984, Michael Eisner woke up feeling a little nervous. It was his first day as chairman and chief executive of the Walt Disney Company. Tall, with dark curly hair, at age forty-two Eisner still had something of the boyish look of the prep school student he once was. Anxious to make a good first impression, he dressed carefully in a suit and tie and got in his car for the trip to Disney. He planned to drive from his home in Bel Air to Interstate 405 North, then onto the Ventura Freeway. The Disney studio was so far out of the Hollywood mainstream that Eisner had only a vague idea where it was—somewhere in Burbank. Soon he realized he was deep into the San Fernando Valley. He called his lawyer, Irwin Russell, from the car to get directions.

When Eisner pulled into the Disney lot, he saw a collection of unassuming, low-rise buildings surrounded by neatly clipped hedges and lawns in a modest four-acre campus. It was nothing like the imposing gated entry to Paramount, where Eisner had been president for the past seven years. Several bushes had been clipped into topiary shapes of Disney animated characters. The animation building that had housed Walt Disney's office was at the intersection of Mickey Avenue and Dopey Drive. Around the corner stood the fading Western set for "Zorro," a Disney-produced television show that hadn't been on the air for twenty-three years. Judging from the nearly empty parking area, he was one of the first to arrive.

As he pulled in, Eisner realized he had no idea where to go. Everything had happened so suddenly. Just that Saturday, the board had voted to appoint him chairman and chief executive, along with Frank Wells, a lawyer and former head of Warner Bros., as president and chief operating officer.

A boardroom coup led by Roy Disney had ousted Walt's son-in-law, Ron Miller. The weekend had been filled with meetings with investment bankers and lawyers talking about takeover threats and bandying around financial terms that were unfamiliar to Eisner, such as "book value" and "return on equity."

Eisner introduced himself to a guard, who summoned Disney's head of public relations, Erwin Okun. Okun led him to Walt's old office on the third floor of the animation building. Lining the corridors were original "cels," hand-drawn and colored frames from the classic Disney animated features: Snow White, Pinocchio, Sleeping Beauty, Fantasia. Lucille Martin, Walt's former secretary, was sitting just outside the office. Somewhat apprehensively, Eisner settled into Walt's chair behind the desk.

Then Frank Wells walked in, and sat down across from him. Wells, age fifty-two, looked as if he'd been sent from central casting for the role of studio executive: tall, ruggedly handsome, wearing glasses, graying at the temples. Their new partnership was something of a shotgun marriage, hastily forged in the months leading up to the board vote. Eisner didn't know him well, but Wells's willingness to take the number two position, ceding the top spot to Eisner, had made a deep impression. They chatted briefly as Wells scanned their new surroundings. But Wells showed no sign of getting up from his chair. "Are we going to sit here together?" Eisner finally asked.

Wells shrugged. "I thought we would."

"I can't work that way," Eisner said. So Wells moved to a conference room next door.

Like much at Disney, Eisner's new office hadn't changed much since Walt died in 1966. The pace at Disney was so leisurely that by lunchtime, the workday was pretty much over, at least for top executives and senior producers. They played cards every day after lunch in a small room off the executive dining room. Afterward, they often had massages from Bob Hope's masseur, who was kept on staff, followed by visits to the steam room and Walt's custom-made thirty-nozzle shower. Employees stopped work early to play softball every Tuesday evening. When a newly hired executive persisted in working evenings and weekends, it was considered so unorthodox that security launched an investigation.

Almost no one was fired. At most studios, numerous employees were hired for the run of a production, then let go when shooting wrapped. At Disney, they stayed indefinitely, awaiting new assignments. Instead of using outside producers, Disney kept them in-house. Disney released a new animated feature every four years, and had produced just three live-action films the year before Eisner's arrival. Typical overhead on a Disney film was twice that of rival studios.

Eisner and Wells had already decided that this was going to change, but on their first afternoon at the company, they tried to reassure nervous employees, speaking from a bandstand that had been built for the film *Something Wicked This Way Comes*. It helped that Roy was with them. Then they toured the lot, meeting every employee they could and shaking hands. Eisner asked one young woman where she worked. "BVI," she replied.

"I didn't know Disney owned an underwear company," he said.

"No," she laughed. "BVI is Buena Vista International," Disney's movie distribution arm.

Much to Eisner's relief, in the many interviews leading up to the board vote, no one had asked him much about Disney, either the company or its products. As he later wrote in a draft of his autobiography, "To be honest, I knew little about Disney, little about the culture or even the actual films. If Disney had not been under siege and under real risk of being acquired and sold off in pieces, I would not have passed the interview process. If Disney Production had not faltered creatively, I would not have passed the interview process. If Roy Disney had not just had blind faith in me, for reasons I will never understand, I would not have passed the interview process. And if Sid Bass had not backed this blind faith, I would not have passed the interview process.

"The fact of the matter [was], I knew far too little about Walt Disney Productions.

" 'So Mr. Eisner,' the interviewer would have said. 'What did you think of *Snow White*?'

" 'I never saw it,' would be my answer.

" 'Oh really? Then tell me, how did you feel about *Sleeping Beauty*?'

" 'Never saw it,' I would embarrassingly respond.

"The questions would continue, but eventually the conversation would reveal that I never saw a Disney film until I was an adult. . . . And I would also have to admit I had never seen 'The Wonderful World of Disney' on Sunday nights. . . . I could have talked about Broadway musicals from my youth, like *South Pacific*, or *Carousel*, or *Oklahoma!*, or *Kiss Me Kate*, or *Where's Charley?* or *The King and I*, or television from my childhood like 'Hopalong Cassidy' or 'The Milton Berle Show' or 'Howdy Doody' but not Disney.

"And I was not really like Walt. That could have hurt me in the [interview] process. It's not that I came from Paramount or ABC, from Hollywood, if you will, but my entire background was different. Walt came from the heartland. From Chicago and Kansas. I came from New York City. Walt was in the majority, a Christian; I [was] a minority, Jewish. Walt lived in homes, on farms, in the American community. I lived in an apartment. Walt walked to public co-educational school, down dirt roads, across pastures, avoiding dogs and bulls and bullies. I walked down Park Avenue to Seventy-eighth Street past red lights and candy stores and bullies to Allen-Stevenson, a private boys' school where I had to wear a tie. I ate dinner every night with the full family, served by candlelight with my tie still on. I suspect Walt did not."

Once at Disney, Eisner had to absorb quickly the basic elements of the Walt story. Disney had always held itself aloof from Hollywood—its glamour and hedonism, its star system and cutthroat dealmaking. Immigrants from Eastern Europe and New York City had created Paramount and the other big Hollywood studios; Walt and his older brother and business partner Roy grew up on a Missouri farm, without electricity or indoor plumbing. An idealized view of life in rural middle America at the turn of the century— the sleigh rides, church socials, farm animals, and trips to the general store— permeated Walt's imagination, showing up repeatedly in Disney films and especially at Disneyland, where Main Street was modeled on downtown Marceline, Missouri, Walt's hometown.

After the family farm failed, Walt's father moved the family first to Kansas City, then to Chicago, where Walt took lessons at the Chicago Museum of Art. He astounded his pragmatic father when he announced in 1919 that he'd decided it would be easier to make a living as an artist than an actor, his other ambition. He moved back to Kansas City, was rejected for a job as a cartoonist at the *Kansas City Star*, and found work at the Kansas City Slide Company, which made ads that were inserted before feature films at movie theaters. He and his friend and fellow artist Ub Iwerks created Walt's first primitive one-minute cartoons. Emboldened by promises from a New York distributor, they founded their own company, Laugh-O-Gram Films, which went bankrupt when they never got paid.

Walt came to Los Angeles in the summer of 1923, and later that year asked his brother and Iwerks to join him in a fledgling animated film business. Roy put up most of the money and managed the business. In 1925, Roy's girlfriend Edna came from Kansas City to marry him. Lillian Bounds joined the company, first as a painter on cartoon cels, then as Walt's secretary. Roy married Edna on April 11, 1925; Lillian was her maid of honor. Walt married Lillian three months later.

Theirs was a hand-to-mouth existence, financed largely by sales of a cartoon featuring an Iwerks creation, Oswald the Lucky Rabbit. Partly due to Walt's exacting standards of craftsmanship, the costs of producing Oswald outstripped the fees they were paid by Universal, Oswald's distributor. Roy dispatched Walt, accompanied by Lillian, to New York to ask for more money. While they were gone, Oswald's producer, who owned the rights to the character, hired away the Disney animators and dispensed with the Disney brothers and Iwerks. When they returned, Roy was waiting anxiously at the station. "Have you got something lined up?" he asked.

"No, but I've got a wonderful idea," Walt replied.

"A mouse had always appealed to me," Walt later explained. "While working in Kansas City, I caught several in wastebaskets around the studio. I kept them in a cage on my desk and enjoyed watching their antics. One of them was quite tame and would crawl all over my desk while I worked."

Walt had started drawing mice on the train returning from New York, and showed his sketches to Lillian. "They were cute little things," she later recalled. She asked him what he was going to call the main character. "Mortimer Mouse," Walt answered.

"That doesn't sound very good," she said. She thought for a moment. "What about Mickey Mouse?" Never again would Walt and Roy allow someone else to own the rights to their creations.

"Steamboat Willie," the first talking cartoon, created a sensation when it was first screened in New York in 1928. Mickey Mouse became a star, and the Disney studio was launched. In part because of Walt's restless imagination, obsession with quality, and lack of interest in profit-and-loss statements, Disney was never on a firm financial footing until *Snow White and the Seven Dwarfs* was released in 1937. *Snow White* cost a then unheard of $1.5 million, financed with the Disney brothers' own money and a loan from Bank of America.

Walt hovered over every aspect of *Snow White*, and even when it was done, he was not satisfied and wanted to remake a few scenes at a cost of an additional $300,000. Roy stopped him. The film brought out the showman and frustrated actor in Walt. The premiere, on December 21, 1937, at the Carthay Circle Theatre in Hollywood, drew four thousand guests and featured costumed dwarfs wielding pickaxes in a full-scale replica of a diamond mine. In the first public appearance of live cartoon characters, actors dressed as Mickey, Minnie, Donald, Goofy, and Pluto greeted guests. A live symphony orchestra, chorus, and soloists accompanied the film. The *Motion Picture Herald* called it "the most extraordinary premiere in cinema history."

Snow White was nominated for an Academy Award for best music and song in 1938, and was given an honorary Academy Award in 1939. It brought millions in profit into the Disney Company and unleashed a golden age in Disney film animation. In the next five years came *Bambi, Pinocchio, Dumbo,* and the film Walt considered his masterpiece, *Fantasia.* The 1950s and 1960s produced *Cinderella, Sleeping Beauty, 101 Dalmatians, Jungle Book,* and *Mary Poppins.* And then, after Walt's death in 1966, the brilliance of Disney animation began to fade.

Despite Eisner's sense that he had little in common with Walt, there were certain elements of the Walt story that especially appealed to him. As he later wrote, "I was fascinated, at a personal level, by Walt's resilience, optimism and relentlessness in the face of the endless obstacles that began with a very difficult childhood and continued in his work life right up until his death in 1966. I was awed, at a professional level, by Walt's immense creativity and originality, both as an artist and businessman stretching over a remarkable forty-year period."

Eisner, too, thought of himself as creative, like Walt, a storyteller at heart. He had majored in literature in college, dabbled in playwriting, and prided himself on his ability to evaluate a script. Walt relied on Roy to oversee the more mundane tasks of finance and administration; Eisner now had Frank Wells.

But Eisner was also well aware that his affluent Park Avenue upbringing was very different from Walt's. Eisner's maternal grandfather, Milton Dammann, was a self-made multimillionaire who became president of the American Safety Razor Company before selling it to Philip Morris. (For a time, his grandfather was the second-largest individual shareholder in Philip Morris.) The Eisner side of the family was also wealthy. Michael's great-grandfather had made his fortune manufacturing uniforms for the army and the Boy Scouts. Michael's father attended Princeton and Harvard Law School and his mother grew up on an estate in Bedford Hills, New York, with fifteen servants and staff.

Despite the family wealth, Eisner's grandparents displayed a frugality often associated with Old Money. The young Eisner was once riding in a taxi during a snowstorm when he spotted his grandmother, in her eighties, boarding a bus outside Bloomingdale's department store. He had the taxi stop, intercepted his grandmother, and insisted she join him. "Why are you wasting money on a cab?" she demanded. His grandfather insisted on crossing into Manhattan on the Willis Avenue Bridge rather than the Triborough Bridge to save the twenty-five-cent toll.

Michael, his sister Margot, and their parents divided their time between an apartment on Park Avenue, the Bedford estate, and a farm in Vermont. Michael knew from a young age that his family was wealthy, especially his grandparents. But discussion of money was taboo, as off-limits as sex. His family had an aversion to people who flaunted their wealth or called attention to their charitable donations—attitudes common in old-line, wealthy, Establishment families, but not in Hollywood or Beverly Hills.

In many ways Eisner idolized his father, Lester, who was handsome, athletic, charismatic, and energetic, though remote from his son. In the summer of 1949, when Michael was seven, his father put him into the family Buick for a drive to Camp Keewaydin, near Middlebury, Vermont, the first time Eisner can remember being alone with his father. Michael's father, grandfather, and uncles had all gone to Keewaydin, founded in 1910 as one of America's first summer wilderness camps for boys. The camp fireplace had been donated by Michael's grandfather, and bore a plaque commemorating his uncle Jacques, a Keewaydin alumnus killed in the Battle of Guadalcanal. Other trophies and plaques cited various Eisners for their prowess in swimming, canoeing, and as "best athlete."

It was dark when they arrived, and a nervous Michael was left alone to sleep in a "wigwam" with other boys. After a day of touring the camp and joining in activities with other campers, the camp leader conferred with Michael's father, and then asked if Michael wanted to box with another boy at Saturday night's wrestling and boxing matches. "Sure," Michael replied, dubious that there was any alternative. He had never boxed. When time for the event arrived, he stepped into the makeshift ring to face an opponent two years older and, it seemed, twice his size. Eisner was soundly beaten in two minutes. He didn't cry.

Eisner spent many summers at Keewaydin, both as a camper and later as a counselor, later calling it "by far the most important experience of my life." As he later wrote in a manuscript for a book called *Camp*, "Team unity is the critical component of our success (it's no accident that the building where I work is called Team Disney), and it was at Keewaydin that I came to understand that success comes when the whole group is paddling in the same direction."

Curiously, Eisner was never allowed to call his father "Dad," "Daddy," or even "Father," but was required to address him by his given name, Lester. This proved embarrassing for Michael when other children questioned whether Lester was really his father. When Michael asked his mother why he had to call him Lester, she explained that his sister had had difficulty pro-nouncing "Daddy" as a toddler, so had been encouraged to refer to him as Lester. This explanation struck even the young Eisner as highly implausible.

Despite his Princeton and Harvard Law School education, Lester drifted through a series of jobs without notable success or fulfillment. The Eisner family uniform business, run by Lester's brother, failed, though it had no discernible effect on Michael's family fortune. Lester ended up as a government bureaucrat, the head of public housing under New York governor Nelson Rockefeller, but resigned rather than comply with a state requirement that he disclose his financial investments, deeming the requirement an invasion of privacy. Lester imposed a strict work ethic, rousing his children early on weekends to perform chores and insisting they work at summer jobs. While Michael and his sister were regularly taken to Broadway musicals, they were oddly deprived of more traditional cultural fare. Michael must have been one of the few children of his generation who was never taken to see any of the Disney animated films; he later said his mother wasn't interested in them. Lester stressed competitive athletics. He regularly woke Michael's sister at 5:00 A.M. for ice-skating practice, and she bore the brunt of Lester's competitive drive as she competed but narrowly missed qualifying for the 1960 U.S. Olympic figure skating team. He paid less attention to Michael, who was a natural athlete and team leader, at least until he got to prep school.

Michael's best friend was a boy named John Angelo, whose father had been killed in World War II. Angelo's and Michael's mothers were best friends, and Lester was something of a surrogate father to John. On one occasion when Angelo came to spend the night with Michael, the boys were put to bed at 9:00 P.M. Michael boasted to his friend that he often stayed up much later, a claim Angelo refused to believe. When his mother came to check on them, Michael asked her to back up his assertion. Instead, she sided with Angelo. "Michael, you know you always have to be in bed by nine," she replied. Michael, feeling betrayed, flew into a tantrum. Years later he asked his mother to recall the episode and correct the injustice by admitting she hadn't been truthful. By then she couldn't remember what he was talking about. But Michael never forgot the incident.

When he entered the ninth grade, Michael was sent to boarding school at Lawrenceville Academy in Lawrenceville, New Jersey, a prestigious, academically rigorous prep school that traditionally fed many of its graduates to nearby Princeton, Lester's alma mater. After a relatively easy time at the nurturing Allen-Stevenson School in Manhattan, Michael found the transition to Lawrenceville difficult. He was away from home for extended periods, the sudden growth spurt to a height of six feet three had undermined his athletic coordination (he failed to make both the varsity football and basketball teams), and he was an indifferent student. His native intelligence and quick mind had always compensated for a short attention span until Lawrenceville, which put a premium on sustained academic inquiry.

It was at Lawrenceville, too, where Michael first felt any discomfort at being Jewish. He'd grown up in a strictly secular household, and Lester was an avowed atheist. It hadn't made an impression on the young Eisner that the family of one of his classmates at Allen-Stevenson changed its name from Lipski to Lipsey. His family had always stressed that the Eisners were of German descent; he'd never seen any irony in the fact that during World War II his family had employed a German housekeeper, who was a surrogate mother to Michael and his sister. But at Lawrenceville, Michael felt the sting of prejudice. He got into a fistfight after another boy called him a "kike," and he overheard plenty of comments and jokes characterized by thinly disguised anti-Semitism. He hated the sense of being different, not just because he was Jewish, but also because his family was wealthy and privileged. He daydreamed about a more "normal" life, like the ones he saw on television— a regular mother and father, a modest house with a yard and picket fence, and a coed public school—just like the lives he saw portrayed on "The Donna Reed Show," and in Doris Day movies, which he loved.

It was exactly this kind of idyllic, bucolic, all-American setting that Eisner spotted on the cover of a college catalog for Denison University in Granville, Ohio. A respected coed liberal arts college whose nineteenth-century, tree-studded campus looks like a stage set for higher education, Denison was nonetheless hardly in the league of Princeton, which Michael's parents hoped he would attend. He didn't tell them he'd applied until after he was accepted. He enrolled there in the fall of 1960.

At Denison, Eisner shed the insecurities of Lawrenceville and rediscovered his inherent optimism, self-confidence, sense of humor, and leadership skills. Eisner was one of only a handful of Jewish students, but he fit in easily with his sixteen hundred mostly white, affluent fellow students. He joined a fraternity, Delta Upsilon, where he was elected president (several fraternities, such as Sigma Chi, barred Jews at the time, though there was little of the overt anti-Semitism that had bothered him at Lawrenceville). More important, he abandoned tentative plans to become a medical doctor and discovered literature and drama, inspired by a professor of nineteenth-century literature, Dominick Consolo. Eisner was creative but not especially scholarly: he wrote a thesis on the presidency of Woodrow Wilson in the form of a one-act play. In his literature and drama classes he found it easy to construct scenes and write dialogue.

Jonathan Reynolds, a playwright and food writer at *The New York Times*, was Eisner's friend and classmate at all three of Eisner's schools. Reynolds grew up on Fifth Avenue and had play dates with Eisner as a child. He recalls Eisner as a natural athlete and leader and an average student. When he spotted Eisner on the Denison campus, he assumed his grades hadn't been good enough to get him into an Ivy League school. But Eisner impressed him at Denison, both as a fraternity president and a budding playwright. Eisner had a play produced on campus, and the subject matter was controversial for the time. "It was about an Irish girl who was expelled from school because she'd written a paper about Walt Whitman alleging that he was a revolutionary and gay," Reynolds recalls. "So she goes back to work in her father's Irish bar. And in the second act, there's a death and a funeral and Eisner insisted that a life-size coffin be placed on the bar." Eisner's play drew a sizable local audience, and Reynolds says he sat there watching and thought, "Wow, this guy has gone and written a play." *

After years of all-boys schools, attractive young women surrounded Eisner at Denison. He gave the starring role in his Walt Whitman play to Barbara Eberhardt, a budding actress he was hoping to date. That gambit failed, but he soon met his first serious girlfriend, Judy Armstrong, from Hamilton, Ohio, who embodied the all-American virtues that had drawn Eisner to Denison. By the time he graduated in 1964, he and Armstrong were "pinned," a serious step just short of engagement.

Eisner moved to Paris to explore the glamorous existence of a young expatriate playwright, but he didn't stay long, moving back to Park Avenue with his parents before getting his own apartment on Sixty-fourth Street. Armstrong had stayed in Ohio. Michael's Christmas gift to her that first year after graduation was returned to him unopened. When he called to find out why, her mother answered. "I guess I should tell you," she said, "that Judy got married yesterday."

Eisner was stunned. He couldn't eat anything at dinner that night. Still, he went out to a party a friend was having. He tried to turn his heartbreak

---

* Many years later, Reynolds had a play of his own produced at an off-Broadway theater. Eisner booked a $35 seat in the front row to accommodate his long legs. Afterward, he sent Reynolds a note saying how great it was that "after all these years, things are working out for you as a writer." Eisner also gave $5,000 to the theater.

into a funny story, regaling the other guests with a dramatic rendering of his rejection. One of the guests, an attractive, down-to-earth redhead from small-town Jamestown, New York, named Jane Breckenridge, listened politely, but found him self-centered and boorish. When Eisner called the next week to ask for a date, she refused. He persisted. After repeatedly spurning Eisner's requests, she relented and agreed to go to the theater with him. They were married in 1967.

Paramount had produced such legendary critical and box-office hits as the *Godfather* films, *Chinatown*, and *Nashville*, but the studio was adrift and losing money when Charles Bluhdorn, chairman of Paramount's owner, Gulf+Western, named Barry Diller the studio's chairman in 1974. He and Eisner had worked together at ABC, and Diller hired Eisner as president two years later. "I hear you've really matured as an executive," Diller said wryly. "You even return your phone calls."

Though they were the same age, Diller had ranked above Eisner at ABC, and their relationship was a mixture of competitiveness, wariness, and mutual admiration from the start, honed during the period that Diller produced movies for ABC's Movie of the Week and Eisner worked under him as director of feature films and development. ABC's movies became a hugely successful feature under Diller, and Eisner eventually rose to head of prime-time programming of ABC, responsible for such hits as "Welcome Back, Kotter," "Happy Days," and "Laverne & Shirley."

Eisner seemed to have a sixth sense for American popular taste. Though he liked to quote Willa Cather and Shakespeare, and mention that he had been a literature major in college, it was Diller (who never graduated from college and got his start in the mailroom of the William Morris Agency) who aspired to higher culture. When Eisner and Diller were young assistants together at ABC, Eisner had once mentioned that *Ethan Frome* was one of his favorite books. Diller said something noncommittal. Eisner subsequently spotted Diller in the elevator carrying several Edith Wharton novels and a Wharton biography.

Coming from television, neither Eisner nor Diller knew much about the insular world of theatrical motion pictures before they arrived at Paramount. But their collaboration produced a now-legendary string of commercial and critical hits: *Saturday Night Fever, Grease, Flashdance, Footloose, 48 Hrs.* Eisner often told how he'd had the idea for *Beverly Hills Cop*, another big hit starring Eddie Murphy. He was stopped for speeding the first day he drove his new Mercedes convertible through Beverly Hills, and as the officer wrote up his ticket, Eisner had wondered what it must be like to be a cop in such an affluent enclave.

Soon after he arrived at Paramount, Eisner met Jeffrey Katzenberg, who had worked as Diller's assistant and was rapidly establishing a reputation for prodigious energy and hard work. When Katzenberg met Diller and recording industry impresario David Geffen at the airport, he whisked them through customs and baggage claim so efficiently that Geffen turned to Diller and asked, "My God, who the hell is that guy?" Geffen was so impressed that he wanted to hire Katzenberg, but ended up becoming his best friend instead.

Diller warned Eisner that Katzenberg had been so aggressive, abrasive, and relentless as his assistant that he had moved him into marketing so he could learn to function better in an organization. Short, lean, with glasses and prominent teeth, Katzenberg exuded restless energy and ambition, which Eisner was happy to harness. Like Eisner, Katzenberg had grown up in a luxurious Park Avenue apartment, though his family wasn't nearly so wealthy or cultured as Eisner's. His father was a self-made stockbroker. While Eisner revered his experience at Camp Keewaydin, Katzenberg had been expelled from a camp along the Kennebec River in Maine for playing poker. He attended one year of college, at New York University, before joining the New York mayoral campaign of John Lindsay. He rose rapidly through a series of jobs, and was willing to handle any task. He eventually served as treasurer for Lindsay's unsuccessful 1972 presidential campaign. After dabbling in casino gambling, a talent agency, and working for a film producer, he was hired as Diller's assistant in 1975.

Katzenberg was smart, intense, and in Eisner's view, unpolished. Eisner cringed when he mentioned he wanted to remake Hawthorne's classic novel *The Scarlet Letter* and Katzenberg asked what it was. Still, Katzenberg got things done. He never had to be told something twice. Katzenberg developed a sixth sense for what Eisner wanted and anticipated his needs. He could finish Eisner's sentences after Eisner had said just a few words. Not that Katzenberg always agreed with Eisner; he could be quite critical, and the two often argued. But he was fiercely loyal. Eisner reprimanded Katzenberg once for criticizing him to an outsider, and never had to do so again. Eventually Eisner promoted Katzenberg to head of production at Paramount. Katzenberg saw Eisner as a mentor and confidant, though the two almost never socialized.

At Paramount, Eisner's touch also extended to television production. Like most of the major studios, Paramount had a television production unit on its lot. FCC regulations barred the networks from producing their own programming, so they bought it from the studios for the initial broadcast, and then the syndication rights reverted to the studios, an enormously lucrative windfall to Hollywood, and one the industry lobbied fiercely for in Washington. Under Diller and Eisner's leadership, Paramount Television had five of network TV's top ten hits: "Taxi," "Happy Days," "Laverne & Shirley," "Angie," and "Mork & Mindy."

Eisner prided himself on keeping costs modest; some thought it bordered on obsession. He preferred to develop ideas generated internally at Paramount rather than high-priced agents and "packagers," a strategy aimed at hitting "singles and doubles," as he put it, rather than home runs. For Eisner, the quality of the story was all-important, not high-priced directors and stars. He looked for stories with compelling characters, clear conflict and resolution, three easily identifiable "acts," and universal themes that could be summarized—that is, marketed—in a sentence or two. This approach, dubbed "high concept" in the parlance of Hollywood, spawned many imitators, but few were as successful as Eisner and Diller.

For all of Paramount's success, Eisner's judgment wasn't infallible; he turned down the script that became *Private Benjamin,* a huge hit for actress Goldie Hawn. But such lapses were rare. And in any event, Paramount had so many hits that Eisner didn't need to waste time lamenting the few he rejected. "It isn't the movies you pass on that make the difference, but the ones you make," he said so often that it became a refrain.

Despite his frugality, Eisner was on occasion willing to take financial risks. After two other studios balked at the high projected costs, and even Diller opposed the project on financial grounds, Eisner signed *Star Wars* writer George Lucas, director Steven Spielberg, and actor Harrison Ford to make *Indiana Jones and the Raiders of the Lost Ark.* With $240 million in U.S. box-office receipts, it became a "franchise," a huge hit that spawned a series of highly profitable sequels.

Nevertheless, Eisner was fanatical at keeping costs low to earn a profit, a curiously iconoclastic view in Hollywood, which had a long and deeply entrenched tradition of rewarding talent, agents, managers, and studio executives before anyone gave much thought to shareholders. After the huge success of *Raiders,* Eisner recorded his philosophy in a twenty-one-page manifesto distributed to Paramount executives. In it, he noted that nearly all of the studio's profits from 1981 had come from *Raiders,* an expensive anomaly in the Eisner canon, and he didn't want anyone at Paramount to get the idea that he was veering from his time-tested strategy that combined high concept and low budgets. "Often the big win comes with a single smash movie," he wrote. "The intoxication of a blockbuster hit can lead to an easy sense the luck will keep striking. Over the past five years, Paramount has either been number one or two in the motion picture business. Success tends to make you forget what made you successful, and just when you least suspect it, the big error shifts the game. Will success lull us into the fatal bad play?"

Eisner proceeded to make his own priorities clear. "We have no obligation to make art. We have no obligation to make history. We have no obligation to make a statement. But to make money, it is often important to make history, to make art, or to make some significant statement. . . . In order to make money, we must always make entertaining movies, and if we make entertaining movies, at times we will reliably make history, art, a statement, or all three. We may even win awards. . . . We cannot expect numerous hits, but if every film has an original and imaginative concept, then we can be confident that something will break through."

But a low budget could never be its own reward. "An apparently no-risk deal is never a valid reason to produce a mediocre movie," he continued. "A low budget can never excuse deficiencies in the script. Not even the greatest screenwriter or actor or director can be counted on to save a film that lacks a strong underlying concept. And we should generally resist making expensive overall deals with box office stars and top directors, because we can attract them later with strong material."

Eisner's memo became gospel at Paramount, and circulated widely in Hollywood. It established him as something of an analytical genius in the movie business, where few of the great impresarios of the past had ever been able to articulate any kind of formula for artistic or commercial success. And he also led by example. Shortly after issuing the memo, he agreed to make *Terms of Endearment* only if director James L. Brooks could do it for a low-budget $7 million, and when costs ran to $8 million, Brooks had to find the additional $1 million somewhere else. Eisner's intransigence led to legendary shouting matches between the two men. In the end, Eisner could easily have afforded to be more generous. The movie was a smash hit, earning over $100 million, as well as the Best Picture Oscar for 1983. But it made a lasting impression on Eisner that Brooks subsequently conceded publicly that the film was actually better for having been made on a strict budget.

If a picture was a huge hit, or seemed likely to be one, others in Hollywood—Diller, for example—lavished praise, relaxed the rules, and sweetened the perks, all to keep the producers and talent happy. None of this came naturally to Eisner. He was stingy with praise. When Diller offered Robert Redford a $750,000 bonus for the successful completion of *Ordinary People*, Redford's debut as a director, Eisner was fiercely opposed. He felt vindicated when Redford snubbed Paramount and took his next film elsewhere.

When Eisner arrived at Paramount, knowing little about the movie business, producer Larry Gordon had helped tutor him. Gordon blended Southern charm with keen instincts for popular culture; the two developed into best friends. Eisner's and Gordon's sons attended school together, where they were close friends, and at Eisner's suggestion, Gordon had sent his boys to Keewaydin, where he and Eisner visited them together. Their wives were also best friends and the families lived close to each other in Beverly Hills.

Eisner and Gordon also had a close and successful business relationship: Gordon had an ongoing production deal at Paramount and one of the most desirable offices on the studio lot. The relationship had yielded spectacular profits for Paramount with the smash hit *48 Hrs.*, starring a young Eddie Murphy in his feature film debut, directed by Walter Hill, and produced by Gordon. But the experience on *48 Hrs.*, as well as earlier difficulties on *The Warriors*, foreshadowed future problems. Two weeks into filming, after Eisner and Jeffrey Katzenberg saw the early footage, they met with Gordon and Hill.

Both Eisner and Katzenberg insisted that "Eddie Murphy isn't funny, and we have to replace him."

"Who in the hell do you think is funnier?" Gordon retorted.

The producer and director held their ground, and Eisner let the production continue. Even after *48 Hrs.* grossed $76 million and made Murphy an instant movie star, the ill will persisted between Hill and Eisner. It didn't help that Eisner and Katzenberg signed Murphy to an exclusive deal with Paramount that excluded Gordon and Hill. When Hill approached Gordon with his next project—a script he had written himself called *Streets of Fire*—Hill was still so upset over the Murphy incident that he refused to let Gordon submit the script to Paramount. "This is going to get me into terrible trouble at Paramount, especially with Michael," he told Hill. But the director was adamant.

Figuring it was better to break the news himself, Gordon called Eisner. "Look, I know you've heard about this, or you will hear about it," he said of the *Streets of Fire* deal. "I just want you to know that it's going to Universal and there's nothing I can do about it."

Eisner's tone was cold. "If you really wanted to, you could," he retorted. "You're just doing this for the money." Gordon tried to persuade Eisner that because Hill had the rights to his own script, he had no choice, but Eisner wouldn't relent. Gordon was furious, and refused to give Eisner the script.

Eisner had his staff get a copy, which told the story of a rock musician kidnapped by a biker gang. Eisner read it and said it was terrible. He was gleeful after he saw a preview and pronounced the film a mess. *Streets of Fire* was a critical and commercial flop. Gordon kept working at Paramount, and he didn't sense any hard feelings on Eisner's part.

Gordon brought to Eisner his next project, which was called *Brewster's Millions*. Eisner agreed that Gordon could direct it, as long as he worked for scale. Their lawyers started negotiating a deal, but kept running into obstacles. Paramount insisted on tight budget controls and the right to replace Gordon if he failed to meet a myriad of what he considered minor requirements. While Eisner insisted these were reasonable measures to protect the studio's investment in an unproven director, Gordon was again offended that after his long and successful track record as a producer, he could still be fired from his new project over technicalities. *Streets of Fire* was then in production at Universal, and Universal executives urged Gordon to do *Brewster's Millions* with them. But Gordon said no, he was still negotiating at Paramount.

As time passed with no resolution, Katzenberg called Gordon. It was a Friday afternoon, and Eisner was out of town. "What's happening with *Brewster's Millions*?" he asked. "We need to wrap this up. It's gone on too long. Just tell us, is this on or off? No hard feelings either way."

Gordon pondered this. "Jeffrey, are you telling me, whether I say yes or no, that nobody's going to be upset?"

"Absolutely not," Katzenberg replied. "Just make your decision."

"Okay then. The answer is no. I'm going to move on."

"Fine," Katzenberg said. "Good luck."

Eisner returned that night, and later that weekend, on Sunday afternoon, Eisner, his wife, Jane, and his father, Lester, walked the two blocks to Gordon's house to see him. Lester Eisner was recovering from open-heart surgery, and wanted to thank Gordon for recommending a surgeon at Cedars Sinai Hospital. Afterward, Gordon walked back with them. While he was at the Eisners', the phone rang, and Eisner answered. Gordon overheard his end of the conversation:

"What? Really? He did what?" There was silence, and then Eisner hung up. He glared at Gordon.

"I guess I'd better go," Gordon said.

"I'll drive you," Eisner said. It had begun to rain.

"Don't bother, I can walk," Gordon said, but Eisner insisted. They drove the short distance to Gordon's house, and as Gordon opened the car door, Eisner said, "I want you to know that this is the last time we'll ever speak. Jeffrey just told me what you did."

Gordon was stunned. "What did Jeffrey say?"

"I know what happened and I'm not going to discuss it."

"Let me tell you what happened."

"I'm never going to speak to you again," Eisner said.

Gordon got out of the car, slammed the door, and Eisner drove away.

Early the next morning, Gordon got a call from the Paramount lot. "The movers are here to get your things," a studio assistant told him. "Where should we send them?"

"You've got to be out of your mind," Gordon exclaimed. "Don't touch anything until I get there."

When he arrived, boxes were stacked outside his office. He called Paramount's lawyer to make the point that his contract said he could be removed from the lot only on ninety days' notice. The lawyer told him that Paramount didn't care what his contract said. Even though it was heresy for a producer to sue a movie studio, Gordon called his lawyer, went to court, and got an injunction barring Paramount from ejecting him.

Then Eisner banned Gordon from the Paramount commissary. He had the court overturn that, too. Gordon's contract guaranteed him an office, but it didn't say which one. He had to move from his luxurious quarters into a dark cramped space. He continued to come to work and eat in the commissary every day for the ensuing ninety-day period, just to make his point.

Eisner honored his vow of silence. When the two men showed up the next summer to visit their sons at Keewaydin, Eisner was standing at the end of a dock on the lake when he saw Gordon approach. Rather than risk an encounter, he dived into the water, still wearing his shoes.

Eisner avoided Gordon for two years, leaving restaurants if necessary, refusing to emerge from his house when Gordon came to pick up his sons. But the following summer, the two were again visiting their sons at Keewaydin, awkwardly trying to avoid each other, when a sudden rainstorm forced the scheduled family picnics into a small cabin. Pressed together in such close quarters, Gordon said to Eisner, "Either we should talk or we should go out into the woods and settle this thing once and for all." Eisner stared at him for a moment, then said, "Okay, when we're back in L.A., we can sit down and talk."

Eisner came over to Gordon's house. Minutes into the conversation, they were screaming at each other. "You fucked me on *Streets of Fire*," Eisner yelled.

"You'll never admit you were wrong," Gordon retorted.

After what seemed like hours of heated argument, they ran out of steam. Nothing was resolved. But they started talking about their kids, their careers. They started talking again on the phone, though the relationship was never what it had been.

Plenty of people had complaints about how difficult Eisner was to work with, but there was no arguing with success. Paramount's phenomenal track record attracted increasing media attention. After *Terms of Endearment* won five Academy Awards, Eisner and Diller were the subject of admiring profiles in *Newsweek*, *The Wall Street Journal*, and *BusinessWeek*. *New York* magazine ran a cover story on Eisner and Diller with the headline "Hollywood's Hottest Stars," written by Tony Schwartz. While the *New York* article was unsparing in its depiction of Eisner and Diller as tough people to work with ("Paramount is the studio that gives you a green light and then dares you to make the picture"), it also hailed it as "the leading studio in Hollywood . . . put simply, Paramount has figured out, better than any other studio, how to make the right movies." It was also one of the first articles to elevate studio executives to the level of stardom previously reserved for actors and directors.

"The one thing you cannot be bad at in this business is choosing material," Eisner told Schwartz. "Yes, it helps to keep your negative costs down, to keep away from the type and not to grab for stars and not to pay ridiculous prices. But you know what? If you pick the right material, all that pales. . . . It's great to have good marketing, and I think we have the best, but you don't need it to sell *E.T.*, and it won't help if you're selling *The Pirate Movie* [one of Paramount's rare critical and commercial flops]. This is a business based on ten to twelve decisions a year. They are very important. Nothing else is close." In other words, what really mattered were the creative decisions made by a studio executive, not the business or financial decisions that anyone with an MBA could figure out.

A quote from Don Simpson, then one of Paramount's most successful producers, responsible for such hits as *Flashdance*, captured the creative Eisner in action: "We went into a boardroom at nine in the morning. There were maybe eleven people in the room. At the time, we had absolutely nothing good in development, which is the real estate of this business. Eisner said,

'We're going to come up with twenty projects today even if we have to stay here until midnight. Leave if you want to, but then don't bother coming back.' Several people looked at him like he was crazy. But by 5:30, we had fifteen projects."

In one anecdote, Schwartz mentioned that he was at dinner with Barry Diller when Diller "casually" mentioned that he planned to stop in at a midnight screening to see how paying customers would react to *Indiana Jones*. Schwartz tagged along, and when they arrived at the theater, Eisner and his wife were already there. The next day, Schwartz got a call at his hotel from an unnamed "caller":

" 'I know you went to Westwood with Diller last night,' the caller told me. 'Did you realize Diller did that just to impress you? He never goes to check audiences. Eisner, on the other hand, is a maniac. He went to two more theaters after he left you. You're missing the story.' "

The "caller" was Michael Ovitz, founder of Creative Artists Agency, already influential but soon to become Hollywood's most powerful agent. Since the falling-out with Gordon, Ovitz had become Eisner's closest friend in Hollywood. Eisner had asked Ovitz to call Schwartz and plant the idea that Eisner was far more important to Paramount's success than Diller.

Ovitz and Eisner had met when Ovitz tried unsuccessfully to pitch a game show to Eisner while he was head of programming at ABC. Ovitz had annoyed Eisner by sending his wife a lavish bouquet of flowers, which Eisner interpreted as an inappropriate effort to influence his decision. Still, he grudgingly admired Ovitz's persistence, and Jane didn't mind the flowers. After the Eisners moved to Hollywood, the two families became close friends, dining regularly at the Palm and other restaurants favored by the Hollywood elite. Eisner often came to dinner straight from his office at Paramount, eager to complain about Barry Diller: Diller was a "horrible person," he was "immoral," and worst of all, "he doesn't even come to work until 11:00 A.M."

Along with the article about Eisner and Diller, *New York* ran a sidebar on Jeffrey Katzenberg, in which he was described as Diller's and Eisner's "golden retriever," a nickname that stuck. But there was no mention anywhere of Martin Davis, the chairman of Gulf+Western, Paramount's parent company. What Eisner had failed to grasp was that in Hollywood, there were times when the only thing worse than bad publicity was good publicity, especially when it slighted your boss. Davis was incensed over the article.

Eisner barely knew Davis, but he was a type of executive that Eisner had never confronted directly before. Davis took aim at anyone beneath him whose success seemed to pose any threat to his hold on power. He had long toiled in the shadow of Charles Bluhdorn, who had built Gulf+Western from an obscure sugar manufacturer into a force in mining, publishing (Simon & Schuster), and entertainment. Davis was brusque, unpolished, and often vulgar. He had a finance background and had little understanding of or respect for the creative process. After Bluhdorn suffered a fatal heart attack at his home in the Dominican Republic in 1983, Davis succeeded him. From his office atop the Gulf+Western building in New York, Davis badgered Diller to get rid of Eisner.

Davis also resented the attention that Katzenberg had garnered in the magazine. On a visit to New York, Katzenberg stopped in to meet Davis for the first time since he'd become chairman of Gulf+Western. Instead of the praise Katzenberg expected, Davis ventilated his hostility toward his Hollywood executives. "You're all overpaid and spoiled," he said. He told Katzenberg he was "a little Sammy Glick." After Katzenberg reported the bizarre encounter to Eisner, Eisner confronted Diller and demanded to know what was going on. Weary of the subterfuge he'd been maintaining, Diller told Eisner that Davis wanted him to fire Eisner. It was hard to believe, given Paramount's success. "Marty's an idiot, but it's true," Diller said.

Eisner talked to Katzenberg about forming a business partnership to produce movies and television, and the two even worked up a business plan. After years of working in Eisner's shadow, Katzenberg was thrilled that his mentor held him in such high regard. "Don't worry," Eisner told him. "Whatever happens, we're partners for life."

Several other possibilities were floating around—a move to CBS, or Capital Cities/ABC, for example—but moving back to television didn't excite Eisner. He and Ovitz strategized about a buyout of American International Pictures, which Eisner wanted to rename Hollywood Pictures. And then, while visiting his sons at Camp Keewaydin in August 1984, Eisner learned of Roy Disney's resignation from the Disney board, and called him. "Are you still interested in coming to Disney?" Roy asked when he returned Eisner's call.

During the 1980s, the era of swashbuckling corporate raiders, Roy E. Disney seemed like the last person to lead a boardroom coup or hostile takeover. Somewhat quiet and shy by nature, with a wry sense of humor, Roy rarely spoke at Disney board meetings. He and Eisner served together on the board of the California Institute of the Arts, a school founded and endowed by Walt and Roy O. (Walt's brother and Roy E.'s father). In those meetings, Eisner never heard Roy say a word. Though he bore a strong family resemblance to his uncle Walt and was the only male heir in the family, Roy had long ago been pushed aside in the Disney hierarchy in favor of Ron Miller, the handsome ex–football star who married Walt's daughter Diane. But Roy's gentle demeanor masked other qualities he'd inherited from his Disney ancestors: determination, persistence, and a strong, even stubborn, will.

After their respective marriages, both Walt and his brother Roy had been slow to conceive children. There was rejoicing in the two families when Roy Edward was born to Roy and Edna in 1930. (It is a somewhat confusing tradition in the Disney family to name sons after their fathers, but to choose a middle name that begins with their mother's initial, in this case "E.")

Roy was a quiet only child who loved books. Walt often read aloud to Roy, and acted out stories. Roy later said the studio's animated *Pinocchio* disappointed him because Walt's telling of the story had been more exciting and dramatic. "For Roy Edward," his father wrote to Roy's grandparents, "I can't think of anything he appreciates more than good story books. He loves that little Indian book you gave him while you were here. I am reading to him from 'The Swiss Family Robinson' a little bit at a time in the evenings. . . . He sits around and reads and is a fine little boy. He said the other day that he thinks Christmas is a 'fine idea.' "

Walt's and Lillian's daughter, Diane Marie, was born in 1933. The couple adopted another daughter, Sharon Mae, in 1936. Walt doted on his two daughters, as did their uncle Roy. In a 1938 letter to his parents, Roy O. wrote, "Gosh, it makes me jealous. I wish we had a little girl at our place, but I haven't been able to talk Edna into it as yet. I thought we might be able to go down and adopt one, if we could find one we could fall in love with. But I think my wife is having too good a time right now and hates to take on the added responsibility."

Old home movies show a young Roy E. frolicking in the backyard pool with his cousins Sharon and Diane, with their parents looking on fondly. When she was ten, Roy taught Diane how to dive. He and his cousins had the run of the Disney studio lot, riding their bikes through various stage sets. Roy loved to watch the animators at work in their cubicles in the animation building. He and his friends got to test-drive the miniature race cars that later appeared at Disneyland.

When Roy was ten, he received an HO-scale model railroad, which he put together in a toolshed behind the house. The next time Walt came over, Roy was eager to show it to his uncle, and the two disappeared into the toolshed for several hours. About a month later, Walt invited Roy to visit. "Come on out and see this," he told his nephew, leading him to a playhouse that Diane and Sharon had outgrown. Inside was an array of HO-scale model trains, with every accessory Roy had ever dreamed of.

Though the close bond between Walt and Roy and their families survived early hardship and near-bankruptcy, it suffered from the pressures of wealth, fame, and success. Walt and Lillian moved from the modest Hollywood bungalow next door to Roy and Edna, first to a larger home in Los Feliz Hills and then to an even larger one they had built on Carolwood Drive in Holmby Hills, an exclusive enclave wedged between Bel Air and Beverly Hills. Roy and Edna moved to the San Fernando Valley, to a spacious home in Toluca Lake. The Kansas-born Edna was famously thrifty and down-to-earth, always doing her own grocery shopping and employing a couple as housekeeper and gardener. Walt and Lillian had a household staff.

Still, Roy E. and his parents made regular visits to his uncle and aunt in Holmby Hills. Still fascinated by model trains but no longer content with HO-scale replicas, Walt had built a coal-fired steam railroad that wound through the five-acre property and traversed a small ravine. Walt had always loved the Central Pacific, so he used the CP logo and called his line the "Carolwood Pacific." The track ran 2,615 feet and included a 90-foot concrete-reinforced tunnel, which neighbors referred to as Los Angeles's longest bomb shelter. The cars and engine were one-eighth scale, and Walt had the coal custom-ground in Scranton, Pennsylvania, also to one-eighth scale. Whenever Roy came over, Walt had him wipe down and polish the cars and haul water for the steam engine. Other kids in the neighborhood—Candice Bergen and Nancy Sinatra among them—joined in the rides, with Walt driving the engine in an engineer's cap.

One afternoon when Roy was eighteen, the passenger cars derailed. Roy, who was tall and lanky, had been dragging his foot on the ground, kicking up dust and gravel, some of which landed on the track. The engine separated from the cars. Walt got off and stalked back to the youngsters. Roy could tell his uncle was angry because of his scowl and cocked eyebrow. Roy still had the incriminating foot on the ground. "I didn't mean to, Uncle Walt," Roy said.

Roy was sentenced to the barn for the rest of the afternoon.

The backyard railroad was the inspiration for the Disneyland steam-powered railroad, a centerpiece for the new theme park, which triggered the first serious breach between Walt and his brother Roy O. Walt wanted to retain personal ownership of the railroad, as well as a planned monorail, through a new company called WED, his initials. WED would also own all rights to the Walt Disney name, always a source of proprietary interest on Walt's part. Publicly traded Walt Disney Productions, in which Walt and Lillian held roughly a third of the shares, and Roy and Edna a fifth, would pay royalties to WED and Walt's salary of $153,000 a year to a personal services subsidiary, Retlaw ("Walter" spelled backward). Roy had never minded being out of the limelight, but he was skeptical about the Disneyland venture and strongly opposed to this potential conflict of interest. He was angered when Walt nearly hired an agent to aggressively champion Walt's interests. He was also surprised, since Walt had never seemed all that concerned with his personal wealth. He was particularly upset that Walt would now claim ownership of the Disney name. It had been bad enough when Walt insisted on changing the name of the company from Disney Brothers Productions to Walt Disney Productions to reflect his creative role. Even so, Roy grudgingly acquiesced rather than prompt a showdown with Walt.

But there was a new distrust that had never been there before. Even though Walt refused to join the board, saying it would distract him from the "real business" of the company, the brothers now vied for influence. Walt installed two personal allies—E. Cardon Walker, who handled advertising and public relations, and producer Bill Anderson—expressly to do his bidding. Employees at Disney were soon divided between "Walt men" and "Roy men."

Ten years later, with payments to Walt's WED and Retlaw soaring, and shareholders threatening a lawsuit (the board had never approved Walt's self-serving arrangements), Roy confronted Walt during a weekend the families spent together at Walt's Smoke Tree Ranch in Palm Springs. The moment the subject of WED was broached, the brothers boiled over. They yelled at each other the entire weekend. "Dammit, I want to be on a par with what other people are making in this industry, Roy," Walt yelled at one point. "If you don't do that, I'm going to leave."

Walt and Roy didn't speak for the next six months. Eventually, after contentious negotiations, Walt Disney Productions bought back WED from Walt, including the rights to use the Disney name, for $60 million. Walt gave Roy a wooden peace pipe, which he hung on his office wall. "It was wonderful to smoke the pipe of peace with you again," Walt wrote his brother. "The clouds that rise are very beautiful." Roy E. later inherited the pipe from his father, and keeps it in his office.

But the rift between the families never fully healed. The huge payment by Walt Disney Productions to Walt, which ended up making the Walt side of the family enormously wealthy, rankled throughout the Roy side. When Roy E. went to work for the company after graduating from nearby Pomona College, his father worried that Walt wouldn't treat his son as well as other employees.

Roy worked in the editing room on one of Walt's early nature documentaries, *The Vanishing Prairie*. They were viewing footage of ducks and geese returning in spring when Walt spotted a sequence in which a duck unwittingly lands on a still-frozen pond and tumbles over and over. "Where's the rest of this, where he hits the other ducks on the pond?" Walt asked. No one answered. "I know it's there somewhere," Walt said. "Roy, go find it."

Roy started poring through millions of feet of film negatives. He couldn't find it. "Where is that film?" Walt asked again at the next screening. Roy meekly said it didn't exist. Finally the director sent a crew to Minnesota where they staged a duck's landing into a group of ducks on a frozen lake, then incorporated the footage into *Vanishing Prairie*, accompanied by the sound of a bowling ball hitting pins. Walt loved it. "See, I told you you had that footage," Walt said. Roy suspected that Walt knew all along that they didn't. "Go find it" was Walt's way of saying "Go shoot the footage. Get this done."

To Roy, Walt's frequent criticism and impatience with him simply reflected how stingy Walt was with praise and how demanding he was with all his employees. When Roy finally got up the nerve to ask permission to make his own nature documentary, Walt agreed, and Roy produced *An Otter in the Family*. During a screening, Walt laughed out loud at one sequence, which Roy knew was high praise—and all that he'd get.

When Roy got married to his childhood neighbor Patty Dailey in 1955, Walt attended the wedding. "Great news! My nephew's marrying a girl with some spunk!" he said. In private, Walt complained that Roy lacked drive and ambition. After Walt complained to Card Walker that Roy would "never amount to anything," Walker dubbed him the "idiot nephew."

By the time Roy was making nature films, Walt had already transferred his plans for the next generation to his son-in-law, Ron Miller. After Miller married Diane in 1954, Walt had talked him into joining the company. Miller had fractured his nose and rib playing for the Los Angeles Rams, and afterward Walt came up to him. "Ron, if you play another year of football, you'll get killed out there and I'll have to raise those kids. Why not come work with me?"

Miller's first job was as a messenger, ferrying architectural plans for Disneyland from Burbank to Anaheim. Then Walt got him into the Directors Guild, and as an assistant director he directed Walt's lead-ins to the weekly Disney television show, which made him nervous. Walt was a chain smoker, and whenever his voice got hoarse Miller stepped in with a glass of water.

Diane recalled that her parents took an immediate liking to Miller. "Ron was very shy. He was not very articulate. He was kind of a fizzle at education," she recalled. But "I think Dad was thrilled with the way Ron came along and grasped" the business. "And actually, Ron had no training for anything else. He was like a blank notebook. Dad could take him and mold him in his pattern. I think the nicest thing I ever did for Dad was that through some quirk of fate I was able to marry a man who fit into Dad's dream."

Miller certainly looked the part: a trim six-foot-five, with dark hair, broad shoulders, blue eyes and a perpetual tan from his frequent golf outings. He and Diane owned the Silverado vineyard in the Napa Valley, a ski house in Aspen, and they and their seven children lived in John Wayne's former house in Encino. He drove a Rolls-Royce and the vintage white-and-gray Mercedes that had been Walt's favorite car.

Although Roy was the largest individual shareholder of Disney, with about 3 percent of the company's stock, the Walt side of the family, allied with Miller, controlled a total of about 11 percent, divided among Walt's widow Lillian, Diane and Sharon, and various trusts, which gave them effective control of the company. Now that Walker was chairman, it didn't help Roy's standing that his father had once tried to have Walker fired. Walker and Miller did little to conceal their low esteem for Roy, brushing aside his ideas for films and excluding him from any role in decisions.

For Roy, the breaking point came in 1977, a year after Miller was named to head the studio. Roy's lawyer and business partner, Stanley Gold, suggested that Roy leave the company, but continue as an independent producer for Disney. In contrast to the mild-mannered Roy, Gold was short, stocky, restless, filled with pent-up energy, and aggressive by nature. His weight fluctuated with his latest diet. He punctuated his speech with profanities. He'd grown up in modest circumstances in south-central Los Angeles, attended public school, Berkeley, and UCLA, and then law school at Oxford and the University of Southern California. When he joined the law firm of Gang, Tyre & Brown as a new associate, he was assigned to work with Frank Wells, one of whose clients was Roy Disney, a former classmate of Wells at Pomona College.

After Wells left the firm to help run Warner Bros., responsibility for Roy's interests descended to Gold. Though Gold bore little resemblance to the polished Wells, Roy recognized in him qualities that he himself lacked.

Gold's first deal for Roy was the acquisition of a ranch in Oregon with Peter Dailey, Patty Disney's brother, and their children. Gradually Gold expanded his work for Roy, eventually forming Shamrock Holdings to manage Roy's assets. Soon Roy was confiding in Gold, not just about financial matters such as Disney's faltering share price, but also his worries about Miller and the studio.

Roy and Gold met with Walker to discuss Roy's departure and to seek approval for a modest production deal. "What do you want to do, Roy," Walker asked sarcastically. "Make *Deep Throat?*"

Roy sat in shocked silence at this mention of pornography. Gold jumped in. "We're just trying not to do *The Love Bug* for the fifteenth time," referring to Disney's 1968 film about a Volkswagen Beetle named Herbie—the last time the studio had a hit.

Roy had always known that Walker didn't like or respect him; he knew that he was the one who had dubbed him the "idiot nephew." But he didn't understand why Walker had to insult him.

On March 4, 1977, the forty-seven-year-old Roy resigned from the company bearing his name with a letter expressing his frustrations. "The creative atmosphere for which the Company has so long been famous and on which it prides itself has, in my opinion, become stagnant," he wrote. "I do not believe it is a place where I, and perhaps others, can realize our creative capacities. Motion pictures and the fund of new ideas they are capable of generating have always been the fountainhead of the Company; but present management continues to make and remake the same kind of motion pictures, with less and less critical and box office success. . . . The Company is no longer sensitive to its creative heritage. Rather, it has substituted short-range benefits . . . for long-range creative planning."

When news of his resignation broke, Roy received hundreds of calls from people curious to know his plans, including one from Michael Eisner. Since he knew him slightly from the CalArts board, Roy returned the call, using the number at the Middlebury Inn that Eisner had left.

By 1984, Disney was ripe for a hostile takeover. Disney stock, after hitting a high of $123 in 1973, a year after Disney World opened in Florida, had plunged after the Arab oil embargo and by 1984 was still hovering at just $50. Though Walker had nominally retired in 1982, ceding his chief executive position to Miller, he kept his office, remained chairman of the board, and blocked nearly every innovation Miller and other executives proposed.

When they wanted to raise the price of parking at Disneyland from a ridiculously low $1 per car, Walker vetoed the move. "The parking lot is the first thing the guest sees," he argued. "Walt wanted them to think that this is the greatest place on earth." Likewise the admission price couldn't be touched. "We have to keep our prices low," Walker argued, "so that guests feel they've gotten good value."

At the same time, costs at the theme parks were soaring. Another of Walt's late visions—the Epcot theme park at Disney World in Florida—had cost $1.2 billion, three times the estimate, even after Walt's original concept of a domed city that would be a "living blueprint of the future" had been whittled down to little more than a perpetual world's fair, at a time when an increasingly sophisticated public had wearied of world's fairs. The 1981 world's fair in Knoxville, Tennessee, was such a flop that the concept had all but died. Roy refused to attend Epcot's grand opening in October 1982.

One reason the Disney live action studio hadn't had a hit since *The Love Bug* was because Walker did not believe in marketing and advertising. *Tron,* an expensive, computer-generated science fiction picture, opened a few weeks after *E.T.: the Extraterrestrial* and *Annie.* The competing studios were spending a then astronomical $10 million each on advertising and marketing campaigns. Walker refused to raise the minuscule marketing budget, citing Walt's adage that the only publicity worth the money was free. When *Tron* finished its opening weekend in a dismal sixth place, Walker still refused to increase advertising, insisting that word of mouth would come to the rescue. Much of the $17 million cost had to be written off.

Disney was also hobbled by its increasingly outdated notion of "family" fare, which had hardly budged in the face of the civil rights movement, the women's movement, the decline of the nuclear family, and a soaring divorce rate. Disney would not produce an R-rated film. The same year as *Tron,* the lewd, ostentatiously sophomoric *Porky's* grossed $70 million. Walker vowed that if audiences didn't want the wholesome G-rated family fare identified with Disney, then the company simply wouldn't make feature films. In 1983, the studio released only three pictures.

As the ultimate arbiter of "what Walt would have done," Walker's influence was pervasive. But Miller had been trying to break out of the creative straitjacket by carving out another brand name, Touchstone Pictures, for riskier adult-oriented fare. In 1962, he and Diane had watched *To Kill a Mockingbird* with Walt and Lillian at their home screening room. When it was over, everyone was moved, and Walt said, "I wish I could make movies like that." Even Walt had felt constrained by the Disney brand. As he put it in one outburst, "I've worked my whole life to create the image of what 'Walt Disney' is. It's not me. I smoke, and I drink, and all the things that we don't want the public to think about." Miller had vowed that someday he would make adult films at Disney.

Walker had resisted for years. "We have our image," he insisted. But once Miller was chief executive, he'd relented. Miller established Touchstone, and tried to bring in some new blood to run it. His first choice was Michael Eisner.

Given his success at Paramount and the attendant publicity, Eisner was an obvious candidate for just about any studio but Disney, which had traditionally resisted hiring outsiders. But Eisner already had two projects under way at Paramount that he'd persuaded Disney to co-finance: a musical version of *Popeye* directed by Robert Altman and starring Robin Williams, and a medieval fantasy epic, *Dragonslayer*. Both were troubled projects that ended up losing money. Still, Miller liked Eisner, thought he had a good sense of humor and creative instincts, and asked him and Jane to join him and Diane for dinner at Ma Maison, home to celebrity chef Wolfgang Puck. Diane found Eisner charming, if a little overeager, like a puppy. Afterward they were standing outside, waiting for their cars. Eisner got a grin on his face and leaned toward Diane. "There's something I've been wanting to ask you," Eisner said. "Is he . . ."

Diane cut him off. "I know what you're going to ask, and no. Dad isn't frozen." She couldn't believe Eisner would ask her about the rumor that her father's corpse had been used for an experiment in cryogenics, which she considered as credible as reports that Elvis was alive. In fact, she told Eisner, Walt had been cremated after dying of lung cancer in 1966.

Despite that jarring note, it was a pleasant evening. Miller liked Eisner, too. They had several subsequent meetings, and Miller suggested that Eisner come to Disney to run motion pictures and television. "Ron," Eisner responded, "I'm bigger than you right now at Paramount. I make three times as many pictures and do really well. So if I come here, I want to be president and chief operating officer. You could be chairman and chief executive. I'd work for you."

Miller seemed to like the idea; Walker was planning to step down as chairman the following year. But he realized it would be tough to sell Card Walker on the idea that an outsider could be COO of Disney. Several days later he called Eisner to report that Walker had objected. "You don't know the theme parks."

"You can handle the parks," Eisner suggested. Miller suggested they meet with Walker.

When Eisner arrived, Miller and Walker had just been arguing about *Splash*, the first live-action film from Touchstone. While *Splash* was hardly another *To Kill a Mockingbird*, Miller also had in development more serious fare, like *Country*, with Jessica Lange, and *The Journey of Natty Gann*, with John Cusack.

But *Splash*, produced by a young Brian Grazer and directed by Ron Howard, was certainly breaking new ground for Disney. It starred Daryl Hannah as a voluptuous mermaid. Even though long blond tresses artfully concealed Hannah's naked breasts, rumors about the film and its subject matter had triggered anxiety among board members. Finally Walker had called Miller. "I'm hearing a lot of things about *Splash*. Can I see it?"

"Sure," Miller replied. After the screening, Walker called Miller into his office.

"That's one hell of a film," Walker said. "Now, if we just take out six or seven scenes . . ."

Miller was exasperated. "Card, you just don't get it."

Miller mentioned his frustrations to Eisner, shaking his head at Walker's reaction. When Walker joined the meeting, the atmosphere still seemed tense. Walker seemed amenable to the idea of hiring Eisner as president, but his demeanor was nonetheless cool. After they firmed up the terms of his potential employment, Walker said with a note of disdain in his voice, "I suppose your kind of people would need a press release." Eisner stared at him. Was "your kind of people" a reference to Eisner's being Jewish? Disney had long been rumored to harbor a streak of anti-Semitism. But Eisner thought not. Rather, he sensed that to Walker, Eisner represented "Hollywood," the studio culture from which Disney had always stood apart. To Walker, Hollywood was filled with people who were vulgar, publicity-seeking, and flashy, whatever their religion or lack thereof.

"You are a public company," Eisner replied, "so yes, you will need a press release."

When he left the meeting, he told his wife, "I don't think they're ready for me."

This, at least, is the version of events Eisner later published in his autobiography (and recounted in interviews with me). Ron Miller, however, maintains that this account is "fiction," and says that Eisner never met with Walker, and that Walker never said anything about a press release or made any reference to "your people." The rest of the account, he says, roughly corresponds to events that Miller described to Eisner on the phone.

Whether or not the meeting Eisner described ever occurred, Walker finally gave in to Miller's arguments on Eisner's behalf. They summoned a business affairs executive to iron out the details. "We're calling Eisner right now and we're making him president and COO," Miller announced.

The executive was shocked. "You can't do that. You've got to give that job to somebody from within."

Walker slammed his fist down on his desk. "That's it," he said. "We're not doing it."

After Eisner and Jane arrived home, the phone rang. "It's not going to work," a dejected Miller said. "Card said, 'We can't do this.' "

Miller felt vindicated when *Splash* opened in March 1984 and was a big hit, grossing more than $69 million, a new Disney record for a live-action film. But it was too late to change the perception of Disney as undervalued and badly managed. The same day that *Splash* opened in theaters, Roy Disney sent a short letter to the company marked personal and confidential: "I hereby resign as a director of Walt Disney Productions." He and Stanley Gold had decided to wage a campaign to take control of Disney from outside the boardroom.

Less than three weeks later, corporate raider Saul Steinberg revealed that he owned more than 6 percent of Disney's shares and planned to buy up to 25 percent, formally putting Disney "in play," and vulnerable to a hostile takeover. After the board bought off Steinberg by paying him "greenmail," and Disney shares plunged, Roy raised his holdings to more than 5 percent. As rumors circulated that Roy himself might make a takeover bid or mount a proxy fight to oust management and directors, Walker, Miller, and Ray Watson (another board member) finally concluded that they had to make some kind of peace with the annoying "idiot" nephew they had so long dismissed as ineffectual. They agreed that Roy could return as a board member of Disney and bring with him two allies, Gold and Roy's brother-in-law, Peter Dailey. Roy would be granted the title of vice chairman of the board. Now Roy and his allies would have three of the board's eleven seats—not a majority, certainly, but enough, they thought, to make a difference.

Gold subsequently met with Miller to discuss finding a position for Roy at the studio, as well as a top job for Frank Wells. "Ron, you've got to get some help," Gold said.

"I'm attempting to," Miller said. He had again called Eisner, and said he was trying to resurrect the deal where Eisner would join Disney as COO. This time Eisner was promising to bring Katzenberg with him, too. "I've been having conversations with Michael Eisner and we're very close to making a deal."

"Do it," Gold said.

But the next day, Gold called him back. "Ron, don't sign Michael yet. Just hold off on that."

Miller assumed Gold was trying to delay so he could keep maneuvering on behalf of Wells. Miller called Eisner the same day. "They're trying to push Frank down my throat," Miller told him.

"Who needs a Frank Wells?" Eisner replied.

But time was running out for Miller. With other corporate raiders accumulating Disney shares and a takeover threat still looming, Gold argued forcefully that the best takeover defense was new management. Miller didn't help matters by separating from Diane over an affair with another woman. It was hardly an endorsement of Disney's much-vaunted family values, and although Miller and Diane subsequently reconciled, it cost Miller the support of Lillian, his mother-in-law, and the Walt side of the family at a critical juncture. When Walker finally retired as chairman, the title went not to Miller, but to Ray Watson, a real estate developer who had advised Walt on Disney World and who had little experience in the movie business. On August 17, the board named a committee of outside directors to review the company's current management. Seemingly oblivious to the fact that he would be the target of the committee's scrutiny, Miller endorsed the idea.

After the meeting ended, it fell to outside director Philip Hawley, chairman of the Los Angeles department store chain Carter Hawley Hale and a personal friend of both Ron's and Diane's, to break the news to Miller that it was an all-but-foregone conclusion that the committee would be asking for his resignation. Miller was stunned. He left the room, then returned with Ray Watson, whom he considered an ally. Miller asked if what Hawley had said were true. Neither Watson nor Hawley said anything. Then Miller broke down and cried.

"What should I do?" he asked, once he'd collected himself.

"I think you ought to get a lawyer to protect your interests," Watson said, "because you're too good-hearted a guy, Ron."

After returning from Vermont and the phone conversation with Roy Disney, Eisner met with Stanley Gold and Frank Wells at Gold's home in Beverly Hills on a Sunday evening. It was Wells who had suggested they approach

Eisner about coming to Disney. "Whatever else you do, get Michael Eisner," Wells had told Gold. "He ought to be running that company. He's hot. He's got a track record. You do everything to get him, and I'll help."

Gold said that what he had in mind was for both Wells and Eisner to join the company, Wells as the top business executive, Eisner the creative head of the company. Just how this would work wasn't clear. After his experience under Diller at Paramount, Eisner didn't want another number two job. But Wells indicated he wouldn't mind reporting to Eisner. While Eisner said he'd be enthusiastic about coming to Disney as chief executive, he alluded to recent articles in the *Los Angeles Times* that suggested that the reporter, Kathryn Harris, had a source in the boardroom. Eisner strongly suspected that Gold had been leaking to the press. He warned them that he would not tolerate boardroom leaks in any company where he was in charge. "I want you to give me your word, Stanley, that you will never breach the secrecy of board deliberations." Gold said that was fine with him, and in any event he denied being Harris's source.

Ray Watson had initially been cool to the idea of Eisner, but Gold worked hard to sell him on the combination of Eisner and Wells. Still, there was resistance from some board members who wanted a more seasoned industry veteran like Dennis Stanfill, former head of Twentieth Century Fox. Eisner met with Watson two weeks later to seek his support. He felt comfortable with the unassuming, even-tempered Watson, who managed by consensus. The two discussed their mutual interest in architecture, and Eisner stressed what an impression *Pinocchio* had made on him when he took Jane and his son Breck to see it at a Bronx, New York, drive-in. "You guys are ripe to be turned around in movies and television," Eisner told Watson. "You're in the same position that Paramount was when I started there, and ABC before that. There are enormous opportunities to ramp up production. The Disney brand name is still a unique, largely untapped asset."

The next day, Wells called Eisner to report on his own meeting with Watson. Watson had been cool to the idea of co-chief executives, so Wells had stepped aside in Eisner's favor. "You need creativity more than anything else," Wells had told Watson. To Eisner, he said, "I think you've got the job." In the cutthroat world of Hollywood, it made a deep impression on Eisner that Wells would sacrifice the top job on his behalf.

Watson wrote his fellow board members that hiring someone with Eisner's reputation and track record "would instantly provide us with the substance and image to show to the world we mean business when we say we are going to turn this company around," and by doing so, ward off any more hostile takeover offers. A few days later, Watson called Eisner to tell him the board was meeting the next day to remove Miller, and that he would recommend that Eisner replace him. Watson would stay on for the time being as chairman, which was fine with Eisner as long as he was named sole chief executive.

Marty Davis, Eisner's boss at Gulf+Western, was visiting Los Angeles that same week, and the next day he summoned Eisner to discuss his Paramount contract. Before Davis could begin, Eisner said, "I think I'm about to be offered the job as president and CEO of Disney." It was satisfying to be able to turn the tables on Davis like that, after all the bad things he'd heard from Diller. Davis was obviously surprised. "I won't stand in your way" was all he said.

As Eisner was meeting with Davis, Miller appeared before Roy, Gold, and other members of the Disney board at the studio, knowing that he was about to be formally relieved of his position. "Don't you have something to say to me?" he said. "Aren't you men?"

Silence was the only reaction.

"I'm very disappointed in this," Miller continued. "I've given my life to this company. I've never worked anywhere else. I've made progress with this company. I think I've taken great strides in leading it as far as it has come. I feel like this is a betrayal." Miller glared at Roy in particular, who as usual said nothing. Then he turned to Gold. "Don't you have anything to say, Stanley? You talk so much all the time. You're really the ringleader of this." Gold, too, remained silent. Then Miller left, and the board voted unanimously to ask for his resignation.

With Watson's memo recommending Eisner on the table before them, the directors turned to the issue of Miller's replacement. Gold expected Watson to promptly nominate Eisner and for the board to confirm him. Instead, director Phil Hawley proposed a screening committee to consider a wide range of candidates, adding that it was essential that Miller's replacement have "corporate experience," a pointed reference to the fact that Eisner had never run a business on his own. "Okay," Watson said. "Fine." Gold was stunned. The old guard had turned the tables yet again.

At Paramount, Eisner waited for the call from Watson. As the hours passed, his confidence waned. Finally, late in the afternoon, Wells called. "How do you feel?"

"How should I feel?"

"Hasn't anyone called you?" Wells broke the news that Miller had been fired, but no successor had been named. Eisner had a sinking feeling. He regretted having spoken to Davis. He hung up, left the studio, and drove to see Gold at the Shamrock offices. "He doesn't have the guts to call you," Gold said, saying that Watson had meekly accepted Hawley's proposal. "No decision was made on you."

"What do you mean?" Eisner asked, incredulous. "Last night Ray told me I was in."

"I don't know what Ray told you, but it's not done. The fat lady hasn't sung the last aria."

That evening, Eisner attended a dinner in Davis's honor at Diller's house. It was a bitter pill, having to pay homage to the man he thought he'd vanquished that very morning. To make matters even more precarious, Diller took Eisner aside to confide that he was leaving Paramount to take the top job at Fox. When Diller's news broke the next week, Davis summoned Eisner and Katzenberg to New York.

After having told Davis about the Disney offer, Eisner hardly expected to be offered Diller's position. Still, it was a shock when, after they arrived in New York, Katzenberg called him at his hotel at 2:00 A.M. The next day's *Wall Street Journal* had just been delivered to Katzenberg's hotel, and in it was an article reporting that Frank Mancuso, Paramount's head of marketing, would replace Diller as chairman. It quoted Davis at some length discussing his unhappiness with Paramount's "market share" and failure to place more new television shows on network schedules. Eisner realized that he was about to be fired.

When he met with Davis at noon the next day, a press release announcing his "resignation" had already been prepared. Eisner had brought along a copy of his contract, which provided incentive compensation and the forgiveness of the loan on his house in the event that he was not offered Diller's job if Diller left, a total of $1.55 million. In his eagerness to be rid of him, Davis readily agreed, saying he just needed Eisner to sign off on the press release. Eisner refused. "I want the check for what I'm owed," Eisner said.

"I can't get a check on such short notice," Davis insisted.

"That's ridiculous," Eisner said. "I'll be back in an hour." He walked out.

Twenty minutes later, Eisner had his check, and approved the press release. He left the building and walked across town to the Park Avenue headquarters of Chemical Bank, where he and his parents had long done their banking. He deposited the check and demanded that it be credited immediately to his account, rather than wait for it to clear. He worried that Davis would try to void the check before it cleared.

The next day, Eisner and Jane returned to Los Angeles on the short-lived luxury airline Regent Air. *New York* magazine's Tony Schwartz had been tipped that Eisner and his wife were flying back to Los Angeles, and he managed to reserve the seat across the aisle from Eisner. Eisner had liked Schwartz's earlier article, and after only brief hesitation, decided to unburden himself. The result was a sequel called "Son of Hollywood's Hottest Stars: Behind the Quake at Paramount That Rocked the Business."

Eisner soon experienced firsthand the fate of deposed studio heads. Michael Ovitz was at Eisner's home one evening when Eisner called Morton's restaurant to book a table, only to be told that nothing was available. "Let me call," Ovitz said, and quickly secured a reservation for Eisner.

"In Hollywood, you're only as good as your job," Eisner commented, sounding dejected.

He didn't intend to stay unemployed for long, and immediately began strategizing with Stanley Gold to resurrect the Disney possibility. Gold's solution to the Disney board's reservations about Eisner's business acumen was to reintroduce Wells, who was a lawyer and had more solid business credentials. Eisner still rebuffed the idea of sharing power as a co-CEO, but he could live with an arrangement where he was chairman and CEO, Wells was president and COO, and both reported directly to the board. Gold got Sid Bass on a speakerphone and Eisner made his case.

"Companies like Disney are always founded by creative entrepreneurs," Eisner began, "but eventually the founder dies or gets pushed out, or moves on to something else. Inevitably the businesspeople take over—the managers—and they focus on preserving the vision that made the company great in the first place. They don't have any creative ideas themselves and they end up surrounding themselves instead with analysts and accountants to try to control the creative people and cut costs. In the process, they discourage change and new initiatives and reinvention. In time, the company begins to ossify and atrophy and die. It's important to have financial parameters and never to bet the house, which is how we always protected Paramount. But in a creative business you also have to be willing to take chances and even to fail sometimes, because otherwise nothing innovative is ever going to happen. If you're only comfortable running a business by the numbers, I can understand that. But then you shouldn't get involved with a creatively driven company like Disney."

When Eisner finished, there was a brief pause, and then Bass spoke. "You're right. We're with you."

Support from the company's largest shareholders was hardly decisive with the board, but it certainly helped; now Gold and Roy could threaten a credible proxy fight to replace the board members. To drive home the point, the Basses bought virtually all the Disney shares that came on the market, increasing their stake from 5.5 to 8.6 percent within a week.

Eisner also reached out to Walt's side of the family, especially Miller, with whom he felt he had a good relationship stemming from Miller's attempt to hire him. After winning the support of the Basses, Eisner stopped by the Millers' house in Encino. Miller was sitting in the backyard, suddenly unemployed, with nothing to do and nowhere to go. He greeted Eisner, who said he was hoping to get the Disney family's support.

"What are they offering you?" Miller asked.

"My salary is the same as yours," Eisner replied ($500,000 a year).

"Stock?"

"Five hundred thousand shares."

Miller was stunned. In his tenure at the company, Miller had been awarded a total of just 25,000 shares. "Michael, they'll never give it to you," he said—500,000 shares was astronomical.

"Well, you've got to start somewhere." Miller was amazed at Eisner's audacity.

"So, do I have your support?" Eisner asked.

"You know what, Michael?" Miller said. "You don't need it."

The key holdout was ex–chief executive Card Walker, who was on a fishing trip in Arizona. Walker was still hostile to Roy and his ally Gold, so Wells flew there to meet him. He proved the perfect emissary for the conservative Walker. Walker was no more enamored now of Eisner than he had been before, but he could see the writing on the wall. "I guess we bet on the wrong horse," his wife had told Patty Disney, referring to Walker's earlier support of Miller. Now Wells stressed that if he and Eisner prevailed, and Walker supported them, he could keep his board seat and its perquisites—trips on the company planes, events at the theme parks, openings, screenings, and, of course, director's fees. Walker not only agreed to support him and Eisner, he volunteered to give the nominating speech to the board.

Wells called Roy from the plane on the way home. "Bingo!" he said.

The board met on September 22, 1984. Eisner invited his friends Larry Gordon and Michael Ovitz to await the final decision with him and Jane. The group made nervous small talk. Finally the phone rang at noon. "Congratulations," Gold told him. "You got it."

"We should open a bottle to celebrate," Ovitz said. "Don't you have some champagne?"

Eisner turned to his wife. "Where is that bottle we got for Christmas?" He left and returned with a bottle of red wine. As Eisner started to open it, Ovitz interrupted him, "Wait! Let me see that." It was a 1982 Château Pétrus. "You can't just open this and drink it," he said. "You have to let it breathe."

Eisner rolled his eyes and pulled the cork.

With Gordon and Ovitz still in the room, Eisner called his lawyer, Irwin Russell, to finalize an employment agreement. "I don't care about salary," Eisner told Russell. "Just get me all the stock and options that you can."

Russell and Disney arrived at a pay package that was even more lucrative than what Eisner had described to Miller: a base salary of $750,000 plus a signing bonus in the same amount; an annual bonus of 2 percent of any profit Disney earned in excess of $100 million (the most Disney had ever earned in a single year); and options to buy 510,000 shares of Disney at $57 a share, its current price. As Eisner had wished, it was the options that made the contract so potentially rich.

That afternoon, Eisner and Wells joined the board for a lunch hosted by Roy at Lakeside Golf Club. Toward the end of the meal, Eisner turned to Roy. "Now that this is all over, what would you like to do?" Roy hadn't given his future role at Disney much thought, but on impulse he said, "Why not let me have animation? It's an arcane thing for you people, and I know the process and the people."

"Great," Eisner said. He and Wells had been talking about shutting down animation, but if Roy wanted it, fine.

That evening, Gold and his wife hosted a small celebratory dinner at his home on Alpine Drive in Beverly Hills. The Eisners and the Wellses were there, along with Roy, Patty, and an investment banker who had advised Shamrock. Everyone was in a festive mood, though not everyone loved the Italian grappa that was Gold's favorite aperitif. Eisner had never met Roy's wife before, and in contrast to the understated Roy, he found her to be acerbic, outspoken, and effervescent. Patty made it clear that it was her decision as much as Roy's to force a management change at Disney, and he made a mental note not to underestimate her, or Roy, for that matter.

As the dinner concluded, Gold made a toast to new management. Wells handed out elegant Mickey Mouse watches engraved with September 22, 1984, the date of the pivotal board meeting. "Thank you," he said to Roy and Gold. "We know you're responsible for our being here."

"Anytime we disappoint you, just tell me," Eisner added. "You got me this job. I'll never forget it. If I ever lose your confidence, let me know, and I'll resign."

TWO

Jeffrey Katzenberg was so eager to begin work at Disney that he'd started meeting with Eisner and Wells the same weekend they got their jobs. These weekend sessions to plot strategy continued, usually at Wells's house, even while Katzenberg was nominally still working at Paramount. And Eisner continued to advise Katzenberg on projects still under way at Paramount. Eisner had committed Paramount to a biblical epic, *King David*, starring Richard Gere as David and directed by Bruce Beresford. Katzenberg was now shepherding the production. Three weeks into filming, Katzenberg sent Eisner the dailies.

Eisner called Katzenberg as soon as he saw them. "What's going on?" he asked.

"What do you mean?" Katzenberg replied.

"Why is Richard Gere wearing a dress and earrings?"

"That's what Bruce said they looked like," Katzenberg explained, referring to the ancient Hebrews.

"I don't see David in a dress," Eisner said. He felt vindicated when *King David* failed at the box office.

But what happened at Paramount was rapidly fading in importance to Eisner. At the weekend strategy sessions, Disney officials not already earmarked for dismissal were summoned to make presentations, among them Stan Kinsey, a young vice president in charge of operations, finance, and new technology. Kinsey, a Stanford Graduate School of Business graduate and Goldman Sachs alumnus, was a golden boy of the previous regime; Miller liked his golf game and had personally sponsored his admission into the exclusive Bel Air Country Club. But the new executives seemed impressed by Kinsey's aggressive plan to reduce the studio's overhead by 30 percent.

Kinsey was also eager to share a more important project he had under way involving a new technology operation that was an offshoot of George Lucas's Industrial Light & Magic, the *Star Wars* director's special effects operation outside San Francisco. He'd been at the Disney animation building one afternoon the year before when three engineers—Lem Davis, Dave Wolf, and Mark Kimball—took him aside. "Can we show you something?" they'd asked quietly. They took him into a darkened room and showed him a computer screen displaying a boat that had been computer generated in vector form. There was no color, but the drawing was almost three-dimensional. "Can we get $12,000 to buy one of these vector graphics machines?" they asked.

"What do the animators think?" Kinsey asked.

"They love it," the engineers said.

"Then why aren't you asking for $12 million?"

Kinsey went into high gear. He'd been a Stanford classmate of Scott McNealy, chief executive of Sun Microsystems, and he called McNealy for advice about workstations that could handle computer animation. McNealy directed him to George Lucas. Kinsey, the engineers, and animator John Lasseter flew to San Francisco to visit Lucas's operation. They were thrilled by the technology—not just that it replaced painstaking human labor, but that the results were so rich, both in color and dimension. The results could be every bit as good as in the golden age of Disney animation, an era that had been lost to prohibitive labor and camera costs. After looking at other computer animation labs around the country, Kinsey and his team zeroed in on Lucas's operation.

Card Walker had balked at the notion that a machine could replace hand drawing. But now Kinsey had another chance. He started to explain how computer technology could replicate the kind of animation that required seventeen cameramen for the opening scene of *Pinocchio*. He was disappointed when Wells cut him off. "We're going to shut down animation," he said bluntly. "It's not making any money." New management seemed far more interested in his plan to cut costs, and Kinsey didn't think the name of the operation he was working with even registered: Pixar Advanced Computer Graphics.

On the Monday after that weekend meeting, Kinsey was at his desk when Katzenberg, still at Paramount, called. "I'm a first impression kind of guy," Katzenberg said, dispensing as usual with preliminaries. "I've never been so blown away by somebody at a first meeting. We're going to take this studio to twenty movies a year. In four years we're going to be the number one studio at the box office." Then he hung up. The call had lasted no more than thirty seconds, but it was electrifying. Disney was barely in the movie business at all and Katzenberg was predicting they'd be number one! What a change from the old regime, Kinsey thought.

Wells, too, was impressed by Kinsey, and started inviting the young executive to join him in his office at the end of the day. Wells would typically open a bottle of wine, pour two glasses, then pick Kinsey's brain about Disney personnel and operations. One evening Kinsey was in Wells's office when George Lucas called. "Is there anyone there worth keeping?" Lucas asked.

"He's sitting right here," Wells replied, smiling at Kinsey. It almost seemed too good to be true.

Though it seemed a foregone conclusion, Katzenberg still had to close a deal to join Eisner and Wells at Disney. Wells rented one of the storied bungalows at the Beverly Hills Hotel as a way to impress Katzenberg, and Katzenberg came to the meeting armed with a hastily scribbled "wish list" for his new job as chairman of the Walt Disney Studio. As opposed to Disney's longstanding frugality, the list was larded with Hollywood status symbols, circa 1984: "2 secy's, beach house, corporate jet, travel-family-etc., screening room, house maintenance? Butler?"

More important, Katzenberg asked for a stock-option package like the ones Eisner and Wells had gotten. "The board will never go for that," Wells insisted. But both Wells and Eisner agreed that Katzenberg both needed and deserved some kind of incentive compensation. So Wells offered Katzenberg an annual bonus amounting to 2 percent of any profit earned by anything he put into production, which would include live-action and animated films as well as television programs. In calculating profits, revenues would be included from "all forms of exploitation," which meant not just ticket sales and broadcast fees, but video, merchandise, and theme park attractions based on his productions. Moreover, whenever he retired or left the company for any reason, Katzenberg would be entitled to a lump sum payment of the estimated future value of his 2 percent profit interest.

Wells seemed proud of this plan, arguing to Katzenberg that the bonus would provide an annuity for his infant twin sons, while confiding to Eisner that he doubted the 2 percent bonus would ever amount to anything. Disney's film studio was largely living on the animated classics of the past. The Christmas release for that year was the 1940 film *Pinocchio*, only a modest success even in its original incarnation. Disney re-released an animated classic every seven years, an interval calculated to reach a new generation of children and parents. Then it was returned to the vault.

Even more than Eisner and Wells, Katzenberg's arrival at the Burbank campus lent a new sense of urgency to the revitalization of Disney. The partnership Katzenberg had envisioned with Eisner while still at Paramount was reconstituted, albeit with Katzenberg as a junior partner. Though they had rarely socialized outside the office, they began having dinner together every Monday night at Locanda Veneta, an Italian restaurant in Beverly Hills, when they were both in town. Katzenberg moved into an office in the animation building next to Eisner's.

One afternoon Katzenberg walked into the boardroom, where plans for the renovations of his new office had been laid out. Katzenberg glanced at the plans, and without acknowledging the presence of the architect, whom he'd never met, said, "Let's have a look at the office." They headed down the hall, and as they walked, the Disney executive in charge of the project said, "Jeffrey, maybe I can take this moment to introduce you to . . ." Before he could finish, Katzenberg thrust his arm up, his hand in the air. Without turning or altering his stride, he said, "We just met." Then he dropped his hand.

Despite the sometimes frenzied schedules and long hours, in the early months and years of the new regime management was surprisingly informal. Many of the best ideas surfaced at Eisner's Monday staff lunches, when the heads of the various divisions sat down together when they were in town. At some of the early meetings, division heads came prepared with the latest numbers and projections, prepared to be grilled by Eisner. So they were taken aback when he opened one meeting by stating "Today we're going to talk about whether Mickey and Minnie should get married." A scenario was developed in which the iconic mice would get engaged on Valentine's Day, shop for rings at Tiffany in April, get married in June and honeymoon in Paris, but the idea struck many as heresy, and Eisner dismissed it. Still, the episode showed Eisner's willingness, even eagerness, to challenge conventional wisdom. "Give me the idea you didn't want to embarrass yourself with," Eisner often suggested. "Give me the idea that you think is going too far," or, "What would you do if there was no budget?"

Stanley Gold's instinct that Eisner's and Wells's skills and personalities would complement each other proved correct. Eisner and Wells settled into a comfortable working relationship, with Wells shouldering most of the administrative burden of running the company and attending to financial affairs, while Eisner oversaw the creative aspects, from film and television production to the expansion of the theme parks.

Eisner and Wells wandered in and out of each other's offices at will, and Eisner felt he could trust Wells with any confidence. Wells was discreet, and from the beginning he never aspired to usurp Eisner or overshadow him. He was a natural manager and mediator, and when other executives had problems with Eisner, they went to Wells. "I'll take care of it," Wells would say, and almost invariably did.

The flurry of changes and the vote of confidence from the influential Basses made an impression on Wall Street. Just one month into Eisner's tenure, Disney stock had surged. One afternoon Eisner got a call from the ever-competitive Barry Diller. Referring to Eisner's stock options, he asked, "Is it really true you've made $3 million on paper?"

"I guess so," Eisner replied, as if he himself had trouble believing it.

The only major division making money when Eisner and Wells arrived was theme parks, under the leadership of Richard Nunis, the only other member of management besides Walker and Miller to hold a board seat. Nunis and other parks executives gave Eisner and Wells walking tours of both Disneyland in Anaheim and Walt Disney World in Florida during their first weeks at the company. On the visit to Disney World, Eisner brought along Ovitz and his family for moral support. Afterward, Ovitz wrote Eisner an effusive thank-you note, stressing "how much we love your family and enjoy your friendship."

While Eisner had complete confidence in his ability to manage the movie and television business, he knew little about theme parks. Just as he had never seen a Disney animated film as a child, Eisner had never been taken to Disneyland. He'd been to Walt Disney World just once with his own children, though they'd been to Disneyland several times. Eisner knew that the shadow of Walt hovered over the theme parks more than any other division in the company. Disneyland had been Walt's idea; he had pursued it even over Roy O.'s objections, and it mirrored Walt's idea of a utopian escape from the real world that would appeal to adults as well as children. The parks were amazingly clean; "cast members," so named by Walt, were clean-cut, friendly, and helpful, every aspect of their appearance and demeanor regulated by a detailed handbook; everything was beautiful but not quite real. Park employees for the most part exhibited an almost fanatical and genuine devotion to preserving Walt's dream, an attitude cultivated in the intensive two-week orientation that included appearing in one of the parks as a character.

No tradition was more hallowed than Walt's habit of personally picking up any scrap of paper or refuse that he detected on his frequent visits to Disneyland. Walt was obsessed by cleanliness at the parks, and it was a tradition among executives to compete with one another to spot trash and pick it up. Now Eisner felt everyone was watching him. "God forbid," he worried, "that I miss a candy wrapper." The moment he saw some paper, he darted to it and bent over, then caught himself. His back was killing him. Eisner had developed severe back pain, which he attributed to stress at the prospect of being judged by park executives. Then he saw some more scraps. Considering that every step of his route had been preplanned, with crews having replaced wilted flowers, cut the grass, repaved sidewalks and painted facades, it looked suspiciously as if the trash had been planted. Was this a hazing of some sort? Eisner decided he just had to keep picking it up, no matter how intense the pain. As soon as the park visit was over, his back pain vanished.

In planning Disneyland, Walt had assembled a handpicked creative team of animators, directors, writers, artists, and set designers from the studio that met secretly to plan a theme park and became known as Imagineers. Originally part of Walt's WED Company, which had created such tensions with the Roy side of the family, they had been merged back into the company but still retained their own cultlike status, occupying their own warehouse in Glendale, where new attractions were developed in conditions of top secrecy. In stark contrast to the theme park "cast members," Imagineers cultivated and flaunted eccentricity. While some looked like refugees from a 1950s sitcom, others had long hair, ponytails, facial hair, and earrings, in one case so many that the Imagineer's earlobe was distended almost to his shoulder. Their leader was Marty Sklar, a former publicist for Walt, whose long tenure and close ties to the master gave him immense stature within Disney.

With the Epcot theme park finished and $300 million over budget, the Imagineers had been targeted for extinction by the previous regime, and it was true that much of their work could be subcontracted more cheaply. When Eisner and Wells arrived, Sklar and his team were at work on a new water ride, in which guests would ride logs down a hurtling flume, culminating in a thrilling drop down a waterfall. Dick Nunis had asked for a water attraction, the kind of ride growing in popularity at amusement parks all over the country, but had balked at the proposed $80 million cost. But Eisner loved the scale model of the water chute, and urged Sklar and Nunis to go forward. "Frank and I often favored the more creative (and costly) solution to the problem," Eisner later said, which coincided perfectly with the attitude of the Imagineers, who had long been criticized for ignoring budgets. Sklar showed Eisner the early models for Disneyland and Disney World, took him into the archives, and regaled him with stories of Walt's and Roy's often contentious relationship. Eisner was "blown away," as he put it. The possibility of more theme parks was already in his mind. The Imagineers had saved their very existence.

In contrast to his excitement over the Imagineers' projects, Eisner was dismayed when he saw plans for two new hotels scheduled to be built on Disney World property. He thought they were the ugliest buildings he'd ever seen. They were cheap, bland, boxy slabs, just as bad as the already-built Contemporary Resort, a forbidding concrete pyramid that looked anything but contemporary. Determined not to get any further into the hotel business itself, the previous regime had contracted out construction and ownership of the hotels to New York–based developer John Tishman. "We have to get out of this deal," Eisner told Wells.

The next day Eisner and Jane were shopping at Knoll International in the Pacific Design Center for furniture for his new office at Disney. His salesman, who was well dressed and spoke knowledgeably about architecture and furniture design, impressed him. Eisner turned to his wife. "I'm hiring him to protect me from bad architecture and design," he said impulsively. And he did, even after learning the salesman had dropped out of college and run away from home at seventeen to go to Israel. Art Levitt Jr. became Eisner's personal assistant. Only later did he learn that Levitt was the son of the chairman of the American Stock Exchange and future Securities and Exchange Commission chairman. Levitt's mother called Eisner. "I just want to thank you," she said. "We've been so worried about Art."

Eisner wasn't sure just where he'd developed such a keen interest in architecture, but it appealed to his imagination and artistic sensibilities. His parents had hired noted architect Robert Stern to design their new apartment when they "downsized" by selling the Park Avenue co-op where Michael and his sister had grown up. His parents were also friends of the noted contemporary art collectors Victor and Sally Ganz, and the Ganzes had treated Eisner to a whirlwind tour of classical architecture during a visit to Rome when he was eighteen. He often stopped to admire two Manhattan classics of modernism, Mies van der Rohe's Seagram Building and Eero Saarinen's CBS Building, commissioned by legendary media executive Bill Paley. Just two weeks after arriving at the company, Eisner convened a meeting with Marty Sklar, and Wing Chao, Disney's resident architect, as well as

Kinsey, who was in charge of developing a master plan for the studio lot, which called for a new hotel on a small parcel along Riverside Drive in Burbank. "Let's make this a Mickey Mouse hotel," Eisner suggested.

"You mean the name, the Mickey Mouse Hotel?" Sklar asked.

"No," Eisner replied. "Make it in the shape of Mickey, with rooms in the legs."

"Like the Colossus of Rhodes?" Chao asked.

"Yeah," Eisner said. "Straddling the street. That's what I'm talking about."

At first no one reacted. Had Eisner gone off the deep end? Then Chao pointed out that it would be difficult to run elevators up Mickey's outstretched legs. No hotel ever got built in Burbank, and they were never quite sure how serious Eisner was. But he had certainly succeeded in breaking the creative ice. No idea seemed too outrageous. Kinsey was impressed. He could see that Eisner and Wells were like right and left arms, one creative, impulsive, irreverent; the other measured, practical, decisive.

At the behest of the Basses and Al Checchi, a former executive at Marriott Corporation who moved to California both to advise Eisner and report to the Basses, Eisner met with Bill Marriott, the corporation's chairman, to discuss a partnership that would supplant the Tishman arrangement. Disney would retain ownership of new hotels, but Marriott would build and operate them in a joint venture. The idea made sense, given Disney's scant experience managing hotels, but when Eisner visited Marriott's design center, his spirits sank. Marriott's hotel designs were little better than Tishman's. Eisner couldn't imagine Marriott agreeing to anything even remotely like a Mickey Mouse Hotel.

Marriott's chief financial officer, Gary Wilson, also impressed Eisner, much as he'd been attracted almost immediately to Art Levitt. In the midst of what seemed a conservative corporate culture, Wilson stood out, with his impeccably tailored suits, monogrammed shirts, and pocket handkerchiefs. In his early forties, Wilson was refreshingly direct and self-confident, and showed both a mastery of financial details and a lively imagination.

Wilson also knew the old Disney culture. He and Bill Marriott had gone to Burbank to discuss a hotel deal with Card Walker, but were actually assessing Disney as a possible takeover target for Marriott. Even though Disney's own hotels—the Disneyland Hotel in Anaheim and Contemporary and Polynesian resorts in Orlando—were booked to capacity and profitable, Walker had brushed aside their suggestion that Disney might want to build and operate more hotels. "Disney is not in the hotel business," Walker maintained. "It's in the park business."

"Why is that?" Marriott asked.

Walker seemed surprised by the question. "That's the way we do things," he said.

Wilson had concluded that Disney was ripe for a takeover, though Marriott's board ultimately decided that Disney was too big for Marriott to digest, and so no offer was made. Wilson disagreed. He and his staff had done some projections showing the dramatic effect on the bottom line of simply raising admission prices and expanding hotel capacity.

Sid Bass had made the same point when Eisner flew to meet him in Fort Worth during his first week as chief executive. On the flight, Eisner insisted that Mike Bagnall, Disney's chief financial officer, take him line by line through Disney's last annual report and balance sheet. Eisner peppered him with questions, some of them embarrassingly elementary. Bagnall didn't actually say so, but it looked to him as if the new chief executive was an idiot. Eisner thought Bagnall could have been a little more deferential.

When they arrived at the meeting, Bass was surrounded by some of his top advisers, including Checchi and Richard Rainwater, a partner of the Basses and their chief financial adviser. After brief introductions, Sid Bass turned to Eisner. "So how do you see the company?"

Eisner spoke extemporaneously, using a black marker to write down some of his points. He reiterated his belief in the need for creative leadership, and stressed the company's potential to ramp up film and television production, especially TV, where the profits for syndication could be huge. These were businesses he knew well from Paramount, including ways to finance films that shifted most of the financial risk onto outside investors looking for tax deductions. He also stressed the importance of new secondary markets for theatrical films, especially home video and cable television. These markets alone, he argued, should boost the value of the Disney library of animated classics to about $200 million. And, as in the past, he felt that new Disney films would be a fertile source for new theme park attractions.

Bass and his advisers left the room for about a half-hour. When they returned, they urged Eisner and Wells to raise the admission price to the theme parks, which Bass said was "ridiculously low," and do more to develop the vast acreage Disney owned around Disney World. Disney ran only three hotels, one in California and two in Florida, which were nearly always fully occupied. Scores of other hotels had sprung up around Disney World to accommodate the approximately 10 million visitors per year streaming to Orlando. There was no reason Disney shouldn't capitalize on the park's success by developing more hotels on its property.

Later, Eisner had dinner at Bass's house, which was filled with modern art. Though Eisner himself knew little about the subject, he knew that Bass was on the board of New York's Museum of Modern Art with Ovitz, and before the trip Ovitz had spent hours lecturing Eisner on modern art in general and Bass's taste in particular. Bass was impressed when Eisner recognized and complimented him on a piece of sculpture by Robert Irwin, an obscure California artist that Ovitz had told him Bass collected.

Despite Eisner's reservations about Marriott's lack of creativity, a joint hotel deal seemed to make sense, and negotiations went ahead. The Basses and Checchi strongly encouraged it. Frank Wells met with Judson Green, a young theme park executive in Orlando, took a cocktail napkin and jotted down terms of a deal with Marriott he wanted Green to negotiate. "Don't drop the ball," he said in parting.

A few weeks later, Chao showed Eisner and Wells some model rooms he and a group of Imagineers had designed for the Grand Floridian, one of the new hotels to be built by Tishman. The hotel was designed with a frilly, fanciful Victorian theme, far more creative than anything Eisner had seen on his visit to Marriott. It confirmed what Eisner was thinking, which was that hotels could be entertainment as much as lodging—the same kind of themed attractions that the parks themselves offered. So sure was he of the concept that Eisner decided then and there that Disney could create its own real estate development subsidiary, make all the creative decisions, and jettison both the proposed Marriott deal and the Tishman partnership. "We're going to hire the best people in the industry," Eisner insisted in a burst of excitement. "We'll make mistakes along the way, but they'll be our mistakes and we'll learn from them." Wells readily agreed.

In getting the best people, Eisner was determined to fire Bagnall as chief financial officer and lure Wilson away from Marriott. After their first meeting with Wilson, Eisner had pulled Wells aside. "This is the guy we should hire," he said. Wilson was intrigued by the possibilities he'd seen at Disney, but chief financial officer was a lateral move, and his goal was to become a chief executive. Eisner persisted. He was so eager to get him that he offered Wilson lavish financial incentives and a seat on the Disney board. Then, when Wilson flew out to meet with Eisner and Wells, Wells volunteered that he only expected to stay at the company for five years before quitting to resume his quest to climb the highest peak on every continent. Wells mentioned that he also harbored political ambitions, and might decide to run for office. Eisner stressed that if Wells stepped down, Wilson would be his logical successor. The prospect of succeeding Wells as president clinched the deal, and Wilson joined Disney in September 1984 as America's highest-paid CFO.

Wilson wasted no time in raising admission prices at the theme parks, over the objections of some of the longtime employees. The increases had little impact on the number of visitors to the parks. Indeed, the only thing that surprised him was how much guests were willing to pay. Hundreds of millions of additional dollars dropped to the bottom line. As Eisner told *New York Times* reporter Aljean Harmetz, "Such a bounty has fallen into my lap. Every day a new asset falls out of the sky."

Wilson hired another Marriott executive, Larry Murphy, to create a strategic-planning department, and for the first time, they began requiring the divisions to produce five-year plans. Wilson was determined to transform Disney into a "growth" company in the eyes of Wall Street, which meant aiming for a 20 percent growth in earnings and a 20 percent gain in the stock price every year. He dubbed this the 20/20 plan.

Wilson's arrival helped soothe Checchi, the Bass adviser who'd worked with Marriott, who was strongly opposed to Disney getting into the hotel business on its own. He thought Disney needed an experienced partner like Marriott, and argued that high-end architecture was too expensive and did nothing to boost revenues. It was also elitist, fundamentally at odds with Disney's populist appeal. But Eisner stubbornly dug in.

"If we're going to imprint our stamp on the world," Eisner wrote in a memo to Wells, "if we're going to do something more than help people have a good time with Mickey Mouse, if we are going to make aesthetic choices, then we've got to upgrade the level of our architecture and try to leave something behind for others. This is going to be highly charged politically inside the company. There is definitely going to be a problem trying to make some of our executives understand that we're not going to be just concerned about the bottom line, we're not going to do schlocky architecture, and we are going to try to make a statement—to make some history. There are some who feel it's going to cost us additional money. I don't think it has to, but even if it costs a few dollars more, I think it's well worth it."

By the end of the year, the deal negotiated by Green with Marriott was ready to be signed. But then Wilson weighed in, agreeing with Eisner and Wells that they should walk away from it. It fell to Wells to communicate this news, both inside the company and to Marriott and Tishman. On a visit to Orlando, he approached Green, the chief negotiator, and suggested they take a walk through the park. "We're going to pull the plug," he said. "Michael and I think we can create more value. We don't need Marriott." Wells realized that

Green was disappointed after devoting almost a year to the project. "There will be plenty more great deals," he said, putting his arm around the young executive. "This just wasn't meant to be."

Tishman responded to Disney's decision by filing a $300 million suit against Disney for breach of contract and asking for an additional $1 billion in punitive damages. Since Disney was on shaky legal ground—it seemed a clear-cut breach of contract—it fell to Green to negotiate a complex hotel deal as the basis for a settlement of the case, in which Disney agreed that Tishman would still own two new hotels and offered him a choice site adjacent to Epcot. Tishman could also set the construction budget as long as Disney determined the design and service standards, an inherent contradiction, but one that left ultimate control with Eisner.

Eisner finally had the chance to indulge his passion for architecture. He asked Michael Graves and Robert Venturi, two prominent architects recommended by Victor Ganz, if they could work together on the project. "Isn't that a little bit like putting Steven Spielberg and George Lucas together?" Graves asked when Eisner called.

"Remember, I did that," Eisner countered, referring to *Raiders of the Lost Ark*, which Spielberg directed and Lucas produced.

Their collaboration was doomed when Venturi, the more senior of the two architects, insisted on a competition to choose a single architect. So Eisner had Levitt organize one. Tishman insisted that his own architect, Alan Lapidus, be included, someone who was far more developer-friendly. Eisner agreed, though he viewed Lapidus with thinly disguised contempt. Lapidus's father, Morris, designed the flamboyant Fontainebleau and Eden Roc hotels in Miami Beach, exactly the kind of "schlock" that Eisner was determined to avoid.* Disney's own Imagineers also contributed a design.

All the models were displayed in a conference room next to Eisner's office in the old animation building. Though Graves's models were sidetracked to Memphis and barely arrived in time, Eisner was immediately drawn to his unconventional but stylishly postmodern plans, one for a giant pyramid, the other a vault, two iconic classical shapes. The pyramid had a giant fountain at its apex. Tishman was aghast. "This design is outrageous and impossible," he said. "The buildings make no sense practically or economically." But Eisner was delighted, and asked only that Graves "lighten them up." The archi-

---

* Though derided by architectural critics at the time, Lapidus's hotels have recently been undergoing a critical reappraisal, and Lapidus has been cited as a role model by a new generation of architects.

tect responded by adding giant dolphins to the top of one pyramid building, swans to the other (inspired, Graves said, by the fountains of Bernini, the Italian Baroque master). Despite arguments and cost-cutting efforts by Tishman that continued throughout construction (some of which had to be countermanded by Eisner), the Swan and Dolphin hotels were essentially built as Graves designed them, down to the smallest details of the interior decor.

During his first week at the company, Katzenberg asked to see what the animators had in development, and they arranged a screening of *The Black Cauldron*, which had been ten years in the making and was scheduled as Disney's animated 1984 Christmas season release. *Black Cauldron* was the work of the Old Guard; the younger animators scoffed at it.

In the years after Walt's death, animation had split into two uneasy camps. The legendary and much revered "Nine Old Men" who worked closely with Walt had mostly died or retired. Their successors were a group of older animators who tried to resist the changes sought by a group of twenty-something renegade artists, most recently hired from the CalArts program, among them John Lasseter and Tim Burton. Lasseter's 1979 animated film at CalArts, *Lady & the Lamp*, had won the Student Academy Award for Animation. He was talented, affable, and wore Hawaiian shirts. Burton, by contrast, dressed formally in black, and sometimes disappeared into a closet, where he'd stand for hours. After some dental surgery, he returned to the office and delighted in dripping blood on his colleagues' desks. Lasseter left Disney shortly before Eisner arrived.

The Black Cauldron was almost completed, and Roy had already seen it. He'd been disturbed by the graphic violence in the opening sequence, in which a flying dragon swoops down on a young boy, sinks his talons into him, and flies off. Roy insisted that a few particularly bloody frames be cut, but he didn't know what else to do. Apart from the violence, "I just don't understand the story," he told the writer and producer, Joe Hale.

When Katzenberg saw it, he was even more dismayed, and blunter about saying so. The dark and forbidding story was unsuitable for small children. Katzenberg didn't see how it could garner a G, or general audience, rating, which had always been affixed to the Disney animated films. It would be a disaster for the Disney brand.

"This has to be edited," he proclaimed as soon as the film ended.

Hale objected. "Animated films can't be edited," he insisted. There was no "excess" footage in an animated film, all of which was painstakingly hand-drawn and colored. You couldn't just cut scenes and add new ones, not with the release just weeks away.

"That's ridiculous," Katzenberg retorted. "You can edit anything."

"No, you can't," Hale persisted. "It's seamless."

"Yes you can, and I'll show you how," Katzenberg said, as tension mounted. "Let's go into the editing room."

As Katzenberg began work, Hale rushed to a phone and called Roy, who was having lunch with Eisner. "He's butchering *The Black Cauldron*," Hale fumed about Katzenberg. Yes, *The Black Cauldron* was dark, but it was an attempt to give Disney animation an edge, to be more contemporary. The animators were in an uproar. Eisner called and got Katzenberg out of the editing room. "What are you doing?" Eisner demanded. "Everybody's upset."

"I'm trying to salvage this mess," Katzenberg replied.

Eisner told Katzenberg to calm down and said he wanted to speak to him in person. For the time being Roy, as head of animation, could deal with *The Black Cauldron*. Katzenberg left the editing room, but not before some succinct parting words: "It's bad. Fix it."

More frantic calls ensued, complaints about Katzenberg that Roy passed on to Eisner. Katzenberg embodied all the animators' fears that philistines had taken control, people who didn't have the slightest understanding of animation and the hallowed Disney traditions. But when he spoke to Katzenberg, Eisner seemed amused by the turmoil. "Good," Eisner said. "That's what you're here for." But he reminded Katzenberg that they wouldn't be at Disney if it weren't for Roy. "Be deferential," he said, "but get in there and fix it."

At the same time, Eisner assured Roy that he'd spoken to Katzenberg and warned him not to overstep his bounds. Still, "I can only control him so much," he said with a shrug. Katzenberg heeded Eisner's advice and invited Roy to have dinner, and Roy found himself agreeing with many of Katzenberg's points. In any event, Katzenberg was head of the motion picture studio, which made him Roy's boss. Roy had agreed to the arrangement when Katzenberg was hired, and he intended to honor it.

In the end, there wasn't much that could be done with *The Black Cauldron*, though it was postponed until the following summer for some rewriting and editing. Despite Katzenberg's insistence, Hale was more right than wrong about editing animated films. Katzenberg managed to cut just a few minutes, and by his own admission, could only make it slightly less bad. Roy received a film credit for "additional dialogue." Still, when Roy appeared on the "Today Show" to promote the opening, he drew a blank when the host asked, "What's *The Black Cauldron* about?" He still wasn't sure. The film grossed almost $22 million, but far less than it had cost to make. Even more discouraging to the animators was the fact that *The Care Bears Movie,* based on the American Greetings teddy bears, was made using cheap foreign labor for just $2 million, but grossed more than *Black Cauldron* at the box office.

Joe Hale was already at work on his next project, *Mistress Masham's Repose,* a sequel to *Gulliver's Travels,* in which Lilliputians come to England and live on a country estate. Roy thought the idea had charm, but when Hale described it, Katzenberg said simply, "I hate it." After the *Black Cauldron* episode, Roy wasn't surprised. Hale was fired shortly after, along with most of the *Black Cauldron* team. *Mistress Masham* languished. More cutbacks were in the offing. Katzenberg asked Roy for a list of people he wanted to save.

After the layoffs and the fiasco of *The Black Cauldron,* Roy felt he was fighting for the future of animation, which he still believed had the potential to once again be the heart of the company. At about the same time as the disastrous screening of *Black Cauldron,* Roy invited Eisner, Wells, and Katzenberg to a viewing of storyboards from a new project called *Basil of Baker Street.* While most animators had been painstakingly toiling on *Black Cauldron,* two dissident animators who had been cut from the *Cauldron* team, Ron Clements and John Musker, both former altar boys from the Midwest, had been developing a story based on a book about mice living under Sherlock Holmes's London flat. They'd used Ron Miller as the model for the villain, Professor Ratigan ("big, hulking, handsome, and personable"), and Miller had been the film's producer until he was abruptly dismissed. Clements, bearded and redheaded, and Musker, taller and more talkative, set up nearly fifty storyboards that snaked through the corridor and in and out of rooms in the old animation building. Unlike live-action features, Disney's animated films had rarely started with scripts; storyboards had scores of cartoonlike drawings that mapped out the story, and dialogue was added later by the animators as they drew. Eisner, especially, seemed puzzled by this. "We should begin with a script, just like with our other movies," he insisted.

As they wandered along the storyboards, neither Roy nor the animators could figure out if the executives were really following the story. Eisner startled them at one point by wondering aloud whether a song in a bar that had already been scored by composer Henry Mancini could be turned over to pop star Michael Jackson. Clements and Musker froze, their dismay evident. Finally Eisner said, "Part of your job is to talk me out of bad ideas."

Eisner found *Basil* cute but confusing. He liked the Sherlock Holmes angle; he'd produced *The Young Sherlock Holmes* while at Paramount. But he thought it lacked dramatic structure, the traditional three-act "beginning, middle, and end" that had served him so well when judging scripts at Paramount. But he and Katzenberg agreed that, at the very least, it would not be another *Black Cauldron*. Roy pressed for a green light, pointing out that Disney risked losing its most talented animators if they didn't have something to work on.

Eisner asked the animators how much more time they needed.

"Two years," Clements said.

"I want it in one. How much will it cost?"

"About $24 million."

"Nope," Eisner said, "$12 million."

In the end, they got the green light and a budget of $10 million.

Katzenberg moved quickly to put his stamp on the animation division. He scheduled his first major meeting for a Sunday at 7:00 A.M. Not yet familiar with Katzenberg's work habits, Roy and the animators took this as an affront. Patty Disney told Roy, "Tell Jeffrey that if he ever makes you do this again, you're going to show up in your pajamas." The meeting got off to a bad start when Katzenberg discovered that no one had stocked the room with Diet Coke.

A few days later, Eisner issued invitations to one of his "gong shows," a first for the animators. He told them he wanted five new ideas from each of them. Clements went to a bookstore and started leafing through a book of fairy tales. One caught his eye: Hans Christian Andersen's "Little Mermaid." Though the fairy tale had a sad ending—the mermaid dies—Clements wrote a two-page treatment in which the mermaid becomes human after meeting her prince. He was also a big fan of science fiction at the time, so his other ideas were all science fiction, including one he jotted down, "Treasure Island in Space."

Eisner and Katzenberg went around the table, and the animators got a crash course in "high concept." When Clements's turn came, he said, "The Little Mermaid. . . ."

"Gong," Eisner and Katzenberg said in unison. "Too similar to *Splash*."

"Okay, how about 'Treasure Island in Space'?"

"Gong." Eisner knew that Paramount was already developing a *Star Trek* sequel with a *Treasure Island* angle.

Pete Young, another animator, suggested "Oliver Twist with dogs." Everybody waited for the gong, but none came. Then Katzenberg said he loved it.

He'd wanted to do a live-action film version of the Broadway musical *Oliver!* while at Paramount, but it had never gotten out of development. Now Katzenberg had the idea that they could do a Broadway musical as an animated feature—with dogs in the main roles.

"Oliver Twist with dogs" got the go-ahead.

Clements left the meeting depressed; he'd been "gonged" after only a few words. But Roy came up to him afterward and said he liked the "Little Mermaid" idea. And the next morning, Katzenberg called to say he'd read all five of his ideas overnight. He, too, said he liked the mermaid idea and suggested that Clements expand his treatment. Clements was amazed and impressed that a high-ranking executive like Katzenberg had actually read his material and reacted to it so quickly.

Another idea Eisner and Katzenberg liked was a project already in development from the Ron Miller era, a live action–animated hybrid based on a book called *Who Censored Roger Rabbit?* Part of the plot hinged on the lack of public transportation in Los Angeles, a theme that resonated with Eisner, who still missed New York's public transport system.

As Katzenberg spent more time with the animators, he started browsing in the Disney animation archives. He was amazed to discover that Disney maintained a vast trove of documentary material that included practically everything Walt had ever written and said. Stenographers had been employed to follow Walt around and take down everything, so there were long transcripts of Walt analyzing the making of all the Disney classic animated films. There were also thousands of archival photos. Disney still employed a staff of sixteen full-time still photographers whose sole responsibility was to document the work of the studio. Katzenberg considered it a monument to Walt's ego; Paramount had had none of this. But since it was there, Katzenberg decided to take advantage of it. In the midst of shelves filled with dusty cartons that looked as if they hadn't been touched in years, Katzenberg began systematically retracing Walt's career in animation. It was all there, neatly cataloged: Walt's files on "villains," "heroines," "lyrics," "music."

He also discovered a book written by two of Walt's disciples called *The Art of Animation*. Katzenberg made a point of rereading it every four to six months. He spent hours in the archives, often in the early morning or late at night when no one else was around; he typically slept just five hours a night. He came to view the experience as the college education he'd never gotten, and a refuge from the stress and hectic pace of the studio.

Far from wanting to shut down animation, as Eisner and Wells had initially proposed, Katzenberg began to see it as a unique Disney asset. Just because Disney had failed to generate a new classic since Walt's death didn't mean it never would again. In any event, Eisner had told him to keep Roy happy, and Roy believed in animation. On a flight to Tokyo to visit Tokyo Disneyland, Katzenberg talked with Roy about how to ramp up production at the animation division. "You need your own Katzenberg," Katzenberg told him. "Somebody like me, to get things done for you." So at the behest of Bob Fitzpatrick at CalArts, Roy interviewed Peter Schneider, whose background was in live theater, not animation. Still, he'd just run the arts program for the Los Angeles Olympic Arts Festival. Roy liked him, so Schneider met with Katzenberg—a 5:30 A.M. interview—and then Eisner. "Either it will work out or we'll fire you," Eisner said breezily. Schneider got the job, but he sensed that Eisner had little interest in either him or the money-losing animation division.

Eisner was far more interested in reviving Disney's live-action film and television divisions, businesses he knew well from his stint at Paramount. He had Katzenberg and Kinsey develop a master plan for the studio, which called for tearing down the old, unused "Zorro" set and building bungalows to house live-action producers on the lot. As live-action film production ramped up, office space grew tight, especially in the coveted area close to Eisner and Wells. So the animators had to move. The decision was highly symbolic, since Walt's office had always been in the animation building at the heart of the studio. Roy objected, but finally agreed when Eisner personally promised that they'd be brought back to the Burbank campus as soon as a new building could be built.

The move was demoralizing. Roy kept his office in the old animation building, but everyone else moved several miles away to a dreary, nearly windowless warehouse in Glendale. Tim Burton left to direct *Pee Wee's Big Adventure* for Warner Bros. Despite assurances that the move was temporary, the animators concluded that their days were probably numbered. Apart from *Basil,* they had so little work to occupy them that they passed the time with chair races, cell-sliding contests, and Trivial Pursuit games.

After hiring Katzenberg, Eisner and Wells moved quickly to remake Disney, especially the studio, into something closer to the Paramount mold. The theme parks, the only division making money, were spared, at least for the time being, and continued under the leadership of Nunis, who remained on the board. Indeed, Eisner was exceedingly careful about board members. He added Wells and Wilson from the company; Sharon Disney Lund represented the Walt side of the family; and Roy, of course, had rejoined at the same time as Eisner. Though Stanley Gold had stepped down as part of the compromise to elect Eisner and Wells, he, too, returned in 1984. With such staunch allies, Eisner had effective control of the board, not that the old guard, represented by Walker, Watson, and Nunis, were likely to challenge his leadership.

In contrast to his handling of the board, and despite the reassuring words to longtime employees in his first-day speech, Eisner was impatient with the leisurely hours and work habits of many Disney old-timers, even though the afternoon card games had vanished the day he and Wells arrived. But firing people was not something Eisner enjoyed. It was the kind of distasteful but sometimes essential task he handed off to Wells. Wells continued to probe Stan Kinsey for information and gossip about longtime employees. As Wells zeroed in on theme parks head Nunis, Kinsey finally said, "I'm not your guy. I don't feel comfortable discussing people like this."

A culture of "survival of the fittest" soon developed. Two people would be assigned the same tasks, and whoever prevailed kept his job, at least temporarily. One afternoon Katzenberg told Kinsey he wanted him to analyze Disney's international distribution, an operation run by Harry Archinal. Kinsey blanched at the request. The genial Archinal had practically invented the business, and was well known and highly regarded in Hollywood and abroad. He had also been especially gracious toward Kinsey when he came to the company. So Kinsey hated the idea of going behind his back. "Why don't you call Harry?" Kinsey suggested to Katzenberg. "Tell him I'm going to be working on this and you want me to help him evaluate the business."

Katzenberg stared at him dismissively. "If you need me to do this," he said, "then you're not the man for the job."

Despite the cool reception he'd gotten at his first meeting with new management, Kinsey had also kept working on the computerized animation venture with Pixar, which went by the acronym CAPS, for Computer Animation Production System. He still believed strongly in the potential to return Disney animation to its glory days by developing new computer technology. But one afternoon a secretary came to his office. "I'm here to collect your files on the technology group," she said.

"Why?" he asked.

"Jeffrey Rochlis wants them," she replied. Kinsey had never heard of anyone named Rochlis. "He's the new head of the technology group."

"Let me get this straight," Kinsey said. "Jeffrey hired this guy without telling me? And he sent you to get my files without introducing himself?"

"I'm just doing what I was told," she said. Kinsey had the secretary take him to Rochlis. "There must be some misunderstanding," Kinsey began. "I'm Stan Kinsey and I'm in charge of the new technology group. What's all this about the files?"

"Jeffrey just hired me to be head of new technology," Rochlis replied.

"Oh really," Kinsey said, his tone controlled but icy. There was an awkward silence.

"Maybe your problem is Jeffrey, not me," Rochlis said. "I would have expected him to tell you what was going on."

The normally mild-mannered Kinsey marched to Katzenberg's office, cutting past the usual line of people waiting to see him. "Sorry guys," Kinsey said, as he entered the office and closed the door. Katzenberg was on the phone.

"What's your problem?" Katzenberg asked.

"What the hell is going on?" Kinsey demanded. "Who is Rochlis?"

"I hired him from Atari [actually Gulf+Western's Sega unit]. You don't have time for this stuff. It's a good fit. Anyway, I go for the best athlete."

"Are you trying to get rid of me?"

"No, no . . ."

"Then I want a raise and a new title right now because I can't believe this."

"Fine, you got the money and the title," Katzenberg said. "Now get rid of the files."

Kinsey complied, and in the ensuing weeks, he heard a stream of complaints from animators and engineers that Rochlis was slashing costs and all but shutting down the technology projects. That February, while on a ski vacation, Kinsey realized that Katzenberg was right: He wasn't the man for this kind of job, or this harsh new regime. As soon as he returned, he sent Katzenberg a memo proposing that Rochlis replace him as senior vice president for operations and that he dedicate himself to the lower-ranking technology job. "If you're not happy, I'll leave in July," Kinsey promised. "I won't cause problems." Katzenberg shrugged, but readily agreed. Rochlis seemed thrilled by the sudden promotion. Kinsey got his files back, and immediately began reviving the computer animation project.

In his new position, Rochlis began a series of meetings with studio executives, among them James Fleming. "You're director of finance," Rochlis said in a friendly tone, as Fleming nodded. "But what would you really like to do?" Fleming lit up at the question, since he had long harbored ambitions for a more creative job. "I'd love to move into marketing," he said.

"You're fired," Rochlis said abruptly.

"What do you mean?" Fleming asked.

"I only want people who love the job they're in," Rochlis replied. "You clearly don't want to be in finance."

Over a thousand Disney employees lost their jobs during Eisner's and Wells's first year. Numerous Paramount executives replaced them, including virtually the entire television production unit under Richard Frank. Eisner stayed aloof from the purge, preferring to let Wells and Katzenberg carry out the mandate to cut costs. After working his way through the studio ranks, Rochlis was dispatched to the Imagineers, whom both Gary Wilson and Wells thought were long overdue for serious cost cutting.

However they felt about Katzenberg's often-abrasive style, holdovers from the prior regime, as well as Roy, were in awe of his energy and productivity. He was more accessible than either Eisner or Wells. A line always formed outside his office, where two secretaries fielded and placed phone calls. Katzenberg used two phones at once, with one party on hold as he finished one call and had a secretary start dialing the next. On his desk was a stack of three-by-five index cards for each call, on which he'd written what it was he wanted to accomplish. While still on a phone he'd use a free hand to wave in the next visitor to his office, squeezing brief meetings in between calls. He tried and usually succeeded in keeping calls and conversations to thirty seconds or less.

Despite his prodigious efficiency, Katzenberg was notoriously late to meetings. Rather than gather at the appointed time, animators in Glendale waited for a call reporting that Katzenberg had left his office, then posted an observer along his route so his progress could be monitored: "He's at the corner of Riverside and Magnolia," someone would report from his car phone. The animators would be waiting as Katzenberg walked through the door of their conference room. He'd hold out his hand and someone would slip a chilled Diet Coke into it. He never said "thank you," not out of any disrespect, they assumed, but because it was a waste of time.

In television, Eisner moved swiftly to revive Disney's long-running Sunday night program, which Card Walker had canceled the year before out of fear that it would compete with the newly launched Disney Channel on cable television. Under various names and networks, "The Wonderful World of Disney" had run continuously for twenty-nine years, and, as Walt had put it, was his "way of going directly to the public." Original movies like *Davy Crockett* were some of the biggest hits in the early days of television, even if, in more recent years, the Disney fare had sometimes seemed stale, predictably saccharine, and attracted mediocre ratings. Eisner had already proven himself with the weekly movie at ABC, and he persuaded ABC chairman Fred Pierce to revive the weekly Disney tradition on Sunday evenings opposite the CBS ratings juggernaut, "60 Minutes."

Eisner was convinced that, just as Walt had hosted the Disney program each week as the voice and face of the company, the new program needed a host to give the program continuity. Walt was hardly a professional actor, but he was a legendary storyteller, and he came across as warm, inviting, and down-to-earth; a natural for the new medium of television. Eisner sounded Roy out about doing it, but he declined, in part out of his inherent shyness and aversion to celebrity. A search ensued: Julie Andrews, Dick Van Dyke, Cary Grant were considered, and Grant was even approached, but turned it down.

The executive in charge of the search brought name after name, all rejected for one reason or another by Eisner. Finally he reported that he'd approached Tom Hanks's agent, and that Hanks was interested. Hanks had co-starred in Touchstone's first hit, *Splash,* and had co-starred in the Paramount-produced hit sitcom, "Bosom Buddies." The executive thought the wholesome, all-American Hanks was a suggestion Eisner couldn't refuse, but he rejected Hanks out of hand as too young. Only then did it dawn on him that Eisner was going to reject every candidate except for one.

Finally Eisner broached the idea to Wells. "I don't want to do it, but I guess I'll have to do it," he maintained, arguing that the chief executive needed to be the face of Disney to show that the company wasn't being run by the "ghost of Walt." He also ran the idea by Sid Bass, who Eisner maintains was enthusiastic.

Without telling anyone else, and using his wife as the producer, Eisner made a short tape with himself as host. The results were discouraging: For someone who was quite relaxed and animated in person, he came across as stiff and awkward; he spoke too fast; he emphasized the wrong words; he looked fat. Even Jane was critical, and one of his sons said his father would embarrass him by going on television. Disney executives, including Katzenberg, were pretty much unanimous that the test was a failure. But the criticism left Eisner even more determined. The company hired a professional director to coach him. He lost weight, changed his wardrobe, and rehearsed his delivery. He even suggested changing his first name to "Mickey" to encourage the audience to identify him with the company, though no one was sure he was serious. Still, one of his first tapings, to introduce the movie *Help Wanted: Kids,* showed scant improvement. "This isn't going to work at all," Katzenberg warned him. Roy, too, was dismayed. If Roy had realized that Eisner was the alternative, he might well have accepted the offer to be the host. "You have to learn how to relax," he told him.

"I'm trying, but it's not as easy as it looks," Eisner said.

Eisner stubbornly persisted in the face of almost unanimous criticism. Walt hadn't been all that smooth, either, he reasoned. When he told Katzenberg during a flight on the corporate jet that he'd made a final decision to host the show, Katzenberg thought he finally understood: Eisner saw himself as Walt's heir.

THREE

Just days after assuming his post at Disney, Eisner had gotten a call from legendary International Creative Management agent Sam Cohn in New York. Cohn represented director Paul Mazursky, who'd made the critically acclaimed and modestly profitable *Bob and Carol and Ted and Alice* and *An Unmarried Woman*. He had rewritten a French comedy about a bum who moves in and takes over the lives of a wealthy couple after they save him from drowning in their swimming pool. Translated to southern California, the script became *Down and Out in Beverly Hills,* and the story appealed immediately to Eisner—a romantic comedy with a populist spin that could be made on a budget—even though Universal had had the rights to the script and had passed on the project.

In his quest for talent at bargain prices, Eisner had the idea to resurrect careers that had fallen into eclipse, in this case, Richard Dreyfuss and Bette Midler. Dreyfuss was just emerging from drug rehabilitation a few years after winning an Oscar for *The Goodbye Girl,* and Midler's *The Rose* had been nominated for four Academy Awards but her career had slowed in years since. Eisner had loved Midler ever since seeing her legendary act at the Continental Baths during the 1960s, while he was scouting for new talent at ABC. He thought she needed to get away from the serious, overblown musicals she'd been making. A nonsinging comic role would be perfect. It fell to Katzenberg to get the movie made on a budget. He signed Dreyfuss and Midler for $600,000 each, with no profit participation (Your client's career is "in the fucking toilet," he bluntly told Midler's agent), added Nick Nolte to the cast as the bum, and the final tab was a modest $14 million.

Eisner and Katzenberg were acutely aware that, as the first live-action feature film to be released under new management, *Down and Out* was freighted with symbolic importance, sending an important message to the creative community, moviegoers, and Wall Street. Released under the Touchstone label created by Ron Miller, it set new standards for raunchy language and sex in a Disney-produced film and garnered an "R" rating. Eisner probably would have cut some of the language and sex had he still been at Paramount, but he wanted to give a director of Mazursky's caliber free rein, in part to overcome the reputation for meddling he'd acquired at Paramount, and because he wanted to mitigate Disney's stodgy image. Still, as he sat through a screening of the film with Roy and Patty, every profanity leaped out, and the relatively brief sex scenes seemed interminable. He found himself drenched with perspiration, apprehensive about their reactions. When the film ended, Eisner turned to Patty. "Well, how do you like your new guys?" he asked, referring to himself and Wells.

"I love it. We're in business again," she said. Roy didn't venture an opinion.

Down and Out in Beverly Hills opened in January 1986, the first major release of the Eisner/Wells/Katzenberg regime. Audiences loved it, as did most critics. "*Down and Out in Beverly Hills* made me laugh longer and louder than any film I've seen in a long time," raved Roger Ebert in the *Chicago Sun-Times*. It eventually earned $62 million in U.S. box-office receipts, which put it ahead of *Splash* as Disney's most successful live-action feature. Eisner's instinct to cast Bette Midler in a comic role was especially vindicated; Midler went on to star in a series of hit comedies for Disney with other talented but moderately priced stars: *Ruthless People* with Danny DeVito, *Big Business* with Lily Tomlin, and *Outrageous Fortune* with Shelley Long. The films were all made on modest budgets and grossed at least $40 million each, which made them not just solid hits, but highly profitable ones. As he had said he would, Eisner had simply shifted his remarkably shrewd commercial instincts from Paramount to Disney, following the manifesto he'd written years earlier to make appealing story-driven high-concept ideas and eschew the blockbuster, mega-star mentality—hitting the "singles and doubles," as he'd put it.

The architectural competition won by Michael Graves had emboldened Eisner to pursue his vision of an architectural legacy with virtually everything Disney built. He had had little contact with Robert Stern while the architect was working on his parents' apartment, but since then Stern's lavish re-creations of turn-of-the-century shingle-style beach cottages had become the ultimate 1980s status symbol in wealthy enclaves like the Hamptons on Long Island. Eisner hired Stern to design the "casting center" where new employees were hired and trained for Walt Disney World (and where I rehearsed for my stint as Goofy). Then Stern built two more hotels, the Yacht and Beach Clubs, both evocative of a patrician New England past. They quickly became Eisner's favorite hotels at the resort, the ones where he himself stayed.

But nothing excited Eisner's architectural ambitions more than plans for an entirely new theme park in Europe. The old regime had just opened Tokyo Disneyland when Eisner and Wells took charge, and Richard Nunis explained that Disney had already tried but failed to negotiate an agreement with the French government for a similar park. As part of that effort, Disney had evaluated nearly twelve hundred potential sites in Europe, and had narrowed the choices to three: two along beaches on the Mediterranean near Barcelona, Spain, and the other in a large beet field east of Paris, near the town of Marne-la-Vallée. Eisner and Wells were both immediately enthusiastic. Tokyo Disneyland had attracted 10 million people its first year and had contributed $40 million to the bottom line. Their only regret was that Disney shared profits with the Oriental Land Company, a Japanese co-owner. "Start negotiating with both countries and see if you can get us a deal," Wells told Nunis.

There was much to recommend the Spanish sites, starting with the weather, but Eisner wanted France from the start. To him, France represented the pinnacle of Western culture, the antithesis of American mass culture that, ironically, Disney itself represented. Since his brief foray to Paris as an aspiring playwright, Paris had been where Eisner wanted to make his mark. Two camps within Disney quickly formed: the traditional parks people, led by Nunis; and Eisner, who was backed by Gary Wilson and Wells. Eisner argued that the weather in Paris wasn't much worse than Tokyo, and the Japanese were willing to wait in lines for hours in subfreezing temperatures. Paris had a much larger population than Barcelona, was a year-round tourist destination, and was more of a transportation hub. Nunis argued that Spain had a far more cooperative government, was offering better locations near beaches, and was already a major tourist destination, Europe's equivalent of California or Florida.

Not surprisingly, Eisner prevailed. In December 1985, he flew to Paris to announce plans for a new Euro Disney on the scale of Disney World: a Magic Kingdom, thousands of hotel rooms, campground, golf course, convention facilities, an office complex, and residential development, all to be built on 4,400 acres fifteen miles from Paris. While he was there, he happened to visit a movie theater on the Champs-Élysées, where he saw the hit French film *Trois Hommes et un Couffin*. Even though he had trouble understanding most of the French dialogue, Eisner loved the visual comedy and the audience's delight in a story of three hapless bachelors trying to care for an infant.

As soon as he returned, Eisner told Katzenberg to get the rights to the film. But a bidding war erupted, and it became obvious that Disney couldn't pursue its usual low-budget strategy. "They are asking for a ludicrous deal," Eisner wrote in a memo during negotiations. "If you add in the cost of a star, you are in the mega-cost picture and maybe we should forget it. On the other hand we could be at the threshold here, if we don't go forward, of passing on the equivalent of *Stripes* or *Tootsie* or one of those movies. The only thing I know is that this movie will be vastly and wildly and spectacularly commercial."

When Eisner felt strongly, he was willing to pay, as he had for *Raiders of the Lost Ark*. Disney ended up paying $1 million, a huge sum for rights to a foreign film.

The architectural competition for the Tishman hotels at Disney World proved just a warm-up for the much grander scale of Euro Disney. Eisner and his team of Imagineers had already embraced the ambitious notion of "reinventing" the theme park. As Tony Baxter, the Imagineer Eisner assigned to the project, put it in an early meeting: "We're building a resort next to one of the most sophisticated, cultured cities in the world, and we're going to be competing with the great art and architecture of Europe. We have to do something unique." No one ever said that no expense was to be spared, least of all the tightfisted Eisner, but that was the message embraced by the Imagineers, encouraged by Eisner to think freely without regard to cost.

This had also been implicit from the beginning, when, at Eisner's behest, Wing Chao assembled a team of prominent architects—Stern, Graves, Venturi, plus Frank Gehry and Stanley Tigerman—who sequestered themselves over an Easter weekend at Stern's offices in New York to brainstorm over a master plan for a European resort. Then Eisner staged an international competition for specific assignments within the master plan, adding a roster of prominent international architects to the competition: Bernard Tschumi, the Swiss architect who was dean of the architecture school at Columbia University; Hans Hollein from Austria; Rem Koolhaas from the Netherlands;

Jena Nouvel and Jean-Paul Vigier from France; Aldo Rossi of Italy; Arata Isozaki of Japan, as well as additional Americans. They made their presentations at Eisner's house in Bel Air over a four-day period, a veritable movable feast of architecture for Eisner, even though he thought most of the designs were far too cool, abstract, and restrained for a theme park.

After choosing six winning architects—Stern, Graves, Gehry, Aldo Rossi, and Antoine Predock—Eisner plunged into planning for the new park with an enthusiasm that eclipsed even his interest in film. He began spending extended periods with the Imagineers in Glendale, sometimes in meetings that continued for days. He seemed to love his time there, finding in the Imagineers kindred creative spirits. The Imagineers eagerly seized on this burgeoning interest, recognizing it as a way to stave off cost cuts and staff reductions.

Eisner obsessed about design details, even the ashtrays in the hotel rooms. He wanted working fireplaces in the hotels and real logs in the rustic Sequoia Lodge. As he described it, "Unlike producing movies, here we could be producer, director, editor, and even the actors in every foot of the film. Designing parks was more exciting than anything one could do in the proscenium world, where two dimensions was the rule." Eisner rented an apartment in Paris during the summer of 1988, moved there with Jane, and took French lessons.

All this personal attention from the company chairman was not to every architect's liking. Aldo Rossi ended up rejecting the assignment. "I am not personally offended and can ignore all the negative points that have been made about our project at the last meeting in Paris," he wrote in a letter to Eisner. "The Cavalier Bernini, invited to Paris for the Louvre project, was tormented by a multitude of functionaries who continued to demand that changes be made to the project to make it more functional. It is clear that I am not the Cavalier Bernini, but it is also clear that you are not the King of France. Aside from the differences, I do not intend to be the object of minuscule criticisms that any interior designer could handle. It is my belief that our project, notwithstanding the specialists, is beautiful in its own right and as such will become famous and built in some other place."

Emblematic of Eisner's approach was the Disneyland Hotel, a turreted, pink wedding cake of a hotel that bore no resemblance to anything designed by the prominent architects. It was solely the creation of the Imagineers, with substantial input from Eisner himself. The fanciful structure had originally been conceived as a grandiose ticket booth at the main entrance, but Eisner insisted that such coveted real estate be used for rooms. The hotel straddles the park's main entrance, just as Eisner had wanted the unbuilt Mickey Mouse Hotel to straddle Disneyland's Riverside Drive.

The plan for the hotel triggered fierce debate. Venturi warned that it would obscure sight lines toward Sleeping Beauty's castle from the park entrance. Wells feared that park visitors would look up and see hotel guests in their underwear. Others complained about the high cost of the design and the need for another hotel. When a vote was taken of the working group planning the park, it was nineteen to two against building the hotel. Eisner's vote was one of the two (Wilson's the other), and so it went forward.

As plans for Euro Disney picked up steam, the *Basil* animation project was nearing completion. It had been renamed *The Great Mouse Detective* because Eisner thought the name Basil was too English. Despite a constant effort to control costs, it was not meeting its $10 million budget. Eisner had trouble understanding why a half-hour of television animation could be produced for a half-million dollars, but a ninety-minute Disney feature couldn't be made for twenty times that. To the Disney animators, this attitude showed a lack of understanding that bordered on contempt. Disney animation featured seamless motion, not the crude, jerky movements of Saturday morning television. Shapes were delicately outlined and richly shaded; they were not "cartoons." Backgrounds were carefully rendered to suggest three-dimensional depth and perspective. The thousands of cels were hand-drawn and colored and sequences were drawn and redrawn until the directors were satisfied. This is why *The Black Cauldron*, for all its shortcomings, had taken ten years to produce, and why Disney produced only one animated feature every four years.

To most of the animators and to Roy, *Mouse Detective* became an ominous experiment in cost control. The same low-cost laborers who did television animation performed much of the hand-coloring. Shapes were boldly outlined in black and filled in with simple flat colors. While Roy was dismayed by the quality of some of the drawing, he told the animators that they had to go along to show Eisner and Katzenberg that they were "team players."

Despite all the cost-cutting efforts, *The Great Mouse Detective* eventually cost $14 million and took two years to produce. By the time it was released, there was little enthusiasm for it within Disney, though Roy thought the film was delightful. Even without much marketing it grossed $38 million, a modest success.

The poor quality of the animation gave Stan Kinsey another opportunity to push for the new computer project he was developing with Pixar, even though it became clear that the price tag was going to be more than $12 million. Rochlis, during his brief tenure as head of new technology, had vetoed it as too expensive. Kinsey couldn't elicit any interest from Katzenberg, Eisner, or Wells, so finally he went to Roy. "I'm going to need your help on this," he said. "I can't seem to get this going. Rochlis is trying to kill it. Can I show you what we're working on? Come up to see Lucas with me and take a look." Roy joined the delegation for their next visit, and he, too, was won over by the potential to reinvent animation. When he got back, Roy tried to make the case to Wells, but Wells and Eisner balked. While willing, even eager, to take creative risks, Eisner was wary about spending money on something no one would see. In this instance Wells agreed. "We're not an R and D company," he said. "It's going to cost twice as much as they say, and I don't believe it will ever save us a dime."

Roy and Kinsey refused to give up. At one of their meetings at Pixar, Ed Catmull, Pixar's acting chief executive, indicated that Lucas was facing a financial restructuring due to his pending divorce, and Pixar needed capital to replace Lucas's stake. Kinsey immediately sensed opportunity in Pixar's distress. Disney was contemplating spending $12 million anyway, and now Catmull indicated that for an investment in the neighborhood of $15 million, Disney could own half the company. "We need the money, and this would be a perfect fit," Catmull argued.

When he got back, Kinsey scheduled an appointment with Katzenberg. On the way to the meeting, he ran into Rochlis, and excitedly told him about the chance to buy Pixar. "I think we should," Kinsey said. "If we do a deal with them, we're going to be funding them anyway. If we owned them, we could negotiate better fees. I'm going to present this to Jeffrey." As they got to Katzenberg's office, Kinsey paused to exchange some pleasantries with one of the secretaries, and Rochlis got into the office ahead of him. As Kinsey walked through the door no more than thirty seconds later, he heard Rochlis say, "I think we should buy Pixar. It's an incredible deal." Kinsey stopped in his tracks. Rochlis was brazenly stealing his idea! Rochlis wasn't interested in Pixar's technology. He'd never even been there.

It turned out it didn't matter. "No, no, no," Katzenberg said. "We don't want to mess with this."

"Do you know the background?" Kinsey asked.

"Yes, Jeff told me," Katzenberg said. "I can't waste my time on this stuff. We've got more important things to do."

Kinsey finally called Catmull and said he couldn't interest Disney in a deal. Eventually it was Steve Jobs, the founder of Apple Computer, who saw the potential in Pixar and bought out Lucas's stake.

In the meantime, Kinsey and Roy doggedly pursued a deal to license Pixar's technology. Roy was convinced that with the investment in this new technology, Disney could both manage the soaring costs of traditional hand-drawn animation and reverse the alarming decline in quality that had begun with *Mouse Detective*. He brought the subject up at every opportunity. Katzenberg resisted. He insisted on comparing hand-drawn cels to those drawn by computer, skeptical that a machine could duplicate the quality. But over time, he became persuaded. And Eisner and Wells relented. "Roy wants to do this, and he believes in it," Eisner argued. "I think we have to take a deep breath and say yes."

Peter Schneider, hired to be Roy's "Katzenberg," had only been at Disney a week when Katzenberg asked him to represent the animation department at a meeting on the Universal lot with Steven Spielberg and producers Kathleen Kennedy and Frank Marshall to discuss the *Roger Rabbit* project. When their initial budget came in at an eye-popping $50 million, the project nearly died. But the producers finally whittled it down to $29.9 million, which at the time still made it the most expensive animated movie ever green-lit in Hollywood.

Despite the price tag, Katzenberg was determined to bring the prestige of Spielberg to Disney, and he also argued that the hybrid of live action and animation would "save" the animation department from extinction. Eisner and Wells were apprehensive, but agreed, largely because of their confidence in Spielberg. But Eisner warned Katzenberg he'd have to ride herd on costs.

The *Rabbit* deal was an unusual partnership, which gave Spielberg and director Robert Zemeckis final creative control and a share in any profits. Disney kept all merchandising rights. Spielberg had recruited director Robert Zemeckis fresh from the huge success of *Romancing the Stone* and *Back to the Future,* and Zemeckis had insisted on hiring the man he considered "the best animator in the world," a commercial artist and animator in London named Richard Williams, best known for the "Pink Panther" cartoons. Part of Schneider's job was to manage Williams and coordinate with the Disney animators. Casting character actor Bob Hoskins in the lead role rather than Harrison Ford, Spielberg's choice, saved some money.

But keeping the budget under control was a nearly impossible task, given that Spielberg and Zemeckis had creative control, which meant de facto control over the budget and schedule (something Eisner had learned in his hotel partnership with Tishman). Williams saw himself as an artist, openly disdainful of the Disney bureaucracy, incredulous that Disney animators were expected to clock in when they arrived at work. On one of his first days at the Disney studio, he gathered all the animators to watch a screening of *The Thief and the Cobbler,* an animated labor of love on which he had been toiling since 1968. Williams told Schneider that in return for doing *Roger Rabbit,* Disney and Spielberg would help him distribute *Thief.* He refused to work in Los Angeles, and to accommodate him and his animators, production was moved to London.

Schneider soon realized that for every day spent working on the film, they fell another day behind schedule. The film had been budgeted for a lock-stop camera, but Zemeckis insisted on a moving camera, which doubled costs. Finally Katzenberg told Eisner and Wells that the budget was nearing $40 million, and Eisner exploded, accusing Katzenberg of hiding the bad news from him. "Nothing upsets me more than finding out about a problem when it's too late to do anything about it," he fumed. He ordered Katzenberg to immerse himself in the project and slash costs or else he'd either take control himself or shut down the production.

In a dramatic gesture even by his own standards, Katzenberg summoned the top people involved, including Williams, Spielberg, Zemeckis, Marshall, and Schneider, to a meeting in New York, halfway between Los Angeles and London. The California contingent had to take an overnight flight while the others flew from London. "This isn't working," he began, once they had assembled. "Michael has given me an ultimatum." Schneider had felt the only solution was to fire Williams, but instead Katzenberg told Williams to finish drawing the two major cartoon characters, Roger and Baby Herman, and relieved him of his management duties, which went to Schneider.

In the wake of the meeting, word coursed through the animation community that *Roger Rabbit* was in serious trouble, which prompted a call to Katzenberg from Kim Masters, a reporter for *Premiere* magazine who was working on an article about the mounting disarray. Desperate to stave off bad press, Katzenberg offered Masters exclusive access to the set, animators, and production process if she'd agree not to print anything until the movie was finished. Everyone breathed a sigh of relief when she agreed.

Eisner remained skeptical of both the costs and the quality of the film. He flooded Zemeckis with production notes and complained to Katzenberg when Zemeckis ignored them. Katzenberg argued that Eisner couldn't simply substitute his judgment for that of major talents like Spielberg and Zemeckis. "I'm doing the best I can," Katzenberg finally said in exasperation. "If that's not satisfactory to you, then I'm not the person to do the job." After that exchange, Eisner stopped speaking to him—the first serious rupture in their partnership.

But the silent treatment only lasted a few days. *Roger Rabbit*'s first screening before a test audience of mostly teenagers was in April. Much of the animation wasn't finished, the teenagers grew impatient, and the film broke halfway through. Desperate to prevent any bad word from leaking, Katzenberg summoned everyone to the rear of the theater. "We have just had the greatest preview ever," he said solemnly. The film and audience reactions steadily improved. Roy was delighted with it, though he took Eisner aside in the parking lot after a screening. "This is too risqué for the Disney label," he warned.

"Why?" Eisner asked.

"You know, Jessica's line: 'Is that a gun in your pocket, or are you just glad to see me?' "

Eisner was happy to oblige him, since he thought marketing the film as a Touchstone release would broaden the appeal to adults. Katzenberg, too, was delighted. "This is going to be the number one film of 1988," he confidently predicted.

Who Framed Roger Rabbit? opened in June to ecstatic reviews. *Newsweek* did a cover story. Rita Kempley, writing in the *Washington Post*, raved that

"Roger Rabbit" took an army of artists, 1,000 special effects and more technology than a nuclear submarine. But this humanimated miracle is more than razzle-dazzle. It's also a landmark of high spirits. You get the feeling that everybody involved was in love with the notion—from director Robert Zemeckis of "Back to the Future" to animation director Richard Williams. Hoskins, who reacted to thin air during the filming while a comic in a rabbit suit read Roger's lines off camera, is wonderful. And the chemistry is there— the effervescent essence of Roger, his unbearable lightness really, at odds with Hoskins' stolid fireplug physique. Indeed, Toontown is a new Wonderland, a rowdy, jellybean and yellow-brick-road-colored piece of property, where the flowers dance and the sun has a face and the theme song is "Smile, Darn You, Smile." And that's the best way to get in the mood for this overwhelming charmer.

Roger Rabbit grossed $154 million, and was hugely profitable despite its final cost, which was pretty much the $50-plus million that had been Spielberg's first budget proposal. Eisner and the Imagineers were soon at work on a "Mickey's Toontown" attraction for the theme parks. *Rabbit* merchandise flew off the shelves.

Though he won an Academy Award for his work on *Rabbit,* Williams seemed indifferent to the critical and box-office success, feeling that the film was no longer the picture he'd envisioned. When Katzenberg asked for changes in his beloved *Thief,* Williams refused. Neither Disney nor Spielberg ever distributed the film, which, in a much-altered form disowned by Williams, was eventually released by Miramax under the title *Arabian Knight.* Williams later contended that many elements of *Thief* reappeared in Disney's *Aladdin.* "We took the best out of Richard," Schneider conceded ruefully.

As *Roger Rabbit* opened, the *Oliver Twist* project, now titled *Oliver & Company,* was nearing completion. In keeping with Disney tradition, the main character was now a kitten, and the action had been moved from London to New York City, but it was still a musical. Katzenberg had the idea to bring in a group of big-name singer/songwriters, each of whom would contribute a song: Billy Joel, Barry Manilow, Huey Lewis. At the suggestion of his close friend David Geffen, Katzenberg brought in lyricist Howard Ashman for the song "Once Upon a Time in New York City." Soon after, Geffen also recommended Katzenberg use the composer Alan Menken. Ashman and Menken had written the lyrics for *Little Shop of Horrors,* which Geffen produced off-Broadway, with Schneider as the company manager. Roy's son Tim earned a writing credit on *Oliver.* Schneider thought the resulting production lacked continuity, and coming from a theater background himself, thought it was the wrong way to approach a musical. Still, it was Katzenberg's idea, and Schneider did his best to make it work. A lot was riding on the project. Much of the animation in *Roger Rabbit* had been contracted out to Williams's people; *Oliver,* by contrast, was entirely a Disney production.

Like *Mouse Detective,* no one at Disney was entirely satisfied with the finished *Oliver & Company,* including Katzenberg. But he was impatient with artistic reservations. "Do you want to win the Academy Award or the Bank of America award?" he asked so often that it became a refrain. In that regard *Oliver & Company* had two marketing advantages: the classic Dickens story and a pop score by well-known composers. Katzenberg insisted that Disney put some aggressive marketing behind it. *Oliver* opened in November 1988 and, to everyone's surprise, grossed $53 million, setting a new record for an animated feature.

Katzenberg was not only emboldened by the success of an animated movie that had been his idea, but also by the growing realization that Disney had a virtual monopoly in animation and that it could be even more profitable than live action. After all, there were no high-priced stars or blockbuster directors demanding a percentage of the gross revenues. With almost no demand for their skills beyond Disney, the animators were barely paid above scale, and lived so modestly that at a retreat for the top artists at the Santa Barbara Biltmore, several asked if they could keep the soap and shampoo from their hotel rooms.

Initially preoccupied with the live-action schedule, Katzenberg began devoting more of his time to animation, scheduling 6:00 A.M. meetings on Tuesdays and Fridays at the animation offices in Glendale that typically lasted three hours. Though invited to attend, Roy resented the early hours and when he came, tended to say little. When he did speak, Katzenberg listened impatiently and then ignored him, at least from Roy's perspective. Though the animators had learned to be deferential toward Katzenberg, behind his back they drew cartoons lampooning him. Many of them were adolescent and scatological. In one widely circulated drawing, Katzenberg is urinating on one of the animators' storyboards, one hand outstretched. The caption: "More Diet Coke!"

Just as Eisner had hired Art Levitt on impulse, he took an instant liking to Steve Burke, who, like Levitt, happened to be the son of a powerful father, Dan Burke, the chief executive of Capital Cities/ABC, which owned the ABC network. A recent graduate of Harvard Business School who'd worked a few years at General Foods and American Express, Burke was energetic, personable, and eager, even if his boyish good looks made him look, to Eisner, like a college freshman. Burke was hoping for work in movies or television, but was offered a spot in consumer products, the division that licensed the Disney characters. Disney generated about $100 million in annual profits on Mickey Mouse watches, plush toys, clothing, and other merchandise.

In his newly created job as director of business development, Burke found most employees were trapped in the what-would-Walt-have-done syndrome, so he launched a contest for new business ideas. First prize was a free dinner for two at a restaurant anywhere in the world, although the winners had to pay for their own transportation. He narrowed the finalists to twelve, then presented them to Eisner and Wells. "Let's just do them all," an exuberant Eisner responded.

One of the winning ideas was a concept for stand-alone Disney retail stores outside the theme parks. Larry Murphy was cool to the idea—"a small business with relatively low margins," Murphy warned—and Wells tended to agree. "Can't a company our size try something every once in a while just because it feels right?" Eisner countered. "What if it does fail? It's still not going to cost as much as one expensive movie script."

Eisner prevailed, and Burke was thrilled that Eisner would take such a risk with a young, unproven executive. Eisner rejected his first two store designs, but approved one meant to look like a working movie set, with scenes from the animated films in the windows and previews of upcoming films playing on monitors inside. Eisner insisted that Burke undergo the theme park "cast training" (he portrayed Friar Tuck) and Burke introduced a version of the training for in-store employees, so they could emulate the theme parks.

The stores were a huge success, with sales per square foot setting new records for specialty retailers. Like his earlier decision to develop his own hotel business and reject Marriott, Eisner decided that Disney could build its own retail store operation under Burke. Burke led a rapid expansion, with Disney stores sprouting in every major upscale retail area in the country, including Fifth Avenue in New York and North Michigan Avenue in Chicago. (The chain reached its peak in 2000, with 742 stores worldwide.) Eisner loved to drop in unannounced, and he and Wells showered Burke with notes containing suggestions and criticism. Burke, just thirty years old, suddenly found himself a featured executive at board meetings. He thought he'd found the perfect job. He loved walking down Main Street in Disneyland with his wife and kids, feeling he was an important part of the company.

Nor was Burke the only young executive whose fortunes soared in the new regime. Bill Mechanic, a young executive from Paramount, had followed Eisner and Katzenberg to Disney, hoping to become a movie producer. After he arrived, he met with Katzenberg. "We've got good news and bad news," Katzenberg said. "We have a great job for you, but it's not what you want."

"What?" Mechanic asked.

"Home video."

His spirits sank. Mechanic didn't even own a video recorder, nor was there much of a market for selling videotapes of movies. They were expensive, and most people rented them at a retail outlet. But with an infant daughter at home, Mechanic thought maybe he could sell the classics as high-priced collectibles. After *Pinocchio*'s theatrical re-release, Eisner and Wells had convened a meeting to discuss releasing *Pinocchio* on video the following summer. At first the very idea of selling any of the Disney classics seemed anathema. If American households were filled with videocassettes of the Disney classics, why would families come to theaters every seven years? The films might lose their aura of exclusivity and seem like any other movie. The fledgling Disney cable channel was also counting on airing the classics to attract viewers. Moreover, mass-marketing videos might cheapen the Disney image. Roy was opposed to the idea, and Katzenberg, too, felt it was a mistake. Wells conceded that "there are overwhelming reasons not to do this, but it's important to have the debate."

After his arrival, Mechanic was the most forceful advocate for pushing ahead with video sales, and as a parent, Eisner was skeptical that Disney videos would become collectors' items, handed down from one generation to the next. He could never figure out where all of his own children's toys and books went, but in time they disappeared. Finally the group decided on a compromise approach: Disney would offer *Pinocchio* for sale on video, but at such a high price—$79.95—that almost no one besides video rental outlets could afford to buy it. This would force viewers to rent copies. And sales would be confined to a limited period, at which point the title would be retired to await a new generation. But initial sales at such a high price were modest.

In August, Mechanic decided to experiment by slashing the price to $29.95 and relaunching *Pinocchio* with a marketing campaign that included network television ads. He ended up spending over $7 million, an unheard of amount for a video. His superiors were too busy to pay much attention, but Katzenberg and Rich Frank, the chief operating officer of the studio, were distressed when they found out the ad budget. "Why are you spending money on a market that's presold?" Frank demanded, referring to the fact that everyone already knew about *Pinocchio*.

"We've got to change consumer habits," Mechanic argued. "It's not that easy."

Pinocchio sold out its 1.7 million units.

So Mechanic asked for *Cinderella,* which was that year's Christmas re-release. *Pinocchio* was one thing, but *Cinderella* was a core classic. Katzenberg, backed by Roy, vetoed the idea. Mechanic took the issue to Eisner and Wells, who agreed the issue needed to be debated. They convened a meeting with Katzenberg, Frank, Gary Wilson, and strategic-planning executives. (Roy couldn't attend, but reiterated his opposition to releasing *Cinderella* on video.)

Mechanic placed two large posters on easels at the end of a long conference table. One showed "emotional issues"—"Could releasing the animated classics on video undermine their uniqueness by making them too widely available in viewers' homes?" and "Might such a move cheapen Disney's image and cheapen the brand?"

"We're not here to talk about theories," Eisner began, pretty much dismissing the emotional issues. The ensuing discussion made it clear that, as with most "emotional" issues, there couldn't be any definite answer; maybe it would cheapen the brand, but then again, maybe it wouldn't.

The other poster was titled "economic issues." Mechanic estimated that four theatrical releases of *Cinderella* over the next twenty-eight years (once every seven years) would generate $125 million in revenue. And $125 million in revenue spread over twenty-eight years had a present value of less than $25 million, given the effect of compound interest over time. By contrast, Mechanic estimated that sales of *Cinderella* videos at $29.95 would generate $100 million that year alone, in addition to the revenue from the Christmas theatrical release. Whatever the emotional issues, put this way, the numbers were compelling. "What are we waiting for?" Wells asked.

Katzenberg wasn't pleased. He pulled Mechanic aside and said he had undermined him by going to Eisner and Wells.

"Hey, I thought I was just doing my job," Mechanic said.

Roy still wouldn't budge on *Cinderella*, but agreed to a compromise: *Sleeping Beauty*. Like *Pinocchio*, *Sleeping Beauty* had never performed all that well at the box office.

Mechanic doubled the ad budget, marketing *Sleeping Beauty* as a regal masterpiece, the equal of *Cinderella*. It sold 3 million units.

In the wake of *Sleeping Beauty*'s runaway success, Katzenberg and Roy gave up their resistance to *Cinderella*, though they still wouldn't let Mechanic release Disney's crown jewel, *Snow White*, or Walt's treasured *Fantasia*. The following year, with the aggressive expansion of distribution into discount chains like Caldor and Wal-Mart, *Cinderella* sold 6 million copies, with revenues of $180 million on top of the $34 million *Cinderella* earned in theatrical re-release. In other words, *Cinderella* alone generated more revenue in one year than the estimate of $200 million Eisner gave the Bass brothers as the value of the entire Disney film library. Home video sales rapidly became Disney's biggest profit center apart from the theme parks. Despite their initial disagreements, Mechanic felt that Katzenberg and Roy became enthusiastic supporters.

The success of *Oliver & Company* and the stream of video income, not to mention the ongoing sales and license fees from merchandise, slowly began to convince Eisner that animation, as Roy had always maintained, might indeed be the heart of the company.

By the end of 1988, just four years after Eisner's arrival, Katzenberg's audacious prediction that Disney would be the number one studio at the box office had come true, even earlier than Katzenberg had dared to hope. *Roger Rabbit* was the summer's big hit (though it didn't quite meet Katzenberg's prediction that it would be the year's number one picture; it was runner-up to *Rain Man*, which won the Oscar for Best Picture). Even though Disney had paid over $1 million for the rights to *Three Men and a Baby*, Katzenberg had kept costs to a modest $11 million by casting lower-priced television stars Ted Danson and Tom Selleck in the lead roles. Eisner's prediction that the film would be "hugely commercial" was right: *Three Men and a Baby* grossed $170 million in the United States after it was released at Thanksgiving 1987.

The following January came *Good Morning, Vietnam,* starring Ovitz client Robin Williams, whose fee had dropped drastically after he went into drug rehabilitation to overcome a cocaine habit (which helped explain the manic performance I'd witnessed at the taping of "Mork & Mindy"). The latest in the line of stars whose careers had faltered, Williams joked that Disney cast its movies by hanging out at the back door of the Betty Ford Center, which offered drug and alcohol rehabilitation. "Vietnam" brought in $124 million.

Even Katzenberg, never bashful about predicting success, could hardly believe Disney's good fortune in the cyclical film business. "We are going to run into a bad streak," he warned in a 1987 *New York Times* interview. "We are going to fail big. Just so the scales get properly balanced, we are going to have one of the all-time big flops."

In television, "The Disney Sunday Movie" hosted by Eisner was only a modest success, but "The Golden Girls" proved a bona fide hit for the Touchstone television studio. Eisner and Katzenberg seemed well on their way to repeating Paramount's success at creating hits for television.

Eisner and Katzenberg also put some of the underemployed animators to work making programs for Saturday morning television and a two-hour weekday block called "Disney Afternoon." Twentieth Century Fox owned the Metromedia chain of TV stations, and Eisner persuaded his old friend and colleague Barry Diller to program "Disney Afternoon" on his fledgling Fox network. "Disney Afternoon" soon became Disney's most profitable television venture, earning $40 million a year.

Eisner, Wells, and Katzenberg had presided over the most astonishing studio turnaround in Hollywood history. In part this reflected both the disciplined approach to costs and sheer hard work. Katzenberg's work schedule was legendary. After a few hours of sleep, he routinely arrived at the office at 5:00 A.M., which tended to overshadow the fact that Eisner and Wells worked almost as hard, often seven days a week, and expected the same of everyone else. Sometimes Wells nodded off from exhaustion, only to awake the minute someone stopped speaking. "Keep going, tell me more . . ." he'd say impatiently.

But if tight budgets and hard work were all that it took, there would have been plenty of rivals for the top box-office crown. Eisner's insistence on the importance of the creative process seemed vindicated. As in many creative businesses, it's very difficult to know whom, exactly, to credit for the decisions that created so many hits. Katzenberg essentially ran the studio. But Eisner created a highly charged environment in which creativity could flourish. He had an infectious enthusiasm, a seemingly unerring sense of what audiences wanted. He read scripts avidly and scrawled copious notes on them. He attended weekly meetings of the top film executives, and commented freely and bluntly. He convened intense creative meetings, locking everyone in until good ideas emerged. As the hits spewed out, the excitement was contagious.

Eisner and Wells seemed to manage the company on impulse. Most important decisions were made at Eisner's weekly Monday lunches of division heads, or during casual visits with Wells, or at his Monday night dinners with Katzenberg. There was never a formal agenda. There was no strategic planning before Wilson brought in Larry Murphy. Eisner would ask for a presentation on animation, then suddenly ask, "What about Disneyland?" Conversation would roam freely through the company's businesses. "You could never get to the point," recalls Peter Schneider. "I'd leave scratching my head, wondering if anything had been decided."

Sometimes Wells, and to a lesser extent Gary Wilson, had to restrain Eisner's bolder impulses. Ever since working at ABC, Eisner had wanted to run a television network, and in 1985, Ted Turner made a hostile run at CBS, the "Tiffany" network, which put CBS in play. Eisner desperately wanted Disney to buy it. The proposed price actually made some sense, but Wells and Wilson insisted Eisner back off, arguing that network television was a declining business because of the rise of cable. In any event, Eisner finally agreed that they already had too much on their hands to absorb something as big as a television network. But it was clear he hadn't given up on the idea.

Other than the weekly lunches, Eisner made it a habit to keep his schedule relatively clear. That way, he could convene meetings and make decisions spontaneously as problems arose. Other executives, however, had tightly packed schedules, which meant that whenever Eisner summoned them, they had to cancel other meetings or fall behind.

It fell largely to Wells to bring order to what was otherwise creative chaos. "Frank could be as abrupt as Michael," says another top executive, "but he was rational. Michael was not rational. Frank was the mediator. He was compassionate. He could calm the warring factions." Another executive maintains that "You had to keep Michael out of the room because you couldn't get anything decided while he was there. Later, you'd call Frank, and he'd get Michael to agree to what you wanted." But no one disputed that the process achieved results. "It was very exciting, intoxicating," recalls Schneider. "There was real, not fake, synergy. One idea would spark another. Everything turned to gold."

Operating income at Disney jumped from less than $300 million when Eisner and Wells took the helm to nearly $800 million in 1987. Though the live-action film and animation studios attracted most of the attention, curiously little of the revenue growth actually came from the company's more creative initiatives. An internal analysis commissioned by Gary Wilson to help understand the company's burgeoning profit found that nearly all of it came from just three sources: raising admission prices at the theme parks; greatly expanding the number of company-owned hotels; and distributing the animated classics on home video (a technological development that had happened since Eisner's arrival). These decisions may seem simple and obvious; Wilson had already laid similar plans when Marriott considered taking over Disney. Still, the creative success of the company lent it a luster that was hard to value in dollar terms, but set the stage for even greater growth, through product licensing, new theme park attractions, and new distribution channels.

Disney's success attracted the attention of the press, including Tony Schwartz, who, after his earlier articles about Eisner for *New York* magazine, had a major best-seller as co-author with Donald Trump of *Trump: the Art of the Deal.* Schwartz approached Eisner about a book on the transformation of Disney. Eisner was hesitant but agreed to record his thoughts on a tape recorder in his car in case he decided to go ahead. These tapes convey Eisner's sense that, as he put it on one of them, he was "working in the world's biggest candy store."

Not everyone thrived at the new Disney. Stan Kinsey left after the CAPS project was approved to start a new entertainment technology company with Don Iwerks, a Disney engineer and son of the legendary Ub Iwerks, Walt's chief artist, who had drawn the first Mickey Mouse cartoon. While he admired what Eisner, Wells, and Katzenberg had accomplished, Kinsey was so disillusioned by the cutthroat politics that he vowed never to work in a big corporation again. Wells, his onetime mentor, wished him luck but also showed a tougher side. "Don't even think about doing anything this company is doing," he warned him. "You'd better be damn careful."

John Lasseter, the animator who worked with Kinsey on the CAPS project, joined Richard Williams's studio and then Pixar, after Disney passed him over for a directing assignment. His first film at Pixar, *Luxo Jr.*, about father and son appliances, won awards at the Berlin Film Festival and the World Animation Celebration, and was nominated for an Academy Award.

Jeff Rochlis met his match in Imagineering, where he was installed in 1987 to rein in costs. His reputation as the Terminator having preceded him, every suggestion was met with surly resistance by the Imagineers. They ridiculed his "Triangle of Success" campaign in which Rochlis demanded that Imagineers wear triangle pins representing "budget, schedule, and quality." The "Pleasure Island" attraction at Walt Disney World went so far overbudget that it was almost as though the Imagineers were trying to defy Rochlis. Marty Sklar kept a stream of complaints about Rochlis flowing to Eisner. Rochlis was fired soon after, and filed suit against Disney for breach of contract. (A judge ruled in favor of Disney.)

Five years into his tenure as chief financial officer, Gary Wilson quit to make a successful bid for Northwest Airlines after Wells told him he was having too much fun at Disney to resume mountain climbing or run for public office. Wilson, however, remained on the Disney board.

Bill Mechanic parlayed his success with home video into the presidency of Twentieth Century Fox (he replaced Joe Roth; Larry Gordon had resigned the post soon after Diller became chairman). As much as Mechanic liked Disney, he knew he'd never run the studio as long as Katzenberg was ahead of him. "They always saw me as the guy pitching videos," Mechanic recalls.

Seeing a second-tier Disney executive like Mechanic jump to the top of a rival studio, overnight becoming one of the top executives in the industry, sent a powerful message in Hollywood. Disney was flooded with résumés. Disney was not only making money; it was the "hot" studio sought after by agents, directors, stars, and executives alike.

In his 1987 letter to shareholders, Eisner had trouble containing his glee. "How does one present an 80 percent increase in net income and pretend such an improvement is nothing special? I'd like to say that the only reason for the delay in writing this letter is my difficulty in communicating how well we have done without sounding too cocky, too confident and certainly too proud!"

In the first four years with Eisner and Wells at the helm, Disney stock, adjusted for splits, leaped fourfold, which made Eisner's contract, so hastily negotiated the morning of the board election, extraordinarily lucrative. In 1988 he was paid his salary of $750,000, a bonus of $6.8 million (2 percent of the profits over $100 million), and he earned $32.6 million by exercising some of his stock options. (He had an unrealized profit of $50.5 million on the rest of his options.) His total income of just over $40 million that year made him the highest paid executive in America.

FOUR

Michael Eisner's outsized compensation was hardly lost on Jeffrey Katzenberg. In stark contrast to his boss's millions, Katzenberg was stunned to discover that, despite the fact he'd made Disney the number one studio at the box office, his own bonus that same year was—zero.

Katzenberg fired off an angry memo to Wells, expressing his disappointment and incredulity that notwithstanding the studio's remarkable string of hits and the success of television series like "Golden Girls," Disney's calculation of his 2 percent of profits still came to nothing. Wells adopted a typically conciliatory but firm stance. He wrote back that Katzenberg was "perfectly reasonable" to have expected a bonus and acknowledged the "enormous success" of the studio. Nonetheless, he insisted that, under Disney's accounting practices, the studio was still running at a deficit, even though that was likely to change as soon as revenues were booked as profit. A confidential memo sent to Frank Wells calculated that the studio's output under Katzenberg since 1984 had accumulated a deficit of over $48 million after deducting distribution and overhead charges. By this calculation, *Down and Out in Beverly Hills,* far from the huge success it appeared to be, earned just $2 million on revenues of $18 million, more than offset by a $6.5 million loss on *Adventures in Babysitting.*

"Many of these pictures still have substantial revenues forthcoming," Wells continued, "and of course, will continue 'forever,' " an evident reference to the 2 percent "annuity" that was part of Katzenberg's original deal. Wells sent a copy of his letter to Eisner, along with the handwritten note, "Probably worth a quick read."

Katzenberg wasn't entirely mollified, especially given the huge disparity between his compensation and Eisner's, which hardly seemed to conform to the spirit of the "partnership" they'd forged. Katzenberg's contract didn't expire for two more years, but he began negotiating a new deal with Wells that would extend his tenure at Disney. The course of the negotiations suggests that it was beginning to dawn on Wells (as well as Eisner, with whom Wells discussed the matter) that the provision in Katzenberg's contract entitling him to 2 percent of all profits from any project he generated while at Disney might turn out to be far more lucrative than anyone had anticipated. Wells immediately asked Katzenberg to relinquish his right to the 2 percent lump-sum payment in the event he left the company. Katzenberg said he might, but only if Disney would guarantee that he'd make 75 percent of whatever Eisner earned (including bonuses and stock options). Wells rejected that out of hand, insisting the board would never tie one executive's compensation to another's. Katzenberg countered by asking that revenue from the re-release of the animated classics be counted toward his bonus and lump-sum payment, his rationale being that he directed the marketing and home video campaigns that had been so effective in enhancing the value of the film library. Wells agreed, but in return, he again tried to get Katzenberg to abandon the 2 percent annuity. Katzenberg refused.

Negotiations continued throughout the year. Katzenberg wanted assurances that if Wells should leave, he would be his successor, given his extraordinary success with the studio. As Eisner had often said, financial executives like Wilson were fungible; creative executives like Eisner and Katzenberg were irreplaceable. In one draft of the new contract, Katzenberg's lawyer wrote, "If Frank leaves, you replace him."

Though Eisner kept his distance from the negotiations, Wells kept him informed, and the issue of Katzenberg's succession annoyed him. "I won't make that deal," he exclaimed at one point. Eisner blamed Katzenberg's demands in large part on David Geffen, who had become a billionaire by selling Geffen Records to MCA Corp. Since their first meeting, he and Katzenberg had gradually become best friends. They spoke on the phone every day and were sharing a vacation house in Acapulco when the issue arose. Eisner complained to Katzenberg's lawyer, Arthur Emil, that Geffen was wielding undue influence on Katzenberg, and Eisner seemed to resent their close relationship.

Though Wells assured Katzenberg that he was his successor, and said he'd even discussed the eventuality with Roy, Stanley Gold, and Sid Bass, Eisner made sure that such language never made it into the final contract. So instead of extending the contract for another six years from the expiration of his current deal, to 1996, Katzenberg said he wanted an option to leave two years sooner, in 1994, in the event Wells stepped down and someone other than he took his place.

Still, there was plenty to reassure Katzenberg in his new deal. Besides an enhanced salary of $750,000, a grant of 500,000 stock options, Disney agreed to pay $4 million toward the new beach house Katzenberg was building in Malibu, and retained the lump-sum payout provision—still a "tremendous concept," Wells wrote, that "should increase by a big amount."

In a handwritten letter to Eisner dated June 26, Katzenberg expressed his appreciation. "The last few months were very difficult for all of us. But they are behind us and I just want you to know that I feel great about where we ended up. Most importantly to me . . . way beyond the dollars and cents of it all, is [the] fact that in the end you came thru [sic] and delivered for me. . . . We've been together a very long time, in fact, in terms of Hollywood time-keeping about 3 lifetimes so far. I not only hope but I'm counting on us stay-ing together *forever*. You've been great. You've handled my crap with extraordinary patience and care and understanding. I'm deeply appreciative and do love you for it. Jeffrey."

After the surprising success of *Oliver & Company*, Katzenberg and Schneider were on the prowl for another Broadway-style musical, and Schneider turned to Howard Ashman, whom he knew from *Little Shop of Horrors*, where Schneider had worked as the show's stage manager. A native of Balti-more with a master's degree from Indiana University, Ashman had begun writing plays while working as an editor at Grosset & Dunlap publishers, and later became artistic director of the WPA, an off-Broadway theater that pro-duced *Little Shop*. Ashman, however, was worried about how he'd be treated working for Disney. He told Schneider he was gay, and asked how "progres-sive" Disney would be. "We're open, tolerant, and very supportive of diver-sity," Schneider assured him. Ashman didn't seem entirely convinced. "It is the Walt Disney Company," he said, though he thought Eisner's decision to permit same-sex dancing at Disney World was a step in the right direction.

After the modest success of *Mouse Detective*, animator Ron Clements re-vived his idea for the Hans Christian Andersen fairy tale "Little Mermaid." This time the animators produced a longer treatment of the story, which in-troduced a villain—Ursula, a giant sea witch—and a happy ending, in which the mermaid becomes human and is united with Eric, her prince charming. Eisner and Katzenberg read the new version the same night they received it,

and Katzenberg immediately recognized the new elements as Walt's prescription for the animated classics: good versus evil, overcoming odds to realize a dream, and a happy ending. "We've got to do this," Katzenberg
enthused to Eisner the next morning.

Splash was now safely in the distant past, and Katzenberg and Eisner gave
some thought to developing "Mermaid" as a live-action project. Writer
Michael Cristofer, who'd won a Pulitzer Prize for his play *The Shadow Box,*
briefly worked on a script, but Clements persuaded Katzenberg to give him
and John Musker a shot at the script. Geffen, meanwhile, kept insisting to
Katzenberg that Ashman was a "genius," and that Disney should find more
work for him. So in 1986, Katzenberg and Schneider met with Ashman and
showed him some of the animated projects in development, including *Little
Mermaid,* which was the script that captured Ashman's interest.

Ashman and his composing partner, Alan Menken, commuted weekly
from New York to California, and claimed an office next door to Clements
and Musker at the animation warehouse in Glendale. Less extroverted and
acerbic than Ashman, Menken had grown up in suburban New Rochelle,
New York, and composed and sang commercial jingles while writing more
ambitious musical scores. His first collaboration with Ashman was for a 1979
WPA production of *God Bless You, Mr. Rosewater,* which led to *Little Shop.*
They and the animators darted in and out of one another's offices, trying
new ideas.

Ashman had the idea to structure the opening sequence as an under-
water montage, for which he and Menken wrote the song "Fathoms Below."
He proposed staging "Under the Sea" as a jubilant calypso number. Ashman
transformed Ursula into a raspy-voiced, overweight octopus who sashays
through the film in a sleeveless black gown, a character modeled on Divine,
the transvestite star of *Hairspray, Female Trouble,* and other cult movie hits
far removed from the Disney canon. Ashman wanted the crab Sebastian to
be a wisecracking Trinidadian. The character of Sebastian let the writers
bring comedy into the script and allowed Menken to write songs that were
clever pastiches of calypso and reggae tunes, just as *Little Shop* had recycled
1950s pop styles.

Katzenberg was dazzled by Ashman's knowledge of theater and music,
and especially his familiarity with the Disney canon. It seemed that everything Katzenberg had struggled to learn in his long hours in the Disney
archives Ashman already knew. Ashman naturally dominated the process;
animators often saw him hovering over Menken at the piano, showing him

how to adapt the melodies to his lyrics. The animators thought of Ashman as the John Lennon to Menken's Paul McCartney.

After the songwriting team had finished five numbers, Schneider summoned Eisner, Katzenberg, and Roy Disney for a run-through. As soon as he heard "Under the Sea," Eisner was convinced Ashman and Menken had created a song that would be a hit on its own, whatever the fate of the movie. Roy was captivated by the undersea theme, and retrieved some undersea footage of a giant octopus from one of the nature documentaries he'd worked on when he first came to the studio (though the real-life octopus bore scant resemblance to the campy Ursula). Katzenberg, too, felt mounting enthusiasm about the quality of the film. *Oliver* had been a first step, but no one had ever approached an animated film as though it were a Broadway musical. Schneider had been right that a musical needed a unifying score and lyrics. *Mermaid* felt fresh, original, and exciting. Still, Katzenberg cautioned that the commercial potential of a film about a mermaid was probably limited by its appeal to young girls.

Early screenings were not as promising as the songs. Katzenberg, in particular, had problems with the third act's resolution of the threat from Ursula. It simply didn't make any sense that the gentle mermaid Ariel would be so easily able to overcome the all-powerful sea witch Ursula. "This just doesn't work," Katzenberg said on several occasions before leaving screenings. This had become Katzenberg's style: something either "worked" or it "didn't work." The animators found it disconcerting, but they had to concede that Katzenberg's broad instincts were almost always right, as opposed to his more specific suggestions, most of which they ignored. It was best for Katzenberg to identify the problems, then let the animators figure out a solution.

At one early screening, kids squirmed during the musical sequence "Kiss the Girl," a gentle lullaby that was still in black-and-white sketches. "We're cutting that song," Katzenberg said as soon as the screening was over.

"You can't cut that song!" Ashman practically yelled.

"Okay. We'll cut it in half," Katzenberg replied. Ashman looked wounded. Everyone tried to change Katzenberg's mind, and finally the lead artist, Glen Keane, got him to leave the song alone for one more screening. Ashman and the others held their breath as the sequence, now in full color, played. No one in the audience budged, and the song stayed. But "Fathoms Below" was cut; unlike a Broadway show, Katzenberg didn't think audiences would sit through a lengthy opening musical number.

In another early screening, Eisner was perplexed by Sebastian's sudden transformation from Ariel's foe to friend. Animators were still relying largely on the old storyboard approach, despite his insistence on scripts. "Why can't these problems be solved at the script stage?" he asked. At his behest, new scenes were created—a beach encounter between Ariel and Sebastian, and, at the climax, a scene where Eric destroys Ursula by crashing his boat into her.

Little Mermaid was the first animated film to use CAPS, the new computer system that Kinsey and Roy had championed, which made it much easier to create and insert new sequences. Even so, *Mermaid* was going over its already high budget of $40 million, and because of costs, the full artistic potential of the new system couldn't be tapped. The colors used for Ariel, for example, were scaled back from eleven to seven, saving nearly $750,000. And in the end, only the scene where Ariel and the Prince head off into a rainbow as the undersea characters wave was computer-generated.

As the film neared completion, Schneider was overseeing the final dubbing and the scoring of the music. Menken showed up for the sessions, but Ashman stayed in New York. "Where's Howard?" Schneider asked. Menken said Ashman didn't want to travel. Both Schneider and Katzenberg thought it was odd, given Ashman's pivotal role in making the film, but didn't give it much thought. Toward the end of the process, Disney scheduled an unusual preview screening at night. The mostly adult audience seemed enchanted, and broke into applause at the end. Katzenberg was elated, and immediately changed the marketing plan. Initially worried that the film would appeal mostly to young girls, the campaign was broadened to target parents as well.

Little Mermaid opened in November 1989. "The heroine of Hans Christian Andersen's story 'The Mermaid' failed in her bid to become human, and became a disembodied spirit relegated to spending centuries in limbo," wrote Janet Maslin in *The New York Times.* " 'The Little Mermaid,' a glorious Walt Disney version of this tale and the best animated Disney film in at least 30 years, is due for immortality of a happier kind. 'The Little Mermaid' is a marvel of skillful animation, witty songwriting and smart planning. It is designed to delight filmgoers of every conceivable stripe." *Little Mermaid* grossed an astounding $110 million at the box office in the United States, $222 million worldwide.

As box-office revenues from *Mermaid* poured in, Katzenberg pressed to boost production of animated films. Eisner and Wells, who had initially considered abandoning animation altogether, and had then banished it to Glendale, took little persuading. Disney animators had traditionally worked on a civilized, if not leisurely, schedule that generated a new film every four years.

With Katzenberg's encouragement, Eisner insisted he now wanted one every twelve to eighteen months. At meetings with the animators, Katzenberg mixed praise with exhortations for more. "Bigger, better, faster, cheaper" became his mantra, often mockingly parodied by animators who resented the increasing demands and long hours.

Many of them took their complaints to Roy, who had emerged as the champion of the division's traditional methods and values. Schneider and some of the other animators used code names to discuss the top Disney executives; Roy was "the Godfather" or "the shepherd," Eisner was "Dad," and Katzenberg was "Mom." Despite his position as head of the division and vice chairman of the company, Roy continued to defer to Katzenberg, and his attendance at the weekly meetings where Katzenberg made most of the important decisions became sporadic. When he did attend, he said little, as was his wont, especially with someone as decisive and opinionated as Katzenberg. Still, he played an active if quiet role in the division. Roy conveyed most of his suggestions through Schneider, and talked directly with many of the animators. He saw rough cuts of all the animated films, and made detailed notes. Roy worried that radically stepping up production would inevitably erode the quality of the animated films.

Eisner disagreed. Ever since director James L. Brooks had grudgingly conceded that budgets and tight schedules had made *Terms of Endearment* a better picture, Eisner was convinced that such pressures and the resulting discipline improved quality. It fell to Schneider to mediate between Eisner and Katzenberg on the one hand, and Roy and the animators on the other. He tried to steer a middle ground. "If cheaper means not squandering money, we are making strides to improve the efficiency and better manage the process," he wrote Eisner in a December 1989 memo. "If cheaper means smaller budgets for our movies, then this is in conflict with 'bigger, better.' With Jeffrey and Roy's desire to make truly top production value movies, it will cost more money. In my opinion, the reason that Disney animated movies were and can again be great is the ability to throw out and redo and make it better. The money spent during the making of 'Mermaid' made a good movie into a great movie."

So budgets rose, but so did production. Employment in the animation division soared. To keep all the animators busy, Roy proposed reviving a long-cherished dream: the making of a new *Fantasia,* a sequel of sorts to Walt's 1940 classic. Walt had always envisioned *Fantasia,* a collection of animated segments set to classical music, as a work-in-progress, something that could be constantly updated and refreshed. Though Eisner explored the idea in a meeting with composer-conductor Leonard Bernstein, he'd been cool to the idea. Katzenberg hated it. Still, Roy persisted.

Then Eisner hit on a compromise. Roy was still resisting the release on video of both the original *Fantasia* and *Snow White*. So Eisner proposed using the proceeds from the sale of *Fantasia* videos to finance a *Fantasia* sequel under Roy's direction. After a meeting with Eisner and family members, Roy agreed. *Fantasia* sold 15 million copies, and Eisner called Lillian, Walt's widow, to tell her that *Fantasia* had finally earned a profit.

But Katzenberg remained hostile to a new *Fantasia*, which became an ongoing source of unspoken friction between him and Roy. As work began on the project, Katzenberg showed no interest in it. Roy and the animators held meetings and reviewed storyboards without him, something that would have been unthinkable on any other feature animation project. Instead, Roy dealt directly with Eisner.

Katzenberg was in any event too busy with his own projects to worry about Roy's. In keeping with the faster pace, he rushed to sign Ashman and Menken to another project even before *Mermaid* was released. The pair turned to a musical retelling of "Aladdin and the Magic Lamp," the tale from the *Arabian Nights*. Ashman had already mapped out the script, and he and Menken had completed several songs, but Eisner didn't feel confident about the mass appeal of a story set in the Middle East. So Katzenberg had them drop work on *Aladdin* and persuaded them to move to another classic fairy tale, "Beauty and the Beast."

Beauty and the Beast had been in development for over a year as a traditional Disney animated fairy tale, and a team of British animators had been hired to give it a fresh look. But now Ashman made it his next candidate for the Broadway musical treatment. Clements and Musker were brought in as producers, and the British team was dismissed. Ashman and Menken went to work on a new score and lyrics, and the musical elements were woven seamlessly into the plot, just as Rodgers and Hammerstein had used music, lyrics, and dance to advance the plots of their Broadway musicals. This time Ashman got his way with a Broadway-style extended musical opening. "Belle," the opening number, was a musical montage that occupied a full seven minutes of screen time, an unheard-of length in an animated feature.

Most of the creative work on *Beauty* was done in New York to accommodate Ashman. Soon after the opening of *Little Mermaid*, he told his partner, Bill Lauch, an architect, that he was meeting in New York with Katzenberg, and "I've got to tell him, and I've got to tell him today." Only Lauch and

Ashman's family knew that he had AIDS, which had been diagnosed more than a year before. Ashman had been very nervous about Disney's reaction, given the stigma of the disease, but the success of Little Mermaid gave him the strength.

Ashman told Lauch that Katzenberg had been great, taking the news in stride. "Okay," Katzenberg had said. "What do you need? We'll do it." Schneider and Eisner were equally supportive. They were surprised, but realized they shouldn't have been, given Ashman's increasing absences in California. At considerable expense, Disney moved the entire Beauty and the Beast team to the Residence Inn, an extended-stay hotel in Fishkill, New York, a Hudson River town not far from Ashman's house. Screenings were held at the hotel. Ashman continued to review storyboards and to sing new lyrics to Menken's songs in an increasingly weak but determined voice. He and Menken listened to a recording of Stephen Sondheim's A Little Night Music, finding inspiration in Sondheim's sophisticated, bittersweet comedy of manners.

Like so many of the classic fairy tales, the original "Beauty and the Beast" has dark overtones and an unhappy ending. As with Mermaid, Ashman proposed changes that transformed the story into something that was both more emotionally satisfying and in line with the Disney formula. He shifted the story's point of view from the pretty but somewhat bland ingenue Belle to the more complex Beast, a kind spirit trapped in a repulsive body, which let the audience share the Beast's deep longing for love and a normal life. The Beast's rival for Belle's affection was changed from the foppish Gaston into a muscular, square-jawed, even sexy suitor whose handsome surface and grossly sexist prejudices made him the psychological opposite of the Beast. From an animation standpoint, Ashman had the strikingly original idea to turn the inanimate objects of the Beast's kitchen and dining room into characters, and then unleash them in a dazzling Broadway-style production number, "Be Our Guest." Still, Ashman didn't always get his way. Katzenberg cut one of his favorite songs, "Human Again," saying it was redundant.

While the CAPS computer system was still in its infancy in Little Mermaid, its potential was fully realized in Beauty. The system made possible much more lavish and realistic background images. At one meeting, Katzenberg criticized the ceiling in the Beast's castle. "Fix the ceiling," he insisted. "Make it French, like Botticelli." While the Botticelli gaffe was widely repeated among the animators, the ceiling was redrawn in dazzling detail.

The renaissance of animation was confirmed in March 1990, when Little Mermaid won two Academy Awards, including Best Song for "Under the

Sea." Ashman and Menken accepted the award. "At home, there's my mom, there's my sister, there's Nancy and Bill. I feel really lucky," Ashman said. Only after the ceremony did Ashman finally tell Menken that he had AIDS.

Even more remarkable than the awards and critical acclaim was the film's effect on the bottom line—not just box-office revenues but sales of home videocassettes, which amounted to 9 million units and $180 million, not to mention Ariel dolls and other merchandise.

That summer, Katzenberg, Roy, and Schneider were flying from London to Paris to help promote the European opening of Little Mermaid. The group was ruminating about coming-of-age stories, and that watershed moment— the birth of a child, perhaps—when the child becomes a man. Katzenberg started telling the story of such a moment in his life. "I'd like to tell that story, set in Africa," he said, the inspiration having just come to him. Katzenberg had been fascinated by Africa ever since he worked on a movie set in Kenya when he was twenty-one. "The animal kingdom is a metaphor," he contin-ued. "A child loses a parent, goes out into the world, tries to avoid responsi-bility, then faces it. . . ." Katzenberg looked at his audience. "Uh-huh," Schneider said noncommittally. "I like the idea of animals," Katzenberg con-tinued. Little Mermaid, Beauty and the Beast, Aladdin all had humans as the main characters.

Not only was this his idea, but the coming-of-age aspect resonated deeply with Katzenberg. At one of the script meetings, he told a story of his own loss of innocence, while working in the 1972 presidential campaign of John Lindsay. As an advance man, he took hundreds of thousands in unrecorded cash campaign contributions, including a cash-filled envelope from a man who subsequently profited enormously from dealings with the city. Cash contributions weren't illegal at the time, but bribery was, and Katzenberg ended up being subpoenaed by a grand jury investigating Lindsay and the businessman. Though no charges resulted, it was a searing education in money and politics for Katzenberg, and as he told the story he choked up and couldn't continue, a rare display of emotion.

The very originality of Katzenberg's idea was as much a risk as a possible virtue. All of the great Disney classics starting with Snow White had been adaptations of tried-and-true classics. When they returned to Los Angeles, Schneider put the idea into development, but with a distinctly second-tier group of directors and animators, since the division's stars—Musker and Clements, animator Glen Keane—were already occupied with Beauty and the Beast and Aladdin. To help oversee the project, Schneider drafted Thomas Schumacher, a producer for The Rescuers Down Under, an artistic success but one of Disney's rare commercial failures when it was released in November 1990. A script slowly began to evolve under the working title *King of the Jungle*.

The enormous success and creative explosion in animation began to overshadow the live-action studio, but there, too, the Disney profit juggernaut continued to roll on, with *Cocktail* starring Tom Cruise in 1988 and *Honey, I Shrunk the Kids* and *Dead Poets Society* opening the same year as *Mermaid*. In *Dead Poets Society*, the prep school English teacher played by Robin Williams was loosely based on Eisner's favorite professor at Denison, and the film won the Academy Award for best original screenplay. Eisner credited marketing head Dick Cook for the idea to open *Dead Poets*, a relatively serious film with appeal to adults as well as teenagers, into a summer schedule crowded with special effects adventures and light comedies. *Dead Poets* alone brought in $236 million worldwide.

In the wake of such unprecedented success, Eisner and Katzenberg embarked on the same strategy as in animation: sharply boost production. In order to accommodate both of Katzenberg's top production executives, David Hoberman and Ricardo Mestres, Disney launched a sister studio to Touchstone, Hollywood Pictures, the name taken from Eisner's earlier plan to reinvent American International Pictures, had he taken over that studio. Walt Disney Pictures, the vehicle for live-action family fare, was placed under Hollywood, reporting to Mestres. Katzenberg had persuaded Eisner, over Wells's strenuous objections, that another studio would enable Disney to capitalize on the explosive growth in multiplex theaters, which meant far more demand for new films and potentially wide distribution. Wells argued that other studios had tried the same strategy and failed, but other studios didn't have Disney's track record. Katzenberg's 1987 warning that a flop was inevitable now seemed just a fleeting moment of self-doubt that had been proven wrong. In the notoriously fickle business of moviemaking, twenty-seven of Disney's first thirty-three films under the Eisner/Wells/Katzenberg regime had been profitable, including nineteen in a row. Disney seemed to have discovered a foolproof formula for hit movies, something that had eluded even the greatest of filmmakers.

The only studio that wasn't sharing in Disney's amazing box-office success was Walt Disney Productions, the old family-oriented live-action studio that had made *Mary Poppins* and *20,000 Leagues Under the Sea*. In addition to putting Walt Disney Pictures under the new Hollywood label, Katzenberg also hired David Vogel, a young executive who'd worked with Steven Spiel-berg on Amblin's "Amazing Stories" TV series, to bring in some fresh ideas. After working at Disney for about a year, he was invited to give a presentation on the studio to Eisner, Wells, Katzenberg, and other studio executives. He spoke for an hour, arguing that *Raiders, Close Encounters of the Third Kind, Ghost Busters, Cocoon*—"These are the movies that Walt Disney would have made today. They're not dog and cat movies. They appeal to the child in everyone, not just children. They're about the triumph of the human spirit." In Vogel's view, even Spielberg's *Schindler's List,* a story about a concentra-tion camp, which had just opened to critical acclaim, could have been a Walt Disney picture.

Eisner was enthusiastic, and even though Vogel didn't get much of a budget to implement his ambitious vision, he at least felt he was on Eisner's radar.

As production rapidly geared up from fifteen to more than thirty films a year, it became harder to stick to the high-concept, low-budget comedies that had made the Disney formula such a success. It was a rule laid down by Eisner that no director could be guaranteed more than $1 million a picture, even as the going rate for top directors rose to the $3 million level. Katzen-berg and other Disney executives constantly had to beg top directors and stars to take a cut to make a Disney film. On some projects, they settled for second-rate scripts and talent, like a project Katzenberg approved called "3000," a dark story about a Los Angeles prostitute, which he insisted be rewritten as a modern-day fairy tale. The project was rechristened as *Pretty Woman.*

At a meeting to present the project to Eisner, Katzenberg explained the concept and said the film would star Julia Roberts, who was virtually un-known, and Richard Gere.

"You've got to be out of your mind," Eisner said. Gere had been the star of the ill-fated *King David.* Eisner had never gotten over the fact that Gere had worn "skirts," as he put it—actually authentic Hebrew garb of the period—which Eisner felt had alienated mainstream audiences and damaged Gere's appeal.

Stung by Eisner's tone, Katzenberg angrily pointed out that Disney didn't have enough films in development that were coming together in time to meet its release schedule.

"If I have to say yes to this movie because we need a movie, then fine," Eis-ner replied. "But this movie is going to be a bomb. It's a failure before I've even seen it." Then Eisner got up and walked out, leaving Katzenberg fuming and everyone else in the meeting speechless.

Just as Eisner had broken the budget mold at Paramount with *Raiders*, he was occasionally willing to gamble on a major "event" picture. *Dick Tracy*, an elaborate take on the famed cartoon strip, starring and directed by A-list talent Warren Beatty, rapidly soared above its $23 million budget and commanded a disproportionate amount of the time and attention of Disney studio executives, especially Katzenberg. Beatty was indecisive, a perfectionist, and insisted on numerous takes of scenes. Notoriously promiscuous, Beatty was having an affair with his co-star, Madonna, even while arranging afternoon trysts on the set with other women. Though charming, Beatty consumed vast amounts of Katzenberg's time: He had to spend an inordinate amount of time on the set and had dinner with Beatty every night, either at the studio or at Hamburger Hamlet in West Hollywood. *Dick Tracy* eventually cost $47 million, which would have been far higher if Katzenberg hadn't kept such close watch.

Pretty Woman, by contrast, already declared a failure by Eisner, was produced for a relatively modest $14 million. Producer Garry Marshall had to fight the usual budget battles, but succeeded in keeping the tone of the film cheerful and upbeat, a modern-day *Pygmalion*, in line with Katzenberg's vision for the film. A scene where Julia Roberts's character uses a trip to the bathroom to inject drugs was dropped; she flosses her teeth instead. Though Roberts's character is surely one of the most virginal prostitutes ever portrayed on film, some Disney executives were concerned that it glorified prostitution. "It's a fantasy!" Katzenberg responded with some exasperation.

Pretty Woman opened in March 1990. Despite Disney's worries, Roger Ebert wrote in the *Chicago Sun-Times* that "It's astonishing that 'Pretty Woman' is such an innocent movie—that it's the sweetest and most openhearted love fable since 'The Princess Bride.' Here is a movie that could have marched us down mean streets into the sinks of iniquity, and it glows with romance." Only after he saw the opening weekend box office did Eisner concede the film might be a hit. *Pretty Woman* grossed $463 million worldwide, the most successful live-action film by far in Disney's history.

Dick Tracy opened three months later, backed by an extraordinary $54 million marketing campaign. Reviews were mixed: praise for the stylish, brightly colored sets and costumes, but tepid reactions to the overall effect. The film grossed a respectable $100 million, which barely covered production and marketing costs. Merchandise tie-ins languished mostly unsold.

Thoughts of turning *Dick Tracy* into an Indiana Jones–style franchise evaporated.

The excitement at Disney over the success of *Pretty Woman*, and the preoccupation with *Dick Tracy*, helped disguise the disconcerting reality that during that same year, something went fundamentally awry with the Disney formula. The nearly unbroken series of profitable films abruptly ended. For the first time, some studio executives began quietly questioning Eisner's judgment, which no longer seemed infallible. After all, he had championed *Dick Tracy*, and dismissed *Pretty Woman*. Most of the studio's live-action films, even low-budget ones, were commercial and critical failures, forgotten almost as soon as they disappeared from screens. The multiplex cinema phenomenon offered more opportunity but also more competition. Word-of-mouth and critical reception, so long the driving forces behind audience demand, began to give way to marketing blitzes, big stars, and "event" films that drew huge audiences to opening weekends. Other studios that year produced mega-hits *Die Hard 2, Back to the Future III, Total Recall*. Even the family audience flocked to the non-Disney *Home Alone* and *Teenage Mutant Ninja Turtles*, films that openly mimicked the Disney formula. By contrast, Disney produced the soon-to-be-forgotten *Marrying Man, Run, Taking Care of Business, Spaced Invaders*—to name a few—and turned down as too expensive the script for the Clint Eastwood thriller *In the Line of Fire*.

In part due to the success of Michael Ovitz and his agents at CAA, costs soared for the kinds of stars, as well as for big-name directors and screenwriters, that could all but guarantee an opening-weekend audience. For Disney, the sequel to the low-budget *Three Men and a Baby* became the high-budget *Three Men and a Little Lady*. The year's big hit wasn't a Disney film at all, but *Home Alone*, produced by Joe Roth, now the head of Twentieth Century Fox.

The previous summer, Katzenberg had handed Dan Wolf, manager of public affairs for the studio, a copy of Eisner's analysis of the movie business while he was at Paramount. "I'd like to do something along these lines," Katzenberg told Wolf. "You know, put out my philosophy." Both were too busy to work on it, though, until Wolf joined Katzenberg the following August, in 1990, at his house in Malibu, where the two spent hours together brainstorming, refining the "singles and doubles" strategy espoused by Eisner. Wolf wrote an eighteen-page draft, but then the project again languished.

Though Eisner had declared the 1990s the "Disney Decade," and renewed a promise to deliver 20 percent annual earnings growth over five years, Roy and other board members worried that such a feat was becoming mathematically impossible given how fast Disney's earnings had already grown. "At that rate, we would have been over the moon by 2000," Roy noted. *Business-Week* questioned Disney's strategy in June of 1990, quoting an analyst to the effect that "There are reasonable limits to how big the pie can get," and noted that former chief financial officer Gary Wilson unloaded his $60 million in Disney stock that year.

As the year drew to a close, Katzenberg felt drained of his usually irrepressible optimism. David Geffen worried that he was depressed, and recommended therapy. Katzenberg even thought about taking a leave from work. That Christmas, he retreated to the Kahala Hilton in Hawaii, where it rained every day. He read biographies of William S. Paley and Samuel Goldwyn. He brooded about *Dick Tracy* and the performance of the studio. As his thoughts proliferated, he returned to the project he'd begun with Wolf, and started calling him from Hawaii every day. New drafts were faxed back and forth. As Katzenberg continued, he grew more excited about this developing "manifesto" and its potential to restore the studio's magic. After he returned to Los Angeles, they polished the draft. Finally he sent copies of the twenty-eight-page memo to Eisner, as well as other Disney executives.

"As we begin the new year," Eisner read, "I strongly believe we are entering a period of great danger and even greater uncertainty. Events are unfolding within and without the movie industry that are extremely threatening to our studio."

As he read, Eisner couldn't help but think of his own industry memo, written at Paramount almost exactly ten years earlier: "Success in the motion picture business is highly prone to prompting complacency and recklessness. . . ."

Eisner continued reading. "Some of you might be surprised to read these words. After all, wasn't Disney number one in 1990? Yes, but our number one status was far from a sign of robust health. Instead, it merely underscored the fact that our studio did the least badly in a year of steady decline for all of Hollywood . . . a year that was capped off by a disastrous Christmas for nearly everyone.

"Since 1984, we have slowly drifted away from our original vision of how to run a movie business. Once we had a fairly strict and pretty successful strategy, which we referred to as our 'Singles and Doubles Philosophy.' At some point we seem to have replaced it with a strategy that might best be called the 'Yes, But Philosophy' "—here Eisner underlined the words and wrote "well said"—"as in, 'Yes, he's expensive, but it's a great opportunity for us' or 'Yes, that's a lot to spend on marketing, but we have too much at stake not to. . . .'

"Our initial success at Disney was based on the ability to tell good stories well. Big stars, special effects and name directors were of little importance. Of course, we started this way out of necessity. We had small budgets and not much respect. So we substituted dollars with creativity and big stars with talent we believed in. Success ensued. With success came bigger budgets and bigger names. We found ourselves attracting the caliber of talent with which 'event' movies could be made. And more and more, we began making them. The result: costs have escalated, profitability has slipped and our level of risk has compounded. The time has come to get back to our roots. If we remain on our present course, there will be the certainty of calamitous failure, as we will inevitably come to produce our own 'Havana' or 'Two Jakes' or 'Air America' or 'Another 48 Hrs.' or 'Bonfire of the Vanities' [all enormous flops] and then have to dig ourselves out from under the rubble."

Katzenberg bemoaned the "blockbuster" mentality that had overtaken the industry, noting that "the shelf life of many movies has come to be somewhat shorter than a supermarket tomato." His proposed solution was basically to go back to the earlier Disney formula.

Eisner had little trouble with these points, nearly all of which he considered his ideas in the first place. But he cringed when Katzenberg began discussing specific projects and naming names, especially *Dick Tracy* and Warren Beatty: " 'Dick Tracy' is a case in point as to how the box-office mentality is affecting the movie-going experience," Katzenberg wrote. We "knew that its success would be for the most part judged by its opening weekend box-office performance. So we did everything that we could in order to get the film [the] audience and recognition we felt it deserved. . . . It seems that, like lemmings, we are all racing faster and faster into the sea, each of us trying to outrun and outspend and outearn the other in a mad sprint toward the mirage of making the next blockbuster. In this atmosphere of near hysteria, I feel that we at Disney have been seriously distracted from doing what we do best." Which was to say, movies like *Pretty Woman*, "the kind of modest, story-driven movie we tended to make in our salad days."

Eisner could hardly miss the similarity to the situation at Paramount that had prompted his own memo: the costly failure of *Reds*, another Warren Beatty epic, and the huge success of *Raiders of the Lost Ark*, which masked a series of other failed movies. Then Katzenberg took a parting slap at Beatty: "When Warren Beatty comes to us to pitch his next movie—a big period action film, costing $40 million, with huge talent participation, [an obvious reference to Beatty's upcoming film, *Bugsy*] . . . we must hear what they have to say, allow ourselves to get very excited over what will likely be a spectacular film event, then slap ourselves a few times, throw cold water on our faces and soberly conclude that it's not a project we should choose to get involved in." *Dick Tracy,* Katzenberg concluded, "was also about losing control of our own destiny. And that's too high a price to pay for any movie." Nor did Eisner like the fact that Katzenberg singled out Steve Martin, Bill Murray, Dustin Hoffman, and Sylvester Stallone—all of whom Disney had negotiated with—as examples of the "celebrity surcharge" that was driving up the cost of movies.

While free with his criticism of past films, Katzenberg exempted the studio's current projects, citing *Scenes from a Mall, Billy Bathgate,* and *What About Bob?* (starring Bill Murray in a package negotiated by Ovitz) as "outstanding projects" while conceding there are "too many of them." And he specifically hailed the $35 million *The Rocketeer* as "the kind of event film we must continue to make."

Eisner began jotting down comments. Where Katzenberg called for films that were "affirmative and uplifting," Eisner wrote "It would be fun for us to do a tragedy once a year or once every other year—even if it is a single or a double." And later, he found it necessary to remind Katzenberg that profit isn't everything. "Even if once in a while we would be successful with low life action 'junk'—so what—we do not need that success," he wrote. By the end, when Katzenberg makes an innocuous observation that "The theater is something special. The products we strive to put into them should be equally special," Eisner can barely contain himself. "This sends the wrong and expensive signal and is contrary to everything you have said so far," he scrawled in the margin.

Katzenberg concluded with a passage that struck Eisner as unmitigated self-promotion: "Passion is the only word that can explain why one would choose to burrow through 10 to 15 scripts every weekend on the chance of uncovering something great. Passion is the only word that can explain why one would spend a 60-hour week at a studio and then, for fun, on the weekend go see three movies. . . . So let's go back to the drawing board and get back to basics. And, as we do, let's not be afraid to admit to others and ourselves, up front and with passion . . . that we love what we do."

Eisner evidently felt a mix of emotions. At the bottom of the page he wrote, "As I finished this paper I really felt good that we are more than basically on the same wave length—I could have written (not as well though) this paper—We agree!" Eisner stopped Dan Wolf in the hall and told him he thought the memo was "great." However sincere at the time, the good feelings didn't last long. Eisner was soon feeling a mix of resentment, suspicion, and anger. Katzenberg's memo was in some ways so similar to his own memo at Paramount that it bordered on "plagiarism," as he later put it. Yet Eisner's name wasn't even mentioned, nor was Frank Wells's. (Katzenberg had cut an acknowledgment of Eisner from an earlier draft.) Katzenberg had usurped the royal "we," speaking of "our" success. He had anointed himself some kind of "genius"; or, "I am Mr. Movie Mogul," as Eisner later wrote.

On the front of the paper, Eisner wrote something that hinted at his real feelings: "I would demand that this paper never get into any hands outside our company, especially the press, but agents and lawyers as well." If that wasn't clear enough, nearly two weeks later, on January 23, Eisner sent Katzenberg a handwritten note: "I told Linda to collect your movie making paper so that it does not get out. I am really nervous, as you know, about the press. I would not let anybody else see it. Nobody needs to . . . We must keep some secrets—OK."

Eisner was still brooding about the memo at his next Monday evening dinner with Katzenberg at Locanda Veneta. "Sometimes I get the feeling that I'm competing with you," Eisner said at one point. A careful reading of Eisner's marginalia might have given him some clues, but Katzenberg was startled. "How could you say that?" he asked. Loyalty was one of Katzenberg's prized virtues; no one was more loyal to Eisner, or more grateful for what he'd done for his career. Katzenberg wouldn't tolerate criticism of his boss. He'd stopped speaking to one of his best friends, producer Irwin Winkler, after Winkler criticized Eisner's outsized compensation the previous year. But Eisner didn't pursue the matter. Katzenberg decided it was just a passing comment, and tried to forget about it.

Despite Eisner's explicit warnings to keep it private, it didn't take long for Katzenberg's memo to surface in the press. *Variety* printed it in its entirety. Perhaps this was inevitable, given that Eisner's copy was one of at least two dozen that Katzenberg had dispatched to Disney executives. Eisner told *Vanity Fair* writer Peter Boyer that he didn't believe Katzenberg had leaked it. On the contrary, Eisner was convinced that Katzenberg had done so. Eisner maintains that he was given a faxed copy of the memo that had his handwritten comments on them, which as far as he was concerned, proved that Katzenberg was responsible. (Katzenberg has denied leaking the memo.)

Eisner's reservations about the memo were quickly vindicated. It was dismissed as "28 pages of banalities," by one studio executive. Everyone mentioned in it was furious. Bill Murray denounced Disney on "Larry King Live," even as he was supposed to be promoting *What About Bob?* Warren Beatty stopped speaking to Katzenberg. Alec Baldwin referred to Katzenberg as "the eighth dwarf—Greedy."

Beyond the furor in Hollywood, the memo appears to have marked a critical turning point in Eisner's relationship with Katzenberg, coming as it did on the heels of Katzenberg's recent successes and attendant publicity. Eisner's resentment was so intense that evidence suggests he wanted to fire his longtime partner. During the same month the memo was written, in January 1991, Frank Wells asked Cheryl Fellows, a company accountant, to undertake a top secret project to calculate the amount of the 2 percent "annuity" due Katzenberg in the event he was terminated or left the company. The project was given a code name: Project Snowball. Fellows was explicitly warned to conceal the project from Katzenberg. She moved from her cubicle into a private office so no one could see her work. It isn't clear where the name Snowball came from, whether this referred to the massive amount of work this required on Fellows's part (as Disney later maintained), or, more plausibly, whether it referred to the rapidly escalating value of Katzenberg's percentage.

With the success of *Little Mermaid* and *Pretty Woman*, Katzenberg's incentive, deemed virtually worthless when it was granted, had soared in value. *Little Mermaid* seemed sure to join the pantheon of Disney classics, which meant revenues in perpetuity from home video, re-releases, and merchandise tie-ins. If Eisner did, in fact, say he wanted to fire Katzenberg, Wells surely would have wanted to know what such a move would cost the company. (Eisner later maintained that he knew nothing about Project Snowball. But when I pointed out the timing, and asked if Eisner told Wells he wanted Katzenberg fired over the memo, he paused, then replied, "I may have.") In any event, as the calculations began, Katzenberg knew nothing about them.

At Disney's conference for Wall Street analysts in Orlando that September, Katzenberg made his manifesto the center of his presentation. To the music of "Also sprach Zarathustra," the theme from *2001: A Space Odyssey,* a video showed a mysterious space object that grew larger until it revealed itself to be . . . "The Memo." Eisner happened to see a rehearsal. "I don't think you should do that," he warned Katzenberg. "The memo is old news." But Katzenberg failed to take the hint, and the presentation went ahead, to Eisner's obvious chagrin.

What was really galling to Eisner was that there was scant evidence that Katzenberg heeded the advice he had so freely dispensed in his memo. It was true that many of the films in the pipeline had been launched before he wrote the memo, but as the months and then years proceeded, Disney's record in live action was, if anything, worse than when Katzenberg wrote the memo. A measure of how far the studio's fortunes slipped was that Disney's highest-grossing film for 1993 was *Cool Runnings,* about a Jamaican bobsled team, which made $69 million.

Just as it was difficult to pinpoint the source of the studio's remarkable success, it was now hard to diagnose the cause of the stunning reversal. No doubt the creation of a new studio, the doubling of production in live action, and the even greater increase in production of animated films stretched the resources of the company and the attention spans of Eisner and Katzenberg. In part it reflected the changed landscape in theatrical film distribution identified by Katzenberg in his memo, which put enormous pressure on opening weekends, hugely expensive marketing campaigns, and the big budget "event" films that, in the wake of *Dick Tracy,* Eisner and Katzenberg had vowed to avoid. The big hits in the years 1991–1993 were Spielberg's *Schindler's List,* more films in the *Aliens* and *Batman* franchises, and *In the Line of Fire,* which Eisner had turned down.

On some level, the demoralizing string of failed films mirrored the deteriorating relationship between Eisner and Katzenberg. In their long and fruitful partnership, they had shared a remarkably similar taste in films. Now their views diverged. Finally Katzenberg confronted Eisner, complaining that Eisner was coming to meetings unprepared; that he wasn't reading scripts, relying instead on brief summaries, or "coverage," written by young assistants; and that his comments were unhelpful and "embarrassing." Eisner interpreted this rebuke as a request that he stay away from the weekly meetings to discuss scripts and new live-action film ideas because he was "undermining" Katzenberg's authority.

Eisner next became convinced that Katzenberg was scheduling screenings of rough cuts without including him. He assented to this diminished role, in part because he was so busy with other parts of the company, especially construction of Euro Disney. But he complained about it to Wells, and viewed it as a worrying indication that Katzenberg's ego was running amok. To Katzenberg, the explanation was simple: He had to keep Eisner at arm's length because his comments were erratic, in large part because he was being stretched too thin. In any event, Eisner's attendance at weekly meetings at the studio did fall off.

The studio did have some hits: Whoopi Goldberg in *Sister Act*, and *The Mighty Ducks*, green-lit largely because one of Eisner's sons played hockey; and the quirky Tim Burton feature *The Nightmare Before Christmas*. But as the money-losing failures mounted, Eisner complained to Wells that Katzenberg had abandoned the fiscal discipline that had made the studio such a success, giving in to agents' demands in a misguided effort to ingratiate Disney with the kind of talent that might deliver a hit. Eisner, of course, could always have overruled him, but he said nothing directly to Katzenberg, and their Monday-night dinners continued as usual. Yet in his mind, blame for the studio's failures increasingly rested with Katzenberg. Eisner's bonus for 1991 sank to $4.7 million, a fortune to most people at Disney, but a fraction of his previous year's pay.

Eisner responded by slashing the bonus pool for the live-action studios in half, a decision communicated by Wells in an unusually harsh memo to executives. Katzenberg protested, and some of the bonus pool was restored, but morale at the Touchstone and Hollywood studios sank.

Fortunately for Disney, animation was more than making up for the failures of live action. In March 1991, Katzenberg and Schneider arranged a preview in New York City of the still unfinished *Beauty and the Beast*, although it wasn't really as unfinished as the work they actually screened. To build anticipation, Katzenberg had chosen a print from two months earlier. The opening sequence, "Belle," was fully realized and in color, but most of the rest of the film remained in black and white. It had the effect of focusing attention on the remarkable score and lyrics. In the audience that night was a far more sophisticated crowd than was ordinarily drawn to children's animated films: press, critics, Academy members who lived in New York. The screening was part of a carefully planned strategy to get Academy Award consideration for *Beauty and the Beast*, though no animated film had ever received a Best Picture nomination. (*Snow White* received a special Academy Award.)

After the screening, David Geffen, Katzenberg, and Schneider rushed to St. Vincent's Hospital to brief Ashman. The hospital, in New York's Greenwich Village, had become the leading AIDS treatment center in the country. But treatment consisted mostly of trying to ease the collapse of the body's immune system and the pain of debilitating afflictions. There was no cure and as yet no effective treatment. St. Vincent's facilities were all but overwhelmed by the epidemic, which had filled its wards with gay men of all ages and from all walks of life. Ashman had entered the hospital the previous December, but had spent Christmas at his home with Lauch and family members. He had kept working even as his health deteriorated. He and Menken resumed work on the *Aladdin* project, and most of the score was finished. Now he had returned to the hospital.

Word that three powerful Hollywood executives had come to see Ashman rippled through the ward. Ashman lay in his bed, blind and frail. He had trouble breathing and could no longer speak. Geffen knelt by the bed and took Ashman's hand. "You're going to recover," he said. "This is going to be cured. A miracle will happen. You have to believe, just as you have inspired so many people to believe in magical things. You must never give up. And I want you to know that you are surrounded by people who love you." They couldn't be sure that Ashman heard or understood the words, but his eyes filled with tears.

A week later, Ashman died. He never saw the finished print of *Beauty and the Beast.*

Lauch, Ashman's partner, recalls that "It was such a satisfying time for Howard, working on those films. He felt like he'd lucked into a format that fit him best. He loved the theater but was sometimes frustrated by it, but here this film company indulged him. And the timing was perfect because he was just hitting his stride. He was really just getting started, and he was grateful."

Katzenberg was devastated by Ashman's death. Since discovering the Disney archives, he'd felt Walt's presence, as though he were an angel watching over the rebirth of animation. He felt that Ashman had joined Walt as a guiding spirit. Katzenberg prayed that he'd find someone to replace him. He later arranged an auction at Sotheby's of original art from *Beauty and the Beast.* Disney donated the proceeds to the Gay Men's Health Crisis, in honor of Ashman.

Ashman's spirit seemed to hover over the wrap party for *Beauty and the Beast,* held in October at The El Capitan Theatre in Hollywood. Katzenberg made sure to invite Lauch and Ashman's mother, though Lauch could not go. Everyone who'd worked on the film gathered at the historic theater, restored by Disney, for the first screening of the finished film. It had deliberately been kept under wraps during the previous weeks to prevent premature gossip and word of mouth. But after the still-unfinished *Beauty and the Beast* became the first animated film to open the prestigious New York Film Festival in September, and was greeted with thunderous applause from a sophisticated, adult audience, everyone at Disney believed they had a potential hit.

Before the film rolled, Roy and the director spoke, lavishing praise on the creative team, especially Ashman and Menken. Then Eisner took the stage to announce that "I decided today to build a new animation studio on the lot." An older building would be torn down to make way for a lavish new building to be designed by Robert Stern. Wild cheering broke out among the animators. They were jubilant. Just a few years ago they'd feared for their jobs. Now they would be returning in triumph from their exile in Glendale.

Peter Schneider had been leading a search for new space for the animation division, and was close to leasing a building being vacated by Lawry's restaurant chain about five miles down the freeway from Burbank. Or so he thought. Katzenberg looked stunned and angry. It was obvious to all that Eisner had told him nothing of any plans for a new building.

Once the excitement subsided, *Beauty and the Beast* unfolded on screen. Several of the musical numbers were interrupted by applause, and the movie earned a standing ovation. The mood was euphoric at the party afterward at the Sheraton hotel.

The Eisners and the Disneys had not stayed for the screening but left early to have dinner together at the Sheraton before the party, leaving Katzenberg behind. During the meal, Eisner gloated over how he'd upstaged Katzenberg with the announcement—or so reported two agents who overheard the conversation from the next table.

A month later, *Beauty and the Beast* opened in theaters to rapturous reviews. Janet Maslin wrote in *The New York Times,* "Two years ago Walt Disney Pictures reinvented the animated feature, not only with an eye towards pleasing children but also with an older, savvier audience in mind. Disney truly bridged the generation gap with 'The Little Mermaid,' bringing the genre new sophistication without sacrificing any of the delight. . . . Lightning has definitely struck twice. With 'Beauty and the Beast,' a tender, seamless and even more ambitious film than its predecessor, Disney has done something no one has done before: combine the latest computer animation techniques with the best of Broadway. Here, in the guise of furthering a children's fable, is the brand of witty, soaring musical score that is now virtually extinct on the stage. . . . By far the songwriters' biggest triumph is the title song, which becomes even more impressive in view of the not-very-promising assignment to create a 'Beauty and the Beast' theme song. But the result is a glorious ballad, as both a top-40 style duet heard over the closing credits and a sweet, lilting solo sung by Miss [Angela] Lansbury during the film's most meltingly lovely scene. For the latter, which also shows off the film's dynamic use of computer-generated animation, the viewer would be well advised to bring a hanky. And Mr. Menken should make room on the shelf where he keeps his Oscars."

Times critic Frank Rich, subsequently reviewing the year in arts, added that "The best Broadway musical score of 1991 was that written by Alan Menken and Howard Ashman for the Disney animated movie 'Beauty and the Beast.' Mr. Ashman, who died of AIDS this year, and Mr. Menken were frequent collaborators off-Broadway but had never worked as a team on a Broadway musical." Eisner himself, in his 1991 letter to shareholders, wrote that "It is amazing how a single creative act can change everything. . . . I know 'Snow White' did it for Walt. Well, 'Beauty and the Beast' is doing it for us. . . . 'Beauty and the Beast' is one of the great movies of all time (he said shamelessly). And it will be around forever."

Beauty and the Beast earned $145 million at the box office, making it the third-highest grossing film of the year (*Terminator 2: Judgment Day* was the leader). The *Times* reported that at some screenings adults outnumbered children by a ratio of ten to one. It sold more than 22 million videocassettes, more than doubling the sales of *Little Mermaid*. *Beauty and the Beast* became the first animated film ever to be nominated for Best Picture, and it won two Academy Awards—for Best Original Song and Best Original Score. Katzenberg had arranged with the Academy for Lauch to accept the award on Ashman's behalf. (The creepy thriller *The Silence of the Lambs* won for Best Picture.)

Beauty and the Beast also won a special award for technical achievement, and in their acceptance speech, engineers Lem Davis, Mark Kimball, Randy Cartwright, and Dave Wolf thanked Roy Disney, who had supported their early conviction that technology could transform animation.

Galvanized in part by Frank Rich's comment in the *Times*, Katzenberg urged Eisner to capitalize on *Beauty and the Beast*'s commercial success and remarkable score to mount it as a Broadway musical. Katzenberg had been badgering Eisner to produce something on Broadway, and the company had made a few modest investments in other shows. But Eisner had resisted. "We don't need to soothe our vanity by becoming Broadway producers," he told Katzenberg, suggesting that it was mostly Katzenberg's ego that was driving the idea.

As he did so often, Katzenberg made his case to Wells, who got Eisner to reconsider, on several conditions: The show had to be done by Disney alone, so it retained full creative control, and Eisner wanted to use people already associated with Disney, steeped in the Disney culture. As Eisner liked to point out, the theme parks already produced more live shows than all of Broadway.

And there was another condition: Eisner himself had to be involved. "I'll only do this if we do this together," he insisted to Katzenberg. Katzenberg didn't understand why he couldn't just go ahead on his own. The Broadway show was budgeted at just $34 million, which included the cost of renovating the theater, no more than the cost of a typical feature film. But as the production evolved, Eisner went to absurd lengths, in Katzenberg's view. Rehearsals for the show were being held in Houston, and Katzenberg flew down almost every week. But Eisner forbade Katzenberg to deliver his production notes directly to the cast, insisting he review them first. Katzenberg largely ignored the edict.

As the show developed, Katzenberg made sure to include Ashman's partner in the planning. Lauch met the director, Robert Jess Roth, and he was especially pleased that Katzenberg restored "Human Again," the Ashman/Menken waltz that had been cut from the film version. He knew Ashman would have been thrilled.

On one of his flights to Houston, Katzenberg was reading a script when he suddenly stopped and turned to Thomas Schumacher, his deputy in animation, who had been enlisted to watch a preview. "Why doesn't Roy like me?" Katzenberg asked. Schumacher wondered what to say. He knew that neither Roy nor most of the animators liked Katzenberg. He decided to speak candidly.

"You dominate," he said. "You showboat. You take all the credit."

Later, Katzenberg asked Schumacher to write down a list of Roy's problems with him. Schumacher's list included rudeness, arrogance, ignoring the artists' concerns, being dismissive of Roy's suggestions, showing no interest in *Fantasia*. When Katzenberg read it, he nodded. "I get that," he said.

Just a year after the spectacular success of *Beauty and the Beast*, *Aladdin* opened to even greater commercial success. At David Geffen's suggestion, Katzenberg had dispatched Schneider to recruit Tim Rice (lyricist for *Jesus Christ Superstar*) to pick up where Ashman had left off. He and Menken had completed the score, and Robin Williams, grateful for the career boost he'd gotten from *Dead Poets*, portrayed the genie for a scale wage of less than $500 a day in a deal brokered by Michael Ovitz. Critics loved Williams as the genie: "Williams and animation were born for one another" (Roger Ebert); a "dizzying, elastic miracle" (Janet Maslin). The film grossed an astounding $502 million worldwide, the highest grossing film of the year. *Aladdin* again won Academy Awards for Best Song and Best Score, as well as five Grammys, including Song of the Year for Ashman and Menken's "A Whole New World."

Thanks in large part to animation, the Walt Disney Company reported record profit of $1.4 billion in 1992, a 31 percent increase from the prior year. Filmed entertainment had revenues of $3.1 billion and an operating income of more than $500 million, a 60 percent rise. The lustrous financial results obscured the fact that for the first time since taking the helm eight years earlier, Eisner's and Wells's judgment had faltered. All of the profit in filmed entertainment came from animation, since the live-action studios actually lost money. In his annual letter to shareholders, Eisner glossed over mounting problems at Euro Disney. "Disneyland was too expensive," he wrote. "Walt Disney World's Magic Kingdom opened and the company's stock fell by half (it recovered quickly, I might add). Tokyo Disneyland threatened the very existence of the Oriental Land Company. And Epcot Center was the mother of all expensive parks. But, like all good fairy tales, the company not only survived, but it is living happily ever after."

Disney's annual report that year also disclosed that Eisner and Wells had exercised stock options on 6.6 million shares and then sold 5.1 million of them. The company attributed the sales to proposed tax legislation that would have eliminated corporate tax breaks on compensation over $1 million; Disney said the company saved $90 million in corporate taxes by having the executives exercise their options before the end of 1992. Of course, the timing was fortuitous, since Eisner and Wells were aware of the dire state of the live-action slate, and the mounting problems at Euro Disney. Eisner realized $197 million on the sale, Wells $60.3 million. Combined with his annual compensation, Eisner earned well over $200 million, again placing him far ahead of any other corporate executive in America. (Sandy Weill, then chairman of Travelers Group, was a distant second at $52.8 million.) Although Eisner vaulted that year onto the *Forbes* magazine list of the four hundred richest Americans, criticism was muted. After all, Disney's market capitalization—and its stock price—had jumped more than tenfold, from $2 billion in 1984 to $22 billion just eight years later.

Nor was Disney's and Eisner's achievement simply financial. In *Little Mermaid, Beauty and the Beast,* and *Aladdin,* Disney seemed to have conjured up the magic it so often talked about, producing deeply moving, critically acclaimed yet accessible films likely to become enduring classics. As Eisner had written while still at Paramount, "if we make entertaining movies, at times we will reliably make history, art, a statement, or all three. We may even win awards." With Roy as vice chairman in charge of animation, Katzenberg the de facto chief executive, and a remarkable team of talented producers, composers, lyricists, and artists, Disney animation had become something like a symphony orchestra, finely tuned, perfectly balanced, and playing at the peak of its virtuosity.

Eisner made that year's letter to shareholders a tribute to animation. "Your company has nothing less than the most talented, inventive, creative, original, resourceful and brilliant people working in animation," he wrote. "I probably sound like the proud parent who indulgently shows off his children, even if they are decidedly not perfect. But 'The Little Mermaid' in 1990 and 'Beauty and the Beast' in 1992 were perfect children, conceived in love, four years in gestation, birthed comfortably and getting better with age." Noting that June 1993 would mark the hundredth birthday of Roy's father, Roy O., Eisner continued that "With all that Roy Sr. gave to this company, perhaps his number one legacy to our company is his son, our Roy, who did nothing less than save the company in 1984—with the help of Stanley Gold, Roy's partner and friend, from the outside, and Ray Watson, the chairman of the company, from the inside."

Roy, Eisner insisted, deserved the lion's share of credit for the astounding success of animation. "The common wisdom was that drawing a movie frame was archaic and too expensive. But Roy bought none of that," which shows "how insightful and downright gutsy Roy was to insist way back in 1984 that we pour major resources into what most people thought was a moribund, money-losing enterprise that would only be relegated to kids' matinees. Roy understood that animation, done right, was magic. And magic is the essence of Disney." Katzenberg warranted only fleeting mention: "One of his major responsibilities was to work with Roy to restore Disney's lost luster in animation.

"We should always remember that we have Roy to thank," Eisner concluded.

FIVE

One afternoon in late 1991, Eisner called Steve Burke, the young head of the Disney stores. "I'm going to St. Louis. Come along, and we'll visit some stores." Once on the Disney plane, Eisner asked Burke what he'd like to do next.

"I'm really happy doing the stores," Burke said. But Eisner persisted.

"After the Disney stores what do you want to do?"

"Gosh," Burke said. "My dream job would be to run a theme park."

Eisner grabbed the phone and called Wells. "He said 'theme parks,' " Eisner said. "I told you he'd say theme parks."

Eisner hung up and turned to Burke. "We want you to run Disneyland."

Burke was thrilled. He started haunting the park with his wife and kids, developing ideas. But months passed, and nothing happened. Finally Wells called to tell him that Dick Nunis had been cool to the idea of naming someone from outside the parks division with no theme park experience. Instead, they wanted him to help run Euro Disney, which was scheduled to open in April 1992, working closely with the French resort's new head, Philippe Bourguignon. Burke didn't really want to move his family to France, but he agreed. Wells promised to bring him back to the United States in a few years.

When Burke met with Bourguignon, he said, "Steve, we're about to lose $500 million." Burke was stunned. Neither Eisner nor Wells had given him any hint. He couldn't believe it. "Let me look at the numbers over the weekend," he said. By Monday morning, he conceded, "You're right."

The costs of building Euro Disney had soared, and even though Eisner always insisted the project was within its budget, that was only because the budget was constantly revised upward. By his own reckoning, Eisner had attended over fifty meetings with the Imagineers, and pored over the design of every aspect of the new park, starting with the Magic Kingdom's centerpiece castle. In both Disneyland and Disney World, the castles had been made of molded fiberglass. Tony Baxter, an Imagineer who'd bonded with Eisner after designing the captivating, albeit expensive, "Splash Mountain" attraction, pointed out that in France, Disney could hardly use fiberglass when the countryside already boasted real castles made of stone. "We can't just do a kitschy rendition of French history right in their own backyard," he argued, and Eisner had agreed.

Instead of using the kind of actual European castles that had inspired the ones in the American theme parks, the Imagineers turned to the fantasy castles in Disney's animated classics, especially the one in *Sleeping Beauty*. The Euro Disney version was built of pink stone, with handcrafted stained-glass windows picturing scenes from *Sleeping Beauty* and a dungeon with a fire-breathing dragon. While undeniably more spectacular than the American castles, it also cost millions more.

Eisner was far more interested in the creative challenges than the practical problems, which as usual were Wells's responsibility. Building Euro Disney was the most ambitious construction project Disney had ever undertaken, and translating the ideas of Eisner and the Imagineers in Burbank, not to mention those of the team of international architects responsible for the hotels, fell to European contractors and Bob Fitzpatrick, the former CalArts president whom Eisner and Wells had installed as head of the project. Eisner didn't mind spending money, as he put it, "on the walls," meaning on something spectacular that guests would see. But operating expenses drove him crazy. On an early visit to the site, Eisner and his entourage were ferried around the beet fields in four Land Rovers. Eisner called Wells. "Why do we have Land Rovers rather than Jeeps? This is just the tip of the iceberg. Nickels and dimes add up, and I can tell you right now we've got to get this under control."

No one at Disney had any experience with building in Europe, let alone dealing with contentious French labor organizations. When they arrived at the steps of the Paris Bourse, home to the nation's stock market, to celebrate the first day Euro Disney shares were publicly traded, Eisner and Gary Wilson were confronted by angry demonstrators and pelted with eggs and ketchup. "Uncle Scrooge Go Home!" read one banner.

Budgeted at $1.3 billion, costs were approaching $2 billion and construction was falling behind when Wells called in a consultant who warned, "You are headed for one of the biggest failures in construction I've ever seen." Eisner and Wells tapped Judson Green, who had negotiated the Marriott deal at Disney World, to rescue the opening and get operations up to speed. Green airlifted over five hundred Disney employees from the American theme parks for a crash effort to prepare for an opening. The task force worked eighteen-hour days for the four months. Disney was also a victim of Eisner's insistence that the company meet its pledge to open at a precise time in April, as Walt had done with Disneyland, and Roy with Walt Disney World. The deadline was an open invitation to blackmail from the contractors, who threatened work slowdowns unless they were given premiums to complete the work on time. One group of contractors demanded $150 million in over-time and "change orders." Euro Disney ultimately cost a staggering $4 bil-lion.

Whatever the cost, Euro Disney did succeed in opening at precisely 9:00 A.M. on April 22, 1992. All the architects were on hand along with stars Can-dice Bergen, Eddie Murphy, and Melanie Griffith. Farmers blockaded the roads. French president François Mitterrand declined to attend, dismissing the expensive new investment with Gallic indifference as "pas ma tasse de thé" ("just not my cup of tea"), a comment that infuriated Eisner.

For all Disney's efforts, it was clear from early reactions that Europeans would not be easily won over by Disney's American version of make-believe. *International Herald Tribune* critic Stephen Bayley wrote, "The Old World is presented with all the confident big ticket flimflam of painstaking fakery that this bizarre campaign of reverse-engineered cultural imperialism represents. I like to think that by the turn of the century, Euro Disney will have become a deserted city, similar to Angkor Wat. . . ." The opening day attendance was just six thousand people, far short of the projected ten thousand. Although attendance through December reached seven million, it fell off drastically during the cold weather. Unlike the Japanese, the French were not willing to wait in lines in the cold. Nice as the hotels were, few wanted to stay so far from Paris. Occupancy at the hotels was just 60 percent, far short of the pro-jected 85 percent. Wells confided that he "dreaded" going to the fax machine every morning to get the previous day's Euro Disney attendance figures. More fundamentally, costs had so far exceeded projections that Euro Disney, now saddled with a staggering $3 billion in debt, would have had trouble earning a profit even under the most optimistic of assumptions.

With the park open, Green returned to run the U.S. theme parks, and Bourguignon, a Frenchman, was named chairman and chief executive of the Euro Disney Resort. Frank Wells called Steve Burke every morning, and Burke tried to sound warnings, as did Bourguignon. But the message didn't seem to get through to Eisner, who continued to predict that the clouds over Euro Disney would disperse as soon as warmer weather boosted crowds and as Europe emerged from the recession that followed Iraq's invasion of Kuwait. Eisner was still intent on adding a second theme park to the site—a European version of the MGM Studios park in Orlando—and the Imagineers were hard at work. But early in 1993, Richard Nanula, the newly appointed chief financial officer, and Larry Murphy, head of strategic planning, who had consistently warned about overspending and optimistic assumptions, flew to Paris with a team from Disney to assess the financial health of the venture. It was even worse than Burke and Bourguignon had warned.

Nearly all the assumptions Disney had made in the early projections and used to determine the budget had been wildly off base. Europeans' vacation habits were dramatically different from Americans', something that might have been anticipated had Disney relied on European data rather than projecting results from Disney World onto a European setting. For one thing, the average middle-class European had far more vacation time than did Americans. But this meant that they spent far less per day to make ends meet. They were not willing to stay in expensive hotels like the ones Disney had built, nor did they eat, drink, attend shows, or buy souvenirs at a rate anywhere near that of Americans. The hotel occupancy rate was less than 50 percent. Unlike Americans, 75 percent of Euro Disney's visitors booked their trips through travel agents. Most Americans called Disney directly to make reservations. The resulting agents' commissions that Disney was forced to pay made a dramatic dent on the bottom line. Given the cost structure, Euro Disney wasn't making money on an operating basis, let alone able to service its massive $3 billion debt.

Warmer weather did not bring a dramatic improvement. Indeed, it was clear to Larry Murphy that under the most optimistic operating assumptions, Euro Disney would not make money. The situation was so dire that Disney was rapidly heading toward breaching its debt agreements, which could cause the banks and other major lenders to force the project into bankruptcy, an almost unthinkable embarrassment.

Determined to force Eisner to face reality, Murphy insisted on two full days at a retreat in Aspen in July, attended by Wells, Bourguignon, Burke, other top executives, and Sid Bass. The first step was to illustrate what had gone wrong, which, simply put, was the massive overspending undertaken largely at Eisner's behest. Murphy and his team prepared charts that compared the initial budget to actual costs, which were more than $1 billion over the original pro formas, and the consequences for debt service and operating margins. Bourguignon and Burke added their pessimistic views; they'd decided they had to be brutally honest or risk losing their jobs when the weak numbers came in.

As the meeting progressed, Eisner became visibly angry. It was the first time anyone in the company had so directly criticized something for which he was responsible. Finally he burst out, practically shouting, "I don't understand this. The pro formas said we could spend this." It was true the pro formas had been revised upward every time Eisner indicated he wanted to spend more. "That's because people told you what you wanted to hear," Murphy said. It was the first time anyone could remember Eisner raising his voice in front of Sid Bass.

Murphy and Nanula outlined a drastic set of remedies: cutting the price of admission, hotel rates, food, and merchandise; slashing operating costs by firing a thousand employees; and restructuring management. Even then, the debt would have to be restructured or, Murphy projected, Euro Disney would lose several hundred million dollars a year in 1994 and 1995.

When Murphy finished, everyone turned anxiously to Eisner, who looked sullen and withdrawn. "He made it perfectly clear to everyone trying to speak the truth that it was unwelcome," recalls one executive at the meeting. Despite his claims to Katzenberg that he always wanted to be the first to hear about problems, Eisner did not like to be told bad news, nor was he used to it. He had presided over a nearly unbroken string of successes, largely by acting on his creative impulses. In many ways, Euro Disney had been the grandest of these. From the beginning, it seemed as if Eisner craved critical acceptance and approval by the Europeans, which was the main factor driving the expensive quest for perfection in building the park. Still, the consequences of doing nothing were worse than the proposed remedy. Eisner reluctantly agreed that the second park would have to be put on hold, and told Burke and Bourguignon to return to Paris and drastically cut costs.

Although Eisner later called this decision a "bitter pill to swallow" and "distressing," he nonetheless demonstrated a characteristic sense of optimism even in the face of dire projections. As he put it, "There was never a single moment—including that moment—when I lost faith in [Euro Disney]. We still had a great park at a great location. We faced a business crisis, a blazing one at that, but I'd faced similar crises, albeit on smaller scales, nearly every week for thirty years. Although others at our meeting probably would have disagreed, my main feeling as we ended was one of optimism."

Be that as it may, it didn't stop Eisner from casting blame for the Euro Disney fiasco on others. Gary Wilson and Frank Wells came in for the brunt of the criticism, Wilson for pushing for so many hotel rooms and for taking on so much debt, and Wells for the optimistic pro formas based on Disney World numbers. Wilson, of course, was conveniently gone, though still on the board. Judson Green replaced Richard Nunis as theme park chairman.

Most strikingly, Euro Disney appeared to drive a wedge between Eisner and Frank Wells. To others, Eisner blamed Wells for everything—from the budget shortfalls, to bad personnel decisions, to skyrocketing operational costs. Wells did deserve some of the blame. Euro Disney exposed managerial weaknesses in Wells that had been apparent to many. He was overextended, he didn't pay attention to details, and he had a short attention span. Still, he had simply been trying to implement the big decisions made by Eisner and his creative team. And he was invariably fair-minded, even-tempered, and good for morale.

At their Monday dinners at Locanda Veneta, Eisner increasingly vented his frustrations with Wells to Katzenberg, going so far as to suggest that he'd have to fire Wells if Wells didn't quit first to climb mountains or run for public office. (Given that Wells reported to the board, not to Eisner, he couldn't have unilaterally fired him.) And Eisner frequently complained about Wells to Ovitz, seeming to ignore the fact that Ovitz and Wells were friends. On one occasion, when Eisner and Ovitz and their wives were dining at the Palm, Eisner arrived late, then immediately said, "That fucking Frank. He's crazy."

"What happened now?" Jane asked.

"He's so scattered. I can't get him to focus." Eisner complained that Wells wouldn't accept responsibility for the Euro Disney mess.

Eisner had also managed to convert his former boss and friend Barry Diller into a bitter enemy. Just as with Larry Gordon, Diller and Eisner had stopped speaking, and were going to elaborate lengths to avoid each other in public. The feud began when Disney bought a Los Angeles television station, named it KCAL, and wanted to air "Disney Afternoon," the block of children's programs being carried by Diller's Fox affiliates, including one in Los Angeles. Eisner had Katzenberg call Diller. In Diller's recounting of the discussion, Katzenberg said, "We want to renegotiate 'Disney Afternoon' and we're taking away the L.A. market."

Diller was shocked. They had a contract. "That's not fair," he protested. "I know you bought an L.A. station, but give us two or three years to replace this. Let's be reasonable."

Diller called Eisner, who refused.

"We were there for you when you needed us," Diller reminded him, pointing out that he'd bought the original programming for "Disney Afternoon." Eisner still refused. "Okay then, we're out of business," Diller said.

Fox promptly dropped "Disney Afternoon" from all its wholly owned stations, and encouraged its affiliates to do the same. Then it developed its own series of cartoon programs, including the wildly successful "Mighty Morphin' Power Rangers." "Disney Afternoon" never recovered from the blow.

Still, that wasn't what put Diller over the edge, even though he felt Eisner had betrayed him. It was when Disney sued Fox on antitrust grounds, claiming that Fox was trying to monopolize children's programming, and then complained to the FCC that Fox was a morally unfit broadcaster, with risqué programming like "The Simpsons" and "South Park." When Disney lawyers approached Diller about a possible settlement, Diller said the only settlement he'd consider was an apology.

Disney ended up dropping the suit in 1992, but Diller told Geffen, "I'm never going to speak to him [Eisner] again."

Frank Wells also felt the brunt of Eisner's temper. Eisner had called Gold at one point to complain about Wells, and asked if he could fire him. "Are you out of your fucking mind?" Gold says he replied. "You're a team. You both report to the board." Eisner didn't bring it up again. One morning after Wells's usual jog around the UCLA track with Stanley Gold, he stopped at Gold's house in Beverly Hills and sat on the terrace. They had juice and coffee. Finally Gold got up to shower and head to the office. "Time to go," Gold said. Wells didn't move. "I'm not going to work," he said.

"What's the matter?"

"I hate it. I hate Michael Eisner," he said. "I can't go in there anymore and take the shit."

Gold yelled to the maid. "Mr. Wells will be spending the day here." He urged Wells to relax, unwind, and take his time. He knew he'd go back for the good of the company.

That spring of 1993, Tony Schwartz called Eisner again, noting that September 22, 1994, would be the tenth anniversary of Eisner's arrival at Disney, a good time to reconsider the book that Schwartz had proposed. "I should have done it when you suggested this before," Eisner said, given the enormous success of his early years at Disney. He still had the tapes he'd been recording during that period, and he told Schwartz he'd consider it.

Eisner later wrote that Schwartz's call came at a time when, for a variety of reasons, he was amenable to the suggestion. "We were enjoying success on a variety of fronts—movies, television, theme parks, and consumer products. It was tempting to keep doing things exactly the way we had. But rather than a sense of confidence, we felt a growing apprehension. The problem, we sensed, was that some of our executives were feeling not just complacent and self-satisfied but bored and restless. The business equivalent of the seven-year itch was setting in. . . . Writing a book, I suggested to Frank, my partner and Disney's president, might be one more way to keep our focus on the challenge at hand. If we committed our intentions to paper—and faced a deadline—we'd feel more compelled to implement significant changes, even if they proved unsettling to the company in the short term. . . . Above all writing a book simply seemed like something fun to do—a new adventure."

Eisner may also have had other reasons. Robert Sam Anson, a journalist best known for his reporting on the civil rights movement and from Vietnam, had just signed a contract to write an investigative book on Disney. Eisner's book might blunt the impact of Anson's book, if not preempt it altogether. Eisner later mentioned to Schwartz that he worried Katzenberg "could conceivably make an alliance with Robert Sam Anson," according to Schwartz's notes. Still, "Jane tells me I'm crazy to do this," Eisner said to Schwartz when he called again to discuss the project further.

After five months of negotiating, they reached a deal. Eisner would be the author and would retain absolute control over the content; Schwartz would receive a "with Tony Schwartz" credit. Eisner didn't want Schwartz to negotiate a contract with a publisher, even though, after the runaway success of *Trump: the Art of the Deal*, Schwartz felt he could have commanded an advance of $4–$5 million for a book on Eisner and Disney. Instead, Eisner proposed that he pay Schwartz an equivalent amount (in later testimony, Eisner said he couldn't remember whether he paid Schwartz or Disney did). Then, when the manuscript was finished, Eisner would negotiate a publishing contract. Schwartz worried he was making a Faustian bargain, but in the end he accepted Eisner's terms.

As Euro Disney's fortunes were spiraling downward, Eisner continued to brood about his relationship with Katzenberg. Late in 1992, he'd called Ovitz. "I've got to get rid of him," Eisner insisted. "I can't take him any more."

He went into a long recitation of Katzenberg's faults. Though used to Eisner's complaints about Katzenberg, Ovitz was surprised, given the extraordinary success of animation.

"I don't think you should," Ovitz said. "Why rock the boat?"

But Eisner persisted. "You've got to find me someone," he said.

Ovitz thought the impulse would pass once Eisner vented his feelings, but Eisner called every day for a week. Finally Ovitz gave in. "Okay, I've got someone for you: Joe Roth."

Roth, then head of the Fox studio, where he'd been recruited by Diller, was leaving to start his own production company, and Ovitz was his agent. In his mid-forties, Roth had rugged good looks, modishly long hair, and was affable and charming, popular with directors and actors. He'd had a mixed record as a producer, but also some big hits, notably *Home Alone.* Columbia Pictures was also recruiting him for a production deal. Ovitz suggested that Eisner keep Katzenberg and bring Roth in as an independent producer working for Disney. If he decided he had to get rid of Katzenberg, Roth would be available, and in the meantime, Eisner could see if he got along with Roth.

Eisner immediately called Katzenberg and told him to work out a deal with Roth's production company, Caravan Pictures. Incredibly, given his conversation with Ovitz, Eisner told Katzenberg that he saw Roth as someone who could fill in for Katzenberg when it was time for Katzenberg to "move up" in the company.

Initially, Roth favored the Columbia deal. But Ovitz had structured the Disney deal so that if Eisner decided to replace Katzenberg with Roth, Disney would have to buy out his company. "Let me assure you," Ovitz told Roth and his then-wife, "at some point you're going to be bought out."

When Eisner, Katzenberg, Ovitz, and Roth had lunch to close the deal, Roth took Katzenberg aside and warned him, "I've got the feeling they want to park me at your place, and I'm not sure that's good for you." But Katzenberg told Roth that hiring him had been his idea.

Geffen, too, tried to warn Katzenberg that Roth was his replacement. Though Katzenberg usually heeded his friend's advice, this time he disagreed, pointing out that he'd be number two at the company in the event Wells stepped aside, and Roth would then report to him.

However much Eisner may have wanted Katzenberg to believe this, it appears to be patently false. Eisner had a habit of writing letters to his lawyer, Irwin Russell, who was also on the Disney board. The letters have the air of unguarded candor, as in this passage describing his feelings at the time about Katzenberg:

> Over the last two years [1992–93] Frank and I have become more and more frustrated with how Jeffrey conducts business and especially with his personal agenda. He has displayed more and more a desire to keep us out of the process, and this has made me particularly unhappy. I never really know where he is or what he is doing. And of course our dismal performance in live action features is what got Frank's attention. We met on several occasions and discussed with Jeffrey our unhappiness with how it was going.

Yet it's not surprising that Katzenberg felt secure in his job and even anticipated a promotion. *Beauty and the Beast* and *Aladdin* were two of the most successful animated films ever produced, and would be generating millions in revenue for the foreseeable future. In 1992, Disney became the first studio to earn over $500 million in a single year. The studio was so profitable that even with the conservative accounting Disney used to calculate Katzenberg's annual bonus, he was earning a significant amount—over $10 million in total compensation in 1991. The 2 percent lifetime annuity that Eisner and Wells thought wouldn't amount to anything when they included it in Katzenberg's original contract in lieu of stock options was beginning to look substantial, so much so that Katzenberg wondered just what it might be worth. After all, he did have the option to leave in 1994.

In April, Arthur Emil, Katzenberg's lawyer, wrote Disney asking for the amount of his bonus under the 2 percent formula. The letter was meant to satisfy his curiosity, but also to drive the point home to Eisner and Wells that Katzenberg's departure would be costly.

Wells, of course, was well aware of the soaring value of Katzenberg's interest, thanks to the ongoing Project Snowball. According to an internal Disney document labeled "Project Snowball, Privileged and Confidential," calculations were made for two "scenarios," one in which Katzenberg left in 1994, the other if he stayed until 1996. For a 1994 termination, Katzenberg would receive $169.4 million; in 1996, $194.6 million. But instead, Katzenberg received a letter from Joe Santaniello, one of Disney's in-house lawyers, which took the startling position—startling to Katzenberg at any rate—that Katzenberg wasn't entitled to any bonus if he exercised his option to leave in 1994, two years before the expiration of his contract.

Katzenberg took the letter straight to Wells and said that he assumed there had been some misunderstanding. He reminded Wells that Wells had been the one who pushed to include the bonus provision, that Katzenberg hadn't been willing to give it up when they negotiated his new contract in 1988, and that he was sure that Wells would "put things right." Wells said he'd look into the matter and get back to him.

In the meantime, Katzenberg was busy negotiating a deal to buy Miramax, an independent production company named after the parents of the two brothers who founded it, Harvey and Bob Weinstein. Bill Mechanic set up a dinner with the Weinsteins and Katzenberg at the Cannes Film Festival in 1992, though he worried that Katzenberg might be put off by the brothers' appearance, especially Harvey, who chain-smoked, was overweight, and sometimes disheveled. The Weinsteins were showing their movie *Sarafina!* a musical starring Whoopi Goldberg as an apartheid-era schoolteacher, and Mechanic stressed to Katzenberg that the Weinsteins had "incredible taste," despite appearances.

As soon as he met them, Katzenberg embraced the idea of extending Disney's reach by acquiring Miramax. The Weinsteins needed capital. At the time, they were producing just 10 percent of their films, acquiring distribution rights to the rest after others produced them. Of course there were risks to the Disney brand. Miramax's biggest critical and commercial success, *The Crying Game,* featured a transsexual. Again, Katzenberg pressed his case to Wells, who was initially skeptical, afraid that the Weinsteins would simply take the money and "retire," as he put it to him. But with plenty of incentives for the Weinsteins built into their contract, Wells was persuaded, and Eisner agreed. Maybe Miramax could salvage the live-action film roster. Disney was able to buy Miramax for $60 million plus the assumption of debt, which amounted to about $40 million more; *The Crying Game* alone had earned $63 million. For their part, the Weinsteins had financing commitments, and, more important, contractual guarantees of independence. "Nobody can tell us what to do," Harvey Weinstein boasted.

Certainly not Dick Cook, Disney's head of marketing and distribution. The usually genial Cook clashed with the Weinsteins almost immediately, so Katzenberg asked Mechanic to oversee them. Mechanic soon had his hands full, reviewing scripts for *Pulp Fiction,* by a new writing and directing talent, Quentin Tarantino, and another film called *Priest. Pulp Fiction* was filled with graphic violence and sadomasochism. *Priest* was about a gay priest in Ireland, likely to rile Catholics, including Patty Disney and her family.

Just days after the deal was concluded with Disney, Harvey Weinstein called Mechanic from London and said he wanted to acquire *Little Buddha,* directed by Bernardo Bertolucci and starring Keanu Reeves. Mechanic was skeptical, but gave in when Harvey insisted that he had to act quickly. Miramax bought the rights. Months later, Harvey called Mechanic after the film was finished. "I just saw it," he reported. "I'm killing Bertolucci and fixing the movie."

"Harvey," Mechanic said. "It's Bertolucci. All you can do is make it shorter."

"A slow-moving and pointless exercise," critic Roger Ebert wrote of the finished *Little Buddha,* which did less than $5 million at the box office.

Even after making the deal with Roth, Eisner continued to talk with Katzenberg about a new contract and about expanding his responsibilities at Disney. Eisner invited Katzenberg and his wife to stay overnight at the Eisner home in Aspen in October, when Disney executives would be having their next executive retreat, to discuss the possibilities. Despite Katzenberg's request earlier that year to calculate his bonus payment, "It never occurred to me," Eisner said, that Katzenberg might actually be planning to leave.

Then, in mid-August, Katzenberg was startled by a letter from Santaniello, the in-house lawyer, asking him to state his "intentions." Katzenberg asked his lawyer to respond by calling Wells to clarify the bonus issue. Wells was less than conciliatory, telling Emil that if he wanted an answer, he should "read the contract."

"I don't have to read the contract," Emil angrily retorted. "It's not the deal that we made."

"Listen, it's not going to be an issue. Jeffrey's going to stay these next two years," Wells said, "so don't get upset about it."

Katzenberg, furious, called Wells and said he couldn't understand why Disney was "playing games" with him. "If the point of this is to leverage me into staying with the company, then this would certainly cause me to do exactly the opposite," he warned. Wells said again he wanted to look at the contract. "Let's come to an understanding first as to what the contract says," he said.

"Okay. We'll go back and look at the contract, but I have to say I know what the deal is, Frank."

The next day Katzenberg met with Wells in Wells's office. He said he'd read the contract and didn't see what the issue was. "If you cannot confirm that the deal is as I understand it, then I'm telling you now I'm leaving." Wells said the problem was Eisner, who had a "misunderstanding" and believed that Katzenberg wasn't entitled to any bonus if he exercised the option to leave in 1994. Katzenberg said he'd have his lawyer write Eisner a letter, but Wells told him to wait. "I'll handle it with Michael. I will take care of this."

Katzenberg thought the matter was settled. As he testified much later, in his lawsuit with Disney, "Frank was the person that, you know, kept Michael Eisner and I working well with each other. He was the one who handled these issues between us . . . he was the peacemaker, the marriage counselor."

Katzenberg had to give notice to preserve his option to leave, so on August 31, Katzenberg's lawyer, Arthur Emil, responded to Joe Santaniello's request for Katzenberg's "intentions" by writing a formal letter to Eisner announcing Katzenberg's intention to exercise his option to leave the next year. Eisner later said the letter "took me by surprise."

The next time Eisner saw Katzenberg, he acknowledged getting the letter, but thought it was a negotiating ploy. He couldn't believe Katzenberg would actually quit and give up his compensation for 1995 and 1996, the two years remaining on his contract. "You really want to give that up?" Eisner asked incredulously, noting that it would amount to $100 million.* According to Eisner, Katzenberg didn't take issue with the amount, saying he could "easily" earn that amount somewhere else. In any event, he said it didn't matter because, "I have no intention of leaving. I'm just protecting myself legally, in case you don't come up with new mountains for me to climb." Eisner told Wells that "there is no chance he will do this."

Still, Eisner must have thought there was at least a slight chance Katzenberg would leave, because he later approached Joe Roth about taking his place as head of the studio. As Eisner described it in a memo to Irwin Russell, "I had had a conversation . . . with Joe Roth asking him if Jeffrey left (which I thought very very unlikely) would he take over. He said yes. But I told him Jeffrey was under contract, did not look like he would ever leave, but you never know. And of course there is always the truck that could hit him."

When Disney executives gathered in Aspen the first week in October, Eisner seems to have determined to use the occasion to get Katzenberg to stay through the end of his contract in 1996, and even to enter into a new longer-term agreement.

Katzenberg and his wife, Marilyn, arrived at the Eisner home on Friday evening, their first visit to the Eisner's lavish Robert Stern–designed "cabin."

---

* Where Eisner came up with such a round number isn't clear. It doesn't correspond to anything in the Project Snowball calculations, which projected Katzenberg's total compensation in 1995 and 1996 would be approximately $44 million. The bonus due him was far more than $100 million.

They admired the view, then settled into comfortable chairs in the living room. According to Katzenberg's later testimony, they had a pleasant conversation, and then Eisner raised the subject of Katzenberg's contract. "I want to make a new deal," Eisner said. "It's time." He added that he realized Katzenberg wanted some new challenges, and he wanted to expand his responsibilities.

In a letter to Irwin Russell describing this encounter, which appears to be the closest thing to a contemporaneous record, Eisner wrote, "Jeff was in Aspen with me and we discussed his future. He asked for Frank's job the first night. Of course I flatly denied this request." (Katzenberg later said he had no recollection of any such conversation the first night.)

The subject of Katzenberg's contract arose the next day, as Eisner and Katzenberg waited on the sidewalk outside a bar and grill called Boogies, and their wives shopped for sweaters. In Katzenberg's account, Eisner volunteered that he was negotiating a new deal with Frank Wells, but he didn't think Wells would serve out his full term. "I think Frank will do this a year or two, then leave to run for governor, or climb mountains. If that happens, I'd expect you to assume the number two job. In the meantime, I'm prepared to make clear that you are number three. I'm prepared to make you vice chairman and put you on the board, if that's what you want. I don't necessarily think that's what you want, but I'd be willing." He pointed out that if Katzenberg went on the board there would be public disclosure requirements, such as his compensation. Katzenberg was naturally flattered.

The mention of vice chairman gave Katzenberg an idea. "Would it be inappropriate if Frank became vice chairman and I became president?"

"I could never do that to Frank," Eisner said, saying it would be perceived as a demotion.

"Well, I would never want you to do that to Frank," Katzenberg said. "Forget it."

"I believe Frank would accept it because he would do anything to keep you in the company," Eisner went on, "but in the quiet of his room he would feel hurt."

"I wouldn't want to take anything away from the guy," Katzenberg said, now feeling almost guilty that he'd asked.

Eisner seemed eager to mollify him. "Of course, if for any reason Frank isn't here; if he decides to run for political office; if he goes off to climb the summit; you are the number two person and I would want you to have the job."

If Eisner's goal was to keep Katzenberg, he succeeded. Katzenberg was enormously heartened by the conversation, especially after the problems they'd been having that year. For the first time he began to look forward to extending his contract under the new deal Eisner was talking about.

Eisner gave a somewhat different version in the account he wrote to Irwin Russell. "I made it clear it was unethical and the like," he wrote of Katzenberg's inquiry about being president. "He backed off and almost pretended he never suggested it. He went on to plan 2. Plan 2! Jeffrey told me three things that he needed to sign on 'forever.' If we made an acquisition then he could run that acquisition which would give him 'a new mountain to climb.' In other words, he felt he had done it all and wanted more to do. He also felt our company lacked forward thinking, maybe guts, entrepreneurial instincts, capital 'balls' or what-have-you; and that we were just not in the league with Rupert Murdoch, Sumner Redstone, Ted Turner and the like. When I would ask him his comments on how and why the value of the company went from $2 billion to $22.5 billion he says nothing. He values Rupert not Warren Buffett.* The second thing he wanted at that time was to be 'anointed,' his word to Frank Wells. I think this meant he wanted it to be known that he was clearly the number three person in the company and was the 'heir' behind Frank. And he wanted on the Board."†

Eisner provides a still different account in his 1998 autobiography, this time making no mention of any Friday-night conversation:

"Much later, Jeffrey would claim that I had promised during our walk to make him president of the company should Frank ever decide to leave. Obviously, I remember the conversation very differently. The only issue in my mind is whether, in my phrasing, or my tone, or my body language, I might have inadvertently given Jeffrey a measure of false hope about someday inheriting Frank's job. What I know with certainty is that neither Roy Disney nor the board was prepared to make Jeffrey president of Disney. I did hold out the possibility—even the wish—in my own mind that he might grow in ways that would someday make it possible to promote him. In any case, I deeply valued Jeffrey as the executive in charge of filmed entertainment, and I didn't want him to leave the company or feel discouraged about his future prospects. I suggested we talk instead about what else we might do to satisfy

---

* Buffett is famous as a long-term "value" investor rather than an aggressive buyer of other companies, like Rupert Murdoch.
† Katzenberg maintains that while these subjects may have been touched upon, Eisner's account is grossly inaccurate, noting that it was Eisner who offered him a seat on the board, which he didn't want.

him. 'I need new mountains to climb,' Jeffrey said again. I promised to give it some thought."

In neither of these versions does Eisner explicitly deny making such a promise. And in an interview with Tony Schwartz, Eisner all but conceded that he did say something to that effect. Schwartz had arrived in Los Angeles that fall to begin work on the long-delayed book collaboration, meeting with Eisner and other executives, sitting in on meetings, immersing himself in the company. Some Disney executives thought he'd joined the company as Eisner's assistant, the latest in the line that had begun with Art Levitt. (Levitt has since left Disney to become chief executive of Fandango, an Internet ticketing service.) Schwartz carried around a laptop computer and typed his sessions with Eisner. When he was back in New York, he often met with Eisner at Eisner's mother's apartment in the Pierre hotel. Though he realized he was speaking to a journalist, Eisner seems to have been relatively candid, as though he enjoyed being able to speak freely to someone outside the company, while retaining full control over anything that would actually be published.

When the subject of whether Eisner promised Katzenberg that he'd succeed Wells arose, Eisner said "I may have," Schwartz's notes indicate (and Schwartz later testified that the notes were a verbatim account of Eisner's remarks). "Only thing I may have said is: if he [Wells] hadn't signed a perfect seven year deal, if he wasn't here . . . if I didn't have this wife, you'd be great, you would be right." And in another interview with Schwartz several months later, Eisner said, "[I] don't know whether I did say he could have Frank's job."

Frank Wells had returned to Los Angeles earlier in the day, and Eisner was eager to fill him in on his talk with Katzenberg. There's no way of knowing just how Eisner characterized Katzenberg's demands when they spoke, but according to Eisner, Wells replied, "Jeffrey really said that? I'm just amazed by his chutzpah." Wells seemed more hurt than Eisner had expected, but nonetheless he evidently put his feelings aside. He and Eisner spent the rest of the conversation talking about ways they could expand Katzenberg's responsibilities.

One possibility they discussed, one that Katzenberg himself had been pushing for, was to acquire a television network, an idea that Eisner had never entirely abandoned ever since giving up on acquiring NBC back in 1984, when it was sold to GE. His main motivation was as a distribution channel for Disney-made television programs and films. Despite his strenuous intention for Disney to build its own businesses rather than acquire others, Eisner made an exception for television networks. True, Barry Diller had defied skeptics by creating a fourth network for Fox, but Murdoch's Fox already owned a critical mass of television stations on which to build the network, and Disney did not. That fall of 1993, Eisner spoke to Dan Burke, Steve Burke's father and chief executive of Cap Cities/ABC about a possible merger. Eisner even dangled the possibility of running the network before Katzenberg. They also discussed expanding Katzenberg's responsibilities for Broadway theater, for records, and video games.

To all appearances, Katzenberg was reassured by what Eisner promised him at Aspen. Yet Eisner wrote his lawyer/confidant Irwin Russell the following April that Katzenberg "was confident that they [the conditions for his staying] would happen which goes to his unrealistic expectation about everything. And I did not dissuade him. He knew we were talking to ABC and I never told him it was a 'no shot' just a 'long shot.' He kind of settled in although we kept having terrible results in our live-action business and he became more secretive. . . . If Jeffrey was on his way to Washington, I wouldn't even know. I would say to my secretary, 'I need to talk to Jeff.' She would find him on the plane. I would say, 'Where are you?' He would answer 'On the plane.' 'Oh,' I would respond. 'Where are you going?' He would simply say 'Washington.' He would never give either Frank or me any more information. We would have to dig and dig. Mostly we gave up."

As his letter suggests, Eisner was troubled by Disney's continuing dismal performance in live-action films. Under Katzenberg's direction, the studio was having a great year thanks to video sales of *Beauty and the Beast* and the continuing success at the box office of *Aladdin*. But the bonanza from animation masked the continued weak performance of live action now that Disney was running both Touchstone and Hollywood studios and churning out forty films a year. There were a few modest successes—*What's Love Got to Do with It?*, a biography of Tina Turner; *The Joy Luck Club*; a remake of *Tombstone* with Val Kilmer and Kurt Russell; and a Walt Disney production, *Homeward Bound*, a low-budget remake of *The Incredible Journey*—but the only memorable work was *The Nightmare Before Christmas*, produced by former Disney animator Tim Burton.

But given the studio's track record in live action, Eisner was increasingly derisive of Katzenberg's manifesto of two years earlier. Unfortunately for Katzenberg, almost every film that he'd singled out for praise—*Scenes From a Mall*, *Billy Bathgate*, and especially *The Rocketeer*—had been huge box-office flops. Eisner attributed much of the live-action failures to his exclusion from meetings and screenings and his belief, as he later put it, that "most successful movie studios and television networks have had at least two strong executives at the top, supporting and counterbalancing one another."

Eisner complained about the Katzenberg manifesto to Tony Schwartz, characterizing it as "insubordination," showing that it was still on his mind two years later. Schwartz's notes read: "wrote the memo, he didn't write anyway, because he was so proud of it . . . he wanted me to read it, thought it was so brilliant . . . so I read it and say, Jeffrey, this is dynamite, putting down a lot of actors, it is also self-serving . . . don't show it to anyone; I wrote on the memo: 'Do not Xerox or send this to anyone' . . . he completely disobeyed me; Frank and I discussed throwing him out . . . from that moment on I knew it was over. It wasn't the memo, fact I told him not to show it, and faxed it, and lied about it . . . I just let him have it; just sits there and stares at you and walked out; everyone I knew was pissed off . . . from that memo on never made a decent movie."

At their weekly dinners, Eisner expressed at least some of these concerns to Katzenberg, but he felt that Katzenberg didn't take them seriously. Katzenberg was baffled. From his vantage, Eisner had approved every movie the studio produced. He had always stressed that Eisner had the right to veto any project he didn't believe in. And he had carried out Eisner's directives, even when he disagreed. A case in point was the movie *Cabin Boy* starring Chris Elliott, a comedian who was performing skits on "Late Show with David Letterman." Adam Resnick, a former writer for Letterman, wrote the script. Katzenberg thought the idea—a pampered rich boy takes to sea with some salty fishermen—was trite, the script terrible, and told Eisner so. Not one person on the Touchstone staff wanted to make the film. But Eisner insisted it would be a comic hit.

When the movie was released, the reviews were scathing and it barely earned $3 million at the box office. Katzenberg was pummeled in Hollywood, yet out of loyalty to Eisner, he said nothing to defend himself. But Katzenberg's shouldering the blame for *Cabin Boy* seemed to generate scant goodwill from Eisner. He complained about Katzenberg to Ovitz, faulting his bad manners, his lack of education, his rudeness. At a meeting with animators developing *The Hunchback of Notre Dame,* Eisner spoke about the historic Paris cathedral and Victor Hugo's classic novel. "How do you know all that?" Katzenberg asked, and Eisner gave him a withering look.

"I went to college," Eisner said.

At Frank Wells's sixtieth birthday party, hosted by his wife, Luanne, and held at the Beverly Hills home of a close friend, Eisner was appalled that Katzenberg left after the first course, citing another business engagement.

Wells didn't seem to care, but he, too, complained to Ovitz from time to time about Katzenberg's lack of polish, aggressive manner, and naked ambition, so different from the urbane aura that Wells cultivated.

In his letter to Irwin Russell, Eisner wrote, "Jeffrey acted like he was staying forever, and both Frank and I were perplexed. On one hand he was doing his job, almost with a voracious appetite. Meetings, meetings, meetings, deals, and more deals; volume at any expense. Frank and I had such mixed feelings that we discussed him all the time. Every day we obsessed over Jeffrey Katzenberg. Basically Frank really did not like him. He treated Frank as a necessary obstacle to getting his agenda done. He never was really polite to him, actually quite rude. He left his surprise sixtieth birthday party after the first course for some meaningless 'business dinner.' Of course he was always rude to those of us inside the company. He left everything early. Jane would never invite him to anything at our house because he was so rude. Why should I be surprised about Frank's feelings. Jeffrey was the only one who never mentioned or wrote to me after my father's death."

It is striking that in his letters to Russell, Eisner never said anything nice about Katzenberg. Even the animators, who were generally hostile to Katzenberg, thought Eisner's condescension toward him bordered on cruelty. Yet from a business perspective, it was hard to fault Katzenberg given the stupendous success of the animation division. Thanks to the recent animated hits and home video sales, the studio had record earnings in 1993 of $622 million despite huge losses in live action and television. Operating income at Disney dropped sharply from $817 million in 1992 to $300 million in the year ending September 1993. Because of the accompanying slide in Disney's share price, Eisner and Wells received no bonuses. It was no longer possible to gloss over the alarming problems at Euro Disney, which in December 1993 reported a loss of more than $1 billion. In his annual letter to shareholders, Eisner acknowledged Euro Disney to be his "first real financial disappointment." "This has been a serious problem, one that has cost an enormous amount of time and anxiety, and one on which Frank Wells has concentrated his—and the rest of our—full attention."

Disney had created a reserve sufficient to fund Euro Disney's losses through March 31, 1994, but Eisner used the annual report to declare that this could not continue indefinitely, and that others would have to bear their "fair share," meaning that the creditors would have to forgive or restructure a large part of the crushing $3 billion in debt. "We will deal in good faith with our fellow Euro Disney shareholders and Euro Disney creditors. But in doing so, I promise all shareholders of the Walt Disney Company that we will take no action to endanger the health of Disney itself."

Given the studio's financial success, especially when contrasted with the performance of the other divisions, it still seemed inconceivable to Katzenberg that Eisner would want him to leave the company. The issues of staying until the end of his contract and the 2 percent bonus if he chose to leave were still unresolved—he'd never heard back from Wells about Eisner's "misunderstanding"—but Katzenberg let them go in the wake of his conversations with Eisner at Aspen and the ongoing efforts to expand his responsibilities, such as running any acquisitions. From a legal standpoint, his letter from the previous fall announcing his intention to leave the following year still stood as his last word on the subject.

At some point during the following spring, Katzenberg's tenure again became an issue. He told Eisner and Wells that he wanted to make a new five-year deal with David Hoberman, who was running the money-losing Touchstone operation. Eisner thought it made no sense to enter into an expensive, long-term contract with Hoberman if Katzenberg himself was leaving, so Katzenberg promised to tell Eisner where he stood by April. But before then, at one of their weekly dinners, Katzenberg said he'd like to stay, but only under a contract that gave him the right to leave with thirty days' notice. In other words, Katzenberg would be free to accept a high-level job at another studio, network, or entertainment company and extricate himself within a month from Disney. Under this arrangement, Katzenberg said he didn't want to be on the Disney board. He didn't want his compensation to be disclosed, as it would be if he were a board member.

To Katzenberg's surprise, Eisner seemed comfortable with the arrangement. Eisner said he understood that Katzenberg didn't want to make a long-term commitment unless the conditions they'd discussed at Aspen were met, and used the occasion to once more express his surprise that Katzenberg was willing to walk away from $100 million by leaving two years before his contract expired.

In fact, as Eisner wrote to Russell, Eisner was only too happy to give Katzenberg the option to leave, or for Disney to fire him, with just thirty days' notice. "I was pleased to hear this," Eisner wrote, "because neither Frank nor I knew if we wanted him to stay at all. And he now did not want to go on the board under this arrangement. Certainly I was thrilled about that. His pontificating on the board would be unbearable. Frank and I were still undecided but he was working hard. If we could only get him back to being a team

player maybe it would work. I think Jeffrey was surprised to hear that I accepted his 30-day out, but seemed OK with it."

As Katzenberg was falling from favor, others, especially Peter Rummell and
general counsel Sandy Litvack, were ascending. Rummell, who'd worked in
real estate for most of his career, both for Arvida before it was acquired by
Disney, and then Rockefeller Center, ran the Disney Development Corporation, which had built the hotels and infrastructure for the theme parks in Orlando and Paris. Rummell, age forty-six, was articulate, personable, and
conversant with architecture and leading architects, which impressed Eisner.
He was in charge of developing a new planned community near Orlando,
called Celebration, and was also overseeing Disney's rehabilitation of the
landmark New Amsterdam Theatre on Forty-second Street in New York. Eisner found both projects a welcome diversion from the intrigues of the film
studio and the woes of Euro Disney. Eisner confided to Tony Schwartz that
Rummell was a "rising star," a possible successor to himself.

In late 1993, Eisner had been meeting in New York with Robert Stern
when Stern suggested they walk over for a look at the New Amsterdam Theatre, built in 1903, home to the Ziegfeld Follies, and once the "jewel of Forty-
second Street." Eisner had resisted efforts to involve Disney in the proposed
rehabilitation of Times Square and Forty-second Street, which had descended into a drug-, crime-, and prostitute-infested urban blight in the decades since Eisner had watched movies and theater there as a teenager. But
negotiations with the Shubert Organization, which, along with the Neder-
lander Group, owned nearly all the theaters on Broadway, to find a theater
for *Beauty and the Beast* had convinced Eisner that Disney needed to own its
own theater if it hoped to make money on Broadway.

Stern took Eisner, Jane, and his son Anders over to the theater, where they
donned hard hats and carried flashlights. Water was leaking through the
roof, forming puddles; bird droppings were everywhere; crumbled plaster
and other debris was scattered over the floors. Still, the potential grandeur of
the theater was evident: remnants of allegorical murals, friezes, and mosaics;
Art Nouveau architectural details.

By the time they finished the tour, the prospect of salvaging a landmark
theater and restoring its fabled grandeur had captured Eisner's imagination.
This was a project that would cast Eisner in the role of Renaissance patron,
not just another corporate CEO. As soon as he got on the company plane that
day, he called Rummell and told him to follow up. "This is going to be much

more expensive than you think," Rummell warned. "And a lot of headaches." But by Monday, Rummell was negotiating with people from the Times Square Redevelopment Project.

Eisner insisted on driving a hard bargain: Disney put up just $8 million of the $34 million budget, using low-interest city and state financing for the rest. Though details remained to be ironed out, in February 1994, Disney's deal to acquire and restore the New Amsterdam was announced at a press conference at City Hall in New York. Mayor Rudolph Giuliani called Disney and Times Square a "match made in heaven" and predicted that Disney's involvement would jump-start the redevelopment of Times Square. In a few months, other companies and developers followed Disney's lead, including Tishman Realty, Disney's partners in the Dolphin and Swan Hotels; Condé Nast, publisher of *Vogue* and *Vanity Fair;* and the AMC Entertainment movie theater chain.

After the success of his negotiations for the New Amsterdam, Eisner named Rummell to head the Imagineering unit, the latest executive to follow Rochlis in an effort to rein in the burgeoning unit, which, besides Euro Disney, was now hard at work on a new theme park to be called Disney's America. Eisner had embraced the idea of a theme park that captured the sweep of American history after Dick Nunis suggested he visit Colonial Williamsburg. Strategic planning had vetoed tidewater Virginia as too far from a major population center, but Eisner liked the concept and Rummell soon turned his attention to potential sites near Washington, D.C., settling on three thousand acres outside Haymarket, Virginia, most of it owned by Exxon, which had abandoned ambitious development plans during the 1991 recession. The tract was twenty miles from Washington, adjacent to hunt country, and just five miles from the historic Manassas Civil War battlefield.

In its determination to capture the complexity of the American experience throughout its history, Disney's America may have been Eisner's most ambitious undertaking, intellectually if not logistically. In January 1994, he convened an all-day meeting with Rummell and the Imagineers. "The most difficult job," he told them, "won't be to tell important stories about our history, or to deliver an enjoyable experience for our guests, but to achieve both these goals without having either one dilute the other. . . . We need to keep working to create a daylong experience that makes our guests laugh and cry, feel proud of their country's strengths and angry about its shortcomings."

Some Imagineers thought it was too great a burden for a theme park to carry. So the idea of a working steel mill, which guests would view from the perspective of a roller coaster running through it, was scrapped as an inherently inconsistent hybrid of thrills and education. So, too, was a Lewis and Clark white-water raft ride against the backdrop of Manifest Destiny. Nevertheless, the Imagineers developed ambitious plans for seven themed areas, including a Native American village, a Civil War fort, Ellis Island, a state fair, and a working family farm. Eager to attract a major potential tourist attraction, the Virginia legislature approved a $140 million bond issue to finance highway improvements and a $20 million marketing campaign to promote Virginia tourism. As in France, Disney could dangle the possibility of a theme park in return for substantial public benefits.

Of course, many of Euro Disney's shareholders and creditors were now regretting their eagerness to entice Disney to a site outside of Paris. Despite Eisner's public warnings that the lenders had to accept their "fair share" of the losses, and that Disney would consider letting Euro Disney go bankrupt, if necessary, the European lenders had been intransigent, saying that salvaging the park was Disney's responsibility. As general counsel, Litvack reported to Wells, but had been complaining to Eisner that Wells hadn't given him sufficient responsibility. Given Eisner's tendency to blame Wells for Euro Disney's problems, this fell on sympathetic ears, and Eisner encouraged Litvack to take on the lead negotiating role in Paris. When a lawyer for the lenders threatened to sue Disney for fraud based on the representations it made at the time of the original financing, Litvack was so angry that he made only a brief rebuttal, then walked out and boarded a plane for Los Angeles, refusing to continue negotiations.

Litvack's dramatic gesture broke the logjam. Negotiations soon resumed, and Litvack arrived at an agreement that essentially divided the burden of reducing the debt by $1 billion among Disney and the lenders. Among other provisions, it gave Euro Disney a reprieve by suspending interest payments for sixteen months and deferring principal payments for three years. "Close the deal as best you can," Wells told Litvack.

Soon after, an anxious Philippe Bourguignon interrupted Steve Burke, who was in the middle of a meeting, and took him into a small room. "Our phones have been tapped," he reported. The offices had been swept for listening devices. "Yours and mine have been tapped. We don't know by whom, or for how long, but they're trying to find out our end game." Burke was in a meeting later that day, about to leave for London, when Wells's secretary called him and said he should call Wells from a pay phone as soon as he landed in London. When Burke reached Wells from a phone at Heathrow Airport, Wells said, "Sorry about this, but our feeling is, if they're tapping you in the office, they could be tapping you elsewhere." He noted that the French government was believed to have voice recognition eavesdropping technology, and the French government was one of Euro Disney's biggest creditors. "Go see Sandy [Litvack] at the Bristol Hotel, take him out into the street, and explain that we may say things we don't really mean."

But before Burke could carry out his mission, an agreement in principle was reached on March 3. Litvack used a pay phone to call Eisner and Wells with the news. "It's too generous," Wells said, on the assumption that someone was eavesdropping.

"The board will never approve it, and in any case, we'll never be able to sell it to Sid Bass," Eisner added.

Litvack was furious, and later called Wells. "We made a good and fair deal and all you did was criticize it."

Wells said nothing, and Litvack was still angry when he hung up. But then Burke arrived at his hotel, and took him outside. Burke told him that Eisner and Wells were bluffing for the benefit of any eavesdroppers.

It's impossible to know if Disney's hard line led to any concessions, but a deal to restructure the debt was announced on March 14, the same day as Disney's 1994 annual meeting, and just in time for Eisner to reassure the Disney board. While the deal brought some immediate concessions, it really only postponed a day of reckoning. The now tainted Euro Disney name was dropped, and the park was rechristened Disneyland Paris.

With the Euro Disney negotiations temporarily resolved, Frank Wells turned his attention to the struggling live-action studios, Touchstone and Hollywood. Contracts for several top studio executives were about to expire, including the Hoberman deal that Eisner and Katzenberg had discussed. And, of course, Eisner had been discussing the Katzenberg situation, as he had confided to Russell, on a daily basis. In March 1994, Wells wrote a detailed critique of the studios and convened a meeting with Katzenberg and Eisner to discuss it.

Wells had two major points: Disney was making too many movies, and Eisner needed to be more involved in the creative process, as he had been in the early years of their collaboration at Disney. "It's not worth being in the business at anything like this profile," the memo read. "I really believe the two of you, working in partnership as you did the first four years, can make 15— plus or minus—movies a year and have spectacular results. But I'm very concerned about going much beyond 15. . . . I seriously do not believe that the true head of production (that is Jeffrey—let's be real clear) can manage more than 15 pictures per year and give each one the individual attention it requires. Particularly as Jeffrey moves into broader responsibilities, we should all agree, starting now, that Michael becomes a true partner in the creative process."

Eisner was dubious. As he described the meeting in another letter to Russell, he confided, "When Frank and I tried to show him [Katzenberg] how badly he had done over the past three or four years in live-action films, he simply said it is all fixed. 'This year we are going to make $250 million in live action. . . . Frank had tried to point out that our success came to an end after he pushed me out of the process and on top of that his desire to release 60 films. Whether that is true or not, Jeffrey displayed the strangest deafness one could imagine."

Shortly after that meeting, Disney released two live-action films: *Angie* and *The Ref,* which did not make any money and received bad reviews. The results only added to Eisner's pessimism.

In his many sessions with Tony Schwartz, Eisner complained constantly about Katzenberg. On March 2, 1994, they were discussing Katzenberg's 1991 manifesto, still on Eisner's mind three years later. Schwartz's typed notes read: "jeffrey katzenberg . . . think I hate the little midget . . . but that . . . since plagiarized four years ago; from that moment decided was genius and loving person, he excluded me." The notes go on to suggest that Katzenberg told Eisner he was "embarrassing" him at meetings and had "agreed to meet with him for a half hour each day, but then talked "about things other than product."

The growing tension between Eisner and Katzenberg, as well as Roy's antipathy toward Katzenberg, were increasingly evident to the animation and studio staffs. Peter Schneider and Thomas Schumacher began nearly every day with a cell phone conversation about the latest quarrel between "Dad" and "Mom." Relations between the two had gotten to the point where Katzenberg issued orders that no one who reported to him was allowed to initiate a conversation with Eisner. If Eisner happened to call one of them, they were to call Katzenberg immediately and report the substance of the conversation. Katzenberg explained the ban to Schneider by saying that Eisner was "meddlesome and crazy."

But Eisner had already asked Schneider to report to him on Katzenberg's activities. He often called Schneider to gather intelligence on Katzenberg, which naturally put Schneider in the awkward position of double agent. As

Eisner later confided to Irwin Russell, "I call Peter all the time, and although he is a political troublemaker, he did know what was going on." Eisner flew into a rage when Schneider told him that Katzenberg was taking cels and backgrounds from the Disney archives for his own personal collection. When Schneider suggested that this was inappropriate, considering that Disney was planning to auction off some of its collection, Katzenberg had argued that Walt Disney himself had a collection he'd taken from archives. "But you're not Walt," Schneider said.

"I'm the Walt Disney of today," Katzenberg replied.

That, at least, was the substance of the conversation that Schneider reported to Eisner, who "went wild" over the reference to Walt, Schneider recalls. Eisner insisted that Katzenberg reimburse the company for the cels (Katzenberg did). Even more than the taking of the cels, Eisner was incensed that Katzenberg would dare to compare himself to Walt. Eisner promptly reported the incident to Roy, further fueling Roy's antipathy toward Katzenberg.

Schneider had lunch every Tuesday in the Rotunda, the executive dining room, with Roy. Given that Roy was such a large shareholder, neither Eisner nor Katzenberg could forbid Schneider from talking to him, but it was clear to Schneider that they resented it. "You're much too political," Eisner warned Schneider at one point. But Schneider, like most Disney executives, felt he had little choice, caught between warring factions in which each piece of information became a test of loyalty.

Eisner was also furious that earlier that year Katzenberg had opened a deep-sea-themed restaurant in partnership with Steven Spielberg called Dive! Although Katzenberg cleared the venture in advance with Wells, who had no objection to it, Eisner thought it was a blatant conflict with Disney's efforts to open its own themed restaurants. It was especially galling to Eisner that, while Dive! was enough of a success that a franchise opened in Las Vegas, a Disney-themed restaurant never got beyond a prototype. As Eisner later expressed it, "my deepest concerns about Jeffrey had to do with the way he conducted himself, and the degree to which he focused on his own agenda."

Eisner concealed these feelings from Katzenberg, and Katzenberg brushed aside his complaints about the performance of live action. "Wait until next year. It's going to be great!"

Katzenberg's optimism sprang in part from ongoing work on *King of the Jungle*, which had now been renamed *The Lion King*. Thomas Schumacher had convinced Katzenberg that *King of the Jungle* should be a musical. Tim Rice, who'd stepped in for Howard Ashman on *Aladdin,* wanted to work with popular composer Elton John, but Katzenberg resisted. It took another phone call from Geffen, a friend of John's and former producer of his records, to get Katzenberg to agree. But once John accepted the assignment, Katzenberg was so enthusiastic that he flooded the composer with press and marketing requests. Finally John called Schumacher. "Make him stop calling," he begged. So Schumacher called Katzenberg.

"Too many people are calling Elton," he said.

"Great," Katzenberg responded. "We'll limit calls to just you and me."

"He'd rather you not call."

"Oh." There was a brief silence. "You mean just you?"

"Me and Denise [Greenawalt]," he said, who was the press person in charge of the film.

Schumacher thought Katzenberg took the rebuff well, and Katzenberg issued a memo saying John didn't want to be disturbed by calls.

For the most part Katzenberg honored his own edict, though it didn't stop his active involvement in the project, which, after all, was his idea. He wasn't satisfied with the development of the script. Countless scripts had been written and rejected, and Katzenberg felt that the story wasn't jelling. Then, in the fall of 1993, during one of the weekly meetings, a story artist mentioned that "You know, what you're really trying to do here is tell the story of *Hamlet.*" Katzenberg paused for a second. Suddenly everything fell into place. "You're right!" he exclaimed. Katzenberg urged that the dialogue be made "more Shakespearean."

In the resulting script, Scar, the king's brother and Simba's uncle (and the voice of Jeremy Irons), became a much more important role. In Shakespeare, Hamlet's uncle kills Hamlet's father, the king, so he can marry Hamlet's mother. The king's ghost returns to exact vengeance. In *Lion King* Scar kills Simba's father, who later returns as a ghost, though the analogy probably shouldn't be stretched too far. Simba, unlike Hamlet, leaves his father's kingdom to find himself, weaving in an element of the biblical story of the prodigal son.

Elton John and Tim Rice had finished their score, which had a troubled history. Katzenberg had initially rejected the music for the opening sequence, "Circle of Life." Even after John rewrote it with a different melody, Katzenberg thought it was "barely suitable for the end credits." But composer Hans Zimmer, brought in to supervise the music, had transformed it using African musical influences in the voices and orchestrations. The directors had wanted to cut "Can You Feel the Love Tonight?," which they thought was an "unearned" moment between Simba and his budding love interest. A version of the film was screened for John with the song deleted. John went ballistic, shouting at Katzenberg on the phone that he'd cut his best song. Katzenberg intervened, and the directors found a way to bring the song into the story much later, when Simba and Nala have established their relationship, and the audience would be yearning for their reunion.

Katzenberg was also working to salvage *Toy Story,* Disney's first joint venture with Pixar. Late that year, John Lasseter and his team came to Burbank and screened some of it for Katzenberg, Schneider, and Thomas Schumacher, who was acting as the Disney liaison to Pixar. While they still liked the idea of toys coming to life, the Disney executives agreed that the project was a "mess," as Katzenberg put it. There was no coherent narrative line. But suddenly Katzenberg had an idea: In the characters Woody and Buzz Lightyear, the retro cowboy and the futuristic spaceman, Lasseter had the makings of a classic buddy movie. "Go out and watch two movies," Katzenberg told Lasseter and his team, *"The Defiant Ones* and *48 Hrs."* Both were classic "buddy" pictures where opposites bond, with 1958's *The Defiant Ones* starring Sidney Poitier and Tony Curtis.

"I get it," Lasseter said. Katzenberg felt it was a breakthrough moment, just like *Hamlet* had been for *Lion King.*

Not that these suggestions, however constructive they may have been, endeared Katzenberg to either the Disney animators or their Pixar counterparts working on the project. In one of the cartoons they drew, which especially amused Roy, Katzenberg stands at the head of a conference table surrounded by animators. They have unzipped their trousers and put their penises on the table. Katzenberg's is so small as to be barely visible.

"Who has the biggest?" Katzenberg demands.

"You do, sir," chime the animators.

SIX

One measure of Eisner's rising stature in Los Angeles was a membership in the exclusive Bel Air Country Club, which he'd joined in the fall of 1993 at the request of his sons who wanted to learn to play golf—much as Roy O. Disney had joined Lakeside so that Roy E. could learn the game. Michael Ovitz helped pave the way. Bel Air had been Ron Miller's club, and though it no longer excluded Jews (Ron Miller had proposed the first for membership, and recalls taking "quite a bit of heat for it") or entertainment industry people, it retained an aura of wealth and inherited privilege. The club was on Bellagio Road in the heart of Bel Air, a few minutes from the Eisner home.

Eisner had neither the time nor patience for golf, though he'd occasionally played with his father and had a decent swing. Six months after joining Bel Air, he had yet to set foot on the course. But on Easter Sunday afternoon, March 27, 1994, a beautiful, warm spring day, he, Jane, and their son Anders decided to play a round. Though Eisner was pleased to discover he could still hit the ball, they were erratic players, with numerous divots, tree and sand trap shots, and balls lost in water hazards and out-of-bounds. So they were late arriving for an Easter dinner hosted by their oldest son Breck and his girlfriend. Everyone gathered around an antique dining table that had once belonged to Eisner's grandmother.

Five minutes into dinner, at about 6:30, the phone rang. Breck answered, then told his father it was Lucille Martin, his secretary. It was very unusual for Martin to interrupt Eisner at a family event.

"Michael," she said. "Frank is dead."

Eisner felt numb. "What happened?"

Martin had only a few details: Wells had been killed in a helicopter crash returning from skiing in a remote area in the Nevada mountains. Only one passenger had survived. Others on the trip, including one of Wells's sons, his mountain climbing partner Dick Bass, and actor Clint Eastwood, had been in a different helicopter.

Eisner said he needed a moment to collect himself. He hung up and gestured for Jane to join him outside the dining room. Conversation came to a halt. "Frank is dead," he said. Jane screamed, then started crying. Eisner himself showed little emotion; "My reaction in crisis has always been to set my emotions aside and to focus on the issue at hand," he has said.

Roy, Patty, and their pet Labrador were returning from their weekend house in San Juan Capistrano when their car broke down, stranding them alongside the road until a truck arrived to rescue them. They, too, were late for dinner at their son Roy Patrick's house, and the meal had barely begun when Martin reached Roy. "My God," Roy said. "Frank is dead."

Stanley Gold was in his car with his family, after an early dinner, when the phone rang. "Are you driving?" his secretary asked. "Pull over."

"What is it?" he asked, but she insisted he stop driving. "I just heard from Lucille. Frank was killed in a ski accident." Gold let his head fall to the steering wheel. Wells was his best friend.

When Michael Ovitz walked into his house that evening, the usual array of notes from a message pad was arrayed on the dining table. He glanced through them and saw one from "M": "Mr. Eisner called. Mr. Wells was killed in a helicopter crash an hour ago." Thinking of the time he'd called Eisner with the news that John Belushi had died of a drug overdose, and Eisner hadn't believed him, Ovitz thought the message was a prank. He immediately picked up the phone and called Eisner.

"He's not dead," Ovitz said.

"He's dead, Michael."

As usual, Eisner's first call was to Sid Bass, whom he reached at a restaurant in Aspen. Then he spoke to Gold, Roy, and Irwin Russell, his closest confidants on the board, and then Ovitz had called. With each, he discussed what immediate steps needed to be taken and the issue of succession. Roy insisted that Eisner not try to find another Wells. "He was unique," Roy said. "You can't clone him." The consensus was to not make any dramatic moves. Eisner called John Dreyer, head of public relations, asking him to draft a press release. He called Sandy Litvack, a sign of Litvack's growing stature in the company. He phoned other board members, the heads of Disney's various divisions, asking them to inform their staffs, and finally, at about 9:30 P.M., he called Katzenberg.

The Eisners were about to set out to try to console Luanne Wells. As usual, Luanne had not accompanied her husband on one of his strenuous outdoor weekends. She was at their beach house in Malibu. Katzenberg suggested he come along. That was the last thing Eisner wanted, and he dismissed the idea as "inappropriate." Instead he told Katzenberg to call his people, and said he'd meet with him early the next morning. "We have to keep the ship on an even keel," he said.

Wells's death was front-page news in the next morning's *Los Angeles Times*, which reported that he and two others were killed when their helicopter crashed in the remote Ruby Mountains in northeast Nevada. "There are no words to express my shock and sense of loss," Eisner said in a prepared statement. "Frank Wells has been the purest definition of a life force I have ever known. His wisdom, his charm, his zest for experience and challenge . . . his naked and awesome intelligence . . . set him apart and beyond. The world has lost a great human being."

As Katzenberg pulled into the parking garage at 6:30 that morning, he noticed Eisner's car wasn't there yet. He cleared his schedule, canceling lunch and dinner plans, in case Eisner needed him, as he assumed he would.

Overnight, Katzenberg had thought of little else but the assurance Eisner had given him at Aspen that if anything ever happened to Wells, Katzenberg would succeed him. Of course he'd never expected anything so sudden, so tragic, as this. Wells had been a mediator between him and Eisner so often, and Katzenberg would miss him. But fate moved in unexpected ways. At age forty-three, Katzenberg was ready for the partnership with Eisner that they'd discussed for so long, and that now seemed within his grasp.

Katzenberg waited anxiously. Surely Eisner knew he was there; he had to have seen his car. Each time the phone rang, he thought it must be the summons from Eisner. As time passed, other studio executives dropped by, shocked and apprehensive and, at the same time, intensely curious about Katzenberg's future. Katzenberg did his best to reassure them, urging them not to let Frank's death distract them from work. Finally he couldn't take the suspense any longer, and dialed Eisner's office. Martin answered.

"Do you need anything?" Katzenberg asked. "Is there anything I can do to help?"

"He's in a telephonic board meeting," she answered. The directors had convened by telephone to discuss the Wells succession issue, and were at that moment making Eisner chairman and president.

Katzenberg was stunned by the news. He was the number three executive in the company; Eisner hadn't spoken to him, and yet he had already convened a board meeting.

Katzenberg tried to turn his attention to his work. As always, there was plenty to do. *Beauty and the Beast* was about to open on Broadway; *Lion King* was in the final edit; Lasseter and the Pixar people were trying to schedule a screening of *Toy Story*.

Finally, at about 11:30, Martin called, and Katzenberg's expectations rose again. But it was just to say that Eisner would be going ahead with his regularly scheduled Monday staff lunch.

Eisner's decision to assume the title of president himself was meant to reassure Wall Street, but also to send a firm message to Katzenberg. That morning, Eisner had again discussed the matter with his usual circle of close advisers: Bass, Gold, Russell—and Litvack. They agreed that, at least as a temporary measure, Eisner should assume Wells's titles. The subject of Katzenberg did come up. Eisner told Roy that "Jeffrey wants to be president," and Roy responded that "I don't think that's a good idea." Although Roy felt Katzenberg's behavior had been improving, he still thought he spent too much time talking about "I" rather than "we," and that he was rude to subordinates. But Roy insists that "Eisner never asked me to make Jeffrey president. Never."

Indeed, Eisner had already complained about Katzenberg on so many occasions—including the letters to Russell—that no one on the board considered Katzenberg even a remotely serious candidate. When he mentioned Katzenberg to Gold, Gold didn't take the suggestion seriously, and rejected it out of hand (though both Gold and Roy maintain that Roy never threatened to quit the board if Katzenberg were made president, as Eisner later said).

As soon as he was off the phone, Eisner went into Wells's office, closed and locked the door, and searched Wells's desk and files.

A little before noon, Katzenberg dropped by Eisner's office, and the two walked to the elevators and then to the executive dining room in the building's rotunda. Katzenberg said nothing about how Eisner had ignored him and Eisner avoided the succession issue. Katzenberg used the opportunity to urge Eisner to continue speaking to the press about Wells, saying his comments in that day's papers were "great" but that Eisner "had to do more" since others would be talking. Given his feelings about Katzenberg, Eisner was alarmed that this was a veiled threat that Katzenberg would start talking to the press, trying to position himself as Wells's successor. Katzenberg's remarks agitated and upset Eisner; he later said he felt "cornered."

As they walked into the dining room, Jody Dreyer (John Dreyer's wife), Eisner's assistant who had replaced Art Levitt, was already there with copies of the freshly drafted press release in hand, announcing that Eisner would assume the title of president. She handed a copy to Katzenberg. Eisner hadn't planned for Katzenberg to learn the news from a press release, or in so public a setting. Katzenberg read the release and said nothing. Roy was also on hand; Eisner had asked him to be there.

The lunch, as Eisner later described it, was "awkward and sad." There are people who instinctively rise to such occasions, but by his own admission, Eisner isn't among them. He felt uncomfortable talking about someone so recently deceased, and his discomfort spread to other participants. Toward the end of the lunch, Eisner confirmed what they'd already read in the press release, which was that he would be assuming Wells's titles and duties as president and chief operating officer. They discussed the release and the likely press reaction, and Eisner stressed that only he and Roy would speak to the press. Much to his relief, Katzenberg agreed to this restriction.

As they left the room, Katzenberg came up to Eisner. "That's entirely appropriate," he said. Eisner was pleasantly surprised that Katzenberg was being so mature about it. As he later put it, he thought he'd "dodged a bullet."

In fact, Katzenberg was devastated, so upset that he hadn't brought himself to look directly at Eisner during the lunch and barely ate. The minute he saw the press release, drafted without his knowledge and without a single consultation, he knew that his nineteen-year relationship with Eisner—one in which he'd invested so much of his energy, his loyalties, his hopes, and his dreams—was dead.

By the time he got back to his office, Eisner's feelings of relief were giving way to guilt about the way he'd treated Katzenberg. He realized he'd snubbed him, that he'd not had the courage to explain his decision to him face-to-face. He called Katzenberg and suggested they have their usual Monday evening dinner at Locanda Veneta, just the two of them. Katzenberg readily accepted, noting that he'd cleared his schedule that day and wanted to help in any way he could. The hopes that had been dashed at lunch stirred again. Perhaps Eisner's decision to assume Wells's titles was temporary.

Eisner was feeling drained by the day's events by the time he met Katzenberg at the restaurant. He brought along the two memos that Wells had been working on—one describing Katzenberg's new responsibilities, and one discussing giving him 1.4 million stock options. Eisner started talking about dividing Wells's responsibilities. Katzenberg could take the record division, the venture with the telephone companies, interactive video. Katzenberg said nothing. As he sat and listened, his expression hardened. He realized that Eisner was dumping what he considered "every money-losing, pain-in-the-ass" business on him. Anything that really mattered—strategic planning, finance, legal—would now be reporting to Eisner. Katzenberg let him go on. "And Jeffrey," Eisner finally said, "we've got to close your deal."

"Why don't we let the dust settle?" Katzenberg suggested, fighting to control his anger and disappointment. Eisner seemed relieved to do just that, and put the folder away.

Katzenberg was now in such a state of disbelief that the rest of the evening passed in a blur as he and Eisner carried on as though it were just another one of their Monday dinners. The promise at Aspen was never mentioned, nor was the presidency of Disney. As Katzenberg later put it, it was as though an elephant were sitting in a third chair at the table, and neither of them said anything about it.

Katzenberg didn't sleep that night. At times he was so angry he felt short of breath. It wasn't just that he had been denied the presidency he felt he'd been promised. It was that Eisner had ignored him. He wouldn't face up to him. He wasn't being honest. That was something Katzenberg couldn't accept.

The next morning, Eisner called Katzenberg to discuss a contract with David Hoberman, the head of Touchstone. Katzenberg couldn't believe Eisner was just going on with business as usual. He said he had to speak to him, and it was "urgent." It was the first time in their nineteen years of working together that Katzenberg had ever made such a demand.

The two met for lunch in a private dining room off the Rotunda. "What's going on?" Eisner asked.

"I don't get it," Katzenberg said, barely able to contain himself. He reminded Eisner of his promise at Aspen that if anything ever happened to Wells, he would be number two. "Tell me that you meant it," he said, "or tell me that you've changed your mind. Just be honest."

"What's the alternative?" Eisner asked, which infuriated Katzenberg.

"If you can't tell me after nineteen years, if you can't tell me, then you've told me everything I need to know about my future. I've hit the ceiling. I have to move on."

"Are you putting a gun to my head?" Eisner's voice rose.

"Just be honest with me," Katzenberg pleaded. He said he couldn't believe that Eisner had come to the previous night's dinner as though nothing had changed, Wells were still alive, and they were discussing some new responsibilities and a contract for Katzenberg. He was "hurt," he said, that Eisner hadn't offered him the presidency Saturday night or Sunday, but that he assumed Eisner's taking the job was a short-term "corporate thing." "I was amazed that you didn't bring it up at dinner last night," he said. "After nineteen years together, I've earned the right to be your partner."

"I'd rather not discuss this now," Eisner said. "Let's concentrate on Frank."

"You can trust me to be as good as Frank," Katzenberg insisted.

The reference to "trust" unleashed Eisner. "I trust you," he said, "but not the way I trusted Frank. Read the newspapers for my view of partnership as I described Frank. We've had terrible problems in this area of trust. I do not want to have to tiptoe around WDI [Imagineering] the way I have to tiptoe around Animation. I can't be shut out in the Parks the way I am shut out in live-action features." Eisner paused to collect himself. "I might consider it down the road, if you earn it. Let's see how it goes."

"I'm not going to audition for you," Katzenberg countered. "Not after nineteen years. You should know me by now."

It wasn't just Eisner who had problems with Katzenberg becoming president, Eisner added, but Roy and other members of the board. "You have a serious problem with Roy," he reminded him. "Why, for someone who wines and dines the press, the Spielbergs, the agents, can't you perform talent relations with Roy?"

"Give me sixty to ninety days," Katzenberg replied. "It's done."

"It will take years."

"Give me the job of president for two years, and if it doesn't work out fire me," Katzenberg suggested.

"No."

They were at an impasse.

Finally Eisner spoke. "Are you saying to me that if I do not commit to you now that within sixty to ninety days you will be president of the Walt Disney Company, you will leave?"

"Correct," Katzenberg answered.

Eisner rose from his seat and walked out, followed closely by Katzenberg. They turned and headed in opposite directions.*

As soon as he got back to his office, Eisner called Sandy Litvack, his latest confidant. He told him what happened, and told him to go see Katzenberg and calm him down. He didn't want a crisis with Katzenberg so soon after Wells's death. Then he called Stanley Gold and told him that Katzenberg was threatening to quit, was "holding a gun to his head." He called Irwin Russell. He was still on the phone when Litvack returned, "shaken," in Eisner's view, by his encounter with Katzenberg. Litvack reported that Katzenberg had flown into a rage, ranting that "I am Michael Eisner! I am better than Michael Eisner was ten years ago! I will be Michael Eisner, if not here, somewhere."

Litvack urged Eisner to fire him that very day.

Instead, Eisner took the opposite tack. He didn't want Katzenberg to control the sequence of events. He'd flatter him, calm him down, defuse the situation. He asked Katzenberg to come to his office. "I'm sorry the conversation was so difficult," he said, referring to their lunch. "You are a fantastic executive," and "you have an outstanding future. Now is not the time to discuss all these things." Eisner said it was all he could do to deal with the funeral, memorial service, and business over the short term. They again discussed Katzenberg's strained relations with Roy and ways he might improve them.

But Eisner's feelings toward Katzenberg were still close to the surface. That evening Eisner called Ovitz. "Drop whatever you're doing and come over," he said. When Ovitz arrived, he, Eisner, and Jane sat in the study, where Eisner's cook served them dinner. Without any preliminaries, Eisner said, "I can't take any more." After summarizing the day's events, he launched into a long tirade against Katzenberg: He lied. He had no character, no integrity, no education. Roy hated him. Frank had hated him. Sandy hated him, and

---

* The account of the lunch meeting is an amalgam of both Katzenberg's and Eisner's versions, including Eisner's description of the meeting in a letter to Irwin Russell written just afterward. While they disagree about the precise wording and sequence of the dialogue, their versions are consistent as to the substance of the conversation.

thought he should be fired at once. Jane said nothing. Ovitz was used to Eisner's complaints about Katzenberg, but he was taken aback by the vehemence of Eisner's feelings on this occasion.

As he had in the past, Ovitz argued against it. Whatever Eisner's feelings about Katzenberg, it made no sense to remove him so soon after Frank's death. There was already enough turmoil and uncertainty at Disney. But Ovitz left feeling he'd failed to persuade him.

By the next morning, Eisner had reconsidered yet again. He called Katzenberg into his office, and was conciliatory. He said he was sorry the subject of naming him president had come up. "I'm not going to address it again for weeks," he said.

"Address it whenever you like," Katzenberg replied. "Weeks, months . . ."

Eisner concluded that Katzenberg was in a "good mood," and called Ovitz to report that a crisis had been averted.

The following Monday, April 4, nearly five thousand people gathered on the Disney lot for Wells's memorial service. A choir from the First African American Methodist Church sang gospel hymns. Wells had become involved with the church while helping organize Disney's relief efforts in the wake of the 1992 riots in south-central Los Angeles. Speakers included Clint Eastwood, who'd been on the ski trip with Wells when he was killed, actor Robert Redford, and Bob Daly, chairman of Warner Bros. and a close friend from their days together at Warner. Daly compared Wells to Clark Kent, "a tall, unassuming man with glasses but a Superman underneath."

Then Eisner came to the podium. "More than anyone I have ever met, Frank was willing to embrace the most creative and theatrical ideas," he said. "Sleep was Frank's enemy. Frank thought that it kept him from performing flat out one hundred percent of the time. There was always one more meeting he wanted to have. Sleep, he thought, kept him from getting things done. He fought it constantly, but sleep, Frank's enemy, finally won."

Perhaps unwittingly, Eisner stressed in his remarks how important it was to him that Wells had never tried to steal the spotlight or challenge his primacy. "He was a man unfettered by jealousy, competition, or personal ambition. His personal agenda was the company's agenda. Every minute of every business day Frank was out for the interests of the Walt Disney Company. He was a man who held a moral compass that was always true."

The last speaker was Wells's son Briant, a handsome, aspiring actor. Briant was haunted by the fact that he and his father had an often stormy relationship, and had argued just before Wells left for the ski trip. "Dad," he said. "I wish we had more time. You are my hero."

Wells's funeral and memorial did nothing to dispel Eisner's preoccupation, if not obsession, with Katzenberg. Less than two weeks later, on April 16, 1994, Eisner confided his feelings about Wells's death and his dealings with Katzenberg in another lengthy letter to Irwin Russell.

> Dear Irwin:
>
> I wanted to memorialize my lunch with Jeffrey if for no other reason than to vent my anger and frustration. I am angry because one day after Frank's death he had the bad taste and audacity to demand Frank's responsibilities and title or else he, Jeffrey, would leave the company. I am frustrated because his stupidity and lack of insights further convinces me he is either stupid, badly advised with the likes of a David Geffen, or totally deluded about his talent and value.

After a lengthy recitation of events leading up to their lunch, Eisner continued,

> That was some lunch, and the event I described at the top of this memo. He "was hurt." He couldn't believe "I hadn't offered him the job as soon as I found out about Frank on Sunday." He was "shocked" that at the dinner last night I only talked about the situation as though Frank were still in the equation. He assumed I only took Frank's job as a very short term "corporate thing" and intended to reverse that very soon. He said I told him last summer if Frank were not around he'd have the job. And certainly Jeffrey did not cause or ask for Frank's death. It was only my loyalty to Frank and Frank's ability that precluded Jeffrey getting the job last summer, a job he now says he never asked for.
>
> I immediately said no. I told him to read the newspapers on my view of a partnership as I described Frank in the L.A. Times and the New York Times. I told him that although I trusted him, it wasn't the same as the way I trusted Frank; and I would have to have that. . . .

On the subject of trust, Eisner reminded Katzenberg of a long-ago grudge.

> In those 19 years (more like 16) there had been three or four Jeffrey Katzenbergs. I reminded him that after he worked for me a couple of months at

Paramount, he went to Barry Diller and told Barry I should be fired. Barry asked him why seeing that we were the top studio the last four years and had 5 of the top 10 television shows. I do not remember his answer. He left that room with his tail between his legs. . . . The lunch ended badly.

Where do we now stand?

I am not quite sure. After my lunch where Jeffrey gave me the take-it-or-leave-it, I asked Sandy [Litvack] to come into my office. I explained the whole thing to Sandy and of course he was so outraged as were you and Stanley Gold. Stanley Gold said, "everybody in the town knows he has failed. Who does he think he is? And fuck him." And we all know how much Roy Disney hates Jeffrey and Stanley made it clear (mostly to Sandy later) that if we backed into giving Jeffrey Frank's job, Roy would quit the board and "go public." At any rate, Sandy went to speak to Jeffrey about his outrageous position.

Sandy came back to me shocked. Jeffrey was shaking with anger and was very upset. He said to Sandy as I understand it, "I am Michael Eisner. I am better than Michael Eisner was 10 years ago. I will be Michael Eisner if not here, somewhere." . . . And on and on. Sandy thought I should dump Jeffrey immediately. But we discussed it and I decided that I would talk to Jeffrey, calm it all down; and put things on my schedule. Frankly I do not believe there are so many jobs open right now although I will not kid myself. Jeffrey will do very well. He will end up a high level executive, but eventually he will fail.

Eisner made it clear that there was now no way that Katzenberg could succeed Wells. "Jeffrey is waiting and probably has deluded himself into believing that he will get Frank's job. He has probably figured out that all the jobs he thought were there for him are not really there right now. . . . Jeffrey cannot assume Frank's position and that is that. . . ." Eisner concluded:

I am not sure why I have written this letter except to get my thoughts down on paper. Maybe this will be interesting to read in a couple of years. In the meantime I am sure the saga will continue.

Michael 4/16/94

The following Monday, all the participants in the "saga" gathered at New York's Palace Theater for opening night of *Beauty and the Beast.* There had been plenty of carping among Broadway veterans about the impending arrival of a show backed by the deep pockets of a giant corporation. Disney had swept away the traditional role of Broadway producers, backers—the whole ritualized development process of backers' auditions and wealthy Broadway "angels" who put up the money for shows. Disney simply financed the show itself, from start to finish.

Eisner had deliberately shunned the Broadway creative community, insisting that the show use artistic talent from Disney's theme park theatrical productions (one exception was the costume designer). One executive involved insists it was because Eisner didn't want to have to deal with the Broadway unions. And there was plenty of skepticism about transplanting an animated musical to the stage.

The audience gave the show a standing ovation, and the buzz was positive. The day after the show opened, the Palace set a Broadway record by selling $700,000 worth of tickets. Reviews were surprisingly good. *Variety*, however, captured the larger point when it wrote that "It will almost certainly be met with varying levels of derision by Broadway traditionalists . . . The complaints, however, will be meaningless where it counts, which is at the Palace box office. Disney's first Broadway show will be packing them in—and thumbing its nose at the naysayers—for a very long time." Whatever the artistic merits, the show was a triumph for Disney—an amazing achievement considering the odds of succeeding on Broadway, especially for a first-time producer. Hundreds of talented people worked on the show, so allocating credit for the success was difficult, if not pointless. But it was Katzenberg who had pushed for it, persuaded Wells to finance it, and talked a reluctant Eisner into going along. Nonetheless, Eisner insisted that Katzenberg's name be deleted from the program credits. Katzenberg pretended he didn't care, but he did. Still, he figured Eisner knew the truth.

The intense strains between Eisner and Katzenberg were increasingly apparent inside the studio, which emboldened other executives to disagree with Katzenberg, and even go around him to Eisner. Another screening of *Toy Story* that month led to a sharp split within the Disney executive ranks. Lasseter had embraced Katzenberg's idea for a buddy movie, and Katzenberg felt the movie, while still seriously flawed, was now on the right track. Schneider disagreed, so much so that they thought it was hopeless. He lobbied Roy to shut the project down and write off the losses. Roy took the matter up with Eisner, who called Katzenberg. "Should we shut this down?" he asked.

Katzenberg wasn't thrilled that once again his deputy, Schneider, had done an end-run around him to Roy and Eisner, but he pointed out that under the agreement with Pixar, Disney's contribution was limited to $21 million, much of which had already been spent. Pixar would have to fund anything over that. So there wasn't much downside risk. He argued strongly that Lasseter should have another chance. Even though Eisner had never been enthusiastic about the concept for the movie, he agreed. "Fine," he said. "Go ahead."

Katzenberg also clashed with David Vogel, who ran the Walt Disney Pictures label. Vogel had steadily gained stature as his low-budget, family-oriented films like *Homeward Bound* proved to be reliable moneymakers. Still, despite his speech to Eisner and other executives in which he'd outlined his ambitious agenda, he felt he was relegated to films with animals, children, and third-tier actors and directors. It was humiliating to be at meetings where others pitched the latest vehicle for Julia Roberts or Bette Midler and he had to beg for the money to make yet another *Benji* sequel. One day Vogel showed Katzenberg a script he liked for a film called *The Mighty Ducks*, about ice hockey. "Nobody cares about hockey," Katzenberg replied, evidently oblivious to Eisner's constant anecdotes about his son who played hockey.

"Fine," Vogel said. "But who cares whether you care about hockey? This is a $10 million film about little kids and hockey, and why don't you just let me make it? I'll either fail or succeed."

Katzenberg resisted, but after Vogel threatened to quit, Katzenberg reluctantly passed the script on to Eisner on a Friday afternoon. On Monday morning Katzenberg walked into Vogel's office. He slapped the script on Vogel's desk and said, "Here's your hockey movie. Michael likes it. Go make it." Then he walked out.

After *Mighty Ducks* turned into a hit, Eisner had Disney buy a professional hockey team and name it The Mighty Ducks. Vogel hoped he might get invited to the opening game, but he wasn't, nor was he given season tickets, as were some of the film's production team. He ended up never seeing the team that his movie had inspired.

Katzenberg may have felt sidelined at the opening of *Beauty and the Beast*, but it didn't deter an ongoing stream of press attention. *Esquire* ran a profile of Katzenberg in May 1994 that, as Eisner told Irwin Russell, "is but another example of his lack of control, use of language, and the wrong image for the Walt Disney Company." Articles in *The New York Times* and *Los Angeles Times* speculating that Katzenberg was Wells's likely successor also irritated

Eisner. But nothing so incensed him as a page-one story in *The Wall Street Journal* that ran on May 16, 1994.

Reporter Richard Turner had gotten the idea for the story after Katzenberg invited some press to one of the Disney soundstages. Katzenberg marshaled a real elephant, bales of hay, a live orchestra, and Nathan Lane and Ernie Sabella to sing a comic duet between the characters Timon and Pumba. A presentation about the making of *The Lion King* featured Katzenberg in nearly every scene. The movie clips looked great; the song with Lane and Sabella was hilarious.

So Turner had called Katzenberg's office to propose a behind-the-scenes story on the making of the film, and Katzenberg agreed. Turner's story opens with a scene in which Katzenberg is meeting with composer Hans Zimmer: "Unaccustomed to hearing edicts from a studio executive, [Zimmer] is about to hear one now," Turner wrote. "The music in one scene, complains Mr. Katzenberg, is too 'dense—it's a lot of information to take in . . . I beg you, please, please, you've got to let it breathe. It's too loud, it's overwhelming the scene.' "

No one disputes that Katzenberg was intimately involved with every aspect of *The Lion King,* but participants in the meeting say that the scene depicted by Turner was a scripted reenactment of a meeting with Zimmer that had already happened, and that exaggerated Katzenberg's contribution. (Be that as it may, Turner emphatically dismisses the notion, saying that he saw many similar meetings in which Katzenberg's comments were critical to the finished film.)

Turner also attended a test screening in Pasadena and a dinner afterward with Katzenberg, Roy and Patty Disney, and members of the creative team. Turner noticed that everyone drank Evian water except Roy and Patty, who smoked cigarettes and had cocktails. The Pasadena audience had obviously loved the film, but Katzenberg and his team were still tinkering with it, especially the ending. Turner found Roy to be a "gentle, kindly soul," and that he made several good creative suggestions, though none made it into the final story.

The article was undeniably favorable for Disney, for *The Lion King,* and above all, for Katzenberg. "Prominent in the Disney formula is Mr. Katzenberg," Turner wrote, somewhat ironically, "who, if not exactly the re-incarnation of Walt Disney, brings his own blend of passion and obsession to Disney's mission of creating Disney animated 'classics' . . . his frenetic presence looms over virtually every aspect of 'The Lion King.' " Thomas Schumacher had a particularly memorable quote: "Jeffrey is the sheepdog and the wolf. He's the sheepdog guarding us, and the wolf hunting us." And at another point, Schumacher says, "He might not always articulate what is wrong with something, but he's like a heat-seeking missile when it comes to homing in on weakness."

Initially, Katzenberg seemed pleased. He called Schumacher the morning the story appeared to congratulate him on his quotes. Just about everyone in animation thought the article was great. But Katzenberg later maintained that even as he read it, he knew there would be trouble. Eisner's name was not mentioned in the story. There was only a passing reference to Roy, even though Katzenberg had asked Turner to include Roy in the article (Turner confirms this). Turner had used the phrase the "re-incarnation of Walt Disney." With Katzenberg in the midst of his sixty- to ninety-day charm offensive aimed at Roy, Turner couldn't have chosen a more loaded, or damaging, comparison.

The Lion King opened on June 15, 1994, with premieres at Radio City Music Hall in New York City and the El Capitan in Hollywood. Eisner and Katzenberg attended a gala and screening at Washington's National Zoo. Critics were largely smitten, though not quite so rhapsodic as with *Beauty and the Beast* and *Aladdin*. Writing in *The New York Times,* Janet Maslin placed *The Lion King* in the great arc of neo-Disney classics that began with *The Little Mermaid,* and found it "as visually enchanting as its pedigree suggests. But it also departs from the spontaneity of its predecessors and reveals more calculation. More so than the exuberant movie miracles that came before it, this latest animated juggernaut has the feeling of a clever, predictable product. To its great advantage, it has been contrived with a spirited, animal-loving prettiness no child will resist. Let's put this in perspective: nobody beats Disney when it comes to manufacturing such products with brilliance, precision and loving care. And films that lure the lunch-box set never lack for blatantly commercial elements. Still, the wizardry of 'Beauty and the Beast' managed to seem blissfully formula-free, while 'The Lion King' has more noticeably derivative moments. Strangely enough, the fact that this film has an original story makes it less daring than Disney films based on well-known fairy tales."

At least one critic found the song "Can You Feel the Love Tonight?" gratuitous—Katzenberg's original complaint—but audiences had no such problem. *The Lion King* soundtrack shot to number one (the first animated soundtrack ever to top the charts), and "Can You Feel the Love Tonight?" became a top 40 smash hit.

The Disney marketing machine was becoming a well-oiled machine. *Lion King* had an unprecedented range of toys and product tie-ins. Burger King did a nationwide promotion; Toys 'R' Us featured two hundred *Lion King* toys and games in a special jungle-themed display. One Wall Street analyst called *Lion King* the "most profitable picture in the history of Hollywood."

After the opening, Katzenberg phoned Roy to congratulate him. "Thank you," Roy said, and hung up.

SEVEN

Michael Eisner had never met Senator George Mitchell, the Senate majority leader, when Stanley Gold introduced them at a May 1994 dinner benefit for the Irish-American Fund where Mitchell was the featured speaker. Mitchell had announced he would leave the Senate the following year, and Gold wondered to Eisner if Mitchell might make a suitable addition to the board.

Gold was only half-serious; Mitchell had no business experience, and certainly none in the entertainment industry. But Eisner lit up at the prospect, even suggesting that Mitchell could replace Wells. In some ways Mitchell's defects could be seen as virtues: There was no danger he'd compete with Eisner on the creative front. Litvack, his recent favorite, could handle the operational issues that Wells had taken care of, functioning more like a chief of staff. Mitchell would round out a triumvirate. Mitchell had stature, he could oversee the myriad issues on the political front that affected Disney, and he could be the company's ambassador to the world, freeing Eisner from most of those ceremonial duties. Eisner had always judged people on impulse, and he liked Mitchell. "I was impressed by his quiet passion, his common sense, and his obvious decency. I especially liked the fact that he communicated such passion about the importance of ethics in public life," Eisner later wrote of his first impression of Mitchell.

Eisner met with Mitchell several times to get to know him better and to air the possibility of his becoming president, but Mitchell resisted. He didn't want to leave his home on the East Coast; he stressed his lack of experience; he was planning to join a law firm in Washington, D.C., where he could stay involved in public policy issues. But Eisner persuaded him to at least join Disney's board as soon as he retired from the Senate.

As the prospect of Mitchell dwindled, Eisner's thoughts turned again to his old friend Michael Ovitz. Ever since he and Wells had first tried and failed to recruit Ovitz during their first year at Disney, Eisner had periodically raised the possibility of Ovitz leaving his agency to join the company. But as Creative Artists' business had surged, the prospect of luring Ovitz had become prohibitively expensive. Recently, however, Ovitz had been expanding his activities, functioning more like an investment banker, a dealmaker, an adviser to corporate chieftains, and less as a traditional agent. His most visible roles had been as an adviser to Japan's Matsushita Electric Corporation in its acquisition of Universal, and to Sony Corporation in its acquisition of the Columbia and Tri-Star studios. He'd also advised Coca-Cola on branding and advertising strategy. Not that he'd given up being an agent—he still represented Hollywood's biggest writers, directors, and stars—all of which led to his being dubbed "the most powerful individual in Hollywood" on the front page of *The Wall Street Journal* in December 1986.

Eisner spent the weekend of July 12, 1994, with Joe Roth and his wife at the Eisner home in Aspen, then traveled with Roth to Pittsburgh, where his latest Caravan picture for Disney, *Angels in the Outfield*, was having its premiere in conjunction with the All-Star game. Eisner used their time together to assess Roth as a possible replacement for Katzenberg, who knew nothing about the Aspen invitation and didn't attend the *Angels* premiere. Roth passed muster. Eisner was reassured that, if necessary, he could replace Katzenberg at the studio immediately.

On the Disney plane back to Los Angeles from Pittsburgh, Eisner discussed the pros and cons of Ovitz with Jane. The pros were that he thought Ovitz could ease the burden on him, and that Hollywood and Wall Street would be reassured by Ovitz's appointment. At the time, probably no one else in Hollywood had the visibility and the respect that Ovitz commanded. Landing him would doubtless be considered a coup for Eisner. The cons, or con, was Ovitz's ego. As Eisner told his wife, "You have to understand, I don't want to feel as if I'm in competition with anybody. My biggest question is whether he could tolerate being number two, and whether he would be a team player." Still, Eisner said he'd readily cede authority to Ovitz. "The truth is that I'm very happy to have all the divisions report to him, so long as he lets me know what he's doing," he told Jane. "If we can agree on that, it could be fantastic."

"My interest is simple," Jane replied. "I want your life to be simpler. Don't you think this could help?"

Later that week, Eisner agreed to an interview with two *Los Angeles Times* reporters, Claudia Eller and Alan Citron, in which his comments were flagrantly at odds with his real feelings about Katzenberg. As public relations chief John Dreyer sat by, Eisner said that there was "no one" he trusted more than Katzenberg. "He is very supportive of the whole company . . . a team player," Eisner said. Eisner volunteered that in their long history together, "We've never had a fight. . . . He is clearly the best golden retriever I ever met. He's the best person to follow through on a project, an idea or slate of ideas. . . . I did 100 percent of the thinking and he was the one to get something done." Eisner was dismissive of Wells's role, and made it sound like he was doing Katzenberg a favor by not promoting him to the presidency. "I don't want Jeffrey at the moment to worry about corporate insurance and that's what Frank Wells did . . . he kept the machine running. I want to keep my stars in star roles."

"I know I'm going to regret having done this," Eisner told Dreyer after the interview ended. Indeed, he had managed to demean Wells's contributions as well as relegate Katzenberg to "golden retriever" status, a point he reiterated in an interview with author Tony Schwartz, whose notes read: "Jeffrey was my retriever . . . he was [the] end of my pom pom; I'm the cheerleader."

Eisner, along with Roy, saw a rough-cut of the animated feature scheduled for the following summer, *Pocahontas.* Though *Lion King* continued to do phenomenal business at the box office, Eisner was worried that Disney animated films would now be held to an impossibly high standard after the unbroken success of *Beauty and the Beast, Aladdin,* and *Lion King.* Both Eisner and Roy had problems with *Pocahontas,* especially Eisner, who worried that the second act lacked momentum. He also wanted Pocahontas to speak English throughout the film (rather than her native American tongue, with subtitles) and wanted changes to one of Alan Menken's songs (Menken was now paired with composer Stephen Schwartz). Eisner passed his comments on to Katzenberg.

A few days later, both Ovitz and Eisner were attending investment banker Herbert Allen's annual media and entertainment conference in Sun Valley, Idaho, an event that had quickly become the epicenter of corporate power, influence, and deal-making, attracting everyone from Katharine Graham to Warren Buffett to Bill Gates, memorialized in lavish Annie Leibovitz photo spreads in *Vanity Fair*. Barry Diller was there; he and Eisner had resumed speaking after Eisner sent him some apples from the Eisner farm in Vermont along with a conciliatory note. David Geffen was there, of course, as was Katzenberg, who was scheduled to speak on a panel chaired by Jack Valenti, chief executive and chairman of the Motion Picture Association of America. Eisner invited Ovitz and his wife, Judy, to accompany him and Jane on the Disney jet.

Eisner used the time on the plane to press on Ovitz the advantages of joining Disney as president, and this time Ovitz responded positively. "I'm ready for a change," he acknowledged. "I think the idea of working together is great. We would make an unbeatable team." But in just what capacity Ovitz would come to Disney remained vague. Eisner liked to use the word *partner*, but in Hollywood generally, and especially with Eisner, "partner" is a loose, ill-defined term, often a euphemism for someone who is in fact subordinate. Coming from the world of agencies, Ovitz was unfamiliar with corporate hierarchies. During his time at William Morris, the agency had no formal titles, nor did CAA during its early years. Ovitz asked at one point if being partners meant they'd be co-chief executives. Eisner recalls that Ovitz said he wanted to be co-chief executive.

However "partners" was defined, any notion of equality was a raw nerve for Eisner, touching on the anxieties he'd already expressed to Jane about Ovitz "competing" with him. It contrasted with Wells's willingness to cede the CEO title, which was so important to Eisner. Nonetheless, Eisner kept selling Ovitz on the idea of coming to Disney, stressing how many opportunities the company faced, and what a great challenge running it would be. He tantalized Ovitz in confidence by mentioning that Disney had commenced talking with GE about acquiring the NBC network—a perfect opportunity, given the early experience of both men with networks. At one point Ovitz asked about the Disney board: "What if they don't approve me?" Eisner laughed at the suggestion. He went down the list of board members, ticking off the various ways they were beholden to him, assuring Ovitz that the board would do what he wanted. Still, by the time the plane landed, Eisner felt he and Ovitz were at an "impasse" over the issue of sharing top billing. Eisner later wrote that he'd been "upset" by the conversation.

Later that evening, walking to dinner, Eisner felt pain in both his arms. He thought it might have been stress brought on by the Ovitz discussion, worrying about replacing Wells, and Euro Disney. He hadn't been sleeping well. He stopped to rest. Of course, the pain might be a symptom of something more serious, though he preferred not to think about it. His father had

had heart problems, and had undergone open-heart surgery when he was sixty-five. Eisner had begun taking cholesterol-lowering medication, and he took regular stress tests, though the last one had been two years ago. He alternated between thinking the pain was in his head and that he was about to have a heart attack. But he and Jane pressed on.

Afterward, he, Jane, and Katzenberg, who had joined them at dinner, wandered into the indoor ice rink. Eisner mentioned the reorganization he and Wells had been planning and the stress of Euro Disney, confiding in Katzenberg in a way he hadn't since long before Wells's death. After the Eisners returned to their room, he felt pain and shortness of breath, and insisted on going to the local hospital. By then the pain was gone. He had an electrocardiogram, which was normal. He decided it was all in his head.

The next morning, Eisner went to a presentation by Tom Murphy, chairman of Capital Cities/ABC. Eisner's talks with Dan Burke the previous year about ABC hadn't gone anywhere, but he remained interested in a network, especially since the FCC was dropping a long-standing rule that barred networks from owning the programming they aired. Murphy stressed ABC's intention to develop its own programming, which caused Eisner considerable anxiety about the Disney television studio's ability to develop and sell programming to the networks. Afterward he called his secretary Lucille Martin, told her he wanted to return to Los Angeles the next day, a day early, and asked her to schedule a stress test for him with his doctor.

That evening, Eisner got a call from his regular doctor saying that Martin had mentioned he was having chest pains. He suggested Eisner have the stress test as soon as he returned the next day, and made an appointment for him at Cedars-Sinai Medical Center. Somehow it made Eisner feel better just to have an appointment. Things were under control.

The next morning, he went to Katzenberg's presentation, which left him agitated, given that at this juncture, almost anything could set him off on the subject of Katzenberg. "As always, he was aggressive and outspoken, but he also interrupted the other speakers and cracked bad jokes," Eisner later wrote of the panel. He complained to Jane and Ovitz, who attended the panel with him, that Katzenberg was an embarrassment and shouldn't be representing Disney. They said he was overreacting. "Jeffrey is Jeffrey," Ovitz shrugged. "He's not doing anything new or different."

At lunch, their wives urged Eisner and Ovitz to talk again, and after that year's *Vanity Fair* photo sitting, Ovitz suggested they take a walk. Ten minutes into it, Eisner paused to rest, and said he'd rather sit down in Ovitz's condominium. They still seemed to be talking at cross-purposes, Ovitz as-

suming that "partners" meant some kind of equality, while Eisner kept waiting for a Wells-like concession that Eisner would be in charge. They hadn't
resolved anything when Eisner and Jane left for the airport. On the plane,
Eisner watched tapes of the pilot for a new NBC show "ER," written by Ovitz
client Michael Crichton and produced by Spielberg. Under the circumstances, a television show about a hospital emergency room was unnerving.

When they landed in Los Angeles, Eisner went straight to the hospital;
Jane met him there after dropping off their luggage. In short order, he failed
the stress test, and an angiogram showed that 95 percent of a major artery
was blocked. The head of cardiac surgery recommended an immediate
open-heart bypass operation. As he was about to be wheeled into surgery, he
made some "last requests" of his wife and sons. "I want to be buried above
ground, not below" was first. "Also, I really don't want you to build the new
house we've been considering because ours is fine, and we don't need a bigger one." Finally, "If it becomes an issue, I think that either Ovitz or Diller
would be good choices to succeed me." He also suggested that if anything
happened to him, Jane should be named to the Disney board.

"Fine, fine," Jane replied.

Early the next morning, at 4:00, Ovitz's phone rang at the Sun Valley condominium. It was Jane. "Michael has had open-heart surgery," she said. She
sounded calm. "He's in intensive care. Can you come down?"

Ovitz and his wife were leaving the next morning to celebrate their
twenty-fifth wedding anniversary on Martha's Vineyard, but he immediately
scrapped their plans and took an 8:00 A.M. flight to Los Angeles, where Ovitz
was on the board of governors of Cedars-Sinai. When he got to the hospital,
he met Jane and went straight to the intensive care unit. Like all postopera-
tive heart patients, Eisner looked terrible, pale, motionless, with a tube in his
throat. Ovitz immediately took charge, which seemed to come as a relief to
Jane. They set up a schedule so that someone—either Jane, one of Eisner's
sons, Ovitz, or Judy—would be at Eisner's side at all times, able to monitor
his condition. Jane went home to get some sleep. Ovitz ordered that no one
else be admitted to his bedside, the only exceptions being Eisner's regular
psychotherapist and Irwin Russell. A security firm policed Eisner's floor and
Ovitz told them to make sure no unauthorized person got in, especially no
one from the media.

Eisner regained consciousness at about 6:30 A.M. A few hours later, Sandy
Litvack showed up with a press release he'd drafted, and seemed furious

when Ovitz wouldn't let him see Eisner. Ovitz himself approved the release. When Eisner finally had the tube in his throat removed, his first questions to Ovitz were about the press coverage. He was obsessed with the idea that Katzenberg might talk to the press.

Katzenberg returned from Sun Valley that morning, and after he got the previous night's box-office numbers, called Eisner at home to report to him on a successful opening for *Angels in the Outfield.* Jane answered. She sounded like she'd been asleep.

"Did I wake you?" Katzenberg asked.

"I meant to call you," she said, and then told him about Eisner's surgery. He was fine, she assured him.

"Who else knows?" Katzenberg asked.

Jane said nothing had been released to the press yet, but key people had been informed: Sid Bass, of course, Michael Ovitz, Stanley Gold, Roy and Patty—they were flying back from their castle in Ireland—Sandy Litvack, John and Jody Dreyer . . .

The inner circle, Katzenberg realized.

When he hung up, he turned to Marilyn. "Wives don't lie," he said.

"What does that mean?"

He explained that in her moment of greatest need, Jane turned to the people Michael trusted most. He wasn't among them. "She's told us everything we need to know," he said.

Katzenberg left early the next morning for Las Vegas, where he was giving a speech at a video industry conference. He used the occasion to argue against cheapening the videocassette market through steep discounting and giving copies away as premiums, as MCA/Universal was doing with its animated feature *An American Tail,* at McDonald's. This was a "Faustian bargain that threatens the video business," he told the conference, a comment that especially upset Universal chairman Lew Wasserman.

Despite Ovitz's efforts to contain them, rumors were flying around Hollywood, even that Eisner had died. At the risk of upsetting him, Ovitz told Eisner he had to prove to the outside world that he was alive and recovering. He and Eisner put together a list of people they considered key opinion makers, and then Ovitz placed the calls and held a cell phone to Eisner's lips. They began with Diller. Eisner could only muster a few words at a time, and it was painful and exhausting. After each call he rested for nearly an hour.

Eisner improved steadily, though his medications had to be adjusted several times, and he was suffering from stress. Visitors began trickling in— Litvack was finally admitted, as was Katzenberg on Tuesday afternoon, though only after Jane insisted he talk only about "happy news." When Eisner's former best friend Larry Gordon called from Hawaii, where he was on location, Ovitz answered the phone, but wouldn't put the call through to Eisner.

Ovitz was also trying to shield Eisner from the press, but he insisted on seeing the papers, and a *New York Times* article by Bernard Weinraub on Wednesday, July 20, just five days after his surgery, especially upset him. "Hollywood sees tension at Disney," the headline read. "Mr. Eisner is secretive and has few close friends," Weinraub wrote. That alone made Eisner apoplectic. By contrast, "Mr. Katzenberg is vocal, and has a range of acquaintances and relationships. . . . He was somewhat disturbed to be treated as less a friend than an employee even while Mr. Eisner was in the hospital recovering from heart surgery." To Eisner, the passage had Katzenberg's fingerprints all over it. Then the article quoted one of Katzenberg's "closest friends"—Eisner knew who that had to be, David Geffen—as saying, "The question is, Does Michael want to share power with Jeffrey? If he doesn't, Jeffrey will leave the company by the end of the year."

Eisner got so agitated that Ovitz called Katzenberg. "You've got to stop this," he said. "You know how crazy Michael gets about this."

"It's not me, it's Geffen," Katzenberg said.

"Then call David off," Ovitz said. "You've got to control him."

"I can't stop him," Katzenberg insisted. "I can't control him."

(Geffen acknowledged that he was a source for the stories.)

The next day, July 21, Eisner left the hospital and returned to his home in Bel Air. He'd been hoping to retreat to Aspen, but his doctors told him the high altitude might impede his recovery. Ovitz and Judy left for Martha's Vineyard, and an abbreviated twenty-fifth wedding anniversary. In Ovitz's absence, Litvack stepped into the breach, speaking to Eisner on the phone, visiting him at home, and generally acting as a go-between.

Eisner, still seething over the press coverage, refused to see Katzenberg, spoke to him only briefly on the phone, relying on Litvack to communicate with his studio chief. Nevertheless, when the *Los Angeles Times* reporters who'd interviewed Eisner before his surgery called Disney to check whether the quotes Eisner gave them before he had his surgery, in which, among other things, he'd praised Katzenberg as a "team player," were accurate, he insisted they were.

The *L.A. Times* story ran on July 24. Despite the praise, Katzenberg was rankled at once again being described as a "golden retriever," and especially at the assertion that Eisner had done "100 percent" of the thinking during their years together.

And even the praise was disingenuous. Eisner told Irwin Russell what he really thought about Katzenberg in the days following his surgery in another letter:

"Where to start?

"I guess the Allen & Co. Sun Valley Conference would be as good a place as anywhere. Jeffrey was there, working the room and being Jeffrey. Of course when he went on the Entertainment Panel he was the 'class clown.' I was embarrassed, but Jane did not think he was so bad." Eisner described feeling arm pain, the flight to Los Angeles, and checking into Cedars-Sinai. "I went from stress test to emergency room to angiogram to operating room to bypass, over the next six hours. Everybody was wonderful; everybody but Mr. Katzenberg.

"I came out of the anesthesia about 6:30 a.m. As you know, all I cared about was the correct way of handling the press release. By 10:30 a.m. I guess it was done, and only Jeffrey had his own ideas. I think Sandy knows what they were.

"But what Jeff really started to do was position the press. We know who he called. He prompted all the media right away to do articles about him, about succession. I think he must have thought my weakness gave him the excuse to press, just the way he pressed the day after Frank died."

Much of what Eisner described in the letter appeared to be hearsay from Litvack, which Eisner seems to have accepted uncritically, never considering, for example, that Litvack might have had his own aspirations to succeed Wells as president. "There were several conversations that Sandy had with Jeffrey that deserve to go into the Napoleonic Hall of Honors," Eisner wrote. "In an early conversation with Sandy, he stated what he expected. He said he wanted it all. He no longer was going to be satisfied with Eisner and Son. From now on it was going to be Eisner and Eisner. He went on and on with Sandy. I do not know if Sandy kept notes, but what Sandy told me was amazing. No CEO could possibly accept anything close to what he was suggesting. Sandy's analysis is that Jeff cannot get enough love or adulation. He is just insatiable."

Eisner also complained in the letter about Katzenberg's speech in Las Vegas, especially that he hadn't cleared it with Eisner. "When I asked Jeff why he did not check with me first, he said I was in the hospital. I told him the speech was on Sunday. I was operated on Saturday. He must have had it written earlier. He said it was a last thing!! And then he said, 'Anyway, if I had to make a speech, I wanted to make headlines.' He said, 'I did not want to just give a speech and not get press.' When Sandy questioned him about this speech, suggesting an industry boycott, after the fact, he had no response. And of course MCA is very upset as they should be. Here is another example of a guy that just 'wants to be King' but does not have the ability, judgment or emotional makeup to even be a Prince. Sandy's view is that unless 'Jeffrey is the bride at the wedding or the corpse at the funeral' he is not happy.

"I decided again to put him on hold, to keep everything status quo until I felt better. The doctors were really adamant that I should put stressful things to the side. . . ."

Among other things, Eisner's doctors suggested he try yoga. He engaged a private instructor, who came regularly to the house. He began a low-fat vegetarian diet. He walked on a treadmill for forty-five minutes, three times a week. For someone like Eisner ("I sort of liked stress"), the effort to reduce stress became in itself highly stressful. Lying on his back on the floor, instructed to meditate, he instead thought about . . . Katzenberg. As Eisner later put it, "After several weeks I quit, rationalizing that my life would be far less stressful when I stopped trying so hard to relax."

Still, trying to continue as chairman, president, and CEO in the wake of his surgery was clearly too much. Jane insisted over and over that he had to find someone to take the burden off of him. He invited Ovitz over for a long lunch, where he again raised the possibility of Ovitz being his "partner." This time he was more concrete: he said he'd give Ovitz the title of co-chairman, which sounded good to Ovitz, who said he'd think about it.*

Ovitz thought Eisner seemed depressed. He looked terrible, and not just because of the physical effects of the surgery. Ovitz didn't know how seriously to take Eisner's offer, because he had made some other suggestions that struck Ovitz as bizarre. Among them, he said he wanted his wife, Jane, to be on the Disney board. "That's ludicrous," Ovitz replied. And he said he wanted to "position" his son Breck to succeed him as chairman. "Michael, this isn't your family company," Ovitz said.

Eisner called Ovitz the next day, saying he'd had second thoughts, and making Ovitz co-chairman "wasn't a good idea. It would never work in corporate America," he said. After that, Eisner dropped the subject of bringing Ovitz to Disney. Instead, he spoke again to George Mitchell, put a feeler out to Bob Daly at Warner Brothers, and made an appointment to see Roger Enrico, chairman of PepsiCo.

Feeling he couldn't take any more pressure, Eisner finally called and asked Katzenberg to meet him at his house on Sunday, August 7. They sat in

---

* Eisner insisted that he never offered Ovitz the title of co-chairman.

the den, Eisner still in his bathrobe. Eisner began complaining about the press, about how stressful it was for him, especially reports that Katzenberg was threatening to quit. Katzenberg interrupted him, and adopted a different tone. "I never told Frank Wells how much I liked working with him and how much I loved him," the normally unemotional Katzenberg said. "I realize I've never told you how much you've meant to me." Eisner seemed taken aback by the sudden shift. Katzenberg continued, thanking Eisner for the experience of working together. It had the feeling of a valedictory. "Now I guess it's time for me to move on."

Confronted with the prospect of the very thing he seems most to have wanted—Katzenberg's departure—Eisner tried to change Katzenberg's mind.

"Have you taken another job?" Eisner asked.

"No, not yet."

"Is it something we can discuss?"

Katzenberg said he'd come to realize that Roy and Stanley Gold were implacably opposed to him, even if Eisner could be persuaded to promote him. "I can fix it," Eisner insisted, according to Katzenberg. He even volunteered to speak to Gold and the rest of the board on Katzenberg's behalf. In the meantime, he asked Katzenberg to pull together his thoughts on reorganizing the company.

Katzenberg wasn't optimistic, and felt confused. Reorganizing the company seemed like a presidential-level task. Had his decision to leave finally brought Eisner around to his view? He didn't know, but he started work on a memo.

For someone who was ostensibly trying to "make it work," Eisner soon sabotaged the effort. A few days later, on Wednesday, Eisner called Katzenberg to discuss *Pocahontas,* specifically whether he'd dealt with the issues Eisner had raised before his surgery. "They're insignificant," Katzenberg replied, which angered Eisner and gave him the distinct impression that they'd been ignored. Katzenberg argued that given his past success in animation, Eisner should trust his instincts. "Jeffrey," Eisner retorted, "we've had this problem on each of 'your' successes, and my notes have been taken. I want this work done." Katzenberg grudgingly said he'd make sure his concerns were addressed.

Eisner then called Peter Schneider, peppering him with questions about what had or had not been done to address his concerns about *Pocahontas.* After brooding further on the subject, he called Schneider again the next day. The conversations confirmed his suspicious that Katzenberg was deliberately trying to keep him in the dark. He was especially angry when Schneider told him that Katzenberg had scheduled a screening for 7:00 A.M. that Friday without telling Eisner. Even if he had invited Eisner, he must have known that he couldn't be there that early. Caught between the two, Schneider reported Eisner's call to Katzenberg, who was furious that Eisner had gone around him. He dashed off a handwritten note:

"Your feeling the need to be calling Peter Schneider and checking up on me and inquiring whether or not your notes are being addressed on 'Pocahontas' does not work for me at all. . . . Your calling Peter again today to ask what has been done, asking had it been discussed with Menken-Schwartz, are we doing a big production number, etc., instructing you to call him tomorrow immediately after my screening to report to you the status, is at best amazing. . . . but what may be even worse is what this says about your lack of confidence and trust in me to do what I said I would do. If this is how you see us dealing with one another in the future, it's not for me."

Furious, Eisner phoned Sid Bass and read him the letter. "It's Friday, a good time to leave a company. Call up Jeffrey and tell him to get out," Bass said.

Next Eisner sent a copy of the letter to Litvack, and told him that Sid Bass had said to fire him. This time, Litvack counseled restraint. "Do it on your schedule. Get stronger. Do it when you have a substitute organization," he said. Eisner called Bass back. He agreed they should wait.

Jane said he shouldn't have any more dealings with Katzenberg while he was trying to recuperate; it was too upsetting.

Finally Eisner called Katzenberg, and said, "Your letter was wrong, out of place, silly, and more importantly, I am not going to deal with you for weeks. It's upsetting me and retarding my recovery. If that's a problem, too bad." He hung up, highly agitated, and called Litvack.

"Call Jeffrey and put a lid on the whole thing," Eisner ordered. Litvack promised that he'd make Katzenberg "feel guilty" about Eisner's health and would "buy time."

"Jeffrey is without guilt and his adviser David Geffen is worse," Eisner replied.

Litvack did speak to Katzenberg, and then relayed the conversation to Eisner. These remarks, it seems, were the last straw. Eisner described the meeting, as relayed to him by Litvack in another letter to Irwin Russell:

Dear Irwin:
    In that I wrote the last letter to you about Jeffrey Katzenberg and his strange, ego-provoked, awkward positions, I thought I would write to you

chapter 2. Actually, putting bewildering personal behavior on paper is therapeutic for me, instructive for Roy and Stanley, eventually for the entire board; and maybe some day even for arbitration. And if for no other reason, Breck feels we are living out a Shakespearean play and it is worth remembering.

Let's call this saga, the post–Michael Eisner quadruple bypass saga, or how I, Jeffrey Katzenberg, planned to increase Michael's stress, selfishly think only of me, Jeffrey, and how I, Jeffrey, can act even worse than I did after Frank's death, a feat everybody would have thought impossible.

After describing the events leading up to the meeting between Litvack and Katzenberg, Eisner wrote:

Jeffrey went on to tell Sandy that he must run the company, totally and completely; and if I did not have more faith in him than I showed in Pocahontas, then it wouldn't work. . . .

Jeffrey told Sandy many more things that I cannot remember, but the total of this conversation and the previous three are enough proof that Roy's feelings are and have been totally correct. Jeffrey's hard work is not enough to overcome his poor judgment. . . .

After continuing in this vein, Eisner summed up:

The conversations Sandy has had with Jeffrey both before and after Frank died and since my operation demonstrate a man of pathological blind ambition, and one with no judgment. Roy is right. He would, left up to his own, destroy the company. When the Wall Street Journal said in an early profile that as a kid "he pushed his little friends faces in the 'dog shit' on the street," they did not know they were talking about Frank and me. Jeffrey is dangerous and being advised by a dangerous man. If there ever was a question about his corporate leadership, which of course there wasn't, there is no question now.

My plan as of tonight is to deal on the Studio level for the time being, corporate governance can wait. I will try to figure out the studio organization without Jeffrey and let him go just before Labor Day. There is obviously no alternative. . . . I will not tell him any of the above, nor acknowledge how outrageous I think he is. . . . Hopefully that will end the Jeff Katzenberg saga, and I and the company can move on to more productive work. Unfortunately he will work the press but that too will pass.

I hope this memo helps to clear some things up; exactly what is the real question!

At the bottom was scrawled, "Michael," and the date, August 14.

Eisner didn't wait until Labor Day. Five days later, he called Joe Roth and asked if he'd run the movie studios. Roth agreed. That evening, he met with Rich Frank and offered him television, home video, and the Disney cable channel. As head of animation, Roy would now report directly to Eisner, not Katzenberg; Peter Schneider would run animation day-to-day. Essentially, Eisner himself would replace Katzenberg at the head of the three units. He was now assuming the duties of three people: himself; Wells, the president; and Katzenberg, the head of the studio. The more Eisner thought about the plan, the better the idea seemed. This was exactly the sort of renewal that he and Wells had been talking about.

Eisner asked Katzenberg to meet with him that Wednesday at 11:00 A.M., ostensibly to discuss the memo about reorganizing the company that Katzenberg had been working on. Katzenberg brought a copy of the memo with him, but Eisner didn't give him a chance to discuss it.

"This is a day I've dreaded for a long time," Eisner began. "I wish it hadn't come to this and that we could have made it work. But I'm not going to be able to give you the job you want and you're not satisfied with the one you have." Eisner handed Katzenberg a press release that Dreyer and Litvack had already drafted announcing his "resignation" and the appointments of Roth, Frank, and Schneider.

Katzenberg read it, then put it down. He didn't seem surprised or upset. "There are two kinds of divorces," he said. "One in which you're best friends, and one in which you're enemies." Eisner said he wanted to be friends. In that case, in the few weeks remaining under his contract, Katzenberg said he'd like to oversee the upcoming releases of *Pulp Fiction*, the first release under the Miramax deal he'd negotiated, and Touchstone's *Quiz Show*, and he'd like to attend the London premiere of *Lion King*, where Elton John was hosting a party in his honor.

Katzenberg also mentioned the bonus that would now be due him, and reminded Eisner of his last days at Paramount, when Eisner had insisted on getting his check from Marty Davis and had walked to the bank to cash it. "It's not that you weren't going to get your money," Katzenberg said. "You just wanted your business cleared up. I'd like the same."

Eisner seemed agreeable. He was feeling almost euphoric now that the long-anticipated deed was done. "The tension seemed to seep out of the room," he later wrote. "Our conversation turned to earlier years and better times together. . . . Jeffrey later described it as the most relaxed talk we'd had in a year."

By the time Katzenberg got back to his office, Steven Spielberg was on the phone from Jamaica, where he was visiting *Roger Rabbit* director Robert Zemeckis. Though the Disney press release supposedly wouldn't be available until 2:00 P.M., it had gone out while Katzenberg was still in Eisner's office. As Spielberg commiserated, Zemeckis called out, "You guys should do something together." Next on the phone was Geffen. "Should I do something with Spielberg?" Katzenberg asked.

"Are you kidding?" Geffen replied. "If I were you, I'd do it in a second." At the Disney studio, Rob Moore, the studio's chief financial officer, raced through the corridor handing out copies of the press release. David Vogel was on the phone, and Moore pressed the release against his internal office window, gesturing frantically for Vogel to read it. Vogel immediately hung up and, on impulse, headed upstairs to Katzenberg's office. In place of the throngs who usually lined up for Katzenberg's attention, no one was there.

Katzenberg was sitting at his desk alone. He had a manila folder in front of him labeled "Michael." Vogel sat down across from him. Katzenberg seemed oblivious to his presence. He pulled out a document from the file and glanced at it. "I guess I won't be dealing with that anymore," he said as he ripped the memo first into halves, and then quarters. He hurled the scraps into his wastebasket. He continued until he'd ripped up every document in the folder. Vogel saw a nineteen-year relationship being reduced to torn scraps of paper.

That evening, Eisner and Jane joined songwriter Carol Bayer Sager and Warner Bros. chairman Bob Daly for a long-scheduled dinner and a meditation session with celebrity guru Deepak Chopra, another of Eisner's experiments in stress reduction. Sager had been emailing Eisner for months, urging him to try meditation, and Chopra had flown in from North Carolina for the occasion.

Daly was already in Sager's living room chanting when Eisner arrived, but paused to commiserate over the hard day he assumed Eisner had had. Eisner found Chopra "smooth, articulate and charming," but before they could even get to the mind-body connection, the New Age physician launched into a rapid-fire discussion of marketing his books and tapes, his publishing deals, and whom he knew in Hollywood. By the time they got around to meditating, Eisner felt overstimulated. As in his brief attempt at yoga, the attempt to clear his mind was in itself stressful. Still, "settling Jeffrey

Katzenberg's future provided enough stress reduction for the next several months," he said.

Perhaps inevitably, this peace of mind was short-lived. Katzenberg did his best to deter his friends and allies from commenting to the press, including, especially, David Geffen, who did remain uncharacteristically silent. Katzenberg was hoping to maintain the aura of goodwill of their last meeting, finish out his tenure with dignity, and, most important, do nothing to jeopardize the lump-sum payment due him when he left the company. As long as that payment was unresolved, Eisner retained enormous leverage over Katzenberg.

Even so, Katzenberg's departure from Disney was a seismic event, not just in Hollywood. Given his prominence and the success of the animated films he produced at Disney, his leaving was front-page news in the major papers. *Newsweek* made the split its cover story. In the *Los Angeles Times,* Spielberg compared Eisner to Machiavelli, which made Eisner furious. Eisner angrily accused Katzenberg of fomenting harmful publicity.

The tone of that phone call worried Katzenberg. He called a lawyer, Bert Fields, and filled him in on the termination bonus in his contract and the background. Fields suggested that Katzenberg give Disney a deadline to make the payment, which he did—September 9, which was two weeks away. In the meantime, Katzenberg learned that he wasn't welcome at the *Lion King* premiere in London. Elton John canceled his party. A Disney lawyer asked Katzenberg how quickly he could vacate his office. Like Larry Gordon years before, he insisted he was staying put until the day his contract ended, on October 1.

Peter Schneider told the animators that they couldn't throw a going-away party for Katzenberg at the studio. Senior live-action executives, also barred from holding an event on Disney property, chipped in $5,000 each to rent a hangar at the Santa Monica airport and throw a decent party. Everyone came, even people who had worked for Katzenberg but had since left Disney. Still, it was a restrained, sad affair. Katzenberg took his wife and twin sons to Disney World over the Labor Day weekend, as he had every year since coming to Disney. There, the Orlando-based animators managed to give him a party, with kegs of his beloved Diet Coke.

Katzenberg's September 9 deadline passed with no word from Disney. The next day, a Saturday, Eisner came to Katzenberg's house. The pretense of goodwill, of "staying friends," had vanished. The conversation quickly deteriorated into mutual accusations. Eisner again blamed Katzenberg for the press coverage, and this time Katzenberg was combative.

"You know how to stop it," Katzenberg countered. "You have not fulfilled one single promise that you made to me in terms of how you were going to deal with this. You've done an assassination job on me. I've yet to be paid a nickel. Deal honestly with me."

Eisner argued that because of "ambiguities" in the contract, he was going to have to get board approval for any payment, and said, "I can't go to the board right now. They're too angry with you." This infuriated Katzenberg, since he believed it was Eisner who had turned the board against him. And whether the board was angry or not, it still had to honor his contract.

That Friday, Katzenberg went into Eisner's office and slammed the 1988 deal memo written by Frank Wells on his desk. He'd highlighted with a yellow marker the passage outlining his bonus. "My eleven-year-old would read this and understand what it means," he said. Eisner seemed flustered, and said only that he was handing the matter over to Litvack.

Any possibility, however remote, of an amicable settlement between Eisner and Katzenberg were dashed the weekend of September 16, when *The New Yorker* magazine faxed Eisner and Katzenberg advance copies of an article by Ken Auletta, *The Human Factor,* which was an account of Katzenberg's ouster. Someone in Katzenberg's office faxed a copy of the article to his lawyer, Bert Fields, with a note from Katzenberg: "Thanks for all your help." But a copy of the fax was mistakenly sent to Eisner's office. As Eisner told Tony Schwartz a few days later, "I can't talk any more to Jeffrey Katzenberg; sending lawyer, everything I ever said to him, he tells Geffen, or media; now bringing up whole financial thing in media. When we got our New Yorker story faxed to us, [he] put on a Bert Fields cover page . . . So Jeffrey is caught in his tracks. I said to Jeffrey . . . 'I would suggest you don't negotiate with me in the newspapers, like you did your last situation . . . finally [I] read this piece. [I] decided it is over forever. I don't care what he thinks. [I'm] not going to pay him any of the money."

Despite the near-total rupture with Eisner, Katzenberg was determined to leave on a semblance of his own terms. He attended the New York Film Festival for the opening of Tim Burton's *Ed Wood.* And he went to Washington for the premiere of Robert Redford's *Quiz Show.* Then, on October 1, 1994, he got into his car parked next to Eisner's, and left the Disney lot for the last time.

Part Two

———

DISENCHANTED KINGDOM

EIGHT

With the vexing Katzenberg situation resolved and his stamina returning, Eisner was determined to reassert his own leadership and reverse the negative press that, he was convinced, was being orchestrated by Katzenberg and his allies. One way to do this in the deal-crazed mid-1990s was to do something big—like acquire a broadcast network. In the wake of the FCC's decision to repeal the so-called fin-syn (financial syndication) rules, which had long prohibited the Hollywood studios from owning a network and vice versa, all three major networks were potentially on the block. Eisner had already talked with Dan Burke about acquiring ABC; Barry Diller had been negotiating with Larry Tisch to buy CBS; and Jack Welch, GE's chairman, had been grumbling about NBC, then in third place among the major networks.

The GE pension fund was a major investor in a private equity fund run by Shamrock Holdings, the Disney investment vehicle run by Stanley Gold. Gold had been hearing from GE people that Jack Welch might be willing to sell the network, which didn't fit with GE's insistence on staying only in businesses it could dominate. After several discussions between Gold and Welch, Gold proposed that they get together with Eisner. In mid-September they all gathered at the executive dining room in the GE Building in Rockefeller Center. It was Eisner's first trip since his surgery.

Eisner was intrigued by NBC as a possible turnaround candidate, just as ABC had been when Eisner had helped elevate it to first from third place. On the flight to New York, Eisner told Gold that Bob Wright, the GE executive Welch had put in charge of NBC, was a corporate finance "suit" who knew nothing about the creative business of network television (a view curiously

189

at odds with Eisner's own oft-stated views that good managers were fungible and could manage any business). Eisner, by contrast, had proven programming abilities. And owning NBC would also guarantee an outlet for Disney-produced entertainment, which had always been the primary strategic rationale for Disney to own a network.

When they met for dinner, Welch said he wasn't yet willing to sell NBC outright, but he was prepared to offer Disney creative control of the network and a 49 percent interest, with an option to later acquire more. And he wanted to give Bob Wright at least two more years to turn the network around. The proposed deal appealed to the bargain-hunter in Eisner: He figured he could gain creative control of a network for just half the cost of buying it all, and secure an outlet for Disney-produced programming. And while he wasn't thrilled with the idea of keeping Wright, he admired Welch for standing behind him.

But after dinner, when Eisner presented the proposal to Sid Bass at Bass's Manhattan apartment, Bass was cool. "I don't think it's favorable," he said of the terms, which pretty much drained the room of any enthusiasm. Half the risk meant half the reward. The next morning Eisner called Welch. "The answer to the proposal is an unequivocal no."

Welch laughed. Still, Eisner felt a sense of disappointment and letdown. Buying NBC would have given Disney a "shot in the arm," Eisner felt, at a time both he and the company needed it.

The very next day, Eisner met with his strategic-planning advisers to discuss progress on Disney's America, the ambitious theme park project planned for northern Virginia. Peter Rummell showed him new financial analyses that projected that the venture would operate at a loss. After the Euro Disney experience with cold weather, the operating season in northern Virginia was cut back to eight months, and attendance estimates were slashed. As at Euro Disney, costs had soared. The Imagineers, as usual, had introduced new attractions and expanded and upgraded others. But more worrying, opponents of the venture, many of them wealthy neighbors with influence in Washington, had succeeded in turning the theme park area into a historical and environmental cause célèbre. Although the site was actually five miles from the Civil War Manassas battlefield, the public perception was that Disney would be defiling sacred ground. Prominent American historians rallied in opposition; a group called Protect Historic America took out a full-page ad in The New York Times calling Eisner "The man who would destroy American history."

Eisner seemed genuinely surprised that Disney would be derided as much as admired for its values; as he told *The Washington Post,* "I thought we were doing good. I expected to be taken around on people's shoulders." Disney had the support of the Virginia governor and legislature, but "the issue was no longer who was right or wrong," Eisner finally decided. "We had lost the perception game."

So after hearing Rummell's projections, Eisner pulled the plug on Disney's America, at least for the time being. (He insisted publicly that "I have no intention of giving up on a historical park permanently.") Though he had yet to break the news to the Disney board, word of the decision soon leaked, and Eisner had to rush two of Rummell's deputies to deliver the news to the Virginia governor before he read about it in *The Washington Post,* which ran the story on its front page the next day.

The decision to scrap Disney's America, widely perceived as a defeat for Disney, seemed uncharacteristic of the combative Eisner, and many at the company wondered if this was a new, postsurgery Eisner. Eisner himself noted that he hadn't fully regained his strength when he made the decision, and said he didn't want to subject the company, or himself, to more "trauma."

Potentially adding to Eisner's distress was the news on October 12 that Katzenberg was forming a new studio with partners David Geffen and Steven Spielberg, a bold move hailed on the front Arts page of *The New York Times* as "the biggest merger of talent since Charlie Chaplin, Mary Pickford, Douglas Fairbanks and D. W. Griffith founded the United Artists movie empire in 1919." After the success of *Lion King,* Katzenberg was widely perceived as the top studio executive in Hollywood; Spielberg, the director of *E.T.* and *Schindler's List,* was the most sought-after director; and Geffen, who had parlayed the proceeds from the sale of Geffen Records into a $2 billion fortune, was the richest man in Hollywood.

Eisner thought the announcement vindicated his intuition that Katzenberg would have a hard time finding another $100-million-a-year job, and he predicted the new studio would fail, as had United Artists eventually. Still, there was no doubt that Katzenberg had assembled a formidable trio, and prominent investors poured money into the new venture, including Microsoft co-founder Paul Allen, who invested $500 million, and Cap Cities/ABC, which acquired an equity stake and made a TV production deal with the fledgling studio. There was no denying that the new studio—soon christened DreamWorks SKG—posed a competitive threat to Disney, at least in the near term. Katzenberg knew all of Disney's secrets, and Disney now faced an exodus of executives from the studio who wanted to rejoin Katzenberg. As animator Randy Cartwright put it to Ron Clements, "I think everybody's salary just went up." This might have happened even if Katzenberg had simply joined another studio in some capacity, but Katzenberg was creating a new competitor altogether. He pointedly said that DreamWorks would be creating an animation division, a direct assault on Disney's lucrative near-monopoly.

Eisner made no public comment on the new venture, and conspicuously failed to call Katzenberg or any of the participants to congratulate them. Still, if nothing else, Katzenberg had succeeded in reigniting Eisner's fierce competitive drive, which had seemed somewhat dormant after his surgery. The stage was set for a fierce battle between Disney and DreamWorks, fueled by Eisner's barely repressed hostility toward his former protégé, his desire to see him fail, and Katzenberg's fierce sense of betrayal.

So when David Geffen approached Eisner at this juncture about settling the still-unresolved issue of Katzenberg's bonus, Eisner was hardly in any mood to discuss it. Each of the DreamWorks partners was contributing $33.3 million to the new venture, and Katzenberg needed the money. "Jeffrey will take $60 million," Geffen offered. After tax, that would leave him with the money for the DreamWorks stake.

"He's not entitled to anything," Eisner countered.

"This is going to get settled," Geffen warned, "and it won't be for $60 million. Each time the price is going to go up." But Eisner wouldn't budge.

By Thanksgiving, Eisner was not only feeling better, jogging in the Vermont woods during the family's annual Thanksgiving holiday, but he was reveling in Disney's record profits for 1994. With *The Lion King, Pulp Fiction,* and November's *The Santa Clause* all hits, Disney's studio became the first ever to earn over $1 billion in a single year. *Pulp Fiction* alone earned $108 million in the United States, far more than the cost of the Miramax acquisition, and the film cemented the Weinsteins' reputation for spotting talent, with director Quentin Tarantino winning an Oscar for Best Original Screenplay. Comedian Tim Allen, star of *The Santa Clause,* was also starring in "Home Improvement," the year's number one–rated television show, produced by Touchstone for ABC, and Allen's autobiography was the number one nonfiction book for Hyperion, the Disney publishing division. Allen was also going to be the voice of Buzz Lightyear in Pixar's *Toy Story.* This was Eisner's dream of synergy come true. *Snow White,* finally released on video, sold 10 million copies during its first week on sale.

That year Disney earned nearly $2 billion on record revenues of more than $10 billion. In his annual letter to shareholders, Eisner sounded a triumphant note. While noting the "shocks and distractions" of the year, including Wells's death, his surgery, and Katzenberg's exit (which he characterized as Katzenberg's "decision not to renew his contract"), he concluded that "Disney is stronger than most have given us credit for. . . . Our critics did not stop us. Frank's death did not stop us. My heart surgery did not stop us. Our studio reorganization did not stop us." Unmentioned was the fact that *Lion King*, *The Santa Clause*, and "Home Improvement" were all put into development by Katzenberg, who was also responsible for the Miramax acquisition.

The failure of the NBC negotiations had only whetted Eisner's appetite for a major deal. That same Thanksgiving weekend, Eisner flew to Orlando, his first visit to Disney World since his surgery. There he told a large gathering of Disney employees that "During the next several years we should make a major acquisition. The trick is not to make the wrong one. You have to be patient. You want to buy something for what it's worth . . . You want to make a choice that complements the Disney brand, where the sum of the two companies is greater than the parts. That's the deal we are looking for."

Over the Christmas holidays, Eisner took Joe Roth, the new studio chairman, on a whirlwind trip to Walt Disney World. Afterward, Roth met with David Vogel, the head of Walt Disney Pictures, saying he now saw Disney-branded "event" movies as a big opportunity. He asked Vogel what he had in development, and immediately singled out a live-action *101 Dalmatians* and a remake of *The Absent-Minded Professor* for "event" treatment. He explained how Disney could market them the way he'd done with *Home Alone*. "Let's make these big," he told Vogel.

Vogel was thrilled. Finally, he thought, the studio head was someone who understood the potential of Disney-branded live-action films. He seized the opening to discuss his own career with Roth. "Someday I want to make adult movies," he said. "I've been here all these years, and I can't do this for the rest of my life." He pointed to *Cool Runnings*, a film about the Jamaican bobsled team that he'd championed for the Disney label, even though it didn't have kids in it, as an example of the kind of thing he could do. "If I'm successful, I want to branch out beyond what's considered appropriate for children," Vogel argued. Roth agreed that if Vogel succeeded during two more years with the Disney label, he'd give him the budget to make adult films.

That spring, Roth enthusiastically reported that he had "great news": John Hughes, the writer of *Home Alone*, had agreed to write and produce *101 Dalmatians*. Vogel tried to conceal his dismay. Hughes was one of the most expensive writers in Hollywood, and his contract guaranteed him 10 percent of the gross on *Dalmatians*. While attaching him to the film would be seen as a coup for Roth, and all but guaranteed it would be an event film, this seemed directly contradictory to Eisner's mandate to hold down costs. After all, *Dalmatians* was a "talking-dog remake," as Vogel described it, and didn't need a star screenwriter.

Vogel pointed out that he'd already commissioned a first draft of a script from writers with experience with animal-oriented, family films.

"Then I guess you'll have to be the one to say 'no' to John Hughes," Roth replied.

Vogel was in an impossible situation. He said he'd find a way to work it out.

Many people experience profound changes after heart surgery, and not long after New Year's, in January 1995, Eisner received a long, thoughtful letter from Larry McMurtry, the novelist who wrote *Terms of Endearment,* which was such a hit for Eisner while he was at Paramount. McMurtry had undergone heart surgery at age fifty-five, just a few years older than Eisner. He wrote that he felt "younger in body but older in spirit," and described symptoms of depression, insomnia, loss of concentration, and an end to his "Type A" ambition. The letter prompted a lengthy and uncharacteristically revealing response from Eisner:

> A lot of what you write I understand and to some extent I have had similar feelings. But I do not have the problem to the extent you describe; only vague shadows of the problem. . . . This was my surface life: Great success at the office . . . Three great kids . . . great wife . . . Type A life . . . Conflict . . . and Mevacor . . . And finally Euro Disney . . . Then I stopped sleeping two years before my bypass . . . and like you, I hated that.
>
> I have had worse problems than Euro Disney. I had had the long arm of parental conflict but I could deal with it. I forgot about the pain under exercise and just accepted it as part of my emotional life. The pain, I believed, was psychologically induced. I was capturing the attention of my father or some other parent. I did not have real pain.

He described the events leading up to his near heart attack and surgery, and continued:

Something has happened to me that is a big deal. I am no longer immortal. I am no longer even young . . . I still go to the office and still am basically the same person, but there is this giant hole which I guess is called middle age. Or actually it is old age . . . 52 is half of 104 and therefore 52 is not middle age. 52 for me is old age. That's the rub . . . I went from kid to old guy in four hours.

I do not like what has happened, but I guess it's better than many I know. I don't have cancer or any other horrible illness that I know about. But I am different. My life has a finite sense to it, and there is certainly a hollowness that comes with such realizations. I try not to think about it, but I think about it all the time. . . . I used to put up with betrayal as a reality in life and now I won't let it in the door even if there is a blockbuster motion picture associated with it.

When all is said and done, I do feel in the hollow of this new life one strange thing that you do not mention. I feel one positive. I feel one rush that offsets all the feelings you related. I feel one enormous explosion which I haven't felt since my first son was born. I died. And I know what that is. Although I feel the ceiling of death, at the same time I accept death for the first time and even look at it without fear. Death has always been for me the feeling of air turbulence, hitting the shoulder of the highway. . . . Not now. It simply is. I have been there and it was okay.

Board member and former Disney chairman Ray Watson raised the delicate subject of Eisner's mortality in a January 13 letter in which he asked who would succeed Eisner if he were suddenly incapacitated or killed, hardly an unreasonable question in the wake of a year in which Wells had been killed and Eisner suffered a near heart attack. And yet Eisner seemed farther away than ever from picking a successor.

"Let me address tonight just your first point, 'The confidential plan on Succession.'" Eisner wrote (though he didn't actually send the letter until October 8, nine months later). "Here's the sad truth. I do not have one. I know a lot of bad plans, a lot of silly ideas, a lot of frustrating plans; but I have no solid recommendations. . . . We have a fantastic group of young executives that need line experience . . . but right now I cannot say who is really in the 'batter's circle.' It is not Rich Frank. . . . It isn't even Sandy Litvack who has become extremely helpful to me."

Eisner wrote Watson that he'd like to have a chief operating officer who could take over for him, but he had no candidate in mind. "This does not make Jane happy," he added. "What I'm doing now looks crazy, no president, no CFO, no treasurer. . . . Right now I cannot say who is really in the batter's circle. . . . Soon I hope to have a first class CFO."

This, of course, would have come as news to Richard Nanula, who was the CFO, and no doubt to Litvack, who increasingly saw himself as Eisner's heir apparent. "If I do die or become incapacitated," Eisner continued, "I suggest you talk to Barry Diller and Michael Ovitz and make a choice. Today I would choose Ovitz (I think because he is a hard worker, and good family man and motivated, maybe too motivated and somewhat untested. Barry is completely the opposite. He has been tested. He is smarter. Much more ethical. . . . He has a real moral compass and great taste. He is not a family man but I believe you do not have to be a chicken to know a good egg. He will adapt to family values quicker than Fred MacMurray. Maybe I would choose Diller. I don't know. I do know there is nobody else. . . . I think my first choice now would be Diller. He is a creative executive. And the fact that he is a homosexual should have no weight. I mention this because some[one] will surely say something about his lifestyle or at least think it. You crossed a much larger hurdle in 1984 naming a Jew."

Eisner closed on an almost wistful note: "Life will go on. And so will the company. And there will be a nice memorial service for me that I wish I could go to, and then the next animated movie will go out, and the company will be peopled by really strong and talented men and women and somewhere in the archives will be files of my years that made some difference."

In the same letter, Eisner also mentioned his belief in moving executives around, the "counterprogramming" he often discussed with Ovitz, and the reorganization he'd been discussing with Wells before he died. As he had demonstrated with Steve Burke, when he moved him from running the Disney stores to Euro Disney, Eisner was convinced that good managers could run anything, and that it was healthy to shake things up before they became stale.

"All the executives that have been doing their jobs for the last 10 years and are bored are being moved around," he wrote Watson. "All the corporate guys must be moved out and around. We needed and are getting a corporate takeover from the inside. . . . I have worked for a decade at ABC and almost as long at Paramount. I saw what happened when people got bored. They cannot. We cannot let them. We must make the changes to keep everybody excited and working hard. . . . This is founding a new company under the same principles and culture. . . . So the pressure on me is great. I feel without me today it all falls apart."

It isn't clear whether Watson shared the letter with any other board members, but that spring, Eisner began implementing an extensive corporate reorganization—the "renewal" he'd been talking about with Wells. Sandy Litvack took Wells's place as Eisner's confidant and sounding board as he talked endlessly about shuffling personnel among the various divisions. To some extent the timing of the reorganization was forced upon him when Rich Frank, who was now reporting directly to Eisner as head of the television division and had parlayed "Home Improvement" into such a success, reminded Eisner that he had a provision in his contract that, if Katzenberg left and Frank didn't succeed him, allowed Frank to leave the company with his retirement benefits and stock options intact. This provision had been retained when Frank accepted the title of chairman of the television group. Since then, he'd been disappointed at the failure to acquire a network, and clashed repeatedly with Larry Murphy, as well as Eisner himself.

When Frank finally told Eisner he had decided to leave, Eisner retorted, "You can't. I won't let you."

"I can and I will," Frank replied.

"If you walk out that door, you're going to have to sue me" to get your stock options and other benefits, Eisner said. But he backed down after Frank promised not to join Katzenberg at DreamWorks, and agreed to pay the approximately $30 million in stock options due him.

Eisner called a meeting of all division heads that afternoon. Michael Johnson, who ran home video international, asked Ann Daly, head of U.S. home video, what was up. "Rich is leaving and they're naming Dennis Hightower," she said.

"That's the most ridiculous thing I've ever heard," Johnson replied.

Johnson knew Hightower well, since Hightower was the head of consumer products for Europe and the Middle East. A former executive recruiter, he was articulate, good-looking, and had earned a Harvard MBA. There was speculation that he was a former CIA agent, but no one had been able to confirm that. He had no television or other entertainment experience. (Hightower later said he could not comment on whether he was working for the CIA, but said he spent eight years working in the military, performing "airborne, infantry, and strategic operations in the U.S. and abroad as a Ranger and a senior parachutist, conducting counterintelligence and collections. You know what that means.")

But then Eisner walked in with Hightower in tow. He made the announcement, adding, "Dennis is the man. He's going to be the next great Hollywood executive." It was another of Eisner's impetuous personnel decisions, further evidence of his firm belief that a good executive can run anything. Hightower's operation in Europe had indeed done well on the strength of *Beauty and the Beast* and *Lion King* merchandise. Still, many thought Hightower was simply fortunate to have been in the right place when such hit movies spurred a consumer products bonanza, and that living in Europe was hardly preparation for running a huge American television operation.

There was dead silence in the room after Eisner spoke. Finally Rob Moore, the studio's chief financial officer, asked, "What does this mean for the rest of us, that you're bringing in a complete outsider?" Eisner gave Moore a cold, piercing gaze, and didn't answer. Johnson thought Moore had just destroyed his career at Disney.

Johnson promptly called his former boss Bill Mechanic, now at Fox, told him Eisner had just named Hightower to Frank's job, and asked if Mechanic would give him a job.

"You're pulling my chain," Mechanic said. "Not even Michael could make a mistake that big."

Frank wasn't consulted on his replacement, and Eisner used the occasion to take a swipe in the press at Frank for harboring ambitions to replace Katzenberg, saying that, "Now at least we have an enthusiastic executive in the job. Dennis is excited to be running TV. He's not disappointed to not be running movies," Eisner told *Fortune* magazine. As for Hightower's other attributes, "Dennis Hightower is a very smart man," Eisner said, adding, "He's very experienced at sitting down with our partners in Luxembourg and Taiwan." As an African American, Hightower also brought welcome diversity to the top executive ranks.

Even more startling, Eisner put chief financial officer Richard Nanula in charge of the Disney stores. Nanula was understandably startled and dismayed to give up a top corporate post to run a chain of retail stores, and considered it a demotion, but Eisner assured him he needed operational experience and that "this will help you in the future, not hold you back."

Moving Nanula created an opening for Stephen Bollenbach, another Marriott executive introduced to Eisner by Gary Wilson. As chief financial officer for Donald Trump, Bollenbach had helped rescue the New York developer from near bankruptcy, and was now chief executive of Host Marriot, a spin-off of the Marriott Corporation. Eisner was well aware that Bollenbach wouldn't give up a chief executive position unless he was Eisner's designated successor, something Wilson had also stressed. So he assured Bollenbach that, if things worked out, he would succeed Wells as president, and agreed that Bollenbach would report directly to Eisner. But the contract didn't guarantee that Bollenbach wouldn't report to someone else, only that if he did, he would be granted an additional 150,000 Disney shares. On those terms, Bollenbach accepted the offer, even though Eisner later conceded that he never actually considered Bollenbach a likely successor. "Given his lack of experience in entertainment and his limited interest in the creative side of our business, I doubted that would happen." (Eisner also testified that he told Bollenbach he would never be president, but this is inconsistent with Bollenbach's statements at the time. In his later testimony, Bollenbach said he hoped Eisner would name him president eventually.)

Indeed, even as he was recruiting Bollenbach, Eisner resumed his courtship of Ovitz. Eisner's interest was reignited by reports that Ovitz was in serious discussions with Edgar Bronfman Jr. to run Universal, which had just been acquired by Seagram, the distilling company controlled by the Bronfman family. To Eisner, Universal posed a unique competitive threat, largely because it had a rival theme park, Universal Studios, adjacent to Walt Disney World, and a hugely successful studio tour in Universal City, something Disney itself had never been able to duplicate, and he hated the idea that Ovitz might end up as a competitor. In May, he and Ovitz had lunch at Eisner's house. "Why would you want to go to Universal when you could come to Disney as my partner?" Eisner asked. His pitch was a skillful blend of the attributes and greater opportunities represented by Disney, and a disparagement of Universal, especially its new owners, the Bronfmans. At Disney, Ovitz would be working with his best friend and trusted confidant; at Universal, Eisner argued, he'd be at the beck and call of ruthless, mercurial family members. "A board gives you much more freedom," he said, and went on at length about how close he was to board members and how they consistently endorsed his recommendations.

Ovitz listened, but he wasn't swayed. With Bronfman, he was negotiating a deal that would give him a package valued at about $250 million, and plenty of autonomy. Eisner had still not defined what he meant by "partner." Eisner left the lunch feeling that Ovitz probably would go to Universal, a view confirmed a few weeks later when Ovitz made the cover of *Newsweek* as the likely new chairman of Universal. But the Ovitz deal had collapsed the night before *Newsweek* hit the stands, when Ovitz concluded that Bronfman had reneged at the last minute on key promises, including ones related to autonomy, and Bronfman concluded Ovitz was overreaching. Suddenly

Eisner's warnings about the Bronfmans all came back to him. Eisner had been far more effective at planting doubts in his mind about the Bronfmans than he realized.

Ovitz's embarrassing setback obviously made him available once again. Eisner sent him a handwritten note, composed during one of his many plane trips, speaking warmly of him and suggesting what great partners they could be. In this note, Eisner revealed that the thank-you note Ovitz had written after their first trip to Disney World had so moved him that he'd carried a copy of the letter with him ever since. Eisner had Irwin Russell get in touch with Ovitz and resume their negotiations. Russell, however, had doubts about Ovitz for the job. His notes of one of their conversations read "Explained doubts were not related to him personally, but whether he could adapt to corporate culture (based on initial discussions) operationally financially disaster if 6 months is found out a mistake." Eisner brushed such concerns aside.

The arrival of Bollenbach, an innovative and aggressive deal-maker, had brought a significant shift to the tone and urgency of strategic-planning meetings at Disney. In contrast to the cautious, even pessimistic Larry Murphy and Nanula, Bollenbach was a product of the 1990s deal bonanza on Wall Street. He pushed for Disney to make a major acquisition, reasoning that it takes the same management energy to digest a big acquisition as a small one. With interest rates low and Disney's cash flow from its recent hits surging, he argued for using as much leverage as possible to boost returns. "We can borrow cheaply and easily and we ought to take advantage of that," he argued to Eisner. While Eisner was still keen on the idea of the two remaining networks, ABC and CBS, Bollenbach was willing to consider even bigger prey—specifically, Time Warner, the huge amalgam of Time Inc. and Warner Communications.

Soon after Bollenbach's arrival, Eisner had dinner with Cap Cities/ABC chairman Tom Murphy at Gabriel's, an Italian restaurant near ABC headquarters on Manhattan's West Side. Though Eisner's talks with Dan Burke a few years earlier had gone nowhere, Murphy was starting to feel some pressure from the consolidation going on in the broadcasting industry. Murdoch's News Corporation was the first to combine its Fox studio and the Fox network under the same corporate umbrella, and Murphy worried the other networks would end up aligning with Hollywood studios now that the fin-syn restrictions had been abolished. This was a subject Murphy had often discussed with Warren Buffett, whose Berkshire Hathaway was Cap Cities' largest shareholder, and with Robert Iger, ABC's president and chief operating officer. Neither Murphy nor Buffett really wanted to sell ABC, but they recognized that at the right price, they'd have to consider it in the interests of their shareholders. But after the dinner, Murphy reported to Iger that "Michael is cheap. There's no way he'll ever pay a price that we'd want."

Herb Allen's annual media conference in Sun Valley was scheduled for July, and Eisner was "absolutely determined" to be there, both to pursue the usual networking opportunities among the nation's media elite and to prove to this rarefied audience that he was back, he was healthy, and that he was as much a player as ever—even more so. After his medical crisis of the year before, it was like "climbing back up on a horse after a bad fall," as he put it.

The day he was scheduled to leave for the conference, Eisner convened a lunch for the strategic-planning group—Larry Murphy and his assistants, Peter Murphy (no relation) and Tom Staggs, joined by Litvack and Bollenbach—to discuss progress on the acquisitions front. Eisner would soon be mingling with every major chief executive and deal-maker, so he wanted to be prepared.

Peter Murphy outlined the case for a network, pointing out that he'd been pushing for Disney to buy one for seven years. CBS was a turnaround candidate, but was expensive at the approximately $80 per share Larry Tisch was asking. Cap Cities/ABC was already the leading network, so there was less upside potential. Cap Cities was a much bigger company, with extensive cable assets. Its stock was trading at $105 a share, which, after factoring in a premium of 15 to 20 percent, meant Cap Cities would cost Disney about $20 billion. Tom Staggs stressed the advantages of the bigger deal, especially gaining the 80 percent of ESPN, the cable sports network, that Cap Cities owned. Litvack hedged, saying he liked ABC, but could also see the case for CBS.

"I still like CBS," Eisner said. "It doesn't cost as much and I think we can fix it."

Bollenbach pressed emphatically for the bigger deal, noting that it solved the issue of how to deploy Disney's enormous cash flow by taking on more debt. "To me the issue is simple. Either we buy a relatively little house and overpay for it, or we go after this big mansion and get a bargain." Bollenbach had already proposed a bigger "mansion"—Time Warner. Time Warner offered Disney a fully integrated media conglomerate, with creative divisions like the Warner studio, cable networks (CNN and Home Box Office), and publishing that competed directly with Disney but also distribution capacity through its huge Time Warner cable operation. "It's big, it has great assets, and we could buy it cheaply, because the stock is undervalued," Bollenbach argued.

Nothing could have better illuminated the fundamental differences between Bollenbach and the cautious Larry Murphy than this admittedly audacious proposal. Murphy's eyes widened in disbelief. "You're talking about the single most complicated, aggressive, unpleasant transaction that we could conceivably undertake," he said.

"This one would be complicated, but I think we could do it," Bollenbach calmly replied.

Murphy was still opposed to the idea of buying any network, though he conceded the need to find an outlet for Disney's programming. But he thought network television was a fundamentally declining business. "The Disney strategy of sticking to our knitting and building our brand has been very successful," he argued. But it wasn't a prescription for 20 percent annual revenue and equity growth, nor did it use Disney's excess cash.

Eisner was inclined to pursue something down the middle—nothing so bold as a Time Warner bid, but perhaps one of the networks. He told the group he wasn't going to go out of his way to make anything happen, but he'd use the Sun Valley conference as an opportunity to feel out the possibilities.

That same morning, Eisner called Ovitz, who was already ensconced in one of the Sun Valley condos. Eisner was hoping to renew their discussions as soon as he arrived. But Ovitz was uncharacteristically discouraged, already packing to leave early. That morning, Bronfman had concluded his search for a new chairman at Universal by hiring Ron Meyer, Ovitz's partner at Creative Artists, who had long toiled in Ovitz's shadow. Bronfman was planning to introduce Meyer at the conference. "I just don't feel comfortable at someone else's coronation," Ovitz told Eisner.

That, at least, is the somewhat tempered version Eisner later recounted. As usual, he gave a more candid account to his lawyer Irwin Russell, one that raised questions, at least in Russell's mind, as to whether Ovitz was suited to be president of Disney. According to Russell's notes of a July 17 conversation with Eisner, Ovitz was "flipped—crazed at the conference—breakdown. Can he pull his act together?"

For his part, Eisner was introducing two of his own executives to the rarefied world of Sun Valley: Litvack and Bollenbach, each of whom naturally interpreted the invitation as a sign of their own likely succession to the vacant Disney presidency. Joe Roth was also included, making his debut as Katzenberg's successor as head of the studio. (This year, however, Jane opted to stay at home.)

When they arrived, Eisner basked in the attention that his own survival and Disney's recent success seemed to have engendered. Herb Allen himself met him at the airport. Like Ovitz, Eisner's quarters were in the high-status condos, not the lodge. Barry Diller and Diane von Furstenberg joined him at dinner. The next morning, he couldn't resist dropping in on Katzenberg's appearance on the Jack Valenti panel. At one point Katzenberg took out a water pistol and sprayed his fellow panelists. It was a relief, really, that Katzenberg's juvenile antics no longer reflected on Disney or Eisner.

Later that morning, Eisner's and Joe Roth's presentation drew a standing-room-only crowd. Eisner adopted a humorous tone, making light of his own surgery and Katzenberg's highly publicized departure. Roth unveiled his new strategy for the film division, which aimed to produce more family-oriented Disney label films (like *The Santa Clause,* which both Vogel and Roth agreed belonged under the Disney label, and *101 Dalmatians*) and to develop several "event" movies each year, much as the animation division had turned its hits into events. Then he showed a five-minute clip from the forthcoming animated feature *The Hunchback of Notre Dame.*

When Eisner returned to the podium, he couldn't resist tweaking legendary investor Warren Buffett, who was in the audience and whose investment vehicle, Berkshire Hathaway, was the largest shareholder in Cap Cities/ABC. Buffett had bought 5 percent of Disney's stock for $4 million back in 1965, but had then sold it a few years later at a modest profit. Had he held on to it, Eisner said, the $4 million stake would have now been worth $869 million. He drew appreciative laughter when he also pointed out that had Disney bought $4 million of Berkshire Hathaway stock in 1965, it would now be worth over $6 billion.

Afterward, Eisner returned to his room to pick up his bags, a little disappointed that he hadn't picked up any takeover feelers at all at a conference filled with deal-makers. Then, on the path to his condo, Eisner ran into Larry Tisch and his wife, and he leaped at the opportunity.

"I've heard the rumors you're about to make a deal," Eisner said.

"They're true," Tisch replied, surprisingly direct. He was close to selling CBS to Westinghouse, which was diversifying into media.

"Wouldn't you rather make the deal with us?" Eisner asked.

"Yes, absolutely," Tisch's wife, Billie, chimed in. Tisch said to call him over the weekend.

Moments later Warren Buffett walked up, and congratulated Eisner on his presentation. Here was another opportunity, since Buffett was a pipeline to Cap Cities/ABC chairman Tom Murphy.

"The funniest thing just happened," Eisner said. "I ran into Larry Tisch and we ended up talking about our buying CBS. Unless, of course, you want to sell us Cap Cities for cash." Eisner was planting the idea that Disney might buy another network, leaving ABC behind.

"Sounds good to me," Buffett said immediately. "Why don't we go talk to Tom [Murphy] about it?" So Eisner accompanied Buffett as he headed toward the first tee, where he, Murphy, and Bill Gates were about to start a round of golf. On the way, they spotted Murphy in a parking lot chatting with Robert Iger, ABC's president and chief operating officer, and his fiancée, ABC correspondent Willow Bay. "Oh God, here comes Michael again," Murphy said. Eisner and Buffett waved and gestured to Murphy to join them.

"Do me a favor," Iger said. "Don't sell the company without telling me."

Iger was only half-serious, but more than anyone else at Cap Cities, he probably had the most at stake. Just a month earlier, Murphy had told him that in September, he planned to announce his retirement and ask the board to name Iger as chief executive. The move would cap a stunning rise for Iger, who, at age forty-four, had been Cap Cities' president for less than a year.

Tom Murphy joined Eisner and Buffett, and the three went for a short walk. "Michael wants to pay cash for Cap Cities," Buffett began. "I think he's right."

Murphy seemed a little taken aback by his abruptness, but he, Eisner, and Buffett briefly discussed the possibility. "I'll have to think about it," Murphy finally said. Just then Warner Bros.' Bob Daly walked by. "Don't sell your company to that guy," he laughed, pointing toward Eisner.

Later that evening, Murphy reported to Iger that "Michael is more serious than I thought. He's going to call me after this conference."

The next day Eisner was in high deal-making spirits when he called Peter Murphy and Tom Staggs from his home in Aspen. "You sent me out on a fishing expedition, and I've come back with two bites," he said. "Now we have to figure out what to do with them." Sid Bass was also at his house in Aspen, so Eisner had Murphy and Staggs fax him a stack of documents comparing CBS and ABC. Just twenty minutes later, Bass called Eisner. "This Cap Cities deal looks pretty good," he said, assuming Murphy would sell at a reasonable price. "We should probably go ahead and make the deal."

The following morning Eisner reached Tisch at the Bel Air Hotel, and arranged for him to negotiate with Bollenbach. The rest of the day passed with no word from Tom Murphy. On Tuesday morning, Murphy called. He was willing to negotiate a deal, but only if it were for Disney stock rather than cash. "I want my shareholders to have a ticket on the horse race, a chance to ride on the future of the new company," he explained. And he didn't want them to have to pay capital gains tax on the proceeds of a cash sale. (There's no immediate tax on a sale for stock.) Eisner was going to be attending his nephew's wedding in Vermont that weekend, so he suggested meeting Murphy in person in New York that Friday. Bollenbach was already meeting Tisch in New York the same morning. Murphy agreed. He and Iger had continued to discuss the possibility of selling the company, and it was clear to Iger that Murphy was deeply ambivalent. Iger, too, would be giving up his dream of becoming a chief executive, just when it seemed within his grasp. "If they meet our price, we'll sell," Murphy concluded. "If not, forget it."

Eisner, Bollenbach, and Peter Murphy met on West Sixty-sixth Street, just outside ABC's headquarters. Bollenbach reported that Tisch had again pushed up the price for CBS, to $80 a share, which was discouraging. After walking around the block, Eisner decided he'd offer $115 a share for Cap Cities, which he considered a relatively modest premium, considering that Cap Cities shares were trading at $106. The meeting went on for two hours. Though retired, Dan Burke sat in as an adviser to Tom Murphy, and argued against an all-cash deal as putting too much debt on the Disney balance sheet. But neither he nor Murphy seemed startled when Eisner broached the price. On one hand Eisner was pleased, but the obsessive bargain hunter in him immediately wondered if he could have offered less, say $110 a share.

The meeting ended with no movement on either side in the cash versus stock debate. Eisner was pessimistic as he headed off to the family wedding, but Murphy had promised to get back to him after the weekend. On Monday night, Eisner and Jane flew to Toronto for the first road company preview of *Beauty and the Beast*. Even though he'd seen it many times, Eisner still loved the excitement of a new opening, and he lingered afterward for two hours discussing details of the show with the director and choreographer.

The next morning Tom Murphy called with a counteroffer: one share of Disney, then trading at $55, plus $65 in cash, or a total of $120. "It sounds like we're getting someplace, Tom," Eisner replied. It was a reasonable compromise, roughly half stock and half cash, and only a small premium to the Disney offer price. Peter Murphy and Staggs wanted to accept immediately. Larry Murphy still resisted. Meanwhile, Diller reported that a CBS-Westinghouse deal was about to happen, which, once announced, would rob Disney of leverage with ABC.

On Thursday morning, Eisner called Tom Murphy from his treadmill, where he was dutifully working to elevate his heart rate. The deal-maker in Eisner was determined to squeeze a few concessions out of Murphy. He tried lowering the stock component. Murphy said no. He tried chiseling $2 off the price, noting that Disney's stock had hit $57 the day before, $2 more than when they'd talked. "Michael," Murphy said. "I told you yesterday the deal that we were willing to make. . . . That's the deal. The only question now is whether you want to make it or not." Stumped, Eisner said he'd call back.

When he got into the office, Eisner called Bob Iger. "I want to talk about your staying on," Eisner said. Iger said he wasn't sure he was at liberty to negotiate before a deal was reached, considering he was president and chief operating officer as well as on the board. Negotiating for a high-level position in the new company might pose a conflict of interest. "Ethically, I'm not sure what my position should be." Nor was Iger sure that he wanted to work in the new company. Given his Cap Cities stock and options, the proposed deal would make him rich; he didn't need the job. Then Eisner took the opportunity to excoriate Iger for negotiating a deal with DreamWorks, which Iger didn't appreciate. He said he'd have to call him back.

Just before noon on the West Coast, Eisner called Tom Murphy. "Tom, I need to get something."

Murphy was firm. "Michael, I've told you what we're prepared to do."

Eisner took a deep breath. "Okay. You've got a deal."

So long opposed to acquisitions, Eisner had just agreed to one which, at nearly $20 billion, was the second biggest in history. When Eisner broke the news to his mother over dinner, he commented, "Pretty exciting, isn't it?"

"Yes," his mother said. "I can't believe Amy's getting married." Amy was Eisner's niece, who had just announced her engagement.

As the lawyers wrapped up the details, Eisner began calling board members, starting with Gold, to report that he had a "handshake" deal with Murphy. Gold was supportive, as was Roy, though Roy took more persuading, worried that acquiring a network would stretch the Disney brand too thin. Eisner also called Ovitz, telling him that he now had a network he could offer him. "This company is going to be too big for me to run," he said. Eisner reminded him that their long and close friendship had begun while Eisner was at ABC.

Despite making Iger his heir apparent, Tom Murphy told Eisner at a private lunch in the Cap Cities executive dining room that one of the reasons he was selling the company was that Iger wasn't ready to succeed him as chief executive. He was still too young and unseasoned (a comment Eisner repeated to Disney board members and Ovitz). Still, Murphy lavished praise on Iger, and urged Eisner to keep him at the network, stressing that Iger was on top of all of Cap Cities businesses. Eisner called Iger again now that a deal had been reached. This time Iger indicated a willingness to stay on, though he realized he was no longer in line to be CEO of Cap Cities. "I'm only forty-four years old," he pointed out, "and this is a chance to be part of a historic merger." He was also determined to protect his colleagues at Cap Cities. He'd been at ABC ten years earlier, when Cap Cities had acquired the network, and he knew how it felt to be among the "conquered" after a merger.

That evening, Iger and Willow Bay were having dinner with the Catholic priest who was going to marry them that October. Divorced and Jewish, Iger was nervous about making a good impression, but he kept getting interrupted by urgent calls on his cell phone. Finally Iger felt he had to tell the priest what was going on, swearing him to silence. He figured if he could trust anyone to keep a secret, it was someone with experience in the confessional. One of the sticking points in the contract his lawyer was negotiating with Eisner was whether Iger would report only to Eisner. Eisner said he had to have the right to bring in a president, and require that Iger report to him. Iger finally agreed, reasoning that he had as good a shot as anyone at becoming president.

The Disney board met by telephone for three hours on Sunday afternoon, August 6, 1995. Eisner stressed that he had intimate knowledge of television programming from his successful tenure at ABC. He'd revitalize ABC the same way he'd awakened the moribund Disney studio. Given Eisner's track record at Disney, the board had no reason to doubt him. The vote to approve the merger was unanimous.

After the board approval, Tom Murphy and Iger met with their chief financial officer and head of public relations, briefed them on the deal, and told them to prepare for the announcement. When they left, Murphy closed the door. "Jeez, I don't know if I've done the right thing," he said to Iger. He seemed sad and forlorn. Even though he'd be remaining as a board member, he realized that, at age seventy, his own long and distinguished executive career was over. It was a sad moment for Iger as well. He'd never worked for anyone other than Murphy and Dan Burke. He barely knew Eisner.

That evening Iger called top Cap Cities executives and broke the news, swearing them to secrecy and summoning them to an early breakfast meeting the next morning. ABC News was told only that there'd be a major corporate announcement during the next morning's broadcast of "Good Morning America." Willow Bay was subbing for Joan Lunden that Monday morning, and co-anchor Charlie Gibson asked her, "On a scale of one to ten, what is this?"

"It's a twelve," she replied.

Soon after, Eisner and Murphy showed up, and Gibson interviewed his outgoing and incoming bosses about the proposed merger. Afterward Eisner and Murphy addressed Wall Street analysts by conference call from Cap Cities' boardroom, flanked by Sid Bass and Warren Buffett, Disney's and Cap Cities' largest shareholders, respectively. "I've been a critic of many deals that have taken place over the years," Buffett said. "I think this is the most sensible deal I've ever seen from both a financial and an operational standpoint, and I'm delighted as a Cap Cities shareholder." As well he might have been, since he'd just earned a premium on the huge Berkshire Hathaway stake in Cap Cities.

At the time, the value of the deal was eclipsed only by the RJR/Nabisco merger in 1989, and was described as a "stunning surprise" in *The New York Times;* a "landmark merger that creates the largest entertainment company in the world" in the *Los Angeles Times;* and "Disney creates a new Magic Kingdom" in *The Wall Street Journal.* Eisner quickly experienced firsthand why giant mergers can be so intoxicating. Congratulatory calls poured into his office: the Sun Valley crowd, from Diller to Gerry Levin, Sumner Redstone to Jack Welch; Disney people, including Luanne Wells and composer Alan Menken; political figures and journalists. Eisner finally spoke to Katzenberg for the first time since he had left the company. Katzenberg had always wanted Disney to acquire a network, and now it had. Eisner was anxious about taking his call, but given the DreamWorks deal with ABC, he'd have to deal with Katzenberg eventually. Eisner was relieved that the conversation was uneventful and that Katzenberg graciously wished him well with the merger. That night Eisner and Tom Murphy continued the round of talk shows, appearing on "Larry King Live" and "Nightline." Ken Auletta, writing in *The New Yorker,* bestowed the highest accolade: "Eisner's triumph has transformed him once again, from the frog back into a prince."

No one was more electrified by the news than Steve Burke, Dan Burke's son, who'd grown up calling Tom Murphy "Uncle Tom." Burke felt he was languishing in Paris, off the radar screen now that Euro Disney had been restructured and renamed as Disneyland Paris. (Despite the "rebranding" effort to shake off the negative associations with Euro Disney, just about everyone outside of Disney kept referring to it by the old name.) More important, his children were reaching school age, and he wanted to move them to the United States. Burke used every opportunity to remind Eisner that he'd promised to bring him back from Paris.

Nothing had yet materialized, but Eisner assured him that now something would. What better person to help integrate Disney and ABC than Burke, who knew both corporate cultures intimately?

One day Jeffrey Katzenberg called, saying he was going to be in Paris and would like to get together. Though Burke had never been as close to Katzenberg as he was to Wells and Eisner, he admired his achievements. He was surprised when, at their meeting, Katzenberg asked him if he'd be interested in joining him at DreamWorks. Burke declined. "Why not at least consider it?" Katzenberg asked.

"I feel a lot of loyalty toward Michael," Burke answered.

"I promise you, someday that will change," Katzenberg said. "Michael Eisner has no loyalty to you."

"Yes he does," Burke insisted.

"Let me tell you something," Katzenberg continued. "Fundamentally, Michael doesn't care about anybody else. Maybe his wife. All Michael cares about is Michael."

With the Cap Cities deal, Disney nearly doubled in size, which also doubled Eisner's responsibilities. In a sense, it was the ultimate public statement that Eisner's heart attack hadn't diminished him, even if it flew in the face of his doctors' advice to reduce stress. As part of that effort, Eisner had been planning to spend the month of August with Jane in Aspen, getting some aerobic exercise by hiking and biking and, to the extent he was capable, resting. Much to Jane's dismay, those plans evaporated. Now his time was consumed with meetings and phone calls. Jane did her best to remind him that he was supposed to be doing less, that he needed more help, that he should hire someone to replace Wells. Eisner listened, but at the same time he embraced the new venture with zest. He was actually enjoying the stress. But he promised her he'd renew the effort to recruit Ovitz. At the same time, he invited Litvack and his wife, Judy, to join them in Aspen the following weekend.

The Litvacks arrived anticipating that Litvack himself was likely to be offered Wells's job. After all, he'd been functioning as chief operating officer, which had been Wells's position. He'd rescued Disney from the brink of disaster with Euro Disney, and he was leading the legal team in the Cap Cities acquisition. He'd made his debut in Sun Valley, mingling comfortably with other top media executives. More to the point, he'd become Eisner's confidant, his closest adviser. Or so he thought.

After a pleasant day of hiking and relaxing, the families had dinner, and then Litvack and Eisner sat down alone together. When Eisner said he wanted to discuss something with him in confidence, Litvack prepared to discuss his own future role at Disney. Then Eisner raised the subject of Ovitz.

Eisner was not so insensitive as to fail to realize how disappointed Litvack was likely to be at the prospect of Ovitz becoming president. "He was conflicted," Eisner later said of Litvack. "He didn't criticize so much the selection of Ovitz per se. . . . But he did criticize the need to bring in anybody because it was quote unquote 'going so well.' I think he liked the fact that he probably thought himself that he was No. 2 and this was changing—this was bringing in the wicked stepmother . . . well, I shouldn't say wicked stepmother. Bringing in an alien force."

Litvack's dismay soon became apparent. As they talked, Eisner brought out a piece of paper and divided it into two columns, one for the "pros," the other for the "cons" of hiring Ovitz. Eisner proceeded to supply the "pros," and Litvack stressed the "cons." Litvack pointed out that Ovitz was Eisner's close friend, and "if things go wrong, you not only lose a colleague, you lose a friend. It could be very messy." Litvack also conveyed his own personal disappointment. "One of the things I've valued most about the past year is that I've been your closest counselor," Litvack said, almost plaintively. "If you hire Ovitz, that's obviously going to change."

Eisner disputed that, saying Ovitz's skills were "complementary," adding, "I don't think your role will be diminished." Still, by the time Litvack and his wife left Aspen, Eisner sensed that Litvack wasn't convinced, and thought he might even quit. But early the next morning, Litvack called him from California. "I want you to know I'm prepared to do everything possible to make it work," he said, swallowing whatever disappointment he must have felt.

Though he didn't choose to share them with Litvack, Eisner could have listed quite a few "cons" in his assessment of Ovitz. Foremost among them was the opposition of Sid Bass, who said he was "firmly against" hiring Ovitz for the simple reason that Ovitz was "unqualified." Moreover, Bass told Eisner that he didn't trust Ovitz, who, at their first meeting, had lied. "That's typical of Ovitz," Eisner had replied.

Irwin Russell, Eisner's personal lawyer who also was chairman of Disney's compensation committee, and who was handling negotiations with Ovitz, had also expressed reservations. Russell had raised questions about Ovitz's stability, as his notes from July indicated, and he'd warned Eisner that he doubted Ovitz understood the level of public scrutiny that would come with being president of a public corporation. Eisner had agreed with him as well, saying Ovitz "would require further education."

Eisner was also continuing to talk to author Tony Schwartz, who was keeping a virtual diary of the critical period during which Eisner agreed to buy Cap Cities/ABC and was recruiting Ovitz. On several occasions he asked

Schwartz what he thought, and Schwartz warned him that hiring Ovitz would be a mistake.

Later that same week, Iger arrived to brief Eisner on his new acquisition. He stayed at the Eisners' house, and was impressed by the Robert Stern architecture. The next day, Iger took Eisner through all the divisions and the key executives who ran them, from the owned and operated television stations, the radio stations, cable networks, and newspapers to the lucrative employment contracts with Peter Jennings, Diane Sawyer, and Barbara Walters. No wonder news didn't make more money, Eisner observed. Iger was mainly worried about prime time, where ABC's lead was slipping. Ironically, it was the Spielberg series "ER" that Eisner could barely bring himself to watch on the flight from Aspen a year earlier that had put NBC in contention, along with the hit comedy "Friends." It turned out that Jack Welch had been right to back Bob Wright as head of NBC. But ESPN results were better than expected. Still, Eisner seemed surprised by the complexity and enormity of the Cap Cities enterprise. "How can I do this alone?" he mused at one point. Afterward they took a brief hike, and then Ovitz and Judy joined the Eisners and Iger for dinner. Eisner mentioned that he and Ovitz were going hiking together the next day.

Watching the body language at the table between the two old friends, it flickered across Iger's mind that Eisner might hire Ovitz as president. He knew Ovitz—CAA and ABC had done many talent deals over the years—but he had little sense as to how Ovitz would function as a corporate executive.

On some level Iger impressed Eisner, even if Tom Murphy hadn't felt he was ready to succeed him as chief executive. He later wrote that he found him "intelligent, thoughtful and unusually open," and that he was relieved to have "a strong leader at the top of ABC." But that's not what he told board members and Ovitz, who as Iger had accurately surmised, was already in intense talks to become Disney's president.

The Ovitz negotiations, under way ever since Eisner briefed him on the impending ABC deal, had gone into overdrive the same day Iger arrived, after Barry Diller called Eisner to warn him that rumors were rife in Hollywood that Ovitz was negotiating to come to Disney. Then Ovitz himself called. "It's all over L.A. that you and I are talking." Ovitz's colleagues at CAA, having just absorbed the near-loss of Ovitz to Universal, were in revolt. Ovitz needed a decision, one way or the other, by the end of the weekend so he could make an announcement Monday morning.

Iger was also correct that his own assessment of ABC had underscored the need for Eisner to hire someone. And Eisner began calling board members to sell them on the idea of hiring Ovitz, even as he and Ovitz hammered out details of the arrangement. None of the board members really knew much about Ovitz, other than what they had read in the press, but his credentials seemed impeccable. The overriding impression was that he was an effective businessman with vast creative contacts, "the most powerful man in Hollywood." And in any event, Eisner stressed that he'd known him intimately for nearly thirty years.

During some of these calls (to Gold, for example), Eisner disparaged Iger, characterizing him as "soft," too "good-looking," and lacking creative skills, which necessitated the hiring of Ovitz. To Ovitz he suggested he might even dismiss Iger, and replace him with Dennis Hightower, who was already running the Disney television division. But Ovitz urged restraint, saying it would be a "disaster" to replace Iger so soon and that he deserved a few years to prove himself. In any event, if Ovitz was going to run ABC as part of his responsibilities, he needed Iger to help make the transition.

Ovitz and Eisner spent the next twenty-four hours in nearly constant contact, either on the phone, at Eisner's house, or on a long hike. Eisner later stressed that Ovitz was giving up an extremely lucrative position running CAA, so his remuneration had to be correspondingly generous, not so much in salary ($1 million a year) but in discretionary bonus and stock option provisions, which provided for an eventual five million shares. The proposed deal provided that Ovitz's total compensation could not exceed 75 percent of Eisner's—significant because Eisner was also in the process of negotiating a new employment agreement. Pegging Eisner's pay to Ovitz's necessarily meant that the more Ovitz made, the more Eisner could be paid.

As usual, the sticking point was just what Eisner meant by "partner." During their hike, Eisner offered him the title of president as well as a board seat but insisted on retaining for himself the titles of chairman and chief executive. Unlike Frank Wells, who had reported directly to the board, Ovitz would report to Eisner. He also refused to give Ovitz the title of chief operating officer, holding that back as something he could earn.

Titles aside, Ovitz suggested that they just split the company's divisions, and Eisner would run half of them, Ovitz the others, for a year. They'd stay in constant contact with each other but not interfere. Then they could assess the results. Eisner was noncommittal, and never said explicitly that Ovitz would be running a division, even ABC. Still, Eisner promised that "each of our operating divisions, including ABC, would report to him as president," which made Ovitz the de facto chief operating officer, whether or not he held the title. Eisner felt sure that however Ovitz wanted to interpret the notion of "partner," he would be a clear number two.

Ovitz later indicated that he understood that he'd be reporting to Eisner, and that Eisner would be the "senior" partner. At the same time, "I must say that at that stage of my life, with the success that I had, I don't think I looked at myself as junior or senior. I looked at myself as reporting to Michael Eisner," Ovitz later testified. And he stressed that in the end, it was all pretty much a matter of trust in his friendship with Eisner. At one point Ovitz asked, "How can this work when you put me on top of people that have been there for a long time?"

"You and I will be the bosses," Eisner replied, according to Ovitz. "They report to us. And we will make it work."

"I relied on his word," Ovitz continued. "I relied on everything he said to me. I was less concerned about the specifics and the documentation issues because I trusted him. . . . I trusted Michael Eisner totally. And I believe that he trusted me."

And so, as Eisner and Ovitz and their wives reached Independence Pass, Eisner and Ovitz shook hands on their new "partnership."

Irwin Russell, who continued to represent Disney, and Bob Goldman, Ovitz's longtime financial manager, hammered out details of the agreement. This in itself was peculiar, since ordinarily Sandy Litvack, as Disney's general counsel, would negotiate on behalf of Disney. This may have reflected Eisner's perception that Litvack couldn't be trusted to negotiate a deal with someone coming in above him, but it also represented at least the appearance of a conflict of interest, since Russell was also negotiating Eisner's compensation. In any event, there was no denying that for such a complicated deal, it was rapidly negotiated and put together in a single weekend. Even though Eisner stressed how much Ovitz was giving up at CAA to come to Disney, there's no evidence that Ovitz actually disclosed his compensation as an agent, or that either Russell or Eisner ever knew how much he made. (Ovitz was actually earning about $20 million a year, he later testified.) Nor did they find out how much Ovitz was going to be paid had he made a deal to go to Universal, other than a vague idea that it amounted to between $250 million and $350 million.

Although Disney's corporate bylaws require that the board of directors hire the president, neither the compensation committee nor the full Disney board reviewed or approved the agreement that weekend. Sidney Poitier, one of the four members of the compensation committee, was awakened in the middle of the night on his yacht off the coast of Sardinia by Russell, who called to tell him Ovitz was being hired. Later, Russell couldn't recall whether he even mentioned "any numbers." Ignacio Lozano, the other committee member, wasn't contacted until the following Monday.

On Saturday night, Eisner hosted a dinner for Ovitz and Judy to bring them together with Sid Bass, who was also at his house in Aspen. Eisner was eager to win Bass's approval, since Bass was still implacably opposed to hiring Ovitz as president, and it was highly unusual for Eisner to go against his wishes. Specifically, Bass was determined to "emphasize the importance of integrity," given his reservations about Ovitz's veracity. Ovitz realized that this was an audition, and, at least in his view, he and Bass seemed to hit it off. Ovitz looked forward to developing a closer relationship with Disney's biggest shareholder; he stressed the opportunities in the rapidly evolving communications technology, a field Bass was investing heavily in, and also the opportunities for Disney to expand its international presence and revenues. Curiously, given Bass's concerns, neither Ovitz nor Eisner recalled the subject of ethics even being mentioned. The mood was ebullient at the dinner, with Jane, in particular, expressing her appreciation to Ovitz and Judy that Ovitz would be helping to take the burden off her husband.

At 1:30 P.M. the next day, after a final conference call with the lawyers and negotiators, Ovitz asked if he could have ten more minutes to think about it. He still didn't quite understand how the partnership Eisner kept talking about was going to work. Nor was he blind to Eisner's faults. He'd been intimately involved with the Katzenberg saga. He'd listened to Eisner criticize Frank Wells. He'd seen Eisner turn against Larry Gordon, against Diller. But Ovitz thought he was different. He called Eisner back.

"Judy and I have talked it through," he said. "I'm putting myself in your hands."

As soon as Eisner had hung up the phone, he called Tony Schwartz. "I think I just made the biggest mistake of my career," Eisner said. "Can I take it back?"

"If you can, do it," Schwartz replied.

NINE

Disney's press release to announce Ovitz's appointment as president was scheduled for Monday morning, August 14, 1995. The day before, Joe Roth flew to Aspen from his vacation on Martha's Vineyard, and then flew with Ovitz on the Disney plane back to Los Angeles. Eisner wanted them to spend some time together, hoping that Roth would become more comfortable with the new arrangement in which he would be reporting to Ovitz. Roth was cool to Ovitz's appointment; he, too, had considered himself a contender for the job and didn't like the idea of reporting to his former agent, someone who had worked *for* him. He warned Eisner that their styles were different, that Ovitz was a "packager," while Roth preferred to develop materially internally.

On the flight, Ovitz tried to assuage Roth's concerns, "I wanted him to be clear," Ovitz later testified, "because I knew he would be fearful of me getting involved in the movie business. And I [didn't] blame him, because I had very strong ties to the filmmakers, having been their agent. And I assured him that I wasn't going to attempt to get in his way of making movies; that I was there to assist him in any way that I could and that I would make myself available as a resource to him and to try to allay his concerns about my joining the company."

On Sunday evening, Eisner asked Ovitz to stop by his house in Bel Air to go over the press release and to discuss how they'd handle the next morning's announcement. Ovitz arrived in good spirits, energized by his new deal and the resolution of his future career direction. Who knew what the future held? If all went well, he himself might be Disney's chief executive in a few years, reaching the pinnacle of an already remarkable Hollywood career.

But the minute he walked into Eisner's dining room, where he and his wife had shared so many pleasant meals with Michael and Jane, he knew something was wrong. What had obviously been an animated conversation came to a halt. Eisner was seated on the left side of the table. Standing at one end of the room was John Dreyer, the head of public relations. Ovitz had expected to see him, since they were reviewing the press release. But seated across the table from Eisner were Sandy Litvack and Steve Bollenbach, the chief financial officer.

Bollenbach glared at Ovitz and said, "Welcome to the company. I just want you to know that I'll never work for you."

Then Litvack chimed in: "Me too. I'm not going to report to you."

Ovitz was stunned. He waited for Eisner to come to his defense. "I had no idea that those statements would be made . . . they were made aggressively and in a way that was, in my opinion, disrespectful," Ovitz later testified. But in an ensuing awkward silence, Eisner said nothing. Ovitz, proclaimed the most powerful man in Hollywood, felt helpless.

Eisner had delayed telling Bollenbach about Ovitz's hiring until that afternoon, adding, "Don't worry, you continue to report to me." Bollenbach's contract provided that if he reported to anyone but Eisner, he'd be granted an additional 150,000 Disney shares. In any event, Eisner later testified that he had never intended to have the chief financial officer report to Ovitz, even though the CFO had reported to Wells. "I wanted to keep a rein on the finances of the company until I had confidence that Mr. Ovitz had adapted to a public company," he testified. And he said he was "kind of impressed" at the way Bollenbach confronted Ovitz that night.*

Litvack was another story. Eisner was surprised that Litvack followed Bollenbach's lead. "I kind of like avoided dealing with that in my own mind," Eisner later said about whether Litvack and the legal department would report to him or Ovitz. "I knew it would be difficult and when it finally had to

---

* Eisner also testified that he told Ovitz while they were in Aspen that the chief financial officer wouldn't report to Ovitz. "I had told Michael that Steve had this contractual commitment to report to me . . . on this weekend he accepted that the CFO would report to me. . . . Mr. Ovitz knew from day one that Mr. Bollenbach . . . was going to report to me directly." In his book, Eisner concedes that he promised that "all operating divisions" (except animation) would report to Ovitz. Ovitz testified that Eisner had never said anything about Bollenbach not reporting to him, and that he considered legal and financial to be among the operating divisions that would report to him, as they had to Frank Wells.

be addressed, which was over that weekend, when Mr. Litvack followed Mr. Bollenbach's lead in saying that he didn't intend to report to Mr. Ovitz, I let that happen."

Ovitz knew immediately that he was facing his first major crisis at Disney. Though not sophisticated about matters of corporate management, he knew that to be stripped of legal and financial responsibilities meant he was not really a chief operating officer, and that it left him dangerously bereft of any management authority. But it wasn't really so much the lines of authority or management implications. In the instant that Eisner failed to put down the rebellion, Ovitz saw with perfect clarity that his best friend had betrayed him.

Ovitz's mind was reeling, "I was wildly confused . . . I was floored when Michael didn't say to them you have to do this," he later testified. But he did his best to maintain his composure and adopt a conciliatory approach. He made some vain efforts to persuade Bollenbach and Litvack to change their minds, trying to reassure them that he'd be supportive if they reported to him. "I didn't want to walk in and all of a sudden have two guys quit. So I tried to dance around it and make it all work," as he later put it. Eisner simply listened. It was obvious they weren't going to budge without pressure from Eisner, so Ovitz suggested he and Eisner leave the room. They went upstairs for a private talk in the bedroom of one of Eisner's sons.

"You did a really good job with that," Eisner told him.

But Ovitz was nearly distraught. He asked Eisner for guidance. "I was looking for his advice and guidance and his support and backing, which I thought would be critical in my first moment at the company," Ovitz recalled. He asked, begged, Eisner to return to the dining room and back him.

"I can't do that," Eisner said. "Look, that's the way it is. If you don't want to do the deal, just tell me so right now."

It was a stunning suggestion: that Ovitz quit even before the deal was announced. At the same time, Eisner had to have known it wasn't a real option. Ovitz couldn't afford to have another deal collapse after being humiliated in the MCA/Universal negotiations. He'd arranged to sell his interest in CAA. There was no way he could go back now. As he later put it, "I had no choice. I could not walk away from the Walt Disney Company. I had given up my business. I had been put in a position that I had made a deal that I had agreed to with Mr. Eisner. I shook his hand. I intended to keep my end of the bargain. I expected him to. I trusted him . . . I'm a team player. I wasn't going to let this guy down. I was incredibly disappointed. I didn't know what to do."

Ovitz said he'd try to make the arrangement work. "Let's just ride this right now," Eisner said. "And see if you can do a little more work on it. If you can't do it, we will figure out how to do this over the year."

It was clear when Ovitz and Eisner returned to the dining room that Ovitz had capitulated, put in the humiliating position of trying to win the approval of Litvack and Bollenbach. "I did everything I could as a salesperson to try to sell these guys into an amiable, decent relationship. . . . I didn't want to get Michael into trouble and I didn't want to upset them. Frankly, I had no idea how to handle this. I was going totally by the seat of my pants." They went over the press release that had been drafted to state that Litvack and Bollenbach would report to Eisner. "Ovitz, who will be nominated to the board of directors, will assume his new duties October 1," the release read. "He will be responsible for three operating divisions of the company. . . . His leadership abilities will augment those of Sandy Litvack, our chief of corporate operations, and Steve Bollenbach, our chief financial officer, who were so instrumental in making the Capital Cities/ABC merger. Both will continue to report to me."

When Ovitz got home that night, he looked stricken. "What's the matter?" Judy asked.

"I just made the biggest mistake of my career," Ovitz said, echoing Eisner's own words to Tony Schwartz. He explained what had just happened.

"We'll do the best we can do," she said. "You can make it work."

Ovitz called his lawyer, Ron Olson, to report on the disastrous evening and to see if Eisner had already breached their agreement. They concluded that Ovitz had no choice but to go forward. He'd built Hollywood's most powerful agency from nothing, largely through sheer determination and hard work. He would not, and could not, fail at Disney.

Ovitz's hiring as Disney president was announced on August 14 to widespread acclaim. "Ovitz Pick Ideal Choice for Global Giant," read the Los Angeles Times headline. "Walt Disney Co. has reached out for the kind of powerful, globally connected executive needed to run the biggest of the new breed of giant entertainment and media complexes," the article gushed. Only that morning did Irwin Russell tell Ignacio Lozano, the fourth member of Disney's compensation committee, that Ovitz was being hired as president, and Lozano didn't recall that any terms were mentioned.

That same morning, Ovitz and Eisner signed copies of a letter memorializing the terms of his employment: a five-year contract with an annual base salary of $1 million; a discretionary bonus of at least an additional $1.5 million; and options to purchase 5 million Disney shares.

Ovitz arrived for work at Disney just after Labor Day. He had expected to occupy Frank Wells's former office next to Eisner on the sixth floor of the Team Disney building, but Sandy Litvack had already moved in. "Why doesn't Sandy move?" Ovitz asked, but Eisner dismissed the idea. Bollenbach, the CFO, and Larry Murphy, head of strategic planning, also had offices on six. Of the various division heads, only Joe Roth had an office on the same floor with Eisner. The others were on five. Ovitz moved into a small office next to Dennis Hightower, who was running television. Eisner told Ovitz that an office on six was being renovated and he could move in when it was finished. Still, Ovitz's presence on five was a signal of his diminished status. At one point, Ovitz suggested building a staircase between floors five and six, so that he and the division heads would have easier access to Eisner and the other top executives. Eisner looked at him like he was crazy. It was a waste of money, he said, and besides, he'd deliberately designed the building so as to prevent easy access to his office.

One of the first things that greeted Ovitz after his arrival was a copy of a newsletter from Roy Disney to all the animators noting that Peter Schneider, who ran feature animation, would report directly to Roy and Eisner, not Ovitz. This, too, came as a shock to Ovitz, another painful reminder of his ever-diminishing status.

The following Monday, Ovitz attended the first of Eisner's weekly staff lunches, which Eisner had often told him was the focal point of his management of the company, extolling the freewheeling, spontaneous exchange of ideas and "synergy" that he was so proud of. But Ovitz was struck by how little exchange there was. Most of the lunch was a stream-of-consciousness monologue by Eisner. No one disagreed with anything he said. As the weeks went by, Ovitz came to think of the lunches as a waste of time. He was sometimes late and excused himself to make phone calls, which annoyed Eisner greatly.

As one of the country's most successful agents, Ovitz was, by nature and experience, a deal-maker. He had revolutionized the motion picture industry by creating lucrative "packages" for his clients, and often negotiated multifilm production deals, "first-look" or exclusivity arrangements, and office and overhead arrangements on studio lots. Ovitz, of course, was nearly always representing the talent, not the studios. The deals obviously gave his clients far more money than they could hope to earn on a single project. What they yielded the studios was often less tangible: ongoing access to creative talent, as well as the cachet of being identified with star directors, actors, and writers through long-term commitments. Ovitz was aware of the pitfalls of such deals—"a killer application as an agent and a disaster if you ran a studio," as he later put it. But naturally, Ovitz's determination to "make things work" immediately manifested itself in a flurry of attempted deal-making.

One of the first people Ovitz contacted about doing business with Disney was Brad Grey, chairman and chief executive of Brillstein-Grey, a television production and talent management company with high-profile clients like Brad Pitt and Jennifer Aniston. Grey had been a client of Ovitz at CAA, and he was already in talks with Disney, as well as other studios, about some television production deals. As Ovitz later explained his reasoning, he wanted to arrange a deal for exclusive access to Grey's projects as well as the talent he managed, and in return, Disney could offer Grey a chance to break out of television and into movies, with a production deal similar to the one that Ovitz had negotiated for Roth when he came to Disney.

"Mr. Grey is an excellent executive," Ovitz explained. "He is the kind of person we needed to come into the Walt Disney Company and bring his company. He represented over 150 writers. Since he was a manager and not an agent, it would have been an amazing opportunity because you would have the opportunity to really get a first crack at the management clients without having to pay for it. . . . My point of view was that ABC was sliding at a geometric rate and having worked in the network business, once a network goes on a downhill road, it can take five years to turn it around and it's all cyclical. So we were watching NBC dominate and I knew, because I represented Les Moonves [head of CBS], that CBS would really start to pick up because he is very aggressive. And I thought we needed to be aggressive."

Ovitz suspected Joe Roth wouldn't be happy about bringing Brad Grey in as a potential movie producer. But he assumed Roth would go along for the benefit of the TV studio and for the company overall, even if some of the cost had to come out of his studio budget. On that Monday afternoon, still Ovitz's first day at the company, Roth was back on Martha's Vineyard, resuming his vacation after talking to Ovitz in Aspen and on the subsequent flight to Los Angeles. He got a call from Jake Bloom, Grey's lawyer, who told him that Ovitz was offering Grey a deal that gave him the right to produce multiple feature films. "I can't make that deal," Roth protested. "I've never even developed a script with Brad."

C 'G C R)

"This is what Ovitz wants to do," Bloom said.

Roth was incensed, both at the proposed deal and the fact that Ovitz hadn't cleared it in advance with him. He immediately called Ovitz, who seemed puzzled that Roth was so upset. "We can do a Caravan deal, can't we?" Ovitz asked, referring to the deal he'd done for Roth.

Though he nominally reported to Ovitz, Roth immediately called Eisner. "Six hours," Roth said.

"What do you mean?"

"It's taken exactly six hours for my fears to be realized," Roth said.

It didn't take long for the Grey news to reach Bob Iger at ABC and Dean Valentine, who was running Disney's TV animation department under Hightower. They, too, were upset that they hadn't been consulted.

As the tempest unfurled, Eisner called Tony Schwartz. "For Christ's sake, here we go," he said.

At CAA, Ovitz had been advising a group of telephone companies on a programming venture called Tele-TV; Disney had been working on a competing venture called Americast. "Why don't we invite the Tele-TV companies to become part of the Americast venture?" Ovitz suggested that same Monday. "That sounds like a terrible idea to me," Eisner replied. He was concerned about the antitrust implications, especially while Disney was still awaiting approval for the ABC merger. "But why don't you check with Sandy Litvack?"

This gave Litvack an opportunity to ridicule the suggestion, but Ovitz reported back to Eisner the next day that "Sandy didn't take a strong stand one way or the other." Suspicious, Eisner checked with Litvack. "I was polite," he told Eisner, "but I was very clear that I did not think it was a good idea." As he had so many times with Katzenberg, Eisner uncritically accepted Litvack's version of the conversation, which confirmed his suspicions, already voiced by Sid Bass, that Ovitz couldn't be trusted to tell the truth. Eisner again wondered if he could get rid of Ovitz.

Later that day, Eisner told Ovitz, "Between Brad Grey and the Telcos, you've just had about the worst two days imaginable. You've got to slow down and take a deep breath. You need to learn to walk before you can run. There's no need to do everything at once, and there's no reason for us to make deals that create headlines, only to have them come back to haunt us later."

"I feel terrible," Ovitz replied. "I really screwed up. I'm sorry."

Still, Ovitz thought the ideas were good ones on the merits. He just had to master the internal politics.

Despite these early missteps, the reservations about Ovitz he expressed to Tony Schwartz and Sid Bass and his own thoughts about getting rid of Ovitz, Eisner recommended that the Disney board approve Ovitz's appointment as president on September 26, 1995. Although Eisner maintained that he had kept all members of the board fully informed about the courtship of Ovitz in various phone calls, it's clear that only a few—Stanley Gold, Ray Watson, and, of course, Irwin Russell—knew anything in any detail. Ignacio Lozano, a member of the compensation committee, testified that he thought Ovitz's hiring was a "done deal" even before the board meeting. Neither the board as a whole nor the compensation committee had met to discuss Ovitz after the announcement and prior to the vote. To the extent most board members even knew the terms of Ovitz's employment, they were reflected in a brief summary of the deal that omitted numerous details. The minutes of the meeting reflect merely that Eisner "reviewed Mr. Ovitz's professional and educational credentials."

Directors later testified that they did discuss Ovitz, albeit briefly. Neither Litvack nor Bollenbach, both board members, said anything about their refusal to report to Ovitz or their reservations about his hiring. No one asked what would happen if Ovitz didn't work out, or under what circumstances he could be fired, and neither Eisner nor Russell volunteered anything on the subject. No one raised any questions about the fact that Ovitz retained an ongoing economic interest in his former clients at CAA, since he still earned commissions on revenue received under agreements he'd negotiated while at the agency. Though Ovitz never concealed this arrangement from Eisner or anyone else, it posed an obvious potential conflict, since Ovitz had a financial interest in having Disney hire his former clients.

The board unanimously approved the appointment of Ovitz as Disney's president. Moreover, it agreed that Irwin Russell should be given a $250,000 payment for his "extraordinary services" in negotiating Ovitz's contract and persuading him to come to Disney.

As he had with Frank Wells, Eisner was happy to delegate to Ovitz tasks that he found distasteful. In one of their first meetings, Eisner went over with

Ovitz a list of executives that he considered "problems." Much to Ovitz's surprise, the list included Joe Roth and Bob Iger. Just as Ovitz had found Joe Roth to replace Katzenberg, Eisner wanted him to line up replacements.

And Eisner wanted Ovitz to fire Dennis Hightower immediately, just months after naming him the head of the television division. Hightower seemed always to be traveling, to European capitals for days at a time, to Houston for video conferences. Rumors circulated that he was still working for the CIA. But perhaps he was just trying to flee the unpleasant reality that he was completely out of his depth in television, and had no one to guide him. In any event, Eisner had been hearing a stream of complaints. Hightower had become an embarrassment to him, and Eisner did his best to ignore him.

"You've got to fire him," Eisner told Ovitz.

"I'm not going to fire him," Ovitz retorted. "You hired him. You fire him."

Eisner looked annoyed. "Then you've got to do something for him," Eisner said.

During their walk in Aspen, Ovitz had made clear that he expected to at least maintain, if not enhance, the lifestyle he'd acquired while at CAA, which included the usual perquisites of a top-level Hollywood executive—personal assistants, access to a corporate jet, a car and driver when in New York, and a virtually unlimited entertainment budget. The same night the board approved his contract, Ovitz had hosted a party at his house for the prominent contemporary artist Chuck Close. To Ovitz, the party served numerous synergistic purposes, cementing his stature as a prominent art collector with stars like Tom Hanks and directors like Steven Spielberg, who might also want to do business with Disney.

Such entertaining was a way of life for a high-profile agent, and it was second nature to Ovitz. Indeed, he felt one of the reasons Eisner had so few personal relationships with creative people in Hollywood was that he didn't do enough of that sort of thing. "Chuck Close was used as a centerpiece for the party because Disney is in the creative business and he is probably one of the four most important living artists in the world today," Ovitz explained. "So to have a party in his honor, people thought it would be very good for a company that was not known to be particularly talent friendly and to try to mix and match a lot of people that had worked in Disney movies, had worked in Disney animation. I had theme park people there. I had people from the Imagineering group and I mixed everybody up with directors. It was interesting. The Imagineering guys loved talking to Spielberg because he was exclusive to Universal and they sat and picked his brain."

The party cost about $90,000, which Ovitz felt was a bargain—less than half what he would have spent had he still been at CAA. He was later criticized for exceeding the $125 per person maximum allowed by Disney, but in fact the limit applied only to noncatered events. Under the terms of Ovitz's contract (as well as Eisner's), catered events were reimbursed in full. In any event, Ovitz left expense account details to one of his assistants. Indeed, at one time or another Ovitz had five assistants, including one who oversaw gifts from Ovitz on Disney's behalf.

To Ovitz, gift-giving was another integral part of doing business in a creative industry where "talent relations" were paramount. But it was not how Eisner functioned. He sent the same Christmas gift to everyone every year— apples from an orchard near the family's Vermont farm, or a wheel of aged Vermont cheddar cheese. Years earlier, Ovitz had accompanied Eisner on a shopping trip to buy a special gift for Eisner's longtime assistant at Paramount, and Eisner had selected a letter opener. As Eisner said in a note to Tony Schwartz, "I knew from the beginning that I had to treat company money as though it were my own. Maybe it is because I came from wealth or my father drummed it into my head, but I had it. I have noticed through the years that most do not. They treat the company like they would the government. It is big and it doesn't matter. Michael [Ovitz] was that way."

Eisner asked both Litvack and Irwin Russell to closely monitor Ovitz's expenses, looking for infractions of company policy—beginning with the Chuck Close party. He sent Russell a handwritten note, saying "Michael is obviously not reporting gifts," and "He told me some of his stock pickers were buying Disney," suggesting that Ovitz might be inappropriately discussing Disney with brokers. (Ovitz later denied any wrongdoing.) It was almost as if Eisner wanted to find infractions. Litvack kept up a steady drumbeat of ethical and other concerns, which fueled Eisner's suspicions that Ovitz was heedless of such issues, and spent Disney's money like it was CAA's.

Eisner addressed some of these concerns obliquely in an October 10 letter he wrote Ovitz while flying cross-country to look at Georgetown University (his son Breck's alma mater) and other colleges with his son Anders. He began by complimenting Ovitz on his work and saying he was "particularly delighted with a personal relationship that will grow and flourish between us." At the same time, the letter was a little like his Paramount manifesto, meant as a reminder to Ovitz that he was working at a public company. "We are the hired managers of this great institution, but subject to and responsible to all the owners," he wrote. "We must remember that, not because either of us think otherwise, but because that will keep us on course, human, humble, vulnerable, sharp, responsible and ethical. . . . We must lead by ethical standards that the whole company sees and buys into. . . . Frank Wells and Barry Diller taught me to act like 'Caesar's wife.' That is good practical advice for all executives, but especially public company executives and doubly appropriate for executives in the public eye."

In addition to the sermon on ethics, he warned Ovitz about his deal-making. "The 'deal' is not the essence of Disney. . . . Operations are the thing. The deal is a means to an end, to get television series made, movies made, theme parks built, consumer licenses awarded, talent connected. But the deal cannot take the lead. . . . I feel about acquisitions exactly as I feel about everything else. We don't need them. We don't need the overly expensive movie or television show. We do not need the actor who has priced himself out of the market. We do not need the acquisition that, even if we feel it fits strategically, is economically ridiculous. I guess what this letter states is all so obvious, but it did take me many years to be able to even state the obvious. What better time to put the thoughts in writing as we begin this new chapter in our lives? Let's find some time to discuss the future. Michael."

Eisner later explained the letter by remarking that Ovitz was "running like crazy, trying to do everything, working, you know, 17 hours a day. I was excited about how interested and committed he was but I wasn't getting his attention completely on some of the things that I thought were important. And therefore I thought by writing a letter that basically complimented him, and told him that I was excited about his being in the company but that these should be things that he should be looking at."

Eisner maintained that Ovitz never replied to the letter or even acknowledged receiving it, though Ovitz later testified that they discussed it on numerous occasions. He was nonetheless oblivious to the possibility that the letter was in any way a criticism. He said he found it "incredibly helpful and very supportive of me. This is the kind of instruction that I had asked him for on that August walk and previously, and I thought he was being wonderfully responsive." At the same time, Ovitz didn't agree with parts of the memo, especially Eisner's professed opposition to acquisitions (which was in any event hard to reconcile with his multi-billion-dollar acquisition of ABC).

"We had some spirited discussions about publishing and recorded music," Ovitz recalled, two areas where Ovitz was supposedly in charge and where he felt it was essential to grow through acquisitions.

Oblivious to Eisner's mounting suspicions and concerns, Ovitz plunged into his new responsibilities, confident that by sheer dint of hard work and enthusiasm he could carve out a role for himself despite the overt hostility of people like Litvack and Bollenbach, and the passive resistance of Roth. Ovitz surpassed even Katzenberg's legendary work habits, arriving early, spending twelve hours at the office each day, including Saturdays and Sundays. And like Katzenberg, he always seemed to be doing two or three things at once, frequently interrupting meetings to use his cell phone, arriving late or leaving early, canceling appointments at the last minute. This was pretty much business as usual in the Hollywood of CAA, but at Disney, where suspicion and resentment of Ovitz were already rife, every slight was tallied, and most were reported to Eisner.

In one incident, Ovitz managed to alienate both Bob Iger and Steve Bornstein, the head of ESPN. He'd told Iger he wanted to know everything about ESPN, and asked to meet Bornstein. Iger told Bornstein to work up a detailed presentation on the sports channel, which Bornstein had built into a hugely profitable franchise. When Ovitz arrived at Iger's office in New York for the meeting, he asked, "What is this? What's this meeting?"

Iger reminded him that he'd requested it. Ovitz looked at his watch. "I see it's on the schedule for two hours. I only have fifteen minutes. Let's start, see how far we get, and then I can read the rest of the presentation."

Bornstein started his PowerPoint presentation. Five minutes into it, Ovitz excused himself to answer a call on his cell phone. "That was Tom Cruise," he said when he returned. "I'm afraid I can't do this now. Give me the deck and I'll read it, then I'll call with any questions."

Ovitz left. Iger, Bornstein, and his staff were stunned. They'd spent weeks getting ready. Bornstein never heard back from Ovitz.

Ovitz also had a habit of sitting next to Eisner at meetings and whispering in his ear—a gesture that was meant to underscore his intimacy with Eisner but one that infuriated others. Eisner later testified that it "drove him crazy," and that he asked Ovitz to stop doing it.

While Ovitz's exact responsibilities remained unclear, he scheduled weekly meetings with strategic planning and Imagineering. He also began planning an ambitious series of trips to Japan, to China, and to Europe, capitalizing on the close relationships he'd forged in the Sony and Matsushita deals, seeking to expand Disney's international business. He also took the time to write personal responses to the thousands of people who wrote to Disney each week, something he felt Eisner had neglected. Such personal touches were essential in the agency world. In keeping with his notion of partnership, he copied Eisner on every letter, every memo, and had one of his assistants give Eisner a copy of his schedule each day. He knew how upset Eisner had become at the idea that Katzenberg was doing things behind his back.

And, of course, despite the fiasco of his early negotiations with television producer Brad Grey, Ovitz kept trying to do deals. Indeed, he had kept trying to negotiate a deal with Grey, but when Grey eventually met with Eisner himself, it was clear Eisner wasn't interested, and Grey did a deal with Universal instead. As Ovitz later testified, Eisner "didn't like the idea" of doing a deal with Grey. "He thought that television shows needed to be developed in-house."

After that, Ovitz was careful to go over with Eisner a list of other creative talent he hoped to bring to Disney—many of them his former clients, such as director Martin Scorsese, actors Sean Connery and Robin Williams; novelists Michael Crichton and Stephen King; and producers Frank Marshall and Kathleen Kennedy. Ovitz scheduled numerous meetings, introduced them to other Disney executives, and gave them tours of the studio. Many did enter into deals with Disney, but in most cases only after Joe Roth approved them.

There were areas of the company where Eisner had willingly ceded responsibility (and blame) to Ovitz—Hollywood Records and Hyperion Publishing, both businesses that lost money and held little intrinsic interest for Eisner. They were the areas he'd tried to hand off to Katzenberg after Wells died. It didn't take Ovitz long to realize that neither business was large enough to be consistently profitable, which meant they had to grow, either by acquiring more talent or, more likely, by buying other companies. Disney had plenty of cash and borrowing power to make acquisitions.

Ovitz pointed out to Eisner that in publishing there were just four "mega authors," as he put it—Michael Crichton, Stephen King, Tom Clancy, and John Grisham—and two of them had been Ovitz's clients. "In the publishing world," Ovitz explained, "new authors go where the big authors are." Ovitz negotiated with Tom Clancy, brought him in for a tour of the studio, and persuaded him to move to Hyperion. But Eisner balked at the advance Ovitz negotiated, though it turned out to be half what Clancy got when he moved to Putnam. Stephen King had a deal for miniseries with NBC; Ovitz wanted to offer him a joint publishing-TV deal at Disney. Eisner never gave him the authority to go ahead. When MCA/Universal put Putnam on the block, Ovitz met with Putnam's chief executive, Phyllis Grann, and negotiated a price of $350 million to acquire the publishing company. The deal would have brought Clancy and at least twelve other best-selling authors to Disney, and in Ovitz's view, would have put Hyperion Publishing on the map. Eisner vetoed the deal. (Putnam was subsequently sold to Pearson of England for $336 million.)

Similarly, Ovitz came up with several proposals to expand Hollywood Records, a business he knew well. He had represented Michael Jackson, Barbra Streisand, and Prince for years at CAA, and as he later explained, there was "zero" chance he'd move them to Hollywood Records, which lacked the worldwide distribution and the clout with radio stations that came from releasing hundreds of titles a year. Hollywood Records had no blockbuster acts, and as a result, no clout. Like authors, Ovitz argued, recording artists were "migratory birds" who went where the top stars were. Ovitz felt his only hope was to offer recording stars the kind of television and film options that Disney could offer. "We've got to book a mega act," he argued to Eisner, and Eisner agreed, or at least that was Ovitz's impression.

Ovitz had represented the Jackson family, including both Michael and Janet, for twenty-five years. He knew that Janet Jackson, then the world's number one selling recording artist, was restless at Virgin Records and was considering a change. Because of his close ties to the family, he was able to negotiate a deal that would have brought Janet Jackson to Hollywood Records in a seven-record deal for $75 million. But when Ovitz brought the deal to Eisner for approval, he rejected it out of hand. "We'll grow our own acts," he said.

"You can't just 'grow' a major music act," Ovitz insisted. "You've never grown a major act," he pointed out, which seemed to annoy Eisner. Ovitz couldn't even return to Jackson with a lower offer. Instead she signed a new four-album, $80 million deal with Virgin, nearly twice as much as Ovitz had negotiated for Disney.

Ovitz's credibility as a deal-maker collapsed as word of the Jackson negotiations spread through the close-knit recording industry. Nor would Eisner allow Ovitz to replace the head of Hollywood Records, despite acknowledging the studio's weak performance and problems with the division head's "work ethics" and other personal issues. He said he expected Ovitz to fix the problems without signing new talent or changing management.

Confronted with these failures, Ovitz began negotiating a $3 billion joint venture that would have merged the Hollywood and Sony labels. Sony president Nobuyuki Idei "has always been obsessed with Walt Disney," Ovitz explained, pointing out to Eisner that Idei's daughter had written her Japanese university dissertation on Mickey Mouse. Sony was interested in Disney's children's label—the only part of Hollywood records with any significant market share—and in return, Disney "would have been a competitor with an amazing catalogue representing some of the biggest artists around." Ovitz also thought the deal would enable Disney to book its recording acts into the theme parks and other venues, as well as give Disney an entrée into Sony's budding video game business—exactly the kind of synergies so often extolled by Eisner.

Ovitz sent Eisner a *U.S. News & World Report* article about the record business to help make his case, and Eisner replied with a memo disparaging the whole idea of the Sony venture. "I read the article you sent me," he wrote. "Maybe I am just reading it the way I want to, but it seems to shout out to me that the concept of building our own record company is possible. It may be more prudent than paying $5–10 billion at this time to us. What really struck me was the following sentence: 'Of this year's five best-selling albums, only one comes from an artist who had a recording contract five years ago.' This tells me the business is moving more and more to new artists and is somewhat less dependent on existing librar[ies]. This isn't to say a library wouldn't be wonderful, but at what cost? If we can find the acts . . . and if we can market to the [Walkman]-toting Generation Xers . . . I think we can make our record company a success while we wait for an acquisition we can digest."

As Ovitz later put it, "Michael didn't want to spend money for artists even if I could get them for a discount, and he didn't want to do any kind of merger or acquisition." He wanted to build from within, adding at one point that "if we could steal a company that would be even better because I don't want to pay for it."

Perhaps Ovitz's most visionary idea was for a "downtown Disney" venture that would have brought a National Football League franchise to a new sports arena and entertainment complex in downtown Los Angeles. He got the idea at a meeting with Imagineers, who were talking about trying to bring a "Downtown Disney" attraction to Anaheim, similar to the one in Disney World, which features adult-oriented restaurants, theaters, and other entertainment. At the same time, Eisner had been talking about a studio tour in California to rival Universal's; Ovitz had even seen mock-ups of a monorail that would connect Anaheim and Burbank, but it seemed wildly expensive and impractical. Out of this hodgepodge of ideas Ovitz hatched the idea to "take control of that whole plot of land where the Coliseum and the Sports Arena is, gate it and turn it into a sports-based attraction and then you would have ESPN that you could tie in, and you could tie in Disney characters," as he described it. "We could put all kinds of entertainment down there but make it a safe kind of Disney experience for the family and build it around sports." The Imagineers did drawings and a model, "a phenomenal design for downtown. It would have stimulated hundreds and hundreds of jobs. It would have revitalized that whole area."

Eisner was initially enthusiastic, or again so Ovitz thought. He began meeting with NFL representatives and owners of various teams, including the Seattle Seahawks and the Carolina Panthers. The NFL was enthusiastic, as was the L.A. City Council. But Litvack was opposed to the idea and then Eisner "for some reason turned off to the downtown Disney idea."

Besides overseeing the recording and publishing businesses, Ovitz assumed he would be in charge of ABC once Disney's acquisition closed the following January. He scheduled weekly meetings with Bob Iger, Ted Harbert, who was in charge of programming, and other top ABC officials. He flew to New York every week, usually on Sunday evening. He spoke to Iger by phone every day. Disney's acquisition of ABC was the main reason he'd come to Disney.

Early in the fall of 1995, Iger, accompanied by Litvack, Bollenbach, and Larry Murphy, spent a week in New York conducting an exhaustive review of ABC's businesses. They took over a large conference room and each division head made presentations. When it was over, the Disney group's main recommendations were to sell the newspaper group (Cap Cities owned the *Kansas City Star* and other newspapers, as well as Fairchild Publications, publisher of *Women's Wear Daily*) and either to sell the radio division or make a large radio acquisition. Ovitz was aware that the radio business was undergoing rapid consolidation as advertisers sought national audiences; several deals were in the works that would have relegated the ABC stations from the second largest in the country to ninth or tenth. The proceeds from the sale of the newspapers could be used to buy more radio, or reduce debt.

When the group returned to Los Angeles, Ovitz presented the recommendations to Eisner. Eisner scoffed at the ideas. He went around the table, asking each executive—Bollenbach, Litvack, Murphy—what he thought. All agreed with him, saying selling any of the assets would be a mistake. Ovitz was floored. "Guys," he finally said, "we just spent five hours on the plane discussing this and agreeing on this." There was silence. Ovitz felt everyone in the room looked at him like he was crazy.

Though Eisner showed little interest in many of the ABC assets (including ESPN, according to Bornstein), he began intervening in nearly every decision at the ABC television network, reading scripts and reviewing pilots. Everyone at ABC conceded Eisner's legendary success as a programming executive; still, it was disconcerting to hear frequent references to the days of "Laverne & Shirley" and "Happy Days," which were ancient history by network TV standards. People were afraid to say anything to Eisner, so Iger bore the brunt of the complaints. Finally Iger spoke up. "It just doesn't work like that anymore," he said after yet another reference to "Laverne & Shirley." Eisner said nothing, but later complained to Ovitz about it, reminding him yet again that he wanted to find a replacement for Iger.

The combination of intense scrutiny from strategic-planning executives (known to other divisions within Disney as "the goon squad"), whom Iger considered arrogant and insensitive, and Eisner's sudden intrusion into the planning process, left Iger dismayed, so much so that he intimated to Ovitz that he was thinking of quitting. Though Ovitz knew of Eisner's ambivalence toward Iger—Eisner "did not feel Mr. Iger was the right executive for ABC," Ovitz later testified—he thought it essential that Iger stay on, both because he was competent and hardworking and because it was important for continuity at the network.

Ovitz flew to New York early on a Sunday, and went straight from the airport to meet with Iger and Willow Bay at the restaurant of the Hotel Plaza Athénée.*

"I can't take this," Iger said. "I'm supposed to run ABC, but I have no authority." He complained that Eisner was "stuck in the 'Laverne & Shirley' era." Ovitz could empathize, but instead, in his words, he tried to "sell" Iger on the idea of staying. "Mr. Iger sat and told me how difficult it was for him to work with Mr. Eisner because Mr. Eisner was micromanaging him and he wasn't used to that," Ovitz later testified. "I spent three hours explaining to him Michael's intentions, explaining to him how brilliant Michael is creatively . . . and that he had great experience in the network area and that Bob should just run with it; it will take some time." (Iger maintains he didn't complain about Eisner.)

---

* Iger recalled that the dinner was at The Mark hotel. Both hotels are on Manhattan's Upper East Side.

Later, Ovitz described the dinner to Eisner, and while he was careful not to betray Iger's confidence, he said he was worried Iger might quit, and that it might be nice for Eisner to give him a gift, some recognition of how hard he was working.

"Why?" Eisner asked. "He's got a contract. He's not going anywhere."

"Don't you want him to be comfortable, happy in his job?" Ovitz asked. Eisner seemed to ponder the notion for a moment.

"Not really," he said.

But Ovitz didn't give up on the idea. He had noticed that Iger had admired one of his watches (Ovitz collected them), so he asked Eisner if he could give Iger a watch. Eisner resisted, but Ovitz wore him down and finally he gave in. Ovitz picked out a stainless-steel Breguet Aéronavale, which one of his assistants was able to buy wholesale for about $3,500.

At a Disney/ABC management retreat in Phoenix, Ovitz asked Iger to meet him and Eisner in Ovitz's suite at the hotel after a long day of meetings. "We'd like to give you a present for being such a great soldier in helping to merge the two companies," Ovitz said. Iger thought Eisner looked extremely uncomfortable. Ovitz handed Iger a box, and he opened it.

Iger was nearly speechless. He did love watches, and he especially liked the Breguet. On the other hand, he didn't need a watch and could afford to buy one himself. He was just doing his job, for which he was well paid. Eisner looked embarrassed. Iger managed a thank you, and left as quickly as he could.

Iger and Willow Bay were married on October 7, 1995, in a ceremony in Bridgehampton, Long Island, attended by television royalty: Oprah Winfrey, Barbara Walters, Diane Sawyer, Peter Jennings, Tom Murphy—and Jeffrey Katzenberg, who had negotiated a DreamWorks deal with Iger. Both Eisner and Ovitz were invited and planned to attend. One of Eisner's secretaries asked for a copy of the list of guests who had accepted. Katzenberg's name was on it. Eisner canceled. "Cover it for me, won't you?" he asked Ovitz.

At the wedding reception, Ovitz discussed with Katzenberg his still-unresolved dispute with Eisner about his bonus. Ovitz had resolved many seemingly intractable disputes in his career as an agent, and he was convinced that prolonging them or, worse, letting them get into court, was disastrous for both sides. "I think I can resolve this in two weeks," he confidently told Katzenberg.

*   *   *

Not long after Ovitz's arrival at Disney, Katzenberg had begun to staff his new animation department at DreamWorks. As the animators had predicted, he set his sights on numerous Disney animators he'd worked with, including artists Andreas Deja (who had drawn Scar in *The Lion King*) and Glen Keane (who'd drawn much of *The Little Mermaid*) as well as directors Ron Clements and John Musker. Most of the Disney animators had not been enamored of Katzenberg, but they now credited him with creating a golden age of Disney animation, and, of course, they responded to the incentive of money. For years, Disney animators had worked for modest salaries. Very few made more than $100,000, which was one reason they resented the huge money Katzenberg had been earning from their work. And now Katzenberg was talking about doubling, tripling their salaries—in a few cases, even talking about deals in the seven-figure range. Suddenly animators were rushing to hire agents, lawyers, and business managers. In this sense, Katzenberg's departure had a direct economic impact on Disney. Even before DreamWorks had created a single animated feature, it had driven up Disney's cost structure by millions of dollars.

Eisner was determined not to let anything interrupt the juggernaut of Disney animation—*Pocahontas* had opened in mid-June and grossed $141 million domestically, *The Hunchback of Notre Dame* was coming out for the summer, to be followed the next year by a musical version of *Hercules*—and an ambitious schedule of animated features was already in the pipeline. To keep star animators John Musker and Ron Clements happy, Eisner finally green-lit their proposal for *Treasure Island* in space, an idea long resisted by Katzenberg that went back to the first animation "gong show" meeting.

Although animation was one area where Eisner had specifically excluded Ovitz, he now asked him to help retain key animators. As Ovitz later described the situation, "Michael would call me constantly. 'Can you save this?' 'Can you handle this?' 'Can you save that?' 'Can you do this?' " Ovitz encouraged animators to display their art in the commissary, and organized gallery-like "openings" every four to six weeks. Even though Eisner ridiculed the exhibits, the animators seemed to enjoy them. Ovitz met with key animators individually and tried to address their concerns. He threw a party for all the animators at his home, featuring guided "art tours" of his art collection. The more Ovitz ingratiated himself with animators, the more Eisner seemed to resent it. When he saw the bill for the party, he criticized Ovitz, saying it was too expensive and a waste of money. "Besides," he added, "Roy didn't like the party. He said it was rude that you wouldn't let people in your house."

Ovitz thought that was unfair; the dinner had been served outdoors, but the house was open, and the art tours took people through the house. Later, Ovitz asked Roy what he thought about the party, and he said he'd really enjoyed and appreciated it. Was Roy being truthful or just polite? Ovitz had no way of knowing. (Roy had criticized the party to Eisner, and said he wasn't aware of any art "tours." Thomas Schumacher did take some animators who wanted to see the art into the house through the kitchen.)

As Ovitz later described the process, "To his credit, Jeffrey was very tenacious at trying to romance these people. And it is not difficult to shake the relationship of a creative person. And Jeffrey was expert at it . . . we were in a constant fight with DreamWorks at the beginning. These kinds of things take up unbelievable amounts of time, because, unlike other people who do it, I never did nor will I ever do what we call 'touch-and-go' relationships, which is where you go meet someone, you salvage it through whatever means necessary . . . and then you just don't talk to them again. Every time I went after one of these people I made them my client, so I had lunch with them once a month. I called them constantly to see how they were doing. I sent them things on their birthday or their anniversaries or things that were important. I helped them if their kids needed to get into a hospital with my connections. That was part of my job. Can you quantify that for shareholders? I don't know that you can do that. No one else at that company was capable of doing it."

Despite Eisner's complaints about Ovitz's tactics, none of the high-priority animators Eisner had assigned to Ovitz defected to DreamWorks. There were some losses, of course. But Deja and Keane both stayed, as did Clements and Musker, although the vastly greater sums they were offered to stay were no doubt more important than Ovitz's ministrations. Still, they enjoyed the attention and felt they weren't being taken for granted.

On another occasion, Eisner called Ovitz, sounding frantic, with the news that Tim Allen had just walked off the set of "Home Improvement." "He's a $250 million asset," Eisner said. "You've got to get him back."

Ovitz immediately left his office and went to Allen's dressing room on the set. He suggested that Allen calm down and take the rest of the day off. The next day Ovitz invited him to lunch, and listened patiently to his grievances, promising to address them. The campaign climaxed with a dinner party Ovitz hosted for Allen at his house, which included Allen's wife, his lawyer, his manager, and a group of his friends. After Allen admired Ovitz's art collection, Ovitz bought Allen a gift: a print by contemporary artist Roy Lichtenstein, a personal friend of Ovitz, that cost about $1,500.

Allen returned to the set, and production of "Home Improvement" resumed without further incident. But when Ovitz asked to be reimbursed for the cost of the Lichtenstein print, Sandy Litvack hit the ceiling, suggesting that it was unethical, which gave Litvack another opening to fuel Eisner's suspicions about Ovitz's ethical standards. (Although Eisner cited this incident as evidence of Ovitz's lack of ethics, it isn't clear what was unethical about it. Eisner evidently reconsidered, since he testified years later that there was nothing wrong with Ovitz giving Allen a gift on Disney's behalf.)

As Ovitz later described the encounter, Litvack "got very upset with me and angry and said I didn't know how to work in a public company and he embarrassed me in front of a number of people and he told me that I was not very bright about these things and in a public company you can't buy gifts for people. And I explained to Sandy that, if it is the rule, I found it to be ludicrous. I would be happy to pay for it myself. But I got Tim Allen to go back to work. He never missed another episode."

Ovitz detested Litvack, but nonetheless he enlisted his help to try to resolve the Katzenberg dispute. Litvack was a lawyer, and in any event, Ovitz had learned by now that if he didn't get his support, his own efforts would be doomed, especially with something so sensitive as Katzenberg. "I knew what a hot button issue this was," he later explained.

The issue had only gotten "hotter" with Katzenberg at rival Dream-Works, overtly competing with Disney and trying to woo its top animators. And it had reached the boiling point when David Geffen, increasingly angry over Eisner's failure to honor Katzenberg's contract, his treatment of Rich Frank (another Geffen friend), and other issues, decided to unload on Eisner to journalist Robert Sam Anson, whose book project on Disney already worried Eisner. "I'm not afraid of Michael Eisner," Geffen told Anson. "That's why he's so angry with me. Because in this town where people are all about business and making money, I am the only one willing to say the truth." And the "truth," in Geffen's view, was that Eisner suffered from "character flaws" and from something "very, very damaged in his background."

"Michael is a liar," he continued. "And anyone who has dealt with him— genuinely dealt with him—knows he is a liar." As for Katzenberg, "Anybody who worked for me who contributed as much as Jeff Katzenberg—I'd call them chairman of the board. But Michael is a very, very ungenerous guy. He suffers when anyone else shares the credit. . . . I've always said that Michael built Hollywood Records and Euro Disney and that Jeffrey's responsible for everything else."

Geffen made the comments on the understanding that Anson would use them in his book on Disney. But after Anson decided he didn't feel up to writing a Disney book and instead joined *Los Angeles* magazine as editor (which Disney acquired through Cap Cities two months later), Anson kicked off his tenure by using Geffen's comments about Eisner in an article for the magazine, "Geffen Ungloved," which ran in the July 1995 issue of *Los Angeles* magazine. Geffen's comments were the talk of Hollywood. Although Geffen was upset that they were taken out of context, he couldn't dispute their accuracy. (Anson's next piece criticized Ovitz. He was fired as editor three months later for supposedly unrelated reasons.)

This was exactly the kind of press Ovitz was determined to avoid, and that he feared Katzenberg and his ally Geffen would continue to generate, since both had strong ties to reporters, in contrast to Eisner, who used John Dreyer to avoid them as much as possible. Litigation—the "insanity" of "facing Jeffrey's rage" in court, as Geffen so vividly put it—had to be avoided.

"It ultimately was just not a good thing for the Walt Disney Company to be in a litigation with Mr. Katzenberg," Ovitz later testified, "because I felt, (a) that Mr. Katzenberg would have an excellent chance of winning based on what I had seen, and (b) that it would be bad press for the company, and (c) if a deal was struck they should honor the deal or settle the deal in some way, shape or form. . . . I knew that it was very important that the company settle this and not let it blow into a press event."

Litvack agreed to help Ovitz make the case with Eisner, though he surely knew this was not a view calculated to win Eisner's approval. Eisner initially rejected any idea of allowing Ovitz to try to negotiate a settlement, but Ovitz persisted (with Litvack's lukewarm support), and after several weeks, Eisner finally gave in. Ovitz called Katzenberg, eager to follow through on the pledge he'd made to him at Iger's wedding.

"Jeff, I want to talk to you about trying to figure out how to stop all these atrocities that are going on," Ovitz said, the Geffen comments still on his mind.

"No problem," Katzenberg replied. "I'll meet you at St. Joseph's in the reception area." St. Joseph's, a hospital in Burbank across the street from the Disney campus, was a place they were unlikely to be seen by entertainment executives.

When Ovitz arrived, Katzenberg was already waiting in a small cafe off the reception area, two Diet Cokes and bags of Fritos on the table. To

Ovitz the drinks and snacks seemed, under the circumstances, like a peace offering.

Katzenberg laid out his case, calmly and without anger. He said he only wanted what his contract guaranteed him—a share in the profits he'd worked so hard to generate while he was at Disney. Exactly how much that would be wasn't clear, given the ongoing enormous revenues being generated by hits like *Beauty* and *Lion King*, but Katzenberg said the exact amount of money wasn't the issue. He simply wanted Eisner to make a good faith effort to honor his contract. Rather than get involved himself, Katzenberg suggested that Ovitz work through Geffen, and then when they reached a deal, Katzenberg and Eisner could meet.

Ovitz thought Katzenberg was reasonable and gentlemanly. "The conversation couldn't have been more productive or positive," he recalled. He said the same thing to Eisner and Litvack, even though it was obvious this was not what Eisner wanted to hear. Still, he and Litvack agreed that Ovitz should proceed, and that they'd be willing to settle the case for up to $80 million. Ovitz felt anything less than $100 million would be a bargain for Disney. He kept Eisner and Litvack informed "every step of the way; I cleared everything I was doing with them."

Geffen and Ovitz met several times, and spoke more often on the phone. Geffen was straightforward: Katzenberg wanted a round $100 million, the amount Eisner had always said he was giving up by leaving Disney. Ovitz was pleased that the number wasn't even higher; he got Geffen to agree to $90 million, at which point Ovitz thought they should go ahead and make a deal. "It's reasonable, and it's the right number, and I'm going to do my best to close this deal," he told Geffen.

Ovitz spent forty-five minutes briefing Eisner and Litvack on the negotiations up to that point. Eisner wanted to hear every detail. When Ovitz finished, Eisner looked at Litvack, and Litvack looked back at him. "I don't want to settle," Eisner said.

Ovitz couldn't believe it. "I'm not a lawyer," he said. "I may not be as smart as you, but can you please explain the rationale? You're going to run up $20 million in legal fees. You could be on the hook for $200 million."

Katzenberg is "misreading the contract," Litvack said. "He's not entitled to anything." Ovitz was furious that Litvack had again turned against him in front of Eisner.

"Well, let's assume I'm misreading it. You get a bonus. I get a bonus. Are you telling me he's different?" Ovitz said.

"Yes," Litvack answered.

Ovitz felt himself getting agitated. He turned to Eisner. "Whatever you want to say, he worked his ass off for you. Now you're going to make him fight you to get his bonus? What kind of message does that send?"

Eisner said the matter was closed; he wasn't settling and he wasn't paying Katzenberg anything. As Ovitz later testified, after nearly reaching a deal, "I couldn't get approval from Eisner. Litvack was very vociferous about it—Originally he backed me in the settlement idea but when it came to spending that money none of them wanted to do it."

Ovitz felt defeated. He called Geffen and then Katzenberg to say he'd failed to sell the deal to Eisner and Litvack. He felt they took the news calmly, but their comments were withering. "It's obvious you report to Sandy Litvack," Geffen said. "This isn't the old you. You could close anything. You could get it done. Now you have no credibility." Katzenberg sounded almost sympathetic. "This is just the beginning," he said. "You have no idea what you're in for."

The charges were devastating to Ovitz, because they rang true. "For the previous thirty years as agent I didn't ever, ever, not settle a deal or make a deal. I had a one hundred percent accuracy rate, a one hundred percent completion rate in settlements," he later testified.

From Ovitz's point of view, it was hard to know what, if anything, Eisner wanted him to do, since nearly every initiative he embarked upon was thwarted, either by Eisner himself, by Litvack or Bollenbach, or by people who nominally reported to Ovitz. As Ovitz later put it, "every time I went to do something, someone pulled the rug out from under me."

Even Ovitz's hard work seemed to backfire. At one point he got a breathless phone call from Jane Eisner. "I wanted you to go to Disney so Michael wouldn't have to work so hard," she said, obviously upset.

"I'm doing the best I can," Ovitz said, "but it's not easy. He won't delegate."

"You're there Saturdays, Sundays. He can't keep up," she said.

"What are you talking about? He doesn't have to keep up."

"It's causing him stress," she said. "If you're there, he feels he has to be there."

"Jane, talk to him," Ovitz said. "That's ridiculous." But it dawned on him that it wouldn't make any difference what Jane said. Eisner saw Ovitz as a competitor to be vanquished, not an ally, friend or "partner."

*   *   *

Unknown to Ovitz, it's clear that Eisner felt he had made a mistake hiring Ovitz even before he began working at the company, and had already decided to fire him. In any event, that's what Eisner told Sid Bass just five weeks into Ovitz's tenure. The only reason he didn't fire him immediately, Eisner told Bass at the time, was because he thought Ovitz would commit suicide.*

It isn't clear where Eisner came up with the idea that Ovitz was potentially suicidal, but it didn't come from Ovitz. Eisner later testified that suicide was on his mind because he and Ovitz had just seen the Broadway musical *Rent,* in which one of the characters commits suicide. Eisner told me that a fragment from the poem "Richard Cory" by Edwin Arlington Robinson, which Eisner had studied in college, was on his mind. (The poem addresses the paradox of a town's leading citizen, Richard Cory, who "one calm summer night / Went home and put a bullet through his head.")

Even then, Eisner indicated to Bass that he was only going to keep Ovitz for another twelve months, and that he'd have to be fired no later than October of the following year. Eisner complained repeatedly to Bass that Ovitz was unethical, untrustworthy, and that he had suggested lying as a "modus operandi."

Eisner had also expressed his reservations about Ovitz to Tony Schwartz, which surfaced in a draft of the book Schwartz was writing:

"Nothing interested [Ovitz] so much as deals. During his first several months on the job, he suggested a litany of possibilities, among them buying the Seattle Seahawks, the Los Angeles Lakers, and the record company EMI. I was loath to dampen his entrepreneurial instincts, but in each case, when we ran the numbers, they did not come close to making economic sense. Faced with these facts, Ovitz would back off, but only after considerable time had been invested in due diligence. . . . The more relentlessly he pursued deals that ultimately made no financial sense, or failed to take account of how his actions would go over with our other executives, or made choices about how he operated that I believed seemed inappropriate in a public company or sent the wrong message, the more prompted I felt to maintain checks and balances on his authority, and to get involved myself. It was a negative cycle that fed on itself."

Evidently, as part of these "checks and balances," Eisner encouraged even those executives who nominally reported to Ovitz to bypass him and consult

---

* Eisner later testified that Bass was mistaken, and the conversation took place later in Ovitz's tenure.

with Eisner. After the Brad Grey incident, Joe Roth regularly consulted Eisner without informing Ovitz. As Ovitz later testified, Eisner "advised Larry Murphy, who was then head of strategic planning, who reported to me, who I held a weekly meeting with his entire staff, to do nothing that I suggested and to report everything in the meeting back to him. Dean Valentine, who was head of television, told me that Mr. Eisner told him that even though he reported to me, that he should not do what I said and he should consider his channel to Mr. Eisner open."

At another point in the draft of his book, Eisner accuses Ovitz of suffering from "fierce insecurity. In an almost manic desire to prove himself at Disney, he sacrificed the humility, patience, and openness that are necessary to learn any complicated new job. Instead, from the first day, Ovitz focused nearly all of his attention on the same things that had always worked for him successfully before: orchestrating high-profile deals, focusing on his image, and cultivating the visible trappings of power."

Despite their long friendship, or perhaps because of it, Eisner failed to communicate the depth and intensity of these feelings to Ovitz himself, much as he had so long concealed his feelings about Katzenberg. The Eisners and Ovitzes continued their social lives together. Jane Eisner and Judy Ovitz remained best friends; they spent time together at Aspen and in Los Angeles.

Indeed, given what Eisner did say, it's no wonder that Ovitz felt Eisner still valued his friendship as highly as ever. In an October 20, 1995, letter to "Board Members, Bass Family and Jane," Eisner showered Ovitz with extravagant praise:

"Michael Ovitz joined me in Paris. Let me just say right here, boy are we lucky!!!! Even though he is going to read this letter; and I do not want to encourage him too much (I want something to continue to do in the company), his coming to Disney was a great coup for us and a saving grace for me. Everybody is excited being with him, doing business with him, enjoying his energy and knowledge, sense of humor and enthusiasm. He comes with training and experience in the business we are in and has quickly gone from deal-maker to program-maker who understands the deal. He has already run a private company, and being a quick study, has quickly adapted to the public institution."

As Thanksgiving 1995 approached, John Lasseter at Pixar was working feverishly to put the finishing touches on *Toy Story*, the fledgling studio's first feature-length computer-generated film. After Katzenberg's departure from Disney, the project had nearly died once again. Although Lasseter had embraced Katzenberg's suggestion for a buddy picture, Katzenberg had been encouraging him to make the story darker, "edgier." After a disastrous test screening near San Francisco, Peter Schneider had pulled the film from the release schedule and insisted that Lasseter and his staff rework it. Lasseter didn't object. He felt the movie had been drifting further and further from the film he wanted to make.

When Lasseter returned with the revised version, Schneider and Thomas Schumacher were so excited that they moved up the release date from spring 1996 to November 1995. The story of a group of toys that come to life, and the fears of the cowboy Woody that he will be displaced by a space-toy astronaut, Buzz Lightyear, the film opened on November 22 and was an immediate sensation, a technological breakthrough, and a compelling and exciting story.

The new, hip magazine *Wired* featured *Toy Story* on its cover, and the article noted that the movie had required a bank of 300 Sun microprocessors and 800,000 hours of computing time. Each frame required 300 megabytes of information. Roy Disney was astonished that the CAPS system he'd fought for ten years earlier had evolved into something so complex and artistically liberating. In one sequence, Buzz Lightyear jumps off a bed, bounces off a ball, rebounds off the ceiling, and spins around a hanging toy helicopter. Unlike the static backgrounds of conventional animation, the walls, ceilings, and objects expand and contract to simulate the high-speed perspective of Buzz. "It's an amazing ride," concluded *Chicago Sun-Times* critic Roger Ebert. "A visionary roller coaster of a movie. . . . I felt I was in at the dawn of a new era of movie animation, which draws on the best of cartoons and reality, creating a world somewhere in between, where space not only bends, but snaps crackles and pops."

Costing $30 million, *Toy Story* was a huge box-office success, grossing nearly $200 million in the United States alone. And it was a windfall for the consumer products division and the Disney stores, since the very concept of the movie was toys, all of which could be manufactured and sold. Eisner reacted swiftly, ordering Schumacher to negotiate a new, longer-term agreement with Pixar to replace the original three-picture deal with one that provided for seven feature films, a fifty-fifty split of revenues, and reserved to Disney control over any sequels and rights to consumer products.

*   *   *

As they had for years, the Ovitzes and Eisners spent both Christmas Eve and Christmas day together in Aspen, alternating between their houses. On Christmas Eve that year, Eisner handed Ovitz a handwritten note:

1996 is going to be a great year—we are going to be a great team—we every day are working better together—time will be on our side—we will be strong, smart and unstoppable. And I think it will be fun because both of our hearts are in the right place and pumping. I have a lot to learn from you and that is something I look forward to. Only a really smart person* realizes that he can always be educated. I am ready for more. Everybody knows we are winners. Every day I am thankful we are together. Here's to 1996, fun, success, and little stress.

Michael, 12/24/95

* I hope I am

TEN

At Disney's live-action operation, David Vogel was pouring his efforts into *101 Dalmatians*, which was now scheduled to be the successor to *Toy Story* as the "event" film for the 1996 holiday season. Though Vogel and Joe Roth had called on Glenn Close during her triumphant Broadway run as Norma Desmond in *Sunset Boulevard*, she had turned down the part of Cruella De Vil, the glamorous but evil dognapper at the center of the plot, as did Sigourney Weaver. But on impulse, after her run in *Sunset Boulevard* had ended, Vogel called Close's agent, stressing the similarities between the two divas, Cruella and Norma. Maybe Close would like to play another over-the-top character. Vogel was ecstatic when she accepted—on condition that John Hughes rewrite a few of her lines. She and Hughes met soon after.

In the first week of January 1996, Vogel flew to London, where filming was set to begin and Close had arrived for hair and makeup. A few days before filming began, Close looked at the script, and saw that none of the changes she'd requested had been made. Vogel frantically tried to reach Hughes, but he didn't return the calls. The producer, former Disney executive Ricardo Mestres, was in the Caribbean and unreachable. It fell to Vogel to take Close to tea at Claridge's Hotel, hoping to smooth things over, but it was clear that Close was hurt and insulted. "David," she intoned in a deep, throaty voice, "no lines—no Cruella!"

Vogel saw the project collapsing before his eyes. "I don't know where John is," he stammered unconvincingly, though it was true. "So let's figure out what you want." Close went over the lines with Vogel, and he didn't think her requests were so unreasonable. Afterward, he called Joe Roth. "John is in hiding," he reported. "You've got to find him." He finally reached Mestres and told him to either get Hughes to make the changes or he would hire someone else. Mestres called Hughes's lawyer. Finally word reached Hughes, who was furious.

"There's a bullet circling London and it's headed for you," Roth reported to Vogel. Given Hughes's stature in Hollywood compared to Vogel's, Vogel knew that if he alienated Hughes he'd probably be fired.

Hughes finally called Vogel, his tone icy. "I hear you have sided with the actress against me."

"Absolutely not," Vogel insisted. "If you don't want to rewrite these lines, it's totally up to you. I'm prepared to shut down this movie and fire the actress and look for a new Cruella. I have a list of actresses who want to do it, and I'll fax it to you."

There was a long silence. Vogel waited anxiously. Did John Hughes really want to go to war with Glenn Close over a few lines?

"All right," Hughes finally said. "I'll talk to you in the morning." The next morning Vogel found five new lines on his fax machine. Close was satisfied. Filming commenced. Vogel had dodged the bullet.

Vogel thought he might get a call from Roth thanking him for a job well done. If this was any other studio, he might even get a bottle of champagne. But he heard nothing.

Disney's acquisition of ABC closed in January 1996. Katzenberg was threatening to file suit against Disney the same day, but Ovitz persuaded him to hold off. Tom Murphy joined the Disney board, as did Ovitz, on Eisner's recommendation. In a note to Ovitz typed by Eisner that same month, he praised Ovitz as "professional, attractive and competent," and added, "like a marriage, we are doing wonderfully to the outside world."

But there were ominous signs. Eisner was upset that Ovitz had wished Sid Bass a happy New Year. "I really must know what you're up to. It's not enough that you have your secretary call to say that you wished Sid Bass a happy New Year. Hearing from a secretary . . . puts me in a dark position." It was one of many indications that Eisner did not want Ovitz to speak to Bass or any board members. Ovitz was warned specifically not to talk to Tom Murphy or Dan Burke. "These small but aggravating problems pale in comparison to how well you are operating," Eisner continued, "but it's just little things like respecting my relationship to my bosses, the Basses and the board . . . you are squeezing the toothpaste from the middle. It's one way to get paste, but not the way for me."

Perhaps because he had so little real authority, Ovitz seemed to obsess over those things he could control. His office renovation was finally completed—at a cost to Disney of over $2 million, much of it due to overtime charges. Much was made of Ovitz's extravagance—the office costs, the many assistants and secretaries, the $76,000 he spent on flowers—even though Eisner later conceded that Ovitz wasn't really to blame.

With the acquisition of Cap Cities, Eisner wanted to move swiftly to put his stamp on the network, and urged Ovitz to find a programming executive to replace Ted Harbert, who'd been at ABC for twenty years. He was also "very concerned about Mr. Iger's ability creatively," Ovitz later testified. Eisner tried to recruit Marcy Carsey, a partner in Carsey-Werner television, the producers of ABC hits "Roseanne" and "Grace Under Fire," but she turned him down. Ovitz canvassed agents, producers, and directors and came up with a short list of candidates. Jamie Tarses was the first name on just about everyone's list. Ironically, Harbert had suggested trying to recruit Tarses to ABC the previous fall, though certainly not as his replacement.

Tarses was the number two programming executive at NBC, which had streaked past ABC in the ratings with Tarses-developed hits like "Caroline and the City," "Mad About You," and "Friends." Intense, dark-haired, attractive, and a smoker, Tarses embodied the hip, young, affluent audience that advertisers coveted and that had flocked to NBC.

As the daughter of TV producer Jay Tarses, creator of the acclaimed 1987 series "The Days and Nights of Molly Dodd," Tarses had grown up in the television business, reading her father's scripts and analyzing shows during dinner-table discussions at the family's home in the San Fernando Valley. "My father hated executives," Tarses told The New York Times. "He would say they were hateful, horrible people who should be shot on sight." After graduating from college, Tarses worked at "Saturday Night Live" in New York and then at Lorimar in Hollywood before joining NBC.

Even as Ovitz was putting out feelers, he got a call from Robert Morton, the executive producer of "Late Show with David Letterman," who was Tarses's boyfriend and a client of Ovitz at CAA. Ovitz had been talking to Morton about luring Letterman away from CBS to ABC, but in this call Morton broached the subject of Disney hiring Tarses to be in charge of programming at ABC. Though she still had eighteen months on her contract at NBC, Tarses was miserable, he reported. She was contemplating a sexual harassment suit against network president Don Ohlmeyer. Also, her immediate boss, programming head Warren Littlefield, had just gotten a new five-year contract, which meant she wouldn't be advancing anytime soon at NBC. She was not only interested in switching to ABC, but under the circumstances, Morton was sure she could get out of her contract at NBC.

Ovitz wasn't really surprised. Rumors about Ohlmeyer's heavy drinking and erratic behavior had circulated for years. He promptly reported this development to Eisner and Iger. Eisner was keenly interested in any gossip about rival entertainment executives, especially a direct competitor like Ohlmeyer, but he was less sure about Tarses, and said he wanted to do his own "due diligence." But he, too, soon reported that she had received glowing recommendations. Eisner authorized Ovitz to make an approach, and he urged Bob Iger to set up a clandestine meeting.

Almost as soon as Iger and Tarses started talking, Tarses said she'd already met with Ovitz. "Really?" Iger responded, trying to disguise his surprise. Ovitz hadn't said anything about meeting with Tarses. Iger thought he was in charge of hiring a new programming executive, but Tarses was acting as though she and Ovitz practically had a deal. Afterward Iger asked Ovitz why he hadn't told him about the meeting. "We just had a drink," Ovitz said. "It was just a social thing."

The courtship continued, with the main sticking point that Tarses didn't want to report to Iger, but directly to Ovitz and Eisner. But Ovitz was impressed at Iger's ability to overcome her objections in a series of meetings in which he stressed his willingness to delegate the authority she needed and his eagerness for Disney and ABC to have a successful woman executive. Finally, when Tarses spoke with Eisner, he was at his most charming and persuasive. "She was so stimulated by the meeting she had with Eisner and the idea of coming to ABC and being able to be a woman in that high a position and have the control of that development budget, that she wanted to leave under any condition," Ovitz later testified. He added that there wasn't much further discussion of the Ohlmeyer situation, just that Tarses kept assuring them that she'd have no trouble getting out of her contract at NBC, a point reiterated by her lawyer and Robert Morton. (Tarses maintains that Ovitz told her to use the sexual harassment charge to get out of her contract. Ovitz denied this in his testimony.)

In Hollywood, recruiting an executive under contract at a rival company was routine. There was even a name for it: "stacking a deal." "That's the way it is in the business. I'm not saying it's proper or appropriate. That's just the way it works," Ovitz said. Still, recruiting Tarses raised the question of whether Disney was trying to induce her to breach a contract, with the added twist of using the threat of sexual harassment. No one seems to have considered that Tarses's threat to sue unless NBC released her from her contract might look like thinly disguised blackmail.

In any event, Disney offered Tarses the job of head of programming, which would make her the first woman to head a network programming operation. In February, when she conveyed the news to NBC and began negotiating to get out of her contract there, Warren Littlefield called Ted Harbert at home on Presidents' Day weekend. "I hear they've offered Jamie your job," he told Harbert. Harbert expressed shock and disbelief. "Well, you ought to look into this," Littlefield urged. Harbert called Iger, who was out, and then reached David Westin, then president of ABC News. Westin said he'd heard something about it but wasn't involved.

Later that evening, Iger returned Harbert's call. Harbert was furious. Iger had to admit that Tarses was coming but said Disney lawyers wouldn't let him say anything to Harbert. Iger felt terrible. Harbert had helped teach him the business and had loyally stood by him over the years. Now Iger felt he'd been disloyal. He told Harbert he didn't want him to quit and tried to assuage him by offering him the position of chairman of ABC, with Tarses reporting to him.

ABC needed to keep Harbert, at least for the next few months. But offering his title to Tarses had breached his contract, which had more than two years to run. So Iger agreed that Harbert could leave after six more months, and still be paid for his entire contract.

Tarses did not file a sexual harassment complaint against Ohlmeyer, and NBC released her from her contract, but only on condition that she not start working at ABC until after the end of the spring development season. ABC executives were barred from talking to her until then. Although she would be given the title of president of ABC Entertainment, she would not be the top programming executive (Harbert still was) as she had expected. After leaving NBC in February, Tarses and Morton headed off for an extended vacation in Tuscany.

In the midst of this awkward situation, Stephen Bollenbach, who'd been the strongest advocate for a big acquisition like ABC, quit in late January to become chief executive of Hilton Hotels Corporation. He'd begun looking for a job soon after Ovitz was appointed, when he realized that Eisner was not going to make him president, let alone name him his successor as CEO. He later testified that Eisner tried to keep him by saying that the job of president "may open up soon." But having been disappointed once, he wasn't inclined to wait.

Since the evening at Eisner's house when Bollenbach had announced that he wouldn't report to Ovitz, the two had been estranged, Ovitz suspicious of him and Bollenbach resentful of Ovitz's presence. Bollenbach had offered to meet with Ovitz and teach him the company's financial structure, but never with any enthusiasm, and Ovitz thought it a hollow gesture, especially after the meeting about the radio stations where he felt Bollenbach had pulled the rug out from under him. One or the other had canceled nearly all their scheduled meetings on grounds they were too busy with other things. But now that Bollenbach was leaving, they agreed to have dinner.

"You may think I don't like you," Bollenbach told Ovitz, "but it's not true. It was just that Michael promised me your job. The day you walked in, he broke that promise. I got upset."

So that was it, Ovitz thought. (However genuine those sentiments, they didn't stop Bollenbach from subsequently criticizing Ovitz to the press.)

With Bollenbach on his way out, Eisner hastily retrieved Richard Nanula from the Disney stores and returned him to his old job as CFO. Ovitz was in Europe at the time, but he called Eisner and all but begged him to realign the reporting structure, and have Nanula report to him. "This is the perfect opportunity to turn the bad press around," Ovitz argued. "This is a perfect opportunity to send a signal to the hundred thousand employees of the company that we have a team and a partnership. This is a perfect opportunity to stop the press cold. You are having everything report up to me. I report to you."

"The fact is that you are not ready to oversee finance in this company and the board would never approve it," Eisner told him, in what Eisner later described as "one of the most unpleasant conversations we had ever had." "I'm feeling more stressed than I ever have in my life."

"That's terrible," Ovitz said. "I was supposed to make your life easier."

The press release announcing Nanula's reappointment stated that he would report directly to Eisner. "It was like another knife in my back," Ovitz said.

To Tony Schwartz, Eisner maintained that Ovitz's attitude about money was "What was a million here or there? That's the way all agents think. Michael said that to me a thousand times while he was an agent. Even what does a few billion dollars mean to Disney. . . . I had to therefore hold the financial reins. I did not want to. I simply had to."

* * *

In early April 1996, Eisner invited Katzenberg to visit him in Aspen, ostensibly to discuss the DreamWorks television production deal with ABC. Katzenberg assumed the real reason for the unexpected invitation was to discuss his still unpaid bonus, and maybe head off the threatened lawsuit. He still didn't want to face Eisner in court. Maybe they could put this behind them, and maintain a civil relationship. Katzenberg cleared his schedule and chartered a plane.

The night before the scheduled meeting, a secretary called Katzenberg to say the meeting was canceled. No new date was offered. Katzenberg felt humiliated. He immediately called Ovitz. "He can't do this to me anymore," he vowed.

Five days later, on April 9, Katzenberg finally filed his suit in Los Angeles Superior Court, claiming that his contract had been breached and that he was owed as much as $12.5 billion for all the projects he developed at Disney. "If Frank Wells were alive, this would never have happened," Bert Fields, Katzenberg's lawyer, told the *Los Angeles Times*, a remark sure to anger Eisner. Respected New York attorney Herbert Wachtell, also on Katzenberg's legal team, said that "I've had many years of experience as a litigator and dealt with many contracts. The provisions of this written contract expressly requiring Disney to pay Mr. Katzenberg the profit-sharing in question are as clear and unambiguous as they can be."

For Katzenberg, bringing the case came as something of a relief, an important step in his effort to get past his Disney experience. He subsequently gave an interview to Bernard Weinraub of *The New York Times*, reflecting on the transition. "I ran the full gamut of emotion," he said of Eisner's decision to let him go. "I was disappointed, sad, angry, scared, philosophical, sad, vengeful, relieved and sad." Of Eisner, he said, "I thought I knew him. I thought I knew the insides of him. I spent more time with him in 19 years than his wife, his children, anybody. And the truth is, either he's changed, which is possible, or I never really knew him, which is possible. . . . I am aware that for a long time I worked like a mercenary soldier. Someone else wrote the music, and I marched to their tune. And if someone poked me in the chest, I would hit them with a baseball bat. And if they hit me with a bat, I would blast them with a bazooka. And I would escalate this until I reached nuclear bomb time. This was the way I was taught. And it's a very angry place to come from in life. It's a hostile, angry and predatory way to live."

*   *   *

Also in April 1996, Disney announced that Dennis Hightower would "retire." Eisner had finally gotten rid of him. Nevertheless, he issued a statement praising him: "While I am disappointed that Dennis has decided to leave," Eisner said, "it does not come as a complete surprise. When I asked him to return to the United States from Paris last year, he made me aware of his plans to retire early and pursue his long-held interest in education." This caused widespread mirth in the television division. The blow to Hightower was softened somewhat by the fact that Gary Wilson tapped Hightower for the Northwest Airlines board. (He's also on the board of Gillette.)

Hightower insisted he was not pushed out, that his division generated 20 percent growth, and about $1.5 billion in operating income, the year he ran it. He conceded that his "hands-on" leadership style necessitated a lot of travel during his tenure at the division, but he said most of the carping about him from fellow executives had more to do with the speeches he was often asked to give as a high-profile black executive. He said Eisner's management style fostered internal dissension. "We had a This Too Shall Pass philosophy about Michael," he said. "And we also had a saying, which was, 'With Michael Eisner, you're the man of the hour for that particular moment.' "

Despite his frequent complaints about Roth, Eisner expanded his duties and put him in charge of television production, even more critical now that Disney had acquired ABC, as well as the film studio.

That same spring, Steve Burke was thrilled when Eisner offered him a job at ABC, first as an executive vice president reporting to Iger, then as head of the ABC-owned local television and radio stations. He and Iger got on well together, and were soon working closely, along with Stu Bloomberg, head of program development. Eisner was spending one day a week at ABC in New York, which gave Burke his first chance to see Eisner in action on a regular basis. Burke still looked at Eisner as a mentor, but what he saw began to give him pause. It wasn't that Eisner wasn't creative—he was—or that his decisions, in isolation, were wrong, but that the whole decision-making process was skewed by Eisner's presence.

With Tarses still in Tuscany, and Harbert's status unclear, the pilot development process was even more chaotic than usual. Everyone was working nonstop to get ready for the "upfront" presentations in April—the first under Disney ownership—when the networks unveil their fall prime-time schedules to advertisers in lavishly choreographed previews, followed by opulent parties, the kickoff for the sale of national advertising time. Everyone felt his or her job was on the line, especially since Eisner himself would spend two days watching the pilots, deciding which ones the network would pick up, and when to schedule them.

It was a critical season for ABC. Its long and lucrative hold on the ratings as the number one network had slipped away. Its top shows—"Roseanne," "NYPD Blue," and Disney's own "Home Improvement"—were aging, their ratings in decline. NBC had broken through on Thursday night with two new dramas, "ER," which Ovitz had brokered for his client Michael Crichton, and "Friends," developed by Tarses. And it still had its Tuesday night juggernaut, "Seinfeld." With its new mantra, "Must See TV," NBC had captured the young, affluent urban audience most coveted by advertisers and Eisner. During the February sweeps week, ABC had fallen to third place. At the winter affiliates' meeting, Eisner had vowed, "ABC will never again come in third in a sweeps."

Then, with the 1996 development season in full swing, the whole unsavory Ohlmeyer affair burst into public view, first in a brief item in the *New York Post*, then a gossip column in *New York* magazine, and worst of all, an article in *Time* magazine, in the April 15 issue. It wasn't clear who the *Post's* source was, but Ohlmeyer mounted a furious counterattack, with Ovitz bearing the brunt of it. He told *Time* that Ovitz was responsible for "rumors and innuendo that have no basis in fact. . . . Michael Ovitz is the Antichrist, and you can quote me on that."

Even by Hollywood standards, this was extreme. Ovitz was shocked, thought the remark was deliberately anti-Semitic, and that Ohlmeyer "was trying to protect himself. . . . Mr. Ohlmeyer had a certain set of problems, which everyone was very aware of, that induced him into this kind of behavior." He was also upset that Tarses, ABC's new programming executive, initially identified by the press as a victim of mistreatment, was now being vilified as a ruthless schemer.

Eisner was apoplectic about the press coverage, especially after General Electric chairman Jack Welch wrote him a letter complaining about ABC's tactics. He made Ovitz apologize. Ovitz denied he was the source of the leak and assured Welch that he'd never told Tarses to use a sexual harassment charge to get out of her contract. Welch, Ovitz testified, "was aware, as was [Bob] Wright, that Mr. Ohlmeyer had a very serious problem at the network that had little or nothing to do with Jamie Tarses. . . . I called him and gave him my side of the story and he was, as usual, very receptive, he was very humble, he said he understood."

Eisner, too, tried to assuage Welch, and later testified, "We had a very pleasant conversation recognizing that these companies are hard to manage." But Eisner didn't exactly defend Ovitz, telling Welch only that he "wasn't so sure" that Ovitz was behind the contretemps. And to Ovitz, he said bluntly that he thought he was, in fact, responsible for leaking and didn't believe Ovitz's denials—yet another example of Ovitz's lying. "He did not back me," Ovitz testified. "He took the side of the press." Eisner also later testified that he realized Ohlmeyer's bold and public criticism of Ovitz marked an ominous turning point for Ovitz. Before, as the most powerful man in Hollywood, nobody dared criticize Ovitz, at least publicly. Now, at Disney, he was seen as wounded and vulnerable, lacking authority and the backing of Eisner; an easy target.

Eisner showed little sympathy for Ovitz's plight. He told Tony Schwartz that Ovitz was to blame for having nurtured such a high profile. "Like a moth to flame, he seemed to love the press, loved courting the press, and especially loved the reaction he was getting in the press," Eisner told Schwartz. "He now had the unheard of thing: a personal publicist that not only got his name in the papers but forced them to give him credit for things which he was not responsible for . . . the ball was rolling. It was like air and water and life." Eisner concluded, "The [Tarses] episode itself became a source of embarrassment to all the parties involved."

Ovitz simply couldn't understand how for almost thirty years Eisner had apparently believed everything he told him, and from the day he started working at Disney, believed nothing. It was bad enough to be called the Antichrist in print, but for Eisner not to support him or believe him was a worse blow.

Still reeling from the Tarses publicity, everyone filed into the ABC screening room, with Eisner and Ovitz taking seats in the rear. Iger and Ted Harbert sat in front with other ABC programming executives. They watched about two dozen pilots over the next two days. When they concluded, Eisner complained that ABC was two or three pilots short of being able to fill the schedule, which was going to force them to renew some clear failures, like "Murder One" and "High Incident." He spent the next two days shuffling programs, rearranging the schedule. He and Harbert had some furious arguments. Harbert bore the brunt of Eisner's ire, but Eisner also complained to Ovitz about Iger.

Ovitz had little to contribute. With Eisner making the critical decisions, even though ABC reported to Ovitz, Ovitz told Eisner that it was obvious that ABC needed more management attention. "One or the other of us has to be in charge." He offered to move to New York for six months and spend full time on the network. "No," Eisner responded sharply. "We'll both do it."

The situation brought to the surface a basic difference in philosophy between Ovitz and Eisner. As Ovitz later testified, "It was a very complex situation. Mr. Eisner is very, very good at television development. It's also very hard to come into television development and just look at pilots without having been involved in the creative process. And Michael and I were coming in to watch pilots and make decisions on scheduling. It actually was Michael. I was just there. And it's very tough for the people who have spent the whole year in development and then not have the boss, which would have been me, but the big boss, which was Michael, come in and view their work and then start to help them schedule when they have been doing it without him the prior year and the prior 20 years."

Ovitz tried to warn Eisner about growing discontent at ABC. "You've got to stop criticizing them," Ovitz said. "It's irritating. Stop living in the past. This isn't twenty years ago." Although Ovitz had always felt that one of his strengths as Eisner's friend had been his ability to disagree with him, anything he now said seemed to irritate Eisner. Eisner told him, "My obligation is to make ABC work and if some feathers have to be ruffled in the course of business, then that would be part of the process."

Ovitz explained, "I felt that that could still be accomplished without ruffling the feathers and trying to keep the individuals that worked for us working with a smile rather than with a frown. . . . It's just as easy to handle them with kid gloves and get a better result than to handle them in a very harsh way."

Although Ovitz felt he had little or no authority at the network, Eisner was quick to blame him for the failures. That spring, Eisner bumped into Sid Bass on Fifth Avenue in New York. Bass had heard about mounting discontent with Ovitz, about restlessness at ABC, and urged Eisner to talk to Bob Iger. He'd even heard that Iger might quit.

Eisner went to Iger's office at ABC headquarters on West Sixty-seventh Street. He walked in and abruptly closed the door. "I know you're unhappy," he said. "I want you to know that Michael Ovitz is not working out as president. At some point, and I can't tell you when, I'm going to take care of this. You can't tell anyone. But I'm afraid I'm going to lose you and Joe Roth if I don't so something."

Iger had been careful never to complain to Eisner directly about Ovitz; he did after all report to him. But now that Ovitz was a lame duck, Iger unburdened himself. He told Eisner the story of the aborted ESPN meeting, and other incidents that had agitated ABC executives. Iger confirmed that Ovitz wasn't someone he felt he could work for and Eisner encouraged him to call him directly, bypassing Ovitz, if he had any problems.

Eisner reported his conversation with Iger to Sid Bass via email:

"I cannot tell you how good your advice was on talking directly to Bob Iger. I told him . . . I was very happy dealing with him directly if I could totally trust him, if he told me the good news and especially the bad, and if he let me give directly to him my ideas on projects, on schedule, on other creative things. I explained I just did not want to be finessed or ignored. . . .

"So far Michael [Ovitz] has been no help. He still looks at the studios the same way he look[ed] at them as an agent—BIG POCKETS! And since Michael Ovitz has joined, between Joe [Roth] and Michael (big spenders), we are spending $80 [million] a year on talent deals. We should spend maybe $8 million or $18 million. You can see what a great problem we have. . . .

"Of course the one problem that Bob and I both have is Ovitz. He does come between the two of us. And finally Bob simply told me, Ovitz was his problem. After two hours of discussion, he finally admitted he did not trust Michael and gave me many examples.

"At any rate, I want to thank you for clearing my mind about what was going on. Not only did it help, but may have set up the future."

From Iger's perspective, the meeting couldn't have gone any better. Though Eisner still barely knew Iger, and had come close to firing him, he was already telling Sid Bass that Iger might be his successor. Steve Burke, for one, could tell that Iger and Eisner had bonded. "We had a really good session," Iger reported to Burke. "Michael totally understands what a problem Ovitz is."

Not long after Iger's conversation with Eisner, Ovitz called Iger to say that he thought he should consider hiring John F. Kennedy Jr. to be one of the hosts of "Good Morning America." "I just saw him on 'Oprah,' " Ovitz said, "and he was great." Iger was a friend of the Kennedys—they and their wives socialized from time to time, both in New York and on Martha's Vineyard—and Iger doubted that Kennedy wanted to be on television. But he said he'd get a copy of the tape and check it out. Oprah's syndicated show ran on ABC, and when he called, Iger learned that the show with Kennedy hadn't aired yet. Iger called Oprah. Were any advance tapes available? She said no. So Iger called Ovitz to say the show hadn't aired. Ovitz insisted he had obtained a tape. Iger concluded he was lying.

Iger reported this to Eisner, who clearly relished any bad news about

Ovitz. "This gives you an idea of what we're dealing with. He says he sees JFK on 'Oprah,' and he hasn't even been on yet," Iger told him.

The Kennedy incident was much repeated by Eisner and Iger as evidence of Ovitz's duplicity and untrustworthiness, both to others at the time and in later testimony. And yet it's difficult to know where the truth lies, or if their conclusions were fair. When asked about the incident years later, Ovitz had no memory of it, even that he recommended Kennedy to Iger. Clearly there was some truth to his account, since Kennedy had taped an "Oprah" show. Ovitz was also a friend of Kennedy—the two had raised money together for the Municipal Art Society, founded by Jacqueline Kennedy Onassis. Ovitz speculated that he might have gotten a tape from Kennedy himself, though if so, he didn't mention it to Iger. Perhaps he saw a promotional spot for the show and confused it with the actual program. Whatever the truth of the matter, the incident in itself was trivial. But the zeal with which Ovitz's detractors seized on the matter spoke strongly to his rapidly waning stature at Disney.

In May 1996, Ovitz and Eisner had dinner alone, and Ovitz couldn't contain himself. He said point-blank that he disliked his job; that Eisner had undercut him at every step; that he knew Iger, Roth, and other people were going behind his back and that Eisner did nothing to discourage it. "You put me in a position, I gave up the agency, I came to the company, and everything I did you negated—everything." He ticked off the failed deals and opportunities. "I don't have a job," he concluded. "Just give me something to run," he pleaded.

Eisner said he wasn't "ready." Ovitz was still a deal-maker, not an "operator," though Ovitz could never get Eisner to clarify what he meant by that. Eisner lectured him again on the higher ethical standards of a public company. Ovitz complained about John Dreyer, head of PR, and his wife, Jody, who was Eisner's assistant, who he felt were trying to undermine him. "Just fire them," Eisner replied.

"How?" Ovitz asked. "They don't report to me." By the end of the dinner, Ovitz felt he'd gotten nowhere. "I wish you'd listen to me when I talk," Ovitz said.

In June, Ovitz put his mounting grievances and frustrations into a hand-written seven-page letter. "For me, it's just not right," he said of his position at Disney. "I really have nothing to do. . . . I am fighting with the outside world. I have no real authority to do anything. You really do not need me. You need someone who can be happy running point but not looking to grow.

My services and talent are lost in this set up. I can think of a lot of people who could help you more than me."

Eisner was inclined to agree. But other parts of the letter infuriated him. Ovitz had mocked the idea of calling the executive offices the "Team Disney" building. "You're a team destroyer, not a team builder," he wrote. "I've had enough trouble inheriting your fights and enemies. Every day somebody complains to me about something. . . . It's okay because it is human and healthy. . . . I've always had one goal, which is to protect you, the company and our relationship. . . . Maybe you cannot have a partner. You have failed with everyone over the years. You hated Diller. You constantly complained about him even when you went to Disney. You couldn't stand Frank [Wells] or his work habits for the first five years and told Judy and me how hard it was.

"We can talk about this and should . . . but nonetheless I do have some feelings, that have been knocked, stamped and jumped on. . . . I do not give up . . . but let's respect each other's feelings."

Eisner stormed into Ovitz's office brandishing the letter—one of the few times he ever came to Ovitz's office, instead of summoning Ovitz to his. "I never badmouthed Frank Wells. Never. And I never badmouthed Barry Diller," he said, his voice rising.

"Sit down and listen to yourself," Ovitz replied. "You know that is a goddamned lie. You can't rewrite history." Ovitz thought of all the times he and Judy and Jane had listened to Eisner rant about Wells and Diller. "Do you want me to put you on the phone to my wife and Jane to prove it?"

"No, no." Eisner backed down. "But we need to talk this out."

"The letter is how I feel," Ovitz said. "Read it again after you calm down. Then we can discuss it."

They did discuss it—ad nauseam, as Ovitz later recalled—but Ovitz wouldn't retract any of it. The more they talked, the angrier Eisner seemed to get.

Still, Eisner spoke warmly of Ovitz and his family at Ovitz's daughter's bat mitzvah in July. Afterward, Ovitz rented the House of Blues restaurant in Hollywood for his daughter's party. He was a friend of actor Dan Aykroyd, who was a part owner of the chain. Afterward, Eisner called Ovitz in and demanded to know whether he'd paid for the event, or gotten it for free. Litvack had brought to his attention that Disney owned a small stake in the House of Blues, and suggested that Ovitz's use of a facility that was partly owned by Disney was a violation of company policy. Ovitz was flabbergasted; he didn't even know that Disney had an interest in the restaurant, and in any case, he'd paid the restaurant its usual charge. He later produced his canceled check to prove it. But he felt he was being shadowed at every step, spied upon, and certain that Eisner didn't trust him. (Indeed, Eisner continued to cite the House of Blues affair as an example of Ovitz's unethical behavior, including to members of Disney's board.) Life at Disney was becoming a nightmare for him. Yet Ovitz felt his reputation was at stake. He had to make it work.

Later that month, on July 31, Eisner's mother died at age seventy-nine. The funeral was held the next day at Temple Emanu-El on Fifth Avenue in Manhattan. Ovitz and his wife attended, and when they emerged from the service, Ovitz noticed that a car idling at the curb was blocking the hearse from pulling up to the entrance. Ovitz went over to the car and asked the driver to move. He refused, and they exchanged some sharp words before a security guard intervened. The car finally pulled away; the hearse pulled up to the temple without further incident; and the pallbearers emerged with the casket. Ovitz later said that he was only doing what he thought any friend would have done under the circumstances.

Even though Eisner didn't see any of this, he later said he was told by Iger that Ovitz pulled the driver out of the car and knocked him to the ground. (Ovitz flatly denied this.) Eisner testified that this was a pivotal moment in his thinking about Ovitz. "Somebody was driving a car and he thought they were in the way of the hearse and he made a giant scene and everybody reported it to me. It just—I was not in the mood to deal with it or to be too understanding about it . . . not only did I not want him to be my replacement, I didn't want him to stay as president."

Apart from the notion, extraordinary in itself, that at his mother's funeral Eisner was pondering the need to fire Ovitz, this seems far-fetched, since Eisner had decided to fire Ovitz long before, as he had made clear to Sid Bass when he worried that Ovitz might be suicidal.

Ovitz hoped that the combination of Eisner's mother's death, and the onset of August, typically a slow month in Hollywood, might bring a respite. He used the occasion of a Disney executive retreat in Aspen on September 6 to denounce leaks to the press. But the very next day, the New York Post reported his comments. Ovitz threw up his hands. It was obvious that he was surrounded by people trying to undermine him. To Tony Schwartz, Eisner excoriated Ovitz's Aspen performance, complaining he hadn't shown up for an afternoon session, that he was "not in sync" with Eisner "on any ethical grounds," and that he was a "cancer" in the organization, and reported that Bob Pfeiffer, the head of Hollywood Records (whom Ovitz wanted to replace) had called Ovitz the "most devious mean motherfucking creep."

It was by now obvious to everyone near the top of the company that Ovitz's days were numbered. To the extent that he had any friends or supporters, no one was going to risk his or her own capital with Eisner to defend him. As Eisner reported to Schwartz, "Iger was not as direct about his unhappiness as Sandy [Litvack] had been . . . still, by the summer he had let me know that he increasingly found Ovitz's involvement at ABC more undermining than constructive. By the time we got to Aspen, a half-dozen other senior executives had communicated similar sentiments to me, either directly or through their body language."

Nonetheless, Eisner told the *Los Angeles Times* that same month that rumors of a rift between him and Ovitz were "ludicrous. I've been in a lot of management in a lot of companies. I'm sitting here at quarter to 10 in the morning on a treadmill feeling extremely comfortable about the trajectory of the company going forward." Eisner told *The New York Times* during the same period that Ovitz was "a talented, strong and effective executive."

With Eisner's public comments and the reality of his relationship with Ovitz glaringly at odds, a glimmer of a solution occurred to Eisner. Ovitz was still trying to salvage a deal with Sony to merge the record division, and in late September, he had arranged a meeting in New York with Idei, Norio Ohga, and Eisner and himself. During the elaborate three-hour dinner, Ohga went on at length about what a good relationship Ovitz had with Sony and how much he respected him. "You're so lucky to have him," Ohga told Eisner. "Good managers are hard to find."

Eisner grew increasingly restless, and looked visibly relieved when the dinner finally ended. Afterward he lit into Ovitz. "It took you three hours to get to two minutes of real negotiation," he complained. "Why couldn't you get to the point?" Ovitz tried to explain that patience was essential when negotiating with the Japanese. "That's bullshit," Eisner said. Still, he seemed impressed. "They really like you. I bet they'd hire you." Eisner seemed taken with this idea. "Why not?" he continued. "You could run their operations here in the U.S. It's a great idea for you." It was obvious to Ovitz that Eisner wanted to get rid of him, and this provided a face-saving excuse.

"I'll think about," Ovitz said reluctantly.

At the end of September, the Disney board was scheduled to meet at Walt Disney World, and Eisner decided the time was at hand to reveal that he was planning to get rid of Ovitz. As usual, Eisner told some directors of his decision in advance, but not others.

Eisner poured out his feelings in a long letter addressed to Irwin Russell and Ray Watson, his closest confidants on the board, along with Stanley

Gold. Ovitz, he wrote, "seems manic and for many reasons is ill-equipped to lead The Walt Disney Company. . . . if I should be 'hit by a truck.' The company simply cannot make him CEO . . . it would be catastrophic! I hate saying that but his strength of personality together with his erratic behavior and pathological problems (and I hate saying that) is a mixture leading to disaster for this company. You, Irwin and Sid Bass know this already and have many examples. Stanley Gold is aware of the problem, but he does not know the boring details.

"His choice was ill founded, unfortunately," Eisner continued. "The mistake was mine, totally and completely. Maybe I suspected it at the time, but my desire to bring in a strong number two executive, my desire to satisfy my wife's honest request that I get help, my desire to appear not threatened by strong executives, my desire to seek experienced help to run ABC, and my desire to do what was right for Disney, all clouded my basic instinct that I was making a mistake. . . .

"Michael does not have the trust of anybody. I do not trust him. None of the people he works with feels comfortable with his directness and honesty . . . he cannot tell the truth. He says whatever comes to his mind, no matter what the reality. . . . Michael Ovitz has not taken any workload off me. He is work. It is necessary to check on everything he does. . . . I had hoped it was me, that I was dealing badly with some kind of Shakespearean threat from inside the company. It is not. I am sure I am not without political anxiety, but this is not that. Michael Ovitz simply is not a corporate executive."

Eisner also addressed the issue of succession should he be "hit by that truck." "If I had to pick a new president today, I might pick Bob Iger. He is certainly steadier than Michael Ovitz by a thousand fold." But then he cataloged Iger's faults: "He will not get the company into trouble. He is a corporate executive. He is not an enlightened or brilliantly creative man, but with a strong board, he absolutely could do the job. He will want to keep the board out of his way just as he tries and succeeds in keeping out Tom Murphy and Dan Burke. I have found that stupid and weak. They could be great help to him, but he resents them for some reason." Eisner then ticked off all the ways that the board would have to curb Iger's authority, including "spending limits on movies and television shows and series." It was hardly a vote of confidence.

"My conclusion: It is looking bad for Ovitz to continue being president past February. And should I not be around to oversee the selection of a new president or CEO, the Board would be wise in not naming him CEO or appointing a CEO that let Ovitz run the company. I think he would leave anyway and should. The results would be disastrous if he stayed. . . . We should all discuss this soon."

The letter itself wasn't dated, although Eisner appears to have put a copy with the handwritten date of October 1, 1996, in his Ovitz file. Although the letter anticipates keeping Ovitz until February of 1997, Eisner later testified that he told the board at its September meeting that Ovitz had to go. Obviously, Eisner wasn't going to inform the full board at its regular meeting, attended by Ovitz, so he pressed the point in various lunches and dinners with directors where Ovitz wasn't present, and testified that he brought it up in an executive session of the board, saying that "You should know that I'm probably going to work from now on at getting rid of him rather than rehabilitate him." He maintained that, one way or another, he told all the directors about his decision on Ovitz.*

Ovitz knew nothing about these conversations, but he'd already experienced a disconcerting and awkward chill in his relationships with most of the directors. One day he'd walked into Eisner's office and overheard him telling Stanley Gold that he had "problems" with Ovitz. That's all Ovitz heard, but it was obvious that both Eisner and Gold were startled by his interruption. Afterward, Ovitz confronted Eisner: "If you have a problem, I'd rather you address it with me, and if you feel you have to talk to Stanley about it, then speak to both Stanley and me. I'd like to correct the issue or whatever it is you have a problem with."

Then, one day when Roy Disney was absent because he was sick, Ovitz called him to see how he was feeling, even though he knew "it would really irritate Michael when I would call him. I figured I was just being polite." Ovitz had made it a practice at CAA to make a personal call to any employee who was out sick, something he also encouraged at Disney. "They thought I had lost my mind," he said, but he persisted, and most people seemed to appreciate it. But when he reached Roy, with whom he'd always had a cordial relationship, "it was like talking to an ice cube." (Roy said he had no recollection of such a call.)

Ovitz expounded at considerable length on his deteriorating relationships with Disney directors when he was later asked to testify about the subject:

---

* Eisner later qualified that recollection, testifying: "I just can't remember whether it was at an executive session or I just let each of the directors know . . . but I know it transpired." Other directors, including Gold and Roy, had no recollection of any discussion of Ovitz at an executive session.

You would have to be a raving idiot, totally insensitive, imperceptive and stupid to not feel the vibrations that you got from some of those people from the beginning—if I put it on a graph . . . it would move down geometrically each month. And I exclude Litvack from all of this because he was, you know, the Cardinal Richelieu of the group. . . . To the best of my knowledge, I believe that Stanley Gold and Irwin Russell knew everything first. Then Tom Murphy and the others . . . and on the other side, I don't believe that Cardon Walker or Bob Stern or Dick Nunis or Ignacio Lozano or Reveta Bowers knew anything first. They knew it eventually . . . that was my perception of it. It was the way I interfaced with these people. It started fantastic and it quickly— I could feel it start to go downhill. I could feel Roy Disney turn on me. I could just feel it. Now why would he do that? I never had any interaction with him to make him do that. So . . . somebody had to be saying it to him . . . so I assumed when I felt him going south on me it had to come from Eisner. And I felt the same thing from the other directors that I mentioned.

At the same time, Ovitz remained convinced that Eisner could also turn the situation around, both with directors and in the media, with just a few firm words of support. "I went to him many times," Ovitz testified, "and asked him to just please, please make some comment that backs me up. I said, 'You've got to back me up. This is the kind of thing that I told you before I got here conceivably could happen. . . .' He could have stopped this in its tracks by just making the appropriate public statements, but he refused to do it."

Nonetheless, on September 30, the same evening he was briefing directors about his decision to fire Ovitz, Eisner agreed to appear with his beleaguered president on CNN's "Larry King Live" via a live satellite hookup from Orlando. Eisner said nothing about his own nearly constant concerns that Ovitz wasn't telling the truth and couldn't be trusted, and instead suggested that false rumors of a rift between him and Ovitz were being planted by unspecified "enemies."

"Michael," King said, "when Frank Wells died, he was a close friend of yours and a great guy. We knew him very— You replace him with Michael Ovitz. First, would you do that again?"

"I actually offered it when Frank Wells was alive," Eisner replied. "Frank and I both wanted Michael to join us and Frank selfishly would say to me consistently that we needed Michael Ovitz in this company."

"Really?"

"Absolutely," Eisner continued. "And I've known Michael Ovitz since he tried to sell me a game show in the early '70s and I got annoyed because he sent flowers to my wife because he thought she liked the show. He hasn't sent her flowers since, by the way."

"So Michael Eisner, you would hire Michael Ovitz again today?"

"Yes. Are you offering him again?"

"No. All things being . . ."

"Yes. The answer is yes," Eisner said.

"I mean," King continued, "that would certainly clear up any rift stories. Have you any idea—"

"By the way," Eisner interrupted, "there has not been one story where one person is quoted directly about any problems inside our company. It's just all baloney. The fact of the matter is, we, together, have almost as many enemies as Saddam Hussein, and so it's very difficult not to have this kind of gossiping."

"So Michael Eisner, what you're saying, before we take a break, is this is enemies involved. These are people who are in competition with you spreading stuff that isn't true?"

"I don't know who's spreading stuff," Eisner replied. "First of all, it's minuscule. . . . As far as we're concerned, it's an irrelevant gossipmongering kind of thing and they wouldn't be interested in us if we weren't doing well. So I guess we should sort of be flattered."

Eisner later testified about the appearance on "Larry King," saying, "I was telling the board that the Ovitz situation was coming to an end. I had gotten myself or we had gotten ourselves into this interview, so I was trying as best I could as I now try to recall this, that I was 'frumping' [apparently, Eisner's slang for evading the truth] . . . I was trying to obfuscate not trying to answer that directly in that I told the board that very weekend that we were beginning to unravel Mr. Ovitz's arrangement and that I had decided by this time that he had to leave the company."

However misleading to the public, Eisner's evasive performance wasn't lost on Ovitz. "Even when we went on 'Larry King' together he never came out and took my back, ever," Ovitz maintained. "He just wouldn't commit himself to do it. He would say he would do it but he didn't do it."

Still, Ovitz was wholly unprepared when he got an unexpected visit from Litvack the following week. Ovitz was on the phone, but Litvack walked in anyway and waited. Ovitz avoided looking at him, figuring he'd leave, but Litvack kept staring at him. Finally Ovitz hung up. "How can I help you?" he asked.

"You can't help me," Litvack replied. He walked to the chair across the desk from Ovitz and sat down. "I'm here to tell you that Michael doesn't want you in the company. You're being terminated."

Ovitz was dumbfounded. He looked away, refusing to meet Litvack's gaze. He couldn't believe what he'd just heard. There was an awkward silence. Then Ovitz said, "Is this you, Sandy, speaking or is Michael aware of this?" Ovitz couldn't believe that Eisner, who even at this juncture Ovitz considered his closest friend, wouldn't face him himself, and instead had sent the one man in the company Ovitz most detested.

"Michael is the one who sent me here to do this," Litvack responded. Ovitz was churning with emotion: hurt, anger, and a sense of betrayal by Eisner, contempt for Litvack, who, he later testified, "took great joy in telling me to leave. . . . I was sure that he was enjoying every second of it."

Ovitz asked again if Eisner knew what Litvack was doing, and Litvack assured him that it was all Eisner's idea. He's "serious," Litvack added.

"If Michael wants to fire me and end my contract with the company, he'd better come in and tell me himself, because I'm not going to accept your word or your position," Ovitz said, becoming angry.

"Well, you are not to be here. And we are . . ."

Ovitz cut him off. "Sandy, you are going to have to pull me out of here. I'm not leaving."

Litvack sat there in silence. Ovitz avoided looking at him. Litvack kept staring at him, and finally Ovitz returned his gaze with a withering look. Litvack got up and left.

Ovitz was stunned by the encounter. He didn't know whom to turn to. He didn't even call his wife, afraid that he'd just upset her. He left the office and walked alone around the Disney campus, his mind racing. On some level he still couldn't believe that Eisner was behind it all. He knew Litvack had detested him from his first day at the company; perhaps he was trying to precipitate something on his own. If Eisner was behind it, he wondered who else knew. If Eisner hadn't told anyone else, perhaps Ovitz could still change his mind. As he later testified, "I wasn't going to let them beat me. I was going to make it work."

Whether Eisner was behind it or not, Ovitz realized he'd have to confront him. He couldn't bear the uncertainty.

Later that afternoon, he went into Eisner's office and closed the door. He asked if Eisner had sent Litvack to fire him, and Eisner admitted he had. "How could you?" Ovitz asked. "After thirty years of friendship, how could you?"

Eisner was silent. Finally he said, "We need to resolve this. We need to put a good face on this."

"Well, I'm not going anywhere," Ovitz replied. "You made a lot of promises to me before I came here. I'm still learning. You can't cut this off right now. You can't fire me. You've got to give me more time to integrate. I'm not giving up on this." With a tinge of bitterness, he added, "I'm just finally understanding how this place runs."

When Eisner didn't reply, Ovitz walked out of the office.

After mulling over the situation, Ovitz wrote Eisner a letter dated October 8. "Michael, I have been reflecting on our situation," he began. "Needless to say, I am as shell-shocked today as I was then. However, after my conversation with Sandy and the many subsequent discussions with you, it seems to me that you would be much happier if I were not with the company. To that end, I guess I should try to explore other possibilities." While hardly enthusiastic at the prospect, Ovitz was now at least willing to explore the Sony possibility that Eisner had been pushing ever since the dinner with Idei and Ohga. Still, he worried that he was being set up for a breach of contract suit if he looked for another job while still employed by Disney. So he added "P.S.: Since Sandy raised his point of view on the company and me, I think I need you to acknowledge this note by signing it so that I do not end up in a problem which I do not want with the company or my best friend."

Ovitz later explained that he added the postscript "because I didn't trust my best friend or Sandy Litvack, period." Asked if he was being sarcastic when describing Eisner as his "best friend," Ovitz replied, "Absolutely not. . . . I had a relationship. Our families had a relationship. And I tried really hard to separate the confused feelings that I had about this . . . but in my body I felt this terrible sense of betrayal by him. And it just festered with me. But I still wrote that. Unfortunately, there is a part of me that is very vulnerable to the people that I allow to get close to me. And it's one of the reasons I don't allow a lot of people to get close to me. And he was one of those few people."

Eisner replied by handwritten note the same day. He was pleased that Ovitz was finally facing up to the reality of the situation and that he might even get another job, which could relieve Disney of an enormous financial obligation.

Michael,

I read your note and I really appreciate the spirit in which it is written—in light of all our conversations, I am sure you realize that I do not object to your trying to work out a deal for yourself with Sony. And if Sony replaces Disney's financial obligations to you so you come out the same or better, and if Sony handles the "Disney and MDE embarrassment equation" by making some strategic deal with us, then we certainly would not stand in the way of you closing your deal. . . . I am committed to making this a win-win situation, to keep our friendship intact, to be positive, and to say and write only glowing things—all this will be assured for both of us if we remain honest and reasonable and direct. Nobody ever needs to know anything other than positive things from either of us. This all can work out! You still are the only one who came to my hospital bed—and I do remember.

Michael

Despite Eisner's plea to be "honest and reasonable," Ovitz doubted his sincerity. All the talk about it being a win-win situation seemed a not-so-subtle warning that if Ovitz didn't leave and find another job, it could be ugly. Eisner himself later described the letter as "This is all just a lot of talk to get him comfortable that I'm going to say good things about him and he could leave and go to Sony and be a winner." And he acknowledged that, even in the letter, he was less than candid, an odd admission given the premium Eisner placed on truth telling, at least in others. "He wasn't the only one who came to my hospital bed, so that wasn't true . . . sincere and insincere is really not the applicable question. The question is could it work, was it possible. . . . I was bending over backwards to make it good for him, because this would have been great for him, and also solve my problem."

Over the next several weeks, Eisner embarked on a campaign to get Sony to take Ovitz off his hands. He seemed to have given no thought to being "honest and reasonable" with the Japanese, and instead embraced a strategy that was flagrantly at odds with reality. "I was actually talking to Sony myself," Eisner later explained, "telling them that I would be very reluctant to lose Michael Ovitz to Sony, that they would have to pay one hundred percent of the compensation that Disney owed him. And that I was only doing it because Michael Ovitz—you can't really keep a number two man from being number one. And that they would have to give us some deal, record deal or something. I was trying to make Sony believe that this was the last thing in the world that I wanted to do."

Eisner characterized his conversation with Idei in comments to Tony Schwartz: "Really did not want this to happen. Never hold back a friend. But if they're going to do it [hire Ovitz], have to do it with my complete knowledge (thinking of Pearl Harbor). I cannot be embarrassed, has to be a big strategic deal that Disney fits into. Conversation about trading my center fielder; he responds thank you very much, yes, interested, I understand."

Schwartz's notes from this period indicate something of a stream-of-consciousness preoccupation with Ovitz: "Iger . . . hates him, doesn't know anything about business, pontificates, devious . . . horrible New York Observer article . . . soon New York Times story coming . . . Jerry Frabrikant [actually Geraldine Fabrikant, a New York Times media reporter] says he calls these people all the time."

Ovitz wasn't at all sure that he wanted to work for Sony, but feeling he had little alternative, he called Idei to postpone discussions of the joint venture and instead suggested that they discuss his personal situation. To maintain secrecy, Ovitz flew first to San Francisco, rather than flying from Los Angeles to Tokyo, but even so, several Disney employees were on the same flight, and quickly deduced that something was afoot. The next day, Ovitz had lunch with Idei and Ohga at an elegant Sony residence in the heart of Tokyo, where they served him a rare Bordeaux wine. In typical Japanese fashion, the Sony executives had a wide-ranging conversation about broad problems Sony faced, what Ovitz might or might not do there, and a vague sense of possible compensation and benefits, further refined in a call to Ovitz's lawyer. The lunch resulted in what Ovitz later described as a "nonoffer offer," more of an expression of continued interest. But at this point Ovitz wasn't paying that much attention, because while reflecting on the plane and as the discussions unfolded, he'd already decided that he didn't want to work for Sony. He was still determined to stay and succeed at Disney. He left Tokyo at 5:30 P.M. and was in his office at Disney the next morning, less than thirty-six hours after leaving.

"When I was in Japan and I was at Sony and I was with these guys I realized how much I wanted the Walt Disney thing to work for me and for Eisner and for everybody else," he later explained. "The asset base of the Disney Company provided me a better platform than the asset base of the Sony Company. And I would rather deal with the devil I knew than the devil I didn't know. I didn't assume for a moment that the politics inside Sony would be any easier than the politics inside Disney. I figured that the only difference was that I didn't speak Japanese." On November 1, Ovitz sent Eisner another handwritten note. "I have decided to end the discussions and recommit myself to you and Disney."

Eisner was beside himself. His money- and face-saving plan was in shambles. Ovitz seemed to be in some kind of denial; staying at Disney was not an option. Eisner had been eagerly keeping tabs on progress between Ovitz and Sony. He'd heard that Sony had offered Ovitz $5 million. Ovitz said they'd mentioned $3.5 million to his lawyer. Barry Diller reported a rumor that Ovitz wanted profit participation and guarantees of autonomy. Angry that the deal had fallen through, Eisner blamed Ovitz for overreaching, just as he assumed he'd done with Universal. He was even angrier when Ovitz insisted he hadn't overreached and had only asked for the same $1 million base pay he received from Disney, and that "no other financial discussion took place." Eisner didn't believe him. But when Eisner said yet again that Ovitz was going to have to leave, Ovitz responded that he was going to "chain himself to the desk."

No one was more surprised by Ovitz's lengthening tenure than Iger, who'd been told in April by Eisner that he was going to "solve" the Ovitz problem. Iger felt he was in a difficult situation, nominally reporting to Ovitz, but knowing that Ovitz had no authority and was about to be fired. Ovitz asked Iger to have dinner with him at Hamburger Hamlet after he returned from Tokyo, hoping to mend their relationship. But Iger was finding it increasingly tiresome to maintain the charade that Ovitz had any real role at the company. At times the dinner became contentious, with Ovitz at one point warning Iger that he should stop acting like he was a lame duck. "You'd better show me some respect," Ovitz warned, insisting that Eisner would never fire him. After dinner, as they waited for their cars, Ovitz said, "I have a feeling I have a problem with you."

"The problem," Iger replied, "is that I never know where the truth starts and stops with you."

Ovitz looked startled, and said nothing.

In an effort to get Ovitz to face reality, Eisner wrote him a long letter dated November 10, cataloging his problems with him and insisting there was no way to repair the damage.

> I am responding to your request that I let you know whether we can continue in this present management structure. The answer we really cannot. We have discussed the problems over and over again. And no matter what we do, the basic facts do not change. You do not provide what the company needs at this time, you do not like being number two in a company, and you don't really understand or like or are capable of managing a public company such as Disney.

Eisner cited the Brad Grey negotiations, and the Tele-TV suggestion during Ovitz's first two days.

> I started to question my judgment in putting us together. By Labor Day I was wondering what it would cost in dollars and embarrassment to end our cor-

porate partnership right away. Of course the Jamie Tarses incident only made me more concerned that I had brought in somebody with very questionable judgment.

Eisner reviewed his memo of October 10 the prior year, adding,

I also tried to talk to you but never could get connected. Even on the plane, I could not get your attention. Once I even told you that "There is no way to talk to you. You are too interested in talking to Laura Landro [who covered the entertainment industry] at the Wall Street Journal." You were late for almost all meetings. And often you lost your temper, to pilots, drivers, little people.

I do not think there is any doubt but that you started off slowly and poorly. You were nervous and wanted to impress everybody. And you would agree that this was a mistake. No matter what I did to try to help and guide you those first few months, it was impossible. Things were getting worse. By January I was really concerned. I wrote to you that "your view that there is a conspiracy with the people around me toward you is ridiculous." I told you that "I find this attitude stressful, disingenuous, and counter-productive." I said that "it was not team playing," and I warned that "the press is getting wind of these stupid issues. It could be ugly. . . . Many think now you come late to most meetings to show your independence. Everybody is looking at this situation, and it is silly. Why is this happening? Could any of it be your fault?" I hoped I could turn things around, but nothing happened.

By spring it was clear to me that you were out of step with our executives. I am convinced that the cadence problem basically was caused by a lack of trust in you. As we've discussed many times, no one knew when you were telling things the way they were. The truth was often hard to decipher.

Eisner ticked off a list of slights and missteps, from not returning phone calls to wanting to fire Litvack and others, of not following through, of being uninterested in details.

Image is always important to you. I had hoped that company operations someday would become as important to you as image. . . . Michael, a leader of a public company has to lead by example. It is in the little things. . . . Your number of secretaries, the out of control renovation of your office, your attitude to costs.

And he faulted him for hosting his daughter's party at the House of Blues.

The problem I will never be able to solve is the endemic one. You have just been too successful in the past to be happy being a number two in any organization, whether small or very large. . . . You said "you really do not need me. You need someone like Frank, someone who can be happy running point but not looking to grow." I don't believe you ever really understood what Frank did or what it means to run a corporation. . . .

Finally, we do not agree on the way to handle the media. I feel distance and honesty and non-manipulation is the way to go. You want to control or handle or humor the press. . . . That is not how we run the company. We are the media. I do not think your instincts in this company towards the media is the way to play it. And your bad press is not John Dreyer's fault.

Where does that leave us? I think we should part ways professionally. I believe you should resign . . . and my concern now is that we end this as soon as possible and do it hopefully in a way which best protects you in the public eye. I had hoped Sony would have afforded you the opportunity, but it did not work out. . . . I do want what is best for you. You have to decide that, but I can assure you that I would like to remain friends, that I will be supportive and positive and I will work together with you to accomplish what has to be done promptly.

Michael

Eisner sent the letter to Sid Bass, Irwin Russell, and Sandy Litvack—but not to Ovitz. "After conversations with the board members that I sent it to we felt that it was pushing it, it was overly histrionic, it was too mean," Eisner later explained. It also meant that Ovitz had no chance to respond to any of the allegations.

The Ovitz situation was so distracting that Eisner had little time to savor Disney's considerable successes. For all the distractions in the executive suite, it was testimony to the depth of talent at the company that movies got made, television shows produced, and new theme park rides conceived. The summer's animated film, *The Hunchback of Notre Dame,* crawled across the $100 million mark by Thanksgiving 1996, just when the Disney studios kicked off the holiday season with *101 Dalmatians,* which had been completed on a budget of $45 million, even with high-priced talent like Glenn Close and John Hughes involved. Though most critics savaged the effort as a pointless remake of the animated original, Close's performance drew praise, as in the *Los Angeles Times:* "Played with great style and enthusiasm by Close, and costumed to perfection by Anthony Powell, Cruella vamps around in outlandish outfits that include the spikiest heels, a stretch limo version of a cigarette holder, and elaborate gloves with fingernail claws. But her zest for lines like 'I live for fur, I worship fur' can't surmount the great wall of blandness that muffles this movie like a cocoon."

More to the point, the film did $136 million in domestic box office, and unleashed an avalanche of plush dogs and other merchandise. Disney promptly began work on a sequel. In its first crucial test, Roth's "event" strategy was vindicated.

Ovitz was nominally in charge of the studio, and though he got none of the credit, he thought the success of *Dalmatians* might buy him a little more time. His latest plan was to use the Christmas holiday, when their families would be together in Aspen, to spend time alone with Eisner and convince him to change his mind. He started work on an elaborate presentation that would highlight his achievements during the year he'd been there, the initiatives he had under way, and the ways he planned to address Eisner's concerns in the future. His wife, in particular, had encouraged him not to give up: "Her advice was I should beat all these people and stay there and not lose my long-term point of view. She was dead set against me leaving. She was very upset with the way I was being treated," Ovitz testified. Ovitz thought that if he could just hang on until December 14, he was convinced he could win Eisner over. That day was Ovitz's fiftieth birthday, and Eisner and Jane were hosting a party for him, as Ovitz had done for Eisner when he turned fifty.

While this might have seemed a long shot at this juncture, Ovitz insisted he still had a chance. "I'm a very tenacious guy," he testified, which was, if anything, an understatement. "They weren't going to stop me. I was going to make this work. I knew if I could get through the middle of December and I made my presentation that he would give me the time that I needed to do it . . . since we were best friends for all those years I actually expected him to do it. And I thought he had an obligation to the company to take the shot to let me do it because . . . you can't decide if someone can do something on a macro basis in 11 months." Ovitz redoubled his efforts at the company, meeting with department heads, trying to keep the Sony joint venture alive, trying to recruit a new executive for Hollywood Records.

Eisner was dumbfounded that Ovitz was continuing to act as though nothing had happened. On Halloween, he'd met with board member Gary Wilson, Ovitz's best friend on the board apart from Eisner himself, in an effort to enlist Wilson's help in getting Ovitz to face reality. He described the failure of the Sony plan, mentioned an aborted effort by George Mitchell to get Ovitz appointed by Clinton as a special trade representative, and finally concluded, "that for the best of the company he would have to be fired. But I couldn't fire him because he wouldn't accept being fired," as Eisner put it.

Over Thanksgiving the Eisners were staying in California rather than going to Vermont. The Ovitzes usually went to Aspen, but with practically no snow in the Rockies that year, they decided to spend Thanksgiving in the Caribbean, on the 170-foot yacht Ovitz owned jointly with Gary Wilson. The boat spent summers in the Mediterranean, winters in the Caribbean, and had a crew of twelve. Although Thanksgiving was Wilson's allotted time on the boat, at Eisner's urging he invited Ovitz and his family to share the holiday with him and his wife. Ovitz unburdened himself about his plight at Disney during their five days together on the yacht. Unknown to Ovitz, Wilson reported the conversations by cell phone to Eisner, and Eisner took notes.

"Gary Wilson. 12/1/96," Eisner's notes read. "Interesting. Hard to put in summary. In and out of focus. Wanted to talk. Got more focused. Attitude in general equals 'wounded animal in a corner.' [illegible] Loyal friend, devastating enemy. Severely wounded. Blames problem on MDE and people around me—Litvack, Dreyer, etc. Feels he can do job has not been given a fair chance—attitude will have dangerous consequences.

"Judy is emotional. Devastated about—feel betrayed—she blames herself—feel she convinced him.

"He was very emotional. Got more lucid.

"Accomplish. He does recognize it will not go. Out of denial. Board meeting started it.

"Gary Wilson judgment [illegible] in two ways he is afraid that he will get screwed and he is embarrassed—a major point—saving face.

"Still came back and wants to stay but will be available to discuss settlement—I must be magnanimous.

"Deal should be sooner rather than later."

Just when it seemed that Ovitz's plight couldn't get worse, Martin Scorsese's first film under his new Ovitz-brokered deal for Disney blew up into a cause célèbre. Just after Thanksgiving, the Chinese government issued a brief statement warning that Scorsese's forthcoming film *Kundun*, about the early years of the Dalai Lama and his flight from Tibet, jeopardized Disney's business in China. Disney hastily issued a terse statement that it would proceed with the film, a stand that earned Eisner plaudits in Hollywood for standing up for freedom of expression.

In fact, Eisner was furious. He couldn't have cared less about striking a blow against Tibetan Buddhist oppression. He'd always thought the script for *Kundun,* written by Melissa Mathison, then Harrison Ford's wife, was boring, and he'd only agreed to make the $30 million film because Ovitz assured him the Chinese didn't care and because Ovitz was so eager to get a prestigious director like Scorsese to Disney. Universal had passed on the project, and Disney had paid Universal $10 million when it acquired *Kundun* and another project in development there.

When Eisner confronted Ovitz with this debacle, Ovitz protested that he had told the Chinese about *Kundun,* and that none of the top officials objected. He pointed out that there were at least two other films about Tibet in production (including *Seven Years in Tibet,* starring Brad Pitt), both more overtly anti-Chinese than the Scorsese film. The Chinese protest had come from some lower-ranking bureaucrat outside Ovitz's circle of influence and wouldn't amount to much.

By now, Ovitz realized that nothing he said would have any effect. Eisner felt it was just the latest example of how everything Ovitz touched turned into a problem for him. He was especially angry because he had clearly delegated responsibility for international operations to Ovitz. China and Japan were supposed to be Ovitz's strong suits. Ovitz had high-level contacts in the secretive Chinese leadership, and he'd traveled to China to negotiate an expansion of Disney's business there, pressing such issues as copyright protection and the possibility of a theme park in Hong Kong. And now this. Eisner had to hire former secretary of state Henry Kissinger to try to mend fences by assuring the Chinese that Disney wouldn't promote the film aggressively, and that it would be a box-office failure. "It will die a quiet death," Eisner assured the Chinese.

For Eisner, *Kundun* was the last straw. Encouraged by Wilson's cell phone reports that Ovitz was finally facing up to reality and was willing to discuss a settlement, Eisner summoned Ovitz to his office the following week and told him that they had to negotiate a settlement of his contract. Ovitz seemed to agree; he said nothing further about chaining himself to his desk. Eisner reported in a letter to Irwin Russell, "I met with Michael Ovitz today who wants to bring our discussions to a conclusion this week. Wants you and Bob Goldman [Ovitz's financial adviser] to settle out his contract immediately and sign it by week's end." Despite Eisner's interpretation of the meeting, Ovitz had still not accepted the fact that he was being fired. Although he was deeply depressed and overwrought, he still clung to the notion that, if he could hang on until Christmas, he'd turn things around, even as he authorized Goldman and his lawyers to begin negotiations on his behalf.

Though Eisner kept various board members informed of these developments in his usual sporadic way, neither the board nor any of its committees appears to have ever met to consider how to resolve the Ovitz situation, even though the bylaws provide for the removal of Disney's president by the board.*

Remarkably, at a December 10 meeting of the Executive Performance Plan Committee, which determined executive bonuses, including Eisner's and Ovitz's, the committee voted to give Ovitz a bonus for 1996 of $7.5 million. Irwin Russell argued that Ovitz "had performed diligently according to his particular mode of operation even though we had determined that it had not been effective for the company." Eisner attended the meeting and raised no objection. Indeed, he'd met with Russell in advance of the meeting, on December 6, and Russell's notes indicate that Eisner thought Ovitz should get the bonus if he "keeps mouth shut."

Ovitz seems to have never given much thought to what he would be paid if he were, in fact, fired, in part because in his own mind, he hadn't accepted that it was inevitable. Still, he was certainly aware that had he taken a job with Sony, or become a trade ambassador, or simply resigned, as Litvack and Eisner had tried so hard to get him to do, he would forfeit what would otherwise be due him under his contract. "I didn't want to leave and I was prepared to work under my contract," Ovitz later explained. "I was prepared to do what I bargained for. I expected The Walt Disney Company to live up to their end of our agreement. I left an incredibly lucrative position to take this position. I did not expect them several months into the situation to make me miserable, my life miserable, and my career difficult."

The key question was whether Disney was firing Ovitz "for cause," which it was entitled to do without breaching Ovitz's contract, and in which case it would have owed him nothing, or whether his firing was a so-called nonfault termination, in which case he was due the full amount stipulated by his contract. Eisner was aware of the distinction, and asked Litvack if Ovitz's firing might be considered for "cause." As Eisner later testified, "I asked Sandy and everybody else I could find, because I didn't want to pay the money. I was annoyed, I'm cheap, and I just didn't want to pay the money. But no matter how

---

* Eisner later testified at trial that the board met in executive session on November 25 to discuss firing Ovitz, though there was no vote and no notes were taken.

many people I asked I could not get anybody to give me anything but an immediate answer that we had no claim on him." But there's no indication that Eisner discussed this with the board, other than informally with individual members, or anyone else other than Litvack. Oddly, Disney didn't seek any formal legal opinion, either from Litvack and other in-house lawyers, or from outside counsel. Litvack later testified that he did discuss this issue with Morton Pierce, Disney's outside counsel at the Dewey Ballantine firm.

It's quite possible that if Ovitz were indeed guilty of all the things Eisner suspected him of, that would have constituted "cause" for firing him. Given Eisner's tortured reading of Katzenberg's contract to support his contention that Disney owed Katzenberg nothing, it seems highly out of character— astounding, really—that Eisner made such few and feeble attempts to avoid paying Ovitz the full amount Ovitz claimed was due him. At the very least, Disney's lawyers could have tried to negotiate a settlement for some fraction of the full amount.

Nothing of the sort happened. As the negotiations continued between Irwin Russell, for Disney, and Bob Goldman, for Ovitz, Ovitz and Eisner met again to discuss the situation, and talked about various "face-saving" possibilities, including Ovitz's suggestions that he remain on the Disney board, and work as a consultant to complete the Sony Records deal. Eisner agreed to Ovitz's requests. But the next day he changed his mind. "I thought that was stupid, like staying on the board . . . all these requests came up, which I thought were ridiculous. I was absolutely committed to not giving him one dime more than we were contractually obligated to."

Both Eisner and Ovitz were in New York the rest of that week, Ovitz for a meeting of the Council on Foreign Relations and to escort Penny Marshall to the premiere of her new film for Disney, *The Preacher's Wife*. Henry Kissinger and he were co-hosting a lunch for Roone Arledge, the legendary head of ABC Sports. On December 11, Eisner summoned Ovitz to a late-night meeting at his mother's apartment in the Pierre hotel. When Ovitz arrived, he showed him a press release announcing his resignation "by mutual consent."

Confronted in writing with the fact that he was being fired, Ovitz was stunned. Everything had been building to this moment, but—just thirteen days until Christmas, and two days before his birthday—Ovitz still thought he'd have another chance to present his case. The rest of the meeting passed in a blur for Ovitz. "I was on autopilot just fighting for my life," he later said. Nor did Eisner recall the substance of their discussion that night. He remembered only that he stressed public relations: "Kind of like, let's say nice things about each other; we will play up the friendship thing." Ovitz did vividly remember one thing: At the end of the discussion, Eisner said he still wanted to be friends, that he hoped this "wouldn't affect their personal relationship." Eisner said that he and Jane were still looking forward to hosting a fiftieth birthday party for Ovitz in Los Angeles just two days later.

Ovitz stared at him, incredulous.

Ovitz left the Pierre at 1:00 A.M and walked the short distance to his New York apartment at Metropolitan Tower, on Fifty-seventh Street. When he got there, a letter had already been hand-delivered to him, confirming the terms of his separation from Disney. It was especially galling that it was signed by Sandy Litvack.

"It blew me away," Ovitz recalled. "I was just amazed that Litvack sent this letter. It was just like poetic justice that it was he who signed this letter. I had always said to Eisner that if he wanted to do something or say something to me, say it to my face and not to write letters to people and talk to board members and go behind my back and tell people who report to me to report to him and not to do what I say and undermine any little authority that I had . . . I was torn inside . . . the fact that I got fired, or whatever you want to call it, the fact that Litvack wanted my job and was very public about it, the fact that Eisner, who I considered my best friend and I trusted, and he betrayed me . . . the fact of the things he did to me when I left are mind-boggling."

After a sleepless night, Ovitz flew to Los Angeles, gathered members of his family, and retreated to Aspen. Judy was devastated, worried about her husband's well-being, her friendship with Jane Eisner shattered. Ovitz spent his fiftieth birthday alone with his family. He didn't want to see or talk to anyone. He had never felt so humiliated, such a failure.

For the first time in years, the Ovitzes did not join the Eisner family for the Christmas holiday. After New Year's, Ovitz's wife and children returned to Los Angeles. Ovitz was too humiliated to face anyone in Hollywood. He stayed in Aspen, alone, for another month. He never set foot in his Disney office again.

ELEVEN

Ovitz's departure from Disney was front-page news in Los Angeles and New York on December 13, 1996. Eisner issued a statement saying "I will miss Michael's energy, creativity and leadership at Disney. We have been doing business together while being friends for many years and I know that both our personal and professional relationships will continue."

Disney made no mention of how much it would cost to settle Ovitz's contract. Although the terms of Ovitz's departure would have to be made public eventually in SEC filings, Eisner was under the impression that Ovitz had promised not to disclose them. He was thus irked to see major news accounts reporting that Ovitz would receive $50 million in cash plus options on five million shares then valued at $40 million, for a total of $90 million. (Ovitz actually received $38 million in cash. Depending on how the options were valued, the deal was potentially worth far more than $90 million. The consensus figure was $140 million.)

Beginning with a piece in that Saturday's *New York Times,* Eisner was infuriated by the perception that Ovitz himself, as well as sources "close" to him, were spinning the story in Ovitz's favor. Bernard Weinraub, writing in the *Times,* said, "Already yesterday, Mr. Ovitz's associates and even some foes were reshaping his image from that of the Disney president who floundered to that of a man put in an untenable position by Mr. Eisner."

In a withering attack on Ovitz in a December 16 email to John Dreyer, Disney's head of PR, Eisner stated his decision to strike back through an exclusive interview with John Huey, of *Fortune* magazine:

"John, I agree with you I will talk to John Huey and discuss with him an article sometime in the March area. I will talk to the others just to say I am not talking on the record or off the record for a while. I want to see what spin MSO puts on the whole thing. Nobody has got the two main points:

"One, he is a psychopath. Basically he has a character problem, too devious, too untrustworthy and only out for himself. In other words, his problems started and ended with a character problem.

"Two, totally incompetent.

"Nobody has either of these two points correct but let's just wait and see what's [sic] happen."

Not surprisingly, the press felt Eisner had been something less than truthful on the many occasions, including the Larry King show, when he had publicly denied there were any problems between him and Ovitz. The Los Angeles Times's Claudia Eller was especially miffed. "Is it any wonder people are so cynical about what comes out of the mouths of Hollywood's most powerful movers and shakers when they have no compunction about intentionally misleading the news media and their shareholders?" She noted that in an interview with the Times in September, Eisner used the word " 'ludicrous' four times to describe rumors of a rift." Still, director Ray Watson loyally defended Eisner in the article, saying Eisner's public comments about Ovitz were "the proper thing and I applaud him."

Eisner steadfastly maintained that Disney wasn't paying Ovitz one penny more than he was entitled to under his contract, given that Ovitz's firing was deemed a "nonfault" termination. Yet this put Eisner in an awkward position: If Ovitz was really a liar, a "psychopath," and unethical, if he had defied orders to meet with the chief financial officer and to take responsibility for Hollywood Records—to name just a few of the charges Eisner leveled against Ovitz to various board members, both verbally and in writing—then why wasn't Ovitz terminated for cause?

Did Eisner simply rely on Litvack's claim that there was no basis for firing Ovitz for "cause," as he testified? Was he influenced by the residual friendship he felt for Ovitz? However understandable in human terms, that should be irrelevant to shareholders.

Though it had actually been negotiated months earlier, Disney unveiled a new, ten-year contract for Eisner soon after Ovitz was fired. His base salary remained $750,000, but his bonus formula, tied to an increase in earnings per share, was potentially more generous. (Eisner had earned a bonus of $8 million in 1996.) But the key element was a grant of stock options for eight million shares that Eisner could exercise between 2003 and 2006, when the contract expired. Disney had hired corporate compensation expert Graef Crystal to advise the company on both Eisner's and Ovitz's contracts, and he valued the Eisner options at the time they were granted at an astonishing $770.9 million. (Placing a value on options is inherently difficult, since no one knows what the stock will be worth when the options are exercised. Disney itself later valued the options at a far more conservative but still enormous $195 million.) *Executive Compensation Report* cited it as the richest option grant ever given a chief executive. Moreover, the contract made it difficult for the board to dismiss Eisner, since the cost of doing so would be so high. Specifically, the contract provided that if the title of chairman or chief executive were taken from Eisner, he was entitled to terminate the contract for "good reason." In that event, he would be entitled to "a cash payment equal to the present value of the remainder of the salary and to the bonus payments" and the stock options would vest immediately.

The combination of the Ovitz payment and Eisner's new contract triggered a storm of criticism. To the outside world, a contract settlement valued at $140 million to Ovitz for a failed year as president seemed incomprehensible. To Ovitz, it didn't compensate for having relinquished his talent agency to endure a year of frustration and humiliation that ruined his reputation.

In a column in *The Washington Post,* economist Robert Samuelson wrote that Ovitz's contract "transcended wretched excess" and that Eisner should pay the settlement out of his own pocket. Both *The New York Times* and *The Wall Street Journal* chastised Disney and expressed disbelief. "Nobody in the real world, not even in the far-out precincts of Hollywood, gets that kind of money for flubbing up after a year on the job," Holman Jenkins wrote in the *Journal.* In *The New York Times,* A. M. Rosenthal zeroed in on Disney's acquiescent board: "Why should a board responsible to the shareholders allow its chairman to pay so much to push out [Ovitz]? Everybody knows that a board of directors is responsible for the well-being of the stockholders, not executives."

In corporate America, in 1997, it wasn't at all clear that board members at major corporations typically gave the shareholders much thought, unless the shareholders happened to be Sid Bass, or Warren Buffett, or other billionaires holding such large blocks of shares that they couldn't be ignored. The long-running bull market, interrupted only briefly by the 1991 recession, had lulled shareholders into complacency and masked a steady erosion of shareholder democracy. Entrenched executives who managed their companies for their benefit rather than for shareholders had helped bring on the takeover wave of the 1980s, when many of them were thrown out by new owners, but the lofty stock prices of the mid- and late 1990s discouraged hostile takeover bids. Corporate governance experts had urged companies to align the interests of management and shareholders by using stock options rather than cash as compensation. The theory, enthusiastically embraced by Eisner and many other CEOs, was that executives would focus their efforts on raising the stock price, which would benefit all shareholders at the same time it lifted their compensation. In practice, few recognized that the interests of someone who owns millions of shares in a company are far different from someone who owns several hundred or thousands.

Nowhere was this more evident than at Disney. From the beginning, Eisner had embraced stock options as his primary means of compensation, and in some years they had made him the highest-paid executive in the country. Eisner often pointed out that he only became wealthy by making shareholders rich. By the time Ovitz was fired, stock options had made Eisner the company's second largest individual shareholder, eclipsing even Roy and other members of the Disney family. Only the Basses held a bigger stake. At the same time that his ownership was growing, Eisner had consolidated power by isolating board members, compromising their independence, and stripping them of any real oversight function. The Disney board had become a travesty of independent governance.

Obviously Eisner controlled the Disney executives who reported to him and who were also members of the board, such as Litvack. Disney maintained that the other twelve directors were "independent," in the sense that they didn't work for the company. But that was defining "independent" so narrowly as to be meaningless. The most egregious example was Irwin Russell, Eisner's personal lawyer, who negotiated Eisner's lucrative contract and who had a professional duty of loyalty to Eisner simultaneous to his duty to shareholders. Yet Russell was also the chairman of Disney's compensation committee. (Incredibly, during the Eisner contract negotiations, Russell represented Eisner, and Ray Watson stepped in for Disney.) Everyone on the board seemed to think that Russell was an inherently fair-minded and decent person, and so no one appears to have raised any questions about such a blatant conflict of interest.

While less egregious, others had obvious conflicts. Director Robert Stern was Eisner's personal architect and was beholden to Eisner for an immense amount of work from Disney, including designing the new animation building. Reveta Bowers was the principal of the prestigious Center for Early Education in West Hollywood, a school attended by Eisner's sons and the children of other Disney executives, who also gave the school donations. Eisner had named Leo O'Donovan, a Jesuit priest and president of Georgetown University, to the board after Eisner's son Breck graduated from Georgetown. He gave Georgetown $1 million and his foundation financed a scholarship. George Mitchell earned a $50,000 consulting fee in addition to his board stipend, and his law firm earned hundreds of thousands in legal fees representing Disney on various matters. Gary Wilson, Ray Watson, and Card Walker (now eighty years old) were all former Disney officers, although, to their credit, Wilson and Watson at least occasionally asked questions, such as Watson's request for information about Eisner's successor.

Even normally passive institutional investors were aroused by the appearance of conflicts on the Disney board. The Council of Institutional Investors urged shareholders to withhold approval of Eisner's new contract and for the five directors up for reelection at Disney's annual meeting in February (Bowers, Roy Disney, Lozano, Mitchell, and Wilson). Eisner was dismissive of the critics, even contemptuous. He referred to "the Wisconsin pension whatever," saying that if the California Public Employees' Retirement System (CalPERS) and the Wisconsin State Board of Investments didn't like the way he managed Disney, he'd personally buy back their shares and added, "I don't have any great desire to have an old-boy crony network of CEOs that just share the same old war stories. Most CEOs don't understand the entertainment business. They don't understand our problems. If they have so much time to spend on our company, what are they doing at their company? I don't see that as an asset. I'd rather have my kindergarten school teacher who taught my kids telling me about our products."

Eisner could afford to be defiant: With the support of the Basses and Roy, and with his own large stake, corporate governance advocates seemed a paper threat. In the end, they mustered just 12 percent of the votes to withhold approval of directors up for reelection and only 11 percent voted against Eisner's contract. Later that year, Eisner exercised Disney stock options, then worth $565 million before taxes, once again earning the title of America's highest paid executive.

When Los Angeles philanthropist Caroline Ahmanson announced she was stepping down from the Disney board, Eisner discussed the vacancy with his wife, and then proposed that Ahmanson be replaced by Andrea Van de Kamp, another influential figure in Los Angeles social and charitable circles. It was a typically impulsive Eisner personnel decision. He'd been impressed earlier that year when Van de Kamp had called on him to raise money for the troubled Walt Disney Concert Hall project, which had been funded by a $50 million bequest from Lillian Disney in 1987 to honor Walt's love of music. Van de Kamp was the new chairperson of the Los Angeles Music Center, which was building the Frank Gehry–designed concert hall, and was head of the West Coast office of Sotheby's, the prominent art auction house.

Vivacious, energetic, and attractive, with shrewd instincts for the role of power and money in Los Angeles society, Van de Kamp had come to her concert hall position with an impressive résumé and an array of influential contacts developed over years of charitable endeavors and marriage to a prominent Los Angeles attorney, John Van de Kamp, former Los Angeles district attorney and two-term California attorney general. She knew she had a crisis on her hands when, in her absence, her fellow board members of the Los Angeles Music Center elected her chairperson in 1996. The Dorothy Chandler Pavilion, home to the Los Angeles Philharmonic, had never been designed as a concert hall; the downtown Music Center was in debt, losing money, and losing its aging audience. But progress on the Walt Disney Concert Hall had ground to a halt. All but $31.4 million of Lillian's gift had been spent, and all that had been built was a parking garage. Architect Frank Gehry, selected by a committee after an international competition, was increasingly pessimistic that his visionary design would ever get built.

Van de Kamp quickly concluded that either she or the board had to raise the money to match Lillian's gift, or return the $50 million.

For Van de Kamp, the deciding moment was a trip to Bilbao, Spain, where Gehry's new building for the Museo Guggenheim Bilbao was about halfway completed. The beauty of the building and how it was transforming the sleepy capital of the Basque region astonished her.

From a fund-raising standpoint, the problem was straightforward: The Walt Disney Company had refused to contribute. Eisner had been critical of the project and said that Lillian hadn't really liked the Gehry design. Nor was Roy Disney involved in a project initiated by the Walt side of the family. When Van de Kamp approached other major corporate donors, their first question was always: How much is Disney giving? They didn't really draw any distinction between the family of Walt Disney, which had initiated the project, and the Disney company. In the end, it would be Disney Hall, which to most people meant both the family and the company.

Van de Kamp began exploring approaches to Eisner. She was warned repeatedly that he was inhospitable to fund-raising. She enlisted the chairman and president of CalArts, who were interested in developing a theater in downtown Los Angeles, and where both Roy and Walt's daughter Diane had served on the board. She contacted Stanley Gold, who invited them to breakfast at his home. "What are you doing here?" Gold began. "I thought that project was dead." Van de Kamp briefed him on the fund-raising problems posed by Disney's lack of support. She knew that the issue of Roy and Diane's relationship remained a tricky one, but she pointed out the hall would bear Roy's last name, too. "I'm not sure I can help," Gold said. "Michael is not interested." Still, he promised to see if he could get them a meeting with him.

It took eight months, but finally Gold called in September 1997 to say that Eisner would see them. As Van de Kamp and the CalArts administrators sat down in his office, Eisner said, "Are we here to talk about a movie? Because I'm against the Walt Disney Concert Hall."

"Should I leave now?" Van de Kamp asked. "Or can I finish my coffee?"

Eisner laughed, and Van de Kamp seized the opportunity to talk about Gehry's Bilbao project, tapping into Eisner's interest in architecture. She seemed to have gotten his attention. She thought he asked good questions, about whether the budget was realistic, how the space would be used, who would cover the operating costs. But then he said, "Why should Disney care about downtown Los Angeles? We're not even located in Los Angeles."

"If this fails," Van de Kamp said, "it has the Disney name on it, like it or not."

Eisner seemed to be wavering. "Well, for any substantial gift, I'll have to go to the board," he said. He said he'd bring the subject up at a board retreat in December. "I'll be biting my nails," Van de Kamp said.

On the way out, Eisner complimented her. "You're a good salesman," he said. "Maybe you should work here." Van de Kamp laughed off the comment. "I'm not looking for a job."

Afterward, Van de Kamp bumped into Roy in the hallway. Encouraged by Gold, he personally pledged $5 million toward a CalArts theater that would also be housed in the building. Diane Disney Miller was delighted that Roy gave the money, though she would have preferred that the RedCat theater be housed in a separate facility. Diane contributed another $25 million from her mother's foundation, and she and her late sister Sharon's children also gave additional gifts. (Sharon died of cancer in 1993.) Then, after the board retreat, and with Eisner's support, Disney came through with $25 million. Still, it irked Diane that Eisner, who had become so wealthy from Walt's legacy, gave nothing personally. Van de Kamp arranged a press conference to announce the Disney corporate grant, and suddenly other corporate coffers opened. Within six weeks, she obtained another $45 million in commitments. Suddenly the new concert hall was a viable project.

The following summer, when Eisner called Van de Kamp, she had a moment of anxiety that he'd changed his mind, and that Disney was canceling the commitment. Instead, she was surprised when he suggested that Van de Kamp join the Disney board. "Jane and I were talking," he said. "You'd be a wonderful representative for culture in Los Angeles on the board," he said. "Jane and I think you'd be perfect." Van de Kamp was flattered by the suggestion. It didn't occur to her that, as the chairman of an institution that benefited from Disney largesse, she might be seen as anything less than independent. Indeed, she found it jarring when Eisner added, "Of course, don't come back to me for more money if you're on the board."

Freed from his preoccupation with Ovitz, his own power now fully consolidated, Eisner showed little or no interest in finding another president. Despite the pleas of his wife and the advice of his doctors, he seemed even less interested in sharing power with a "partner." As he indicated in his letter to Ray Watson, his chosen successor within the company was now Bob Iger, someone he barely knew, who had been with the company just over a year, and whom he had freely criticized, even in the letter to Watson when he suggested that he was naming Iger his heir apparent. Conspicuously absent from Eisner's succession planning were both Sandy Litvack, who was continuing to function both as chief operating officer and Eisner's main confidant, and studio head Joe Roth, whose duties had expanded to include both live-action film and the television studios. Litvack had outlasted all of his obvious challengers for the presidency: Katzenberg, Ovitz, Bollenbach. But Eisner resisted naming him president, later testifying that he never considered him a viable candidate. Litvack wasn't physically imposing and lacked the polish that Wells had had. Eisner couldn't see him representing Disney to the outside world. Perhaps, as so often happens in corporate suites, serving as Eisner's hatchet man had earned Litvack Eisner's contempt as much as his gratitude. Still, Litvack was generously paid; his options alone were valued at nearly $20 million in Disney's 1997 SEC filing.

To outsiders, Roth seemed the most obvious candidate. He was handsome, urbane, and articulate. Just about everyone liked him, both inside Disney and in Hollywood's creative community. In the wake of Ovitz's departure, Eisner and Roth had several conversations about Roth's future at the company, and the possibility that he might succeed Ovitz as president. In one of these meetings, Roth nominated himself, volunteering that "I could be president. I could function as a kind of junior partner. We could be a creative team." But Eisner made clear that he didn't want a real partnership, least of all a creative one.

"I want someone to take all the shit," he said. "I need someone to make the trains run on time," a job description that relegated a president to little more than a glorified administrative assistant. Roth readily agreed that he wasn't the person for that kind of job.

Of course Roth had no way of knowing that Eisner had begun criticizing him almost immediately after he became head of the studio, or that he'd asked Ovitz to line up a replacement. Eisner was suspicious and resentful of Roth's popularity, which he attributed to his profligate spending. Indeed, Eisner had diagnosed Roth's eagerness to be liked as a need to overcome the harassment and ostracism he'd experienced as a child after his father was one of the plaintiffs in a landmark 1962 Supreme Court case that banned organized prayer in the public schools.

In the same email to Sid Bass in which Eisner lauded his meeting with Iger, Eisner compared Roth to Katzenberg: "Joe's ego simply cannot deal with having a boss. Not only does he not come to me or anybody else, but he is more into 'hiding the fact' than Jeffrey ever was. As a result I am again frustrated. If he was succeeding I would be accepting of this arrangement. . . .

"Unfortunately, we lost $60M[illion] over the last three movies, we spent $90M more than what was prudent this year starting with 'Nixon,' and continuing with all our recent dogs. Not only has Joe not asked my opinion . . . about the current films (ideas, scripts or rough cuts) but I have not seen any of our summer releases. I am seeing them in the theaters on opening weekends. . . . 'Spy Hard' cost $18M I think with a marketing budget going from $20 to $27M—Wow!—with 'The Rock' costing $72M with $40+M on marketing etc. etc. Last year we were OK with Joe because he had no problem limiting marketing spending ($5M–$6M) on Jeffrey's 'dogs,' but there are no 'dogs' in Joe's mind on Joe's films, and therefore he chases every film. . . . Anyway, down the road I am going to have to teach Joe the realities of life."

Eisner had strategic planning meticulously document Roth's spending and gave hard scrutiny to the studio's profit-and-loss statements. He found plenty of fodder for his theory that Roth was buying market share and personal popularity. Still, Eisner kept expanding Roth's duties, consolidating under him the divisions he'd separated after Katzenberg's departure, starting with television after Hightower was fired.

Given that Eisner was badgering him to cut costs, Roth seemed annoyed that David Vogel insisted that he honor his promise to let him make some adult films with larger budgets. After the success of *Dalmatians* and *George of the Jungle,* Disney's live-action version of the popular cartoon series, starring Brendan Fraser, Vogel told Roth that "I've honored my part of the bargain."

So Roth gave him the moribund Hollywood Pictures label, which he would run along with the Walt Disney label. Just two weeks into his new position, Vogel got a call from Jeremy Zimmer, an agent representing M. Night Shyamalan in September 1997. "Night's written a spec script," Zimmer said. "We've already sent it to New Line. If you can clear your lunch schedule, you should read it. You won't be wasting your time."

Vogel knew this was agent-speak for a hot script. Vogel had been following Shyamalan's career since reading his first script, *Praying with Anger*, and then had attended a screening of his film *Wide Awake*, made by Miramax. They'd had lunch at the Four Seasons Hotel in New York, and Shyamalan had complained about Harvey Weinstein's heavy-handed editing of *Wide Awake*, lamenting that it wasn't the film he wanted to make. Shyamalan promised Vogel he'd show him his next project.

Vogel spent the lunch hour reading the script for *The Sixth Sense*. It opened conventionally enough with the shooting of an esteemed child psychologist, Malcolm Crowe, by a demented former patient. Crowe seeks to atone for his failure with this patient by treating a troubled young boy named Cole Sear. Sear's disorder is that he "sees" ghosts as if they are real people. Caught up in the suspense of whether Crowe can cure the young Cole, and whether Cole and Crowe are in jeopardy, Vogel was unprepared for the script's startling final revelation: that Crowe is, in fact, already dead, murdered in the opening scenes. He is one of the ghosts that Cole sees.

Vogel had often said that a film executive could hope to read a spec script that was perfect once or twice in a career. *The Sixth Sense* was perfect. Vogel called Zimmer at 1:30 P.M., the minute he finished reading. "I want it," he said.

"New Line has already made an offer," Zimmer said. It was reportedly $2 million, plus Shyamalan could direct.

Vogel's mind raced. How could he close this deal? He couldn't get into a bidding war—$2 million for a spec script was already off the chart. "I'm going to say some things on the phone," Vogel said, "but at some point you either let me buy this or the deal is off the table." Then he offered a guarantee that if Shyamalan brought the project in on a $14 million budget, it wouldn't be killed by the studio, and he agreed when Zimmer asked for a "pay and play" provision, which guaranteed Shyamalan the right to direct.

Zimmer accepted. Vogel's head was spinning. Joe Roth was out of town, so he couldn't immediately consult him. He had never green-lit a project on his own before, let alone given a director commitment to the screenwriter, a rare promise. When he outlined the deal terms to the senior vice president of business and legal affairs, Phillip Muhl, he was initially floored. "I'm getting this bargain basement!" Vogel argued. "This script reads like perfection beyond perfection, and it's the most controllable deal." Kathleen Kennedy and Frank Marshall, already under contract to Disney, were set to produce, and they were great with kids. Vogel said Shyamalan would likely hire a talented but less expensive actor for the lead—Kevin Spacey, maybe—for $1 million. He'd easily bring this in for $10–$14 million total. "If this is not the moment in my career to try this," he told Muhl, "then it never will be. This is what you wait for." That night, Vogel took Shyamalan to the Four Seasons Hotel in Los Angeles to celebrate.

When Joe Roth returned, he read the script and said he liked it "okay." But Vogel could tell he wasn't enthusiastic. Eisner wasn't going to like the $2 million price tag. Vogel realized that by unilaterally negotiating the deal, he had gone way out on a limb. Yet he had no way of knowing that as far as Roth was concerned, he'd gone too far.

Since Roth's presentation at Sun Valley two years earlier, Disney's live-action film strategy had undergone a fundamental shift. Gone were the modest "singles" and "doubles" of Eisner's Paramount and early Disney days; gone was the philosophy of the Katzenberg manifesto. In their place was a star-driven, blockbuster mentality that had swept Hollywood since the success of Paramount's *Titanic* and Warner Bros.' *Batman* and its sequels. The theory was that audiences, especially overseas, wanted action- and special effects–packed vehicles with major stars that could be mass-marketed and quickly recoup their admittedly high costs. Fees for major stars soared to $20 million a picture, plus profit participation. Studios catered to stars with production deals that gave them office space, support staffs, cars, and other perks as well as multi-million-dollar fees in return for "first looks," or options, on their film projects. Rather than swim against this tide, Disney had embraced it—reluctantly, on Eisner's part. Internal Disney documents show that by mid-1996, Disney had more than forty such deals costing Disney about $50 million a year in overhead. Among the beneficiaries were producers Jerry Bruckheimer ($5.6 million a year) and Kathleen Kennedy and Frank Marshall ($6.6 million); directors Michael Mann ($2.5 million) and Martin Scorsese ($1.7 million); television personality Oprah Winfrey ($1.8 million); and smaller deals for actors John Cusack, Michelle Pfeiffer, Diane Keaton, Sandra Bullock, Tim Allen, and Robert Redford.

One of the few of these deals to yield significant results was the agreement with Jerry Bruckheimer. With his understated manner and casual good looks, Bruckheimer had long worked in the shadow of the flamboyant Don

Simpson, a key producer for Eisner since his Paramount days. Their last collaboration for Disney was the action thriller *The Rock,* starring Nicolas Cage, which grossed $139 million in the United States in 1996, shortly after Simpson died of a drug overdose. Since then, Bruckheimer had emerged as the embodiment of the expensive, action-packed "event" film producer. He'd come into his own with *Con Air,* another prison escape thriller starring Cage, and then *Armageddon,* about a meteor that threatened Earth. Costing $140 million before marketing and advertising, *Armageddon* was the most expensive film Disney had ever made. But it was family-oriented, modestly budgeted hits like the live-action remake of *101 Dalmatians* and *George of the Jungle,* both of which happened to be David Vogel's projects, that produced nearly all of the studio's profits. Eisner proclaimed that 1997 was the most profitable year ever for the live-action studio.

But was it? An internal Disney study reached a different and much more sobering conclusion: Because of soaring overhead costs evidently ignored by Eisner, 1997 was not the most profitable (1988 was), and wouldn't have been profitable at all if not for the huge success of *101 Dalmatians* and *George of the Jungle.* Particularly grating to Eisner was that *Kundun,* which opened in December 1997, grossed less than $6 million in the United States, although at least Eisner could assure the Chinese that, as he'd predicted, the film was a box-office failure.

The studio's dismal performance in 1996 had caused a loss that year of $180 million, and at the time the internal memo was written, the 1998 slate was on course to lose over $100 million. "Over the last seven years, the live action business has destroyed approximately $575 million in value," the memo starkly concluded. "Expensive films like Armageddon, even with aggressive revenue assumptions, have difficulty achieving a positive return as the impact of high up-front investment more than offset future cash flows."

Pressed by Eisner, Roth produced a five-year cost-reduction plan that called for staff reductions, a smaller slate of films, and merging Hollywood into Touchstone, reserving the Hollywood name for some releases. Despite the success of *Dalmatians,* Vogel had fallen out of favor with Roth, who proposed getting rid of him. Roth predicted that merging the studios alone could save $40 million, even as it marked a retreat from the ambitious production schedule launched in the heady days of the Katzenberg era.

Eisner replied in a letter dated April 6, 1998, that expressed some of his frustrations. "I would save Vogel," he wrote. "David (even with his drawbacks) can be helpful in relieving some of your burdens." But he criticized Roth's spending and failure to move more quickly to cut costs. "Everything is reaching for the sky. And overhead is still a big problem. We really have got to move on this. A $260M live action overhead for the year is really off the map. What is Miramax, $40M? I think you would have to agree the entire industry is out of control, but we are joining right along. We have to get off the train. We are spending $166 million in cash on development this year . . . the target we gave the board was $80 million. . . . It is certainly against the strategy of singles and doubles I am comfortable with, or better said, what the 'old' business was like. I understand the new market of event films, but aren't we also now into event overhead and event development? We really have to bring our cost down almost $350 million a year to get back into smart business."

Animation remained a separate division, run by Peter Schneider reporting to Roy. Although Schneider largely escaped Eisner's criticisms for overspending, there, too, costs were soaring, and there was no disguising the fact that Disney's new golden age in animation was waning. *Pocahontas, Hunchback,* and *Hercules,* the three immediate successors to *Lion King,* paled by comparison, both critically and commercially. Internal Disney documents show that by 1997, *Lion King* had generated nearly $1 billion in profit, including international, home video, and merchandising; *Hercules* eked out less than $30 million, and lost money if overhead was taken into account.

Cost increases were even more alarming. *Lion King* had total costs including overhead of $74 million; *Hercules* cost $179 million. Of that amount, "artist labor" amounted to over $100 million, thanks to the competitive bidding for artists by DreamWorks. Budgets for the forthcoming *Mulan, Tarzan,* and the computer-generated *Dinosaur* were all above the $100 million level—the cost of a Jerry Bruckheimer action film.

Animation's ambitious production schedule was hurriedly scaled back, but it didn't save that much in overhead costs, since so many animators had been signed to lucrative multiyear contracts to keep them from defecting to DreamWorks. Many idle animators were assigned to Roy's *Fantasia* project, which was now called *Fantasia 2000,* aiming for a release date to celebrate the new millennium. Progress on the film had been painstakingly slow, as Roy and his creative team sifted through the vast archives of classical music. According to Eisner, some years earlier, he met backstage with Leonard Bernstein after a performance of the New York Philharmonic. Smoking a cigarette and draped in a cape, the maestro looked frail to Eisner, but he was enthusiastic, especially when Eisner suggested a segment using music from the Beatles. But Bernstein had died in 1990. In his place, Roy recruited James Levine, the Metropolitan Opera's principal conductor and music director, as the film's music adviser.

Although Roy had spurned Eisner's Beatles idea as inappropriate for a film featuring classical music, Eisner kept close tabs on the film's progress, and after a trip to his son Eric's high school graduation, insisted that Edward Elgar's "Pomp and Circumstance" be one of the compositions featured in a segment. "Everyone can relate to 'Pomp and Circumstance,' " he said at a meeting with Roy and the animators, noting that he'd just heard it at his son's graduation. Roy said nothing, but everyone could tell from the strained look on his face that he didn't like the idea. Eisner proceeded to outline a plot for the segment: all the classic Disney heroes and heroines—Cinderella and Prince Charming, Ariel and Eric—march in a wedding procession carrying their future babies, which they would present in a ceremony. There was dead silence in the room. "Okay," Roy finally said, with notably little enthusiasm.

When Eisner left, the animators were in an uproar. "Pomp and Circumstance" might have been classic graduation music, but the animators (and many critics) deemed it mediocre even by Elgar standards. Roy hated the idea. The mass wedding procession seemed like something out of a Korean religious cult. And showing the hallowed Disney characters as married with babies implied they had engaged in sex. The very thought was unsettling. Still, Roy reluctantly concluded they would have to try to implement Eisner's idea.

Several animators were assigned the task, and came up with a mythological Greco-Roman setting for the ceremony, with classical architecture and gardens. Various characters paraded by carrying babies or pushing them in perambulators and strollers. When they unveiled the segment to Roy and the other animators, there was stunned silence. "This is an appalling abuse of the characters," one animator said. "It's terrible." The animators flatly refused to continue work on the segment. Roy and Schumacher finally conveyed the news to Eisner, who reluctantly gave up the idea of the babies. "I don't care what you do with it, but you have to use 'Pomp and Circumstance,' " he finally said. Roy concluded it was the price he'd have to pay to get the film made.

Just as the original *Fantasia* had been a commercial fiasco, Eisner knew that a sequel featuring short episodes of traditional animation set to classical music would never be another *Lion King* or *Beauty and the Beast*. The success of animation had spilled over into so many other Disney businesses. The theme parks and especially the Disney stores needed new hit characters, and they weren't getting them. The only bright spot was Pixar, which had created Buzz Lightyear and Woody in *Toy Story*. But Pixar's success was a double-edged sword, since Disney didn't own the company.

In the course of renegotiating the Disney relationship with Pixar, Roth presented Eisner with a proposal that would both solve the issue of succession and address the faltering performance of the animation division. It was admittedly bold: Disney should buy Pixar (as it could have done years earlier) and merge its own animation division into it. "Make it all digital," Roth urged. "That's the future." As part of the deal, Eisner should make Steve Jobs, Pixar's chairman, president of Disney. "Jobs is a darling of Wall Street," Roth argued, "and you'd get John Lasseter, the greatest creative mind that's come out of Disney."

That idea went nowhere.

By late 1997, Peter Schneider and his top deputy, Thomas Schumacher, were increasingly absorbed by the stage production of *The Lion King,* Disney's second venture in live Broadway theater, even as they struggled with running the animation division. *Beauty and the Beast* had opened at the Palace Theater, but now Disney had finished renovating the New Amsterdam. Elton John was also developing a popular musical version of the Verdi opera *Aida,* but Eisner insisted on *Lion King* as a musical. He was convinced that anything *Lion King* would be a success.

Schneider and Schumacher insisted that the $20 million show had to be different, original, and not just another variation on *Beauty and the Beast,* which cost $14 million to mount. Schumacher brought in Julie Taymor, a director he knew after trying to hire her for a Los Angeles arts festival, and asked her to come up with some ideas. She had never seen the film or heard the sound track. At a meeting in Orlando, she introduced the concept of elaborate puppets and masks, so that humans could play the animal characters. Language and music would dominate, especially African music. "What's so visual on the screen will be replaced by music," she suggested. And she wanted to add to the story to include Simba's "lost years," when the young lion would leave the wilderness and confront the big city. "Julie, we're simply not going to do this," Schumacher said, insisting that the show remain true to the original. But he loved the look, the music, and the images she suggested.

For Schneider and Schumacher, working on the Broadway version of *The*

Lion King was the most fun they'd ever had. They knew it was a success at the first preview in Minneapolis. Before it began, Schumacher announced there were some problems with the sets, and there would be some pauses. But there was a sense that something original was being born. The music started, and the first animals started parading down the aisles toward the stage, and the audience went wild, cheering and applauding.

The Lion King garnered an avalanche of rave reviews when it opened in the refurbished New Amsterdam in November 1997. "A gorgeous, gasp-inducing spectacle," *Time* reported; Vincent Canby in *The New York Times* called it "one of the most memorable, moving and original theatrical extravaganzas in years. . . . 'The Lion King' is told with a theatricality that frequently takes the breath away, and with a sophistication that has little to do with the usual Disney cuteness."

The day after the opening, the New Amsterdam box office set a record by selling $2.5 million in advance tickets.

At that spring's Tony Awards, the big rivals for the top prize of Best Musical were the lavishly produced *Ragtime* and *Lion King*. *Ragtime* was the favorite, in part because of lingering resentment on Broadway toward Disney. Schneider and Schumacher had booked a car so they could make a quick getaway the moment *Lion King* lost. Eisner didn't come, partly to avoid questions about Ovitz, partly because he didn't expect it to win.

Ragtime swept the awards for best book, actress, and score, but then, at the end, Schneider and Schumacher were stunned when *Lion King* won as Best Musical. They raced to the stage, but the show was running late, and all they could say was a few thank-yous before the broadcast ended. They ran off the stage, and couldn't stop laughing. Backstage, surrounded by reporters, Schneider said, "We're thrilled and shocked."

In some ways, the Broadway production of *The Lion King* marked the pinnacle of the Eisner years at Disney. It was both a critical and commercial success, both wildly original and entertaining.

It was so exhilarating, so successful, that Schneider wondered what could come next. It was in the nature of the creative process that you couldn't simply repeat yourself and succeed, at least not for long. Even as *The Lion King* played to sold-out crowds, Eisner pressed Schneider about the next show, *Aida*, which was having problems in development. He worried about feature animation. If Schneider had a criticism of the Disney culture, of both Katzenberg and Eisner, it was that they never knew how to celebrate or enjoy success in a true, meaningful way. It was never enough. There was always tomorrow to worry about.

*   *   *

In the wake of *Pulp Fiction,* the Weinstein brothers were favorite sons at Disney, and Eisner frequently prodded them to expand their reach. As Miramax racked up profits and the Disney studios floundered, Harvey Weinstein was sometimes embarrassed when Eisner taunted Joe Roth in his presence, asking why Roth couldn't run the Disney studios as successfully as the Weinsteins ran Miramax. After Katzenberg left, the Weinsteins had to report to Roth (he took charge after Bill Mechanic left), and it hardly helped their relationship. Still, the Weinsteins were generally allowed to do whatever they wanted, including Bob Weinstein's Dimension films, aimed at younger audiences.

Eisner had often encouraged Harvey Weinstein to create a Miramax cable channel, a venue for Miramax's growing film library and for original programming that would compete with the increasingly successful Home Box Office. In the summer of 1997, Weinstein brought Disney a deal in which Miramax would acquire a half interest with Cablevision in two existing channels, Bravo and the Independent Film Channel (IFC), and would create a third Miramax channel. The cost of the deal for Disney was $312.5 million.

But Peter Murphy, head of strategic planning, balked.

"This is pure gold!" Weinstein protested.

"We're not ready," Murphy replied. Pressed by Weinstein, he acknowledged that he liked the deal, but "the powers that be"—meaning Eisner—had said no.

Weinstein pressed the case with Eisner, but made no headway. "We're not moving in that direction," Eisner said, meaning cable. Weinstein reluctantly abandoned the idea; the channels were later sold to NBC for $1.4 billion.

Whatever the merits of the deal, Disney was still struggling with the Cap Cities acquisition. The ABC network's first full year under Disney ownership was little short of a disaster. Tarses had arrived to begin her new job in June. Eisner had a meeting with Harbert to persuade him to stay, but he couldn't really explain what his duties as chairman were, so Harbert exercised his option to leave. Putting aside the management turmoil—the messy hiring of Tarses, Ovitz's firing, and the departure of Harbert—the network that had fallen to third place was barely ahead of the Fox network, which ran only seven hours of prime-time programming a week. The fading "Roseanne" was in its last year; co-star John Goodman had quit the previous spring. Neither Eisner nor Iger had liked the dark drama "Nothing Sacred," about a

Catholic priest, but deferred to Tarses. It quickly floundered against the NBC comedies on Thursday night. "Spin City," a DreamWorks production starring Michael J. Fox, broke into the top ten, but of course it rankled that it was a Katzenberg production.

Apart from the alarming decline in the ratings, the idea that Disney could quickly reprogram ABC into a haven for family-oriented comedies was in shambles. Although she paid lip service to ABC as "the family network," Tarses showed barely disguised contempt for the lower-brow, working-class comedies that had been the backbone of the ABC lineup, preferring edgier, younger, urban comedies like "Over the Top" with Tim Curry and "Hiller and Diller" with Kevin Nealon, both of which soon failed.

The network seethed with resentments, jealousies, and turf battles. Just as Ovitz had been a marked man from the beginning, Tarses came to the job already enveloped in controversy from the Ohlmeyer matter. With Ovitz gone, only Iger could protect her, but he was in New York, and she was alone in Hollywood. Eisner had distanced himself. Harbert had naturally resented her. Development head Stuart Bloomberg, a close friend of Iger's, saw her as blocking his own initiatives. The knives were drawn, and the complaints flowed freely: Tarses didn't return phone calls; she was petty and vindictive; she was fragile and emotional, sometimes crying in front of colleagues. When her boyfriend, Robert Morton, was fired from the Letterman show (but still being paid to develop shows for Letterman's production company), ABC gave him a $2 million per year production/development deal, which triggered howls of nepotism. Harbert said he had no choice, given that Ovitz had already approved the arrangement. ABC programming executives seethed when Morton started showing up at network meetings, pontificating on branding and other corporate strategies. It didn't help that Tarses had to carry the burden of being the first woman president of a network at the same time as she was perceived as lacking any real authority. Rumors that she would be fired or demoted circulated almost constantly.

Partly as a way to lay these rumors to rest, Tarses agreed that a *New York Times Magazine* reporter, Lynn Hirschberg, could follow her around during the 1997 development season, culminating in that year's "up front" presentations to advertisers. She failed to mention this to Iger. The ABC presentation that year was at New York's Radio City Music Hall. As the curtain rose, Tarses was seated at center stage, her back to the audience, wearing her trademark Armani pantsuit, watching a big-screen episode of "NYPD Blue." As the spotlight focused on her, she swiveled her chair around, stood up, and moved to a podium. "What . . . you were expecting someone else?" she said.

There were awkward laughs at the reference to the rumors of her demise. Then she introduced ABC's new branding campaign: "TV is good," which left advertisers scratching their heads. When had TV been "bad"?

Eisner and Iger congratulated Tarses at the party afterward at a Rockefeller Center restaurant, but Eisner was unimpressed with her, later badgering Iger with derogatory comments and complaints. Then Tarses gave the go-ahead for "Arsenio," as a mid-season replacement, without consulting Eisner. Eisner had hated the pilot, in which Arsenio Hall plays a sports broadcaster. Iger ordered her to cancel the show. She resisted, ignoring Iger's calls for three days. When he flew to Los Angeles, she stood him up at an eight o'clock breakfast meeting, later claiming she had overslept. Then, in late June, Iger told her that he was promoting Stu Bloomberg to chairman of ABC, and she would have to report to Bloomberg.

Just two weeks later, on July 7, Tarses's photo was on the cover of *The New York Times Magazine*: "Jamie Tarses' Fall, as Scheduled" by Lynn Hirschberg. To just about everyone in Hollywood, it was a devastating story for Tarses, the worst of it being Tarses's own words:

"Someone said this job was supposed to be fun. Maybe at some point that's going to start."

"It's no wonder that I feel a little paranoid and beat up."

"I never had a mentor, and sometimes, like today, I think that would be really helpful. Men have an easier time having mentors. I always felt I had to do it on my own."

"Sometimes I wish they would just fire me. It would be so much easier."

And so on. At ABC, there was a collective intake of breath. Any one of the quoted comments would have been enough to get her fired.

At one point in the story, Tarses calls Iger in New York, as Hirschberg listens in: "Hey Bob," she says. "How are you? Really? What's wrong? What lawsuit? Can't tell me? That's OK." She then discusses whether to make an offer for another season of "Roseanne." The problem was that Iger had no idea a reporter was listening, and was stunned to see the conversation in print. He wanted to fire Tarses immediately, but Eisner stopped him. "Wait," he urged. "Be patient. Do it on your schedule, not hers."

Just two weeks later, at an annual television writers' conference in Pasadena, Bloomberg and Tarses appeared together onstage, with Tarses announcing, "I am staying at ABC. I am deeply committed to it and I am very, very excited." Bloomberg added, unconvincingly, "We are having a really good time."

And so Tarses stayed. Despite the soap-operatic management turmoil,

Eisner liked to say that all the network needed was one breakthrough hit. London-born Michael Davies, who was developing "alternative" series for Disney's Buena Vista television unit, thought he had one, a curious hybrid of game show and adventure, about a group of contestants, or "castaways," on a desert island.

Davies was so low in the Disney hierarchy that he was pretty much left on his own. Even so, he felt he wasn't making a very good impression. In contrast to the hardworking ethos of the place, he was erratic. He stayed out late, going to bars and restaurants. He dressed in mismatched jackets and pants, with his tie askew. He traveled to London frequently to visit his friends in British television, though he did make deals with many of them, buying U.S. rights to shows like Charlie Parsons's "The Big Breakfast," a live two-hour talk show. Davies had been a fan of Parsons ever since "Network 7," another show produced by Parsons. "Network 7" used a variety of formats, one of them a variation of the castaways idea, in which four people—a soap opera star, a TV drama star, an ex-convict, and a stockbroker—were stranded on an island. The resulting special mixed elements of *Lord of the Flies, Robinson Crusoe,* and "Gilligan's Island." It was just the kind of thing that appealed to Davies.

One day Parsons mentioned that he wanted to revive his island idea with a show called "Survive," this time with an elimination element. Davies leaped at the idea, and the two developed a pitch explaining the logistics and rules. At ABC, they met with Bloomberg, who passed. So did CBS and NBC. But Lauren Corrao at Fox loved it. "I want this," she said. She recruited a producer named Mark Burnett for the show and assigned Fox business affairs to wrap up a contract.

Then, in September 1995, Disney's acquisition of ABC was announced. Under pressure from Disney, ABC took a look at everything Buena Vista had in development, and Davies was told to move "Survive" to ABC. Corrao was furious. Bloomberg gave Davies $130,000 to develop the idea, though he warned that it would be a "tough sell." Davies and Parsons built their own plastic model of a tropical island setting, complete with a tribal council setting. It was admittedly cheap-looking, but workable, they thought. They expanded their treatment and did a sample video. Parsons and his partner, Waheed Alli, flew from London to Los Angeles for a meeting with Jamie Tarses. They explained the concept: the teams, or "tribes"; the physical contests; the elimination angle—one person would be voted off the island after each episode until there was just one winner. The possibilities for intrigue, politics, and betrayal were tremendous, which, when they thought about it, wasn't all that different from life at ABC. They showed her the island model and then the video, which concluded with the slogan "Action. Bravery. Commitment." followed by the ABC logo.

"How do you pilot it?" Tarses asked. "Naturally, you can't really pilot it," Davies explained. "This is something no one's ever done before, but you can't really do just one episode and then cancel it because of the way it's set up. You just have to film the whole series." Davies realized it was an unorthodox approach. In prime-time television, the networks depended on pilots to evaluate a show's chances of success and, more important, to preview for potential advertisers. Plus, the show would be expensive, at least by the standards of the cheap alternative programming Davies was supposed to be developing. The total cost to ABC would be $13 million for the first season.

Tarses looked skeptical. Still, she complimented their effort and didn't reject it out of hand. She didn't seem to balk at the price. Davies thought she had asked good questions and that she liked the idea. Parsons wasn't optimistic. "This is going to be a hard sell," he said, and Davies agreed.

In fact, Tarses later claimed that she loved "Survivor." Could she greenlight it on her own? It was only her second week on the job. In her version of events, she explained the concept to Iger and said that it would be hard, if not impossible, to create a pilot. Iger said he'd have to think about it. The next day, he said no. "I'm obsessed with game shows," Tarses later said. " 'Survivor' was the neatest thing I'd ever heard. It was going to cost $13 million. I went to Iger. I needed his support. He said no. I begged him. He vetoed it. He would not give me the money I wanted to do this. They wouldn't let me," she said. (Iger flatly denies this, saying Tarses never mentioned "Survivor" to him and he knew nothing about the show.)

Tarses never formally rejected "Survivor." When ABC's development deal with Parsons expired, ABC didn't renew it. Davies was disappointed but not surprised. Parsons sold the idea to Swedish television, and "Expedition: Robinson" aired the following year. While it attracted large audiences, its success was marred by the suicide of one of the participants. Eventually Parsons sold rights to a U.S. version to Mark Burnett, the same producer Fox had wanted to bring to the show.

At the urging of Bloomberg and Tarses, Iger had brought Davies to ABC from Buena Vista in late 1997 to be in charge of "alternative" programming. Under Iger's leadership, ABC had scored a big success with "America's Funniest Home Videos," which wasn't a traditional scripted show, and had launched "That's Incredible!" which featured real people performing stunts that ranged from the amazing to the ridiculous. Iger encouraged Davies to come up with some new, preferably cheap, "base hits" that could be plugged into the ABC schedule. This was a variation on Eisner's "singles and doubles" strategy for the movie business.

Tarses was eager for Davies to develop "alternative" comedies, so he bought the rights to "Whose Line Is It Anyway?" a British improvisational show, and developed "The Man Show," with comedian Jimmy Kimmel, who'd worked with Davies on "Win Ben Stein's Money." "The Man Show" was something of a cross between a variety show and *Animal House,* and the brazenly lowbrow show featured plenty of young, bikini-clad women jumping on trampolines and chimpanzees trained to perform scatological stunts. Eisner walked out of a screening. Iger just looked at Davies and shook his head. "Gutsy," he said, "but you must be out of your mind." "The Man Show" was sold to Comedy Central, where it ran for six seasons. But after the failures of other Davies-backed shows like "Puppies Present," hosted by a dog, Davies was marginalized within Disney as someone who belonged in cable. He seemed an embarrassment to Tarses, whose primary interests were traditional comedies and drama.

Later that year, in September 1998, a tape of a new British television show arrived at Davies's home, sent by one of his friends in London. As he watched it, he was excited. Eisner had repeatedly expressed an interest in reviving the venerable game show "$64,000 Question," and Davies had been trying to find a way to remake the show ever since. The new show solved the problems he'd encountered with "$64,000 Question." It was also a "ladder" show, in which winnings rose the longer the player kept delivering correct answers, and with each question, the winnings were at risk. But there was a critical difference: Contestants could quit and take their winnings after they saw the next question and the multiple-choice answers, removing a large element of uncertainty from the bet. And it had another wrinkle, a so-called reality element. A contestant could place a phone call to someone for help in answering a question. In the taped episode Davies watched, a young woman called her father, and they ended up in tears. Davies himself was so moved by the moment he had to brush away his own tears.

He summoned his new assistant at ABC, Andrea Wong. She loved it, too. The pair rushed from their office and bumped into Tarses and Bloomberg. "My God, you have to see this," Davies exclaimed, practically dragging them to the nearest television. But when it was over, Davies's spirits sank. Both said they "liked" it, but it was obvious that neither "loved" it. "This might work on cable," Tarses said. When Davies said he wanted it for prime time, they both looked at him like he was crazy. "This is so good, someone else is going to do it," he warned.

Davies wanted to get on the next plane to London to lock up the rights. Bloomberg said no. Davies called Paul Smith, the show's creator and producer at Celador in London. "I want it for ABC," Davies said, though he had no authorization.

"Everyone wants it," Smith replied. He was thinking of an auction. Davies knew he had to stop that. ABC would never get into a bidding war. He called his friend Ben Silverman, the most aggressive agent he knew in London. Silverman was at William Morris, the agency that had represented Smith when he produced "TV's Bloopers and Practical Jokes" twenty years earlier. "I want this," Davies said. "If you get me this show, I will get you a package and you've got a deal here." Davies could hardly believe he was making promises he had no idea whether he could keep. And after fruitless pleas to Tarses and Bloomberg, he had to call Silverman back; ABC wouldn't give him the money for a prime-time commitment, only a pilot.

Shortly after, Eisner and Iger convened a meeting of top ABC, Touchstone, and Buena Vista executives to discuss development projects and the upcoming season. Davies wasn't specifically ordered not to speak, but Tarses made it clear he was not to bring up any of his offbeat "alternative" ideas, which would only distract from the important scripted dramas and sitcoms. After Bloomberg and Tarses made their presentations, Eisner went around the table, randomly asking people what they were working on. Suddenly his gaze landed on Davies. "What do you have?" he asked.

Davies took a deep breath. He felt he only had one shot, so he'd have to choose between "Survivor" and the British game show, "Who Wants to Be a Millionaire." Tarses was glaring at him. He knew he was about to commit corporate suicide. "Actually, I brought a tape," he said. "You know how you're always asking about the '$64,000 Question?' This is a game show, and it's doing huge numbers in Britain. This is the show we've been talking about for six years." He got up and handed a tape of the show to Eisner. Tarses said nothing.

The next day, he got an email from Eisner, who had watched the tape. "I can't believe I like it, but I really like it."

Iger, too, watched the tape, and called Davies. "I want this on the air."

After the meeting, Tarses said nothing to Davies. When they passed in the hallway, she looked the other way. When he said "hello," there was no response. The silence extended for weeks, then months. Davies never formally quit ABC, nor was he officially fired. One day Bloomberg, who remained friendly, called to discuss a severance deal, and shortly after, Davies left.

Eisner's long-awaited autobiography, *Work in Progress,* written with Tony Schwartz, was published in the fall of 1998 by Random House. It was heavily edited by Disney people, including Sandy Litvack and John Dreyer. Some readers maintained that while Eisner stressed his low-budget, "single and doubles" movie strategy, Disney had in fact embarked on the same big-budget, event-driven schedule that he criticized in others, *Armageddon* being just one example. Others pointed out that, for all Eisner's talk about the importance of "creativity," there were few concrete examples. Numerous characters—Dennis Hightower, for one—entered the story, only to vanish without explanation after being fired, or pushed out, or resigning.

Almost the entire chapter about Ovitz was cut, deemed too controversial. The Katzenberg sections were heavily sanitized, since the Katzenberg lawsuit was still pending. Even so, the book managed to infuriate people, either by not mentioning them at all, or mentioning them with faint praise. Eisner's relationship with author Tony Schwartz had also become strained. On more than one occasion, Eisner had threatened not to publish the book. He had come to feel that the book had lost much of his voice, and certainly his sense of humor. But in the end, he expressed appreciation to Schwartz, taking a swipe at Joe Roth and Bob Iger. "I appreciate all the hard work you've done," Eisner wrote Schwartz in an email. "It really has been fun and rewarding. I wish all the execs here, Joe and Bob especially, worked the way you do."

For someone so eager to psychoanalyze the people around him, Eisner's book is surprisingly unreflective. There is little sense of what motivated him, what satisfaction he derived, or what meaning he found in his career. Yet there are flashes of what seem to be inadvertent self-revelation. In his acknowledgments, Eisner begins by noting that "I don't praise people enough, partly because receiving praise so embarrasses me. Except when it comes to my children, I am too stingy with compliments and too slow to express my appreciation, even though I know how much people need it and how often they deserve it." He doesn't offer any explanation for why praise would embarrass him, or why, if that were so, he bestowed false praise on people like Ovitz, Katzenberg, and others he intended to fire or push out. At the end of the book, Eisner describes a harshly competitive, almost Hobbesian philosophy seemingly at odds with the sunny optimism he so often invoked to describe his own nature: "Life is a race that I began when I was born, but didn't truly appreciate until I nearly died. The race is about getting it all in." And later, "I spend far less time looking back in regret than I do looking forward with anticipation. There is so much to be done."

TWELVE

A cting on Eisner's mandate to cut costs, in July 1998, Roth merged the Touchstone, Hollywood, and Disney studios under the Buena Vista Motion Pictures Group headed by David Vogel, whom Roth had wanted to have fired just a few months earlier. Vogel wrote Eisner a note thanking him for the promotion and for including him in a recent management retreat. "I want to assure you that Walt Disney Pictures will always be foremost on my mind," he said. Eisner was always telling him that he was the only executive who understood the Walt Disney brand, and Vogel wanted to assure Eisner that he could do adult live-action films at the same time. He had one of his assistants hand-deliver the note to Eisner's office.

Joe Roth confronted him almost immediately. "Are you corresponding with Michael?"

Vogel assumed Roth or one of his assistants had seen his own assistant carrying the note. "Yes," he replied, and told Roth what was in the note.

"I'd appreciate it if you wouldn't go behind my back," Roth said.

"Why would I go behind your back?" Vogel indignantly responded. "Michael makes everybody miserable. He makes you miserable. He made Jeffrey miserable. Why would I want that?" Vogel was not going to get close to Eisner only to have his head chopped off, as he put it. He'd had plenty of opportunities, but had remained loyal to Roth. In the intrigue-filled corridors of the Team Disney building, Roth obviously didn't trust him, or anyone else for that matter.

The Sixth Sense wasn't helping Vogel's relationship with Roth. After committing to star in *Armageddon* as part of a two-picture deal with Disney, Bruce Willis had negotiated the right to choose from every leading man role in development at the studio. So Vogel, after buying the rights to *The Sixth Sense*, had sent the script to Willis's agent, Arnold Rifkind, as he did all the scripts he acquired. He didn't imagine that a star of Willis's stature would be at all interested in a small-budget thriller from an unknown writer-director. So Vogel was shocked when Rifkind called producer Kathleen Kennedy and said, "This is our movie."

The next day Rifkind called Vogel. Willis wanted to play the role of Malcolm Crowe, the child psychologist. "The script is good, but Night's not directing," he said.

Vogel realized the star treatment was starting. "He has a pay-and-play commitment," Vogel explained.

"How could you be so stupid?" Rifkind asked.

This infuriated Vogel, who'd only guaranteed Shyamalan the chance to direct in order to get the script. "Who the fuck do you think you are?" he exclaimed. "This guy wrote it, and that's how I got it."

Both he and Joe Roth, who was dismayed that Willis had chosen *The Sixth Sense* rather than sticking with his action picture franchise, figured that Willis would walk when he found out Shyamalan was directing. In some ways, it would be easier if he did. Because of Willis, the budget would vault the film into the "event" category. But Rifkind backed down, and Willis stayed attached to the project. Since he had other commitments, the shooting schedule got delayed. But by the summer of 1998, filming was under way.

About three-quarters of the way though the production, Vogel got a call from Roger Birnbaum, head of Spyglass Entertainment, an independent producer. "I just wanted to tell you that *Sixth Sense* is my baby now." Spyglass had bought all foreign and domestic rights to the film from Disney. "In terms of going forward, you have to run all your budget overages by me first."

Vogel was reeling. Roth sold his movie, without even telling him? Not just foreign, but domestic rights, too? To reduce risk and recoup some of their investment, studios often sold some rights to the films they had in development or production, but rarely both foreign and domestic. So all Disney would get was a distribution fee. Birnbaum added that he expected a producer credit on the film.

"Roger, you're wrong," Vogel countered. "You may be picking this up, but you have to wait until I'm done and stop talking to me like that. It's upsetting to me. I may be getting screwed out of this, but not yet. It's still mine."

Minutes later, Kathleen Kennedy and Frank Marshall were on the line. No one had told them, either, and they were furious.

Vogel wanted to run upstairs and confront Roth. But he held back. What was the point? He knew Roth was competing to succeed Ovitz as president of Disney, and he was under pressure from Eisner to cut costs drastically. Roth would just say that he'd never really liked the script, and that Willis had driven up costs.

The next day, Vogel and Roth met to discuss something else. Vogel was still in shock. Neither said anything about *The Sixth Sense*. But after that, Vogel felt their relationship was never the same. What camaraderie had existed faded. Roth pretty much left Vogel alone.

Miramax's Harvey Weinstein also bore the brunt of Eisner's crackdown on big-budget event movies. Just as Disney was selling off foreign and domestic rights to *The Sixth Sense* to reduce costs, Weinstein approached Eisner with a cherished project: a multipicture deal to turn J. R. R. Tolkien's *The Lord of the Rings* into a film. Rights to the beloved classic were held by British producer Saul Zaentz, who had been notoriously reluctant to give them up. But Zaentz had developed a close relationship with Weinstein when Zaentz co-produced the wildly successful *The English Patient* with Miramax (winner of the Academy Award for Best Picture in 1997). After Weinstein introduced Zaentz to New Zealand director Peter Jackson, Zaentz was captivated by Jackson's grandiose vision for a Tolkien epic, and readily agreed to sell the rights to Miramax for a Jackson-directed production.

Miramax spent about $14 million to develop the project, but because of the projected budget, Weinstein needed Disney and Eisner's approval to go ahead. He arranged a meeting with Roth to show him the concept, some storyboards, and "animatics," models of the computer-generated sets and a few battle sequences that Jackson had created. Weinstein made the pitch for two films, with a projected budget of no more than $180 million. Expensive, yes, but $90 million per film was substantially less than *Armageddon* or other Bruckheimer projects. "Joe, this will be the movie of our lifetimes," Weinstein enthused to Roth. "We'll sell foreign, we'll get half our costs back off the top."

Roth called Weinstein after he took the project up with Eisner. "Michael passed," he said.

"He what?" Weinstein replied, incredulous.

"He said we're not going to spend this kind of money."

Weinstein called Eisner. Eisner wouldn't back down. From his point of view, Weinstein was asking him to risk a huge sum of money on an unproven director, with no finished scripts, no sure market, no partners. This was not the kind of low-budget, independent movie Miramax was supposed to be doing. Besides, he didn't think *Lord of the Rings* would translate well to film.

An earlier animated version had failed. There was a limited audience for the fantasy genre.

"You're making a terrible mistake," Weinstein practically screamed. "This will be the franchise to end all franchises."

After Eisner's rejection, Weinstein reluctantly let Jackson shop the project to other studios. All turned it down. But then New Line, a division of Time Warner, agreed to reconsider. After sitting through Jackson's presentation, New Line's chief executive, Robert Shaye, committed to three films with a combined budget of $350 million, an even more ambitious venture than Weinstein had dared to contemplate.

New Line was so eager to do the project that it agreed to reimburse Miramax's costs, and Weinstein insisted on keeping the right to 5 percent of the gross. When Weinstein reported the deal to Eisner, he just shrugged, which angered Weinstein. Here he'd acquired the rights to one of the most sought-after literary properties in the world, Eisner had killed the project, and now he didn't seem to care that Weinstein had brought him a 5 percent stake. "You don't believe in this," Weinstein finally said in exasperation. "So give me half the five percent." Eisner agreed; Weinsteins' contract specified that the brothers would each be paid 25 percent of any revenues Disney received, "without limitation."

Still, Weinstein was seething. This wasn't the first time he felt Eisner had thwarted him. Eisner had rejected his cable deal. He wouldn't invest in the Broadway musical *The Producers* when Weinstein wanted to help out Mel Brooks. (Weinstein put his own money in the show.) He blocked a deal to buy One Times Square for Miramax headquarters. But this was a feature film that Weinstein desperately wanted to make. It didn't matter to him that Eisner was fully within his rights. Weinstein had had to grovel before Eisner, only to be turned down.

Lloyd Braun, the thirty-nine-year-old president of Brillstein-Grey Entertainment, was intrigued when he got a call from Joe Roth inviting him to breakfast to discuss Disney's troubled Touchstone TV studio. Brillstein-Grey had thrived in the year since Ovitz left Disney, producing "Just Shoot Me" and "NewsRadio" for NBC, and the late-night "Politically Incorrect" with Bill Maher for ABC. Braun, a lawyer and manager who numbered Cher and "Seinfeld" co-creator Larry David as clients, was probably best known as the character named Lloyd Braun whom David kept writing into "Seinfeld" plots.

Another one of Braun's clients was TV writer-producer David Chase. Braun had been trying to develop a new series with him for Brillstein-Grey. But none of Chase's ideas seemed quite right. "I know you've got a great show in you," Braun persisted. While walking Chase out of the office after another disappointing pitch session, Braun said, "These ideas you're coming up with aren't coming from the heart. Bring me something controversial, different."

"Like what?" Chase asked.

"I don't know," Braun said, thinking for a moment. "You know, I've always wanted to do a modern-day *Godfather*. Set in today's world. You know, a guy who lives with his kids and deals with everyday life except he's in the Mob."

"That's interesting. Did you know I was Italian?" Chase asked.

"No, but that's even better."

Two days later, Chase was back, with a proposal for a series about a suburban New Jersey Mob family, set in the present, a family beset with all the problems of any other American family, as well as a dark, parallel existence in the Mob. Despite the "high concept"—a modern-day *Godfather*—it wasn't an easy idea to sell. The three major networks passed on "The Sopranos." On a long shot, Chase sent the treatment to Chris Albrecht at Home Box Office, the pay-cable channel that was developing various series deemed too sophisticated for the networks. Albrecht wasn't sure if the script was "edgy" enough, but went ahead and ordered a pilot.

When Roth called Braun, rumors of chaos at Disney's television studio were swirling. The marriage between the studio and the ABC network had been ill-fated. Although one of the driving forces of the acquisition was to provide an outlet for Disney-made programming, it was almost as though ABC, with Tarses at the programming helm, went out of its way to reject Touchstone-made pilots. Those that did get on the air, like "Hiller and Diller," were flops. The fate of Touchstone-produced "Ellen" was uncertain after its star, Ellen DeGeneres, came out on the show as a lesbian. ABC wants to "forge our identity as a network that takes chances," Tarses told the *Los Angeles Times*, a comment that sent shudders through Disney's upper ranks.

But during their breakfast together, Roth was charming and persuasive, hinting at changes to come and potential opportunities for Braun. They hit it off instantly. At a second breakfast, Braun arrived to find that Eisner had joined Roth. The pleasantries were barely over when they started arguing about ABC and Disney's TV studio. Braun was characteristically candid. The relationship between the studio and the network was "dysfunctional," Braun said. "You should merge the studio and the network. As it is now, there's a terrible rivalry. There's no sense of the common good. People won't pull for each other. They root for each other to fail." Somewhat to Braun's surprise, Eisner listened. In the middle of the discussion, Eisner interrupted Braun and asked, "How do I get you to do this?"

Braun saw the offer as an interesting challenge. He joined Disney as chairman of the Buena Vista Television Group in March 1998, reporting to Joe Roth. From the beginning, he faced the problem he'd already identified: Far from favoring Disney productions, ABC resented any pressure to pick up Touchstone pilots. Braun often compared the mood at ABC to occupied France under the Nazis. At the same time, the other networks were highly suspicious of the studio's relationship to ABC, assuming that it was steering its best projects to its sister network and offering them warmed-over rejects. Braun was in a catch-22: He couldn't sell to the other networks and ABC seemed hostile to any Disney product. Braun became convinced that it was urgent to merge the studio and network, and pushed the idea at Eisner's staff lunches. By the summer of 1999, Eisner seemed to agree, and began sounding it out with Joe Roth (who favored the idea) and Bob Iger (who opposed it).

Bringing Touchstone and ABC together posed some delicate management issues, starting with who would be in charge of the merged division. Roth, who was close to Braun and had brought him into the company, was a strong advocate for Braun. Bob Iger, as head of ABC, and by now Roth's chief rival for the Disney presidency, was suspicious of Braun as a potential Roth ally. Eisner suggested that Braun, as head of Touchstone, report to Stu Bloomberg and Jamie Tarses. Braun rejected that idea out of hand—he had little respect for Tarses, and there was no way he would even consider reporting to her. When Braun once tried to circumvent Tarses by going directly to Bloomberg, she said, "If you think by going directly to Stu you will get what you want, you're mistaken. Stu has no power here." Braun countered that he should run the combined network and studio, with Bloomberg and Tarses reporting to him.

It was Roth who suggested a way out, proposing that Braun and Bloomberg run the combined network and studio together, with Tarses reporting to the two of them. The idea was that Braun would be the senior partner for the studio, Bloomberg the senior partner for the network. "It's the only possible solution," Roth argued to Eisner. Clearly, it further marginalized Tarses. Braun was open to the idea, but Iger still resisted, saying Braun and Bloomberg couldn't work together.

Braun barely knew Bloomberg, but he called and invited him to his house in Brentwood. "I know what you've been told," Braun said, "I'm a viper. It's not true." As the discussion continued, they discovered they had much in common. Despite Iger's skepticism, Bloomberg was won over. At the end of the afternoon, the two shook hands and agreed to work together.

Braun arrived at ABC that summer, moving into a new office down the hall from Tarses and Bloomberg in the ABC Entertainment complex in Century City. He also kept an office at the TV studio. Tarses's reaction was predictably hostile. As with Davies after the "Millionaire" meeting, her demeanor toward Braun was glacial. At meetings, she ignored him, sometimes swiveling her chair so she didn't have to face him. She didn't copy him on emails or memos. It was as if he and his position didn't exist.

The cold shoulder extended through the ranks below Tarses. Braun's presence was barely acknowledged. Finally Jeff Bader, the head of scheduling for the network, came into his office and confided that Tarses had ordered that no one who reported to her was to speak to Braun. "If she sees me in here, I'll be fired," he said, half-seriously.

Braun also detected a certain coolness from agents and producers he'd dealt with for years, in some cases for twenty years. Finally one confessed that Tarses had warned him that if she found out that he returned a phone call from Braun, his projects would be dead at ABC.

Braun finally called Eisner. "This is an unmitigated disaster."

Eisner urged him to hang in. "I need you there," he insisted.

A few weeks after the merger of ABC and Touchstone, Steve McPherson, Braun's former deputy, now head of Touchstone, set up a meeting with Tarses and executives in ABC's drama department to pitch a new crime drama that producer Jerry Bruckheimer, with Joe Roth's encouragement, had developed for Touchstone. The idea was a fresh spin on the tried-and-true police drama: a series about a forensic team in Las Vegas that gathers evidence for police forces and prosecutors. Called "CSI: Crime Scene Investigation," the series had been created by a young, hyperkinetic screenwriter named Anthony Zuiker, who'd grown up in Las Vegas and had driven a hotel tram. He'd sent several scripts to Bruckheimer, who liked Zuiker's tone and sensibility, and called to ask him if he had any ideas for television.

Zuiker spent weeks trailing forensic detectives in Las Vegas, and his vision for a crime drama jelled. Las Vegas seemed the perfect setting: flashy, photogenic, running twenty-four hours a day, with 30 million visitors a year, an inexhaustible source of stories. The idea also tapped into a public fascination with forensic evidence triggered by the O. J. Simpson murder trial, which had the nation debating the significance of a bloodstained glove. The idea also had momentum at Disney, since Bruckheimer was Disney's most successful producer, and Bruckheimer had the enthusiastic backing of Roth, Braun, and McPherson.

Dressed in black, bursting with energy, the thirty-one-year-old Zuiker gave one of his trademark pitches. To his amazement, and to the dismay of Bruckheimer and McPherson, it fell flat with Tarses and her head of drama development. ABC passed.

Zuiker was furious. He prided himself on his pitches. He promptly named his production company "Dare to Pass," explaining, as he put it, "Dare to pass on me and this is going to show up somewhere else." More determined than ever, Bruckheimer and Zuiker shopped it to other networks, even though it was late in the development season. Braun and McPherson saw this as an opportunity to show that Touchstone wasn't a captive of ABC, and could sell potential hits to competing networks. CBS had closed its development slate, but McPherson convinced the network to have one more meeting. After another performance from Zuiker, drama development chief Nina Tassler made an exception. She'd loved the hit series "Quincy," about a coroner, and as she put it, she loved a good autopsy. Tassler ordered a pilot.

As the production company for the series, Disney/Touchstone still had the opportunity to earn big profits on "CSI." Network licensing fees almost never cover the cost of producing a series. But the production company retains the syndication rights to resell the show after its initial network run. If a program is a hit, the syndication fees can be huge when the show is sold for rebroadcast. Syndication revenues are the lifeblood of the TV production industry.

But Iger had already proclaimed his lack of interest in producing shows for rival networks. Why, he reasoned, should Touchstone incur a deficit to produce a show that ABC didn't think was good enough to put on its schedule? Within days of CBS picking up the "CSI" pilot, Iger convened a meeting to address the issue of whether Touchstone should produce a show for a rival network. ABC's chief financial officer had worked up three scenarios: "high," "medium," and "low," depending on how "CSI" performed in the ratings, purporting to show that even under the "high" scenario, "CSI" would lose money for Touchstone. "What's the deficit per episode?" Iger asked. McPherson explained it was about a million dollars. "We can't do that," Iger said. "Michael won't understand how we can spend a million dollars a show to subsidize CBS."

The potential flaw in Iger's reasoning was that ABC's judgment might not be infallible, and that "CSI" could be a hit on another network. Braun and McPherson were both upset, and insisted on meeting with Eisner to press the case. They argued that it would be devastating to Touchstone's ability to sell to other networks if it pulled out of "CSI" now that CBS had picked it up. Besides, "CSI" might be a hit. Why give up the potential syndication revenues? In contrast to Iger, Eisner often wanted Touchstone to sell shows to other networks. But the "CSI" situation seemed to bring out his competitive instinct to inflict failure on a rival. In the final meeting, Eisner said he didn't care if "CSI" was a hit if it was on a network other than ABC. He also warned that Bruckheimer was a profligate spender, and the deficits would probably be a lot more than one million per episode. Besides, he didn't think CBS would be willing to pick up the production costs, and if Disney pulled out, the show would die, creating a hole in the CBS lineup. Braun was ordered to call Bruckheimer and pull the plug.

The unflappable Bruckheimer took the news calmly. He was disappointed but gracious. But Eisner and Iger underestimated his determination, and that of Les Moonves, the head of CBS. Instead of dropping "CSI," as they had anticipated, CBS lined up another producer, Alliance Atlantis Communications, which presold some foreign rights to raise $800,000 per episode, an amount that nearly covered the projected deficit. CBS financed the rest, minimizing the potential loss. CBS placed "CSI" as the centerpiece of its Friday night schedule for fall 2000.

That February 1999, Eisner had asked Steve Burke to come into his office in New York on one of his many visits to ABC headquarters. Despite his many ties to the city, Eisner was tiring of the frequent travel and didn't see why ABC's headquarters should remain on Sixty-seventh Street. "I want to move ABC to Los Angeles," he said.

Burke was startled; nobody had mentioned the possibility. "Why?" he asked. "Ad sales is in New York, soap opera production is in New York, news is in New York."

"Everybody should be together," Eisner said. "My Monday lunches are the way I run the company. I need everybody there. That's the problem with ABC."

This didn't make any sense to Burke, who felt that ABC's distance from Burbank was the least of the network's problems. "Think about this for a minute," Burke said. "Bob Iger and I can fly out there for your lunch. Prime time is the issue, so have Jamie Tarses come to your lunch. Why uproot five thousand people?"

Eisner shrugged, saying he needed people close by so he could be more involved.

On some level, Burke had an emotional attachment to ABC, where his father's portrait hung in the lobby of the headquarters building. "You're going to destroy a whole culture," Burke warned. "You're saying there's nothing worth keeping."

On February 12, Iger issued a memo saying that ABC headquarters would be moved to Burbank, so ABC executives would be "adjacent to Disney senior management"—meaning Eisner.

Predictably, Eisner's decision caused an uproar at ABC. Several top executives quit. Morale plummeted. When Burke expressed his reservations to Iger, Iger agreed with him that it was a big mistake. Burke pressed him to stand up to Eisner on the issue, but Iger said it would be pointless. Eisner was stubborn, and his mind was made up. Burke wasn't surprised; he'd already sensed that Iger wasn't willing to contradict Eisner, not as long as he still thought he had a shot at being president. Burke's high regard for top management had begun to slip.

Burke had reservations about moving his family to the West Coast, but he was willing to consider it. Then Peter Murphy, the new head of strategic planning (no relation to his predecessor, Larry Murphy), convened what Burke thought would be a routine budget meeting to discuss the ABC radio stations, which reported to Burke. Eisner attended. Like nearly everyone else at ABC, Burke was wary of the strategic-planning department. One of Ovitz's arguments little more than a year before had been that the ABC radio network either had to grow through a big acquisition, or be sold. Eisner had rejected both alternatives. But Burke was now negotiating a deal to combine the ABC stations with those owned by Westwood One, which would give ABC the critical mass to make radio a success.

At the meeting, Peter Murphy launched into a thirty-page flip-chart presentation that concluded the ABC radio stations should be sold outright, and that Disney should abandon the radio business. As Burke realized where the presentation was going, he became increasingly angry. No one had warned him about this or shown him the data. No one had consulted him.

"Wait a minute," Burke finally interrupted. "You've never set foot in a radio station. Now you're using this budget meeting to tell me to sell the division?"

Murphy just looked at Eisner, who had obviously known what was coming.

"I'm leaving," Burke said, starting to walk out.

"Sit down. You're not going anywhere," Eisner ordered.

Burke stayed, quietly fuming. He'd had all the freedom he wanted to run the Disney stores, and at Euro Disney, he had been geographically so far away that he was pretty much left alone. His father's management style at ABC had always been to choose good executives, then trust them to run their businesses. But working at ABC was no longer fun. It seemed like every decision was second-guessed by Eisner, with strategic planning pulling strings behind the scenes.

Coming on the heels of the decision to move ABC to Los Angeles, the radio meeting was tough to take. Burke went to Iger and said he wouldn't relocate to L.A. "Wait," Iger urged. "Don't make any decisions until I talk to Michael." Later, he came back and said Burke could stay in New York and be in charge of all the ABC operations, in effect replacing Iger. Iger himself would move to L.A. in some new higher-ranking capacity reporting to Eisner. Iger seemed excited; it would position him for the presidency. Burke said he'd think it over.

On one level, Burke wanted to stay. The new job would keep him in New York. Turning around ABC would be an interesting challenge, if he really had the freedom to do it. But he concluded that he never would, not as long as Eisner was in charge. Burke was grateful to Eisner for launching his career. But, he thought, that was a different Eisner—relaxed, confident, willing to take risks, willing to delegate. Burke still respected his creative instincts, but Eisner's management style had become the antithesis of what Burke had learned from his father and Tom Murphy.

So when a headhunter called Burke, he took the call for the first time in his career. He began talking to Comcast, a large cable company based in Philadelphia. He told Iger he'd decided to leave the company. Iger seemed surprised. "You've really made up your mind?" he asked. Burke insisted he had. A big affiliates meeting was coming up in Orlando, and Burke said he'd be happy to go ahead with his presentation at the meeting. "I'll handle this any way you want," he offered.

The next day Burke got a terse voice message from Iger. "Michael and I have talked. He's very upset. We've decided there's no further need for you here. You can leave tomorrow."

Burke placed several calls to Eisner, who didn't call back. He cleaned out his office, and left. He'd already gotten a job offer from Comcast. Still, people at ABC were stunned that he'd leave Disney and the chance to run ABC for what seemed a lesser job at a much smaller company.

The next week *Time* magazine ran an article on Disney, pointing out Eisner's lack of a successor, noting the recent resignations of Burke and also Geraldine Laybourne from TV, Richard Nanula, and Larry Murphy. But Burke told *Time*, "The whole situation is a lot less sexy and nefarious than people believe. Eisner is the most interesting combination of entertainment and business talent in the entertainment business—maybe in any business— and the company still has one of the greatest collections of business talent I've ever seen." After the article appeared, Eisner returned Burke's call.

"I'm sorry this turned out this way," Burke said, "but I appreciate every- thing you did for me. I hope we can get beyond this."

"Why didn't you tell me?" Eisner asked. "I made your career." Eisner said Iger had assured him everything would be okay, that he had Burke under control.

Burke conceded that he should have earlier dealt directly with Eisner. Maybe he'd made a mistake communicating through Iger. Still, it wouldn't have changed anything because Eisner himself was the problem.

"Thank you for the comment in *Time*," Eisner added. "But I'm still mad at you."

In anticipation of ABC's move to the West Coast, Eisner commissioned a new ABC building from Italian architect Aldo Rossi, who had snubbed the Euro Disney competition, to be built on the Burbank campus. Iger was pro- moted to a new position in Los Angeles, though still not to the Disney presi- dency. He would oversee ABC, but also be responsible for international, the same as Ovitz's ill-fated assignment, and an area in which Eisner was rela- tively uninterested, in part because he didn't enjoy foreign travel. To replace Iger in New York, Eisner tapped Steve Bornstein, the head of ESPN.

Given the success of ESPN, Bornstein was an obvious choice, even a pos- sible rival to Iger. A native of New Jersey, he'd worked at the Public Broad- casting affiliate in Columbus, Ohio, before joining a still-fledgling ESPN in 1980 and became president and CEO ten years later. Under his leadership, ESPN had become even more wildly profitable than anyone had expected; in 1999 its operating profit was a remarkable $750 million. The number of households with cable had soared during Bornstein's tenure from 50 to 90 million. With its heavily male, eighteen to forty-five viewership, a much coveted audience for advertisers, ESPN could command steep advertising premiums. But Bornstein's masterstroke was a $9 billion deal with the Na- tional Football League that guaranteed ESPN eight years of Sunday-night football games for the full season, and secured eight years of Monday-night football for ABC as well as the broadcast rights to two Super Bowls, the most coveted event on network television.

The contract not only conferred a near-monopoly on the most important sports programming, but under a little-noticed provision in ESPN's agreements with its cable operators, securing a full season of NFL games gave ESPN the right to raise its subscription fees 20 percent per year. Bornstein moved aggressively to do just that, and ESPN was able to double its per subscriber fees, from one dollar to two dollars. Still, at the time, a record $9 billion deal for sports programming seemed audacious and risky. Bornstein was grateful that Eisner backed his NFL strategy, something that the more cautious Cap Cities/ABC leadership had been reluctant to do. And Eisner let Bornstein launch *ESPN* magazine in partnership with Hearst, another idea that Cap Cities' Tom Murphy had resisted. The magazine was an immediate success. Eisner was willing to spend money when he believed in an idea. Indeed, in Bornstein's view, he sometimes seemed too willing. Eisner insisted on launching ESPN retail stores, though Bornstein opposed the idea. "Men don't shop in malls. It's that simple," he argued. The effort was abandoned after a handful of test stores failed abysmally.

More important, Eisner let Bornstein run the ESPN business with minimal interference. Eisner came to ESPN headquarters in Bristol, Connecticut, from time to time, and he loved to talk about his enthusiasm for sports in his letters to shareholders. He boasted about ESPN's burgeoning profits in meetings with analysts. But Bornstein knew that Eisner didn't really care that much about sports. He knew real, dyed-in-the-wool sports fans, and Eisner wasn't one.

The dynamic changed when Bornstein arrived at ABC. Nominally he was in charge of the network, but Iger oversaw ABC entertainment and Eisner intervened in all the major programming and scheduling decisions. The blurry lines of authority were exacerbated by the ongoing war between Tarses and Braun. Bornstein thought Tarses was in way over her head, immature, and that she was manipulating Bloomberg, the third member of the triumvirate. It was a mess. Bornstein warned Iger that he'd have to fire Tarses, but Iger resisted. "She's never going to thank you," Bornstein warned. "You're just putting off the inevitable. You're going to have to do it eventually."

ABC prime time was taking up so much of Eisner's attention that he didn't have much time for any of the other divisions, such as the live-action studio under Joe Roth, or animation under Peter Schneider. Despite Roth's efforts to cut costs, to eliminate costly talent deals, to reduce overhead, Eisner was convinced that spending remained out of control and that Roth lacked the capacity to say no. Schneider had been restless ever since the *Lion King* triumph on Broadway, and was threatening to quit. Eisner's solution was to move Schneider from animation to become head of the Walt Disney live-action studio reporting to Roth, with Thomas Schumacher succeeding Schneider at animation. Schneider's orders were to keep costs down, to monitor Roth, and to report directly to Eisner—in effect, to spy on Roth.

News of Schneider's ascension came as a blow to David Vogel, who now reported to Schneider, even though he retained his titles as president of the Walt Disney Studio as well as Touchstone and Hollywood. He went to see Roth. "So I'm fired," he said.

"No, no," Roth assured him. Schneider "had to get the studio, but he'll be far too busy to bother you."

Right, Vogel thought. He wished Roth would just have the decency to level with him. For whatever reason—buying *The Sixth Sense*, he suspected—he was being hung out to dry.

The next Monday, Schneider and Vogel had lunch at the Rotunda, the Disney executive dining room. Schneider announced that he would be making all decisions involving the Disney label, and Vogel would carry them out. "If you're not happy with this, I'm prepared to move into your office," Schneider said. As he said this, Schneider was gripping the table so hard that it shook.

"Give me a week to rearrange the company," Vogel said. He'd been running Touchstone and Disney as a single entity.

"That's not fast enough," Schneider replied.

Vogel had always maintained a respectful distance from Eisner; he'd promised Roth he wouldn't go behind his back, and he honored the promise. Still, Eisner had often complimented him at meetings, and once sent him a note that no one understood the Disney label as well as Vogel. But now Eisner ignored him. Roth invited Schneider to all studio meetings, even Touchstone ones where Vogel was in charge. Schneider said, "I like this" or "I don't like this," effectively controlling the entire development slate.

At one meeting he interrupted Vogel in front of the entire staff, and said that he had little respect for anything Vogel had produced. "Well, I can see that all of our movies aren't perfect, but what about *101 Dalmatians*? It did well."

"No," Schneider said sharply, and proceeded to criticize one Vogel project after another. Everyone present fell into shocked silence.

Schneider told Vogel he no longer had the authority to buy anything on his own. Then he began emailing orders to Vogel's staff, copying Vogel. "I realize you want things done, but there's a chain of command and I'd appreciate it if you'd stop emailing my staff and then cc'ing me later," Vogel wrote back.

When Schneider returned from a trip, he summoned Vogel to his office. "I'd appreciate it if you'd give up the title of president of Walt Disney Pictures," Schneider said. "I can't get anything done."

"Peter, you do realize you're voiding my contract?" Vogel asked.

"Yes, I know, but I hope you'll stay on at Touchstone."

"Thanks, but no," Vogel replied.

He left and called Roth, who was out of the office. He reached him on his cell phone. Vogel told him what had just happened. "Noooo . . ." Roth said, drawing out the vowel.

"Yeeeees . . ." Vogel replied, mimicking him.

Roth said he'd call Schneider and call him back.

"Peter would like you to stay," Roth reported when he called Vogel back. Vogel cut him off. "Joe, I'm gone." Two weeks later, Vogel left.

A few days later he was at home when Eisner called. He was chuckling when Vogel got on the line. "So, I just want you to know that you're a great executive. I mean, this happened to me at Paramount and look how I ended up. So you'll be fine."

"Well, okay." Vogel couldn't resist adding, "I've left you with two of Disney's biggest pictures: *Inspector Gadget* and *The Sixth Sense.*" Then he hung up.

Sacrificing Vogel was evidently the price Eisner had to pay to install Schneider as a watchdog on Roth. Two of Roth's movie projects, in particular, had aroused Eisner's suspicions. The first was a thriller about a whistle-blower in the tobacco industry, *The Insider,* based on a story in *Vanity Fair* by journalist Marie Brenner. The second was the latest "event" movie from Jerry Bruckheimer, *Pearl Harbor,* an epic being directed by Michael Bay.

Eisner had been hostile toward *The Insider* from its inception. One of the main characters in the true story, Lowell Bergman, was an investigative reporter and producer for CBS's long-running news magazine, "60 Minutes," and a central thrust of the article was that CBS had suppressed Bergman's work out of fear of offending the powerful tobacco industry. Eisner was appalled at the idea of a film that portrayed a rival news organization in a negative light. " 'Sixty Minutes' will track us down forever," he warned Joe Roth. Roth thought that was ridiculous—the last thing CBS wanted was more publicity on the matter.

And there were other reasons for *The Insider* that Roth found compelling. The project had attracted acclaimed director Michael Mann (*Heat, The Last of the Mohicans*) and screenwriter Eric Roth, who had written the successful, award-winning *Forrest Gump*. Mann was a personal friend of Bergman's and was passionate about the project. It was an opportunity to get both highly sought-after talents into further projects for Disney. Roth also thought the subject of big tobacco and the plight of a whistle-blower was dramatic, urgent, and important. It was the kind of story that would help earn the kind of prestige that, apart from Miramax, had been conspicuously lacking at Disney.

Despite Eisner's concerns, Roth green-lit the project. Eisner saw a rough cut and praised it, though he again stressed that any facts about CBS had to be accurate. *The Insider* opened in November 1999 and garnered lavish critical praise, especially for Russell Crowe's portrayal of whistle-blower Dr. Jeffrey Wigand. But just as Eisner had feared, there was a storm of controversy. CBS didn't let the film pass without comment, and veteran "60 Minutes" correspondent Mike Wallace was vehement in his denunciations of his portrayal. Even worse, from Eisner's perspective, was the fact that the film earned less than $7 million in its opening week. He was so dismayed that he called "60 Minutes" producer Don Hewitt to complain that it was bad enough Disney had ever agreed to make the film, but to make matters worse it was a box-office flop.

This, in any event, was the account of the conversation that infuriated just about everyone who had worked so hard on the film, especially Michael Mann, who was convinced that Eisner and Disney were deliberately underselling the movie, in the same way they had made sure that *Kundun* was a flop. Neither Eisner nor Hewitt would reveal just what Eisner said in the call to Hewitt (while acknowledging that such a call was made), and Disney denied that it wasn't promoting the film. Still, suspicions were fanned again after *The Insider* garnered seven Academy Award nominations, and Disney mounted what Mann considered a tepid campaign with members of the Academy. *The Insider* was shut out at the awards ceremony.

More important, the whole controversy vindicated Eisner's original instinct that *The Insider* was a mistake, even as he was growing more worried about *Pearl Harbor*. After the success of *Armageddon*, Roth had moved swiftly to sign director Michael Bay to another project with Jerry Bruckheimer. But nothing Roth offered Bay captured his interest, a task made more difficult by the fact that Bay didn't read scripts, or, so far as Roth could tell, much of anything else. Bay had come from the world of fast-paced television commercials, which didn't put much premium on the written word. Still, after the success of *The Rock* and *Armageddon,* Bay was being avidly courted by other studios, so Roth convened weekly meetings with Bay, his agent, his lawyer, Bruckheimer, and Disney executives to hammer out an idea for Bay's next film at Disney. Ten ideas were presented and rejected. The effort seemed to be getting nowhere, and Bay had stood up to leave when Todd Garner, the studio's cohead of production, tossed out two words: Pearl Harbor.

Garner was a frustrated screenwriter, and he'd been dreaming of a Pearl Harbor epic for fourteen years. His idea was to use the devastating Japanese attack on Pearl Harbor as a background for a story that would reunite two brothers and the Hawaiian woman they both loved. Bay nodded. "Yeah, I like it," he said.

The next day Garner pitched the idea to screenwriter Randall Wallace, one of Hollywood's star writers in the wake of his script for *Braveheart,* which won the Academy Award for Best Picture and was nominated for Best Original Screenplay. Wallace was a military enthusiast and liked the idea. The story had all the elements of the sensationally successful *Titanic*—a love affair set against a historical tragedy—and the wartime verisimilitude of *Saving Private Ryan.* Joe Roth assigned the project to Bruckheimer to produce.

It went without saying that the combination of Bruckheimer, Bay, and Wallace meant that *Pearl Harbor* would be expensive. Ben Affleck, still popular from the success of Miramax's *Good Will Hunting* and Touchstone's *Armageddon,* was signed to play one of the brothers, with Kate Beckinsale as his love interest, at which point the heroine became a British nurse rather than Hawaiian. Preliminary budget figures for *Pearl Harbor* came in at $200 million, a number that left Eisner aghast. "Why are we using Michael Bay? I could give this to my son and make it for $70 [million]," he told Roth. He railed at Roth for letting costs burgeon out of control. Roth let him continue until he seemed to calm down, then asked, "Tell me what you'll make it for."

"Get rid of Bruckheimer and Bay. Make it for $70 million," Eisner said.

Roth was appalled. "You can't do this on the cheap. You have to go all out, or it won't work." They argued until Roth volunteered to go back to Bruckheimer and Bay, looking for some cost savings. The producer and director were skeptical, but finally came back with a lower number: $140 million, the same as the budget for *Armageddon.* Garner wanted to cut the ending of the film, the Doolittle raid on Japan that ended the war, which wasn't part of his original idea and would have saved millions. "It's called Pearl Harbor, not Hiroshima," Garner argued. "This isn't about Japan."

Eisner vehemently disagreed. "That's the American victory, the Americans have to win at the end. That's why we're making the movie."

"Everybody already knows the Americans won World War II," Garner countered, but Eisner wouldn't back down.

Eisner finally agreed to $140 million, but then told Roth he wanted no producer or director guarantees, insisting that they not be paid until Disney itself had turned a profit.

Though not unprecedented, such deals were rare in Hollywood, and hardly ever used with top-level producers like Bruckheimer. Major talent on a film—producers, directors, writers, and stars—typically earned a percentage of a film's revenue, usually expressed as either a percentage of the "gross" or, more often, a percentage of "net profits." At the same time, they were guaranteed a minimum fee. Since most films never earned any "net profits," these guarantees were their de facto salaries. Though he had been operating within this system for much of his career, Eisner had long chafed at the notion that the studio put its money at risk, but that talent earned a guaranteed sum no matter how poorly the film performed at the box office. While this wasn't an indefensible position, it ignored decades of economic history. Just as autoworkers don't bear the risk of failure of a new car model, talent in the movie industry had used its leverage to insulate itself from the commercial failure of a film. Eisner may have thought this was unfair, but management controlled the making, distribution, and marketing of films.

Bruckheimer and Bay were predictably insulted. Bay said he was quitting. But Bruckheimer countered with a compromise: Disney could earn back its investment before any guarantees, but then the producers, director, and actors should get a percentage of the gross above the cost of the film. Eisner couldn't fault the logic, and somewhat to Bruckheimer's surprise, he agreed, though it meant Disney would be giving up some of its profits if the film was a big hit. Bruckheimer patiently lured Bay back, arguing that *Pearl Harbor* was such a sure thing that they'd more than make up the money by sharing in the proceeds on the back end. Reluctantly, Bay agreed. Bruckheimer stressed to Affleck that this was his opportunity to break through as a romantic action hero. Everyone finally got on board. At times Bruckheimer felt more like a diplomat than a movie producer.

Shooting began, and then there was another snag. After the first dailies were screened, Peter Schneider stood up, said, "I don't understand this movie," and walked out. Then he convened a meeting and announced that he was shutting down production unless the actors in the thirteen major roles gave Disney options on their next films. Everyone there was stunned. "You can't ask them for options after they've just given up their guarantees," Garner argued. He was increasingly convinced that Schneider was trying to kill the movie. "I don't care," Schneider said. "Either we get the options or we shut it down." He and Garner got into a shouting match before Schneider finally walked out. Garner had never trusted Schneider, especially after he savaged David Vogel at a staff meeting. (Schneider said he didn't recall such an incident, and maintained that cost overruns, not options, were the reason for shutting down production.)

Garner met with business affairs people and tried to negotiate the options. It was impossible. Actors Affleck, Josh Hartnett, Cuba Gooding Jr. all had deals for other projects they couldn't just cancel. Finally Garner went to Eisner. "This is impossible," he argued. "I can't work for Peter. He's a horrible person. I can't stay if this continues."

"Go back to your office," Eisner replied, "because Peter isn't leaving."

Still, Eisner gave up the options demand, and production continued. Garner managed to spend as much time as possible on location in Hawaii, away from Schneider and the studio.

The Insider may have flopped in its early November 1999 release, but just two weeks later, *Toy Story 2* opened to lavish praise and grossed more than $80 million over the Thanksgiving weekend, a record for the period. "The first question about 'Toy Story 2' is whether it's as wonderful as the original," Joe Morgenstern wrote in *The Wall Street Journal*. "The answer is absolutely, improbably yes; Pixar, which releases its films through Disney, has done it again."

The sequel's enormous success vindicated Roth's decision to rescue the film from direct-to-video and have John Lasseter rework it as a theatrical release. Now Lasseter was eager to embark on what would be the crowning achievement of a trilogy: *Toy Story 3*. Lasseter had the story already blocked out. The creative team from *Toy Story 2* was ready to go.

Eisner had reluctantly agreed that *Toy Story 2*, even though it was a sequel, would count as one of the pictures in the new Disney-Pixar deal. But now he dug in. Eisner stubbornly insisted that a third *Toy Story* would not count, and would not displace the already-agreed-upon *Cars* as the last of the Pixar films under the current agreement. "I want *Cars*," Eisner insisted at meeting after meeting called to discuss the issue.

Disney's consumer products division was clamoring for another *Toy Story*. Schneider and Schumacher urged Eisner to reconsider, if for no other reason than to keep Lasseter happy. Steve Jobs himself weighed in. But Eisner was at his most implacable. What was the point of a deal if you just changed it every time something was successful? He invited Lasseter to visit at Aspen, and afterward assured Schneider and Schumacher that he'd defused the situation. But nothing had really been resolved.

Joe Roth wasn't the only division head with whom Eisner had become disillusioned. Apart from the ongoing woes of Euro Disney, the theme parks had been Disney's most consistently profitable division under Judson Green. But it was obvious that Eisner accorded the division little respect, attributing the positive results far more to the creative efforts of the Imagineers than to the parks' executives. At one point he referred to the executives working under Green as "monkeys."

"What do you mean by that?" Green asked.

"They don't have any brains; they're not that smart. It's a simple business."*

Green let the remark pass, but it didn't occur to him that Eisner might think the same about him. But then, just before Thanksgiving, Eisner summoned Green to his office. Paul Pressler, the young, energetic executive who had succeeded Steve Burke at running the Disney stores, had just gotten a job offer from toy company Mattel. Pressler was handsome, charismatic, a personal favorite of Eisner. "Nothing personal; I don't want to hurt you, but I'm promoting Paul to president" of parks and resorts, Eisner informed Green. "You can stay as long as you want, but you won't have any responsibilities."

Green was stunned. He'd had no warning. He had delivered the results Eisner and the financial planners had asked for. Eisner had even praised him in his autobiography for the "special passion" he'd brought to building the Animal Kingdom, and for his creativity as a jazz pianist. Although Pressler was well liked within the company, and had brought some creative ideas to the Disney stores, his division had been faltering from a dearth of new products.

---

* Eisner denies saying this.

Green agreed to remain in the largely titular position of chairman of parks and resorts until he had completed negotiations for a new theme park in Hong Kong. Then his long Disney career would be over. With his departure, the only executive left from the pre-Eisner era would be Dick Cook.

Much as Joe Roth enjoyed his position at Disney, and at times had enjoyed working with Eisner, Eisner was making his life increasingly miserable. Eisner confronted him with increasingly contradictory and therefore impossible demands: to slash production, reduce costs, and yet maintain market share and continue to be the number one or two studio at the box office. There was constant tension between Eisner's belief in a low-budget "single and doubles" approach and the new pressures of costly "tent pole" or "event" movies with big stars and special effects. Roth concluded it made sense to stay only if he had a reasonable chance of moving up to president, or succeeding Eisner as chief executive. Given Eisner's reaction to his earlier suggestion that he be named president, both possibilities seemed remote.

Roth's contract would expire on January 1, 2000, so toward the end of 1998, with little more than a year remaining, he gave Eisner notice that he planned to leave the company when his contract expired. Eisner invited him to lunch and said he didn't believe him. "I'm not really unhappy," Roth said, "but you don't want me to do what I want to do. You don't want to make me president."

This was true—Eisner was increasingly leaning toward Bob Iger, and had already broached the possibility to him. But Eisner didn't say anything.

A few months later, Roth reminded Eisner of his decision to leave. "I haven't changed my mind," he said.

"You won't really leave," Eisner said again.

"Why not?"

"No one will answer your phone calls," Eisner said.

"Michael," Roth answered, "that's called projection."

Eisner thought for a moment. "Maybe that's true, but you'll see."

The dispute between Jeffrey Katzenberg and Michael Eisner over Katzenberg's bonus finally went to trial on April 16, 1999. "I've been waiting five years for this," Katzenberg told the press, his wife, Marilyn, at his side, as they gathered in a makeshift courtroom at his lawyers' offices in Century City. Serving as an arbitrator in the case was distinguished former judge Paul

Breckenridge. In the intervening years, Disney had conceded that it owed Katzenberg something. How much was the issue, and the subject of the trial. Under pressure from the judge originally assigned to the case, Sandy Litvack and Katzenberg's attorney, Bert Fields, had negotiated a settlement in 1997 in which Disney agreed to pay Katzenberg $117 million, which Disney insisted was all that it owed. Katzenberg maintained that the company owed him more, plus interest. Disney and Katzenberg would have a trial before an arbitrator to determine the total.

The settlement itself was a major breakthrough, given the stubbornness with which Eisner held to the view that Katzenberg had forfeited his bonus by leaving early. No doubt Eisner genuinely believed this; perhaps Wells had told him this in order to mask his own mistake in granting Katzenberg such an open-ended bonus. The bonus concept had been Wells's idea in the first place, negotiated in a bungalow at the Beverly Hills Hotel as an "annuity" for Katzenberg's twins. No one had expected it to amount to much, but that's hardly an excuse for such a vague, poorly drafted, potentially limitless liability that Wells imposed on the company. Eisner may have been right about Wells's deficiencies as a business executive, and right to be incredulous that there was no penalty for Katzenberg quitting before the end of his contract. But that didn't change the contract.

During the discovery process, it had become increasingly clear that Eisner's understanding about the bonus was untenable. The language of Katzenberg's contract, the history of the negotiations, and the extensive analysis contained in Project Snowball all supported Katzenberg's claim that he was entitled to a bonus. Although Eisner had always maintained he knew nothing of Project Snowball, the document itself had his initials typed on it, indicating he had received it.

Moreover, Katzenberg's lawyers had subpoenaed all the notes taken by author Tony Schwartz for Eisner's autobiography, replete with unguarded and devastating evidence of Eisner's hostility toward Katzenberg: the concession that Eisner might have offered him Wells's job; his petulant outburst that he wouldn't pay him anything; not to mention plenty of indiscreet remarks about Ovitz and others still at Disney.

Schwartz was horrified at having to turn over the notes, but he could not claim that Eisner had been a confidential source speaking to a journalist. Disney lawyers resisted the subpoena on his behalf, but the court ruled the notes had to be handed over, and Schwartz had to give a deposition, in which he swore that the notes reflected a near-verbatim account of what Eisner had told him. Schwartz wished that he hadn't written so much down, especially things that he knew Eisner would never allow in the book. Yet he had had no way of knowing it would come to this.

As a result, it seemed incomprehensible that in the ensuing year and a half, having already conceded the key liability issue, Disney and Katzenberg could not settle the case. Katzenberg dreaded the thought that everything about his career at Disney would become public. He knew Disney lawyers would try to put his actions in the harshest possible light, suggesting that he had tried to capitalize first on Wells's death and then Eisner's heart attack to advance his own interests, not to mention revealing his compensation at Disney. For Disney, the stakes were even higher. By going to trial, Disney and Eisner risked all the negative publicity it had hoped to avoid, as well as an order to pay far more than it thought Katzenberg deserved.

Yet Eisner remained intransigent. Since Katzenberg's acrimonious departure, their relationship had deteriorated, if such a thing were possible. Eisner blamed Katzenberg for the ruinous competition for animators from DreamWorks. Eisner and Pixar's Steve Jobs accused Katzenberg of stealing the idea for DreamWorks's animated feature *Antz* from the latest Pixar project, *A Bug's Life*. Pixar had been talking about *A Bug's Life* before Katzenberg left Disney, though Katzenberg maintained he'd never heard of it. A Dream-Works film executive, Nina Jacobson, who had no knowledge of the Pixar project, first suggested *Antz*. Then Katzenberg had had the audacity to move the release date for *Antz* ahead of *A Bug's Life*.

Stanley Gold viewed the approaching trial as an impending train wreck. He repeatedly urged Eisner to settle, even though it was obvious that this wasn't advice Eisner wanted to hear. Even Litvack, who had helped derail the earlier Ovitz-brokered settlement, now pushed for a settlement. At their lawyers' behest, Eisner and Katzenberg met to try to resolve the dispute, but the meeting quickly descended into acrimony, and Katzenberg walked out. At another point, Katzenberg appealed directly to Disney board member Tom Murphy, who spoke to Eisner. Lawyers for the two sides again met to negotiate, but Katzenberg was furious that Disney's lawyers wouldn't budge. His lawyer, Bert Fields, said he wasn't going to waste any more time on settlement talks.

Finally Gold reached out to David Geffen. Though he didn't know Geffen, Gold urged him to call Bruce Ramer, his former partner at the law firm of Gang, Tyre, who was Steven Spielberg's lawyer. "Ask Bruce if my word is good," Gold urged him. After talking to Ramer, Geffen agreed to meet with Gold, and Gold visited him at his Malibu beach house. He was surprised to discover that he was comfortable with Geffen. Geffen summarized the case from Katzenberg's point of view, emphasizing the many ways that Eisner had mistreated him. He stressed that Katzenberg was determined to go to trial and that he would win.

Much of what he heard from Geffen was news to Gold. Thus far, he'd only heard Eisner's point of view. For the first time, he began to wonder if everything Eisner had told him was accurate. Gold told Geffen that Disney maintained that its maximum additional liability was $30 million.

Geffen said he'd take $150 million.

Gold said he couldn't get there. "I want to settle this, but I don't think I can sell the deal," he said.

"Stanley, let me assure you, it will cost you more the next time," Geffen insisted. "This is the lowest that number is ever going to be."

The trial date arrived with no resolution. Katzenberg was the first witness. He was calm on the stand, recounting the history of his employment contract and the origins of the bonus provision. He described the crucial meeting with Wells when Wells said Eisner had a "misunderstanding" about Katzenberg's contract, but that he would take care of it. His lawyers introduced numerous documents to support his position: the contract itself; notes taken by Arthur Emil, Katzenberg's lawyer in the salary negotiations; Wells's notes; a copy of the notes Irwin Russell took of his 1988 conversation with Wells about Katzenberg's contract.

The portly, aging Russell was Disney's first witness. His demeanor was nervous and uncomfortable. Asked about the language in his notes confirming that Katzenberg's bonus would "continue" even if he left before the end of his contract, Russell testified that he had forgotten to write the word *loses* before the word *bonus*.

"These were very quick notes strictly for my own purposes," he testified.

"You had enough time to write the word *loses,*" Fields injected.

"Maybe, maybe not," Russell said.

Eisner was the star witness. As his testimony began, he seemed calm, if slightly irritated that valuable time was being wasted in a court proceeding. The key issue was whether Disney had breached Katzenberg's contract by refusing to pay him his bonus, in which case it owed him the bonus plus interest. Thus, any motive on Eisner's part to breach the contract, such as personal hostility toward Katzenberg, was also an important element of the case.

On the critical contract issue, Eisner insisted that he never agreed to continue Katzenberg's 2 percent bonus, notwithstanding various deal memos in Wells's handwriting that contained the provision.

"You never heard or saw the name Project Snowball?" Fields asked.

"No," Eisner said. "Not that I recall."

Fields handed him a memo addressed to him, titled "Project Snowball."

"I don't think I ever saw this memo," Eisner said.

Fields handed him another one, labeled "Project Snowball, Highly Confidential, from Frank and Cheryl F. to Michael Eisner." "You didn't see that one either?"

"I don't recall seeing it, no."

After more testimony on the 2 percent bonus, and how Wells and Eisner had long assumed it would be worthless, Fields abruptly switched subjects, turning to notes taken by Tony Schwartz for Eisner's autobiography. "Did you consider yourself the cheerleader and Mr. Katzenberg merely the tip of your pom-pom?"

"No."

"Didn't you say that to Mr. Schwartz? That's how you looked at him?"

"Mr. Schwartz has that in his notes, I believe. I don't believe I said it. If I said it, I'm quite sure it was in humor. . . ."

"You don't think Mr. Schwartz made that up, do you?"

"I don't know."

"Do you think he made it up?"

"Probably not."

"So you probably said it?"

"In humor," Eisner finally conceded.

Fields continued: "Did you tell Mr. Schwartz that you hated Mr. Katzenberg?"

"In one conversation when he pushed me on things that Mr. Katzenberg had [done], I did say that."

"You said, 'I think I hate the little midget'?"

Eisner looked uncomfortable. "I think you're getting into an area that . . . is ill-advised," he warned. "I don't think it's productive, Mr. Fields, to ask what he was referring to that prompted that response. It was completely private. It has never been in a rough draft or in my book, which only looked at the bright and light side of my relationship with Mr. Katzenberg predominantly, and if you pursue this line of questioning, it will put in the public record those things that I think are not necessary to be in the public record."

"Didn't you say on more than one occasion that you hated Mr. Katzenberg to Mr. Schwartz?"

"I probably did hundreds and hundreds of hours of interviewing Mr. Schwartz . . . Probably out of humor. Out of gross unpleasantness. I did not hate Mr. Katzenberg. I still do not hate Mr. Katzenberg. We had a very long and fruitful relationship. There were things that I'm sure that I did that provoked his dislike and hatred of me and vice versa at any one moment in time. But to characterize it as me hating him is absurd and is going down a direction that I think is not in your client's best interest or mine, but particularly your client's, but that's up to you."

Fields turned to more of Schwartz's notes. "Did you say to Mr. Schwartz, 'I don't care what he thinks. I am not going to pay him any of the money'?"

"I would say again, in anger I said that."

With that, Fields rested. He had gotten exactly what he wanted out of Eisner: an admission of personal animus toward Katzenberg that meant he wouldn't pay him any money, even if he owed it. Eisner seemed surprised by Schwartz's notes (and later contended that he was surprised), which, if true, was an inexcusable lapse on the part of his lawyers, who should have reviewed them with Eisner before he took the stand.

The thankless task of extricating Eisner from this evidentiary mess fell to Disney lawyer Lou Meisinger. "What were the circumstances, Mr. Eisner, which caused you to tell Mr. Schwartz, in substance, that you didn't care what he thinks, 'I am not going to pay him any of the money'?"

"I was particularly annoyed with a practice that he had of negotiating with the press, you know, talking about company business to the press, bringing up the whole financial arrangement in the media," Eisner explained. "I get that very day a misdirected fax that was sent from Jeffrey Katzenberg to Bert Fields, thanking him for all the help of talking to the media on the New Yorker story, which inadvertently went to me, which annoyed me." With respect to Katzenberg's bonus, "I now was saying to Tony Schwartz, screw that. If he's going to play this game, this media game, this deceptive game, this disingenuous game, and do the kinds of things I was angry about him for doing anyway . . . [not] keeping his word, being rude, things like that . . . I simply was not going to pay him his money. And I was aggravated and I'm sure . . . this was just one of the dark sides of an otherwise effective executive. . . . There is occasion when somebody does something that goes toward the dark side that makes you so aggravated that you get annoyed."

Oddly, given Ovitz's deal to settle the case with Katzenberg for $90 million, Eisner also testified that he never received any settlement offers. "We never got a figure, period, and the figure that was kind of out in the ether was so much higher, catastrophically higher . . . that we never had a definitive conversation that I know of."

The press, of course, had a field day with remarks like "the little midget" and "the tip of my pom-pom." Kathryn Harris, the former *Los Angeles Times* reporter now working for Bloomberg News Service, summed up, "Michael Eisner is a charming, intelligent and facile executive who shouldn't be allowed near a witness stand . . . far worse . . . was the ebbing of Eisner's credibility—that most precious commodity in a witness, and certainly in a chief executive who has fused his likeness to a company."

With Wells dead, there will always be an element of mystery about the Katzenberg bonus: exactly what Wells told Katzenberg and Eisner, and what he meant in drafting the contract language. Even so, Breckenridge ruled swiftly in favor of Katzenberg, finding that the evidence made the conclusion "inescapable" that Disney had in fact breached his contract, and thus owed him interest. The precise amount would be the subject of further proceedings.

Geffen called Gold after the verdict. "I told you so," he said, though his intention wasn't to gloat. The next day, Gold visited Geffen at his newly restored palatial estate in Beverly Hills, formerly owned by Jack Warner. As Geffen had warned, the cost of settlement had now gone up—to $200 million. On Saturday, the negotiations continued at the Four Seasons Hotel. Katzenberg's lawyers and an expert witness gave Gold a presentation on the value of Katzenberg's bonus and the interest calculation. After conferring with Eisner and Litvack, Gold called Geffen to say he'd failed to persuade them. Geffen reminded Gold that the longer Disney delayed, the higher the ultimate cost would be.

The second phase of the proceedings began on May 25. This time Gold sat in, and Litvack replaced Meisinger as Disney's lead attorney. A series of expert witnesses made clear how open to interpretation was Wells's promise to pay Katzenberg a percentage of "all proceeds" from his work at Disney. Did this include the sale of plush toys in India and China—the subject of much testimony? Eisner was again slated to take the stand. Gold didn't like what he was hearing in testimony.

Over the July 4 weekend, Gold again met with Geffen at Geffen's beach house in Malibu and dropped any argumentative pretenses. He wanted a deal. As Geffen had promised, the price to settle had risen yet again. This time he and Gold agreed on a number: $275 million. Still feeling burned from his experience with Ovitz, Geffen asked, "If I shake hands with you on this, does this mean we have a deal?" Gold assured him it did. But when Geffen called Katzenberg to announce the momentous news, it was Katzenberg who balked. "I'd always expected something that began with a three." Then, "Okay, I'll take $280 million," he said—$5 million more than the deal Geffen had just shaken hands on.

Now it was Geffen's turn to be furious. "Jeffrey, you can't do this to me. I've given my word." But Katzenberg, sensing another imminent victory in court, stuck to his guns. Finally Geffen agreed that he would personally pay the extra $5 million if it meant so much to Katzenberg.

The final settlement was, in fact, $280 million; Disney agreed to pay the extra $5 million, sparing Geffen from reaching into his own pocket. The settlement was announced on July 7 without specifying the amount.

The irony of the settlement wasn't lost on Ovitz. The merits of many of the deals he negotiated but failed to consummate for Disney were debatable. But this much was incontrovertible: He could have settled the case for $90 million. Now Disney was paying $280 million.

Michael Davies had left ABC, but he wasn't about to give up on "Who Wants to Be a Millionaire." With the backing of both Eisner and Iger as well as Bloomberg, he knew that "Millionaire" had momentum, no matter what Tarses thought about it. He still believed that the show was destined to change his life, so he persuaded Paul Smith to make him an executive producer. Smith agreed that "Millionaire" needed someone like Davies, who could steer it onto an American network, and who understood American sensibilities.

It took months of negotiations with ABC to complete a deal. Although Davies wanted Regis Philbin to be the host, someone he'd already lined up for his "$64,000 Question" project, ABC initially held out for someone with more gravitas, who would give the show a more serious image—both Phil Donahue and Bob Costas were suggested. But Philbin called and practically begged to host the show. He was just the kind of reassuring presence Davies wanted, someone who wouldn't intimidate a post "Jeopardy" audience. Besides, Disney's Touchstone studio was already producing "Live with Regis and Kathie Lee," so it had a relationship with Philbin.

Another sticking point was how "Millionaire" would be broadcast. Paul Smith felt that a critical element of the show's success in Britain was that it was an event—it was "stunted," meaning it ran every night for two weeks, and then stopped. Smith insisted that ABC commit to eleven episodes, which it would run on successive nights, but the network resisted. Davies eventually got ABC to agree. The entire development cost was a modest $1.9 million, plus $1 million in prize money, a relative bargain for eleven prime-time episodes. Davies further narrowed the financial risk by lining up sponsors: *People* magazine, AT&T, McDonald's.

ABC scheduled the first run of "Millionaire" for the week of August 16, 1999, as a summer replacement, a time of traditionally weak viewership when it could afford to risk eleven consecutive nights. Davies had spent weeks reviewing old 1950s game shows for inspiration, and used the British version as a model for the set design, which was built at a Sony television studio on West Fifty-third Street in Manhattan. Paul Smith flew in from London to oversee the first tapings, armed with his 120-page program guide containing the game's rules and production instructions.

Davies nearly panicked after the first run-through. After he'd gone to the mat for Philbin, the host was terrible, forgetting the rules and mispronouncing words and names. But everything came together for the first taping, on a Sunday. The contestants were visibly nervous, and the live audience lent an air of electricity. The first contestant was an accountant from Maryland who was also a member of the high-IQ group Mensa. Philbin rose to the occasion, deftly underscoring the tension with just the right touch of humor. His rendering of "Is that your final answer?" gave every contestant an anguishing moment of doubt and the audience a vicarious thrill. The brainy accountant took home only $1,000.

Davies, Smith, and the rest of the show's crew spent most of the night editing. "Who Wants to Be a Millionaire" debuted the following night. Exhausted, Smith slept through the first airing. The show had had little advance publicity because ABC didn't want to spend to promote it. When Davies got in the next morning, the overnight ratings showed a strong 7.2 rating, 13 share. The second night it was 7.7 and 14. Then, in the third episode, a contestant correctly identified Lake Huron as the second-largest Great Lake, but was erroneously dismissed from the show. Davies and the producers hastily agreed to do the right thing and bring the rejected contestant back for another chance at the million dollars. But the inadvertent mistake brought an avalanche of press coverage. Within two weeks it was the highest-rated program of the summer.

Davies could hardly believe the show's immediate success; it was like a dream. After seeing the ratings, Iger sent an email to everyone at ABC: "This is the kind of out-of-the box creative thinking we have to do to succeed." That same morning Eisner called Davies at the studio to congratulate him. Davies knew his gamble had paid off—not just his belief in "Millionaire," but his whole crazy decision to devote himself to a career in nontraditional, "reality" television.

For the first time in years, ABC had a huge hit. And not just any hit, a bona fide, once-in-a-decade cultural phenomenon. "Millionaire" landed on the front Arts page of *The New York Times*. "The Virgin Mary, Arnold Schwarzenegger, leprechauns—nothing could stop Regis Philbin and his mind-numbing multiple choice show," wrote Lisa de Moraes in *The Washington Post*.

Eisner had said repeatedly that all ABC needed was one big hit to turn it around. Now that he had one, he was determined to put it to good use. ABC promptly ordered another series of "Millionaire" episodes, and scheduled them for the November "sweeps" period, the critical time when A. C. Nielsen measures the nation's television viewership. In the meantime, Iger asked Jeff Bader, the chief of scheduling, to do an analysis of how ABC should capitalize on the "Millionaire" phenomenon for next year's regular season.

Both Michael Davies and Paul Smith had always felt that "stunting"— running the show on consecutive nights at infrequent intervals—was essential to build suspense, maintain viewer curiosity, and keep "Millionaire" an "event." Andrea Wong, Davies's successor as head of alternative programming, also worried about overexposure and argued strongly that "Millionaire" should be scheduled during sweeps periods, almost guaranteeing ABC a ratings boost. The show had never been conceived as a weekly staple. But now the ABC executives were told to study the alternatives and their financial implications.

Bader, Lloyd Braun, Stu Bloomberg, and Patricia Fili-Krushel, the president of the ABC Television Network, met with Iger to present the recommendation that "Millionaire" be retained for sweeps periods and special events, but it fell to Bader to make the case. He argued that "This will be a disaster if 'Millionaire' is overexposed," and launched into the reasons why Smith and Davies thought "Millionaire" had to remain a sweeps event. He'd barely begun when Iger interrupted.

"I'm sorry, but this is not negotiable," he said.

"What do you mean?" Braun asked.

"Michael and I have already decided. We're going to run 'Millionaire' three nights a week."

There was stunned silence. None of the ABC executives had even considered the possibility of so many episodes in a week. Bader looked to his colleagues for support, but no one said anything.

"I'll take full responsibility for the decision," Iger said.

Afterward, the group filed out. "Thanks, guys," Bader said. "You might as well go and get the gun because I'm going to be fired." The other executives apologized for not coming to his defense, but clearly Iger's mind was made up. They and others suspected that Iger's strategy was to use the short-term success of "Millionaire" to propel himself into the Disney presidency. It was also yet another example of how seemingly arbitrary decisions were being made from the top, without any real consultation with the people running ABC day-to-day.

As the ABC executives had speculated, the huge success of "Millionaire" did come just as Eisner was contemplating naming Iger president. Although he'd mentioned the possibility the previous fall, he'd done nothing further about it, and had later backtracked, saying he was worried that Roth and Litvack would leave if Iger became president. Still, he'd encouraged Iger to be patient, and the success of "Millionaire" gave him a strong rationale for Iger's promotion.

So it was all the more devastating when Iger, vacationing in Martha's Vineyard that August, got a worried phone call from Tom Murphy. Murphy, Stanley Gold, and a few other directors had again raised the issue of succession with Eisner, and Eisner had seized on the question as an opportunity to launch a long catalog of Iger's weaknesses and faults. He'd said that Iger "can never succeed me," that he lacked "the stature" to lead Disney. "Bob," Murphy told him, "I hate to tell you this, but you have to leave." Iger was devastated by the advice from his old mentor. He didn't say anything to his wife because he didn't want to spoil the vacation. But he decided he'd have to leave the company. He was expecting a bonus of about $1 million in January. Then he'd announce his resignation.

Lloyd Braun thought the success of "Millionaire" might be the last straw for Tarses, and soon afterward he read a gossip item on the Internet reporting that she was about to be fired. It was a difficult time for Tarses; she and Robert Morton broke up; she was spotted at a restaurant making out with "Friends" star Matthew Perry after denying they were having an affair; she had failed to show up for a week of budget meetings in New York and had to send a written apology. Iger met with Tarses, and she emerged from their meeting triumphant. Iger issued a public statement of support, calling the rumors she would be fired "totally untrue."

Braun was dismayed. Even before "Millionaire's" success, Charlie Parsons and Mark Burnett were again pitching the other "reality" show they'd developed for ABC, "Survivor." Andrea Wong loved the idea and was desperate to get it on the network's schedule. Braun, too, had always liked it, and was especially eager to get an outdoor, action-oriented show on the schedule that would attract young male viewers. His deputy at Touchstone, Steve McPherson, was also enthusiastic.

Admittedly, "Survivor" posed some unusual issues. ABC would have to commit to all thirteen episodes. There would be no pilot. Nothing quite like this had been tried on network television. On the other hand, that was part of its appeal. Wasn't this the "thinking out of the box" that Iger had called for? Davies, Burnett, and Wong recommended "Survivor" again to Tarses and Bloomberg. (Braun stayed away from the meeting so as not to antagonize Tarses.) This time they didn't reject it out of hand. But they wouldn't make the commitment either. They told Wong that if she could line up sponsors without a pilot, she could move ahead. She'd heard that Toyota was looking for something unusual, so she started trying to pique the carmaker's interest.

Braun was worried that Burnett would shop "Survivor" to another network while ABC tried to line up sponsors. By now he was convinced that Tarses was trying to sabotage every idea he supported, but he decided he'd try again to surmount the problem. He had stopped going to programming meetings to avoid Tarses, but now he returned. Tarses glared at him, then looked away. He decided to ignore this, and ask a question. Everyone in the room froze. Tarses pretended she didn't hear it. So he asked again. This time she gave a curt answer, while looking the other direction. Braun got up and walked out. Afterward, he told Mark Pedowitz, the lawyer in charge of business affairs for Touchstone Television, that he'd had enough, and he was quitting. "I'm finished. Iger just gave her a vote of confidence. No one cares what's happening at this place. Fuck this."

Word of Braun's unhappiness filtered up to Iger, and a few days later, he called a meeting. "You are going to behave like adults," Iger told Braun and Tarses. They met in Stu Bloomberg's office. "This is ridiculous," Iger began, and lectured them like grade school students. "You are going to get along, and that's it."

Tarses was twirling her hair around a finger, avoiding looking at Braun.

"I've spoken to Jamie," Iger continued. "I know she wants to say something."

"I realize I've made some mistakes," she began, still not looking at Braun. "Maybe I haven't behaved in a mature way. But it's been hard for me. The rules changed. If you would show me more sensitivity, maybe this would work."

"Lloyd, do you want to say something?" Iger asked.

"Yes, I do," Braun said. "Jamie, I don't believe one word you just said."

Braun had prepared a written list of the problems she'd caused him. He pulled a piece of paper out of his pocket and started reading: the agents she'd told not to work with him, the ABC employees ordered not to speak to him. He continued for five minutes.

Iger grew increasingly agitated. "Are you saying you quit?" he asked Braun.

"I'm saying this isn't going to work. It's my duty to say this. You decide how to handle it."

"This meeting is over," Iger announced.

That afternoon, Braun and Bloomberg met with Howard Stern, who was pitching a new show. The meeting went well; it was actually fun. It reminded Braun why he was in the television business. "Stu, this is what it will be like if Jamie is gone. I don't understand why you defend her. She undermines you."

"What do you mean?"

Braun filled him in on the threats Tarses had made to agents if they dealt with Bloomberg rather than her. "Call the one agent you trust," Braun urged him. "Call and ask if this is true."

Bloomberg called Iger that night. "She's got to go," he said.

Tarses was fired with two years remaining on her contract, and "resigned" on August 27, bringing to a close a tumultuous two years. "I can't tell you how happy I am," she told the *Los Angeles Times*.

The movie sensation of 1999 looked like it was going to be *The Blair Witch Project,* an independent horror film that opened that summer. M. Night Shyamalan was dismayed that it would swamp his film, *The Sixth Sense,* which got pushed forward to August from the fall and had a modest marketing campaign that drew little attention to the fact that a major star like Bruce Willis was in the film.

The Sixth Sense opened on August 6, to generally strong reviews (though *The New York Times* critic hated it). Most critics were careful not to give away any of the surprise twists Shyamalan had been so careful to work into the screenplay. It was the number one film its opening weekend, attracting the usual crowd of eighteen- to thirty-four-year-old fans of the horror genre. But then old-fashioned word-of-mouth took over, a phenomenon so rare that it was practically forgotten in Hollywood. As *New York Post* critic Rod Dreher pointed out, "I can't remember the last time so many people stopped me cold to tell me how knocked out they had been by a movie. Grown men relate stories of having trouble sleeping. . . . Audiences can't get enough of this movie, and they're telling their friends and family all about it."

The Sixth Sense was ultimately nominated for six Academy Awards. Completed at a cost of $35 million, it earned just under $300 million in the United States alone, the most successful live-action film in Disney's history.

David Vogel had been right when he told Eisner that he'd left Disney with one of its biggest pictures. Vogel hadn't found another job and had pretty much stopped looking. He had decided he no longer wanted to rely on the Machiavellian instincts he found necessary to continue as a movie executive. A few studio people called to congratulate him on the film's enormous success, but he heard nothing from any of the top Disney executives, including Eisner, Roth, and Schneider. Of course, Vogel was one of the few people who knew that Disney had sold off the profits to Spyglass, and would earn only a 12.5 percent distribution fee. He wondered what Eisner thought now.

In September 1999, Eisner summoned Steve Bornstein to an urgent meeting, saying he needed Bornstein to step in and run Disney's floundering Internet ventures. Bornstein had been at ABC barely six months, and now Eisner wanted him to move to California. The only experience he had with the Internet was setting up the successful ESPN site, which was run by a Seattle company called Starwave, in partnership with Microsoft's MSN network.

From the early days of the Internet, the new medium had posed a challenge to the "old media" companies like Disney. The Internet was a hybrid of distribution and content. Would consumers pay for content, as they did for cable television? Or was the Internet more like a broadcast network, where revenues came from advertising? Was it both? No one "owned" the Internet, but companies like America Online and Yahoo! were "portals," selling access to the Internet's vast possibilities. Amazon and eBay were content sites, drawing users to the shopping services they provided. How could traditional media companies protect their markets? Simply as a defensive measure, every media company was forced into creating Internet sites that corresponded to their newspapers, magazines, and networks, profitable or not— and most were not, given that they generated little revenue from either users or advertisers.

At Disney, these issues were constantly on the agenda for strategic planning, first under Larry Murphy and then, after his departure, under Peter

Murphy. Like many executives of their generation, both Eisner and Frank Wells had been initially technophobic, slow to embrace new advances and impatient when they failed to work as promised. But with the rise of the personal computer and Internet access, Eisner had become a voracious user of email. Its speed and convenience perfectly fit his impulsive personality, especially when he was suffering from insomnia. Soon everyone at Disney carried BlackBerries, constantly scanning them for urgent messages from Eisner, who used a variety of email pen names—Michael Rust, Michael Breckenridge. Eisner also relied on Bran Ferren, an eccentric Imagineer who at least gave Eisner the illusion that he was abreast of the latest high-tech developments. Others thought Ferren lacked depth and scientific rigor, while conceding that he was adept at spinning fanciful visions of the future that seemed to appeal to Eisner.

As usual, Eisner's strong inclination was to build an Internet business from within. He'd summarily rejected Ovitz's proposal to buy a minority interest in Yahoo!. Then Larry Murphy, working with Tom Staggs and a new chief technology strategist, Kevin Mayer, examined various options, and in August 1997 recommended a partnership with Yahoo!. Staggs had negotiated a potential deal with Yahoo! in which Disney would acquire a 10 to 15 percent stake in Yahoo! for $180 million in return for Yahoo! giving prominent access to all of its sites. The logic seemed compelling to Murphy.

At a meeting to sell Eisner on the deal, Murphy argued that while the portals were likely to emerge as the dominant forces on the Internet business, Disney had arrived too late to establish its own branded portal without a massive and risky investment. The alternative was to leverage Disney's existing sites and strong brand name to create a partnership with one of the leading portals. Murphy considered $180 million a modest sum to gain a stake in the leading portal. Murphy and his team had chosen Yahoo! over AOL, with whom they'd also had brief negotiations. AOL had suggested that Disney buy AOL outright, or even that AOL might buy Disney. Eisner personally called AOL chairman Steve Case to complain about the suggestion and reject any such possibility. But the notion that AOL might try to buy Disney, farfetched on its face, seemed less preposterous as the value of AOL stock climbed into the stratosphere.

Murphy was well aware of Eisner's preference for developing businesses within Disney, which had been a constant refrain ever since he'd rejected Marriott and decided that Disney could build its own hotels. But Eisner had made a major concession by buying ABC. So Murphy was both disappointed and surprised that Eisner not only rejected the Yahoo! proposal but also seemed annoyed by it. "Why do this with anyone else? We'll do this ourselves," Eisner insisted. He derided Murphy and his team as "wimps." "Go back to the drawing board and come up with a plan to do this ourselves," he demanded.

Murphy told Yahoo! that Disney would pass on the deal. But the more he studied the alternatives, the more discouraged he became. After six months, he argued again that Disney could not enter the race alone and hope to catch up. Eisner still balked at the price of an acquisition. In the months Murphy had been studying the alternatives, Internet mania had driven stocks to extreme levels. Even as he was slightly envious about the fact that Disney stock was languishing by comparison, Eisner thought the values were absurd for companies that hadn't earned any profits and had no clear strategy for doing so. He was determined not to pay cash, and equally determined not to use Disney stock, backed by the hard assets of the company, to buy into someone else's "vision." But there was also the nagging worry that a Yahoo! or AOL might make a bid for Disney, using its stock to pay for it.

At a company meeting in New York called the "Digital Future Summit" attended by Eisner and Sid Bass, Eisner listened to various strategies, including buying one of the major portals, but decided once again that Disney should build its own. It already owned a stake in Starwave, which ran the ESPN and ABC sites, and in June 1998, Disney swapped its Starwave position plus $70 million in cash for a 43 percent stake in Infoseek, the third most popular Internet search engine after Yahoo! and Excite.

To merge the Internet assets and run the new portal, named "Go," Eisner tapped Jake Winebaum, an executive at Disney who'd started *Family PC* magazine and had been running the Buena Vista Internet Group. The Go venture was troubled from the outset. As Murphy had predicted, it was hopelessly behind Yahoo!, AOL, and the Microsoft portals. It never gained the critical mass of users necessary to attract advertisers and content. Its operations were far-flung, from Seattle to Sunnyvale to Burbank to New York to Bristol, Connecticut, where ESPN ran its site. The divergent cultures of Starwave and Infoseek were hard to meld. Nonetheless, in the summer of 1999, Disney announced that it would acquire the remaining 53 percent of Infoseek by issuing a tracking stock for the Go assets. (Owners of tracking stocks are allocated earnings from a line of business, so the stock mirrors the performance of that business, in this case the Internet.) It was a clever way for Disney to capitalize on the Internet mania in the stock market, since it sim-

ply issued stock to acquire the rest of a company valued by the market at
$2.8 billion. Still, it assumed all its liabilities, and Infoseek had lost more than
$42 million in the last six months alone.

Then Winebaum left in 1999 to start a new website, Business.com, even
before the tracking stock was issued. In September 1999, Patrick Naughton,
formerly an executive vice president at Infoseek and now one of Winebaum's
top deputies, was arrested for possessing child pornography and soliciting
sex with a thirteen-year-old girl over the Internet. For a family-oriented
company like Disney, it was a public relations disaster, and Naughton was
fired. (He was later convicted and sentenced to home detention, probation,
and a fine but no jail time, in return for helping the Federal Bureau of Investigation create computer programs to detect sexual predators.)

Eisner's answer to the mounting problems had been to recruit Bornstein
to replace Winebaum. Bornstein refused. He said he didn't feel he really understood the Internet, notwithstanding the success of ESPN online. He
didn't want to move to California. Eisner tried a second time. He reminded
Bornstein of his conviction that a talented manager could run anything, and
insisted, "We are going to be the number one portal."

"How?" Bornstein asked.

"We're Disney," Eisner replied. "We're storytellers. Anyone can get email
to work, and do the technical stuff. But we can make it a better experience
than AOL or Yahoo!."

Bornstein wasn't swayed. He thought this was the Eisner of the ESPN
stores, blindly optimistic in the face of common sense. Bornstein had already
established a reputation building ESPN, and now he had a chance to turn
around ABC. Why venture into a business he didn't have any feel for? But
then Tom Murphy called him. Like many Cap Cities employees still at ABC,
Bornstein revered Murphy. "When the chairman of the company calls and
asks you to do something, you've got to do it," Murphy said.

But Bornstein had one other reservation: Bob Iger. Rumors persisted that
Eisner was going to name Iger as president. Bornstein did not want to report
to Iger. "ABC is still a problem," Bornstein said. "It's your most important
asset. If you promote Bob and move me to the Internet group, who's going to
manage ABC?"

Eisner scoffed at the idea of promoting Iger to president. "That's impossible," he said. "I'd end up with another Ovitz problem. There's not room at
the top of this company for two people. We'd be stepping on each other's
toes."

Bornstein said he wanted Eisner's word that he would not name Iger president, and Eisner gave it. Finally Bornstein agreed to take the Internet position.

When he took up his new post, he was stunned to discover the extent of the problems. Organizationally, it was a mess, with two thousand employees in nine countries. The various Disney sites, separated from the operating divisions that created them and merged into Go.com, had no common purpose and no one championing them. Technological issues were far more complicated than Bornstein had imagined. He was at a loss to see how Disney's motley collection of assets could be forged into a profitable business operation. His first recommendation to Eisner was to admit defeat and shut down the portal, focusing instead on four areas where Disney could make money by operating its own sites: the Disney brand, ESPN sports, Disney travel, and ABC news.

Bornstein, blunt and direct, didn't yet know Eisner well enough to know that his suggestion was heresy. Disney didn't admit defeat. Eisner derided Bornstein's pessimism, arguing that "You're running a railroad while the planes are flying overhead"—a refrain Eisner taunted him with in one form or another nearly every day. Eisner insisted that the Internet was the future and that Disney had to dominate it. The public offering for the tracking stock was scheduled for November.

Bornstein found himself scratching his head, plagued by self-doubt. Did everybody else know something he didn't? It was one thing for a start-up to be losing money, but Go.com didn't even have a plan. He couldn't see how, given the cost structure and revenue base, Go.com would ever make money. Still, he thought of himself as a company man. He'd do his best.

The next installment of "Who Wants to Be a Millionaire" blanketed the ABC prime-time schedule during the November 1999 sweeps period. Originally scheduled for fifteen hour-long episodes, ABC at the last minute asked for eighteen, and Davies had to complete a marathon Sunday session in which the three additional episodes were taped in one day. Not only did the new episodes have momentum from the previous summer, the show fulfilled its full creative and dramatic promise when John Carpenter, a thirty-one-year-old Internal Revenue Service employee, had the opportunity to win a million dollars. His question: "Which of these U.S. presidents appeared on the television series 'Laugh-In'? A. Lyndon Johnson; B. Richard Nixon; C. Jimmy Carter; D. Gerald Ford." As suspense mounted, Carpenter used one of his lifelines to call his father. "Hi, Dad. I don't need your help. I just wanted you to know I'm going to win the million dollars." He correctly answered Richard Nixon.

New York Times cultural critic Frank Rich wrote that when historians looked back on the approaching millennium, they would find "a country drunk on a TV quiz show called 'Who Wants to Be a Millionaire.' . . . Not only is the 'Millionaire' viewership huge, but in an era of 'niche' audiences, when every fractionalized demographic in the nation is pandered to by its own cable channel, 'Millionaire' is gathering Americans from all walks of life around the electronic hearth in the way 'I Love Lucy' once did. Low-attention-span kids and surly teenagers watch. Parents watch. The elderly watch. Who could imagine a happier ending to our long siege of White House sexual revelations and workplace massacres? At last, a G-rated cultural value that unites the entire American family—greed! All brought to us by the wonderful world of the Disney Company, which has finally found a dirt-cheap entertainment formula that pleases Wall Street without offending any major faith."

Thanks to "Millionaire," ABC was so far ahead in the ratings race during the November sweeps that it was able to declare victory even before Nielsen had tallied the final results. On the last night of its run it drew more than 30 million viewers, and averaged over 24 million, dominating every demographic group. "Millionaire" also boosted the ratings of shows adjacent to it on the schedule, especially "The Practice," a law drama on Sunday nights from producer David E. Kelley that also won that year's Emmy for best drama.

The case for placing "Millionaire" in the regular ABC schedule now seemed stronger than ever, and ABC announced that it would begin airing "Millionaire" three times a week beginning in January. Without mentioning Eisner or Iger by name, Bloomberg and Braun told *The New York Times* that "virtually every senior executive at ABC and Disney had weighed in" on the scheduling decision. "We decided if we were going to do this, it was take no prisoners," Braun said, describing the decision to milk "Millionaire" for every bit of profit as quickly as possible. ABC doubled the ad rate for "Millionaire" and Disney estimated that the decision would boost ABC profits by $50 million a year.

With ABC suddenly in the ascendancy, the case for Iger's promotion to the Disney presidency seemed compelling, despite Iger's plan to quit in January. Under pressure from Wall Street to name a successor, or at least a strong number two executive, Eisner had again broached the possibility that fall.

This time Iger was skeptical. "Are you sure?" he asked. "You seem to be hot and cold on me."

Eisner had looked startled. "What do you mean?"

Iger felt like mentioning the call from Tom Murphy, and Eisner's remarks to other board members, but he remained silent.

Eisner himself seemed ambivalent about the prospect of any successor. With a characteristic mix of humor and irritation, he complained to *The New York Times* about constant speculation about his successor. "Everybody looks at me and says, 'Oh, well, he is 57. He must be nearing death, so why doesn't he have six successors lined up outside his office? Nobody asks Sumner Redstone, who is 117." (Redstone was born in 1923.)

In December, after the sweeps results, Eisner again brought up the possibility of naming Iger president, and invited Iger and Willow Bay to join him and Jane for dinner. Iger figured that if Eisner offered him the job in front of witnesses—both Bay and Jane—he had to mean it. But again Eisner vacillated. "Every time I think of naming a president, I feel like I'm competing with myself," Eisner said.

"That's ridiculous." Iger countered. "I'm not trying to take your job. It's enough to be president of the Walt Disney Company."

On December 10, Eisner had lunch with Gerald Levin, chairman of Time Warner, at Levin's private dining room in Time Warner's Rockefeller Center headquarters. Since Eisner had rejected Bollenbach's plan for Disney to acquire Time Warner, Disney and Time Warner had frequently been at loggerheads, especially after Disney acquired Cap Cities/ABC. Disney and Time Warner were both fierce competitors and important business partners. Time Warner owned the nation's largest cable system, paying Disney to transmit the ABC network, ESPN, the Disney Channel, and other cable channels. Disney was trying to persuade Time Warner to distribute its new soap opera channel, SOAPnet, and Time Warner was balking. It was also resisting the higher fees Disney was charging for ESPN.

More fundamentally, Time Warner had embarked on a different strategy for growth: "vertical integration," meaning it would own businesses that both created and distributed "content." Disney had taken a step in this direction by acquiring ABC, in part to ensure access for its television productions, but Eisner was hostile to the Time Warner concept.

Eisner felt little affinity for his counterpart at Time Warner. In contrast to the often impulsive and combative Eisner, Levin was a self-styled philosopher and visionary, contemplative, introspective, and sometimes cryptic in his pronouncements. Eisner found this pretentious and off-putting. Still, Levin had been prodigiously effective at corporate political maneuvering, having emerged on top first at Time Inc. and then Time Warner after the notoriously fractious merger of Time, Inc. and Warner Communications.

By the time of the Eisner-Levin lunch, the "irrational exuberance" of the Internet boom, to quote Federal Reserve Board chairman Alan Greenspan, was in full force. Levin told Eisner he was "nervous" that a big Internet company was likely to try to take over either Time Warner or Disney, or even both of them. Levin argued that stock valuations of "old media" companies like Time Warner and Disney were depressed, whereas the stock prices of dot-com companies were so high that they could buy almost anything, using their stock as currency. Both Time Warner and Disney, he suggested, were in "jeopardy."

"We'd never do a deal using that currency," Eisner said, referring to the inflated stock of the dot-com companies. He added that Levin was crazy to even consider exchanging Time Warner's solid assets for the speculative frenzy of Internet stock. Levin pointed out that he and Eisner might not have a choice if a dot-com company made a tender offer for stock and shareholders accepted it. "One of us is going to be taken over," he warned. "Mark my words."

Eisner and Levin discussed the fact that one way to ward off such a possibility was for Disney and Time Warner to merge themselves—something that, unknown to Levin, Eisner had at least briefly considered at Bollenbach's urging. Just who raised this possibility is a subject of dispute. Eisner maintains that it was Levin's suggestion; Levin that it was Eisner's. (They were the only ones in the room at the time.) Neither, it seems, took the idea all that seriously, given that the delicate question of who would run the combined companies—Eisner or Levin—wasn't addressed. Still, the combination of Time Warner's cable systems with Disney's cable channels and broadcast network made for an intriguing possibility.

Given the magnitude of such a potential merger, Eisner nearly forgot to mention the impasse the two companies had reached over their cable negotiations. It was only as he was leaving that he brought up the ABC issue. "Gerry, I don't want to fight with you over this," Eisner said, sounding a conciliatory note. "I hate this deal, but I'm not going to stop it. Just get it done." He and Levin shook hands, and Levin took the handshake as a sign that they had an agreement to settle the dispute.

But Levin's fear that an Internet company might be stalking Time Warner or Disney stuck in Eisner's mind. The very idea angered him, and not least because, as an unreconstituted "old" media executive, he would be superfluous in such a company. One Friday afternoon, he was talking to Peter Murphy when Murphy said he had to get to a meeting. "With?" Eisner asked.

"The head of strategic planning for AOL," he said.

Eisner practically exploded. "Get him out of here! He's a Trojan horse. Cancel the meeting. Get rid of him."

Late that night, Eisner reached Steve Case, AOL's chairman. He was still furious. "Our company is not for sale," he said. "But if you're interested, call me directly. Do not send some emissary." Case started to argue with him, but Eisner insisted they had nothing to discuss. The conversation lasted less than ten minutes.

On Monday morning, Case called Eisner. "Have you calmed down?" he asked. "I thought you were going to have a heart attack."

"Just go away," Eisner replied.

"It is a good idea, you know, AOL and Disney," Case persisted.

"Go away!" Eisner yelled.

Late in the year, as Eisner sat down to draft his annual letter to shareholders, he had the approaching millennium to consider as well as the discouraging prospect of sharply lower earnings and a sagging stock price. And this was despite the remarkable success of "Millionaire," *The Sixth Sense*, the rapid climb of ABC in the ratings, and the continued burgeoning success of ESPN. The biggest reasons for the decline in financial results were areas in which Eisner had scant interest: consumer products and home video. But soaring costs in the more creative areas of the company also took their toll: live-action film, animation, and theme parks, where spending continued to build expansion parks like California Adventure at Disneyland and TokyoSea in Japan in an effort to create "destination" resorts and induce guests to stay longer.

"The last ten years comprised a spectacular decade for Disney," Eisner wrote. "Unfortunately, in financial terms, it ended on a down note." With the continuing dearth of animated hits, Disney was feeling the aftereffects of the *Lion King* bonanza. The company now had more than seven hundred Disney retail stores, no longer novel as they were a fixture in malls and shopping areas across America, with nothing fresh to sell. And Disney was also reaping the inevitable repercussions of the decision to release its classics on video. While the decision had yielded enormous short-term profits, the library was now exhausted. All the classics had been released. Roy's concerns about the future value of the library were being borne out.

The creation of the Go tracking stock had also failed to mask the mounting losses from Disney's Internet venture, not that anyone really expected Internet ventures to show a profit in those heady days of 1999. But as Bornstein kept stressing, he couldn't see how Go would ever make a profit. Eisner sidestepped the issue in his letter, writing "There can be little question that the Internet is the next major development in the realm of information and entertainment. During the coming years, broadband transmission will make it possible for the Internet to become a true entertainment medium. . . . In Go.com I believe we have brought together a collection of assets and skills that will allow us to seize the opportunities that emerge as the Internet evolves and grows in the years ahead."

Eisner could honestly extol the virtues of the ABC acquisition, noting that the cable assets alone were probably worth the $19 billion Disney had paid. "The full value of a single show like 'Who Wants to Be a Millionaire?' is almost impossible to calculate, since it is profitable in itself, helps position the entire ABC network (it played a key role in ABC's remarkable November sweeps win) and provides a promotional platform for all of Disney. Our ABC properties have become so integrated into our company that I simply can't imagine Disney anymore without them."

And Eisner had his usual optimism about the future. "In January there's 'Fantasia 2000,' which is a remarkable continuation of a completely distinct Disney legacy. For Memorial Day weekend, there's 'Dinosaur,' which is truly like nothing you've ever seen before. Further down the road, 'Kingdom of the Sun' and 'Atlantis' are looking to be wonderful additions to the Disney animation legacy. Then there are our new theme park projects, each of which is dazzling. On the Internet, Go.com is an exciting venture into an entirely new world of information and entertainment. I'd like to tell you which of our upcoming films and TV shows will be the next 'Sixth Sense' or the next 'Who Wants to Be a Millionaire?' but that's impossible to predict. However, I believe that these kinds of mega-hits are in the pipeline, and when they break through, their impact will reverberate throughout the company."

Eisner said nothing in his annual letter about his decision to name Bob Iger as Disney's president, but in mid-December he began to prepare other top executives for the announcement, a delicate task given that Eisner's decision ended any lingering hopes on the part of Joe Roth and Sandy Litvack, not to mention reneging on the promise Eisner had made to Steve Bornstein. Eisner told Litvack of his decision, and tried to placate him by naming him vice chairman. But then Eisner publicly repudiated the notion that Litvack was his heir apparent or in line for further advancement. Afterward, Litvack seemed deflated. He congratulated Iger. "I always felt like I wanted to be a member of Michael's club," Litvack said, somewhat wistfully. "And then I discovered there wasn't any club." Litvack announced in October 1999 that he would leave at the end of the year.

By mid-December, Roth, too, had decided to quit, and began forming plans to build his own production company. One afternoon Peter Schneider came into his office and announced that he was going to quit. "This isn't working," Schneider said. Roth had never trusted him, for obvious reasons, and the two had never felt comfortable working together. "I wouldn't if I were you," Roth replied. "I'm going to resign and then you can have the damn job."

Given how often Eisner had complained about Joe Roth, he seemed surprisingly reluctant to have him quit. Roth was spending the Christmas holiday with his family in Barbados, and he told Eisner that when he returned, he planned to resign. During the vacation, Eisner called him every day, just before dinner, urging him to reconsider. But when Roth got back, he walked into Eisner's office and said his decision was final. Eisner reminded him that under his contract, Disney had an option to extend it.

"You said you'd never exercise it," Roth replied. Eisner nodded. But then, after lunch, he walked into Roth's office and handed him a letter exercising the option and offering him stock options on 7.5 million shares, then walked out.

Roth glanced at the letter, then followed Eisner back to his office. "I told you not to do this," he said indignantly. "I'm going to make my own money."

Eisner abandoned his attempts to keep Roth, and once he'd reconciled himself to the idea that he was leaving, asked his advice on a replacement. "Put Dick Cook in my place," Roth urged. Cook, who was in charge of marketing and distribution for the studio, was the last of the pre-Eisner studio executives still at Disney. "He's solid, reliable, he can run the studio."

"No, he's not creative," Eisner countered. "I'm putting in Peter Schneider."

"No one likes him," Roth warned.

Eisner announced that Schneider would succeed Roth as chairman of the studio on January 7, 2000. A few days later, Eisner conceded that Roth had been right about Schneider, at least among studio executives like Garner who'd been reporting to Roth. When Eisner met with them to tell them of his decision to promote Schneider, he'd met stiff resistance. "I've been trying to tell you this for weeks," Roth told him.

"I didn't believe you. I thought you were just being political," Eisner said.

"This is why I'm leaving," Roth said. "I tell you the truth, but you won't listen."

Eisner said nothing to Steve Bornstein of his decision to name Iger president. Bornstein only learned about it just before the news was released on January 24, and was taken by surprise. Stunned, he went to see Eisner in his office. "I feel incredibly abused," he began.

"I guess you're fucked," Eisner replied.

"You gave me a commitment," Bornstein reminded him. "You disregarded it."

"I changed my mind," Eisner said.

THIRTEEN

The long-awaited *Fantasia 2000* premiered at Carnegie Hall in New York in mid-December 1999, with James Levine conducting a live performance by the Philharmonia Orchestra of London, flown in by Disney for the occasion. On New Year's Eve, Disney ushered in the millennium with a $2,000-per-person black-tie benefit screening in Pasadena, also featuring a live performance by the Philharmonia. *Fantasia 2000* opened commercially on New Year's Day in the giant screen Imax format at just fifty-four theaters. Roy, credited in the film as executive producer, used the occasion to pay tribute to Walt. "What better way to recognize the vision of one man who began building on a dream in the twentieth century than by sharing the magic with everyone as we enter the new millennium," Roy said.

Dick Cook, the studio's head of marketing and distribution, was doing his best to make *Fantasia 2000* an "event" movie. Roy seemed delighted with all the promotion and related festivities. But Thomas Schumacher, the head of animation, had serious reservations. Each of the eventual seven "premieres" in the United States, Europe, and Japan, featuring Levine and the Philharmonia, cost more than $1 million. Excerpts from the original *Fantasia* seemed grainy on the huge Imax screen. And in an avalanche of press about the arrival of the millennium, *Fantasia 2000*, an old-style sequel to a 1940 classic, drew scant attention. Though it initially attracted crowds to Imax theaters, the seating capacity was so limited that total revenue was modest (less than $3 million for the opening weekend). Schumacher also worried that by the time the film opened nationwide, curiosity and interest would have been exhausted.

The critical reception was also tepid. *Fantasia 2000* contained a few segments as dazzling as anything Disney had produced—a sophisticated homage to Broadway caricaturist Al Hirschfeld, set in an animated New York City to George Gershwin's "Rhapsody in Blue," and the concluding episode, a vision of Earth's destruction and renewal set to Igor Stravinsky's "The Firebird Suite." But not surprisingly, considering that every episode had a different director and group of animators, it was inconsistent. " 'Fantasia 2000' often has the feel of a giant corporate promotion whose stars are there simply to hawk the company's wares," wrote Stephen Holden in *The New York Times*. The film "is not especially innovative in its look or subject matter . . . despite its science fiction title, the movie is really a compendium of familiar Disney attitudes and styles, one that looks to the past more than to the future." The Eisner-inspired "Pomp and Circumstance" segment, now featuring Donald Duck trying to board Noah's ark with the procession of animals, came in for particularly harsh criticism, confirming the animators' view that the piece didn't belong in the film.

By the time *Fantasia 2000* opened in wide distribution later that spring, Schumacher's fears were borne out: Public interest had evaporated. By Disney's reckoning, the film had cost $90 million and made roughly $60 million in the United States, and Eisner was impervious to arguments that at least $60 million would have been incurred anyway since so many animators were under contract. He didn't say anything directly to Roy, but told others that the film was "Roy's folly," and that it had convinced him that Roy had little, if any, talent.

On January 10, Eisner was startled by news that AOL and Time Warner were merging in a stock swap valued at $165 billion, the biggest merger in history. AOL's Steve Case would be chairman of the combined companies, and Gerald Levin chief executive. Ted Turner, CNN's founder, Time Warner's largest shareholder and a board member, told *The New York Times* that he had voted to approve the deal "with as much excitement as the first time I made love 42 years ago."

Eisner realized that this was what Levin must have been worrying about at their lunch the previous month. Indeed, Case had first approached Levin the previous October, about the same time he was making overtures to Disney. Now Levin had decided to merge with AOL instead, trading Time Warner's hard assets for AOL stock, which Eisner viewed as little more than inflated paper. Although he thought it was a terrible deal, Eisner was worried about the implications. Disney's own Internet venture was going nowhere, and now Time Warner had secured the biggest Internet service provider. Along with its massive cable operations, Time Warner was aggressively expanding into other distribution methods, exactly the kind of vertical integration Eisner opposed, on both philosophical and financial grounds. And then there was the still-unresolved issue of the Disney-owned channels being carried on Time Warner's cable system.

The idea that a combined AOL and Time Warner might use its distribution power to freeze out Disney products became a near-obsession with Eisner, bringing out his fiercest competitive instincts. He talked to Iger and emailed him constantly about the threat. It also brought Iger his first major test as Disney's president. Unlike Ovitz, Iger secured the title of chief operating officer as well, the same title as Frank Wells. Iger's standing in the company had never been higher. In the wake of the success of "Who Wants to Be a Millionaire" in the November sweeps, and the Super Bowl earlier that month, ABC had vaulted back into first place among the networks. But Iger knew he would still have to prove himself and overcome Eisner's deep-seated anxiety about being upstaged by a strong number two. It hadn't been lost on Iger that Eisner refused to let a Disney photographer take a picture of him and Iger together to accompany the press release.

So if Time Warner posed a competitive threat, it was also a leadership opportunity. Eisner decided that it was best both for his and Disney's image that he appear to be above the fray. Iger convened a strategy meeting at ABC headquarters in New York, where top executives argued that the very source of Disney's anxiety—the power of a combined AOL/Time Warner—could be turned to Disney's advantage by threatening to raise antitrust objections, a sensitive topic in light of the government's recent antitrust case against Microsoft. Eisner suggested that Disney go to Time Warner and demand assurances that Disney's programming would be treated the same as Time Warner's. If not, he said, Disney would lobby against the merger in Washington.

Iger broke the news to Time Warner in a telephone call to Levin and Joseph Collins, the chief executive of Time Warner Cable, who had been handling the negotiations with Disney. "We're concerned about the AOL deal," Iger said. Their cable deal was now "off the table."

Levin and Collins were surprised and angry. "We had a deal," Levin said, referring to his handshake with Eisner.

"The world has changed," Iger said. "The players have changed. It's AOL and you. It's a more complicated world."

A relatively discreet business dispute over cable access had escalated into something much bigger. Levin argued that Disney was "abusing" the cable negotiations by tying them to the merger. But Iger wanted new terms, and, in what he considered an effort to be "deadly candid," he added, "We feel you'll be hard-pressed to cause trouble because of the merger process you have to go through." The conversation came to an abrupt close.

Iger followed up by instructing Anne Sweeney, the president of the Disney Channel, to send a new "term sheet," which, he concedes, was "aggressive." In addition to all the previous requests, it removed some assurances that Time Warner had sought with respect to ESPN, asked for about $100 million more in fees, and contained numerous nondiscrimination clauses—guarantees that Disney programming would get equal treatment. Disney's focus on the merger was also made explicit in a provocative letter of February 18, 2000, from Sweeney to Time Warner's Collins, in which Sweeney said that she was "even less optimistic that we will be able to bridge the material differences between us."

Time Warner executives estimated the additional cost of the proposed new deal at $300 million. Its officials were further galled by the emphasis on equal treatment in programming; in their view, Disney conspicuously favored its own programming on its networks. Time Warner responded with a term sheet of its own. It rejected nearly all of Disney's requests and lowered the price it was willing to pay.

One morning during the first week of March 2000, Eisner, still preoccupied with the AOL merger with Time Warner, got out of the shower with a plan for escalating the campaign. He went straight to his computer and drafted an email outlining the strategy he thought Disney ought to follow, which was to launch an attack in Houston, where Time Warner owned the cable system. Full-page advertisements in the *Houston Chronicle* warned that cable subscribers were at risk of losing ABC because of Time Warner's refusal to agree to a deal. Disney offered to subsidize the installation of satellite dishes if subscribers switched to a rival service. Disney gave away vouchers for fifteen thousand satellite dishes in less than three weeks. To test the effect of the Houston campaign, Disney declared a unilateral truce on April 1. It suspended the satellite-giveaway program and the public relations blitz. And it proposed new terms for the retransmission agreement, softening the position it had staked out in February.

But Time Warner's bargaining position got tougher. With Levin and Collins angered by what they considered Disney's betrayals and bad faith, Time Warner unveiled the ultimate threat: If Disney didn't agree to an eight-month extension of the existing retransmission agreement, Time Warner would cease transmitting ABC when the current extension expired, on April 30. In other words, Time Warner threatened to use what Iger thought of as a "tactical nuclear weapon"—taking ABC off the air.

Iger didn't know how seriously to take this threat. Still, Disney scrambled to head off the crisis as the April 30 deadline approached by trying to extend the agreement for another month by letter and fax. April 30, a Sunday, also marked the beginning of the May "sweeps" period, which would determine whether ABC remained the number one network. Time Warner didn't respond. ABC network and station executives, worried about the effect on ratings, were pleading with Iger to make a deal. Eisner was so absorbed by the affair that he couldn't sleep; he was on the phone to Iger at 6:00 A.M. Sunday, April 30, which was 3:00 A.M. in California.

Late Sunday afternoon, Iger organized a conference call of the roughly thirty executives involved in the crisis. He took a roll call, gave an impassioned speech ("We will stay the course," he said), and assigned battle stations. Each station manager was told to record a message to viewers to be aired at 11:00 P.M. Disney, meanwhile, made one last effort—an offer that Iger insisted be simple and clear. Disney faxed Time Warner a one-paragraph document giving Time Warner "unconditional and unequivocal consent" to transmit ABC's programming through May 24. After the 11:00 P.M. local news, Tom Kane, the general manager of WABC in New York, appeared live on TV to warn cable viewers about the possible loss of the network. At midnight, the Disney-owned channels, including ABC and ESPN, went dark on Time Warner's cable systems.

On Monday morning, Iger woke at his usual time, 4:30 A.M., and worked out at the Reebok Sports Club across Columbus Avenue from ABC headquarters. He reached the office at six, and shortly afterward left for Los Angeles, just as ABC's phone lines were becoming jammed with callers, many of them from other media. In an approach modeled on James Carville's all-out defense of President Clinton during the impeachment inquiry, he began a nonstop schedule of media appearances as soon as he landed in Los Angeles, attacking Time Warner for depriving people of the channels. In New York, Houston, and Los Angeles, Disney offered free satellite dishes to the first thousand callers willing to drop Time Warner and switch to DirecTV.

Late on Monday, Time Warner executives were still hoping that Disney, facing a possible ratings disaster, would capitulate. But with public anger at Time Warner mounting, Disney didn't consider the option. Even without Time Warner's 3.5 million affected cable viewers, Monday night was a ratings coup for ABC. The network had scheduled a special "Celebrity Millionaire," and that show alone pulled a rating of 22.1 (each point represents about a million homes). In the New York area, where the signal was missing from more than a million households, the show exceeded the national average.

On Tuesday morning, Iger spoke to New York senator Charles Schumer. Schumer told Iger that his household was among those that had been blacked out by Time Warner the previous night: "My daughters are complaining that they couldn't watch 'Celebrity Millionaire.' " He wouldn't take sides, he said, but added, "TV signals should not be pulled off the air because of corporate battles." He said that he had already spoken to Levin and had asked him to extend the agreement with Disney for six months and get ABC back on the air.

In times of crisis, Levin had often called upon Time Warner's co–chief operating officer, Richard Parsons. Parsons had been in Washington on Monday, tending to merger issues; when he got home that night, his wife, who had been watching the news coverage, said, "How could you be so stupid?"

The battle essentially lost, Time Warner capitulated. "Work something out," Levin told Parsons. "We've got to get this behind us."

At 3:21 P.M., ABC reappeared on the Time Warner systems, even though none of the underlying issues had yet been settled. Then Iger called Parsons, saying, "This wasn't good for either of us, but it was worse for you." Eventually, Disney got almost everything it wanted in a deal it valued at $3 billion.

The victory was an early triumph for Iger, and vindication of Eisner's firmly held belief that "content" was what mattered. In the end, "Millionaire" had trumped Time Warner's access to millions of cable homes. Parsons promised that Time Warner would never again unilaterally stop carrying a broadcast signal. "We've apologized to our customers," he said. "Our customers pay us thirty-two dollars a month to get a cable service that includes ABC, and they don't care about our problems with Disney. They don't care about the legal issues. And one thing we learned is that there's no PR in the world that will overcome the 'Millionaire' show."

"Millionaire" had now proven itself to be more than a ratings juggernaut. Its soaring popularity made it a potent competitive and political weapon. But in the euphoria over the showdown with Time Warner, no one stopped to consider the implications of Eisner's "content" strategy: What if ABC hadn't had a mega-hit like "Millionaire"? Phrased another way, what if Time Warner had dropped ABC and viewers didn't care?

The implications of the show's success didn't stop with the victory over

Time Warner. As a result of the previous summer's decision to schedule "Millionaire" three times a week for the upcoming 2000–2001 season, Eisner and Iger had slashed ABC's development budget, the rationale being that with "Millionaire" occupying so much of the schedule, ABC didn't need to order many new pilots. And in the chaos of Tarses's final days and abrupt departure, ABC's development efforts were in any event already faltering. For the 2000–2001 season, there were only six comedies and five dramas in development—less than half the usual number. By the time the final decisions about the new season were made that year, there were so few options that the show's frequency was increased from three to four nights a week.

As ABC prepared for the annual upfront presentations for advertisers in New York in mid-May, it was riding the wave of its "Millionaire"-driven ratings success, just as the continuing Internet-driven boom in new dot-com companies, all competing for public attention, drove demand for advertising through the roof. Rarely had the stars been so favorably aligned for network television. At that year's ABC upfront presentations at Radio City Music Hall, hosted by Bloomberg and Braun, the ABC executives reveled in it. As the lights dimmed, smoke billowed across the stage and a hydraulic platform ascended, transporting "Millionaire" star Regis Philbin toward the heavens. "Go ahead, take a good look at me," Philbin proclaimed, "the guy who saved the ABC television network."

ABC raked in nearly $2.5 billion in upfront ad sales for the 2000–2001 season, a new record for a single network.

On May 31, "Survivor," twice turned down by ABC, made its debut on CBS in the 8:00 P.M. Wednesday time slot. After watching heavy promotions of the new show on the Viacom-owned MTV and VH1 cable channels, ABC decided to crush it from the outset by using the heavy artillery of "Millionaire." ABC added an additional episode of "Millionaire," already running on Tuesday, Thursday, and Friday, to the 8:00 P.M. Wednesday time slot.

"Survivor" was exactly the show that Mark Burnett and Charlie Parsons had pitched to ABC, right down to the desert island setting (actually the Malaysian island of Pulau Tiga) and the tribal council setting with tiki torches that looked like they might have been purchased at the nearest Kmart. The sixteen contestants carefully chosen for their demographic mix contended with bugs, rats, contrived physical challenges, and one another's treachery in a Darwinian contest to "outlast" one another. Whether this was "reality" in any true sense of the word was open to question. But it was undeniably unlike anything ever seen before on American network television, far more original and risky than the game-show-with-a-reality-twist "Millionaire."

The overnight ratings from the eagerly watched head-to-head matchup between "Survivor" and "Millionaire" stunned Disney executives, including Eisner and Iger, who claimed never to have heard of the program until it showed up on the CBS schedule. ABC claimed victory, with 16.8 million viewers for "Millionaire." But "Survivor" not only managed to attract 15.5 million viewers, an astounding number for an unknown summer replacement, but it beat "Millionaire" in the critical eighteen- to thirty-four-year-old demographic most coveted by advertisers. "Millionaire" failed to deliver a knockout punch, and a barrage of press hailed "Survivor" as the breakout hit of the summer.

Was its debut a onetime event and ratings fluke? While top ABC and Disney officials ducked questions, it fell to ABC spokesman Kevin Brockman to argue the case that " 'Survivor' is a good stunt—but it's a stunt."

The next week, on June 6, ABC again programmed an episode of "Millionaire" directly against "Survivor." The results were devastating to ABC. "Millionaire" shed a million viewers, while "Survivor" jumped to 19 million. ABC abruptly canceled the following week's episode, and two weeks later, "Millionaire" lapsed into summer reruns, leading *The Washington Post* to report that "Survivor" had "demolished" "Millionaire."

Over the summer, "Survivor" became a national fixation. One contestant, Richard Hatch, became an instant celebrity when he came out of the closet in episode two and then went on to defeat former Navy SEAL Rudy Boesch and river guide Kelly Wiglesworth. Amid an avalanche of press, intellectuals struggled to define the appeal of the new "reality" genre. ("You grudgingly have to admit it's a lot more interesting than another episode of 'Friends' or 'Frasier,' " Robert Thompson, a professor at Syracuse University, told *The Washington Post*. "It's a cross between a frat party, a Club Med vacation, and a Girl Scout camp-out.") In its final episode in August, "Survivor" attracted an audience of 50 million, easily surpassing the peak episode of "Millionaire," and larger than any other program except the Super Bowl.

At Disney and ABC, the euphoria of the previous spring vanished with stunning speed, even before Braun, Bloomberg, and their colleagues had a chance to savor their success. "Millionaire's" defeat at the hands of "Survivor" was humiliating. For Andrea Wong and Lloyd Braun, who had championed the series, it was especially agonizing. Eisner insisted publicly, if implausibly, that he would turn down "Survivor" again if offered the opportunity because it was "low brow," didn't measure up to ABC's standards, and would cheapen the Disney brand. The enormous viewership for "Survivor" also gave CBS the chance to promote its fall lineup, including the other prominent ABC reject, "CSI." Apart from "Millionaire," ABC had failed to create a single new bona fide hit, though "The Practice," "The Drew Carey Show," and "Dharma & Greg" benefited from proximity to "Millionaire."

Of course ABC still had "Millionaire." The network hoped for another ratings sweep when the new season debuted that fall. (Unlike ABC, CBS opted to maintain "Survivor" as a thirteen-week "event," and the next install-ment wouldn't be aired until after the Super Bowl the following January.) But "Survivor" had dealt "Millionaire" a serious blow. It had lost the momen-tum of TV's "hot" smash hit. Next to "Survivor," it seemed staid and pre-dictable. Young people abandoned it in droves, leaving "Millionaire" and its aging host to cater increasingly to an audience of couch-bound retirees.

In the November 2000 sweeps, ABC eked out a victory in total viewers, but lost the key eighteen- to forty-nine-year-old demographic to NBC, the focus of all the headlines with its hit shows "Friends" and "ER." Because of "Millionaire," the age of the network's average viewer leaped from forty-one to forty-nine years. Michael Davies came under increasing pressure to create special episodes to inject some freshness into "Millionaire," not just "Celebrity Millionaire," but also shows featuring sports stars, college kids— anything with a twist. Braun dutifully articulated the company line: "Mil-lionaire" "is going to be a staple of the network for quite a while."

At the same time the network's fortunes were faltering, the consumer prod-ucts division continued its precipitous slide, with operating income drop-ping from nearly $900 million in 1997 to just $386 million in 2000. Disney hired Andy Mooney, a Scotland-born Nike marketing executive, to try to res-urrect the Disney brand, which was still suffering from a dearth of product spin-offs from animated hits. Eisner made a point of introducing Mooney to Roy, stressing that Roy was the custodian of the Disney image, and urging Mooney to work closely with him.

In the fall of 2000, Mooney asked Roy to speak to the creative people who worked with the consumer products division, who had gathered for a retreat at California Adventure, Disney's newest park, not yet open to the public. Mooney spoke first, stressing the importance of the Disney brand. But Roy immediately contradicted him. "Branding is for cattle," Roy said, arguing that what was important was creating stories and the products they generated.

That Christmas, Mooney had the idea of creating a mountain of all-white plush toys in the Disney stores. This meant that Disney would have to produce a "white" version of a plush Mickey. Store managers warned Mooney that this was heresy; Mickey was black, period. Mooney thought this was ridiculous. Roy complained to Eisner and Iger, who nonetheless backed Mooney.

Mooney and Roy began clashing over nearly everything Mooney proposed. When he wanted to launch a "princess" line of merchandise, Roy argued that it was inappropriate to portray and market characters like Cinderella and Snow White together when in the fairy tales they inhabited separate worlds and never knew each other.

For Roy, the last straw came when Mooney began marketing Disney-themed vintage T-shirts in upscale clothing boutiques like Fred Segal and Barneys and trendy clothing chains like Hot Topic. One shirt showed Snow White with the caption "Hangs out with seven small men." Another showed an archival drawing of Tinker Bell eyeing her derriere in a mirror. Roy sent Mooney a handwritten note: "You are positioning Tinker Bell as a prostitute." The shirts were hastily withdrawn, and Iger made Mooney apologize.

Iger was increasingly annoyed with Roy, who even urged that Mooney be fired. But the dispute over such seemingly minor details was a symptom of a far deeper disenchantment between a management determined to boost revenue and profits, and Roy, who felt the Disney company was abandoning the creative heritage he had spent his life trying to protect.

Despite those disquieting signs, Disney was enjoying an excellent fiscal year. The combination of a strong ad market, ESPN's continuing success, and ABC's rating performance contributed to a 39 percent jump in Disney's operating income for fiscal year 2000, which ended in September. The Miramax and Dimension units had proven to be a wildly successful acquisition, with hits in 2000 like *Scary Movie* ($157 million gross domestically) and *Scream 3* ($89 million) as well as continuing revenues from 1998's *Shakespeare in Love* and 1997's *Good Will Hunting*. The Weinsteins had seized on their success to renegotiate their contract, and had expanded their financing commitment to $700 million.

The theme parks also contributed a strong performance, partly due to millennium celebrations and a healthy economy leading to robust tourism throughout the summer. Still, in contrast to Eisner's early years at Disney, where raising the admission prices and building hotels had made the theme parks a spectacular engine of growth, it was increasingly clear that the theme parks were becoming just another cyclical business, ebbing and flowing with consumer confidence and the strength of the economy, which were factors beyond Disney's control.

Cost containment at the studio and in animation helped to mask the fact that the projects hailed by Eisner just a year earlier had been commercial and critical failures. The much-anticipated *Dinosaur,* Disney's first computer-generated animated feature, meant to show that Disney could match the technical prowess of its partner Pixar, opened a week before the Memorial Day weekend to mixed reviews and a $39 million opening weekend at the box office, a disappointment considering *Dinosaur*'s $128 million budget. It wasn't the technology that was at fault. *Dinosaur* featured actual locations filmed as backdrops, with computer-generated dinosaurs and other characters imposed onto them. The opening sequence, a sweeping, panoramic excursion through a tropical, prehuman world, was uniformly praised, as was the realism of the computer-generated dinosaurs. But the story left many viewers and critics cold. Apart from elements of the standard Disney formula (the orphaned protagonist, the wise-cracking sidekick, the up-lifting ending), *Dinosaur* was criticized for its graphic depiction of carnivorous T. rexes devouring other animals, and for the stark devastation of a meteor impact.

Whatever the shortcomings of *Dinosaur,* they paled next to *Kingdom of the Sun,* which was little short of a disaster. It had now been rechristened *The Emperor's New Groove,* a transparently desperate attempt to make the story, set in the Inca empire, seem more hip. The original drama and musical score had been almost entirely discarded in favor of a lighthearted comedy. *Groove* was now scheduled for a Christmas release, with *Atlantis* pushed back to summer 2001. Only *Remember the Titans,* a Jerry Bruckheimer production based on the true story of the integration of a Virginia high school football team, made on a non-Bruckheimer budget of just over $30 million with no big stars, turned out to be a solid hit, grossing over $100 million.

Still, the success of *Titans* was just what Eisner needed to feel that his decision to get rid of Joe Roth and his return to the low-budget "singles and doubles" strategy had been vindicated. He extolled "this wonderful—and moderately budgeted—motion picture" in his annual letter to shareholders. Peter Schneider had green-lit the project on the proviso that the script, which was riddled with profanity, be rewritten to eliminate all four-letter words, so the film could be marketed under the Disney label. However odd it seemed that no member of a 1971 Virginia high school football team ever swore, it nonetheless was precisely the kind of "family" entertainment Eisner wanted more of.

Eisner's real excitement was reserved for *Pearl Harbor,* which he was forcing Peter Schneider and Bruckheimer to bring in on the sharply reduced budget of $140 million. "Coming Memorial Day weekend, we have as close to a sure thing as you get in this business—'Pearl Harbor,' produced by Jerry Bruckheimer and directed by Michael Bay, the same team that brought us 'The Rock' and 'Armageddon,' with an all-star cast headed by Ben Affleck," Eisner wrote shareholders. "Wait a second. I take back that this is a 'sure thing.' That is bad luck. It is not a sure thing. It's an absolutely fantastic, probably successful film that should surely draw a significant audience."

In contrast to the rosy optimism about the Internet expressed by Eisner just a year earlier, in the 2000 letter to shareholders he sounded a cautious, even defensive, note. Disney's Internet group was now characterized as "embryonic and evolving. But, unlike many Internet businesses, ours is based on solid assets that should help power this cylinder to performance down the road. Yes, the Internet Group currently posts losses, and yes, that really concerns me and our management. . . . In many ways, today's Internet environment is reminiscent of Disney's early days. Walt and Roy achieved moderate success experimenting with silent cartoon shorts. Then came what we today would call a 'killer ap'—in this case, synchronized sound. The Disney Studios produced the first sound cartoon, starring Mickey Mouse, and overnight, Disney became a household name. The Internet is still in its infancy, but we are closer to the day when it will be transformed into a true entertainment medium . . . and our company will once again be poised at the cutting edge—and helping us out will be Mickey Mouse."

It could be argued that this is exactly the kind of visionary thinking a chief executive should possess, but it was also what Steve Bornstein, the person in charge of the Internet Group, who was somehow supposed to wring a profit out of the assets, found so frustrating. The truth was that Mickey Mouse was not going to rescue Go.com.

In February 2000, Bornstein convened a meeting at the Team Disney building to confront the future of Go.com. He saw no way out of the financial morass, and he was tired of arguing about it with Eisner. "Let me be blunt about this," Bornstein said. "We cannot compete and win." The portal strategy was a failure. Go.com was never going to be another Yahoo! or AOL. It was a hodgepodge of Internet assets that Disney had cobbled together on the cheap. Building a portal "was a flawed objective carried out with a poor strategy," he argued. Bornstein argued again that Disney should maintain its websites as line extensions of its various brands—ABC, ESPN, the Disney channel, the theme parks—but abandon the idea of a portal and a separate Internet division.

Bornstein knew this was the equivalent of corporate suicide. After the meeting, Peter Murphy came up to him. "I've never seen anyone at Disney show that kind of courage or conviction," he said. Bornstein wasn't looking for protective cover. This was his conclusion and he was ready to take responsibility for it. He knew it wasn't what Eisner wanted to hear. He had done what he could for Go.com, but he wasn't going to remain in a hopeless quest. He knew his future at Disney was probably doomed, no matter how successful he'd been at ESPN. Disney was not a culture where anyone could admit defeat and expect to survive. His relationship with Eisner was already damaged. Now it was probably beyond repair.

In a public concession of defeat, Disney exchanged the tracking stock for regular Disney shares in January 2001. In its own way, Disney's failure marked the end of Internet euphoria, and the stock market bubble that accompanied it. It was the first major concession of what was becoming obvious, but still unspoken: For all its promise, the Internet was yielding few business models that made any sense. Go.com tracking stock ceased trading on January 29; the NASDAQ composite average had hit an all-time peak ten months before, in March 2000.

In the ensuing months, the bottom fell out of the technology sector as a whole, and the Internet segment in particular. AOL Time Warner was especially hard hit, fully vindicating Eisner's belief that Time Warner had exchanged valuable hard assets for a grossly inflated stock. Although Eisner had long argued that chief executives should be measured by what they did—the movies they green-lit, the TV pilots they bought—as opposed to the things they turned down, rebuffing an offer from AOL was arguably Eisner's best decision of the decade, since the consequences would have been ruinous.

Still, it is faint praise to say that things could have been worse. The AOL Time Warner disaster didn't change the fact that Eisner, too, had been seduced by the promise of the Internet. Disney had squandered the assets it built up in Starwave to buy Infoseek at the peak of the market, and had poured more millions into trying to make the unwieldy combination work. Ultimately Disney's foray into the Internet cost it over $1 billion on paper, and when it bought back the Go Network's shares, Disney had to take a write-down of $790 million.

Somewhat to Bornstein's surprise, Eisner said he didn't want him to leave the company. Despite the optimism about ABC in his letter to shareholders, and his decision to make Iger president, with primary responsibility for ABC, Eisner was nervous about the network's faltering prime-time development and its dependence on a single hit, "Millionaire." So he asked Bornstein to assume a new position as president of ABC, Inc., which inserted him into the management hierarchy under Eisner and Iger, but over Alex Wallau, president of the ABC Network, as well as Stu Bloomberg and Lloyd Braun.

Bornstein was dubious that what ABC needed was yet another executive in the management hierarchy, which was already plagued by confused lines of authority and turf battles. It was hard to differentiate his duties from Wallau's. He was especially concerned that he wasn't given authority over the cable operations, including ESPN, which he'd supervised before going to the Internet operation. Iger retained responsibility for those operations, which were the biggest profit centers. But Eisner insisted that Bornstein would actually run the network, so he accepted.

Iger was obviously unhappy with the choice, which put Bornstein into the ABC hierarchy between him and Iger's close allies Wallau and Bloomberg. It was clear that Eisner had pitted Bornstein and Iger against each other, and there was immediate speculation within the company about who would emerge as the survivor.

Already wounded by the Internet experience, Bornstein had his work cut out for him. By the end of the 2000–2001 season in May, ABC had fallen to third place in the key eighteen- to forty-nine-year-old demographic, behind NBC and CBS. CBS, on the strength of "Survivor: The Australian Outback" and its breakout weekly hit "CSI," won the competition for total viewers. A barrage of press faulted ABC for ruining "Millionaire" by overprogramming it. Braun bore the brunt of the criticism, and was widely quoted defending the decision. Iger generally escaped criticism, leading Braun and Bloomberg to wonder what had happened to his assurance that he would take "full responsibility" for the decision to program "Millionaire" on multiple nights of the week. Braun and Bloomberg made a joke of it, with one or the other saying "I will take full responsibility" as they passed each other in the halls. (Iger confirmed that he and Eisner made the decision, and said he has never shunned responsibility for it. He noted that "Jeopardy!" and "Wheel of Fortune" ran successfully day in and day out, and so there was no reason not to do the same with "Millionaire.")

ABC rushed to order more pilots—thirty-four, as opposed to eleven the previous year—and slashed the rapidly fading "Millionaire" to two episodes a week for the 2001–2002 season. In a move that brought ABC News's celebrity interviewer Barbara Walters to tears, the network bumped Walters's long-running "20/20" newsmagazine from its traditional Friday-evening slot.

At this juncture, Eisner was plainly worried about ABC, and at board meetings, distanced himself, stressing that the network was Iger's primary responsibility. Indeed, he annoyed nearly all the ABC executives by pro-claiming, as he did repeatedly, that "I could solve ABC's problems if I devoted one day a week to the network."

Despite the success of the low-budget *Titans,* and the praise lavished on it by Eisner, Peter Schneider's tenure as chairman of the studios had been person-ally and creatively unfulfilling, and he talked increasingly to Thomas Schu-macher about leaving. His premonition that it would be hard to duplicate the excitement and success of *The Lion King* on Broadway had been borne out. It seemed like all he did was fight with producers like Bruckheimer and other Disney executives trying to carry out Eisner's cost-cutting mandate. He didn't want to end up like Katzenberg and Roth, bitter toward Eisner. He wanted to stay friends with Roy, who had done so much to support him when he ran animation, and it was becoming increasingly clear that Eisner would make that difficult.

Moreover, in contrast to animation, where he'd gotten along well with the animators and other executives in the division despite his sometimes prickly and exacting nature, many people in live action seemed to resent him. Todd Garner made no secret of his disdain. Still angry over the *Pearl Harbor* clashes, Garner quit Disney in April, as soon as work was finished on the film, to join Roth at a new studio Roth would soon name Revolution. So did Rob Moore, the studio's chief financial officer, who had clashed with Schneider within five days of Schneider's arrival. Others who had stayed seemed barely to tolerate him.

Bruckheimer, now Disney's most important producer, was always pro-fessional and courteous, but the bruising experience over *Pearl Harbor* had alienated him from Schneider, and he treated him like a transitory studio ex-ecutive who would be gone long before Bruckheimer stopped making films for Disney. It hadn't helped Schneider's popularity that he'd been forced to fire staff members. Even though he'd taken live action from a loss to a profit of $350 million in a year, he wasn't enjoying himself. Schneider's plan was to wait until *Pearl Harbor* opened on Memorial Day weekend 2001, then announce his resignation in the wake of what he expected to be a huge hit.

And he wasn't the only Disney executive confident about *Pearl Harbor*. Audience surveys at preview screenings were positive. Awareness of the film among potential ticket buyers was a remarkable 92 percent, higher than for any other film scheduled for release that summer. Despite "taking back" his prediction that *Pearl Harbor* was a sure thing in his annual letter to shareholders, Eisner couldn't restrain himself, in part because he was so eager for a hit. The week before *Pearl Harbor* opened, he sent an email to all Disney "cast members":

"There are no sure things in the entertainment industry, but this comes close. It better, because I've already predicted this in the annual report letter I wrote in December. And, I've been on CNBC and CNN in the last two weeks proclaiming it a smash. I've been telling anyone who would listen that this will be our biggest live-action film ever."

With Eisner's credibility on the line, little was left to chance. "Synergy" was squeezed from Disney's assets: ABC ran a one-hour special hosted by David Brinkley. "Good Morning America" featured the movie every day for a week, with co-host Diane Sawyer calling it "the movie event of the summer" and reporter Jack Ford hailing it as "the biggest summer blockbuster of all time" before the film opened. The History Channel (co-owned by Disney with Hearst and General Electric) obligingly ran three Pearl Harbor episodes as well as a "history vs. Hollywood" segment that focused on the film. The E! Channel, also co-owned by Disney, lavished coverage on the film.

Was the opening of a $140 million Disney movie legitimate news? As Frank Rich noted in *The New York Times,* the fiftieth anniversary of Pearl Harbor ten years earlier received little coverage. But it's hard to fault Disney and ABC for blurring the lines when its rivals were doing the same. NBC ran a two-hour National Geographic special hosted by Tom Brokaw on Pearl Harbor to coincide with the film's opening, and MSNBC ran a special about the making of the movie that could have been produced by Disney public relations. *Newsweek* did a twelve-page cover story. In addition to all the free publicity, Disney spent about $70 million marketing the film in the United States.

For the premiere, the Navy brought the USS *John C. Stennis* aircraft carrier from San Diego to Honolulu. Disney screened the film on board. Navy SEALs parachuted onto the deck as F-15 fighters flew in formation overhead.

Veterans of the Pearl Harbor attack were flown in as special guests. The Honolulu Symphony Pops provided music. After the screening, Disney staged a fireworks display. The tab came to $5 million.

Given all the hype that preceded it, it was indeed news when *Pearl Harbor* opened to scathing reviews and disappointing box office, at least by the inflated standards of the preopening publicity fueled by Eisner's boasts. The headline in *The Wall Street Journal* was "Snore-a! Snore-a! Snore-a!" Roger Ebert wrote that *Pearl Harbor* was "a two-hour movie squeezed into three hours. Its centerpiece is 40 minutes of special effects, surrounded by a love story of stunning banality."

No studio had dared challenge the *Pearl Harbor* juggernaut, so it was the only major movie opening over the lucrative Memorial Day weekend, traditionally the start of the summer movie season. It earned $75 million over the Memorial Day weekend, a more-than-respectable opening, but the box office plunged in ensuing weeks. Especially galling for Eisner was that the big hit of the summer, and the top-grossing film of the year, was *Shrek,* a computer-generated fairy tale based on a William Steig novel produced by Jeffrey Katzenberg at DreamWorks, which had opened just a few weeks earlier.

With benefit of hindsight, it's hard to know what besides wishful thinking could have led to such hubris at Disney about *Pearl Harbor.* The film faced obvious hurdles, starting with a running time of close to three hours. Its length, its romantic plot, and the backdrop of tragedy invited unfavorable comparisons to the wildly successful *Titanic.* And surely Disney executives could sense that, however earnest and patriotic, or dazzling the special effects, the "storytelling"—the quality to which Eisner paid so much tribute— was flawed. Todd Garner, whose idea it was, had said he didn't like the finished script or film. But by then no one was listening to him.

Schneider's plan to exit under the halo effect of a summer blockbuster was ruined. He decided to wait until the release of *Atlantis: The Lost Empire,* the latest animated feature, scheduled for June, even though he had never liked the film. Directed by the same team that produced *Beauty and the Beast, Atlantis* was a departure from the musical genre, an attempt to appeal to pre-teenage boys with an *Indiana Jones*–style adventure film, a quest for the lost continent. *Atlantis* garnered admiring reviews, but was hopelessly eclipsed by the success of *Shrek,* which took direct aim at the Disney canon with its edgy, irreverent send-up of the fairy-tale genre. *Atlantis* didn't earn back its nearly $100 million cost and became the latest in a growing string of animated disappointments from Disney.

These developments were especially worrisome to John Musker and Ron

Clements, who were deep into work on *Treasure Planet*, another attempt at an action-adventure animated feature. Their target audience of preteen and teenage boys apparently still associated hand-drawn, 2-D animation with children's fare and wanted no part of it. And other animators feared for their futures. Schumacher met with two thousand employees in groups of fifty or less to discuss plans for cost cuts, more computer-generated projects, and other "drastic changes," including layoffs and salary reductions. Morale plummeted.

When Schneider announced his departure on June 20, the press made almost no mention of a career that had included some of Disney's greatest successes. Instead, his resignation was perceived as confirmation that *Pearl Harbor* was a failure and Schneider was taking the fall. Disney had to issue a statement denying that Schneider had been fired for *Pearl Harbor*. After the Katzenberg and Ovitz fiascoes, Disney's credibility was nonexistent, even though, in this case, it was true.

Eisner never got over what he considered the injustice of the press reaction to *Pearl Harbor*. In a sense he had a point: The film eventually grossed nearly $200 million in the United States, and another $253 million in overseas markets. Ironically, Bruckheimer, Bay, Affleck, and the others who waived their guarantees ended up making more than if they had stayed with their original deals—not that any of them wanted to repeat the experience. Still, even Eisner conceded that *Pearl Harbor* didn't perform well enough to justify the enormous drain on resources that went into making the film. Just as *Dick Tracy* had marked a turning point during the Katzenberg era, *Pearl Harbor* marked the end of the Roth "tent pole" strategy, and yet another attempt to recapture the early success of Eisner's "singles and doubles" philosophy.

Disney did not announce a replacement for Schneider as chairman of the studios, instead naming Nina Jacobson and Dick Cook as co-heads of the studio. Eisner pledged to be more personally involved in running the studio.

Since the success of the ABC acquisition, Eisner had shed some of his hostility toward mergers, especially since Disney wasn't internally generating the 20 percent growth he'd promised shareholders. Despite Eisner's aversion to having Ovitz do a deal to expand Disney's faltering Hollywood Records business, Disney looked into the possibility of acquiring EMI Records, the venerable British record company. But the talks didn't result in a formal proposal. Steve Bornstein advocated buying DirecTV, the television satellite company originally launched by Hughes Electronics, which was acquired by General Motors. In 2000, GM decided to put DirecTV on the block, and Bornstein thought it made a perfect strategic fit with Disney. As had been proven in the showdown with Time Warner, satellite offered a potent competitive threat to cable. If Disney owned a satellite distribution company, cable companies could never freeze out its "content." Satellite also offered broadband possibilities that would enable movies-on-demand and interactive television. Bornstein was convinced that the lines between "content" and "distribution" were blurring as technology made new creative endeavors possible. But Eisner was cool to the idea. He insisted the world was still sharply divided, and that Disney should remain a "content" company. Satellite was a means of distribution that Disney knew even less about than it did cable. Just as he knew that Eisner wasn't a real sports fan, Bornstein could tell that the technical aspects of satellite distribution simply didn't interest Eisner.

Still, Eisner had the strategic planning department under Peter Murphy continue to pursue other acquisition possibilities, and that spring, Eisner first mentioned to Stanley Gold that the Fox Family cable channel, jointly owned by Rupert Murdoch's News Corporation and Hollywood entrepreneur Haim Saban, might be for sale. Gold was enthusiastic, commenting at a board meeting that "this has big potential outside the U.S."

Fox Family had been on the block four years before, in 1997, when Disney could have bought the channel (but not the programming) for $2 billion. But Eisner had dismissed the possibility because the cable channel had an ongoing deal to air Christian evangelizer Pat Robertson's "The 700 Club," repugnant to the secular Eisner. Since then, Fox Family had made significant strides, overtaking the Disney Channel in Europe with its 1993 hit series "Mighty Morphin' Power Rangers."

But Fox Family's main appeal to Disney wasn't so much the Power Rangers and other programming owned by the channel as it was the channel's wide distribution and the opportunity to "repurpose" programming that had already aired or been produced for the ABC network. Just as the SOAPnet channel had allowed ABC to rerun its daytime soap operas, Fox Family could be used to amortize the high cost of network programming by providing another broadcast outlet, another source of revenue. The channel could rerun established ABC programs; it could also be a development laboratory, airing new programming that, if successful, could then move to ABC. When strategic planning ran the numbers, they found it easy to project 20 percent annual growth rates, even before taking into account Disney's vastly superior marketing and economies of scale. Indeed, the strategy seemed so foolproof that no one at ABC itself was consulted about the possible acquisition, even though, strategically, it would be vitally important to ABC.

Eisner did mention the possible deal to Gold, who was a close friend of Saban. "Can I be helpful?" Gold volunteered. "I know Saban very well. I can get you there." Eisner said he'd appreciate that. "Just give me the numbers," Gold suggested. "I can be a messenger." Eisner said he'd get back to him.

· A few days later, Eisner called. "He wants $5.5 billion," he said of Saban. "I can't get there. I can go to $5 billion, but not $5.5."

"Should I see if that gets a response?" Gold asked.

"Yeah, why don't you."

Late the following night, Gold met Saban at his house in Beverly Hills. "We can go north of $5, but not $5.5," he said. Saban was noncommittal, but the next day, when he spoke to colleagues, he could barely contain his glee.

The next morning Gold briefed Eisner. "Talk to Iger and Murphy," Eisner urged. When Gold reached Iger, Iger said there would have to be a caveat to any offer. Fox Family had bought the rights to most major-league baseball games, a liability that was estimated to cost $700 million over the remaining life of the contract. Bornstein and others at ESPN thought the deal was grossly overpriced, considering that most games aired in the afternoon, when the potential audience for baseball was small. The deal had proved a huge financial drain for Fox. Iger told Gold that Saban should understand that Disney's offer for something over $5 billion contained the proviso that Disney would not assume the major-league baseball contract. If so, it would have to cut the price by a billion dollars.

So Gold called Saban. "Just so there's no misunderstanding, if we have to eat the baseball deal, we're a billion lower."

Saban was silent. Then he said, "Oh, Stanley, you're going to love baseball."

"Haim, it's not whether I love baseball or not," Gold said. "You should call Michael," Gold added.

Several weeks went by, and Gold heard nothing further. Then he got a call in mid-July from Peter Murphy, who was with Eisner at Herb Allen's annual Sun Valley conference. "Michael met with Haim and Murdoch, and we're about to do a deal," Murphy explained.

"How much?" Gold asked.

"Five point three billion dollars."

"That's without baseball?" Gold asked. Murphy said nothing.

"Peter, is it with or without baseball?"

There was silence again. Finally Murphy said, "With baseball."

"What the hell is going on?" Gold exclaimed.

"You know Michael," Murphy said.

That Sunday, Steve Bornstein learned that Disney was buying Fox Family, the first that anyone at ABC had heard of the deal.* On Monday, July 23, Bornstein briefed key ABC executives, including Mark Pedowitz, the lawyer in charge of business affairs for the network.

"What are we going to do with it?" Pedowitz asked.

"They want to repurpose ABC shows," Bornstein explained, meaning Disney would rebroadcast shows that had already aired on ABC.

"Didn't anyone realize we don't have the rights to do that?" Pedowitz asked, evidently the first time anyone had asked him about the legal feasibility of rerunning programs produced by others who retained the syndication and rebroadcast rights.

Bornstein just looked at him and shrugged.

At Fox Family's Westwood, Los Angeles, offices, Saban met with staff members to announce the deal. He was exulting over the $5 billion-plus price tag, especially since there were no other bidders. Eisner had brought up the baseball rights but had quickly given in when Saban had bluffed, and told him he had to take it or leave it. Saban told them the deal had been concluded in less than an hour's meeting with Eisner.

After reaching a handshake deal in Sun Valley, Eisner and Iger flew to Aspen, where Eisner was hosting a retreat for about thirty top executives. They had already assembled when Eisner and Iger, accompanied by Peter Murphy arrived, looking, as one executive there put it, like "cats who had just swallowed canaries."

Many at the meeting were astounded that Disney was spending over $5 billion to acquire a cable network and its programming and that Steve Bornstein and others at ABC had not been consulted. Others argued that Disney should be investing in distribution systems, either cable systems or satellite. Comcast, where Steve Burke was now a top executive, had just made a hostile bid for AT&T's cable systems, the country's largest. Bornstein tried to revive the idea of buying DirecTV, which made far more sense to him than

---

* Murphy insisted that Bornstein had been consulted, but Bornstein said he learned of the deal only after the Sun Valley conference. Murphy also denied saying "you know Michael" or anything else about Eisner in his conversation with Gold.

paying $5 billion for the Family channel. "Why don't we make a bid with Microsoft?" he asked.

Eisner was dismissive, arguing that Disney knew nothing about running a satellite or cable distribution system, but could easily program a cable channel. In any event, Disney wouldn't be able to absorb another big acquisition now that it was buying Fox Family.

The Fox Family announcement coincided with the retreat, but the main purpose of the gathering was to enhance "synergy" among the top executives and foster a closer sense of teamwork. To this end, the group had been going on hikes and bike rides, and Disney had hired a consultant who had been conducting in-depth interviews with the executives, and would be presenting his conclusions at the retreat. The interviews had been revealing in ways neither the Disney executives nor the consultant had expected. The consultant asked questions about whether Disney executives liked and trusted their colleagues and worked well together. Some were less than candid, because they didn't trust the consultant, who they suspected would be reporting everything to Eisner. Others revealed as little as possible, sitting through the interviews with barely disguised impatience. And some were honest: no one trusted anyone else, least of all Eisner himself.

The experience had left the consultant exasperated. As the Disney executives sat in a circle, he said, "The results of my research indicate that you guys are not a good team. You're not a team at all. You're not even a group."

"Wait a minute," Bornstein interjected. "How could we not be a group? Three people in a room are a group."

"You guys are so bad you're not even a group," the consultant insisted.

Eisner disputed that. "How can you say that? You haven't been to my Monday lunches."

The session quickly devolved into arguments about the ways in which Disney management did or did not function as a team, which pretty much proved the consultant's point. Later, Eisner dismissed the whole experiment as a waste of time. Away from Eisner, several of the participants later conceded the issue. "What Michael likes is to put six pit bulls together and see which five die," one said.

By late summer, Stanley Gold and Roy were growing increasingly concerned about Disney's overall financial performance. All key financial measures at the company, including return on equity, return on assets, and return on in-

vested capital, had been steadily declining since 1995—each of these measures by more than 50 percent. The notion of Disney as a "growth" company
was becoming increasingly hard to defend. Despite annual five-year strategic
plans that confidently predicted a return to 20 percent annual earnings
growth, Disney's earnings for fiscal year 2002 were likely to be no better than
they'd been in 1994 or 1995.

ABC's performance was especially worrisome. The ratings of "Millionaire" collapsed, and with it went the lead-ins to ABC's other programs. It was
especially galling that two of the biggest hits on television—"Survivor" and
"CSI"—had once been in ABC's grasp and had vaulted CBS past ABC in the
network rankings.

So it had rankled Gold that as chairman of the executive compensation
committee, he was asked to have his committee approve a new, $9 million,
three-year contract for Stu Bloomberg. As far as Gold was concerned,
Bloomberg was responsible for ABC's faltering prime-time schedule. This
was very much on Gold's mind when he arrived for the board dinner the
night before the meeting in August 2001, held under a tent canopy in the gar-
den behind Eisner's Bel Air home.

Gold expressed his feelings to several directors. (Roy was at his castle in
Ireland.) "Did you see the board package?" Gold asked them. "Did you see
this Bloomberg contract? It's a piece of shit. It's outrageous." And he used the
occasion to question more broadly Disney's performance. After dinner,
some of the directors and the Eisners moved into the living room for drinks
and coffee. As the directors said good-bye to Jane and shook Eisner's hand at
the front door, Eisner pulled Gold aside. His face reddened in anger. "What
the hell are you doing?" Eisner demanded.

"What do you mean?" Gold asked.

"You're talking to everybody. You're causing trouble. Everybody tells me
you're upset."

"I'm just talking to other directors," Gold retorted. "And I am upset."

"Your behavior is outrageous," Eisner said.

Gold protested that he felt it was his obligation to speak up, and that it
was overdue. For too long the board had passively accepted whatever Eisner
told it and rubber-stamped his decisions.

This seemed to infuriate Eisner. "Are you saying you're losing confidence
in me?" Eisner heatedly asked. "Are the two of you? Because if you are, then
I'll resign. Is that what you want?"

"No, but I'm getting close," Gold replied.

Later that night, Eisner sent an angry email to Roy, saying that Gold had been trying to undermine him and stir up trouble on the board. He also emailed Gold, telling him that the Bloomberg contract, as well as a generous deal for Lloyd Braun, was Iger's doing.

Roy phoned Gold from Ireland to ask, "What's this all about?" Roy read him Eisner's email attacking him. Gold related the night's exchanges, and said Eisner had asked if he and Roy were losing confidence in him. He reminded Roy that Eisner had promised years earlier at their victory dinner that he would resign if he ever lost their support. Had the time come to take him up on that? Gold, angry, was beginning to think so, but Roy was reluctant to do anything so drastic. He counseled patience.

The next morning both Eisner and Iger came to the committee meeting, which, in addition to Gold, was attended by committee members Andrea Van de Kamp, Sidney Poitier, Murphy, and Ray Watson. Gold began by saying he was against approving the contracts. "They make no sense, and it's not fair to shareholders," he said. "They have the worst record in the business." Iger mounted a stout defense of Bloomberg and Braun, though failing to mention just who had been responsible for programming "Millionaire" four nights a week and for slashing the development budget, which meant ABC had practically nothing in the pipeline. He concluded by saying that the upcoming season "is great," and would prove the worth of the contracts.

Andrea Van de Kamp looked at Gold and rolled her eyes.

Eisner immediately jumped to his feet, furious. "What are you looking at Stanley for?" he demanded of the startled Van de Kamp.

Gold intervened. "Michael, these numbers make no sense. Anyone can see that."

Eisner sat back down. Despite Gold's concerns, there was little likelihood that other board members would defy Eisner. Rather than antagonize Eisner and waste his vote as a protest, Gold decided he'd go along with the rest of the committee. The committee voted unanimously to approve the contracts. Still, Gold felt he'd made his views clear.

On Tuesday morning, September 11, 2001, Bob Iger's personal trainer arrived at his Brentwood home as usual at 4:30 for his morning workout, finishing at 5:45. Iger was walking to the shower when ABC News president David Westin called from New York. "Do you have your TV set on?" he asked. "You won't believe this, but a plane just hit the World Trade Center."

Iger had a TV in his shower, and turned it on to see smoke and flames billowing from Tower One. "Oh my God."

"It doesn't look like an accident," Westin said.

"I'd better get into the office," Iger said. "Call me when you know."

Fifteen minutes later, the second plane hit. Iger called Eisner from his car, waking him up. "Turn on the TV," Iger urged. "I'm rushing to the office to set up a command post. I'll call you as soon as I get there."

By the time he arrived, a third plane had hit the Pentagon, and a fourth was reportedly en route toward Washington. Iger called Eisner again, and they discussed the obvious: If the World Trade Center, the Pentagon, and possibly the White House or Capitol were targets of terrorist attacks, would Walt Disney World be next?

FOURTEEN

After he had spoken to Eisner, Iger got theme parks chairman Paul Pressler and the head of security on the phone. Disneyland Paris was nearing the end of its day, Walt Disney World had opened at 9:00 A.M., and Disneyland and the new California Adventure park hadn't yet opened. "This is horrific," Iger said. "We have to protect the people in our parks."

The parks had contingency plans for a wide range of potential calamities, from hurricanes and earthquakes to crazed gunmen. Though invisible to guests, surveillance cameras were strategically placed throughout the parks, leaving little chance that an incident wouldn't be instantly detected. There had been some accidents over the years, even a few deaths, but no catastrophes. Still, no one had contemplated the prospect of a passenger jet being deliberately crashed into one of the resorts.

Pressler and Iger made the decision to stage an orderly closing of Walt Disney World and not to open Disneyland or California Adventure. Eisner agreed. Rumors swirled throughout the day that Disney was a target, including its two cruise ships, which were in the Caribbean. Later, Iger spoke directly with Attorney General John Ashcroft, who assured him that the government had no evidence that any Disney properties were a terrorist target. Still, who could know for sure?

The decision to close the American theme parks left thousands stranded in Disney hotels, and Disney waived hotel charges for guests. In part to give them something to do, all the parks opened at their usual times the next day. But already, cancellations were pouring in. It dawned on Iger that the attacks of September 11 would have a serious impact on Disney's financial prospects.

Iger was also on the phone a dozen times that day to David Westin at ABC News, both to learn more about what was happening and to discuss ABC's ongoing coverage. It thrust Disney into the uncomfortable but not unprecedented position of both managing the news, as the parent of ABC, and being the subject of news, as a company that was a possible terrorist target. Generally speaking, ABC News tried to cover Disney as it would any other company, although this line between "church and state" had always made Eisner uneasy. It was understood that investigative pieces aimed at any of Disney's businesses were off limits.

September 11 brought new strains to this co-existence. With anxiety about another terrorist attack at its peak, Westin told Iger that ABC reporter Brian Ross had a story that Spanish prosecutors had obtained what they characterized as surveillance videos of the World Trade Center, the Golden Gate Bridge, Sears Tower, Disneyland, and Universal Studios. Iger was stunned, first because he'd been assured by Ashcroft and other government officials that they had no evidence that Disney was a target, and second by the prospect that ABC News was about to label Disneyland a target, which was the worst possible publicity given that people were already afraid to travel. Suddenly Iger was thrust into the awkward role of news editor. He pressed Westin on whether Williams had actually seen the tapes.

All Williams had was the World Trade Center footage, and Iger argued that it was reckless to label Disney as a target when the government continued to insist there was "no credible evidence" that it was. But given the statements from Spanish prosecutors, Williams stood by his story. "Just treat us fairly," Iger pleaded. After delaying for two days, ABC ran the footage of the World Trade Center and identified Disneyland as an "al-Qaeda objective."

When Iger again confronted Ashcroft in the wake of the ABC broadcast, the FBI agreed to show the footage to Iger and other Disney executives. There were indeed scenes of Disneyland and various attractions, including "Pirates of the Caribbean" and "The Many Adventures of Winnie the Pooh." The voice-over was in Arabic. But the comments were innocuous, and the scenes looked like standard tourist videos. Iger was annoyed with ABC News, since this was hardly what he would call surveillance, nor did it indicate that Disney was an "al-Qaeda objective." Still, the damage was done, and further coverage by ABC would only reinforce the impression that Disney might be a target.

Despite Stanley Gold's concerns about an acquisition of Fox Family that included the major-league baseball deal, when the proposed acquisition came before the board for approval, he and Roy both voted for it. In part this was because they weren't prepared for a full breach with Eisner, and dissenting on such a cornerstone of the CEO's strategy for the company would have been a declaration of war. The pro forma financial statements prepared by strategic planning and finance also impressed Gold. Even with the baseball deal, the financial projections showed 20 percent annual compounded growth easily within reach. To reach these numbers, Disney planners simply took the Fox Family results and superimposed over them the equivalent results for the most successful cable channels, such as the USA Network. The assumption was that Disney, with its marketing prowess, economies of scale, and programming skills, could bring Fox Family to those levels and beyond. As Eisner stressed to the board, "We know programming."

This, of course, had been before September 11. The terrorist attack, which had suddenly threatened the health of the global economy, may not have been precisely an "act of God," but it was an unforeseen material change in circumstances that might have justified Disney's canceling the deal. While the precise economic impact couldn't be immediately foreseen, it was obviously substantial, both for Disney itself and the Family channel, which depended on advertisers and cable operators for its revenue. The stock market, after remaining closed for the duration of the week of September 11, had reopened on Monday, September 17, and reflecting a crisis in investor confidence, dropped nearly 700 points, a record in total points, though not as a percentage decline. Disney shares were hard hit, dropping from over $23 on September 10 to $19.25 when the market reopened. They continued their downward spiral the rest of the week, and by Thursday were below $17.

The reasons were obvious. With its theme parks heavily dependent on air travel and consumer confidence, Disney faced a potentially serious decline in tourism. A remarkably strong advertising market had buoyed financial results at the increasingly weak ABC network, but the collapse of the tech bubble and now a likely drop in consumer spending clouded the outlook for ad revenue. At Fox Family, programming activities had ground to a halt once the sale was announced. Fox had agreed that any spending over $10 million had to be approved by Disney. Over the summer, as decisions had to be made to acquire programming for the fall and winter, nothing was approved, and so nothing new was ordered.

At the very least, Gold thought he could get Saban to cut the price substantially to complete the deal. He asked Eisner if he should again contact Saban to feel him out, but this time Eisner was insistent. "Stay out of this," he warned. "I'll handle it." On the Monday after the attacks, the same day the stock market reopened, Disney went ahead with a $1 billion issue of corporate debt, all of it purchased by its investment bank, Goldman Sachs. It was the first new debt issue since the attack, and Disney said at the time that the proceeds would be used to finance the Fox Family acquisition, though its SEC registration also indicated the possibility of buying back shares.

Two days later, on September 19, Eisner got a startling call from Sid Bass, long his staunchest ally and closest confidant about Disney, even though Bass had never held a board seat. Along with the holdings of his brothers Lee, Robert, and Edward, and their father, Perry, the Basses remained Disney's largest shareholders, even though they maintained they had ceased to invest as a group within the meaning of the securities laws, and therefore no longer had to disclose their combined holdings. In the early 1990s, the Basses had decided to go their separate ways with their vast fortune, and the Disney stake had been divided among them. By 2001, none individually held more than 5 percent of Disney's shares outstanding, which would have required a filing with the SEC. Still, their interests remained closely aligned, and Eisner had retained the staunch support of Sid. Both Gold and Roy were well aware, as was Eisner, that the Basses and Eisner together held a controlling stake in the company, as they had ever since the Basses had thrown their support to Eisner in 1984. As long as he had the support of Bass, Eisner could pretty much afford to snub other shareholders, money managers, pension fund advisers, and even directors, since they served at the pleasure of the company's largest shareholders.

But now Bass told Eisner that he faced a looming crisis from the continuing collapse of the stock market and the plunge in value of Disney shares. The Basses were facing margin calls on vast holdings in technology shares they had bought using borrowed money and other shares, including Disney, as collateral. The value of their holdings had fallen so low that the margin lenders were demanding that the debt be repaid. Long known as shrewd "value" investors, in large part from their wildly successful investment in Disney, Sid Bass, like many such investors, had grown impatient with the solid but unspectacular returns attained through value investing in the late 1990s, when the NASDAQ was soaring 80 percent in a year. In 1999 he had fired his investment manager and plunged heavily into the technology sector, less than a year before it hit its peak in March 2000.

Now Bass told Eisner that he, his brother Lee, and their father had no choice but to sell a combined 135 million shares in Disney, representing a 6.7 percent stake in the company and virtually their entire position. (Neither Robert nor Edward was involved in the transaction, and in any event, had already reduced their Disney stake.) Such was the urgency of the Basses' plight that they needed the proceeds by the close of business the next day.

Eisner was startled but impressed with how calm Bass seemed. The news set off a frenzy of calls to Disney directors and Goldman Sachs. With Disney shares hitting a low that day of $17.50, the Bass stake had a value of $2.2 billion, and there was no telling how much news of the forced liquidation would further depress the price. A stake of 135 million shares was far too large to simply dump on the open market, especially with investor confidence already precarious. When Eisner broke the news to Stanley Gold, Gold was upset. According to Eisner, he was "hysterical." With Roy and related entities holding a stake of approximately 30 million shares, the fall in the stock price had already cost Roy millions. This news could lead to a further rout. Gold argued forcefully that Disney itself should buy back the shares, which would demonstrate confidence in the company's future, help put a floor under the stock price, and would also, he argued, be a good investment.

Other directors disagreed. So did Tom Murphy and Warren Buffett, whom Eisner consulted. Having just issued $1 billion in debt for the Fox Family acquisition, the Disney balance sheet couldn't support another $2 billion in debt—certainly not if it hoped to complete the Fox deal. Some resisted the idea because they weren't sure Disney shares were a good investment, given the changed economic circumstances, and, as one put it, "the lack of strategic direction." They were also suspicious of Gold's motives. He represented Roy's interests, and Roy had a large financial stake in propping up the stock price.

Already irritated with Gold and Roy for their dissent on the board, Eisner fanned the directors' suspicions by alleging that Gold and Roy, like the Basses, were facing their own margin calls, which he claimed Gold had admitted. Eisner knew that Gold and Shamrock had substantial investments in Israel, and the Israeli market was hard hit after September 11.

Ultimately, Eisner compromised, agreeing that Disney would buy 50 million shares from the Basses at a below-market $15 a share. Gold called that morning. "Did you buy it all?" he asked Eisner.

"No, fifty million shares," Eisner said. Before he could explain, Gold slammed down the phone. Eisner was furious. Here he was, worrying about a bomb going off in one of the theme parks, and all Gold seemed to care about was the stock price.

(Gold acknowledges that his conversations about buying the Basses' stake with Eisner became heated, that he raised his voice and used profanities to make his point, that he hoped to boost Disney's share price, and that

Shamrock faced margin calls. But he argues that buying the shares was as much in Disney's interest as Shamrock's. He says Shamrock often uses leverage in its investments, and that it had no difficulty meeting its margin calls. In contrast to Bass, who had to sell Disney shares to meet the calls, neither Gold nor Roy nor Shamrock sold or divested any Disney shares to meet a margin call. Gold maintains that their Israeli investments have in the aggregate been highly successful. He also points out that, had Disney bought the shares at $15, it would have been a good investment.)

At 10:00 A.M. on Thursday, Disney announced that it had bought the 50 million shares and Goldman Sachs had bought the remaining 85 million at $15 a share, well below the market price, enabling the Basses to realize proceeds of about $2 billion. Disney spent $750 million on the buyback, most of the $1 billion it had just raised in the debt offering. Once trading resumed, Disney shares dropped another 16 percent, then rebounded to close at just under $17 a share. Loyal to the end, a spokesman for the Basses stressed that they "have a deep and abiding confidence" in Eisner "and in the future of Disney."

The sale was a huge embarrassment for the Basses, puncturing their carefully cultivated reputation for financial acumen. Sid Bass had proven no more immune to the seduction of the technology bubble than had millions of less sophisticated investors. Such a failure of judgment, of course, raised inevitable questions about his unwavering support for Eisner.

For Eisner, the most important relationship in his corporate life was irrevocably changed. Although the Bass spokesman said the sale left the brothers with a cumulative stake in Disney of approximately 4 percent, or just under 100 million shares, it was no longer anywhere near enough to constitute a controlling stake. Overnight, Sid Bass ceased to be relevant to either Eisner or Disney's future. The years Eisner had spent cultivating his relationship with Sid Bass had yielded an all but unassailable grip on the chief executive position. In twenty-four hours, it was gone.

Disney's acquisition of the Family channel closed on October 24, 2001, at a price of $5.2 billion—a mere $100 million off the price agreed to the previous July. Gold was incensed, convinced he could have driven a much tougher bargain after September 11.

Now that Disney owned the Family channel, critical decisions had to be made about what to do with it. Would it be part of the cable network group under Anne Sweeney, which included all the cable channels except the ESPN brands? Or, given that the strategy for the new channel was to "repurpose" programming from ABC, should it be part of the ABC Network division? Though arguments could be made for both alternatives, and Iger wanted it in the cable group, Eisner assigned the Family channel to Bornstein in his capacity as president of ABC Inc.

It didn't take Bornstein long to realize that he'd been dealt another losing hand. The plight of the Family channel was dire. Sixty percent of the so-called carriage agreements, in which cable operators agreed to carry the channel, had expired or were about to. Because of a change in ownership of the channel, some had the option to cancel. Cable operators were paying Family, on average, seventeen cents per subscriber to carry the channel. Disney's pro formas for the channel had projected nearly immediate increases to twenty cents. But now operators were threatening to drop the channel entirely. And in return for carrying it, they were asking for discounts on the fees they paid for ESPN and the Disney channel. The leverage was supposed to work the other way—to keep ESPN and other Disney-owned channels, cable operators were expected to cough up more for Family. Things got so desperate that Disney had to ask televangelist Pat Robertson to lobby some carriers, such as EchoStar Communications, after the satellite broadcaster tried to drop the Family channel. In a letter to EchoStar, Robertson wrote that he couldn't believe the company would deny its subscribers "quality family programs" at the same time as it provided "five channels of pornographic material."

There were other problems. The Family channel's programming assets— eight hundred Power Ranger episodes and a film library—had been repeated so often that viewer fatigue had set in. Due to cost cuts and spending restraints, there was nothing in the pipeline when Disney took over. And despite its "family" name, the channel had no clear identity. It was an awkward amalgam of children's programming, baseball broadcasts, vintage films, and Pat Robertson's "700 Club," all appealing to different audiences.

As soon as the deal closed, Iger and Bornstein convened a meeting to plan strategy for the new channel. As they started to explain the "repurposing" concept, Mark Pedowitz raised his hand. "You can't do that," he said, explaining that ABC didn't have the rights to rerun most of its shows on the Family channel, a point he'd already made to Bornstein. "And it's not going to be easy to get them. There are profit participants." Even Touchstone executives were wary of the concept. Both Braun and McPherson argued that reruns on ABC Family would undercut the syndication value of the shows it owned, which were the most valuable assets any TV studio owned. Discussions got so heated that the meeting nearly aborted.

For the ABC and cable executives, it seemed almost inconceivable that a deal had been concluded without confronting and resolving this most basic of issues. Murphy and his strategic planning staff seemed to think that TV producers would simply relinquish those rights. Of course, had anyone asked ABC about the strategy, these points would have been raised. But no one had. It was an egregious failure of the kind of due diligence routinely conducted before a major acquisition. To the ABC executives, it simply confirmed the arrogance of the strategic planners, and Eisner's blindness to potential obstacles once his mind was made up. When they raised the repurposing problems with Eisner, he seemed irritated and said, "You'll just have to find a way to work it out." (Eisner said that contrary to the perceptions of the ABC executives, he, Iger, and Murphy were not surprised and were fully aware of syndication rights, but expected to gain repurposing rights over time.)

The programming executives at the Fox Family channel, now rechristened ABC Family, waited for guidance. Several deals had been close to completion before the spending freeze, including some movie packages and more episodes of an original series, "State of Grace." But now Bornstein told them that their marching orders were to "repurpose" ABC shows. Their choices were severely limited, since, as Pedowitz had warned, his effort to get the rights to do so with outside producers were stalled. Desperate for programming, Family took leftovers from ESPN—hours of cheerleading and ice-skating competitions, such as the Hershey Kisses Challenge. From ABC News it took anything about missing persons for a series it cobbled together called "Vanished," and forged another series out of old "20/20" segments about unsolved mysteries. The quality was embarrassing, and little of this made any sense for a so-called family channel.

Finally Eisner insisted that Family re-create the once-successful concept of a block of Friday night family-oriented comedies, which ABC had branded as "TGIF." The problem was that Family didn't have the broadcast rights to enough family-oriented comedies. Over Touchstone's objections, it had acquired the rights to rerun the ABC shows "According to Jim" and "Alias," but that was it. So it added its old episodes of "State of Grace" and patched together a block of the three shows and called it "TGIF."

Tom Cosgrove, a scheduling executive from Fox, pointed out to Bornstein that "Alias" and "State of Grace" weren't even comedies. "This doesn't make any sense," he said.

Bornstein looked annoyed. "I don't care. Just put them on," he ordered. He was under orders from Eisner and Iger to make this work.

Two weeks after the block started running, Cosgrove tried again. "Look," he told Bornstein, "this isn't working. Ad sales can't sell it. The ratings are terrible. The affiliates are complaining. The producers are saying it's going to hurt syndication. We can't keep this on."

Bornstein was angry, because he knew Cosgrove was right. "Fuck syndication!" he said. "Tell ad sales to do it right and sell the damn shows."

But a week later, he conceded defeat. "Take it off the air," he told Cosgrove.

It was obvious that Bornstein was under stress and unhappy in his position. At meetings with Family executives, where the news was invariably bad, he would pull out a mesh bag and down several pills. (He was suffering from migraine headaches.) Staff members started placing bets on how long a meeting would run before Bornstein pulled the bag out.

Despite Iger's insistence to Gold and other directors that the 2001–2002 ABC season would justify the lucrative new contract for Stu Bloomberg, ratings at the flagship ABC network nosedived. It had fallen to fourth place in the key eighteen- to forty-nine-year-old demographic and lost 22 percent of its household audience in a year—a startling decline. The shows that emerged from the truncated development period of the "Millionaire" era were especially weak: "Bob Patterson," starring "Seinfeld" veteran Jason Alexander, was canceled before the end of the season, as were "What About Joan," "Thieves," and "Philly." *San Francisco Chronicle* TV columnist Tim Goodman saluted Bloomberg and Braun as the "worst executives of the year (or more)."

The fate of "Millionaire" was painful. Having failed to stem the public mania for "Survivor," ABC aimed its former ratings juggernaut at another embarrassing reminder of its own misjudgment by placing "Millionaire" in the same 9:00 P.M. Thursday time slot as "CSI." "CSI" crushed the fading "Millionaire," which barely finished third in the time slot. At the end of the sweeps period in November 2001, "Millionaire" was cut to one episode a week, Braun talked openly about canceling it altogether, and blamed the faltering show for the network's alarming ratings slide, which angered host Regis Philbin. He accused ABC of using "Millionaire" as "cannon fodder" against a hit like "CSI" and told *The New York Times* "if 'Millionaire' is the reason why ABC is no longer No. 1 in viewers, I'll eat my hat."

The network's performance was so bad that someone at Disney had to be held accountable, but who? Clearly not Eisner. In an interview with *Fortune* magazine, he repeated the boast that had so annoyed Bornstein. "I would love, every morning, to go over and spend two hours at ABC. Even though my children tell me that I'm in the wrong generation and I don't get it any-more, I am totally convinced that I could sit with our guys and make ABC No. 1 in two years."

Bornstein had only been in his job for six months, so he could hardly be blamed. That left Braun and Bloomberg. Though Braun had been most visi-bly on the firing line, bearing the brunt of the press criticism for the "Mil-lionaire" fiasco, it was hard to fault him. While he, too, had championed his share of failures, he had backed both "Survivor" and "CSI." Susan Lyne, the ABC executive hired by Joe Roth to work at the studio, now running ABC's movies of the week and miniseries, had argued that ABC had made a funda-mental mistake by trying to turn its back on the middle-American, family-oriented comedies that were ABC's historic strength and consistent with the Disney brand. Braun had embraced the strategy, and in November, he made a presentation to the board, describing the new direction and attributing the network's failure to the disastrous, Tarses-inspired decision to imitate NBC with programs aimed at young, affluent, urban singles.

That left Bloomberg. Although Bloomberg was a close ally of Iger, and Braun was not, Eisner now derided his taste in programming as "morose" and "dark," apparently on the basis of Bloomberg's support for "Once and Again," a ratings failure but critical success, and the earlier "Nothing Sacred," about a controversial priest.

The day after Christmas, Lyne was on vacation in Florida when she got a call from Bornstein. Earlier, he'd mentioned that he thought she and Angela Shapiro, head of ABC Daytime, were talented executives who could handle more responsibility. Lyne had helped create for ABC fragile hits, such as "My Wife and Kids" and "According to Jim." "Stu is going to be replaced," he told her. "Do you want the job?"

Lyne had always liked Bloomberg, but if he was out, the opportunity to succeed him was an exciting challenge. After she said she was interested, Iger called to discuss her deal, apologizing for the modest salary increase, which was nowhere near what Bloomberg had earned. "I can understand that you'd think it was unfair," Iger conceded, but after getting the board to approve Bloomberg's contract, "I can't go back to the board and ask for more," he said. Forty-eight hours later, Lyne was on a plane to Los Angeles to take up her new duties.

That same day, Braun heard the rumor that Bloomberg was about to be fired and would be replaced by Lyne. Braun liked Lyne and enjoyed working with her. Still, it was startling and disappointing that he had never been con-sulted on the choice or even informed of it ahead of time, despite being co-chairman of ABC Entertainment. (Bornstein hadn't consulted him out of deference to Braun's friendship with Bloomberg.)

On Monday, January 7, 2002, Bloomberg was summoned to a meeting with Eisner. According to his later accounts of the meeting, Eisner thanked him for "taking the bullet" on "Millionaire," acknowledging implicitly that he knew it hadn't been Bloomberg's decision to air it four times a week. He was also granted an extraordinary exit package: His $9 million contract would remain in effect, and would simply be transformed into a production deal. As he returned to his office in the ABC building, Bloomberg passed marketing head Alan Cohen. Cohen had just gotten a new job at Fox. "I'm leaving," Cohen told him. "I'm fired," Bloomberg replied.

That same day Disney announced that Bloomberg was "stepping down" and would be replaced by Susan Lyne as president of ABC Entertainment, reporting to Braun, who was now sole chairman. Iger pledged his full "support and leadership" to Lyne, who responded that she was confident Iger wouldn't "micromanage me. He has no interest in reading scripts or hearing pitches or any of the day-to-day stuff. He just wants to know that there is a strategy and a focus to the work we're doing." She didn't sign the contract offered her, but its provisions went into effect anyway as her lawyer tried to wring some concessions from Disney.

That Bloomberg was fired months after signing his lucrative new contract wasn't lost on Stanley Gold. At the January board meeting, he confronted Eisner in the corridor. "What the hell is going on?" he asked, demanding an explanation for the continuation of Bloomberg's contract, which he'd criticized in the first place.

"Don't get upset, Stanley," Eisner said. "We would have had to pay him that much in severance anyway."

"Don't bullshit me," Gold responded. "Don't insult my intelligence by telling me we would have had to pay somebody that kind of severance."

Although Disney's weak results for the fiscal year ending in September and the ensuing months could in part be blamed on September 11, Eisner couldn't ignore the plight of ABC in his annual letter to shareholders, which was released a few days before Bloomberg's firing.

"Our broadcasting business also faces challenges that were partly caused by the overall economic environment," Eisner wrote. "Because of the softness in the economy, advertising rates were down for all of the broadcast networks. ABC was the number-one rated network in primetime during a very healthy overall ad market in 2000. But, this year, it has suffered the one-two punch of a down economy and a drop in ratings. This is why we are heavily focused on developing new shows that will help propel ABC back to the top. Of course, there is no formula for creating great content. But, it is what we must do to reap the considerable rewards of owning a broadcast network. Both Bob Iger and I grew up professionally at ABC. This is a business we understand, and one of our top priorities is to develop the kinds of programming that will underpin resurgent long-range success. . . .

"Primetime does present a problem, and we are determined to solve it, so here's a little primer on the network television business. . . . You can move from the number-three or number-four network to the number-one network in two years by having one new hit, say, every six months. When I was at ABC in the '70s, we went from last to first. NBC in the '80s had the same kind of success and pushed ABC out of the leadership role. Under Bob Iger in the '90s, ABC recaptured the lead. Now we have to do it again." In other words, there was nothing wrong at ABC that a few hits wouldn't cure.

Not to mention the success of cable. Despite the ongoing turmoil at the Family channel, Eisner hailed the channel's "remarkably seamless" integration with Disney. "I anticipate a remarkably swift integration into the company, followed by rapid growth and increases in profitability."

Despite this optimism, other divisions of the company were hardly firing on all cylinders. At the theme parks, Disney's California Adventure had opened to weak attendance and tepid reviews. The "second gate" at troubled Disneyland Paris, promised in the previous year's letter, was still under construction. The once-thriving Disney stores had not turned around despite a redesign. Still grappling with a dearth of new products, results were weak, and Eisner announced the closing of fifty-one stores.

And despite the optimistic forecasts for ABC Family, in the quarter ending December 31, 2001, Disney recorded a loss of $362 million for the channel after writing down some of the programming assets acquired in the deal, conceding that the programming rights weren't worth what the company had paid. (Family's revenues also dropped an alarming 27 percent.)

On February 28, 2002, Eisner made a rare visit to Capitol Hill to testify before the Senate Commerce Committee, which was holding hearings on how "content" could be protected from digital piracy, a subject of obvious importance to Disney. It was also a matter of personal interest for Eisner, who had been in New York the previous weekend, and was infuriated to discover that videos of a Disney movie opening that Friday were already being sold on the street. Digital copying over the Internet was an even more serious threat to Disney's burgeoning DVD business.

Eisner's prepared remarks were carefully crafted to draw attention to the problem without stepping on the toes of Disney's many partners in the technology sector. But in the ensuing panel discussion, which included News Corporation's Peter Chernin, and an executive from Intel representing Silicon Valley, Eisner was far more pointed in his criticism: "It is very hard to negotiate with an industry whose growth, they think . . . is dependent on pirated content."

In response to questions from Senator Ben Nelson of Nebraska, Eisner identified one such company: "As a matter of fact, there are companies— computer companies, that their ads—full-page ads, billboards up and down San Francisco and L.A., that say—what do they say?—'Rip, Mix, Burn.' To [get] kids to buy the computer. They are selling the computer with the encouragement of the advertising that they can rip, mix and burn. In other words, they can create a theft and distribute it to all their friends if they buy this particular computer."

This, of course, was an explicit reference to "Rip, Mix and Burn" television ads for the Apple iPod, showing how easy it is to burn CDs with Apple's iTunes program. Steve Jobs, Disney's partner in his role as chairman of Pixar, was also Apple's chairman.

Thomas Schumacher, head of Disney feature animation, was at his office in Burbank when he got a call from Steve Jobs. "Do you know what Michael just did to me?" he practically shouted.

"No," Schumacher said. He'd heard nothing about Eisner's testimony.

Jobs was irate, saying that Eisner had attacked Apple in congressional testimony.

Schumacher tried to calm him down. "I can't believe this," he said. "It's a shock."

Then John Lasseter called from Pixar headquarters. He was even angrier, saying Eisner had betrayed Jobs.

Schumacher immediately called Eisner, saying that Jobs and Lasseter were livid about his testimony. "I don't know what they're talking about!" Eisner exclaimed. "I didn't say anything."

Schumacher called Lasseter. "John, Michael says he didn't say anything. There's been some misunderstanding."

Lasseter seemed slightly mollified. "Well, I'll double check," he said.

Minutes later he was back on the phone to Schumacher. This time he was

screaming. "I'm holding the transcript! Let me read it to you: 'They are selling the computer with the encouragement of the advertising that they can
rip, mix and burn. In other words, they can create a theft and distribute it to
all their friends . . .' He's saying Steve wants to steal his content!"

Confronted with the transcript, there wasn't much Schumacher
could say.

Although Eisner continued to boast that he could personally turn ABC
around, he shrewdly distanced himself from what was an increasingly troubled asset. In February, Iger assumed more visible responsibility for ABC, announcing, "Michael and I have decided that ABC is our No. 1 priority, and we
decided that my time may best be spent focusing on ABC." Iger elaborated in
remarks to the *Los Angeles Times* suggesting that he had not been involved
enough in decision making at the network. "I spent two full years managing
the merger process. . . . I got less and less involved instead of wanting to become more involved. . . . I didn't have the time or the ability to focus during
those years because I was given so much more to do."

Just what this meant quickly became apparent to Steve Bornstein, who'd
accepted his position with the explicit promise from Eisner that he would be
running the network. After he negotiated a deal to bring comedian Jon Stewart to the network for a late-night replacement for the faltering "Politically
Incorrect with Bill Maher," Iger backed Lloyd Braun's preference for Jimmy
Kimmel, the host from "The Man Show." Kimmel was hired.

Iger also stepped into negotiations to bring David Letterman and his
late-night talk show to ABC, an idea Braun had proposed after learning that
Letterman was disgruntled with CBS president Les Moonves. Letterman
hadn't yet been able to renew his contract at CBS, which was expiring in six
months, and under his contract, Letterman was free to negotiate other offers.
When Braun first mentioned the possibility to Eisner and Iger, both had dismissed the possibility. But when Braun raised it again several weeks later, Eisner seemed intrigued.

A move by Letterman to ABC would mean displacing ABC's acclaimed
late-night news program "Nightline," hosted by Ted Koppel. The news division had some hugely profitable interviews, such as Barbara Walters's exclusive 1996 interview with Monica Lewinsky, and the news division as a whole
wsa reliably profitable. But it often balked at the idea of promoting other
Disney ventures, persisted in making unflattering references to Disney (an
investigative piece on sweatshops that mentioned Disney products especially

infuriated Eisner), and, in general, was sanctimonious, in Eisner's view. Its ability to appeal directly to the public by invoking its mission of public service journalism—a higher, nobler purpose than making money—also meant that it was difficult, if not impossible, for Eisner to control the New York–based news division from Burbank.

Braun argued that for an investment of roughly $100 million over three to five years, ABC would gain a profitable franchise ("Letterman" earned more than $50 million a year in ad revenue for CBS, the "Tonight Show" with Jay Leno was making about $150 million, compared to "Nightline's" profits of barely $10 million). Acquiring Letterman would give ABC's entertainment division a huge boost, and provide a strong lead-in to the next morning's "Good Morning America." Although "Nightline" was drawing a respectable 4 million viewers, that was far fewer than either Letterman or Jay Leno, and it attracted a much older audience. While the prospect seemed a long shot, one of Braun's strengths was closing talent deals.

Eisner said to go ahead, but Braun was immediately worried about the Koppel factor. He stressed that they had to tell Koppel, and try to get him involved in planning a new approach for "Nightline." But Iger rejected the notion, arguing that confiding in anyone from the news division was inviting leaks.

Still, Braun felt so strongly that he followed up with an email reiterating the need to reassure Ted Koppel, to the effect that "We are not going to succeed if Ted comes out against this. Let's work out with Ted how 'Nightline' moves."

He received no reply. (Iger said that it was Braun, not him, who wanted the negotiations cloaked in secrecy. But several people at Disney saw Braun's email.)

Iger may well have been correct that briefing Koppel on the negotiations risked a leak. But he evidently failed to consider that the negotiations were likely to leak anyway, whether or not Koppel was told in advance, especially if others at CBS learned that Letterman was talking to ABC. On March 1, ABC's pursuit of Letterman was front-page news in *The New York Times*, which reported that ABC "had made a strong bid" in a "move that would displace Ted Koppel and 'Nightline.' "

That same morning, ABC News president David Westin summoned his irate executives, anchors, and journalists to say that neither he nor Koppel knew anything about the talks. He denounced the possible move of "Nightline" as a "tremendous blow" with "ramifications for the entire news division." A furious Koppel, who learned of the deal when reporters called for comment, huddled with top producers to plot strategy. It didn't help that the only expression of support from Disney came not from Eisner or Iger but in a response from Alex Wallau, the president of the ABC Network. Wallau said only that Koppel was "one of the most respected journalists in America" and "We are hopeful that 'Nightline' and Ted will continue to make significant contributions to ABC in the years ahead."

Letterman issued a far stronger statement of support for Koppel than Disney did, saying he wouldn't join ABC if it meant displacing Koppel. Moreover, Letterman stated that he had cause to wonder how Eisner and Iger would treat him, if this was how they treated Koppel, one of their most respected on-air talents. A full week after the story broke, Iger apologized to Koppel. "The way the story unfolded we could have been more respectful to the people involved and for that I have apologized," he told the *Times*.* But the negotiations continued, with ABC offering Letterman $31.5 million in annual salary and an array of other guarantees. Iger and Braun flew to New York on March 11 to make their final pitch.

With considerable drama, Letterman announced on his show of March 12 that he would stay at CBS, and that he hoped Koppel and "Nightline" would remain on ABC "for as long as that guy would like to have that job." Although ABC was also handicapped in its courtship by its faltering prime-time ratings, just as CBS's were surging, in the end, Braun was right that the deal was doomed without Koppel's endorsement. Once Letterman made his decision to stay at CBS, Koppel broke his silence and issued a scathing indictment of Disney management:

"We hope the corporate leadership of Disney understands that it would not be reasonable to expect all of us at 'Nightline' to continue our work in a climate of ongoing uncertainty. There must be a great many talented comedians who would welcome the opportunity to take over the 'Nightline' time slot. Our hope is that Disney will send a clear and unmistakable signal to them, to us, to the advertising community and to all of our loyal viewers interested in the robust future of network television news that 'Nightline' can count on serious corporate backing."

Disney remained silent. Koppel had won round one. But even though he'd bought some time, he had hardly endeared himself to either Eisner or Iger. The prospect of "serious corporate backing" was remote.

Even as Disney professed support for Koppel and "Nightline," Iger was

---

* Iger also told me that no one would have criticized the strategy had Letterman agreed to come to ABC.

negotiating a more radical approach to the news division: spinning it off into a new company that would merge ABC News with CNN. At least initially, the new company would be 70 percent owned by CNN, and 30 percent by Disney. A reminder of the synergies that might have been realized had Disney and Time Warner merged, it offered economies of scale and an estimated $200 million in annual cost savings, while ridding Eisner of an increasingly unwanted stepchild from the ABC acquisition.

While Iger and Jamie Kellner, chief executive of Turner Broadcasting, worked out the financial details, ABC News president David Westin met with Walter Isaacson, his counterpart at CNN, to focus on the logistics of merging two global news organizations with high-profile correspondents and anchors. They knew the publicity would dwarf the Letterman negotiations. But by midsummer they'd pretty much worked everything out, even the locations of foreign bureaus. So far, nothing had leaked. All they needed was board approval.

ABC did have a solid success that spring with its latest entry into the reality genre, "The Bachelor," developed by ABC's Andrea Wong and outside producer Michael Fleiss. Ratings for the six one-hour episodes built steadily as a thirty-one-year-old single Harvard graduate, Alex Michel, winnowed a file of twenty-five potential brides to just one, Amanda Marsh, and then proposed marriage on national TV. Though the premise arguably pushed the boundaries of the ABC/Disney brand, and drew a few protests from feminists, its final episode drew 18.2 million viewers, nearly beating "CSI" on CBS. Susan Lyne announced that the runner-up, Trista Rehn, would launch a companion series, "The Bachelorette."

At Disneyland Paris, the much-delayed "second gate," a Walt Disney Studios theme park, opened on March 16. Completed at a cost of $533 million, the park was a budget version of the larger Disney-MGM Studios, including the Aerosmith "Rockin' Roller Coaster" but not the much costlier "Tower of Terror." The idea, as with all the new theme parks at existing Disney locations, was to induce visitors to stay longer, a critical need at Disneyland Paris, where hotel occupancy rates remained low. Still, the new park saddled the already troubled enterprise with even more debt payments at a time when the existing debt wasn't being serviced by attendance at the original park.

Eisner attended the opening, and invited the entire board to a preopening dinner on Friday night and to Saturday's opening ceremonies. Instead of the board dinner at Disneyland Paris on Friday, Andrea Van de Kamp, Stanley Gold, and Gold's wife, Ilene, chose to dine at a bistro in Paris.

The next day, the few board members toured the new park with Eisner and afterward gathered for cocktails and a buffet at one of the new restaurants. Van de Kamp found herself chatting with Bob Iger, and mentioned that she had some concerns. "I'm not sure there's enough here," she said. "There's not enough substance to keep people for a full day. People are already leaving, and the park has only been open a few hours." Others came up, and the conversation shifted as they mingled with other guests at the reception.

Minutes later, Eisner spotted Van de Kamp and strode toward her. "I understand you've been griping," he said, his tone cold.

Van de Kamp was startled, first that Iger had already reported something she felt she'd told him in confidence, and second that Eisner seemed so angry. "I was just expressing some concerns and observations," she replied. "We're here to look. We invested a lot of money in this. As a director, I think it's appropriate to share my concerns." But when she reported the exchange to Gold and his wife, she wondered why she was being so defensive. Eisner was the one behaving inappropriately, in her view.

Later, Eisner complained to Gold that he and Van de Kamp had skipped the Friday dinner. "Most of the board didn't come at all," Gold countered.

Eisner liked to boast that Disneyland Paris was the most popular tourist attraction in Europe, with 12 million visitors a year, more than the Eiffel Tower. Disney's goal for the Disney Studios attraction was to increase that by 50 percent, to 18 million a year. But by the end of the year, that looked hopelessly optimistic.

After returning from Paris, Gold had lunch with fellow board member Tom Murphy in New York at Café des Artistes, near ABC's former headquarters. In Gold's view, ABC was floundering, the Bloomberg contract had been a fiasco, and the Family acquisition was a disaster. Roy was reporting that morale at feature animation and at the theme parks, the parts of the company he cared most about, was slumping. Gold had told Eisner he was "close" to asking for his resignation. Now he was even closer, and had decided to sound out other board members. "Michael doesn't know what he's doing," he said. "I think it may be time for a change."

To Gold's surprise, Murphy said, "Let me shake your hand. I'm proud of you for speaking your mind. Finally someone is willing to speak the truth." Murphy, who had been close to Warren Buffett since Buffett acquired his large stake in Cap Cities, added that Buffett had told him that he wouldn't consider investing again in Disney as long as Eisner was chief executive. Murphy suggested that Gold speak next to Ray Watson.

When he returned to California, Gold called Watson, now the longest-serving member of the board. They met for lunch at Sai Sai, a Japanese restaurant in the Biltmore Hotel in downtown Los Angeles, far from Burbank and Hollywood, as they did every year for a private discussion. "Things are bad," Gold said. "I believe Michael has lost his way." Like Murphy, Watson readily agreed that it might be time for a change. Management is in "chaos," he said, adding that Eisner had "no sensible plan" for solving the problem or finding a successor.

It came as a surprise to Gold when, less than a week later, he got a call from Eisner. "I know you're talking to people," Eisner said icily.

Gold realized his confidence had been betrayed. He assumed Watson had told Eisner, since Gold had heard nothing after his lunch with Murphy. Still, he couldn't be sure.

With Iger making the decisions for the ABC network that spring, Steve Bornstein had little choice but to focus on the troubled Family channel. With the "repurposing" strategy in turmoil and the plight of the Family channel worsening by the day, he turned to Angela Shapiro, a veteran of ABC Daytime, whom he considered one of the company's most talented creative executives. She was attractive and vivacious, and popular with her staff. "Why me?" Shapiro asked. "I know nothing about it. I don't even watch cable." She was also candid. Earlier, she'd warned that "I'm not a corporate politics person. If you ask me what I think, I'm going to tell you."

Bornstein insisted that he needed someone creative to take charge. Shapiro sat in on a Family channel meeting, where she quickly realized the strategy was a shambles. "What's the brand identity?" she asked. No one knew. "Who's the target audience?" No answer.

Iger, too, tried to persuade Shapiro. She liked Iger. Like many people, she'd been smitten with his candor, sensitivity, and creative instincts when she first came to ABC. They discussed ABC Daytime, and found they agreed on nearly everything. Shapiro warmed to the idea of working with Iger on the Family channel.

Still, she had one major reservation: She was not going to report to cable division head Anne Sweeney. Shapiro and Sweeney had clashed repeatedly after SOAPnet was launched. As a cable channel, it reported to Sweeney's cable group, but it also had to work closely with ABC Daytime, run by Shapiro. Sweeney, the ambitious and polished administrator, and Shapiro, the more freewheeling creative executive, were polar opposites. Sweeney seemed to reject everything Shapiro and her staff suggested. As long as she didn't have to repeat the experience with Sweeney, Shapiro was willing to at least consider taking the job.

"Who will I report to?" Shapiro asked Iger. "I can work with anyone except Anne Sweeney." Iger promised her she wouldn't report to Sweeney.

When Shapiro described the meeting with Iger to Bornstein, she stressed Iger's promise, and said she wanted the same assurance from him. But she didn't mind reporting to Bornstein. "If you're the head of both ABC and this channel, then I'm sure we can get the job done," she told him. Bornstein assured her that the channel would stay tied to ABC, even though the repurposing strategy was in doubt. "I guarantee this will never go to cable, and Anne Sweeney will never run it," he pledged.

Shapiro had another meeting with Iger, which she later described to her staff. "Michael and I really think you should take the job," Iger told her. "You're perfect." Iger stressed that it would be Shapiro's task to devise a new creative strategy for the channel. She asked specifically if it had to be a "family" channel, and Iger assured her she could change the channel's name to reflect a new identity. Creatively, the channel was a "blank slate."

It seemed like an exciting challenge. Linked to the ABC Network, the channel could experiment with all sorts of original programming, and if something really took off, it could move to ABC's prime-time schedule. When Shapiro accepted the job, she insisted that Iger's promise that she would not report to Anne Sweeney be written into her contract, which guaranteed that she would report to the head of the ABC Network division, and not to the cable networks group. (Disney maintains that Shapiro's contract was ambiguous on that issue.)

In late April 2002, Bornstein was summoned to a meeting in Iger's office. Iger began by talking about how hard it was to be age fifty-two with a baby at home. Despite their differences, he and Bornstein often bantered about the fact that they had much younger wives. Unlike Iger, Bornstein and his wife didn't have children (the tables were later turned when Bornstein's wife gave birth to twins). Iger said he'd been at the beach that weekend as part of a "baby group." The conversation idled to a close, and then Iger turned to the real reason for the meeting.

"This isn't working out," Iger said.

"No, it isn't," Bornstein readily agreed.

Angela Shapiro was at the airport waiting for Bornstein. They were scheduled to embark on a goodwill tour to introduce Shapiro to media and advertisers. Shapiro had just boarded the corporate jet when she got a call from Zenia Mucha, the head of corporate public relations, telling her that Bornstein wouldn't be showing up, and she should go ahead on her own.

After the plane took off, Bornstein called Shapiro. "I had a meeting this morning," he reported. "I'm not here anymore."

For the man most responsible for building ESPN, once perceived as a possible successor to Eisner, it was a dizzying fall from grace. It wasn't as though he hadn't seen it coming. Bornstein had resisted both the Internet and subsequent ABC assignments, but had taken both out of a sense of corporate duty. At ABC, wedged in the cumbersome management hierarchy between Eisner and Iger above him, and Braun, Lyne, and Wallau below, it was hard to see what authority he had, yet he was blamed for two doomed missions, first the Internet operation and then the Family channel. With his departure, yet another threat to Iger—or, for that matter, Eisner himself—had been dispatched.

Two weeks later, Susan Lyne and Braun stepped onto the stage at Disney's New Amsterdam Theatre to unveil ABC's lineup for the 2002–2003 season—the third executive team to greet advertisers in as many years. With Eisner and Iger in the audience, Lyne and Braun outlined the strategy that had evolved from Braun's earlier presentation to the board, a return to ABC's "roots" as a haven for family-oriented comedies like the Eisner-era "Happy Days" and "Laverne & Shirley" or, more recently, "Roseanne." This year, Braun and Lyne had twenty-nine pilots to choose from, far more than the previous year's impoverished development slate. Yet twenty-five of them came from Disney's own Touchstone studio, fueling the perception that Disney was inhospitable to promising shows from other producers. Besides the mid-season entries of "George Lopez" and "According to Jim," ABC touted "8 Simple Rules for Dating My Teenage Daughter" and "Life with Bonnie," starring Bonnie Hunt as a talk-show host. Of course, ABC could not simply return to a past of scripted comedies. It planted the second installment of its new reality hit, "The Bachelor," on Wednesday night against NBC's acclaimed "The West Wing."

Disney executives were especially hopeful about "8 Simple Rules," starring comedian John Ritter as a sportswriter who must take a more active role raising his teenage daughters, especially after his wife goes back to work. The program had a special resonance for Eisner, since Ritter was a star of "Three's Company," a huge ratings success for ABC twenty-five years before, during Eisner's tenure at ABC. Ritter hadn't had a hit series since, and had been reduced to guest star appearances on other shows. Initially, ABC wanted

"Roseanne" star John Goodman for the role, and even made Goodman an offer. But when those negotiations foundered over the issue of Goodman's salary demands ($200,000 per episode), ABC executives reviewed tapes of Ritter's recent appearances on J. J. Abrams's "Felicity" as well as "Ally McBeal" and "Law & Order," and liked what they saw.

Braun was so impressed by the pilot that he and Susan Lyne placed "8 Simple Rules" in the critical time slot of 8:00 P.M. Tuesday, when it would serve as the lead-in to a comedy block that included "According to Jim," "Life with Bonnie," and "Less Than Perfect." Eisner had used Tuesday night to rebuild the ABC schedule when he was in charge of programming, and "8 Simple Rules" inherited the slot once occupied by "Happy Days." Viewer reaction to the new Tuesday lineup would thus be a referendum on ABC's new strategy of family comedies with broad appeal.

Still, the new schedule was hardly the unfettered work of Braun, Lyne, and their staff. ABC announced that a remake of the 1960s hit police drama "Dragnet" would air once "NFL Monday Night Football" ended its season. "Dragnet" was hardly original, but Braun and Lyne were eager to get something from producer Dick Wolf, famous for "Law & Order." Eisner liked it, as did Fred Silverman, the former ABC programming head and Eisner's former boss, whom Eisner had retained that spring as a consultant to the network. That meant that at least seven high-level executives had a say in the ABC schedule—Eisner, Iger, Silverman, Bornstein, Wallau, Braun, and Lyne, as well as Jeff Bader, who was in charge of scheduling.

At least the schedule had some semblance of coherence. But Braun and Lyne didn't want to overpromise, or suffer from inflated expectations. "We want to be as aggressive as we can in the fall with our new shows but at the same time be realistic that we can't expect to fix things all at once," Braun told the press.

One of the new shows that didn't fit Braun and Lyne's "back to basics" theme, but was undeniably original, was a show from LivePlanet, Ben Affleck and Matt Damon's new production company, called "Push, Nevada." Iger was especially enthusiastic about the unusual drama, which featured a fictional IRS agent in a peculiar town in which viewers looked for clues and could win a prize for solving the mystery. Iger said he thought it could be the next "Twin Peaks."

Produced by Disney's Touchstone division, Disney did own the repurposing rights for "Push, Nevada," and Eisner thought it was perfect for demonstrating the inherent synergies in the Family channel acquisition. At one of his first meetings with Shapiro, he urged her to run episodes of the series on the channel. "Are you kidding?" she asked. "There's a guy stark naked, seen from the rear end. You can't put that on a 'family' channel."

Eisner said he didn't see why not. "Get edgy," he urged.

Shapiro resisted. "Push, Nevada" had such low ratings that Eisner stopped mentioning it. It was soon canceled.

Soon after, Shapiro had a testy exchange with Peter Murphy, head of strategic planning, who called demanding to know what her "vision" was for the channel. In a version of their encounter soon circulating within the Family staff, Murphy demanded an immediate answer, adding that he was under pressure from the board. Shapiro said she needed time to research the issue, but Family staff members were indignant. Murphy and other members of top management must have had a vision when they bought the channel. Otherwise, what were they thinking?

In light of Gold's intensified scrutiny and the recent weak results, preparation of Disney's new five-year forecast, which would be presented at the June 2002 board meeting, took on unusual importance. In May, Eisner and Iger convened a series of meetings with division heads to review the targets, and prior to those meetings there were numerous rehearsals. At the Family channel, responsibility for the plan fell to Angela Shapiro, but for the financial aspects she relied on Jim Hedges, chief financial officer for the ABC TV Network, and Spencer Neumann, who reported to Alex Wallau. Neither Hedges nor Neumann could get Murphy or anyone else at strategic planning to give them the projected numbers that had been used to justify the purchase. Finally, strategic planning delivered the targets, but the Family executives couldn't figure out how they had been derived. All projections are necessarily somewhat conjectural, but the assumptions are supposed to be based on fact.

In reality, the Family channel was falling far short of the projections from strategic planning. Hedges and Neumann worked with their numbers, but couldn't come up with anything close to the strategic-planning targets. Tensions mounted. Finally Shapiro and her staff were told that Iger was taking the unusual step of attending the next rehearsal for their presentation, an ominous sign that Peter Murphy and his staff weren't happy.

Shapiro was out of town, so she participated by phone. There were at least ten people in the room. Iger had a copy of the latest projections from Neumann and Hedges. "You've got to go back and rework these," he ordered.

Neumann and Hedges said they had tried, but couldn't get to the numbers.

"We can't be this far off," Iger insisted.

"We don't know how to get even close to these numbers," Shapiro interjected over the speakerphone, a point reiterated by her staff.

"We can't present a number to the board that is hundreds of millions lower than we just gave them a few months ago," Iger insisted.

"Bob, I've never presented numbers I can't deliver," Shapiro replied. "You should know that I'm having a very hard time with this."

Still, the Family staff went back to the drawing board, and came up with numbers that, while still short of what strategic planning wanted, were as aggressive as they felt they could possibly justify. (Iger confirmed that Family executives and Murphy were at loggerheads, and that he intervened. He said it's entirely appropriate to push executives to produce better numbers, he has done so many times, and that it often produces better and more accurate results.)

All of this was in preparation for the meeting in late May 2002 where Shapiro had to present plans for the channel to Eisner, Iger, chief financial officer Tom Staggs, and Peter Murphy. At the meeting she stressed the creative approach she was hoping to develop for the channel, which would be aimed at younger women. She obviously wished she could leave it at that, but she couldn't avoid the numbers. "Michael, the finance people will take you through the numbers, but you should know that they're incredibly aggressive." For good measure, she repeated, "Corporate has made me feel that it's imperative that we reach these numbers, but you should know that these numbers are incredibly aggressive." She stressed the word *incredibly*.

As she paused, there was silence in the room. Finally Eisner spoke. "Angela, I need you to look at me. Either you are totally exaggerating, and these numbers are not aggressive, or you're saying that we really overpaid for this channel."

Shapiro paused to ponder her alternatives as everyone at the meeting practically held their breath. There was no good response.

"I'm waiting for an answer," Eisner said.

Shapiro took a deep breath. "I had nothing to do with the purchase of the channel," she said. "I can't speak to the reasoning or the purchase price. All I can tell you is that these numbers are more than incredibly aggressive."

Eisner frowned, then seemed resigned. He stood up. "I hear what you're saying. I don't envy you," he said. "You have a really bad job." Then he walked out.

*   *   *

ABOVE: Disneyland town square, 1966. Modeled on Walt Disney's Missouri hometown, Disneyland's Main Street embodied the idealized values of rural Middle America at the turn of the century, values that became inseparable from the Disney brand. © *Bettmann/Corbis*

RIGHT: Ron Miller (left), Walt's son-in-law, and Roy E. Disney, Walt's nephew, at the studio, 1967. After Roy quit the Disney board and helped oust Miller as Disney's chief executive, in 1984, the rift deepened between the "Walt" and "Roy" sides of the Disney family. © *AP/Wide World Photos*

Walt on the Carolwood Pacific, the miniature backyard train that became Walt's model for Disneyland. Walt's daughters, Diane and Sharon, his nephew, Roy, and neighborhood kids such as Nancy Sinatra and Candice Bergen were frequent passengers. © *Globe Photos*

Michael Eisner at the Disney/MGM Studios, Orlando, 1989, with Mickey Mouse and Roger Rabbit. The movie *Who Framed Roger Rabbit?* mixed action with animation and symbolized the kind of innovative commercial hit that characterized Eisner's early years as chief executive.

Eisner as host of *The Wonderful World of Disney*. When Eisner told Jeffrey Katzenberg during a flight on the corporate jet that he'd decided to step into Walt's shoes as host of the weekly television show, Katzenberg finally understood that Eisner saw himself as Walt's heir.

LEFT: Urbane and considerate, Disney president and chief operating officer Frank Wells, shown here in 1987, was the ideal foil to Eisner's impulsive creativity. Many cite his death in a 1994 helicopter crash as the turning point in Disney's remarkable good fortune, but even before, tensions simmered between him and Eisner. © *Jacques Tiziou/Corbis Sygma*

BELOW: Roy E. Disney in his office in the Animation building, just after the release of *Beauty and the Beast.* "Roy understood that animation, done right, was magic," Eisner wrote in his 1984 letter to shareholders. But the relationship would soon sour.

Jeffrey Katzenberg, chairman of Disney's movie studio, based *The Lion King* on his own coming-of-age experience. A prodigiously creative and hardworking executive, he resented being called Eisner's "golden retriever" and was furious when Eisner reneged on what he believed was a promise to make him president after Wells's death.

The castle from *Sleeping Beauty*, the centerpiece of Euro Disney in Marne-la-Vallée, France, under construction in 1991. "We can't just do a kitschy rendition of French history right in their own backyard," Disney Imagineers argued, so no expense was spared. The castle featured stained-glass windows and stone turrets, rather than the fiberglass used for its Florida counterpart. Euro Disney (later renamed Disneyland Paris) was a financial disaster and caused the first serious rift between Eisner and Wells.
© *Dominique Aubert/Corbis Sygma*

In 1995, Eisner hired his best friend, superagent Michael Ovitz, to be Disney's president. The night before the news was released, Ovitz told his wife it was "the worst decision of [his] career." If anything, that was an understatement. Ovitz was fired sixteen months later at a cost to Disney of $140 million. Ovitz's career was in ruins, his friendship with Eisner shattered. © *Los Angeles Daily News/Corbis Sygma*

Eisner shakes hands with Thomas Murphy, the much-admired chairman of Capital Cities/ABC, on July 31, 1995, the day Disney announced its $19 billion takeover, which brought the ABC network and ESPN into the Disney conglomerate. The acquisition, the largest ever at the time, nearly doubled Disney's size and vastly expanded Eisner's influence and responsibilities. Murphy joined the Disney board. © *AP/Wide World Photos*

The Eisner family—sons Anders, Breck, and Eric; Eisner and his wife, Jane—in June 1995, less than a year after Eisner's heart surgery. Even Eisner's fiercest critics acknowledge his devotion to his wife and sons. Minutes before his surgery, Eisner asked that Jane be named to the Disney board, and he once told Ovitz he was grooming Breck to be his successor. © *Dave Allocca/Time-Life Pictures/Getty Images*

Julia Roberts starred in Touchstone's *Pretty Woman,* which grossed $463 million for Disney in 1990. Like many movie stars, she became close friends with Joe Roth, who succeeded Katzenberg as chairman of the Disney studio. Roth kept Disney at the top of the box-office rankings in the mid-1990s, but Eisner was suspicious of him almost from the start. "Down the road I am going to have to teach Joe the realities of life," Eisner wrote in an email to a major shareholder, Sid Bass, complaining about Roth's spending. © *AP/Wide World Photos*

Eisner; John Lasseter, former Disney animator and a prolific creative force at Pixar; and Steve Jobs, chairman of Pixar and Apple Computer, at the 2001 premiere of *Monsters, Inc.* Relations were already deteriorating between Eisner and Jobs despite the remarkable string of hits that began in 1995 with *Toy Story.* "I'm furious with Michael," Jobs told a Disney executive. "How can I be a partner with someone like that?" © *Frank Trapper/Corbis*

Glenn Close as Cruella De Vil in *101 Dalmatians*, the 1996 live-action remake of Disney's much-loved animated feature. Production nearly halted when screenwriter John Hughes failed to deliver five new lines requested by the actress. "David," Close told Disney executive David Vogel, "no lines—no Cruella!" © *Globe Photos*

Host Regis Philbin and a contestant on ABC's "Who Wants to Be a Millionaire," the game show that helped launch the era of reality TV and also propelled Robert Iger into the vacant Disney presidency. "Take a good look at me," Philbin told advertisers at a presentation in 2000, "the guy who saved the ABC television network."

Director M. Night Shyamalan and actor Bruce Willis discuss a scene in *The Sixth Sense*, which became Disney's biggest live-action hit ever. But David Vogel, the studio chief who acquired the script and championed its production, discovered too late that Disney had sold off both the foreign and domestic rights to the film. Disney earned only a distribution fee.

Thomas Schumacher, director Julie Taymor, and Peter Schneider with their Tony Awards for *The Lion King*, which won Best Musical in 1998. Schneider succeeded Roth as chairman of the studio, and Schumacher oversaw animation, but *The Lion King* created an intimidating new standard of success. Schneider left the company to produce Broadway shows, and Schumacher moved to New York to head Disney's theatrical ventures. Disney's latest production is *Mary Poppins*, which opened in London in December 2004. © *Mike Segar/Reuters/Landov*

Eisner and president Robert Iger in front of Disney's new "Team Disney" headquarters, designed by noted architect Michael Graves, in 2001. Eisner often disparaged Iger to Disney directors, and after one such incident Tom Murphy urged Iger to quit. © *Kim Kulish/Corbis*

Producer Jerry Bruckheimer and Johnny Depp on the set of *Pirates of the Caribbean: Curse of the Black Pearl.* Although Bruckheimer was Disney's most reliable and successful producer, Eisner rejected his TV series, "CSI: Crime Scene Investigation," that launched a hit franchise for rival CBS. Eisner also second-guessed the early footage of *Pirates,* complaining about Depp's gold teeth, mangy hair, and effeminate mannerisms. *Pirates* became the summer smash of 2003, just when Eisner was fighting for his survival. © *Globe Photos*

John Ritter and Katey Sagal, stars of ABC's "8 Simple Rules for Dating My Teenage Daughter," in July 2002. Ritter's tragic death in September 2003 triggered a crisis for the show, one of ABC's few hits. Eisner wanted the show to return with Sagal as a pregnant widow; the show's executives called the notion exploitative and in bad taste. © *Robert Galbraith/Reuters/Corbis*

Diane Disney Miller, Walt's daughter, in front of the Walt Disney Concert Hall, a stunning architectural and cultural monument in downtown Los Angeles, financed in large part with a bequest from Walt's widow, Lillian. Diane was annoyed when Eisner told a national TV audience that he had "discovered" Walt's grave (her father had been cremated), and refused to support him when Roy called for his ouster. "I think it's time for you to go. You've done some wonderful things, but it's time," she told him. © *AP/Wide World Photos*

Stanley Gold, Ilene Gold, Patty Disney, and Roy E. Disney outside the Golds' home in Beverly Hills. Gold was Roy's business partner, lawyer, and closest adviser, and after Disney directors tried to force Roy off the board in late 2003, both he and Roy resigned in protest. They soon after launched "Save Disney," a campaign to get shareholders to withhold their votes from Eisner. *Silvia Mautner Photography*

When Disney director Andrea Van de Kamp refused to do Eisner's bidding, Eisner orchestrated her removal from the board. "You are so loyal to Stanley, it's like you've carried his babies," Eisner complained. Her ouster brought fellow director Reveta Bowers, head of the prestigious Center for Early Education in Los Angeles, to tears at a board meeting. "How can you do this to this distinguished woman?" Bowers asked. She stepped down the same year. © *Berliner Studio/BEImages*

ABOVE: Stanley Gold and Roy Disney in Philadelphia in March 2004, at a rally for shareholders opposed to Eisner's leadership. "There's a pretty long list of changes we'd all like to see," he told the audience. "For instance, I think the short list would include management."
© Najlah Feanny/Corbis

Disney's chief financial officer, Tom Staggs, at an investor conference at Disney World, December 2003. Staggs helped to minimize Disney's losses in its disastrous Internet venture. © AP/Wide World Photos

Disney's new chairman, former senator George Mitchell, addressing shareholders at the annual meeting in Philadelphia in March 2004. After 45 percent of Disney's shareholders withheld their votes of confidence in Eisner—the highest ever recorded for a sitting CEO—Eisner agreed to relinquish his title of chairman. Mitchell initially said he didn't want it. "You're the only guy I can work with," Eisner insisted. "Anyone who can bring an end to six hundred years of fighting in Ireland can handle the Walt Disney board." © *Tim Shaffer/ Reuters/Corbis*

Disney president Robert Iger was assigned the thankless task of countering the "Save Disney" rally with his own press conference scheduled for the same time. His event was sparsely attended, but, ultimately, his loyalty was rewarded. Under continuing pressure from shareholders to designate a successor, Eisner made Iger his heir apparent three months later. Gold and Roy denounced the choice. © *Tim Shaffer/Reuters/Corbis*

Angela Shapiro, a former head of ABC Daytime and a highly regarded creative executive, encountered turmoil and confusion when she arrived at the newly acquired Family channel. " I don't envy you," Eisner told her at one meeting. "You have a really bad job." She left in October 2003. © *AP/Wide World Photos*

Lloyd Braun, chairman of ABC Entertainment, and Susan Lyne, president, during the summer of 2003. Both suffered from the popular perception that Eisner and Iger made all the critical decisions at the network, which languished in the ratings during their tenure. Ironically, both were fired just months before two shows they championed—"Lost" and "Desperate House-wives"—emerged as ABC's biggest hits in years. © *AP/Wide World Photos*

In 2003, the Will Rogers Institute named Eisner its "Pioneer of the Year." After several similar benefits in his honor, Eisner suddenly announced in 2004 that he would retire as chief executive in 2006, twenty-two years after coming to Disney. But was he really leaving? "I don't want to be irrelevant," he said. "I'm not going to ask the board to be named chairman. I'm not going to beg for it. But the board might come to me. Then I'd have to consider it. Will I continue to play a creative role? That's up to Disney."
© *Gregory Pace/Corbis*

Early in the summer of 2002, Pixar's Steve Jobs invited Disney's Thomas Schumacher to visit Pixar's new animation facility in Emeryville, just outside of San Francisco, which featured a badminton court in the lobby. Jobs and Lasseter were obviously proud of their new creation. At the end of the tour, Lasseter said, "I'll see you guys back at the studio," and walked toward his car. "I'll give you a ride back," Jobs told Schumacher. It was obvious he wanted a chance to speak to him alone.

The relationship with Disney is "going so well," Jobs began, ticking off the amazing string of successes: *Toy Story, Toy Story 2, A Bug's Life,* and the previous year's *Monsters, Inc.* "I love you," Jobs continued, "but I'm furious with Michael." He reminded him of Eisner's stubbornness over the sequels to *Toy Story,* and again brought up Eisner's testimony in Congress. "How can I be a partner with someone like that?" Jobs asked. "I don't trust Michael. I don't know who I can trust."

It was an awkward half-hour ride, since there wasn't much Schumacher could say without seeming disloyal to Eisner.

When he returned to Disney headquarters, Schumacher sought out Eisner. "Michael, let me tell you, they're really pissed off."

Eisner brushed aside his concerns. "They'll get over it. Steve Jobs and I will take a walk."

Schumacher wasn't the only Disney person to whom Jobs reached out that summer. One day, Roy Disney bumped into Dick Cook, chairman of the studio, in the parking lot. Jobs had refused to negotiate directly with Eisner. So Cook was acting as an intermediary. "Steve Jobs would love to talk to you," Cook reported, "but he doesn't want to call you directly."

So Roy called Jobs. As he had to Schumacher, Jobs aired a long list of grievances against Eisner. "He'll say one thing one day, another the next, and then he'll deny saying it at all," Jobs complained. Roy had heard much the same thing from Lasseter. "I just don't see how the relationship can continue as long as Eisner is there," Jobs concluded.

Roy empathized with Jobs, and the next time he was in San Francisco, he had dinner at Jobs's home in Palo Alto. Roy had an Eisner story of his own to match every one that Jobs told. He shared his observation that when Eisner and Wells came to Disney in 1984, it had been like the scene in *The Wizard of Oz* where the Munchkins are freed from the Wicked Witch of the East, and sing, "Ding, dong, the witch is dead." Now Eisner had become the witch. Jobs nodded in agreement. "I'll never make a deal as long as Eisner is there."

When he returned to Los Angeles, Roy briefed Gold on the dinner, and said he was gravely worried about the Pixar relationship. Though they didn't want to reveal that Roy had met with Jobs, they began injecting concerns about the Pixar negotiations into their periodic letters to the board. But it didn't seem to do any good.

Later that summer, Shapiro convened a retreat at the new Grand Californian Hotel at Disneyland to forge an identity and a new brand for the Family channel. Now that "repurposing" had been discredited as an overall programming strategy, and Bornstein was gone, the staff felt liberated. Using reams of market research, they examined the landscape of cable channels to find a demographic that was underserved, and while there were no obvious holes, they targeted two: baby boomers, a group now in its forties and fifties, and thus neglected by the major networks and their advertisers, and women aged eighteen to thirty-four, a key advertiser demographic. The group could find no rationale for a broad "family" channel, which made little sense given cable's appeal to narrower interests, and the wide range of alternatives already available.

In the weeks after the retreat, Shapiro settled on the women's idea, a segment she knew well from her experience in daytime. The eighteen to thirty-four age group also complemented Disney's existing properties, since the Disney channel drew young viewers and ABC was skewing older. Her team named the prototype channel "Pink," and created a logo, branding and marketing campaign, and sample schedules. In August, she and her staff members met with Iger and Disney's general counsel, Alan Braverman, in Iger's conference room to unveil the new concept. "This is what we can be," Shapiro concluded.

Braverman looked awkward. "There's one problem with this. We have an agreement with Hearst that we won't compete directly with Lifetime." Co-owned by Disney and Hearst, Lifetime was the leading cable channel aimed at women, though its audience skewed older than the target for "Pink." The room fell silent. Were there loopholes? Braverman said he'd research the agreement.

Soon after, he delivered the verdict: "Pink" was out.*

So the Family staff went back to the drawing board, and developed another concept, still aimed at the eighteen- to thirty-four-year-old, post-MTV

---

*Braverman said the decision was a business, not a legal, decision, and that he and other executives were well aware that "Pink" posed a threat to Lifetime.

demographic—a "Pink" that would appeal to both men and women. It would be fun, sexy, with lots of reality, led by ABC's "The Bachelor." The leading competitor for that demographic was Comedy Central, but it skewed male. The new channel was dubbed "XYZ," an amusing alphabetical counterpoint to ABC.

Shapiro gave another presentation in Iger's conference room, this time with Eisner present. Everything was done in blue and green, the colors of XYZ's new logo. "This is fantastic!" Iger exclaimed. "You've nailed it." Eisner, too, said he loved it. He picked out the logo from several prototypes: slanted, spray-painted letters with a 1980s graffiti look. Even Braverman liked the idea.

Now that she had Eisner's and Iger's backing, Shapiro organized a second presentation for Anne Sweeney and members of her cable group. When she and her staff finished, Sweeney spoke up. "I'm not sure, but I think our affiliates are telling us we have to keep this a family channel. This may be tough."

"What do you mean?" Iger asked.

"I didn't know this was the direction you were moving in. All the contracts say this has to be a 'family' channel or the affiliates can opt out," she said.

Once again the room fell silent. Sweeney suggested that Shapiro could try to slip the new programming into Family's prime-time slots, without any marketing or advertising support. Perhaps the cable operators wouldn't notice or, by the time they did, ratings would be high enough that they wouldn't care. But Shapiro argued you couldn't raise ratings if you couldn't market the new shows. Braverman said he'd review the contracts. A few days later, he delivered the verdict: no to XYZ.

Shapiro and her staff couldn't believe the issue of the channel's name change was only being confronted now, and not before the acquisition. Hadn't someone reviewed the affiliate contracts?* Discouraged, she and her staff locked themselves in a room for twelve hours. What could they do creatively if they stayed with the concept of "family"? Maybe they could stretch it. Just about anything could be a "family" these days—friends, boyfriends, girlfriends. They decided to try to recast "XYZ," a hipper, younger bookend to ABC, but still a "family" channel, in the broadest sense.

There seemed to be no alternative. In anticipation of the new name and brand, Shapiro began running "Bachelor" episodes and another reality show developed at Disney's Buena Vista studio and by Fisher Entertainment called

---

* Braverman said that he was well aware of the affiliate agreements, and that "XYZ" was rejected for content reasons, not because of legal impediments.

"The Last Resort," which featured couples trying to save their relationships at a tropical resort. Admittedly, scenes of scantily clad couples in hot tubs stretched the notion of "family" fare. But the channel still had vestiges of its previous identity, such as a morning block of Power Rangers and shows aimed at young boys.

Shapiro lobbied hard to introduce the new "XYZ" channel name and eighteen to thirty-four brand identity. But Sweeney and her staff said affiliates were threatening to use any name change as an excuse to drop the channel or to renegotiate their contracts with lower fees. "Who?" Shapiro asked. "What affiliates might we lose? Tell us what the risks are."

No one at the Family channel got any answers. "XYZ" hung in limbo as the channel's identity became even more confused. Shapiro may have negotiated a contract that guaranteed she wouldn't report to Sweeney, but it was obvious to the Family staff that she was being blocked at every turn.

Earlier that year, Dick Cook, now co-heading the film studio with Nina Jacobson, called Jerry Bruckheimer about a new project. "You won't be excited, but take a look," Cook told him—hardly a ringing endorsement. The project had begun life as another attempt to carry out Cook's idea to mine the theme parks for movie ideas. First there had been the *The Country Bears,* based on Disneyland's singing bears, and Disney vice president for production Brigham Taylor had sketched out an idea for *Pirates of the Caribbean,* initially as a cheap, direct-to-video project. (*The Haunted Mansion,* another venerable theme park attraction, was also in development.) But during a meeting to discuss whether Disney should invest in *Master and Commander: Far Side of the World,* an expensive seafaring adventure starring Russell Crowe (Disney passed), Taylor mentioned his pirate idea, and suggested Disney might do its own adventure movie set on the high seas. Jacobson had encouraged him to develop a script.

After talking to Bruckheimer, Cook sent over a new script by Jay Wolpert based on the pirate ride. As Cook had predicted, Bruckheimer was underwhelmed. "It's not a movie I'd go see," he told Cook, and Bruckheimer had long adhered to the self-imposed standard that he'd only make movies he'd want to see. But Bruckheimer knew two writers who were fascinated by the pirate genre, Ted Elliott and Terry Rossio, who had just written *Shrek.* Cook said he'd show them the script. Ironically, they'd already pitched a pirate movie to Disney and had been turned down.

After seeing the script, the writers called Bruckheimer with a fresh idea:

make the pirates cursed (the same idea they'd pitched to Disney before). The pirates would already be dead, trying to return a stolen treasure to earn their final resting place. Visually, they'd look mortal, but would turn into skeletons in the moonlight. Now Bruckheimer's interest was piqued. He called Cook to say he was interested in something that would merge the pirate and supernatural genres.

As the new writers went to work on the script, Bruckheimer flew to St. Tropez to meet with actor Johnny Depp. Depp, the sultry, iconoclastic star of the cult classics *Ed Wood, Edward Scissorhands,* and *What's Eating Gilbert Grape?* was hardly an obvious choice for a Disney action-adventure. Depp had turned down the chance to star in such mainstream hits as *Speed* and *Titanic.* Nor had his films been big commercial successes. But Depp and his companion, French actress Vanessa Paradis, now had two young children, and Depp had hinted that he was interested in performing in films his children might enjoy watching.

It would be hard to imagine a more striking contrast between the bohemian, irreverent Depp and the conventional, buttoned-down demeanor of Dick Cook. But the two had met six months earlier, and had gotten along surprisingly well. Cook stressed that he hoped Disney and the actor could work together. Still, a pirate movie conjuring up dated images of Errol Flynn with earrings and bandanna was hardly what Depp had in mind. Bruckheimer stressed that this wasn't going to be a conventional pirate movie, especially if Depp took the lead role of the renegade pirate, Jack Sparrow. Bruckheimer wanted to reinvent the genre.

With Depp at least interested, Bruckheimer approached director Gore Verbinski, someone he'd been talking to since *Con Air.* A former rock guitarist, Verbinski had moved from directing music videos to the cult horror hit *The Ring.* "I thought the pirate genre was extinct," Verbinski told Bruckheimer. But the more Verbinski thought about it, the more intriguing the project sounded, especially if Depp committed to it. With Bruckheimer attached, he knew he'd get a big budget. If they failed, they'd fail big. He liked the element of risk. When else would he get the chance to do a big-budget pirate movie?

With Depp still uncommitted, Verbinski met the actor in London. Depp was having some trouble with the notion of working for Disney, which symbolized everything he wasn't. "What can we do that will really freak the studio out?" Depp wondered.

"Pirates are gross and disgusting," Verbinski pointed out, encouraging Depp to use his imagination.

"Yeah! That's great," Depp said. Then he had an inspiration: Jack Sparrow would already have had his nose cut off, leaving nothing but a bloody wound. "I could play the whole part without a nose!" Depp enthused.

"Uh-huh," Verbinski replied, noncommittal. He knew that would never fly, but why make an issue of it? "See how liberating this could be?" Verbinski continued, noting that there was another "straight" part, the romantic hero, which meant the Sparrow character could be as eccentric as Depp wanted.

Images started popping into Depp's mind: Lee Marvin in *Cat Ballou.* Rock stars. Keith Richards prancing around the stage as lead guitarist for the Rolling Stones.

"This could be the end of our careers," Verbinski mused, "but let's have fun."

Once Depp committed to do the film (for a relatively modest fee, but also a cut of the gross), Verbinski turned to Orlando Bloom for the role of the "straight" romantic lead, and sent a script and cover letter to Geoffrey Rush, whom he wanted for the part of Barbossa, the villain and pirate captain. "Barbossa is both treacherous and charming and requires a commitment to that wondrous archetype of villainy that has been missing from cinema for so long," Verbinski wrote Rush in a cover letter with the script. "As I look across the landscape of contemporary actors I cannot think of anyone else but you who has the ability to make Barbossa simply delicious. This is a big pirate movie that turns the genre on its head."

Rush loved the reference to "simply delicious."

All that remained was the issue of budget. Eisner had groaned when Cook presented him with the notion of a $120 million period costume drama on the high seas—a recipe for disaster. Every recent pirate movie had failed, including 1980's *The Island,* based on a Peter Benchley novel that Eisner had tried to buy while he was still at Paramount. Thankfully he'd been outbid by Universal. *Cutthroat Island* with Geena Davis was a 1995 flop. Why would this be any different? Eisner rejected the idea out of hand.

Bruckheimer called him repeatedly. Finally Eisner agreed to attend a meeting at Bruckheimer's luxurious offices in Santa Monica, but he was still determined to kill the project. Bruckheimer had assembled storyboards, and drawings of the major scenes: the island of the dead, the Caribbean port under siege, the skeletons under water and on the moonlit pirate ship. After getting a tour and running commentary from Verbinski, Eisner sat down. "I love it," he said. "Why does it have to cost so much?"

"Your competition is spending $150 million," Bruckheimer countered, ticking off projects like the *Matrix* and *The Lord of the Rings,* franchise films that were allowing Warner Bros. to dominate at the box office. Disney desperately needed a franchise of its own.

Eisner shook his head in exasperation. "The theme park is a drawback," he said, "Country Bears" still in mind. "Let's move this away from the park."

If only he knew, Verbinski thought. With Depp as Jack Sparrow, there was no danger that anyone would confuse this film with the charming but tame Disneyland ride.

It was no wonder Eisner was worried about a $120 million budget for a pirate movie. As the summer of 2002 unfolded, forces beyond their control buffeted Disney and Eisner. Economists confirmed that a recession had begun even before the terrorist attacks of September 11. Investor and public confidence had been shaken by an unprecedented series of corporate scandals beginning with Enron in the fall, and continuing with WorldCom, Tyco, Adelphia, and HealthSouth. It was the dark side to the booming 1990s. The stock market decline that began with the bursting of the Internet bubble in the spring of 2000 had turned into a rout, with the technology-heavy NASDAQ index losing an unprecedented 80 percent of its value.

Eisner's view of the AOL Time Warner merger was vindicated when AOL stock turned out to be the inflated paper he had always claimed it was. In the midst of an SEC investigation into accounting fraud at AOL, Gerald Levin was forced to resign. A shareholder initiative to withhold support for the reelection of chairman and director Steve Case garnered about 22 percent of the total, not enough to force his ouster, but a shocking vote of no confidence nonetheless. Bowing to the inevitable, Case resigned on May 16, 2003.

By these standards, Eisner and Disney seemed like pillars of ethical and prudent behavior. However much Disney had lost on its own failed Internet venture, it paled in comparison to Time Warner, whose deal with AOL was now widely derided as the worst deal in business history. And yet Eisner was drawn into the vortex. A common theme in the egregious cases of corporate fraud was a passive and often compromised board of directors that failed to protect shareholder interests. Disney's board had always been something of a special case. Not only was its independence compromised by numerous conflicts of interest, but as long as Sid Bass had remained, in effect, a controlling shareholder and staunch ally of Eisner, the board had served as little more than a figurehead of corporate governance, with Bass and Eisner making all the critical decisions. Now Eisner faced calls for reform at a critical time, just as Bass had relinquished his grip and Gold and Roy were beginning to assert their independence.

Perhaps Eisner could turn the calls for reform to his own advantage. At the June board meeting, he announced that Disney had hired Ira Millstein, a senior and respected partner at Weil, Gotshal & Manges in New York, and an expert on corporate governance, to help draft reforms that would govern the Disney board. While no one could argue that reforms were in order, the undertaking also carried an implied threat to anyone who decided to support Gold and Roy. After all, there were any number of "reforms," such as shrinking the size of the board, that could be used to get rid of Eisner's critics.

At the June 2002 meeting Eisner unveiled his latest five-year plan for Disney's return to annualized 20 percent growth. The plan depended heavily on the performance of the new Family channel, projecting an 88 percent annualized growth in operating income for the channel. The other pillar was ESPN, with a projected 75 percent annualized growth. In addition, Eisner predicted that theme park revenues would return to their peak 2001 levels and that all the ABC network needed was a "stroke of creative lightning." But even as he unveiled the projections, it was clear that Disney's results were falling hopelessly behind the results forecast for the current 2002 fiscal year, which would end in September.

Disney had some successes to its credit, notably *Lilo & Stitch*, the first animated feature to emerge from the animation unit in Orlando. And the latest film from M. Night Shyamalan, the supernatural *Signs*, starring Mel Gibson, opened nationwide on August 2, and made $117 million in its first week. But two successful films couldn't compensate for the continuing slump in tourism and the turmoil at ABC. In July, Disney released its fiscal third-quarter results and its stock plunged to an eight-year, split-adjusted low of $13.75 a share—lower than it had been in the wake of September 11, when Sid Bass had faced a margin call.

Under the new Sarbanes-Oxley Act passed by Congress to combat corporate fraud on the scale of Enron and WorldCom, Eisner and Tom Staggs, as Disney's CEO and chief financial officer respectively, had to personally certify the accuracy of Disney's financial results by August 1. In reviewing its filings, Disney discovered it had failed to make certain public disclosures, including relatives of directors employed by Disney, required by SEC Regulation SK. Toward the end of July, Eisner reached Gold at his apartment in New York. He sounded almost gleeful when he told him that Millstein had advised him that, under new rules being considered by Disney, Gold was no longer "independent" because his daughter had a job in the consumer products division of Disney.

Surprised, Gold had no ready response, but he had his lawyers consider the issue. They responded that at the very least the issue was premature. The New York Stock Exchange was examining the question but hadn't promulgated any new rules. Eisner agreed to hold off at least temporarily, but Gold now had to share his pivotal position as chairman of the nominating and governance committee with George Mitchell, who was rapidly emerging as a staunch backer of Eisner on the board. Gold thought it ironic that Mitchell was being hailed as "independent" while his law firm had earned $2 million in fees from Disney, while Gold's daughter's job paid $86,000. (Mitchell also received a $50,000 annual "consulting" fee from Disney in addition to his $45,000-a-year director's fees and stock options. He also served at one point on eight other corporate boards, six of which paid fees to his law firm.)

The growing conflicting tensions within Disney burst into public view on August 8, when *Los Angeles Times* reporters James Bates and Claudia Eller reported that "Key directors are increasingly impatient with its lagging financial performance and stock price. . . . According to sources close to the board, relations have become increasingly strained between Eisner and two of Disney's most powerful board members, Roy E. Disney and Stanley Gold. . . . Tensions have risen in recent weeks, including some pointed exchanges between Eisner and Gold, sources said."

Eisner was convinced that Gold had planted the story. He fired off a stream of emails to Gold accusing him of leaking the story. Gold hotly denied the accusation, but agreed in an email to keep his differences with Eisner "in house."

Gold was furious that Eisner had obviously given Ray Watson permission to present Eisner's side to the press, even as he tried to silence him. "Disney director Ray Watson said the board as a whole supports Eisner," the story read, quoting Watson: "We have no interest in going out and bringing an unknown into this company and this difficult industry when we believe we already have the best CEO in the business."

Gold was particularly upset given Watson's remarks to the contrary during their lunch, when Watson had criticized Eisner. He quickly fired off a sharply worded letter to Watson:

Dear Ray:

    I was surprised to see you quoted in the Los Angeles Times on Thursday. . . . While you are certainly entitled to your opinion, and I respect that, I am mystified as to how you arrived at that conclusion since our lunch just six months ago. At that time, I shared with you my doubts about the Company's performance and the current leadership's ability to improve that performance. At that lunch, you said that the Company was in chaos and that Michael and the senior management had no sensible plan to extract us from this chaos.

I respect your right to change your mind; you did so in 1984 before supporting the Eisner/Wells team. What I would like better to understand is how your position changed so as to permit you to conclude that Michael is the best CEO in the business? Certainly, it can't be the quantitative performance of the Company during those six months. . . .

But there is plenty of blame to go around. We, the Directors, are guilty of not discussing the real issues affecting the Company. We have not fully and critically addressed the failed plans of our executives or the broken promises that management has made to the Board and the shareholders over the last five years. We are too polite, too concerned with hurting each other's feelings, when our real job is (a) to protect the shareholders and (b) to coalesce around a management team and a plan that we believe will get us out of our current malaise. . . .

I hope you will receive my comments in the spirit in which they are offered . . . serious concern by a Director who believes that we, the Disney Directors, have long been too compliant and uncritical of management's failures. We can no longer accept as fact that all of the bad things that happen to Disney are out of management's control and all of the good things are a result of having "the best CEO in the business."

Kindest personal regards,
Stanley P. Gold

Gold sent copies to Eisner and each member of the board.

Andrea Van de Kamp, for one, was startled by the tone of Gold's letter. She knew he was concerned, but thought the letter was harsh and would likely prove ineffective with other board members. She called Bob Iger to discuss it. "We're really upset," he told her. "Michael is frantic."

Eisner's counterattack was swift. The day Gold sent his letter, Disney disclosed that Gold's daughter, Jennifer, worked in Disney's consumer products division. Disney also disclosed that Ray Watson's son, Ray Jr., worked at the Disney channel, and that Reveta Bowers's son, Craig, had previously worked in Disney's Internet group. The most startling disclosure was that John Bryson's wife earned $1.35 million a year as an executive at the Disney co-owned Lifetime channel. Under the guidelines being developed by Ira Millstein, Gold would be forced to step down as co-chairman of the governance and compensation committees.

These developments were especially unsettling to Reveta Bowers, who had long endured criticism that she was only on the board because Eisner's sons had attended her school. Informed that she would no longer be considered independent (even though her son was no longer at Disney), and therefore that she could no longer serve on the nominating or compensation committees, she told Eisner she wanted to resign. Instead, he persuaded her to wait until the end of the year, when she wouldn't stand for reelection.

A week later, on August 16, 2002, Eisner and Gold met for lunch at the Lakeside Golf Club, the scene of the celebratory lunch on the day Eisner and Wells were named chairman and president. Eisner began by again accusing Gold of leaking to the press, which Gold hotly denied. "Bruce Orwall told me he spoke to you," Eisner insisted. Orwall covered Disney for *The Wall Street Journal*.

"Let's take a fucking lie detector test," Gold said. "I have not spoken to Bruce Orwall. So either he's lying or you're lying. Which one is it?"

(Orwall told me he never told Eisner that Gold had spoken to him. "I never said anything of the sort," Orwall said.)

Eisner dropped the matter, and turned to the real reason for the lunch. He asked Gold to resign as chairman of the powerful governance and nominating committee. Gold refused. He said the person who should be resigning was Eisner. He reminded Eisner of his repeated promise to step down if he lost Gold's and Roy's confidence.

"I never said that," Eisner said.

Gold was incredulous. Eisner had said it many times over the years, to him, to Roy, to their wives, and to others as well. "Let me ask you, Michael," he said. "Are you going to go out as a gentleman, or are you going to be carried out on your shield?"

"Let me assure you, I'll be here long after you're gone," Eisner retorted, before angrily walking out.

Gold followed up with a letter to the board the following Monday, in which he refused to relinquish his position on the committee. He quoted the New York Stock Exchange guidelines to the effect that employment of a relative "does not preclude the board from determining that a director is independent. Such employment arrangements are common and do not present a categorical threat to director independence. I think that when the Board considers this, it will conclude that the Company's employment of my daughter has not and will not compromise my independence. Furthermore, as demonstrated by the current disagreements between us, questions about my independence from management cannot be of real concern to any director. . . . I have stated my views directly to you and to other Board members about the Company's lack of performance, its lack of accountability and its poor allocation of capital resources. While I do not expect that everybody will agree with that point of view, I think that management's attempt to muzzle me for holding or articulating independent views flies in the face of the new rules on independence. A hallmark of independence is the willingness to speak up."

Word of a split within the board coupled with Disney's "reform" measures, clearly aimed at Gold, triggered press coverage. With Eisner's permission, Gold invited *New York Times* reporter Laura Holson to his Beverly Hills home, where he sidestepped questions about his relationship with Eisner, saying only that the Disney family "owes a great debt of gratitude to Michael for what he has done. But my goal is to try to get the Disney Company to perform at a level of efficiency it hasn't seen for a number of years." He went to some length to deflect Eisner's suggestions that he was pressuring him in a desperate effort to boost Disney's stock price because Shamrock had suffered reversals in the stock market. While he acknowledged losses in investments in L.A. Gear and Grand Union (both had gone bankrupt), he cited other gains, and said Shamrock had $1.7 billion in assets with a "manageable" amount of leverage.

The day after the article appeared, Sid Bass weighed in, writing Gold a letter, copied to all the directors, expressing his outrage that Gold was pursuing his campaign in the press. After the sale of so much of his Disney stake, Bass no longer had the power he once wielded. Still, he had a long history as an investor in Disney, and he had influence with directors, most of whom wouldn't have been on the board had Bass objected.

"You as a board member have the right and the privilege to your opinion about the management," Bass said to Gold.

> By the same token, it has been my opinion that every board member has a fiduciary duty not to make statements to investors, investment bankers, and the press which will damage the company. . . . Your public behavior has become a counterproductive distraction at a time when everybody's energy should be focused toward thoughtful and candid dialogue and analysis.
>
> I too am disappointed in the performance of the company in the last few years. Some of that disappointment comes from outside events, a recession and terrorist attacks. Some of that disappointment comes from unwise deci-

sions of management. I measure managements according to what I think I could reasonably expect from myself. Some of the decisions I could have made better, and some poor decisions I spoke against before they were made. I also remember speaking against making Beauty and Lion King into Broadway productions, to name only two very poor opinions of mine that were fortunately ignored by management.

I am not addressing the merits of either side of a debate, but how a debate is properly waged. While I may argue against your summary opinion of management, I respect your opinion. I do not respect or tolerate your current public behavior while you remain an important member of the board of directors. Here you must play by the rules or step down and play by any rules you choose. Not to make that choice is below the high principles that I have seen in your behavior over all these years.

Gold promptly responded to Bass with another letter of his own, also copied to board members:

I have not talked to the press at all, with the exception of Laura Holson at the New York Times. I cleared that discussion with Michael prior to speaking with Ms. Holson. I know that you and Michael find it difficult to believe that I have not spoken with the press, but that is the truth. He has accused me on several occasions of talking to the press, including Bruce Orwall of The Wall Street Journal. He told me that Orwall had told him that I had spoken with him. I denied it, because it is not true. . . .

With respect to employees, investors and fund managers, let me set the record straight. You cannot go anywhere in this town—or any other city for that matter—without someone approaching you to complain about Disney's performance and management's inability to address the problems. I have had fund managers tell me they won't buy a share of stock in the Company while Michael Eisner is CEO. I have had employees (senior executives) tell me the company would be much better off with a new management team. Morale at the company is at an all-time low. I have not leaked this information—it is common knowledge. I have not made it public and I have not even encouraged it.

Sid, it is a fact that everyone in the financial community is well aware of the depths to which the Company has fallen. Financial performance has been stagnant for at least five years, capital has been squandered on numerous investments and projects, and lastly, perhaps more importantly, the creative side of the Walt Disney Company has been lost or abandoned. Rather than taking responsibility for the factual realities, the answer of management is to attack anyone in sight, including me. I am afraid that when you, of all people, join in this chorus you are merely acting as Torquemada's adjutant.

The problem at the Walt Disney Company is not Stanley Gold, it is not leaks (real or imagined) or unprofessional conduct, but instead it is poor performance, lack of credibility and accountability and poor capital allocation. When anyone, much less a Director simply trying to professionally discharge his fiduciary duties, raises these issues, the Company's defense is character assassination. Today they are focused on me; in the past they have used this tactic on others; and there will be new victims in the future. Is it no wonder that many directors are afraid to speak up lest they find themselves the focus of Michael's wrath?

Sid, I value our long friendship and would be pleased to discuss this with you at greater length at your convenience.

In the midst of these mounting tensions, Eisner sought to reassure the board. By email to all board members dated August 22, he wrote, "Dear All,

"I just got back from my second movie today from our upcoming slate. I am really pumped as my kids would say. It makes the press flack and answering questions about executive longevity seem not so important because it is the exhilaration of the product that puts things in perspective. . . ."

Eisner lauded the upcoming *The Santa Clause 2* starring Tim Allen in a reprise of his successful 1994 role, and director Spike Lee's *25th Hour*, which Eisner stressed was made for a modest $14 million. But his most revealing comments were reserved for Pixar:

"Yesterday we saw for the second time the new Pixar movie 'Finding Nemo' that comes out next May. This will be a reality check for those guys. It's okay, but nowhere near as good as their previous films. Of course they think it is great. Trust me, it's not, but it will open." *

With Eisner increasingly irritated by Steve Jobs's refusal to extend the agreement with Disney on terms Eisner considered even remotely reasonable, and jealous and resentful of Pixar's admiring press, it was almost as

---

* Eisner said that early screenings of *Nemo* were disappointing, but that the film improved dramatically by the time it opened. Still, others said Eisner was never enthusiastic about it.

though Eisner wanted *Nemo* to fail, however irrational, considering that Disney would reap 50 percent of the profits on top of its marketing and distribution costs. Eisner also went out of his way to stress the success of ABC Family: "As for ABC Family, we have a meeting next week during which the head of the network, Angela Shapiro, will present her revamped vision. Specifically, Angela will take us through the programming mix (original as well as re-purposed material from ABC), the schedule, and the marketing that will help define the network. Angela is doing a great job as ABC Family starts to really perform."

A showdown loomed at the Disney board meeting set for September 24, where directors would be asked to vote on various reforms, on the independence of directors, on committee membership, and on a new "action" plan that was being submitted for approval by Eisner. Gold knew he lacked a majority on the board that would support him, and without it, directors were unwilling to risk alienating Eisner. Even Tom Murphy, who had decided to support Eisner despite praising Gold for speaking his mind, said it was pointless to vote with him as long as he remained in the minority. Though he continued to meet privately with other directors, Gold's campaign had stalled after his meeting with Watson, now that Eisner knew what he was doing.

Still, Gold pressed ahead, sending a detailed, eight-page letter to directors in early September analyzing Disney's disappointing results, the failure to meet goals of previous five-year plans, and stressing the need for greater diligence by directors in light of Enron and other scandals. "Management shares tidbits, rumors and feel-good messages regarding new movie releases and television pilots rather than factual comparisons to summary targets," Gold wrote. "This Board needs to carefully consider past performance, measure management against its promises and projections, and get independent assessments and data about strategic issues. We can no longer make decisions predicated solely on management's 'trust me' attitude and ad hoc conclusions."

Gold asked for the appointment of a special committee of the Board (with himself as a member) to commission a "diagnostic review" of Disney by outside consultants. Though cloaked in different terminology, it was essentially the same thing as the "management review" that had preceded Ron Miller's ouster in 1984, and the implications for Eisner of adopting such a proposal were obvious. Gold asked that the proposal be placed on the agenda and asked for time to make a presentation to the board.

As Gold's letter-writing campaign continued, Eisner met with each of the board members individually, shoring up his support. When he met Van de Kamp for lunch, he warned her that there was no middle ground. "If you vote for that side," he said, referring to Gold and Roy, "you're off the board."

"Don't be like that," Van de Kamp said. "You're just upset. Stanley is not your enemy. He's worried about performance. Present a plan. Give the board a strategy. Tell us what you're going to do to bring us out of this mess. Don't divide us."

On September 23, Gold took an 8:00 A.M. flight from Paris, where he was racing in an amateur Formula 1 Grand Prix race (he took first place), to be at the Disney boardroom by 5:00 P.M. the same day, when the critical meeting was scheduled to begin. Roy had also made it a point to attend. On the agenda that evening was a motion to remove Gold as chairman of the powerful governance and nominating committee and replace him with George Mitchell. But despite Eisner's warning to Van de Kamp that support for Roy and Gold could cost her her board seat, she resisted. A compromise was reached in which Gold stayed, at least for the time being, as co-chairman with George Mitchell. But Gold's influence was effectively diluted by the addition to the five-member committee of Judith Estrin and Monica Lozano, two of Eisner's staunchest backers on the board. Along with John Bryson, another Eisner loyalist, and Mitchell, they constituted a four-person majority loyal to Eisner.

Gold's presentation was first on the agenda when the meeting resumed at 9:00 the next morning. He and his colleagues at Shamrock had prepared carefully, hoping to get directors to confront the reality of Disney's recent financial performance. But Gold wanted to get the facts on the record. As long as Eisner and his executives controlled the flow of information, the board couldn't be expected to hold them accountable. And Gold thought the facts were glaring, which would be obvious even to the less financially sophisticated directors.

Gold emphasized that by every standard economic measure of performance since 1995—return on invested capital, return on equity, return on assets, and the price/book value ratio—Disney was at a seven-year low. "In all respects," he maintained, "the financial results of the company have been declining for a sustained period of time and currently sit at the lowest levels in years." He noted that with the acquisitions of Cap Cities/ABC and Fox Family as well as other investments, Disney had deployed an additional $24 billion in capital. Yet operating income was now lower than it had been before the acquisitions. Since 1995, the compounded annual return of Disney stock was 1.9 percent, lower than Treasury bonds and significantly behind major stock indices as well as media and entertainment sector indices. "The conclusion is inescapable. Our company has steadily and increasingly underperformed for a sustained period of time (not just the last 12–24 months as management would suggest) and the market is correctly punishing our stock price." He called for "decisive action now" to reverse these trends.

Gold walked the board through a detailed series of PowerPoint slides comparing management's assertions to actual results. Among other data, he noted that Eisner's five-year strategic plans had failed to meet projections every year for the past six years, falling short, on average, by 23 percent the first year, 33 percent the second, 47 percent the third, and 55 percent the fourth. He also highlighted the startling dependence of the Disney Studio on its relationship to Pixar, showing that Pixar's contribution to the studio's operating income ranged from 97 percent in 2000 to 47 percent in 2001, with 2002 projected to be 39 percent. "Is management confident we can extend the Pixar relationship or replace its recent contributions to studio EBITA [Earnings Before Taxes, Interest, and Amortization]?" Gold asked.*

When he finished, Gold asked if there were any questions. There were none. Gold couldn't believe that after an hour and a half, there wasn't a single question. It fell to Tom Staggs to argue that Gold had carefully chosen years calculated to show Disney's results in the worst possible light. No one else spoke, as Eisner sat in stony silence. So Gold called for a vote on his proposed "diagnostic review." George Mitchell asked him to withdraw the request, indicating that Tom Staggs would prepare a written response to Gold's presentation and present it to the board "in due course." Gold agreed, realizing he lacked the votes to force the issue.

Next Eisner rose and, ignoring Gold's remarks entirely, presented his "action plan," a revision of June's five-year plan necessitated by the continuing deterioration in Disney's financial performance. The essence of the plan was two-pronged: that Disney's long-term profitability derived from the strengths of its brands, primarily Disney and, more recently, ESPN, and that after a period of large capital investments—especially in new theme parks, in acquiring the rights to professional sports, and in buying ABC Family— Disney could boost profits by slashing spending and reaping the cash flow

---

*Disney said the correct Pixar numbers were 45 percent, 35 percent, and 29 percent, respectively.

from those earlier investments. The key to the plan was protecting the Disney and ESPN brands by building a "protective moat" around them.

At the end of the presentation, Eisner said that in light of all the recent publicity about divisions within the board, it was important that the directors send a public message that Eisner and his management team had the board's full support. He called for a vote of confidence, and urged that it be unanimous.

At this, Roy made a rare comment in a board meeting: "I couldn't vote for that. You don't have my support," he said.

Eisner's face colored in anger, but before he could say anything Mitchell suggested that Eisner, Iger, and other executive directors leave the room so the board could continue the discussion in executive session. A heated discussion ensued, in which both Roy and Gold reiterated their opposition to any vote of support for Eisner. Finally Mitchell suggested that Eisner's recommendation be tabled rather than go forward with a vote that would only formalize the split within the board. Instead, he said he would craft a statement from the board expressing its "overwhelming support" for Eisner.

Eisner and the other executives returned. It fell to Mitchell to break the news that no vote had been taken. But even before he could finish, Eisner spoke in anger: "I can't live with this," he said, glaring at Gold and Roy. He brandished a piece of paper. "They're undermining me, leaking to the press, and this proves it. While we were in this room I've been emailed by someone at the *L.A. Times* about something we talked about three hours ago." He read from what he said was a copy of an email he'd just received from Richard Verrier, a reporter for the *L.A. Times,* urging Eisner to give him an interview because "we'll be talking to the other side." Gold started to deny the accusation, but Eisner plunged on. "Stanley and Roy are trying to get rid of me. They don't think I can run this company. But who do you think can? Bob?" He turned toward Iger. "Bob can't run this company," he said dismissively.*

There was an awkward silence. Eisner sat down. Several other directors looked shell-shocked. Mitchell quickly adjourned the meeting.

The next day Roy sent Iger a short handwritten message of condolence. "I've never seen anyone treated so badly," Roy said.

Iger reported this to Eisner, who immediately phoned Roy. "I know you sent Bob a note," he said accusingly.

---

* Four directors confirmed this account. Eisner said he meant that Gold and Roy didn't believe Iger could run Disney, and that this was also Iger's interpretation of the remark.

FIFTEEN

For all Eisner's concern over leaks, the article in the *Los Angeles Times* by Verrier and James Bates had sketchy details of the September 24 board meeting. Although "sources" described a "blunt meeting during which Chief Executive Michael Eisner was repeatedly questioned about whether he could meet a series of financial targets," it also stated that "details of the much-anticipated meeting at Disney's Burbank headquarters remained mostly under wraps." Most of the information in the article appeared to come from Disney itself. The company announced the appointments to the nominating and governance committee, and Eisner said, "Today, we furthered our commitment to ensure that Disney remains among the most progressive boards in America on governance issues."

Reveta Bowers, the much revered head of the Center for Early Education, also continued to feel the brunt of the independence issue. Although Bowers's son no longer worked at Disney, the Center had been the beneficiary of Disney largesse. The school's library was called the Disney library, because the Disney Foundation had funded it. More recently, Eisner had indicated that Disney would donate $250,000 toward a younger children's library decorated in a Winnie-the-Pooh motif. But Disney wrote a letter saying that it was improper for Disney to contribute to an organization headed by a director. More to the point, the chairman of the Center's board was Susan Disney Lord, one of Roy's daughters, which meant Bowers's loyalty to Eisner couldn't be taken for granted in the looming battle with Roy and Gold. (Bowers told me she sided with neither Eisner nor Susan and "I always voted my conscience.")

That summer, Susan, who was also on the school's building committee, noticed that both the Winnie the Pooh theme and the Disney name had been dropped from the building plans. When Susan asked Bowers what had happened, and what had happened to the promised Disney gift, Bowers said, "Michael pulled it." *

In the wake of the contentious September meeting, Eisner asked Roy to have lunch with him, anxious to see if there was any way he could mollify him, and drive a wedge between him and Gold, whom Eisner perceived as the real troublemaker. The two met in a private dining room off the Disney commissary. "Roy," Eisner began. "I don't understand this. You have a great life. You've made a fortune. I protect you. Why are you doing this?"

"I agree with Stanley," Roy replied.

"What do you mean you agree with Stanley? What, exactly, do you agree with?"

"You shouldn't have bought ABC."

The response made Eisner furious. "We'd be gone by now! Taken over! There wouldn't be any Disney!"

"Pixar hasn't been taken over," Roy said, pointing out that it was small, but so successful creatively that its high stock price made a takeover prohibitively expensive. "They're Disney people, you know."

The comparison to Pixar also annoyed Eisner. "What else don't you agree with?"

"Andy Mooney," Roy replied, referring to the head of consumer products who had put Tinker Bell on T-shirts.

"Why?"

Roy felt the discussion was getting nowhere, so he saw no point in answering. But he took advantage of the occasion to remind Eisner of his oft-repeated promise that if he lost Roy's support, he'd resign.

"I never said that," Eisner replied, leaving Roy speechless.

Eisner stressed once more to company confidants that he wanted Roy monitored more closely than ever, and that he wanted every conversation reported to him. One day Eisner gestured toward several thick binders on his desk, and said that he had collected every email Roy had sent and received. Some animators blanched at the thought, wondering how discreet they had been. They certainly hadn't expected their emails to wind up on Eisner's desk.

---

* Eisner insisted that he was only trying to adhere to the highest standards of corporate governance.

As instructed, Thomas Schumacher had dutifully reported his conversations with Roy to Eisner, but the tensions between the two were growing intolerable. Schumacher was caught squarely in the middle of the intensifying feud. That fall, Eisner demanded that Roy be excluded from animation meetings, even that the locks be changed on his office and that he be barred from the lot.

Schumacher considered Roy a friend. Roy and Patty had hosted Schumacher and his partner, Matthew White, at their castle in Ireland. Roy had shepherded Schumacher's career, backed his decisions, and championed animation. So Schumacher refused. "Michael, I cannot betray Roy and I won't do that." (On Eisner's orders, he did warn Roy to stay away from animation meetings, but Roy ignored him.)

Just as Schumacher reported Roy's conversations to Eisner, he reported Eisner's remarks to Roy, including Eisner's demand that Roy be barred from animation meetings and from the studio lot. Despite these distractions, Schumacher tried to concentrate that fall on the finishing touches to *Treasure Planet*, the much anticipated—and expensive—animated feature from Clements and Musker.

Treasure Planet cost $130 million—$10 million underbudget. It opened on November 17, the key pre-Thanksgiving kickoff to the holiday season. Warner Bros.' *Harry Potter and the Chamber of Secrets* had already opened to critical acclaim and huge box-office revenues. Most reviewers hailed *Treasure Planet*'s arresting visual imagery—"A Treasure for the Eyes" was the *Chicago Tribune*'s verdict—but overall, critics wallowed in an anti-Disney backlash. A. O. Scott in *The New York Times* was especially devastating. Calling *Treasure Planet* "brainless" and "mechanical," he added that the movie "is less an act of homage than a clumsy and cynical bit of piracy, designed to steal time and money from schoolchildren and their harried, Pottered-out parents during this long holiday weekend. . . . The adventures that youngsters act out on the French fry–littered seats of the family minivan will surely be more exciting, and imaginative, than the film itself."

Treasure Planet director Ron Clements was skiing with his family at Mammoth Mountain when the bad news came in: *Treasure Planet* grossed just $12 million in its opening weekend. The following Sunday, Schumacher called him with even worse news: Disney was announcing that it would take a $74 million write-down on *Treasure Planet*, the biggest financial write-down in animation history. Under SEC rules, Disney had no choice, but animators interpreted the write-down tantamount to an announcement that Disney had no faith in the film, even as it was just beginning its U.S. release, and before it opened in international markets. Until Disney branded it a failure, Clements, Musker, and Schumacher had hoped that *Treasure Planet* might still gross $100 million or more worldwide. Now, box-office receipts plummeted.

Not since the early days of the Eisner/Wells regime, when Eisner and Katzenberg had banished the animators to Glendale, and they had feared for the future of the division, was the animators' morale so low. The Paris animation studio had been shut down after *Hercules*. The only 2-D projects still in production were *Brother Bear* and *Home on the Range*. Once again, rumors circulated that Disney would abandon hand-drawn animation altogether.

The more cynical observers among the animators, and there were many, couldn't help but notice that Eisner now shifted the blame to Roy for the failure of *Treasure Planet*. The *Los Angeles Times* reported that Eisner had "raised a red flag" about the movie and it was Roy who intervened to have Eisner green-light the project. This came as news to the animators. While Roy, as usual, had supported their efforts on the film (using his sailing expertise, for example, to make sure that the sailing knots used on the ship in *Treasure Planet* were accurate), he had nothing to do with green-lighting the project, as far as they knew. How convenient that the write-off took place, and Roy could be blamed, just as the boardroom showdown was intensifying.*

The decision to write off *Treasure Planet* was the last straw for Schumacher. A year earlier, he had told Eisner he didn't plan to stay beyond the end of his contract, which expired in March 2003. Given the lead time of four years for most animated features, Schumacher was making decisions that should be made by his successor. There had been some discussion of his staying on in an advisory capacity in animation while continuing to oversee Disney's theatrical operations based in New York, but now he decided it was better to make a clean break from animation. As the Christmas holiday approached, Schumacher met with Eisner and told him he'd move to New York to run the theatrical division, but added, "You don't want me running animation. I'm too loyal to Roy. The longer I'm in animation, the longer you'll have Roy around."

Eisner didn't disagree. David Stainton, head of television animation, was named to succeed Schumacher as president of feature animation. Roy attended a hastily organized farewell for Schumacher on January 3. After Schu-

---

* When I asked Eisner about this, he said that Roy wasn't to blame for *Treasure Planet* and that he had never suggested to the board or anyone else that he was.

macher left work that day, someone else packed up his office, and he never returned to the animation studio where he'd spent the last fifteen years.

After his promotion, Stainton met with Roy. "I might as well tell you," he said, "that Michael wants to know everything you tell me."

This was hardly news to Roy. "Don't worry," he said. "I've been there before."

In the fall of 2002, CNN's Jamie Kellner made a presentation to the AOL Time Warner board on the status of the negotiations to merge CNN with ABC News. It went without saying that the key board member was Ted Turner, who'd made his reputation and much of his fortune by founding CNN, and remained AOL Time Warner's largest shareholder even after the merger. Kellner had met with Turner several times as the discussions continued, and while Kellner couldn't quite say Turner was enthusiastic about the deal, he had conceded that the merger made financial and strategic sense. So it came as a surprise when Turner announced that he opposed the merger.

Other directors, fresh from accusations that they had been far too passive in approving the AOL merger, jumped in with questions: "What if the Pope were killed? Who would break the story first?" Kellner wasn't prepared for such a barrage; this was just a preliminary discussion to introduce the directors to the concept. But when it ended, he called Iger to report that he'd met stiff resistance. Ultimately, the merger proposal was shelved. Whatever the merits of the deal, Time Warner wasn't in any position to consider another controversial merger.

As 2002 drew to a close and Eisner sat down to write his annual letter to shareholders, his tenure as Disney's chairman and chief executive was at a low point. Disney stock had sunk to $14.14 on October 7, 2002. Much of the blame could be laid on the weak economy, the plunge in tourism, and the ongoing aftershocks of September 11, all factors beyond Eisner's control. But as Gold's boardroom presentation had made clear, the downward spiral had begun long before September 11, which had only intensified the decline. The tone of this year's letter was far from the gleeful optimism of the earlier letters, which had established the tradition of Eisner's chatty, personal, optimistic assessments of the company's progress. Now they were as much a burden as a welcome opportunity to highlight Disney's achievements.

There was of course no mention of any boardroom dissension—

something that would have been of real interest to shareholders—but much of the 2002 letter was nonetheless devoted to restating the "moat" strategy that Eisner had unveiled at the September board meeting. Predicting 25 to 35 percent earnings growth in 2003, and "continued strong growth in 2004," Eisner wrote "we believe this performance will result from the strategic action plan that was unanimously endorsed by the Disney Board of Directors in September. . . . The past years have been disappointing in terms of earnings and stock price, but they have also been an exciting period of investment in our key brands . . . investment that I am confident will pay off well in the years ahead. These investments have protected, buttressed and built our Disney and ESPN brands to secure their competitive advantage for a very long time. . . . What these expansions and investments in Disney and ESPN have in common is that they all build on the uniqueness and relevance of these brands. In so doing, they have created a protective moat around these assets." He added that "We now have a wide-ranging infrastructure supporting Disney and ESPN that will allow us to hold down capital expenditures while we seek to increase cash flow by building audiences for the branded businesses we have created."

Conspicuously missing from the brand analysis was ABC, which had now been entirely eclipsed by its younger sibling, ESPN. While acknowledging that the 2001–2002 prime-time season had been "lousy," Eisner lauded the new season as "very encouraging," singling out "8 Simple Rules," "Life with Bonnie," "Less Than Perfect," and "The Bachelor" as "solid successes," and pointed to the continuing strength of "My Wife and Kids," "George Lopez," "Alias," "The Practice," and "NYPD Blue." He also promised that ABC had "a number of great new shows for the mid-season and fall of 2003."

Eisner, Iger, and television executives Braun and Lyne did have genuine reason for optimism after years of crushing disappointment. During the November sweeps period, ABC had its best showing in years, coming in second to NBC in the key eighteen to forty-nine demographic, a dramatic improvement from the prior year's fourth-place finish. Though "Monday Night Football" and "The Bachelor" accounted for much of the success, the strategy of a block of family comedies won Tuesday night for ABC, with "8 Simple Rules" among the week's top ten shows. The only cloud on the horizon was the Fox network, which announced the next installment of its surprise summer reality hit, "American Idol." "Idol" would air on Tuesday nights beginning in January.

Eisner also called attention to the ongoing governance "reforms" that he was pursuing with Ira Millstein's guidance: "To help make sure that The Walt

Disney Company continues to serve the best interests of its shareholders, we are instituting new rules for board governance, which will reduce the number of board members and enhance the independence of the board. This should further enhance accountability and encourage the flow of fresh ideas at the highest levels of our company. The steps we took along these lines earned praise from a number of business analysts, including *BusinessWeek*. We intend to maintain a leadership position in this all-important area. I am pleased to institute these board governance reforms because, after all, I am a Disney shareholder too. By far, my largest personal holdings are in Disney stock, and I added a considerable amount to these holdings during the past year. I did so quite simply because I believe in this company."

Still, there were limits to the reforms Eisner would champion, especially when they affected his power and prerogatives. He was furious when Gold, as co-chair of the governance committee, wrote a November 10 letter to board members that proposed splitting the office of chairman and chief executive officer, even though many corporate governance experts—including Millstein, Disney's own lawyer on the subject—were publicly advocating such a separation of powers. (Millstein had nonetheless exempted Disney from the requirement, saying the matter could be addressed when Eisner retired.) Van de Kamp further alienated Eisner by supporting the motion, on the grounds that she felt Eisner was spending too much time as chairman manipulating the board and not enough time running Disney. But the measure was defeated in committee by a vote of five to two.

Indeed, Eisner had little fear from the governance committee now that Estrin and Lozano had diluted Gold's influence and Mitchell was co-chairman. At the December board meeting, Eisner proposed that Gold be designated a "nonindependent" director, which would require him to step down from the governance committee. This was not, as originally anticipated, because his daughter worked for Disney (the NYSE never implemented such a rule) but because he was beholden to another board member, Roy, who effectively employed him as chief executive of Shamrock. At the same time, John Bryson was proposed as "independent," despite his wife's $1.35 million position at the Disney co-owned Lifetime, which meant Bryson could serve on the committee.

"You must be kidding," Van de Kamp blurted out. "This makes no sense." She argued that Bryson and Gold were either both independent, or neither was. "The shareholders won't accept this," she maintained.

Nonetheless, the measure to designate Gold as nonindependent and Bryson as independent was put to a vote and easily passed, with only Van de

Kamp, Gold, and Roy voting against it. (Robert Stern, Eisner's architect, was also deemed nonindependent.) Ten minutes later, a typed list of committee assignments was circulated. Bryson was now chairman of the governance committee, and Van de Kamp was dropped.

Eisner didn't stop there. That same month, he called on Reveta Bowers at her office at the Center for Early Education to explain that it would be improper for any Disney employee to contribute to the Center if she remained on the board. Two of Disney's top executives—Bob Iger and Tom Staggs—had children at the school and were important potential donors. But if Bowers stayed on Disney's board, their contributions would be limited to a modest amount. "Now you're hitting me in my bread box," Bowers said, stressing her previous decision to step down from the board. When Bowers reported the conversation to others, including Van de Kamp, she was uncharacteristically angry.

At Christmas, Van de Kamp noticed that she didn't receive the usual Eisner holiday gift—a wheel of Vermont cheddar cheese or apples. She wondered if this was an oversight, and called to ask Patty Disney if she and Roy had received anything.

"Yeah, the aged cheddar," Patty replied. "Do you want one? I have several years' worth in the refrigerator." Van de Kamp demurred, but sent Eisner and Jane a thank-you note anyway, as she did every year, just in case the gift had gone astray. She heard nothing in reply.

After the New Year, Eisner phoned and asked Van de Kamp if she could meet with him in his office on January 20, 2003, which happened to be the Martin Luther King Jr. holiday. After the absence of a Christmas gift, and after hearing about his meeting with Reveta Bowers, she was somewhat apprehensive. Still, she was hardly prepared for the outburst from Eisner that ensued.

"You're a terrible director," he said. "You come late to meetings; you're not prepared; you're too busy." Van de Kamp was shocked. She'd been a conscientious director and not once in four years had Eisner or anyone else complained. "You are so loyal to Stanley it's like you've carried his babies," Eisner said.

Van de Kamp's mind reeled. What was Eisner suggesting? That she had occasionally voted with Gold because she was having an affair with him?

Van de Kamp reached over and put her hand on Eisner's arm, looking directly at him. "Michael, stop this right now. The best thing I have in my life is my marriage." She paused, but he said nothing further, so she continued. "What you're really upset about is that I don't always vote with you. That's the real issue."

"It's not that you haven't always voted with me," he said, but then proceeded to cite every instance in which she had voted against him. She was amazed that the chief executive of a multi-billion-dollar corporation could remember each and every vote; she'd even forgotten some of them. And he'd always gotten what he wanted, her occasional votes to the contrary notwithstanding.

This struck her as petty and vindictive, and she said something that she knew would wound him. "Why don't you show you can lead this company without Frank Wells?"

Eisner flushed in anger. "It's a done deal. The nominating committee has met and has decided not to renominate you," Eisner said. "I want you to go on the Disney Foundation Board and I want it to be your idea," he continued, urging her to "resign" from the Disney board to take up the new post. "If not, this will be embarrassing to you and to me."

Van de Kamp felt her anger rising. Had Eisner simply said he wanted her to leave, she would have stepped down. But he had badly misjudged her if he thought she could be threatened and intimidated. "I'm not embarrassed," she said sharply, rising to leave.

"I don't want you talking about this to anyone, including other directors," he warned her. "If you do talk to anyone, I request that you call me."

When she reached her office in Beverly Hills, Van de Kamp was still shaken by the encounter. Despite Eisner's injunction, she sat down and typed an email describing what had just happened and sent it to all her fellow directors. Apart from Roy and Gold, only Bowers responded, calling to say that she was "horrified" by Eisner's pressure tactics.

Van de Kamp contacted a lawyer to see if she had any grounds to sue Eisner, but he couldn't find any. As the January 28 meeting approached, there was a flurry of calls among directors concerned that Van de Kamp was being purged as a warning to any director who dared question Eisner or sometimes vote against him. Bowers, in particular, lobbied other directors on Van de Kamp's behalf. Tom Murphy, Ray Watson, Sidney Poitier, and Gary Wilson expressed some sympathy for Van de Kamp's plight. But no one else did, or, if they were sympathetic, they didn't dare speak up.

Other than telling her she was a "terrible director," Eisner never told Van de Kamp why she wasn't being renominated. But others told her the reason Eisner volunteered was that she faced a conflict of interest since Disney had given money to the Walt Disney Concert Hall, and she was chairman of the Music Center. Van de Kamp was amazed. The Disney gift predated her service on the board, and there had been no Disney gifts since then. Indeed, it was because of her skill in securing the donation that Eisner had asked her to join the board. Even Ira Millstein had conceded when the issue arose in December that she was "independent" and some of her recent votes certainly confirmed that. Van de Kamp had a legal opinion confirming that she was "independent" within the meaning of proposed rule changes.

The night before the board meeting, Gold called Van de Kamp. "This is going to get ugly tomorrow," he warned. "You can still avoid this if you take the bribe of the Foundation job and go quietly." Van de Kamp looked over at her twenty-two-year-old daughter. What kind of example did she want to set? She felt she was being attacked for trying to do the right thing. Someone had to stand up to Eisner's bullying. "I can't do it, Stanley," she said.

For Van de Kamp, the next day began with a 7:30 breakfast meeting of the finance committee. No one said anything to her. Then she met alone with George Mitchell. He apologized for not responding sooner to her request for a meeting, explaining that he had just attended the Super Bowl in San Diego as Eisner's guest and they'd gotten in late the night before. She noticed that he wouldn't make eye contact. She asked him to reconsider her expulsion, arguing that she was being purged for speaking out and daring to question Eisner. She was being used as an example to the rest of the board. "Well, I don't know enough about the situation," Mitchell said. Van de Kamp wondered: What didn't he know? But it was clear Mitchell wouldn't come to her rescue.

Afterward she bumped into Tom Murphy, who'd also been at the Super Bowl with Eisner. "This is terrible, Andrea," he said. "I spent two days trying to talk Michael out of this. It's no use."

Then she met with the nominating committee, now chaired by Bryson. Estrin, Lozano, and Wilson were also present. "The way I've been treated is an abomination," she said. "You should be ashamed of yourselves. Speaking as a former member of this committee, I want you to know that I would never have done this to you." No one said anything.

Next, Eisner spoke to the committee and argued for Van de Kamp's ouster. Besides generalized claims that she wasn't a good director, he claimed that she leaked to the press and had allied herself with Gold against him. He didn't place any emphasis on an alleged conflict of interest over Disney Hall.

"This isn't right," Wilson said as soon as Eisner left. He argued for keeping Van de Kamp, who he thought was a fine director. Eisner's accusations were inaccurate—there was no evidence that she had leaked to the press—and unfair. But he thought the committee should be unanimous. He was prepared to support Van de Kamp, but not if the other members of the committee wouldn't back him. Bryson, Estrin, and Lozano immediately lined up behind Eisner and voted to eject Van de Kamp. Wilson reluctantly went along with the majority.

At the next day's meeting of the full board, the issue finally came to a vote. Gold moved to reinstate Van de Kamp to the list of directors, a motion that Roy seconded. Sidney Poitier, who rarely spoke at board meetings, spoke in her defense. Then Van de Kamp made an impassioned speech. "I was asked to serve on this board to be an independent director, and now I'm not being renominated because that's exactly what I am—an independent director," she began, as she later recalled the speech. "The performance of this company has not been wonderful. I, along with some employees and shareholders, are concerned. Michael Eisner has cost this company a lot of money: $140 million on Michael Ovitz, and this board did nothing; $280 million on Jeffrey Katzenberg—this board did nothing. We have terrible relations with creative people in Hollywood because of Michael Eisner's arrogance. Many of the best executives have left the company. We've just fired all these people, yet Michael Eisner is getting a $5 million bonus. How do those people feel?

"The process which led to my not being renominated has been outrageous and we should all be embarrassed. How we've conducted this has been a terrible example, both to ourselves and to the outside world. People look to Disney for leadership, and we have failed them."

As Van de Kamp sat down, Bowers burst into tears. "How can you do this to this distinguished woman?" she asked once she had collected herself.

Gold, Roy, and Van de Kamp herself raised their hands in favor of the motion to keep Van de Kamp on the board. Bowers started to put up her hand, and Eisner glared at her. She started to lower it, paused, and then defiantly raised it. Poitier, too, looked like he was going to raise his hand, but after seeing Eisner's reaction to Bowers, he kept his down. He abstained, as did Robert Matschullat, a former vice chairman of the Seagram Company who had just joined the board. "I'm staying out of this," he said. Leo O'Donovan, the president emeritus of Georgetown University, said he was "concerned" about the process, but wouldn't vote against the nominating committee's recommendation. No one else supported Van de Kamp. The vote was twelve to four to defeat Gold's motion, with two abstentions.

Van de Kamp stayed for the duration of the meeting. She was a director until the annual meeting in March, and she intended to do her duty. But when the meeting ended and the others started discussing their transportation arrangements for the annual meeting, she got up and left. No one said anything to her then, but the next day she got a call from Gary Wilson, who had been sitting at Eisner's side and voted to dismiss her. "Your speech was brilliant," he told her. "I'm sorry I couldn't support you." (Curiously, there was no mention of Van de Kamp's speech in the minutes of the meeting.)

With Van de Kamp gone, the board proceeded to strip Gold of his co-chairmanship and membership on the nominating and governance committee and compensation subcommittee, leaving Eisner loyalists in charge of all key board positions. Judith Estrin replaced Gold as chairman of the compensation committee, which promptly approved the special $5 million bonus for Eisner. Gold was nearly apoplectic. It was bad enough that Staggs and Murphy had gotten $1 million bonuses for the Family channel deal, but now it was becoming abundantly clear that Disney had grossly overpaid for the cable acquisition. Despite his vocal protest, the compensation committee approved the bonus.

Van de Kamp wasn't the only board member who wasn't renominated that year. Sidney Poitier was over the retirement age of seventy-two, and Disney declined to waive it, as it had routinely done in the past. As an architect for both Eisner and Disney, Robert Stern had been deemed nonindependent. Bowers had already decided to step down after she was deemed nonindependent. Disney, too, officially ascribed Van de Kamp's ouster to unspecified "corporate governance" initiatives related to director independence.

But when the New York Stock Exchange actually filed its corporate governance proposal with the SEC later that year tightening the requirements for independent directors, it specifically exempted officers of "charitable organizations." Under the rules actually enacted, both Bowers and Van de Kamp would have met the new standard for independent directors.

The NYSE also clarified the issue of the employment of directors' children and spouses. Under the rules enacted, children and spouses had to earn more than $100,000 per year and be living at home with a director. Gold's daughter earned less than the threshold and no longer lived at home. Ironically, it was John Bryson, whose wife, Louise, earned $1.35 million from the Lifetime channel, who was ultimately deemed nonindependent. Nonetheless, he remained on the board.

The new library for young readers opened at the Center for Early Education the following spring, notwithstanding the absence of any donation from Disney. In place of the planned Winnie-the-Pooh theme, Reveta Bowers contributed her own teddy bear collection to decorate the room.

*   *   *

As Spencer Neumann, Jim Hedges, and Angela Shapiro had warned the previous May, ABC Family wasn't even coming close to meeting the aggressive
financial projections that had been incorporated into the five-year projections presented to the board. But perhaps there was a silver lining to the
Family debacle, at least in a purely financial sense. About the same time as the
January board meeting, chief financial officer Tom Staggs launched a confidential, high-priority project to determine the net present value of the Family channel. If the value of ABC Family were far less than Disney paid for it,
the valuation could be used to generate significant tax savings.

A small group of finance executives from the Family channel and Disney's tax department began working with an outside consulting firm that
specialized in valuation. By this point, no one inside Disney was pretending
that the channel and related assets were worth anywhere near the $5.2 billion
Disney had paid Murdoch and Saban. Still, even they were startled by the
conclusions.

According to the internal valuation report that resulted, the net present
value of the cable channel was $1.378 billion. The calculations were complex,
but the report estimated that Disney could realize about $400 million in tax
savings, which would go directly to the bottom line. Based on this analysis,
$3.2 billion of the purchase price was allocated to the channel, the rest to the
programming and other assets, which meant that Disney had overpaid by
approximately $1.8 billion for the channel alone. (Disney had already writ-
ten off $308 million of the value of the library.)

Staggs was enthusiastic about the potential tax savings. Another staff
member declared that "this is one of the smartest things I've ever heard of."
But, he added, "You're never going to get this. It would mean going to the
board and saying our valuation was wrong." The timing was especially bad,
since Gold and Roy were now rigorously criticizing the Family deal.

In March, staff members were notified that the project had been terminated before the outside firm completed its work. When they demanded an
explanation, they were told that Staggs had presented the plan to Peter Murphy, who had vetoed it, declaring that strategic planning's rosy projections
were inconsistent with the valuation. Peter Murphy stressed that valuation is
an "art" and that the low valuation produced by the Family executives was
flatly wrong. He insisted that the channel is worth the $5.2 million Disney
paid, noting that the channel's ratings for December 2004 were the highest
ever.

People working on the project were nonetheless dumbfounded. One staff member declared that "this is outrageous. Someone should go to the board." But cooler heads prevailed. "They'll just say our valuations are wrong. Then you'll be screwed," another person warned. Nothing more was said about it.*

That March, Eisner and I had our dinner at Nobu in Manhattan, where we discussed my writing this book and touched briefly on Eisner's life and career. At the time I knew little about the tempest that was brewing in the Disney boardroom or the events leading up to it. Eisner didn't volunteer anything about it, though surely it was on his mind. Just weeks later, in Denver, Disney's board was scheduled to hold its first annual meeting since Gold and Roy opened their campaign for a management review.

Both were planning to attend the meeting and confront Eisner with more tough questions. But the night before the meeting, Denver was blanketed by a snowstorm, and only a handful of shareholders arrived for the meeting. Neither Gold nor Roy could make it, nor could most of the board members.

Instead, Disney directors met by phone. Items on the agenda included Disney's relationship to Miramax founders Harvey and Bob Weinstein and the ongoing negotiations with Pixar. No action on Miramax was proposed, but directors reviewed a net present value analysis of Miramax prepared by strategic planning that suggested Miramax wasn't making any money. Groundwork was obviously being laid to get rid of the Weinsteins, or at least sharply reduce their compensation.

Pixar continued to be a thorn in Eisner's side, and was now demanding a new deal in which it would receive as much as 92 percent of the profits, and Disney a small 8 to 12 percent as a distribution fee, with numerous other issues still unresolved, including the fate of the two films Pixar still owed under the current arrangement. Eisner warned that the terms being proposed were so onerous that it might not make sense for Disney to continue the relationship, especially if it had to give up profits on Pixar's next two films. Eisner also posited a theory that all creative streaks in the movie business come to an end eventually, as Disney's had in animation after Walt's

* There are rules requiring a write-down of assets under certain circumstances. Valuing intangible assets such as goodwill is the subject of the Financial Accounting Standards Board Statements 141, "Business Combination," and 142, "Goodwill and Other Intangible Assets."

death, before reviving under Eisner, Katzenberg, and Roy. Pixar's string of hits was defying the odds, and Pixar was headed for a fall, he predicted, as he had warned in the email about "Finding Nemo." Maybe then Jobs would be more reasonable. Eisner told the board that he was "hopeful" a new deal could be worked out.

Even Gold and Roy had to concede that the new terms being proposed by Pixar were onerous, but Gold argued that Eisner was to blame for letting such a successful partnership reach this juncture. While he hadn't talked to Jobs himself, he knew from Roy that it was Jobs's distrust and personal antipathy toward Eisner that were the root of the problem. "Forget the terms of what was or could be," Gold told Eisner and the board. "This is bad management. It's abysmal that we're fighting with a creative content partner, and it's abysmal that you've allowed this relationship to deteriorate."

"It's impossible to negotiate with Steve Jobs. Jobs is a Shiite Muslim," Eisner blurted out, at which point Gold started to raise his voice. Mitchell had to step in to quell the dissension.

In the wake of this exchange, Eisner began testing a radical new idea with other Disney executives and confidants: force Roy off the board. At least some who heard the idea were dumbfounded. Roy was the largest individual shareholder, the vice chairman of the company that bore his name. He was still the face of Disney to much of the public, a direct link to Walt, and immensely valuable at the many premieres, openings of new attractions, and employee recognition dinners where Roy represented the soul of Disney. He was still chairman of feature animation, and the animators revered him. In any event, how could Eisner get rid of him?

Eisner reminded them that Disney had a policy that called for the mandatory retirement of directors at the age of seventy-two, with the exception of former chief executives, who could stay until seventy-five. Roy would be seventy-three by the next board meeting. "Of course, we've ignored that rule," Eisner mused in one encounter with Disney executives where he floated the prospect. Indeed, Disney was legendary for not enforcing any mandatory retirement policy. The legendary "old men" of animation had stayed as long as they liked. John Hench, an Imagineer who helped Walt design Disneyland, was still working until his death at age ninety-five. Lucille Martin, Eisner's secretary who had worked for Walt, was careful never to reveal her age, but must have been in her eighties. Tom Murphy and Ray Watson were both over seventy-two.

Some of those who heard the idea discussed it among themselves, and then discarded it as too far-fetched to ever happen. Eisner had a tendency to test controversial ideas by dropping them into conversations, and usually they just disappeared.

On March 23, Miramax dominated the 2003 Academy Awards, with three of the nominees for Best Picture: *Chicago, Gangs of New York,* and *The Hours.* The musical *Chicago* won, along with Best Supporting Actress and four other awards, and was a huge box-office success, earning $306 million worldwide and rescuing Miramax's fiscal year. Another Oscar winner was the provocative documentary filmmaker Michael Moore, for *Bowling for Columbine.*

The glittering success of *Chicago* masked a multitude of problems between the Weinsteins and Eisner and Disney, a relationship that, at this juncture, both sides agree was dysfunctional. The Weinsteins were fuming when Disney issued a press release announcing that Disney had garnered forty-four Academy Award nominations, failing to mention that forty of those were for Miramax films. Chafing at the lack of recognition, Bob Weinstein asked Eisner if Disney might consider taking out an ad in the trades, congratulating Miramax and the Weinsteins. Eisner rejected the idea, saying that wasn't the Disney way. "We don't want any of our executives to stand out," he said.

"Except one," Weinstein thought, though he didn't say so. Paradoxical as it was, considering that Disney owned Miramax, the Weinsteins were convinced that Eisner resented their success and visibility.

Despite the huge success of Miramax films like *Pulp Fiction, Shakespeare in Love,* and *Good Will Hunting,* the Weinsteins, especially Harvey, were a constant irritant to Disney executives. After Roth's departure, Bob Weinstein refused to deal with the genial Dick Cook, so the brothers reported to Peter Murphy, the head of strategic planning, whom they held in thinly disguised contempt. But their real problem was Eisner and his insistence that they stick to their low-budget, independent agenda for Miramax just when Harvey Weinstein was chafing to make glamorous, big-budget, big-star event films that he felt he'd earned the right to produce.

This ongoing contest of wills had only intensified after Eisner rejected *Lord of the Rings.* Costs for *Gangs of New York,* the Martin Scorsese–directed epic starring Leonardo DiCaprio, which lost out for Best Picture to *Chicago,* soared to over $100 million and was a constant struggle between Weinstein and Disney executives. To keep costs down, Miramax sold off foreign rights for $65 million.

But the bitterest dispute was over *Cold Mountain,* based on the best-selling novel by Charles Frazier. This was the latest project from acclaimed director Anthony Minghella, director of *The English Patient* and *The Talented Mr. Ripley*, both for Miramax. With stars Jude Law, Nicole Kidman, and Renée Zellweger attached to the project, and a script calling for elaborate re-creations of Civil War battles, projected costs were in the $80–$100 million range. Eisner was opposed to such an expensive period drama, but Weinstein pried permission from Disney to go ahead as long as he found a partner, which he did at MGM.

Just as filming was getting under way in Romania (rather than the American South, to hold costs down), and with the budget at over $80 million, MGM dropped out, stranding Miramax with the bill. Disney informed Weinstein that it wouldn't accept the full cost and told him he couldn't proceed without a partner. No other studio was interested. Faced with the choice of obeying Disney's orders—it had a contractual right to kill the project—and stranding Minghella and the cast and crew in Romania, or defying Disney, Weinstein went ahead with the movie. He promised Disney he'd find a partner, and in any event, even if he didn't, he felt he could sell foreign rights for half the cost. In any event, the gambit worked, since Disney kept paying the bills.

Just weeks before the Academy Awards ceremony, buoyed by Miramax's forty nominations, Weinstein laid down the gauntlet by bringing in lawyer Bert Fields to represent him in contract negotiations, knowing that hiring Eisner's nemesis in the Katzenberg dispute would infuriate him. Disney had the right to opt out of the Weinsteins' contract in September 2005, and using that provision as leverage, was trying to renegotiate their deal, which Disney deemed overly generous. For good measure, the Weinsteins also hired famed Manhattan litigator David Boies.

Then, just six weeks after *Chicago*'s victory, and as Disney was lobbying the Bush administration in Washington, D.C., over sensitive cable industry licensing fee issues, the Drudge Report carried an item on May 11 that "The Walt Disney Company is set to spend millions financing a new explosive Bush-bashing documentary from Michael Moore—a documentary which claims [Osama] bin Laden was greatly enriched by the Bush family!" Moore himself was quoted as saying that the film would demonstrate how "the senior Bush kept his ties with the bin Laden family up until two months after Sept. 11."

Eisner and other Disney executives were beside themselves. *Kundun* had been bad enough, but this promised to be offensive to the White House. It was no secret that Harvey Weinstein was an ardent Democrat and liberal activist and fund-raiser, but now his activism was spilling over into Disney's business. Eisner promptly called Weinstein, who confirmed the Drudge Report. "Harvey, I really don't want you to make this movie," Eisner said. Disney followed up with two letters stating explicitly that Miramax could not release the film.

Weinstein was in a difficult position. Contractually, he felt he had the right to make the film. The budget of $6 million was well below the level at which he had to seek Disney's permission. Though Disney maintained it had the right to cancel Miramax projects that were politically partisan, Weinstein conceded only that Disney had the right to approve films designated NC-17 because of sexual and violent content. Still, Disney owned Miramax, and the Weinsteins were in contract negotiations. Rather than defy Eisner outright, Weinstein offered a compromise. "Let us make it," he said. "If you don't like it I'll buy it back."

Disney responded by having Peter Murphy send Weinstein a letter. "We are pleased that Miramax has on its own concluded that it will reduce its involvement in this film. As you described to me, your plan is to provide only interim bridge financing for the project. Michael Moore and Wild Bunch will sell off all distribution rights at Cannes or through other means in order to raise permanent, take-out financing. Miramax would then have no interest in the film. In the meantime, you have told us that Miramax will publicly state that it does not control distribution of the film."

Though divested of his leadership positions on the board, Gold kept up the letter-writing campaign that he'd begun with his first missive to Ray Watson and then pursued in the month leading up to the September board meeting. He zeroed in particularly on the continuing failure to turn around the ABC prime-time schedule. After the promising start in the fall, culminating in its surprisingly strong November sweeps finish, ABC's worst fears had been realized when "American Idol" proved a ratings juggernaut for Fox, demolishing ABC's Tuesday schedule. In the February sweeps, ABC again fell to fourth place. It was especially painful that "CSI," the CBS hit rejected by Disney, was the nation's number one show, and a spin-off, "CSI: Miami," was also in the top ten.

On April 3, Gold wrote to George Mitchell, copying Eisner and all the directors:

"I am enclosing a recent article from USA Today [describing] the failure of our television season this year. We received approximately 50 emails last fall touting our progress and success in primetime television. When that success turned hollow, i.e., this year's rating average for primetime will be less than last year's, which was a disaster, we get no information, no explanation, no ownership of the problem, we just switch to a new subject. There are a number of people on this board who said to me that if Michael and Bob [Iger] can't turn the 2003 primetime season around, they would have to go. The jury is in on this one. We are worse off than we were last year and this board refuses to discuss this issue.

"I fear that our inability to discuss difficult problems and make hard decisions is an abdication of our fiduciary duty. The shareholders of the Disney Company have lost $50 billion in the last three years. Our board's unwillingness to deal with the substantial issues of this business borders on the incompetent. . . ."

It fell to Iger to compose a reply to Gold's letter, in which he maintained that ABC prime time was 8 percent ahead of the previous year in the "critically important" eighteen to forty-nine age group, and that, excluding the Super Bowl, ABC was "even with last year" in an "extremely close race" with just .6 of a ratings point separating the rival networks. "We had a great first half," he wrote, while conceding that "the second half has been disappointing. But in no fair sense can the season be characterized as a failure. . . . The new comedies have been successful," and "We are clearly in the midst of a turnaround." Iger lambasted Gold for singling out the midseason replacement "Lost at Home," claiming that he had used "one review to discredit the show," which is "grossly misleading." Noting that the show had only aired three times, he insisted that "the numbers are fine. . . . It is not a hit but it is not a failure. It has real potential and we own it."

The April board "retreat" was held at Disney World, where Epcot's new attraction, "Mission: SPACE," was nearing completion. Walt himself had long dreamed of a ride that would simulate space travel. Costing $150 million, "Mission: SPACE" used a huge centrifuge much like those used by NASA astronauts to simulate the gravitational force of liftoff and then the weightlessness of space travel. Imagineers had grafted the special effects onto a narrative of a trip to Mars, including travel through a meteor belt and a rocky landing on the red planet, all seen through cockpit screens. The ride would have been deployed much sooner had Disney found a corporate sponsor to help absorb the development costs, which Eisner had insisted on before agreeing to proceed. Compaq Computer had finally come aboard, only to have the deal put in limbo when it was acquired by Hewlett-Packard. But now HP had picked up the sponsorship, and the ride was scheduled to open in October. Board members sampled the ride, then had dinner in the courtyard entrance to the swooping pavilion that houses it. (They had to dine after the ride, since motion sickness was an unfortunate side effect for some. Some directors refused to go on the ride.)

Gold did succeed in getting the plight of ABC on the agenda for the two-day retreat that began on April 28. After Iger's presentation, in which he reiterated many of the points in his letter, he left the room. Even Mitchell had to concede that Iger hadn't turned ABC around, and as a result, he and other board members didn't see how Iger could be considered Eisner's successor. Eisner again expressed reservations about Iger, saying he had "doubts" about his creative abilities and "If I had to choose, it would not be Bob." Then Eisner also left the room, and the board continued the discussion, agreeing that they should look more closely within the company for a possible successor to Eisner and consider outside candidates as well. When Eisner returned, Mitchell said that it was the sense of the board members that if Iger didn't turn around ABC within a year, Eisner should replace him.

The attacks from Gold and the discussion of succession—a topic he invariably found unnerving—left Eisner irritated and anxious. Gold had stopped short of asking outright for his resignation. Eisner knew Gold didn't have the votes on the board, so he decided to call his bluff. He said he was tired of his criticism. "So what do you want, Stanley?" he asked in front of the board members.

Gold looked uncomfortable, and said nothing.

"Do you want me out? Is that what you want? Tell me." Eisner persisted.

"No, I don't want you out," Gold conceded. "You're the only person who can run the company. But you don't listen to me."

"I listen to you," Eisner countered. "I just don't always do what you want. That's your problem." *

Even as ABC continued to struggle with its "back to basics" strategy, Eisner could sense that his return to the tried-and-true, low-budget "singles and doubles" strategy at the movie studio was paying off with hits like *Bringing Down the House.* And opening the first week in May 2003 was *The Lizzie McGuire Movie,* a feature film based on the Disney channel's "Lizzie McGuire Show," starring Hilary Duff.

If anyone embodied Disney's approach to "synergy" in the entertainment

---

* Gold says that he meant that Eisner was the only person at the company who could run it, given his failure to groom a successor, not that there was no one else who could run it.

business, it was Duff. Set in a middle school, where the thirteen-year-old Lizzie struggles with all the anxieties and tribulations of adolescent girlhood, "Lizzie McGuire" had become a sensation among preteen girls, simultaneously boosting the ratings of the Disney channel and creating an all-new market: so-called tween girls, falling somewhere between childhood and adolescence. Too narrow for conventional network programming, it was an ideal niche for cable. "Lizzie McGuire" clothing and paraphernalia were also a big hit for Disney's consumer products division.

Conventional wisdom held that preteen girls comprised too small a market for feature films, that girls would go to boys' movies as dates or friends, but that boys would shun girls' movies. But Disney's *The Parent Trap*, starring Lindsay Lohan in a 1998 remake of the Disney classic starring Hayley Mills, had unexpectedly grossed $92 million, showing that the market existed. As a result, *The Lizzie McGuire Movie* was immediately put into development. Hilary Duff would also make her singing debut, and there were plans for a sound track recording from Disney's struggling Hollywood Records as well as a future Hilary Duff debut album, positioning her as the next Britney Spears. Hopes were even high for a Hilary Duff series on ABC prime time that would chart Lizzie McGuire's course through high school.

There was only one cause for concern in this whirl of Disney-generated marketing opportunities: Hilary Duff was the daughter of Susan Duff, an exceptionally demanding and tenacious stage mother. It wasn't lost on Susan Duff that Disney had built a marketing empire on the back of her good-looking and infectiously cheerful young daughter. Susan controlled every aspect of Hilary's career, including approval of her costumes, hairstyles, makeup, songs, choreography, housing, transportation, and diet. During filming in Rome, where the fictional Lizzie is taking part in a postgraduation class trip, filming came to a halt during a night scene involving 200 extras and a crew of 150 while Susan negotiated with a producer over an extra fifteen minutes of shooting time. After arguing for at least that long, Susan finally said, "So. What are you willing to do to smooth things over and make Hilary happy?"

"What do you suggest?" the producer asked.

"Well, Hilary would very much like to swim at the Wall Center when we get to Vancouver," Susan said, referring to the film's next location. The Sheraton Vancouver at the Wall Center, the Duffs' preferred hotel, had been booked, but a membership at the adjoining spa seemed like a small price to pay, so the producer agreed and filming proceeded.

The *Lizzie McGuire* director, Jim Fall, heard little from Disney management during shooting, but after a screening of the nearly finished film in

Burbank, Dick Cook came up and said, "I can smell a hit, and this is it." He proposed a sequel, and offered Duff a two-picture deal, including $3.5 million for a sequel plus a $500,000 bonus if *The Lizzie McGuire Movie* grossed $50 million. Susan said they wanted $5 million. She also wanted a producer credit for herself, and wanted Disney to pay her cell phone bills.

In the midst of these negotiations, Susan acquired a script for a *Cinderella* remake in which the Cinderella character falls for a boy over the Internet and wins his heart at the school dance. She shopped the project to every studio but Disney, and Cook was furious when he found out. He withdrew the two-picture offer, and the Hilary Duff *Cinderella Story* went to Warner Bros. Still, negotiations for a *Lizzie McGuire* sequel, as well as another season of cable programs, proceeded. As the opening of *The Lizzie McGuire Movie* approached, Cook increased the offer to $4 million plus the $500,000 bonus.

Lizzie McGuire opened on April 26, 2003. Reviews were beside the point: The screenwriters realized that the very qualities that critics like Roger Ebert lamented—"The Lizzie McGuire Movie celebrates popularity, beauty, great hair, lip gloss and overnight stardom"—were exactly the things that the target audience (and their mothers) obsessed over. *Lizzie McGuire* earned more than $17 million, the film's cost, in its opening weekend. Within three weeks, the gross had exceeded $40 million, and it seemed sure to surpass the $50 million mark. Susan demanded Hilary's $500,000 bonus.

Cook refused on principle. She'd get the bonus when gross passed the target, and not before. But he reiterated the $4 million offer. Susan said she wanted $4.5. Cook refused to budge, and gave her a deadline of May 8. The designated hour came and went, with no word from Susan or Hilary's lawyer or manager.

The next morning Susan called. "Okay, we'll take the deal."

"You missed the deadline," Cook replied.

That same day, May 9, Disney announced that negotiations for a sequel and an extension of the television series had ended. "Disney thought they'd be able to bully us into accepting whatever offer they wanted to make, and they couldn't," Susan told *Entertainment Weekly*. "We walked away from a sequel. They walked away from a franchise."

While Cook officially made the decision, the tactic had all the hallmarks of Eisner's stubbornness, determination to stand on principle, and to drive a hard bargain that had been on display throughout his career. But Roy Disney, for one, thought that Susan Duff had a point. He lamented the loss of

Duff in a conversation with Gold, noting that both Justin Timberlake and Britney Spears had once been in the Disney fold.

From Disney's point of view, the "Lizzie McGuire" franchise was already waning, with or without a new deal with Hilary Duff. She was getting too old for the "tween" market, and too expensive for an uncertain future as a teen star. Cook was vindicated in one sense: Box-office receipts fell off drastically for *The Lizzie McGuire Movie*, and it never reached the $50 million gross that would have triggered the bonus. Still, it's hard to see what was so important about missing a deadline by a day, when the two sides were so close to reaching a deal, and Susan had ultimately capitulated to Disney's demands.

Although Hollywood Records released Hilary Duff's album, *Metamorphosis*, her next film project—a remake of *Cheaper by the Dozen*—went to Twentieth Century Fox.

"Lizzie McGuire" continued in reruns, but the once-promising marketing juggernaut expired. Disney turned to its next candidate for cable crossover stardom, the Disney channel's Raven-Symone, star of "She's So Raven," who'd begun her acting career as a three-year-old in "The Cosby Show." Even better, as Eisner pointed out, Disney should promote an animated character, who made no demands and had no mother—Kim Possible, the tween superhero of "Kim Possible."

On June 11, 2003, Eisner has invited me to a creative meeting of the feature animation team, led by Schumacher's replacement, David Stainton. Eisner usually attends these meetings once or twice a month. Roy isn't there, although Stainton says he would have been welcome. (Roy says he was told to stay away from the meetings after Schumacher left.) This is a lunch meeting. The group picks up sandwiches and beverages and sits around a conference table. On an easel are boards with upcoming release schedules: *Teacher's Pet* and *The Incredibles* for 2004, *Heffalump* for 2005.

Stainton notes that *Heffalump* is based on a Winnie-the-Pooh character. "We've never done a heffalump," he says. "Consumer products wants more characters."

Eisner nods. "Get consumer products behind this," he urges.

Pam Coats says she has a new title for another project, *Angel and Her No Good Sister*. Dolly Parton is the voice of one of the characters.

"It's cute," Eisner says. "But it feels small . . ."

"I like it," Stainton injects. "It's automatic conflict."

Eisner nods. "I like it. The title changes the whole movie."

They turn to a discussion of the script. "We don't want you to shoot this down," Coats tells Eisner. He'd read two acts of *Angel* and hadn't liked it. The story revolves around a "curse of the blue egg." In the current version, Coats explains, "Elgin says, 'Love can overcome the curse.' He gets knocked out; they haul Elgin to Rose . . ."

"What do you mean, knocked out?" Eisner asks. "He can't be unconscious for three days. He can't be in a coma or on life support . . ."

Someone explains, "It's a *Gulliver's Travels* thing."

"He can't be out cold," Eisner continues.

"It keeps the love story alive," Coats practically pleads.

"Well, I like the *Gulliver's Travels* angle," Eisner says, though he doesn't sound convinced.

Three features are vying for the Christmas 2006 release date: *Gnomeo and Juliet, Fraidy Cat,* and *Wilbur Robinson.*

"I'm not in love with any of them," Eisner says.

Stainton points out that *Gnomeo and Juliet* has Elton John writing the score.

"Can we get three hits out of Elton?" Eisner asks.

Stainton volunteers that "Chris [Montan, president of Walt Disney Music] is beating up Elton on this. He likes the first two songs. Elton is on his game."

The discussion turns to Christmas 2007. Eisner has just read a script for *Rapunzel.* "Someone told me a woman with long hair is old-fashioned," Eisner says.

"That's why this has to be a *Legally Blonde*–type comedy," replies Mary Jane Ruggels, another creative vice president.

"*Sleeping Beauty* was 1938," Eisner says. "The ending was forced. Like *Treasure Planet*—it just ended. It wasn't funny or clever. Are you sure you can save this? Is *Ice Queen* better?

"You mean *Snow Queen*," Ruggels says.

"I love the *Taming of the Shrew* idea," Eisner says. "Take Martha Stewart. She's tough, smart—a worthy adversary. If she was a doormat of a woman, no one would be after her. Marlo Thomas used to call me about marketing 'That Girl.' She said, 'If I was a man, I'd be president of the network.' "

Eisner expresses some reservations about the team assigned to *Snow Queen,* then adds, "John Lasseter. If we make a new deal with Pixar . . ."

Stainton jumps in: "You mean *when* we make a new deal with Pixar."

"I said to John, you can have *Snow Queen*. He loved it. John said, 'I want to do a princess movie.' "

Eisner asks for the *Snow Queen* synopsis.

"The Snow Queen is a terrible bitch," Ruggels says. "When her suitors try to melt her heart, the Snow Queen freezes them."

"Each one should be a phony, but different," Eisner says of the suitors.

"Then along comes a regular guy," Ruggels continues.

"This is perfect!" Eisner exclaims. "I'm afraid to hear more."

"The regular guy goes up there, he's not that great, but he's a good person. He starts to unfreeze her . . . she melts."

"It's great," Eisner says. "Finally. We've had twenty meetings on this."

"We'll have a treatment in two weeks," Ruggels promises.

"Can we have this for 2006?" Eisner asks.

"No way," Coats says.

More ideas are tossed around: *Frog Princess, Rumpelstiltskin, You Don't Know Jack About the Beanstalk, Hansel and Gretel* (with a twist: the kids are obnoxious, the witch likable), *Mother Goose* as a sassy, Queen Latifah type; and something, maybe *Aida,* that would feature an African "princess." Eisner worries that *Aida* is still too live-action. "What's the Howard Ashman piece we can layer on?" he asks, one of several times Ashman's name has come up in the meeting.

"This is good," Eisner concludes, "a good start." He gets up to leave. "I love *Snow Queen*."

As the July release date of *Pirates of the Caribbean* approached, Eisner was clearly nervous. Disney had the opportunity to market a line of *Pirates* products—Depp, Rush, and Orlando Bloom had even been measured for Pirate dolls based on their characters—but in the end, consumer products passed, in part on grounds that the plot was too convoluted for the film to be a hit.

Much like *Pearl Harbor,* it had been a nearly constant battle to get *Pirates* to the screen, which wasn't all that surprising considering the stars and director were gleefully undermining Disney's straitlaced image right from the beginning. At Depp's insistence, the first table read of the script was held not at Disney's headquarters or at Bruckheimer's office, but in the windowless Viper Room in West Hollywood. The place was dimly lit and even at 8:30 A.M. reeked of cigarettes and alcohol. The Disney executives looked uncomfortable, much to the delight of the *Pirate* cast.

During the first days of production, Depp showed up with gold-capped teeth, heavy eyeliner, a braided goatee, and sideburns for a hair and makeup test. "I'm nudging toward Keith Richards here rather than Errol Flynn," Depp said in an aside to Geoffrey Rush.

"Fantastic," Rush said. He could practically see the Disney executives' jaws drop at the sight of Depp.

Disney executives were indeed taken aback. "We should talk about the teeth," Brigham Taylor, the production chief, said to Nina Jacobson, the studio head, as they walked out of the test. The hair, the braids, the capped teeth—they had to go. Depp flatly refused. A meeting was convened with Depp and the Disney executives, with Bruckheimer mediating. "Look," Depp protested. "You do your thing, this is mine. This is my circle, and you're not allowed inside my circle."

"We just want the audience to see more of you," Taylor diplomatically countered.

Finally a compromise was reached. Depp agreed to reduce the gold teeth to three in return for keeping the braided goatee and the eyeliner. But when filming began, Depp slipped some of the gold caps back on.

Even after the hair and makeup test, Disney executives were unprepared for the sashaying gait, slurred speech, and stoned demeanor that Depp brought to the role. When Taylor saw the first dailies, he called Jacobson. "Everyone has to talk about this. It's a significant choice he's making here. I mean, what are we buying with our money?"

Taylor sent the dailies to Cook and Jacobson, who was out of town. When they all spoke by phone, Cook was amused by Depp's eccentric portrayal. "I think it could be great," he said. Jacobson was worried. "I think this could be genius or it could be a crazy risk. I've got to talk to Johnny and find out why." Eisner himself weighed in after seeing the dailies: "We've hired the sexiest actor in the world and he looks like this?" Not to mention the stereotypically gay mannerisms. Eisner launched into an account of his *King David* story, in which Richard Gere had worn a skirt and earring, with disastrous results at the box office. But as Disney executives continued to worry, filming proceeded, and Depp brought a consistency and level of conviction to the role that in the end brought them around, albeit grudgingly in some cases. Cook promised Eisner that camera angles could be used to minimize the teeth and facial hair.

Director Gore Verbinski firmly backed Depp, but he was fighting his own battles with Cook, Jacobson, and Taylor, mostly about the budget. He quit or came close to quitting at least four times, and there was talk on the set that

Disney would fire him. After one meeting with Verbinski, Bruckheimer, Cook, Jacobson, and Taylor that had devolved into a shouting match, Bruckheimer told Verbinski that it was the worst meeting he'd ever endured as a producer, which was saying a lot. There were numerous compromises: Verbinski got the expensive ship-to-ship battle he desperately wanted but not an interior shot of the longboats rowed by the pirates. The budget eventually pushed toward $150 million.

There was only time for one test screening of *Pirates*, which was in Anaheim, close to the theme park that inspired the film. The audience seemed captivated and laughed knowingly at visual references to the ride—the dog outside the jail holding the key in his mouth, the redheaded prostitute in the sequence where the town is burned. But it was hard to draw many conclusions from one test. (In a subsequent London screening, the references to the Disneyland ride passed without any audience recognition.)

Eisner was worried about the expense, Depp's portrayal, the length, but most of all the title. He disliked *Pirates of the Caribbean* and was afraid associations with the theme park ride would hurt the movie with the key teenage demographic, who would assume the movie was for children. He also wanted something that would lend itself to sequels if the film was a hit, like *Raiders of the Lost Ark*. Finally he agreed to settle for a subtitle: *The Curse of the Black Pearl*.

This brought howls of protest from just about everyone, even Taylor and other Disney executives. The *Black Pearl* was the name of the ship commanded by Barbossa, and thus figured in the plot. But the ship had nothing to do with the pirates' curse. Verbinski thought it was nonsense. Eisner refused to back down. *The Curse of the Black Pearl* remained the subtitle, although on most posters and trailers the words were so small as to be barely visible.

Pirates of the Caribbean opened on July 9, a Wednesday rather than the usual Friday, and after the critical July 4 period. Conventional wisdom was that a summer blockbuster had to be out by Memorial Day, July 4 at the latest. Reviews were mixed: Elvis Mitchell in *The New York Times* found it "an often frenetic, colorful and entertaining comic adventure," while critics in Chicago and Los Angeles panned it. But nearly everyone found Depp's performance to be riveting. "Depp and Rush fearlessly provide performances that seem nourished by deep wells of nuttiness," wrote Roger Ebert in the *Sun-Times*. "Depp in particular seems to be channeling a drunken drag queen, with his eyeliner and the way he minces ashore and slurs his dialogue ever so insouciantly. Don't mistake me: this is not a criticism, but admiration for his work. It can be said that his performance is original in its very atom. There has never been a pirate, or for that matter, a human being like this in any other movie."

Like Disney executives, the critics—most well past their own rebellious youths—failed to gauge how unerringly Depp's performance tapped into the irreverent instincts of moviegoing teenagers. Audiences burst into applause even before the movie was over. Verbinski kept the pace so brisk that audiences didn't have time to puzzle over the convoluted plot that had worried Disney's consumer products people.

Pirates of the Caribbean joined *The Sixth Sense* as that increasingly rare phenomenon—a movie with "legs." Backed by Disney's marketing muscle and across-the-company promotions, *Pirates* had a good opening weekend with minimal competition. But ticket sales kept surging—*Pirates* was among the top five grossing films for a record twelve weeks. Many teenage boys saw it multiple times. Eventually, *Pirates* grossed $305 million in the United States, and $348 million internationally. And this time, Disney hadn't sold off the profits.

Disney moved swiftly to capitalize on its new franchise, signing Verbinski, Depp, Rush, Bloom, and the winsome Keira Knightley to two sequels, to be shot simultaneously, like the *Lord of the Rings* trilogy. Verbinski assured me that he and Depp will have more surprises for audiences—and for Disney. "We've already grafted the pirate genre with the supernatural. I think we're fair game to go into everything from the Orient to sea monsters," he said. "We have a wonderful opportunity to tie up loose ends and open the thing up, take the genre to a wild place. You don't do something because it's a sure thing. You don't do something for the bank. That's the one that flops. That's a riskier proposition than doing something completely original. It's risky to be safe."

For all of Eisner's efforts to establish Disney as a "growth" company with 20 percent annual profit and market capitalization increases, the only division that indisputably met the criteria was ESPN, now run by Steve Bornstein's affable former deputy, George Bodenheimer. Besides the steep increase in fees charged to cable operators, ESPN had aggressively expanded the brand, and now boasted ESPN2, ESPN Classic, and ESPNews. Still, there were concerns at ESPN's Bristol headquarters. Bornstein's eight-year, $9 billion deal with the NFL would expire in 2005. Any renewal would cost even more.

Ironically, ESPN was exactly what Eisner had always said he disdained: a distributor of content owned by others. True, ESPN had packaged that content in some original ways, with shows like "SportsCenter" and "Pardon the Interruption," which were essentially sports talk shows. In July, ESPN's programming head, thirty-three-year-old Mark Shapiro, hired conservative radio star Rush Limbaugh to add a provocative element to pregame football coverage. (Limbaugh was fired just a few weeks into the show after making what was deemed a racially insensitive remark, and then began treatment for what he described as an addiction to painkillers.) Despite these efforts, ESPN was essentially dependent on the rights to actual sports events. When it lost the rights to NASCAR racing, ratings suffered.

So the previous December, Shapiro spread the word that ESPN was looking for an original sports-themed dramatic series, something that would be "appointment TV" for the heavily male audience coveted by national advertisers. After all, the E in ESPN stood for "entertainment," and a successful original series would lessen ESPN's dependence on sports programming owned by others. Shapiro read over seventy scripts and treatments before focusing on "The Red Zone," a pilot script by John Eisendrath, a former *Washington Monthly* reporter who was also a writer for ABC's "Alias." Eisendrath had originally written the script for the FX channel, which opted for "The Shield" instead.

Shapiro and other ESPN executives met with Eisendrath in Hollywood several times, and Eisendrath pressed his view that traditional fictional series about sports had never worked. A fictional sports event could never compete with the suspense and excitement of a real game. He wanted to do a series that used sports as a backdrop, a series about men caught up in a macho culture that didn't sanction fear or emotion. In other words, professional football.

By February, Shapiro was so enthusiastic that he ordered eleven episodes, to be produced by Disney's Touchstone studio, with plans to run each episode five to six times a week. Shapiro conferred regularly with Eisendrath over the story lines. In the script for the second episode, which was about drug usage by players, there was a reference to Hall of Famer Lawrence Taylor, the former linebacker for the New York Giants who admitted to years of drug use while in the NFL. Shapiro said he was worried about how the NFL would react, adding, "Look, we're portraying a fictional world, and the NFL is already not terribly happy." So any reference to an actual NFL player was banned (though references to real players in other sports were okay). Eisendrath thought that was ironic, given that ESPN itself had covered the Taylor story.

Even then, Shapiro pressed Eisendrath about the fictional drug addict on the team. "Do we have to keep seeing that?"

"Well, he is an addict," Eisendrath responded. "He's going to get help, but it's not realistic to think he'll be cleaned up by episode three." Shapiro agreed.

By episode six, one of the players was coming out of the closet, a process extending over five episodes. "That's too much," Shapiro argued. "Our viewers don't want to watch that." ESPN had held focus groups in which it tested the plot lines for all eleven episodes. Shapiro said no one was interested in a gay theme.

Eisendrath laughed. "You've got fifteen guys, total strangers, sitting around—you're not going to get them to raise their hands and say, 'Gee, I want more of the gay character.' "

Shapiro agreed to four episodes focusing on a gay character.

The new show, "Playmakers," debuted on ESPN on August 26. It was undeniably original and provocative. Eisendrath was impressed that Shapiro had the courage to put it on the air, and that Bodenheimer and ESPN backed him. It was also a ratings success, especially for cable, drawing an average of 2.2 million viewers, five times what ESPN had been getting for the time slot. "Playmakers" looked like a bona fide hit.

And then NFL commissioner Paul Tagliabue saw a promotional spot for the show during ESPN's broadcast of an NFL preseason game. The spot showed one player in a crack den, another getting an injection, and two others hiding cocaine in the glove compartment of their car. Tagliabue picked up the phone and called Eisner.

On September 9, Eisner has invited me to join him at the weekly studio meeting, where the feature film slate is reviewed, budgets are discussed, and deals are proposed. In the wake of *Nemo, Pirates,* and a surprise hit, *Freaky Friday,* a remake starring Jamie Lee Curtis and Lindsay Lohan, the film division is heading toward a record $3 billion in revenue. After a disappointing 2002, this box-office bonanza couldn't have come at a better time for Eisner. It has helped him blunt the ongoing criticisms from Gold and Roy, and strengthened his hand with the board, demonstrating that he hasn't lost his touch, and is precisely the kind of "creative" chief executive the company needs.

The meeting I'm attending isn't where movie ideas are green-lit, which remains the prerogative of studio chairman Dick Cook and president Nina Jacobson, along with Eisner—decisions like that are made in Eisner's office, or Cook's, in meetings to which I haven't been invited. Still, "The key to the studio is in this room," Eisner tells me as we enter a conference room on the second floor of the Team Disney building, adjacent to Cook's office. Unlike prior studio chairmen, from Katzenberg through Roth, each of whom had an office on the sixth floor near Eisner, Cook has opted to keep his office on the second floor with the other studio executives.

Cook is in Toronto on this day, where Touchstone's *Veronica Guerin* is being shown at the Toronto Film Festival. Jacobson is in charge. When he is in town, Eisner attends these meetings regularly, and this week he congratulates Brigham Taylor on his recent promotion to senior vice president on the strength of *Pirates of the Caribbean,* whose story was his original idea. Responsibility for theme park–derived movies seems to have fallen to him. He's at work on *The Haunted Mansion,* also inspired by a Disneyland attraction, starring Eddie Murphy, due in October.

Jacobson asks people to introduce themselves for my benefit. Brad Epstein, a studio production chief, is working on *Ladder 49,* about a group of New York City firemen starring John Travolta and Joaquin Phoenix, and *Confessions of a Teenage Drama Queen.* Eisner mentions that he's flying to Florida to have lunch with Travolta. "He lives on a runway in Florida. He has his own hangar," Eisner says, shaking his head in disbelief that anyone would want to live in such a place. "How is Travolta?" Eisner asks Epstein. Travolta's weight has been fluctuating, a subject avidly chronicled in the tabloids.

"He looks fantastic," Epstein assures him.

"This will be a good movie for him."

"There is an issue," Epstein continues, "over who dies in the fire. Who's the hero? Travolta is wondering, 'shouldn't I be the one'?"

Eisner sidesteps the sensitive issue of whether Travolta's character might be overshadowed by Phoenix, and the introductions continue. Jacobson emphasizes the importance of so-called below-the-line elements, such as schedule and budgets, and Eisner jumps in to remind everyone that "some creative things happen by holding the line." He launches into an anecdote about Shelley Long and the making of *Outrageous Fortune* that, judging from the looks around the table, all have heard before. Eisner explains that a scene in the movie called for a set for a drama school, and instead the scene was shot with Shelley Long speaking into a telephone. "It only cost a dollar!" Eisner exclaims. "It was a very creative way to do what would have been a clichéd scene. Sanity on costs leads to better movies."

"If the filmmakers had their way, the sky would be the limit," Jacobson adds. "*Matrix II* is an example." Eisner readily agrees that the *Matrix* series from Warner Bros. has become overburdened with expensive special effects.

Jacobson mentions another project in development about a NASCAR racer played by Dennis Quaid. "The script has been tough," she says. "But it's a great story of men learning to become fathers."

"When will we release this?" Eisner asks.

"Summer of 2005."

"Why not next summer?

"I wish we could."

"Let's discuss it."

"It's impossible."

Next up is *Princess Diaries 2*, "You have to change the name," Eisner says. "How about 'Curse of the Black Dress'?" Everyone laughs at the reference to *Pirates*. " 'Princess in Love'? *Princess Diaries 2* should be the subtitle."

"*The Santa Clause 2* worked," someone points out.

"We got away with that one," Eisner says. "*Princess Diaries 2* is so boring."

"I like *Princess in Love*," Jacobson says. "The script needs some work, we have some issues on length. . . . It's testing so big, more than it really deserves. It's one hour and fifty-two minutes, not too long, but too long for the material."

"It's way too long," Eisner says.

"It's a struggle," Jacobson says.

Jacobson mentions that they've gotten a good script for a feature film version of "Kim Possible," the animated girl action-hero, which, like *Lizzie McGuire*, should have a guaranteed preteen audience. She says the movie could be ready for summer of 2004.

"Who's in it?" Eisner asks.

"You have to find a girl."

"Do we get Hilary Duff?" Eisner asks.

"No, you get a great new girl and create a franchise," Jacobson says.

"Any girl can do this," Taylor adds. "You can create a Kim Possible."

Next up is *The Ghosts of Girlfriends Past*, a remake of *A Christmas Carol*, starring Ben Affleck as Scrooge. The twist is that the ghosts are his past, present, and future girlfriends. Eisner says he's just read the script. "I like it," he says, "but it's going to be tough to pull off for three reasons: one, he [the main character] is hateable."

A discussion ensues. Eisner mentions that he'd been planning to attend the much-hyped "wedding of the century" between Affleck and Jennifer Lopez until it was abruptly canceled. The whole affair hasn't exactly enhanced Affleck's appeal.

"Two," Eisner continues, "can you play Don Juan jokes for two hours?"

Jacobson agrees the jokes are a problem. "It's too ribald. It's got to be PG-13. This is supposed to be a romantic comedy."

"You know," Eisner muses, "sometimes *A Christmas Carol* is very boring. Going back to the ghosts stops the action. You want to know what happens next." He pauses, then continues. "I like the Ghost of Christmas Present. Could she be Queen Latifah? But Christmas Past, Christmas Future, they're very boring." No one responds, so Eisner resumes.

"Three: it's one note. It's a clever idea."

"It's very well written," Jacobson adds.

"Is it too clichéd? He's so bad. There are no surprises once you know the gimmick."

"That's what a romantic comedy is," Jacobson says.

"It could be fun," Eisner allows, though he doesn't sound convinced. "This could be a revival for Ben." (Affleck's most recent film, *Gigli,* had been savaged by critics and was a box-office flop.) "Is he negotiating like he's had some failures?" he asks.

"Unfortunately, we got him before that," Jacobson says.

The group moves through numerous projects: *Dark Water,* a thriller; *Guardian,* a Coast Guard story being considered by Ashton Kutcher; *A Lot Like Love,* a British script, maybe for Orlando Bloom; *Flightplan,* a Jodie Foster thriller about a mother whose baby disappears on a plane in midflight. "The script went to Johnny Depp yesterday," Jacobson says, but "would you be comfortable with Sean Penn? He's gettable."

"What do we have for summer?" Eisner asks, then answers his own question. "*The Woods* [the latest Shyamalan thriller], *Princess Diaries 2, Mr. 3000* . . ."

"Maybe *The Ladykillers,*" Jacobson adds.

"This does not stand up to this summer," Eisner says. "*Flightplan* might do it."

"Or *Ghosts of Girlfriends,*" Jacobson suggests.

"We have to have something," Eisner says.

Some more ideas are tossed out, including *The Greatest Game Ever Played,* about a golfer in the 1920s. Eisner looks dubious. "Do they play in those funny pants? Who cares about golf in the 1920s?"

Jacobson agrees. "Golf is boring. But it's about character."

"Of the whole list, it makes me nervous," Eisner says. He asks to read the script.

Eisner thanks everyone again for a "fantastic summer," but adds, "Now

I'm nervous. I don't want to go from $700 million to $200 million." His anxiety seems palpable, and I'm reminded of Peter Schneider's comment that Eisner can't relax and enjoy success, because he's too worried about what's next.

"I'm seeing *The Alamo* tonight," Jacobson says, sounding hopeful. *The Alamo* is slated for Disney's big Christmas 2003 holiday release. "It's the director's cut. It's three hours."

"It won't end up there?" Eisner asks, sounding alarmed.

"I hope not. I hear it's really good."

"Unless it's *The Godfather,* people don't want that much history. By the way," Eisner adds before leaving. "Do we want to do another Western with Kevin Costner?" (Disney has just released *Open Range*).

"I can take a breather," Jacobson says.

Eisner has recently met with Costner. "Costner has this idea. He said it's a family movie. It's an elephant thing. He said it's three hours.

"I said, 'We'll do seventy-two minutes.'

"He said, 'Why?'

"I said, 'Because it's an elephant movie! Elephant movies are difficult.' "

Everyone laughs. The staff seems in a good mood. "Congratulations on the summer," Eisner says again. "It's fantastic."

Perhaps Eisner was right to be worried about next year. Later that day I ask if I can accompany Jacobson to see *The Alamo* but am told Directors' Guild rules prohibit any outsiders from seeing the rough cut. Later, Eisner mentions that he'd seen it, and I ask him how it was. "It's a mess," he says, shaking his head.

Nor would *Ghosts of Girlfriends Past* come to the rescue for either the holiday or summer seasons. As Affleck's reputation continued to take a drubbing in the tabloid press in the wake of his messy, highly public breakup with Jennifer Lopez, Jacobson killed the project, and Eisner agreed.

Two days after my meeting with Eisner and the studio executives, a new episode of "8 Simple Rules" was being shot at Touchstone's Studio Six, on the Burbank lot. Although it was the second anniversary of the World Trade Center attacks, there was no pause in the shooting schedule, and "8 Simple Rules" was shooting the fourth episode in the new season.

That afternoon, John Ritter and the rest of the cast were making some promotional spots. As usual, Ritter was entertaining everyone in the cast, acting like a puppet. "Is your hair on straight?" director James Widdoes asked. Ritter grabbed his scalp, moved it back and forth, contorting his face. Everyone was laughing. The teenage cast members had come to think of Ritter as the father he played in the show.

They were about to start blocking that afternoon's scenes when Ritter came over to Widdoes. "I'm feeling a little sick to my stomach. Can I go upstairs and lie down for a while?" Widdoes said fine, they'd use his stand-in. "Feel better," he said.

When executive producer Flody Suarez got the news, he told an assistant director to get the nurse. He thought it might be food poisoning, and at about 5:00 P.M. Ritter checked into St. Joseph's Hospital, across the street from the studio. Suarez hurried over to see him and poked his head into the room. Ritter looked pale. "Are you just lying there, or can we do one more promo?" Suarez quipped. "Fine," Ritter grinned.

Ritter's wife, Amy Yasbeck, showed up, as did his close friend and lawyer, Bob Myman; Steve McPherson, head of Touchstone, and others. After the doctors performed an electrocardiogram, Suarez called Susan Lyne, who'd already received an email from McPherson saying they'd shut down production early because Ritter wasn't feeling well. Now Suarez told her the EKG "hadn't gone well." A half-hour later, he reported that "It's much worse than we thought," and the doctors were trying to prepare Amy for the worst. The next time Suarez called Lyne, he was sobbing. Ritter had died in surgery, the victim of a torn artery. He was fifty-four.

The stunned, grieving cast and crew gathered spontaneously the next morning on the soundstage. People were sobbing. Suarez ordered food and coffee. People took turns paying tribute to Ritter, and it seemed everyone had a story about how their lives had been touched by his generosity and humor. Both Braun and Lyne spoke briefly. Though no one broached the subject of what was going to happen now to "8 Simple Rules," Lyne assured everyone that no one would lose their job.

Still, the issue had to be faced. "8 Simple Rules," despite having been overshadowed by "American Idol," was ABC's most promising show, and the linchpin of the Tuesday-night schedule. The few precedents weren't encouraging. Freddie Prinze, star of "Chico and the Man," had killed himself during the show's second season in 1977. Redd Foxx, star of "The Royal Family," had died in 1991. Both shows had been canceled. Lyne and Braun both assumed that "8 Simple Rules" would suffer the same fate.

On Monday afternoon, after Ritter's emotional funeral, attended only by family and close friends, Lyne and Braun sat down to discuss the show's fate. Both had been struck by the reaction of the cast to Ritter's death, as if he were their real father. "Should we be listening?" Lyne asked. "Is there something here?"

Braun was thinking along the same lines. "Are we crazy? Or should we think about addressing this directly in the show? What happens when a young father dies? How do you pick up the pieces?"

So Braun and Lyne floated the notion to Suarez, Widdoes, and executive producer Tom Shaydac. Nobody really wanted to talk about it, but no one vetoed the idea, either. Amy Yasbeck and Bob Myman seemed supportive. Amy, in particular, knew how important the jobs were to the cast and crew, and felt Ritter would have wanted the show to continue without him. Obviously, ABC had to tread a fine line between empathy and exploitation. On Tuesday, ABC announced that the production would go into "hiatus," but was careful not to say that the show was being shut down permanently.

Two days later, Eisner weighed in with an email to Braun and Lyne. Not only did he want to continue the series, but he proposed that Cate, Ritter's wife in the show, played by Katey Sagal, be pregnant (she'd had a pregnancy scare in an earlier episode). Then she could give birth for the May sweeps week. Iger weighed in with an email: "This is a great idea. Let's discuss."

"Oh my God," Braun told Lyne. They were both appalled. It had been hard enough to approach Amy about continuing the show at all, but to suggest that Ritter's character would be leaving a baby behind was going too far. It seemed unspeakably exploitative to capitalize on Ritter's death by making his wife pregnant and having her give birth during the May sweeps.

At first they said nothing, hoping Eisner's idea would die the natural death they felt it deserved. They didn't want to reject it immediately, knowing that would provoke Eisner. But he brought it up again. So did Iger. Finally Braun said he thought it was tasteless. "Audiences will love it," Eisner insisted. "Who cares what the critics say?"

More calls and emails ensued, with Iger continuing to weigh in on behalf of Eisner's idea. Finally Braun wrote, "I cannot endorse this." This prompted Iger to accuse Braun of being "insubordinate" in an email that was copied to numerous people involved in the show.

Eisner himself was also furious, and summoned Braun and Lyne to his office to confront the matter. Iger was out of town, so he participated by phone. Both Braun and Lyne were feeling emotionally drained from Ritter's death and its aftermath. Lyne took the lead, trying to sidestep the issue of whether the idea was exploitative of a tragic situation. Eisner had already told them he thought that objection was "ridiculous." She pointed out that if Cate were pregnant, she'd be getting bigger and bigger during the season.

The writers couldn't introduce another love interest; they couldn't have a pregnant mother dating. And it would shift the focus of the show away from the teenage girls to the mother and baby, which was a totally different show.

But the more she talked, the angrier Eisner became. "You just don't get it!" he yelled. He was scathing, attacking Braun and Lyne as elitists, saying both lacked the common touch. "You're not TV people," he said contemptuously. Braun shot back, saying pregnancy was a "terrible idea" and in "terrible taste."

Finally Eisner screamed at Braun, "You're a creative wimp."

"Oh really?" Braun shouted back. "Why is that? Is it because I have the guts to disagree with you? What if I'm right? Maybe I'm saving your ass."

Suddenly there was silence. Eisner looked like he might explode, his eyes bulging. Lyne and Braun had heard reports of Eisner's explosive temper, but they'd never experienced it firsthand, and had discounted them as exaggerations, until now. Finally Braun got up and put on his jacket.

Eisner collected himself, but there was no point in continuing the meeting. As they walked out into the corridor, Braun confided in Lyne, "Let me tell you, I am not going to do something that I find morally reprehensible to keep this job. If this means I'm gone, then I'm gone."

On September 11, 2003, the same day as Ritter's death, it fell to Angela Shapiro and the Family channel's new head of finance, Reinaldo Del Valle, to present the financial numbers for the channel, which were little short of disastrous. Shapiro did her best to emphasize the good news, and there was genuine progress to report. By the upfront presentations to advertisers that spring, she and her staff had been able to introduce a total of three hundred hours of original programming. Despite the "Family" name, she had been gradually skewing the programming toward women aged eighteen to thirty-four with more romantic comedies. The channel was actually getting better ratings than MTV with an afternoon block aimed at teenage girls. But it was awkward. During the presentations, a reporter had asked how the new programming fit the "Family" label. "Well, I call it kind of family, but not the traditional family, if you know what I mean," Shapiro said. What else could she say? Not the truth—that it made no sense but she was carrying out orders.

Despite mounting uncertainty over the future of the channel and her own status, Shapiro had continued to acquire new programming. At the September 11 meeting, Iger suggested yet another name change for the channel, this time to the US Network. Disney owned a half-interest in *US* magazine with *Rolling Stone* publisher Jann Wenner, and the magazine already had a strong brand identity and appealed to the target eighteen- to thirty-four-year-old women's audience. Anne Sweeney said nothing, but Shapiro loved the idea.

The next day, Iger asked Shapiro to come to his office. He asked her to sit down, and joined her in the comfortable seating area across from his desk. According to reports of the meeting from members of Shapiro's staff, Iger said, "Let me explain something. The board hates me. I may lose my job. I'm connected to the network and to ABC Family, and they're both losers. So I'm going to say something that you're going to hate. I have to put ABC Family under the cable group."

Staff members were incredulous, since they all knew Shapiro had been explicitly promised she would not report to Anne Sweeney. Iger had given her his word. When they asked her what happened, she reported that Iger had said that "things change and I need to save my job," adding that "You don't understand how important Michael's job is to me and now I feel I may not get it."

Shapiro kept lobbying Iger to change his mind about having the Family channel report to the cable division and to keep it tied to the network, much as NBC was successfully linking the Bravo channel to NBC. Though conceding the idea made operational sense, he stressed that the underperforming Family was doing nothing to help ABC's bottom line. Family's embarrassing shortfall could be buried in the successful cable division. Family executives concluded the decision was being driven by accounting issues, not what was best for the channel.

When I asked about this, Iger conceded that the move may have breached Shapiro's contract, but said he had an obligation to do what was best for Disney and for the channel. He had always argued that Family belonged in the cable group. The ABC Network had too many management problems of its own to oversee another channel. And there were economic efficiencies in terms of allocating overhead and other costs. Despite perceptions of some Family executives, he said the move had nothing to do with covering up a mistake, burying Family's results, or concealing anything from the board. Eisner added that the channel was moved because the "repurposing" strategy wasn't working, so it made no sense to keep Family with ABC.

Finally Shapiro told Iger she didn't see how she could stay at the company, so he asked Eisner to intervene. Eisner, too, tried to talk her into staying, but Shapiro countered that it wasn't even the breach of contract, but the breach of trust when Iger broke his word.

Eisner suggested that maybe she'd misunderstood Iger. Maybe Iger hadn't really promised, but had used some variation of the "elastic go" that Eisner himself employed. Shapiro insisted there had been no misunderstanding.

In the midst of these discussions, word reached Tom Murphy that Shapiro might leave the company. Concerned, he spoke to Iger. "She's the most creative person I know. Why would you try to push her out?"

"She and Anne don't get along," Iger replied.

Next Murphy called Shapiro, who he knew from her time at ABC. "What's going on?" he asked.

Shapiro filled him in on her contract provision, Iger's promise, and the decision to move the channel under Sweeney, as well as Iger's ambition to succeed Eisner. She was incensed when Murphy told her Iger had characterized the problem as a "girl thing." She said it was nothing of the sort.

"Angela, I've known Bob Iger forever," Murphy said after hearing Shapiro's explanation. "I have to tell you, he's lost his soul."

Angela Shapiro told Iger on Friday, October 3, that her decision to leave was final. Her lawyer would work out the details with Alan Braverman, Disney's general counsel. Shapiro didn't want to sue Disney; she was hoping to leave on amicable terms. After all, she'd been there for eight years, and until she was assigned to the Family acquisition, she had loved working at ABC. They agreed that Shapiro would stay until she negotiated her severance, and they'd announced the change to the staff the following Tuesday.

When Shapiro arrived at the office on Tuesday morning, everyone on her staff had already gotten a voice message summoning each at a specific time for meetings with Sweeney. She faced a barrage of questions about what was going on. Shapiro was irritated that she hadn't been able to make the announcement before the calls, but she called the staff together, told them the channel was moving to the cable group, and that she would be leaving. Still, she tried to reassure them that there wouldn't be any drastic changes and their jobs were secure.

When Shapiro returned from her meeting with Sweeney, she was visibly shaken. She reported that she had offered Sweeney her help and support, but had been brushed aside. In short order, Sweeney had vetoed the "US" name, dispensed with the strategy for reaching teen girls and women, and declared that the channel would be "gender neutral." Romantic comedies already in development would be marketed to men.

Shapiro's assurances to her staff that everything would be all right were largely undermined by their individual meetings with Sweeney, especially since someone from human resources was present at all of them. Sweeney told them all variations of the same message: that the channel should always have been in the cable group, and there would be a series of meetings to "see where you fit in." Sweeney added that she'd be reviewing their program development efforts, and repeated what she'd told Shapiro, that the channel would now be "gender neutral."

The following Monday, Sweeney and Iger met with Shapiro's staff. According to several people present at the meeting, Sweeney said, "Angela and I have worked closely from the beginning. It was her idea that we meet with each of you separately. Let me repeat what I told each of you in those meetings. We'll be reviewing the programs in development. As I said, I'm so proud to take over this channel. You've done a remarkable job and I'm so proud of all your hard work. You're going to be part of an even stronger team."

The Walt Disney Concert Hall finally opened to the public in October 2003 with a series of three gala benefit concerts, culminating in a star-studded musical tribute to Hollywood and a dinner outside the hall under a huge tent. After the project was nearly abandoned for lack of funds and interest, the new concert hall managed to garner rave reviews both for the stunning architecture by Frank Gehry and the acoustics: "Its silvery cascades are one of the most beautiful sights anywhere in the U.S. *(Time)*; "Disney Hall is a defining masterwork" *(Newsweek)*; "A serene, enobling building" *(The New Yorker)*. Though she didn't live to see its completion, Lillian Disney would surely have been proud that a fitting memorial to Walt's genius had risen in downtown Los Angeles. "Walt and Frank [Gehry] are the perfect match, an artistic marriage made in heaven," Steven Spielberg told the opening-night crowd. Lillian's own love of flowers was reflected in the bold floral-print carpeting laid throughout the hall and in a sculpture of a rose made from broken Delft tiles.

Walt Disney Hall was a source of pride to just about everyone connected to it: Diane Disney Miller, who had worked so hard and given so generously to preserve Gehry's vision; Roy, whose gift helped build the RedCat Theater; Eisner, who agreed that Disney would give $25 million; and Andrea Van de Kamp, the Music Center chairwoman, who had rescued the project from the brink of financial collapse. It fell to Van de Kamp to organize the gala and oversee the seating chart for the dinner. Then, the following Monday, the hall was hosting another glittering event, the premiere of *Matrix 3*, the latest in the action-adventure-science-fiction series from Warner Bros.

Three days before the hall's opening, Eisner called Diane to complain that Disney Hall was going to premiere a film from a rival studio. "We need to fix that," Eisner told her. "Can you do something about it?"

Diane dutifully called the hall, where she learned that *Matrix* producer Joel Silver was a close friend of Gehry, and, more to the point, Warner Bros. was underwriting the event with a generous gift. Diane decided the premiere was a good idea, and a good deal for the hall. In any event, Walt Disney Hall was a memorial to Walt, and not to the Disney Company. It was meant to encourage artistic expression from whatever source. Gehry had specifically banned the kind of Disney corporate trademarks that were planted all over the architecture at the theme parks and at Disney's headquarters. The *Matrix* premiere stayed on the schedule.

Faced with making the dinner seating arrangements, Van de Kamp had a delicate task. Apart from her own feelings about Eisner, he and Roy were barely speaking, and there was always the danger that lingering tensions between the Roy and Walt sides of the family might flare up. Eisner had asked Roy to accompany him to the premiere, but Roy had declined, saying he and Patty were going to be sitting at Van de Kamp's table. So Van de Kamp carefully placed her table, Diane's three tables, and Eisner's two tables at distant points under the tent.

The price for a table was high—$25,000 to more than $100,000 for tickets that included all three gala events. Despite his recent disparagement of her performance on the board, Eisner called Van de Kamp to complain that he didn't see why he had to pay for a table when he had been responsible for a $25 million gift. Though she felt she had been grossly mistreated, Van de Kamp decided not to argue with him, or point out that no other major donor asked for or received a free table. So Van de Kamp arranged for a second table at no additional cost. (Eisner paid for the first.)

Somehow it all came off. The Philharmonic played excerpts from classic film scores and the audience applauded the splendid acoustics. Tom Hanks and Catherine Zeta-Jones were gracious co-hosts. And at the dinner, none of the three warring factions—Eisner, Roy, and Diane—even saw each other.

A few weeks later, on November 4, Eisner was scheduled to speak at what was shaping up to be the East Coast equivalent of Herb Allen's Sun Valley conference, a media conference co-hosted by investment bankers the Quadrangle Group, management consulting firm McKinsey & Co., and accountants PricewaterhouseCoopers. When I show up at the Wall Street Regent Hotel in Manhattan, I learn that the conference is ostensibly off the record and closed

to journalists, but a number of prominent journalists are already there—
Tina Brown, founder of the defunct, Miramax-financed *Talk,* who has resur-
faced with a talk show on CNBC; my *New Yorker* colleague Ken Auletta;
Norman Pearlstine, my former editor at *The Wall Street Journal,* now editor
in chief of Time Inc.; and PBS talk-show host Charlie Rose, who is serving as
a moderator. The gatekeepers don't seem to mind after I explain I'm working
on a book and that Eisner knows I'm in the audience.

Right away, I bump into Brian Grazer of Imagine Entertainment, who re-
minds me that he produced *Splash,* Touchstone's first live-action hit, for Ron
Miller. Then Richard Snyder, former CEO of Simon & Schuster, who, like
Eisner, detested their mutual boss Marty Davis at Paramount, recalls the day
Davis fired Eisner. Everyone there, it seems, has an Eisner story.

Eisner and Rose take the stage. Eisner begins by lauding the ABC acquisition to this deal-oriented audience, praises the "momentum" in Disney's
media networks, and predicts "substantial" growth at the theme parks due to
pent-up, post–September 11 demand.

"Wouldn't Comcast and Disney be the perfect merger?" Rose asks, referring to the giant Philadelphia-based cable company where ex-Disney executive Steve Burke has been named president.

Eisner rolled his eyes. "That's a terrible idea," he retorts. People laugh.

"Why?" Rose asks.

"I don't think content and distribution belong in the same company,"
Eisner says, repeating his oft-stated conclusion on the subject. "Content is
evergreen . . . distribution is replaced by better technology. Content people
come from a different planet. They don't get along well."

Rose asks about the just-announced deal in which General Electric is acquiring Universal's entertainment assets.

"I like it," Eisner says. "A competitor with a smart owner. I want to see GE
planning in Ronnie Meyer's office," referring to Universal Studios chief Ron
Meyer, Ovitz's former partner. "That's a joke," he adds. "But you don't want
stupid competitors."

"What about Miramax?" Rose continues.

"It's fabulous," Eisner says. "Harvey [Weinstein] is staying. He's bigger
than life. He's delivered incredible material to our library."

"Is he happy?"

"I think so. He says he is."

"Pixar?" Rose asks. Wall Street has been eagerly awaiting the results of the
Disney-Pixar negotiations, especially after the enormous success of *Nemo,*
which had grossed $865 million worldwide by the end of 2004.

"Disney hasn't announced anything," Eisner replies, looking uncomfortable. "We are in conversations. . . ." He stops. Zenia Mucha, sitting in the front row, is scowling and vigorously shaking her head.

"What if they go away?"

"My PR person worked for George Pataki," Eisner answers. "She says don't answer that one."

"The Ovitz lawsuit," Rose continues, bringing up another contentious subject.

Eisner rolls his eyes. "Why am I doing this? I can't talk about that."

Rose mentions that AOL's Steve Case is his "hero," a "genius." "Who else has the vision?" he asks Eisner.

"Barry Diller," Eisner answers promptly. "He spotted assets that were undervalued," referring to the collection of Internet assets Diller has forged into a single company. "He had a strategic vision. He's exercising it prudently and brilliantly."

"You used to work for him."

"Anyway, he turned out to be right. People thought he was desperate to be a movie guy but he was putting together assets . . ."

"Criticism of your stewardship, the stock price . . . is there a misconception about what happened to Disney?"

"Disney is a great company. . . . I've never seen the company in twenty years in better shape. We're focused on the future, we're strategically positioned. . . . We didn't make any stupid acquisitions that brought us to our knees. We were cautious, we've come through the storm."

Rose brings up another awkward issue—succession. "Sandy Weill [chairman of Citigroup] just retired."

"I'm 140 years younger than Sumner [Redstone]!" Eisner exclaims. "I'm younger than Rupert [Murdoch]! Why don't you ask them about succession? Look, I like what I'm doing. We have excellent people in place. Bob Iger, the president, is highly respected along with five other people who could run the company."

"Do you have a retirement date in mind?"

"No," Eisner says emphatically.

Rose asks him about the need for a "rebirth," the need to "redefine" Disney.

"That's true," Eisner says. "Disney cannot become a museum. It has to reinvent itself creatively while standing for certain values. Disney has the brand, the culture, the type-A personality to be around forever. We are managing from decade to decade, not quarter to quarter. It's a long marathon. We have to step back. We have to put out great products, and get them to the public."

After Eisner's presentation, I join him and his entourage backstage, and he offers me a ride uptown in his chauffeured SUV. Once we're in our seats and maneuvering through traffic, I ask him to name the five people at Disney who, along with Iger, could succeed him as chief executive. He gives me an annoyed look. "There aren't five people," he says, then pauses. "There are twenty."

As we continue uptown, Eisner mentions that he just had lunch with Sandy Litvack, his former chief administrative officer and general counsel. "Sandy told me you interviewed him," he said. As it happens, I had interviewed Litvack that morning. "Sandy told me you can't be trusted."

"Really?" I say.

"I decided to go ahead anyway. Everybody has a dark side," Eisner continues. "It's just a matter of finding out what it is."

The comment gives me pause, and I find myself still thinking about it days later. I've heard others repeat similar comments from Eisner about a "dark side," and it was something he mentioned several times during his testimony in the Katzenberg lawsuit. I wonder: Does everyone have a "dark side"? Do I? Even if I'm not the best judge of my own character, I don't assume that everyone else has a "dark side."

I realize that by mentioning Litvack's remark—assuming Litvack said it—Eisner has simultaneously positioned Litvack as someone I can't trust, and has ingratiated himself with me. He has cleverly attempted to turn me against Litvack—exactly what so many current and former Disney executives have told me happened to them.

By the time we reach the ABC building on West Sixty-seventh, Eisner's cheerful mood has returned. He's eager to tell me about a recent animation meeting similar to the one I attended the previous summer. "We had two fabulous ideas," he says. "One is a documentary, a 'mockumentary,' really, with animals talking. You interview a wolf, a cow, a prairie dog. . . . I've been talking about wolves, something with wolves, but it always sounded like 'Rin Tin Tin.' But then I thought of *Best in Show* [a 'mockumentary' about dog owners by Christopher Guest]. And I thought, an animal mockumentary!" Eisner sounds genuinely excited. "Two. I've always loved *White Christmas* [sic]. You save the lodge with a show. Here you've got a circus going under. The animals put on a show, a benefit!

"We've totally refocused animation," Eisner continues, as he gets out of the SUV. "I brought all the best animators, Glen Keane, everybody, into the office last Wednesday. I said they weren't leaving until we had two great ideas, and I'd stay as long as it took. It took an hour!" Eisner says, as he heads into the building.

That evening I join Eisner, his assistant Chris Curtin, and Mucha for dinner at Ouest, a "hot" restaurant on the Upper West Side. I've noticed that Eisner gets reservations anywhere on short notice, which reminds me of the anecdote in which Ovitz was able to book a table at Morton's when Eisner couldn't. Eisner is, as usual, good company at dinner, though it's difficult to interview him as he hops conversationally from one topic to another. But tonight he's prepared to discuss the September 24 board meeting at which Gold threw down the gauntlet.

The background, he explains, is that Disney faced a "perfect storm": the beginning of a recession, September 11, the Iraq war, aging ABC programs, having to spend $9 billion for the NFL football package. "This gave my enemies for fifteen years the pleasure of a fall." Then Sid Bass had to sell his Disney stake. "People got caught in the bubble," Eisner observes. "Sid Bass was brilliant. I hope I can be so graceful. It was financially devastating for him. Not for a moment was anyone blamed."

After Gold's presentation to the board, Eisner says, "I presented to the board the real situation, division by division. I had to reinvent the movie business. I had to promise the board I would run it personally. Nina and Dick could handle it day to day, but I would decide what to make. I promised the board.

"Anyway," he continues, "the perfect storm. I've been there before so many times since the 1960s. 'All My Children'—no one was watching. Bad press. There were rumors I was going to be fired three weeks after I got to Paramount. I've been there, walking the plank. On the cover of *Time*, both ends! It's ludicrous. Still, the board meeting was a new experience. Stanley was the one board member against me. Ray Watson told me Stanley was unhappy I didn't make him president.

"As long as I've been doing this, criticism doesn't bother me. I read a review every morning. Everyone's an expert. Even my kids call up: 'What were you thinking?' I don't care.

"I was invigorated by the rebirth we had to do. It's fun to go from the floor to the ceiling. When someone threatens you, you either run away or you're invigorated by it. I handle crisis well. Success is the hardest to endure, not failure. . . . My job is like a baseball coach. Getting fired is no dishonor. You just had a bad season."

Later, the conversation turns again to the question of succession, and his decision to name Bob Iger president. "Bob looks 'straight,' " Eisner observes, "but there's more there. He did 'Twin Peaks' and 'Cop Rock.' You're looking for some theatricality. . . . He's a tireless worker. People like Bob."

But it's clear Eisner isn't comfortable describing Iger's promotion, and says that Iger had no reaction when Eisner told him he was making him president. "Bob and I are both 'cool' people," he says by way of explanation. "We're not 'high-fivers.' " Eisner also makes clear that Iger is by no means his heir apparent. Besides the five (or twenty) Disney executives who Eisner believes could succeed him, Eisner mentions that there are a number of ex-Disney executives who should also be considered.

"I see these companies," he says. "They have a successor, and then there's a shark frenzy. You become a lame duck the minute you say so. No one respects you."

It took a Herculean effort to get "8 Simple Rules" back on the air, and not just because Eisner and Iger didn't like the script. At the first table read, actress Kaley Cuoco, one of the teenage daughters, had the first line. Every time she started to speak, she burst into tears. "I'm so sorry," she said. Just about everyone on the set ended up crying, including Susan Lyne.

The show returned in an hour-long episode that aired on November 4, which was also sweeps week. Braun had banned any laugh track, with the exception of some faint laughter in the opening segment, before Ritter's character, Paul Hennessy, suffers a fatal heart attack while on an errand to buy milk. Two new characters, the grandparents, played by James Garner and Suzanne Pleshette, arrive to rally the family and help the children and their mother confront their devastating loss. No one is pregnant.

Considering the delicacy of the situation, and the inherent difficulty of treating subjects as profound as death, remembrance, and grieving on a sitcom, the episode was remarkably successful. The show "was done as tastefully as television permits, blending scenes of sorrow with wry touches of comic relief" *(New York Times)*; "a heartfelt, emotional farewell" *(Los Angeles Times)*. And from a commercial standpoint, the gamble paid off: "8 Simple Rules" attracted over 20 million viewers, giving ABC a huge boost during the critical sweeps week.

In the wake of the reviews and ratings, Lyne and Braun waited in vain for any congratulations from Eisner or Iger. Finally Lyne asked Eisner what he thought of the show, hoping for at least a modest compliment. "I didn't like it," he said, complaining that it was "lugubrious." Neither he nor Iger said anything positive to either her or Braun, leaving them both angry and dispirited.

Braun was also furious when he discovered that NBC had picked up a new reality show from Mark Burnett, the "Survivor" producer, that Braun thought he had locked up for ABC. A year before, Braun and Andrea Wong had pitched an idea to real estate mogul Donald Trump. Though Trump had declined, opting to create another show, "The Apprentice," with Burnett, he insisted they offer the show first to Braun and ABC. Two minutes into the pitch—aspiring business tycoons vie for a job in the Trump organization— Braun jumped up from his sofa and said, "Done. I'll take it. We want it." He and Burnett shook hands and hugged each other to seal the deal.

Then "The Apprentice" was turned over to business affairs and ABC's bureaucracy. At $1.5 million per episode, with a projected fifteen episodes, ABC didn't have the money in its budget for Braun to approve the show on his own. It would need Iger's approval (budgetary discretion was crucial to Eisner's and Iger's ultimate control over the network). ABC negotiators tried to get Burnett to lower the price. Exasperated, he took the show to NBC, where programming head Jeff Zucker, who had virtually unfettered authority to make programming decisions, immediately bought it. Braun was furious when he found out, both because ABC had lost the show and because Burnett gave him no advance warning that he was going to NBC.

After the blowup in Eisner's office, the email from Iger accusing Braun of insubordination, and now this, relations between Braun and Iger, never warm, deteriorated even further. There was palpable tension between the two in every meeting. Morale at ABC suffered as speculation swirled that Braun would quit or be fired. Finally, on a Thursday just after the November sweeps, Iger asked Braun to dinner at Vincente, a popular restaurant near Iger's Brentwood residence. Braun agreed. But he came prepared with a litany of complaints that he had discussed with Lyne. "I don't know how this will play out," he told her. "I can make these just from me, or from both of us. It's your call."

Lyne said she'd back him, and that he could say they were from both of them.

When Braun arrived at the restaurant, he held out his hand, but Iger refused to shake it. "I hope you're up for this," Iger said, "because I'm going to let you have it." They were seated, and Iger continued, "This is the most dysfunctional relationship I've ever had. You don't respect me. You don't like me. It's unacceptable."

"Really?" Braun said. "Well, maybe you need to know why. Do you want to know?"

"Yeah," Iger said.

Braun pulled out some notes he made and said he had several major problems. "Lack of character; incompetence; taking credit for things you had nothing to do with; and running away from decisions you made." Saying that Lyne agreed with him, Braun started citing specific allegations in each category, from the mishandling of "Millionaire" to "8 Simple Rules," as Iger grew visibly more angry. Braun said Iger deserved little or no credit for ABC's few successes.

"What about 'Bachelor'?" Iger countered.

"You did shit on 'Bachelor'!" Braun exclaimed, his voice rising. "You didn't even know about it until we were half done shooting it."

At this point Iger was so angry that he gestured with his arm, hitting a passing waiter who was carrying coffee. The waiter stumbled, spilling coffee down Iger's shirtfront, ruining his tie.

"Can we just go home?" Braun said. "Nothing good is going to come from this."

They got up without having eaten and left. They waited in silence on the sidewalk for the valets to bring their cars.

Braun stayed home the next day. He consulted his lawyer, saying he expected to be fired. Eisner replied to his email, proposing a meeting, saying that given how Braun had treated Iger in recent months, a meeting would be a good idea. But he refused to see Braun alone, arguing it would just turn into another personality conflict.

Accounts of the ill-fated dinner spread rapidly through the ranks at ABC. Susan Lyne and others worried that things had blown up so quickly that Braun hadn't been able to get his message across. Lyne was so worried Braun would be fired that she went to see Iger that Friday. She spent two hours with him, trying, in a measured and calm way, to underscore how important Braun was to the network and how much he did to boost morale. At the same time, she was candid in her assessment of Iger. Echoing sentiments that were widespread at ABC, she told him that his presence at the network had become a "dark cloud" because he always seemed negative, and that he kept demanding that they fix things while conveying skepticism that they could. "The Bob Iger who hired me, who got me to ABC, who was trained and guided by Tom Murphy, is gone," she said, her tone one of sadness more than criticism.

It was a sobering message. Iger looked anguished, and finally said, "You don't know how hard it is to do the job that I have. Working for Michael is very different from working for Tom."

Over the weekend, Eisner sent another email to both Braun and Iger. "Can we all please just take a deep breath and calm down?" he wrote. And then, on Monday, Iger struck a conciliatory note, acknowledging that it was healthy to discuss their differences, and joking that he'd ruined his tie.

Braun went to the Giorgio Armani boutique in Beverly Hills, picked out a tie, and sent it to Iger with a note: "A fresh start requires a new tie."

Braun and Iger had lunch the next day. The tone was civil, conciliatory. They agreed to try to work together. That weekend, Eisner invited Braun to meet him at his home. "How did it get to this point?" Eisner asked, referring to Braun's relationship with Iger.

"It's not productive at this point to get into it," Braun replied. "I dealt with this with Bob. I didn't run to you. It got horrible, but let's just leave it at that."

Eisner pressed him for more details, but Braun held fast. He didn't want to get between Iger and Eisner.

The next week, Iger told Braun that Eisner had told him about the meeting. "He said you wouldn't trash me," Iger reported.

Part Three

———

DISNEYWAR

SIXTEEN

On November 20, 2003, a week before Thanksgiving, Roy Disney met with John Bryson at the bar in Pasadena where Bryson broke the news that Roy would not be renominated to the Disney board. After Roy abruptly ended the discussion and walked out, Bryson called Eisner. "Roy seemed shocked," he reported. "Roy said it was like we stuck a knife in his heart."

Eisner felt uneasy. This didn't sound good. He wondered if Bryson had been the right person to handle this. Had he been too blunt? If Eisner had been the one to deliver the news, he would have soft-pedaled it a little, left some "air" in the situation, maybe given his famous "elastic no."

"I think we've got a problem here," Eisner said. "I'd say we tested the water and the water is cold."

"Yeah," Bryson agreed. He said he had told Roy that he would discuss the matter with the committee and get back to him.

After the call, Eisner spoke to public relations executive Gershon Kekst, a longtime adviser who was also concerned about Roy's reaction. "I don't see why you'd want to put the Disney name into the battle," Kekst said, urging Eisner to back off. Zenia Mucha, Disney's head of public relations, also advised that alienating Roy was a mistake.

Eisner called Gold, hoping to defuse things a little. "Stanley, I think we need to discuss Roy," Eisner said. "I'm not sure Bryson gave him all the information about this. Maybe it's not a done deal."

"Have Bryson call me," Gold said coolly. He told Roy the decision wasn't final, and he thought something might be worked out to salvage Roy's board membership.

After Bryson spoke to his fellow members of the nomination and governance committee—Lozano, Estrin, and Wilson—he reported that the committee remained firm in its determination to force Roy off the board. If the rule were applied inconsistently—forcing off Murphy and Watson, but giving Roy a reprieve, or not applied at all—Disney might be open to criticism.

In this matter Eisner has portrayed himself as simply bowing to the will of the committee. Other board members confirm that at this juncture, they were so annoyed with Gold and Roy and what they considered their disruptive tactics that, having come this far, they were determined to press forward. But given Eisner's influence over the committee and the board as a whole, there can be little doubt that had Eisner wanted to keep Roy on the board, he could have. There were obvious alternatives: as chairman of animation, Roy was a management director, and thus not subject to mandatory retirement; or the board could simply have raised the mandatory retirement age to seventy-five for all directors, which would have given Roy three more years.

When Gold actually spoke with Bryson, the conversation went nowhere. Bryson said the committee had again discussed the issue and concluded that Roy would not be renominated. The committee's decision was final.

Even so, the committee's decision would have to be approved by the full board. Though the board had never overruled the committee, it was theoretically possible that Roy could prevail. But Bryson and Eisner quietly contacted the other board members to brief them and make sure they were on board. Eisner was confident he wouldn't have to worry about a board revolt.

When Roy returned from the drink with John Bryson, Patty Disney could tell her husband was in shock. All four of their children gathered on the yellow floral sofas in the formal living room at the Toluca Lake home, and along with their parents, discussed for hours what had happened and how Roy should react. In the ensuing days, Roy met regularly with his advisers at Shamrock—Gold, of course; Clifford Miller, the PR adviser who had helped advise them in 1984; an outside lawyer, David Robbins; and a younger executive, Mike McConnell, a former investment banker and teacher who had helped prepare the September 24 boardroom presentation. "No one can force me off or make me quit," Roy declared at the outset. "I'd rather leave first."

The board's action galvanized the extended Disney family in ways Roy hadn't anticipated. On impulse, he picked up the phone the day after Thanksgiving and called Diane, who was with Ron Miller at their Silverado vineyard in Napa Valley. The cousins rarely spoke, and had not been close since the events of 1984 that culminated in Miller's ouster. But Roy was working on "Destino," an unfinished animated short begun by Walt and Salvador Dalí in 1945. Diane had sent him an image of Walt and the surrealist painter, and had mentioned that she'd met Salvador Dalí at their house. Roy had written back that she should be interviewed for the DVD version of the film.

When Diane answered the phone, Roy said he wanted to thank her for the Dalí image, adding that the short had turned out so well that some people were talking about it as a possible Oscar nominee. But then he said he had some bad news. "I've been asked to step down from the board," he said, describing the painful meeting with Bryson.

Despite the strains in the family, Diane felt an immediate wave of sympathy for her cousin. He was so much more invested in the Disney company than she and Ron were, and she could tell how dispirited he was. "That's terrible," she said. "You shouldn't be treated like this."

"Well, they'll probably call me the 'idiot nephew' again," Roy said, sounding even more dejected.

"Roy," Diane said firmly, "I want you to know that in our family, that was never said."

"I think it came from Card Walker," Roy volunteered.

"I do, too," Diane agreed. They chatted for a few moments, and Diane asked Roy to keep her informed.

By then, Roy, Patty, and their four children had all agreed that Roy had no choice but to resign rather than be forced off. Roy and his advisers labored over Roy's letter of resignation. In contrast to Gold's presentation to the board, Roy didn't want to dwell on Disney's financial performance, its slumping earnings, or stagnant stock price. These things, per se, weren't as important to him. He had always felt, as Walt had, that if you provided quality products that the public enjoyed and wanted, then profits would follow. Roy didn't like to think in financial terms; indeed, he felt Eisner's drive for short-term profits, a near-obsession over 20 percent annual growth, was at the root of many of Disney's problems. In Roy's sometimes romantic view, Disney at heart was a creative company, and creativity had to be the engine of profit growth.

On November 30, 2003, the Sunday after Thanksgiving, Roy had the letter hand-delivered to Eisner, who was at his apartment in the Pierre hotel in New York. Copies of the letter were faxed to *The Wall Street Journal, The New York Times,* the *Los Angeles Times,* and other media outlets, as well as to all board members. Open warfare had begun.

*   *   *

In New York, Eisner was watching a football game on television. He was feeling far more relaxed than usual. He'd taken a day off, and he and Jane had visited the branch of the Smithsonian Museum on Fifth Avenue, and then he'd walked five miles through the city. He was beginning to think about his annual letter to shareholders, and there was a board meeting the next week when he could expect another awkward confrontation with Gold and Roy. But for now he could relax.

Then a chime went off on his computer signaling an urgent email. When he went to the monitor, he saw a message from Zenia Mucha: "Urgent. Call me. What are we going to do about Roy's resignation?"

Resignation? What was she talking about? Then Eisner thought he heard something at the entrance to the apartment. When he got to the entry, he saw an envelope had been thrust under the door.

> Dear Michael,
>
> It is with deep sadness and regret that I send you this letter of resignation from the Walt Disney Company, both as Chairman of the Feature Animation Division and as Vice Chairman of the Board of Directors.
>
> You well know that you and I have had serious differences of opinion about the direction and style of management in the Company in recent years. For whatever reason, you have driven a wedge between me and those I work with even to the extent of requiring some of my associates to report my conversations and activities back to you. I find this intolerable.
>
> Finally, you discussed with the Nominating Committee of the Board of Directors its decision to leave my name off the slate of directors to be elected in the coming year, effectively muzzling my voice on the board—much as you did with Andrea Van de Kamp last year.
>
> Michael, I believe your conduct has resulted from my clear and unambiguous statements to you and to the board of directors that after 19 years at the helm you are no longer the best person to run the Walt Disney Company. You had a very successful first 10-plus years at the company in partnership with Frank Wells, for which I salute you. But, since Frank's untimely death in 1994, the Company has lost its focus, its creative energy, and its heritage.

Roy identified various ways in which Eisner had "failed": ABC prime time; the Family channel; his "micromanagement" and resulting "loss of morale"; his "timidity" in building new theme parks "on the cheap"; a "creative brain drain"; poor relations with creative partners such as Pixar and Miramax; and the lack of a succession plan.

> Michael, it is my sincere belief that it is you who should be leaving and not me. Accordingly, I once again call for your resignation or retirement. The Walt Disney Company deserves fresh, energetic leadership at this challenging time in its history just as it did in 1984 when I headed a restructuring which resulted in your recruitment to the Company.
>
> I have and will always have an enormous allegiance and respect for this Company, founded by my uncle, Walt, and father, Roy, and to our faithful employees and loyal stockholders. I don't know if you and the other directors can comprehend how painful it is for me and the extended Disney family to arrive at this decision. . . .

> With sincere regret,
> Roy E. Disney

On one hand, Eisner wasn't surprised. Events had been pointing to something like this for over a year. In a sense it was a relief. The gauntlet had been thrown, and Roy had been forced into the open. It was also exciting. Eisner felt his adrenaline pumping. He felt he was at his best in a crisis, calm and focused.

Bob Iger was planning to enjoy a rare quiet Sunday afternoon with his wife at the Neue Galerie, the museum of Austrian art and culture on Fifth Avenue, but he had barely walked in when he felt his cell phone vibrate. He went outside to take the call. It was Eisner. Roy had resigned. He had just read Roy's letter and had spoken to Zenia Mucha. Bruce Orwall was calling from *The Wall Street Journal* seeking comment.

It was a lot for Iger to absorb. He saw his Sunday evaporating. Eisner asked him to join him at the Pierre as soon as possible. They'd have to draft a press release and plan strategy. He was also summoning Mucha; Alan Braverman, the general counsel; and his own assistant, Chris Curtin. They were all in New York for the upcoming board meeting. They quickly decided that Roy was trying to make Eisner the issue, and therefore Eisner himself should stay above the fray. Instead they would portray this as an attack on the company and its entire board, an issue of corporate governance, with Roy trying to block needed reforms, not of management's performance. They would not respond to Roy's specific allegations, since that would inevitably put the spotlight on Eisner and management. George Mitchell, the presiding director, was chosen to issue the statement the group drafted.

Whether he yet realized it, Mitchell was being drawn into a precarious position. As a director, he owed a fiduciary duty to shareholders—not to Eisner or other Disney executives. He was now being asked to lend his reputation, bolstered by his Nobel Peace Prize for negotiating a truce in Northern Ireland, to defend Eisner and Disney management against Roy's charges. Mitchell issued a statement:

> The Governance and Nominating Committee recently informed Mr. Disney of its judgment that the mandatory age limits of the company's Corporate Governance Guidelines, which had previously been unanimously approved by the Board, should be applied to him and two other Board members, Thomas S. Murphy and Raymond Watson. It is unfortunate that the Committee's judgment to apply these unanimously adopted governance rules has become an occasion to raise again criticisms of the direction of the Company, and calls for change of management, that have been previously rejected by the Board.

The group spent considerable time trying to anticipate what would come next. Where was Gold in this picture? How would they deal with him at the board meeting? The situation promised to be exceedingly awkward now that Roy had resigned. How could the board discuss a counteroffensive, with Gold telling everything to Roy, not to mention leaking to the press? Somehow, Gold would have to be neutralized.

And, in typical fashion, Eisner ruminated on his long relationship with Roy, amazed that after all he had done to protect Roy, and to show him respect, Roy—the "idiot nephew"—would now turn against him. Eisner remained convinced that it was all Gold's doing, and that Gold was acting out of selfish motives—still bitter that he hadn't been offered Wells's job; angry that Eisner wouldn't buy back the Basses' Disney shares; disgruntled that Eisner wouldn't "listen" to him.

For the next week, Eisner's apartment in the Pierre became the "command center." The inner circle, joined by outside PR consultants and lawyers, met every day to plot strategy. But no one was really worried, least of all Eisner. What could Roy and Gold do? This wasn't 1984. Roy and Gold weren't up against a weakened chief executive like Ron Miller; they didn't have the threat of a hostile takeover behind them, or the support of anyone else on the board. There wasn't going to be any boardroom coup, not with this board. It was too late to mount a proxy contest to elect new directors; Disney's 2004 annual meeting was in March, and under Disney's bylaws, the deadline for submitting the names of alternate candidates was less than three weeks away. Anyway, Disney shares were so widely held that a proxy contest would be prohibitively expensive, and probably doomed.

All Roy had, really, was the Disney name.

At the Shamrock offices in Burbank, discussion turned to how Stanley Gold should react. By remaining on the board, he would continue to have access to confidential financial information, as well as insights into the board's thinking. But he would also be muzzled by confidentiality agreements and fiduciary obligations. Roy argued that Gold would be isolated, excluded from important committee meetings and "executive sessions." Before Roy resigned from the board in 1984, he'd been the only dissenting voice, and it had been frustrating and lonely. Far better for Gold and Roy to be free to wage an all-out campaign. In Roy's view, the decision to purge him from the board was a declaration of war. They needed to wage it with every means at their disposal. Still, the group decided that they'd gauge the reaction to Roy's resignation before making a final decision.

The official Disney response, coming as it did from Mitchell, speaking on behalf of the board, convinced Gold that there was no point in his remaining. The following day, he resigned, issuing a letter that, in contrast to Roy's, was focused on criticism of his fellow board members.

"It is with regret that I resign effective immediately," Gold began,

and second Roy Disney's call for the removal of Michael Eisner as Chairman and CEO. I am proud of my more than 15 years of service and my role in reshaping the Company in 1984 by bringing Frank Wells and Michael Eisner to the Company. I do, however, lament that my effort over the past three years to implement needed changes has only succeeded in creating an insular board of directors serving as a bulwark to shield management from criticism and accountability. . . .

As for the decision to oust Roy from the board,

The real reason for the committee's action is that Roy has become more pointed and vocal in his criticism of Michael Eisner and this board. This is yet another attempt by this board to squelch dissent by hiding behind the veil of "good governance." What a curious result.

Roy has devoted a lifetime to Disney as both an employee and director. He has served with renewed vigor during these times of malaise, disappointment and instability at the Company, trying to maintain the morale of employees, focusing on the magic that makes Disney special and attacking bonuses to the CEO and increased compensation for board members while the company falters and shareholder value erodes. . . .

The board seems determined to devote its time and energies to adopting policies that . . . only serve to muzzle and isolate those directors who recognize that their role is to be active participants in shaping the Company and planning for executive succession. Further, this board isolates those directors who believe that Michael Eisner (when measured by the dismal results over the last 7 years) is not up to the challenge.

Perhaps acting independently, from outside the boardroom, not hamstrung by a recently enacted board policy barring board members from communicating with shareholders and the media, I can have greater success in shaping the policies, practices and operations of Disney than I had as a member of the board.

Eisner may have succeeded in barring Roy from any meaningful role at the animation division, but the company's animators were among the first to rally to his cause. Dave Pruiksma, the supervising animator for *Beauty and the Beast* (he also drew Mrs. Potts and Chip) and *Lion King* (he drew Pumbaa), and Academy Award nominees Tim Hauser, a writer, and Steve Moore, a director, issued a letter the day after Roy's letter became public. It was not just an endorsement of Roy, but a window into the thinking of a critical contingent of Disney's creative artists, as well as confirmation of the crisis in morale that Roy had been trying to bring to the board's attention:

We, the undersigned members of the animation community, wish to lend our full support to Roy E. Disney and Stanley Gold as they seek to uphold the traditions of excellence that once defined the Disney name. [Roy] protected the Feature Animation division from the new studio brass, who did not sense its continued potential. Without Roy, the Little Mermaid, Beauty and the Beast, Aladdin and The Lion King would never have come to be, let alone the company's artistic renaissance and financial turnaround.

But after a string of critical and box office successes, animation artists were increasingly locked out of leadership roles. In the new corporate template we became little more than factory workers or unskilled laborers at the studio we had helped rebuild. Micro-managers from outside the medium fostered a highly toxic work environment, spawning a creative malaise that continues unchecked.

The unique traditions of visual storytelling, humor and personality animation on which the Walt Disney Studio had thrived, gave way to politically correct sloganeering, stale one-liners and film seminar formulae to which audiences have refused to respond. Mr. Eisner's rejection of Walt Disney's heritage has been a colossal failure. Yet this is a man who has been paid over $700 million in compensation since 1996, while the feature animation department has been decimated by pink slips.

Now, skilled craftsmen go unemployed while the executive ranks swell. A unique American art form, the Disney cartoon feature, hangs precariously in the balance—reduced to the production of cheap direct-to-video franchise extensions made by committee.

Without Roy, who will protect the 70-year Disney legacy from becoming no more than a hollow brand?

Within two weeks of the letter's appearance, 4,500 present and former Disney animators—nearly everyone who had worked there—had added their names as signatories.

The letter's salvo at Eisner, especially its harsh attack on micromanagement, did not go unnoticed, nor did it earn the animators any goodwill from Eisner. Weeks later, on January 12, Disney announced that it was shutting down its Orlando animation unit, where *Lilo & Stitch* had been created.

On Thursday evening, December 4, 2003, a phalanx of limousines blocks the driveway to the Century Plaza Hotel, a curving high-rise in the middle of Century City, long the favored venue for Hollywood celebrity tributes and fund-raising benefits. Tonight, Motion Picture Association chairman and chief executive Jack Valenti is presenting the Pioneer of the Year award to Eisner, a benefit for the Will Rogers Institute, considered among the film industry's highest honors. Previous honorees have included Cecil B. DeMille, Jack Warner, Darryl Zanuck, and Sumner Redstone. Only now, nineteen years into his tenure as Disney chairman, is Eisner receiving the honor. He had previously declined invitations, insisting he found such events embarrassing, not to mention the fact that he was too young. But at the behest of Dick Cook, eager to enhance goodwill with the film community, and given the need to burnish his own public image, Eisner has relented.

The timing seems auspicious: Every guest is handed DVDs of *Nemo* and

Pirates, whose huge box-office success is propelling Disney toward a record $3 billion year at the box office, as well as boosting just-released fourth-quarter earnings in which profit more than doubled and operating earnings rose 54 percent. But as women in evening gowns and men in business suits pass through security checks and gather for cocktails, everyone is buzzing about Roy Disney and Stanley Gold, who were certainly not on the guest list.

"Michael, I know it's been a long week," Phil Collins, the singer and composer of the score for *Tarzan,* among other Disney projects, says into the microphone as he kicks off the entertainment. "We're here to help you forget all that."

At the center of the ceremony is a filmed tribute to Eisner, with testimony from Steve Martin, Tim Allen, John Travolta, and both Harvey and Bob Weinstein of Miramax (despite their ongoing disputes). Even Jeffrey Katzenberg had gotten a call from a secretary in Eisner's office, asking if he would participate by contributing a segment to the tribute to Eisner. Katzenberg could only wonder what was going through Eisner's mind. He and Eisner weren't on speaking terms, and he was also insulted that a secretary had made the request. He didn't return the call. (Eisner says that he expressly said that Katzenberg was not to be asked, but that someone in his office must have been overzealous.)

There are other conspicuous absences. By tradition, other media and entertainment chief executives gather to pay their respects, but few are in attendance. A topic of speculation is the amount of last-minute arm-twisting Dick Cook and others at Disney had to perform to fill the tables. There is star power in evidence: I'm seated next to Jamie Lee Curtis, star of *Freaky Friday,* and at the same table as Diane Lane, star of *Under the Tuscan Sun,* both Disney productions, along with Disney's studio president Nina Jacobson. Curtis is funny and charming. "You sure have something to write about," she observes as we sit down. A few tables away I see Demi Moore and Ashton Kutcher, who is starring in a forthcoming Disney film. But I don't see anyone I recognize who isn't in some way beholden to Disney. Eisner is at a central table in the well of the ballroom, in front of the stage, surrounded by Jane, his sons, Bob Iger, and Willow Bay.

Jack Valenti, in dinner jacket and his trademark white coiffure, bounds onto the stage, seeming to defy the passage of time, and notes that he first met Eisner as a "tall, gangly twenty-something at ABC," who had "a fresh, assertive manner spilling over with a torrent of a dozen creative ideas a minute."

Within Eisner, he continues, "stir the molecular contradictions of business executive and creative artist, a marriage of fire and chaos, which Michael has brought into fluid harmony. That this unseemly combination has worked to the long-term interest of the Walt Disney Company is beyond doubt. Let me phrase it this way—in a manner that every Wall Street fiscal analyst (at least those not under indictment) can understand: If you invested $10,000 in the Disney company on the day that Michael became its leader and never sold a share, you would have today the tidy sum of $220,000! And that was before *Nemo* was found on DVD. When Michael became Disney's chief, its market cap was $2.1 billion. Today, December 4, 2003, it's $48 billion. . . .

"Finally, there is another side to Michael and Jane Eisner. Beneath a canopy of anonymity, they have given millions to causes that count to them—and to this country. They have never sought gratitude or press headlines for this. They give because they care, without a need for public plaudits.

"I count Michael as one of the great giants of our industry."

To warm applause, Eisner rises from his table and comes to the stage. "Let me just say to Phil Collins that it's been a great week." He mentions that his son has just been hired to direct a big-budget film for Paramount, that his two other sons have joined him for the dinner, along with his wife, and so, "to say that I have had anything but a wonderful week would be an understatement. Let me say that I do believe what we do is very important. The entertainment that we deliver, the movies that we make are the cultural legacy on which our country is founded and on which it stands. What we do . . . is a testament to individual creativity. This country stands above any place in the world . . . the hope we have for the future is the creativity that evolves out of the democratic process.

"I thank Jack. I thank the Motion Picture Pioneers and intend to be here in thirty years in my wheelchair applauding some other person who will be getting this award."

As Eisner is making his way back to his table, pausing to shake a few hands, people are streaming toward the exits. Curtis has already excused herself, leaving before Eisner's remarks. As the lights come up, I expect to see Eisner surrounded by well-wishers, but the only people near him are his wife and sons, and by the time I work my way to the table, his sons have also departed, as have Iger and his wife. As Eisner gazes at the rapidly emptying room, I step into the breach, and he thanks me for coming. It's the first time we've met since Roy's resignation. I congratulate him on the award, and ask how he's feeling. "Great," he replied. "I'm at my best in a crisis. I love a good fight." He does seem energized, and eager to talk, but then Jane takes his elbow.

"It's time to go," she says, leading him toward a rear entrance.

*   *   *

"I've always believed that good news shouldn't wait," Eisner wrote that year in his annual letter to shareholders. Buoyed by the box-office success of *Nemo* and *Pirates,* Eisner could extol a 36 percent gain in Disney's stock price and an over 50 percent improvement in cash flow, a welcome change from the previous two years' glum results. He devoted considerable space to Mission: SPACE at Disney World; to *Pirates;* to ESPN, reporting overall ratings gains of 13 percent for ESPN, making it the number one basic cable network; and to the Disney channel, the number one cable channel among kids aged six to fourteen.

As for the struggling ABC Network, Eisner wrote, "The network is slowly but surely dealing with its financial and ratings performance issues. In 2003 we stabilized its primetime ratings and established a solid foundation for future growth." He praised ABC's "strategic emphasis on comedy," and noted that "this strategy plays to ABC's historic strengths, since the network was known for its strong comedy lineup throughout its years as the number one network."

The only mention of ABC Family was that it had been "integrated into our cable organization so that all of our cable holdings can work more effectively together." And there was no mention at all of Roy Disney or Stanley Gold.

Cold Mountain opened on Christmas Day 2003. Weinstein had never found the partner he promised Disney. He had managed to sell the foreign rights— no small feat for a film about the American Civil War—but only for $30 million. Reviews were generally admiring, but not positive enough to turn it into a major hit. The film grossed a respectable $95 million in the United States, but didn't make back its costs, confirming Eisner's apprehensions that a Civil War costume drama would have limited appeal. Still, it came close to turning a profit, and may well do so over time. The real issue was that Eisner, Peter Murphy, and Dick Cook felt that Harvey Weinstein had brazenly defied them and breached his contract. It hardly enhanced the tone of their ongoing negotiations.

During the first week in January 2004, Steve Burke, now president of Comcast; Brian Roberts, Comcast's chairman; other top executives and a group of investment bankers and advisers gathered at the Marriott hotel near the

Philadelphia airport, a site where they were unlikely to be noticed. In case anyone did, the ostensible purpose of the meeting was to discuss Comcast's "strategic direction." But this was clearly no routine meeting. Among those attending were major deal-makers, including the Quadrangle Group's Steve Rattner, who'd hosted the media conference where Eisner was interviewed by Charlie Rose.

When Burke left Disney to join Comcast, the cable operator had 4.5 million subscribers. By 2002 it had nearly doubled, to 8.5 million. Then it had doggedly pursued and ultimately succeeded in buying the cable assets of distressed AT&T, making Comcast the largest cable operator in the country, with 21.3 million subscribers. Despite widespread skepticism on Wall Street, Comcast had successfully integrated AT&T's far-flung cable operations, an undertaking directed by Burke, and its stock had nearly doubled from its low in 2002. Comcast was now seen as a major deal-maker, and with the AT&T merger behind it, was ready for something new.

Alone among the biggest cable companies, Comcast was an almost pure "distribution" company, exactly the kind of company that Eisner had derided as being from a "different planet" from "content" companies like Disney. Time Warner, the second largest cable operator, had major content holdings in its Warner Bros., HBO, and CNN operations, and Fox under Rupert Murdoch had DirecTV as well as its studio and network operations. By contrast, Comcast derived 95 percent of its revenue from cable, with the remainder coming from its modest part-ownership of the E!, Outdoor Life, and Golf channels (E! in partnership with Disney). But now Comcast had 21.5 million subscribers, with 20 million considered the critical mass necessary to launch a profitable cable channel. That meant that Comcast could launch programming on its own cable systems.

This had taken on more urgency the previous summer, when France's Vivendi put its Universal Studio on the block. Roberts and Burke had spent three months analyzing the Universal assets, and had grown increasingly excited about the potential for a Comcast-Universal combination. But once General Electric entered the bidding, the price soared. Roberts and Burke thought it was too expensive, and Comcast never surfaced with a bid.

Nevertheless, the experience had fundamentally changed Roberts's and Burke's thinking about the future of Comcast. They met with investment bankers to consider the options, which were limited: Fox, Time Warner, Viacom, Sony, Universal, and Disney. None was for sale, and all posed formidable obstacles—except possibly Disney. It was, of course, a company that Burke knew well, but he initially opposed the idea. He argued to Roberts and

Comcast's board that the theme parks offered limited synergy and, post-September 11, was going to be a tough business. It was not a business that held any interest for Comcast, and yet it produced 40 percent of Disney's cash flow. Network television also looked to be a wasting asset. Not to mention an entrenched management and a board that seemed to be Eisner's captive.

But then Roy and Gold resigned, suggesting instability on the Disney board. Shortly after, Dennis Hersch, a partner at the prominent New York law firm of Davis, Polk & Wardwell, and a longtime adviser to Comcast, said he knew someone who was close to George Mitchell, the Disney board's presiding director. This person had reported a curious conversation with Mitchell in which Mitchell had allegedly said, "I've got a problem. Michael Eisner is exhausted. He's looking for a graceful exit." Mitchell had further ruminated that Eisner should have left two years ago, adding that several Disney board members agreed with this assessment.

Was Mitchell suggesting that a merger with Comcast might be the "graceful exit" Eisner was looking for? This was electrifying news to Roberts and Burke. He had assumed that Eisner would be a nearly insurmountable obstacle to any deal, but this suggested he might even welcome it. Still, knowing Eisner, it was hard to believe. How should they proceed? Comcast's board met for dinner in Philadelphia on December 16, and after hearing about the latest developments, agreed that Hersch should have the intermediary approach Mitchell again to gauge the board's appetite for a Comcast-Disney merger. To preserve confidentiality, no one but Hersch would know the identity of the intermediary, who was someone close to Mitchell. The first approach was made the next day, on December 17.

A week or so later, Roberts, Burke, and Hersch had lunch to discuss the results of the latest contacts with Mitchell, which included several conversations with the intermediary. Hersch had stressed the success of Comcast's merger with AT&T, and reported that Mitchell had agreed that "this makes a lot of sense," referring to the marriage of content and distribution. "Murdoch is putting a lot of pressure on us," Mitchell had added, referring to Rupert Murdoch and the vertically integrated News Corporation.

As the Comcast executives and their advisers gathered at the Philadelphia Marriott in January 2004, it appeared that the Walt Disney Company might indeed be for sale. Burke swept aside his reservations about the theme parks and the network, and argued that under these circumstances, this was a unique, probably once-in-a-lifetime opportunity to acquire a major entertainment company and one of America's most esteemed brands, not to mention a chance for Burke to run the company where he'd once worked.

"What do we do next?" Roberts asked. "Let's go out there," Burke suggested, and meet with Eisner in Los Angeles.

The intermediary again approached Mitchell, and this time reported that Mitchell had replied, "Michael doesn't want a meeting. Maybe there's another way. . . . Maybe I should do it," Mitchell had told the intermediary. "I don't know . . . Can you give me some more information on Comcast?" Then, in another conversation, he said, "Well, why doesn't Comcast just write a letter to me and the board. We can take it from there." At this juncture, Mitchell reported the contact to Eisner, who wrote an email to Disney board members. "I want you to be aware of Comcast chatter," he said. "On January 15, George Mitchell reported that a friend came to him and asked as a favor if they could have dinner with George and me. Last week the friend came back asking for lunch just with George. He responded in accordance with guidelines for directors. The guidelines are: call Michael if you want to discuss this issue, but Disney is very comfortable with its current strategy."

There was concern at Comcast that Mitchell, however skilled a politician and diplomat, was out of his depth in the rarefied world of mergers and acquisitions. They were also in the highly unusual position of negotiating through not one but two intermediaries, the identity of one of whom they didn't even know.

"Does Mitchell understand this?" Burke asked, somewhat skeptical. "He's not an investment banker. A letter from us will have to become public. In effect, it's a bid."

"Yes," Hersch insisted. "He's got a lawyer advising him." Indeed, Mitchell had said, "Let me assure you," that such a letter would be "welcomed" by the Disney board.

Academy Award nominations were announced on January 27, and Disney/Pixar's *Finding Nemo*, received four—Best Animated Feature, Best Original Screenplay, Best Original Score, and Best Sound Editing. Roy Disney was also nominated for Best Animated Short Subject, for "Destino." *Nemo*'s worldwide box office was approaching $1 billion, eclipsing Disney's *Lion King* as the highest-grossing animated film ever.

For Disney however, the ongoing, runaway success of *Nemo* was double-edged. While it was boosting the Disney studio's revenues to a record $3 billion, it had also, as Eisner had feared, emboldened Pixar and its mercurial chairman, Steve Jobs, to demand more from Disney in the already contentious negotiations to extend their agreement. Just two weeks before, Disney had rejected the latest proposal, in which Pixar wanted exclusive rights to sequels, in addition to earlier demands for a far greater share of the profits and to include the films *The Incredibles* and *Cars* in the new deal. But Eisner and Dick Cook expected Pixar to come back with a revised proposal.

Instead, two days after the Academy Award nominations, Jobs called Cook and told him he was terminating discussions. He issued a statement to the press: "After ten months of trying to strike a deal with Disney, we're moving on. We've had a great run together—one of the most successful in Hollywood history—and it's a shame that Disney won't be participating in Pixar's future successes."

Eisner in turn issued a conciliatory response: "We have had a fantastic partnership with Pixar and wish Steve Jobs and the wonderfully creative team there, led by John Lasseter, much success in the future. Although we would have enjoyed continuing our successful collaboration under mutually acceptable terms, Pixar understandably has chosen to go its own way to grow as an independent company."

After calling Cook, Jobs called Roy Disney. He conceded that Disney was the logical partner for Pixar, but said, "I can never make a deal with Disney as long as Michael Eisner is there."

Roy commiserated with him. "When the Wicked Witch is dead, we'll be together again."

I am scheduled to see Eisner in New York the next day, and am surprised that, in the wake of the Pixar news, his office calls to confirm rather than cancel. The press had been uniformly negative for Eisner, even though Disney had dispatched both Iger and chief financial officer Tom Staggs to make the argument that Pixar was asking Disney to give up more potential revenue from *Incredibles* and *Cars* than it could hope to earn from distributing future Pixar films. When I arrive I can tell Eisner has been shaken by the Pixar setback, which he says he doesn't want to talk about. He invites me to join him that afternoon at a "table read" of a new Broadway musical version of *Tarzan*. "This is what I really care about, not all this shit," he says, referring to the press coverage of the Pixar breakdown.

Rarely if ever have I heard Eisner use any kind of expletive. Then he does talk about Pixar, sounding exasperated. He argues that he was in a no-win situation: had he done a deal on Pixar's terms, he would have been criticized for giving away the store; now that talks have broken down, he's being criticized for not saving the deal. "I said to Steve Jobs, 'We'll make the same deal as any other studio going forward.' I'll give you the letter we gave them! His board members can't believe they let this deal go. Every [Disney] board member emailed me," Eisner asserts. He says the Disney board, including Roy and Gold, unanimously rejected the terms proposed by Pixar. "Is it a ploy?" Eisner asks rhetorically. "It could be. I told the board, sixty-forty he'll still make a deal."

The Pixar situation has played into Roy's and Gold's hands, and the two have been widely quoted in the media commenting on the breakdown of the negotiations. "This just proves, sadly, that we're right," Roy told the *Los Angeles Times*. "Our point is that if we had cultivated this relationship for the past five years you would never have gotten to where you are now. This is bad long-term management."

Eisner continues to dismiss Roy and Gold as ineffectual gadflies, but the strategy group is meeting every day for at least fifteen minutes, in person or by phone. Eisner seems genuinely baffled, if not hurt, that Roy has publicly turned against him.

"Roy did nothing in animation," Eisner tells me, stressing the word *nothing*. "Jeffrey Katzenberg and I did it. I spent my life encouraging people to be nice to Roy. Frank Wells would say, 'Roy wants to do this.' I'd say, 'Why not?' Jeffrey never learned. I told him, 'Be nice to him. If you can be nice to Jack Nicholson and Warren Beatty, you can be nice to Roy.' Jeffrey said, 'I don't have time.' "

"I spent seventeen years indulging him," Eisner says of Roy. "Little things: Could I be on the 'voice' committee [which determines the voices appropriate for the animated characters]? I came down on anyone who didn't respect him. After fifty years, he thought he'd earned respect. The reality was, I demanded it. It was in our interest. I had him at the theme parks, I made him the Holy Ghost of the Trinity of Disney. But I never let him do anything."

Eisner tells me an anecdote about his grandparents. "My grandfather rescued Jews from Germany. Then Hungary. He brought Jews to this country. My grandmother would say, 'They never even sent me a thank-you note! They weren't appreciative.' I thought, you don't do it for the appreciation. You saved their lives! They're assimilated. Don't expect them to thank and honor you. Just let them be." He adds that his grandmother always tipped waiters before rather than after the meal. "You get better service," she'd told him.

In contrast to his grandmother, Eisner says he neither sought nor expected any thanks from Roy. Still, he never thought he would turn against him. "Roy and Patty do not know what I had to do to change Roy's image in the company," he says. He launches into the saga of *Fantasia 2000*, his attempt to get Leonard Bernstein involved before the maestro's death, and describes how the animators "revolted" against his idea for the "Pomp and Circumstance" sequence, and the idea that Disney characters might have babies. "I can't really blame Roy for *Fantasia*," Eisner concedes, but then proceeds: "All my ideas disappeared. So I gave up. Bernstein would have made it commercially successful. *Fantasia 2000* lost a fortune. Stanley saw in a board meeting that it lost $100 million. He called me up. 'Never let my client do something like that again,' he said." Eisner said Gold often called, urging him to keep a close eye on Roy. "You know Roy, he doesn't care about money. Roy cares about art," Gold said, according to Eisner.

"We could not have picked two better adversaries," Eisner says of Roy and Gold. "It's not like they're Warren Buffett and Tom Murphy. . . . Stanley says, 'Now I'm free and can talk,' but they've been talking all along." Eisner confirms that Ray Watson reported on his lunch meeting with Gold. "Stanley told Ray, 'You, Tom [Murphy], and I are going to go in and fire Michael,' " Eisner says. "I thought, what ingratitude after what I've done. . . . You see your true friends when you're in the foxhole."

I ask Eisner about the "reforms" that stripped Gold of his power and forced Roy off the board. "I didn't set a trap," Eisner says. "We put in strong rules, we had to. I've led the charge. The shareholders were expecting this. You want current, up-to-date governance. True, a lot of the new rules caused Stanley to become impotent. He could not be on the compensation committee, or governance. Stanley feels he was marginalized. The board, having been abused by Stanley, had to deal with this."

As for Roy, he was over seventy-three, "and the committee said, no exceptions," Eisner says. "We talked about making him a director emeritus, but he couldn't be a voting member. Some board members said to the committee, 'Is it worth it? Why not give him another year?' The board disagreed." Eisner says he was concerned at the time, but now that Roy has resigned, "I'm glad it happened," and Gold's resignation "was a gift. We finally had a board meeting that was intelligent and calm."

It's a brilliant, sunny winter afternoon as I ride with Eisner in the SUV to Times Square and a "table read" of the musical *Tarzan,* which Disney hopes to open on Broadway in the fall of 2005. He seems in a pensive mood. "This business is changing," he observes. "I'm not sure you're going to see another chief executive in Hollywood like me. I think I'm probably the last of the creative types to run a company like this. They want MBAs, accountants." He shakes his head.

Eisner brings up the subject of ABC, and acknowledges that prime time isn't showing any signs of improvement. "We turned around the studio," he reminds me. "The board insisted that I step in and personally oversee it, and I did. I could do the same thing at ABC, if I spent one day a week there and focused on it."

"Why don't you?" I ask, which seems an obvious question.

"Because I can't pull the rug out from under Bob," he replies, sounding frustrated. Since he has delegated responsibility for the network to Iger, he explains he can't undermine him by substituting his judgment. "But if things don't improve by May, there's going to be a big change," he says somewhat ominously. There have been persistent rumors that Eisner will replace Iger, even that Eisner has approached Peter Chernin, the highly regarded president of Twentieth Century Fox, about coming to Disney. Iger has heard it so many times, that he has asked Eisner if it was true. Eisner has denied it.

The situation was increasingly frustrating for Iger, who called various executives outside of Disney to complain. In one of these conversations, he said "I just feel every time I pick up a magazine I read there isn't any successor. I'm invisible. No one takes me seriously. I'm miserable." (Iger said that while he may have mused with people from time to time about quitting, he doesn't recall ever saying he was "miserable" and in fact has enjoyed his tenure as Disney's president.)

When we arrive at the rehearsal studio on Forty-second Street, Thomas Schumacher is in charge, and the creative team has gathered—composer and songwriter Phil Collins, writer Henry David Hwang, director and set designer Bob Crowley. The "table read" features a full cast, a small orchestra, and the performance is far more polished and professional than I'd expected. There are about forty people in the audience, which responds with prolonged applause. Though everyone, including Eisner, seems aware that Disney's remarkable string of Broadway successes is bound to end sometime, the buzz in the room lends *Tarzan* the feel of another hit.

Afterward, the creative team gathers with Eisner in an adjoining room. "I think it's great," Eisner begins. "It's further along at this point than any show we've had before. I have one idea. I finally figured out why the movie didn't make $200 million. There's a flaw . . . the ending of the movie is unsatisfying. It turns into a TV show."

In both the Disney animated film and in this musical, Tarzan, having been raised by apes, discovers he's human and falls in love with Jane. The climax comes when he has to decide whether to return to England with Jane or remain with his ape family; Tarzan chooses the apes, and Jane impulsively stays with him in the jungle—a predictably happy ending.

"We should not do the Disney [film] ending," Eisner continues. "Do the ending in the book—the apes send Tarzan back to England. Let the apes conclude that he is now the man and should go back into his jungle. . . . Man is the animal, the animals are men. This is what [author Edgar Rice] Burroughs did. Why did we do it this way?"

This pronouncement seems to leave the group speechless. "It did do $175 million," Schumacher finally says, somewhat defensively, of the animated *Tarzan,* which was released during his tenure as head of feature animation.

If Tarzan returns to England, "then what happens?" Schumacher asks Eisner.

Eisner shrugs. "That's for the sequel."

"The end does have a problem," Schumacher concedes. "We know there's something wrong at the end."

"I don't like the ending," Eisner persists. "It's too much. It has an obligatory feeling."

"It's been unconventional, and then it turns into . . . *Beauty and the Beast,*" Schumacher observes.

"Well, that's my big idea," Eisner says. "It's only five pages at the end. Otherwise, it moves."

"You mean that's your cherry bomb in the pond," Schumacher says.

The Tuesday after the Super Bowl, ESPN's Mark Shapiro called John Eisendrath, the writer for "Playmakers." Despite the success of the series, Eisendrath was worried. He knew Tagliabue had complained strenuously to Eisner. Indeed, the NFL had gone further. Denver Broncos owner Pat Bowlen told *The Wall Street Journal* that the show was "horrible" and he couldn't understand why ESPN "would go out and crap all over" the NFL.

"They're killing it," Shapiro said, sounding dejected. "The NFL is too important a partner to us and we can't do it."

"Can I take the show somewhere else?" Eisendrath asked.

"No, because the NFL will get mad if we let it go."

(While conceding that Disney was facing critical contract negotiations with the NFL, Iger told me the show was canceled not because of pressure from the league but because "it wasn't very good.")

At ABC, Lloyd Braun and Susan Lyne were working feverishly on developing the 2004–2005 ABC season. Despite Eisner's oft-repeated claim that he could turn the network around, it was too late for anyone to salvage the current season. Barring a miracle, ABC seemed destined for a fourth-place finish, even in the eighteen- to forty-nine-year-old demographic where it had been third the prior year. It was especially demoralizing to Braun that "The Apprentice," the show ABC lost to NBC, was an instant hit, attracting upwards of 20 million affluent viewers and saving NBC's all-important Thursday night lineup.

The previous summer, Braun and Lyne had run their own version of Eisner's "gong show," gathering everyone at ABC for a retreat at the Grand Californian Hotel at Disneyland's California Adventure. Even Iger was responsible for pitching a drama, comedy, and "alternative"—meaning, reality—idea. Iger pitched a show he called "Stacey's Mom," based on a Fountains of Wayne music video he showed. The premise was that the mother was the "hot mom" in the neighborhood, and teenage boys come over to be around her rather than her kids. The idea made it into development, but was never ordered as a pilot.

Braun pitched an idea he called "Lost." He described the show as a cross between *Cast Away,* the 2000 movie starring Tom Hanks as a survivor on a desert island, and "Survivor." (Like "The Sopranos," many of Braun's series ideas have come from feature films.) But, Braun explained, "not a guy alone on a desert island with a soccer ball, but rather a group of people who find themselves thrown together and now have to make a life together and form a society. A world where no one knows who anyone really is, where, at the end of the day, everyone has to figure out, 'how the hell do we get off this island?' "

"Lost" was one of dozens of ideas to emerge from the meeting that got circulated to Hollywood agencies and producers to see if any attracted any interest. A few weeks later, veteran producer Aaron Spelling said he wanted to do "Lost," and ABC ordered a pilot script from a Spelling writer. When the script arrived in December, Braun hated it. A rewrite in January was, if anything, worse. Warned that the show would have to be delayed a year, Braun insisted he'd get a new writer and salvage it. With ABC in fourth place, "We have to swing for the fences," he told Lyne. "I have a feeling this is going to be a home run." She agreed.

Braun turned to J. J. Abrams, the creator of "Felicity" and "Alias," the closest thing ABC had to a hit, and did everything he could think of to interest him in the project. Finally Abrams agreed to think about it over the weekend. Heather Kadin, who worked in ABC's drama department, introduced him to a promising young writer named Damon Lindelof. They hit it off, and at their next meeting Abrams was excited. He and Lindelof had a new idea: Besides the group of castaways, the survivors of a plane crash, there would be something else on the island—a sinister, unseen presence. But it was now February, too late to complete a full script. Braun and Lyne would have to green-light the project without a script.

The year 2004 was the first in which Braun and Lyne had been granted the authority to approve the new schedule. In prior years, Iger had retained the right to make the final decisions in consultation with Eisner. This year, eager to distance himself from the floundering network, which was clouding any possibility he'd ever succeed Eisner, Iger had ceded control, at least in principle. Lyne had reservations about approving a show like "Lost" without a script. Still, she admired Braun's passion for the show, and agreed with his argument that ABC had to try something different, something that, in his words, would "make noise," that would be "so big, so different, you can't avoid it."

Lyne threw her support behind "Lost," and Braun, in turn, backed her favorite project, "Desperate Housewives," a combination of soap opera and satire about a group of suburban women from creator Marc Cherry. Lyne had been looking for a show that would appeal to women, a group she felt the networks were ignoring in their rush to air procedural police dramas. HBO's popular "Sex and the City" was finishing its run, leaving open Sunday evenings for a must-see women's show. Lyne had even hired "Sex and the City" director Charles McDougall.

When Braun and Lyne met with Iger to go over all the projects they'd approved, he was amenable to "Desperate Housewives" but critical of "Lost." "This is a waste of time," he said. "It might work as a miniseries, but not as a series." "Lost" also kindled bad memories of "Twin Peaks." Just as "Twin Peaks" creator David Lynch had never known who killed Laura Palmer (and as a result, the show devolved into an incoherent mess), the creators of "Lost" either didn't know or wouldn't say who or what the mysterious presence on the island was.

Iger's response was a clear invitation for Braun to kill it, but instead Braun openly defied him, despite the new spirit of cooperation and collegiality that both were supposed to foster. Braun urged Abrams to finish the script, began casting the show, and assigned a team of preproduction people to shepherd it. Steve McPherson, head of Touchstone, was so hostile to the project that Braun threatened to banish him from casting sessions.

Eisner was similarly dismissive. At one of their meetings with Iger, he came in through the connecting door to his office and sat down. "What have you picked up?" he asked. When they described "Lost," he frowned and said, "That's never going to work." He argued it was just another "crazy" Abrams project. He and Iger frequently criticized "Alias" as needlessly complicated and faulted them for "coddling" Abrams. On another occasion, Eisner gave Braun and Lyne a list of the pilots they'd ordered on which he'd graded them on a scale of one to ten, one being the worst. Eisner gave "Lost" a two.

Finally the new pilot script was done. Braun and Lyne thought it was brilliant, but the price tag for the two-hour episode, which involved staging an elaborate plane crash, was a whopping $12 million. Braun persuaded Abrams to make a two-hour pilot, so that if it didn't work as a series they'd still have a made-for-TV movie for their money. He and Lyne did everything they could just to keep production moving forward. "If we're pregnant enough, they won't shut us down," Braun argued. At the same time, he realized that he was living dangerously. If Eisner or Iger decided they wanted to get rid of him, he'd handed them the ammunition: He had green-lit a $12 million pilot that didn't even have a script.

Pixar's surprise announcement that it was withdrawing from talks with Disney lent new urgency and momentum to Comcast's planning for a bid for Disney. As Jobs had intimated in his phone conversation with Roy, perhaps new management at Disney, unburdened of the strained Eisner-Jobs relationship, could salvage a Pixar deal.

On Thursday, February 5, 2004, the Comcast board met over dinner to discuss a formal bid for Disney. By now there had been numerous discussions between Mitchell and the intermediary. In a one-hour presentation, Roberts and Burke emphasized that this was a unique opportunity, since it was unlikely that any of the other major entertainment companies would ever be for sale. He also stressed that after years of investment in broadband technology, the cable systems were now in a position to profit from entertainment content, especially by offering video on demand and creating new cable channels. A major issue was how much it made sense for Comcast to pay for Disney. The film library, the cable channels, and especially ESPN offered major synergies to the cable operators. The theme parks, none. And it would probably have pained Eisner to know that Comcast valued the ABC Network at zero. Based on this analysis, Comcast felt it could get to the mid-twenties per share, but not much higher. Brian Roberts summed up, lending his support to the merger on the right terms and the right price, and the board gave its unanimous approval to move forward.

But in a surfeit of caution, on Thursday, February 6, Comcast again reached out to Mitchell. After all, at this juncture there had been two intermediaries positioned between the Comcast executives and Mitchell himself.

This kind of "telephone" approach was not only unorthodox, but inevitably risked a misunderstanding. This time, the intermediary called Mitchell from the Davis, Polk offices in New York. Hersch told the Comcast executives that he had conveyed the message "We're coming. Are you sure?" Mitchell, through the intermediary, had answered "Yes, we want you to do this."

On Monday afternoon, February 9, Roberts, Burke, Larry Smith, Comcast's CFO, and six of their advisers met at a conference room in the Westin Hotel in Philadelphia, across the street from Comcast's headquarters, to make a final decision. That Wednesday, Comcast was scheduled to meet with Wall Street analysts, and it felt it would have to disclose its interest in Disney then. After numerous discussions of the timing, coming just weeks before the potentially contentious Disney board meeting the first week in March, the Comcast executives had concluded they had to act swiftly.

Roberts was still worried about the accuracy of the messages from Mitchell. Another of the investment bankers—not Hersch or the usual intermediary—volunteered to call Mitchell. He stepped out of the room and used his cell phone to call Mitchell, who was in London that evening. Mitchell answered.

"We're ready to go tomorrow," the Comcast banker told him, referring to the letter Comcast was going to send the Disney board. "Once you put this out, it will be huge news," he said. "Gigantic."

"I understand," Mitchell replied. "We see this as a positive thing. We'll look at it carefully."

After the banker reported on the call, Burke said, "Okay, now's the time. Do we go?"

"I've got to call Michael," Roberts said. He felt he owed Eisner a personal call, especially since Comcast hoped to characterize the offer as "friendly." Because they worried about the quality of a cell phone connection, and Roberts wanted privacy, he stepped out of the room to use a nearby pay phone. Dennis Hersch followed him and waited anxiously outside.

Roberts went into the phone booth and dialed Eisner at his office. Eisner happened to be at his desk. In less than five minutes, the call was over and Roberts emerged from the booth shaking his head.

"You're not going to believe this," he said. "Michael said he wasn't interested. He didn't even hear a price. I couldn't get the words out. He's not interested at any price."

No one had expected this—not in the post-Enron era of heightened fiduciary duty to shareholders. At the very least, they thought Eisner would consider selling at some price. But he hadn't given them a chance.

As Roberts recounted the conversation, he had asked Eisner, "Are there any conceivable ways you could see putting our two companies together?"

"No," Eisner had said firmly. "I like the hand I've been dealt."

"Is there any conceivable way you'd sell?"

"No," Eisner had said curtly.

That's as far as Roberts had gotten in his script. The conversation was over in a matter of minutes.

Comcast executives spent the next day huddling with their investment bankers, lawyers, and public relations consultants. On the one hand, Eisner's reaction suggested they'd be in for a fight. There was no suggestion that Eisner wanted to retire, or was looking for a graceful exit, as Mitchell had first suggested. But by this point, the group wasn't putting that much emphasis on Mitchell's encouragement. They felt the deal made sense, and when both Disney and Comcast shareholders had a chance to consider this, Disney would have to negotiate.

On Wednesday morning, they released a letter from Roberts to Eisner, which had just been delivered to Eisner, who was at Disney World preparing for presentations to Wall Street analysts. "Dear Michael," the letter began.

"I am writing following our conversation earlier this week in which I proposed that we enter into discussions to merge Disney and Comcast to create a premiere entertainment and communications company. It is unfortunate that you are not willing to do so. Given this, the only way to proceed is to make a public proposal directly to you and your board."

Roberts proposed a deal in which Disney shareholders would receive .78 shares of Comcast for each share of Disney, or a total of about $54 billion at the previous day's closing share prices. The letter extolled Comcast's 21 million cable customers, 5 million high-speed Internet customers, and the possibilities of video on demand and broadband video streaming of Disney content. "We hope that the Disney board will pursue the opportunity that this proposed combination presents to your shareholders," Roberts concluded.

The Comcast team waited anxiously for any signs of a Disney boardroom revolt. They didn't have to wait long. That same morning, Barry Diller called Brian Roberts to report that he'd spoken to Eisner, who had consulted him about fending off the Comcast offer. On Diller's recommendation, Disney had hired famed takeover defense lawyer Martin Lipton, of Wachtell, Lipton, Rosen & Katz in New York. Clients who hired Lipton rarely had any intention of negotiating a friendly merger, let alone embracing a hostile offer. Moreover, Lipton had represented AT&T in Comcast's long, hostile, and ultimately successful pursuit of AT&T's cable assets. They felt Lipton still resented Comcast from that battle.

Later that day, after its board met by telephone, Disney issued a distinctly cool response to the Comcast offer: "The Walt Disney Company Board of Directors has received and will evaluate the unsolicited proposal from Comcast Corp. In the meantime, there is no action for Disney shareholders to take. Today and tomorrow, the company will present to institutional investors and analysts at a previously scheduled conference its broad array of unique and valuable businesses, as well as the strategies being deployed to fully realize the long-term value of those assets."

Roberts, Burke, and the rest of the team realized that something had gone terribly awry, despite all of their preliminary communications. Confronted with the reality of a bid from Comcast, Mitchell had evidently panicked and retreated into fortress Disney. Comcast's line of communication through the intermediary went dead.

The Comcast bid also encountered immediate, and more fundamental, obstacles. In Orlando, where Eisner, Iger, and other top Disney executives were meeting with Wall Street analysts, Disney officials were furious at the timing of the Comcast bid, in the belief that it had been deliberately timed to overshadow Disney's presentations. But the presentations gave the company the opportunity to boost its stock price, which, in the face of an all-stock takeover bid, is by far the most effective defense. Disney accelerated the release of its quarterly results, which were buoyed by the effects of *Nemo* and *Pirates*. Disney shares rose 16 percent in two days, both from the improved results and as arbitragers jumped in, expecting a higher offer, either from Comcast or another bidder.

Despite the efforts of Roberts and Burke to explain the rationale for the offer, both to Wall Street analysts and to major shareholders, investors reacted far more harshly than Comcast's executives and advisers had expected. The stock of a company making a hostile offer almost always declines, and they had expected some negative reaction at first. But after years of capital investments and the $51 billion AT&T acquisition in 2002, Comcast shareholders had been looking forward to a period of increased cash flow and higher earnings, not another big new acquisition. They questioned a cable operator's ability to run a major creative business, overlooking the fact that, in Steve Burke, Comcast had a seasoned executive and a Disney veteran ready to take the helm. In just two days of trading, Comcast shares dropped an alarming 12 percent.

Since Comcast had made an all-stock offer for Disney, this meant that a

.78 share of Comcast was now worth $23.53, while Disney shares had jumped to $28. The total value of the offer had fallen from $54 billion to $48 billion in just two days. The possibility that Comcast might increase its offer made its shareholders even more irate, leading Comcast to issue a statement stressing that "at the right price, this is a great deal, and we are going to be disciplined about the price." Comcast had left some room for a slight increase in the event Disney decided to negotiate a friendly deal. But those hopes were dashed on February 16, when the Disney board unanimously rejected the Comcast bid: "We are committed to creating shareholder value now and in the future and will carefully consider any legitimate proposal that would accomplish that objective," the board said. Further, "the interests of Disney shareholders, which represent the fundamental priority of the board, would not be served by accepting any acquisition proposal that does not reflect fully Disney's intrinsic value and earnings prospects."

Even so, the Comcast team was surprised when Disney, on George Mitchell's behalf, issued a further public statement that any reports that Mitchell might have encouraged a bid from Comcast or suggested that any directors were unhappy with Eisner's performance were "a complete fabrication."

When I asked Mitchell to elaborate, given the Comcast team's detailed chronology of numerous communications, Mitchell replied by email: "I received a telephone call from a friend (who was later referred to as an intermediary) who asked if I would be willing to set up a meeting between Brian Roberts, his father, Michael Eisner, and me. After briefly considering the suggestion I called him back and declined. Later he called again and asked if I would be willing to meet with Brian Roberts. I again declined. I told him that if Brian had anything to say he should call Michael and say it directly to him. That is what happened. As it turned out, the Comcast bid, when it was made, was so low that it was rejected by Disney's shareholders and its Board, and by the market."

Among those galvanized by the Comcast bid was Diane Disney Miller. Though she had vowed to stay out of the battle between Roy and Eisner, a corporate takeover threat was another matter. She was especially concerned after reading news reports that Comcast distributed pornography. (Like virtually all cable companies, Comcast carries adult-themed pay-per-view programming, and cable channels that sometimes broadcast material with explicit sexual content.) So, over the President's Day weekend, she wrote a letter to the board and sent each a copy by Federal Express after getting their addresses from Roy's office. After expressing her opposition to the Comcast bid, she continued, "I would hope that the independence of this company was almost as important to you as it is to us. I cannot believe that any of you would want to see this company suffer the same fate as befallen other recent victims of media 'mega-mergers.' Comcast, specifically, seems especially unsuited to Disney, a company which has always been dedicated to quality family entertainment."

So far, Disney's public relations department could have drafted the letter. But then Diane veered in another direction:

"We hope that the Board of directors will act to do what is best for the company. One of the greatest perceived weaknesses of the company has been Michael Eisner's unwillingness to identify and nurture anyone who might be deemed a successor to him. We believe all Disney shareholders would, like us, be relieved to know that someone very uniquely qualified to head the company was being groomed to replace Mr. Eisner when his contract terminates in 2006. We believe that the Walt Disney Company is the most magnificent entertainment company that the world has ever known, and that it will never be equaled. It is a company full of talented, creative people who value being a part of the business that my father and uncle built. It is a company that deserves to stand alone, to remain independent, as it has always been."

On Tuesday, the day after the holiday, Eisner called. "Good letter, Diane," he said. "If you could just change that last paragraph."

"But Michael," she replied, "you've been there twenty years. Even university presidents don't stay that long."

"Can't you just say you support management?" he persisted.

"I can't say that," Diane said. "I think it's time for you to go. You've done some wonderful things, but it's time."

"What are some of the issues that need to be worked on?" he asked.

"I don't want to get into it, Michael."

"Just give me one thing."

"Okay, the Ovitz thing." The Ovitz firing followed by the huge payoff had always grated on Diane. She knew Ovitz had been Eisner's best friend, and by hiring him, she felt Eisner had begun to treat Disney like his own private club.

"Oh, Diane, I can explain that to you," Eisner said. "He didn't really make that much off of it." He started to explain how Ovitz hadn't sold his options when he could have, but Diane cut him off.

"The point isn't how much Michael Ovitz made off it, it's what the Disney company paid out for it. Anyway," she continued. "I just think it's time for you to move out of the way for someone else." She added that she wouldn't have gone about it the way Roy did, but "it seems everyone perceives Roy as their hero."

"It's the name!" Eisner exclaimed in evident exasperation. "It's that Disney name! We've taken polls and Roy's popularity is so high."

"Well, I don't want you to think that I'm being swept along in the same stream as Roy and Stanley, because I think it's destructive to the company."

Eisner seized on this opening. "Diane, please just change that last paragraph. I'll write it for you."

"Michael!"

"I'll fax you a proposed rewrite of the letter."

Diane had no intention of changing her letter, and in any event, Eisner never sent a fax, and she heard nothing further. She was disappointed that, as time passed, none of the other directors responded to the letter. She thought she'd at least receive the courtesy of an acknowledgment or reply.

Though overshadowed by the bid from Comcast, Disney executives faced a potential revolt by institutional shareholders. Roy and Gold—taking as their model Howard Dean's grassroots, Internet-based campaign for the Democratic presidential nomination—had launched a website, SaveDisney .com, as the centerpiece of their effort to unseat Eisner. They became the first dissident shareholders to attempt to use the Internet to democratize the notoriously unresponsive system of corporate governance. "Shareholder democracy," while lauded as the centerpiece of democratic capitalism, had in fact become an oxymoron, with the vast majority of corporations firmly in the grip of their chief executives and acquiescent boards.

Roy and Gold's initial effort had been criticized as cumbersome and ineffective, but in January they had introduced a redesigned site, with color graphics, streaming audio and video, and links to other sites. With many Disney animators at their disposal, the site was illustrated with original work. The first day, Roy and Gold posted a cartoon showing Eisner dressed as the evil queen from *Snow White*. "Who's the greediest of them all?" Eisner asks as he gazes into a mirror.

In a more serious vein, they used the site to unveil the focus of their effort: a "vote no" campaign to withhold shareholder support for Eisner and the three directors they deemed most under his influence: Mitchell, Judith

Estrin, and John Bryson. As Disney executives had noted at the outset, Roy and Gold's resignations had come too late to mount a genuine proxy contest, which would have offered shareholders an alternative slate of candidates for the board. But in recent years, shareholder advocates had used similar withholding campaigns to express their displeasure. The most prominent example had been at AOL Time Warner, where 22 percent of voters withheld their support for chairman Steve Case, who had orchestrated the devastating AOL Time Warner merger.

It is difficult, if not impossible, for such efforts to actually evict directors. Brokerage firms, for example, routinely vote shares they hold for their clients in favor of incumbent management directors unless instructed otherwise by shareholders, most of whom never respond. Even most mutual funds and institutional shareholders lack the time and resources to evaluate the thousands of proposals that surface in proxy statements. Given that such efforts had never succeeded, there was no incentive to buck the status quo other than to register a protest. Roy and Gold had no expectation or even hope of gaining a majority of "no" votes. Their goal was 10 to 20 percent; enough, they thought, to force the Disney board to heed shareholder displeasure and take at least some action.

On January 27, Roy and Gold used the website to issue an open letter to shareholders:

"Now is the time for all Disney shareholders to take the first step in bringing needed change. . . . Join us in voting NO on the re-election of Michael Eisner, George Mitchell, Judith Estrin, and John Bryson as directors. . . . By just saying NO you will send a message the Board of Directors cannot ignore . . . you will force the Board to recognize the widespread conviction that serious changes in both senior management and the Board are necessary."

Besides their usual criticisms of Eisner, the letter took aim at Mitchell, noting the more than $1 million in fees his firm had received from Disney; at Judith Estrin, chairman of the compensation committee, for approving "excessive" 2002 bonuses of $40 million for Eisner, Iger, and three other executives, a year when the stock declined 16 percent; and at Bryson, whose "wife was being paid millions of dollars as an executive of Disney's 50 percent owned Lifetime Channel."

Of course, an audience of Disney shareholders was one thing. The far more critical audience were the proxy advisory services, especially the most influential of these, Institutional Shareholder Services (ISS) and Glass, Lewis & Company, as well as the large corporate and public pension plans, such as CalPERS, the California pension fund managers. On February 2, as the

Comcast executives were sounding out Mitchell about a possible bid, Gold, Roy, and their colleagues from Shamrock made a critical appearance at ISS, stressing Disney's poor financial performance and its unresponsive board. Mitchell from Disney explained the reforms the board had implemented and its intentions to institute more formal and detailed succession planning.

It took ISS just nine days to reach a decision, making it the first major independent shareholder services firm to weigh in on the Roy and Gold campaign. On February 11, the same day as the Comcast bid, ISS issued a stinging rebuke to Eisner's leadership. The firm noted the stock price was where it had been in 1998, and questioned Disney's "uncertain" prospects.

> The recent announcement of the Pixar-Disney divorce and the failure of Disney's retail operations lead one to ponder future growth and strategy at a company whose chairman and CEO has been distracted by boardroom drama. . . .
>
>   Sadly, it has often appeared that reconstituting the board was aimed more at quieting healthy boardroom dissent rather than creating it. . . . Board ties to Disney management are omnipresent. The lines between management and board are blurred. The latest revelation of the SEC investigation and potential settlement over non-disclosure highlights the depths to which non-independence and nepotism were the norm at Disney. . . .
>
>   At the end of the day, all roads lead back to Eisner. For 20 years Disney's revolving door for board members and management has had one constant—Mr. Eisner. The boardroom battles and management departures, which pre-date the Disney/Gold campaign, are disappointing, expensive, distracting, and not in the best interest of shareholders. If there ever were a case of separating the roles of Chairman and CEO, this company is the poster child.

ISS recommended that shareholders vote "withhold" for Eisner, though it spared the other directors at least temporarily, saying shareholders could wait a year to see if reforms take hold, and if not, "Shareholders may be best served by boardroom change."

Disney issued a statement saying it found ISS's recommendation on Eisner to be "inexplicable and unjustified," and hailed his "commitment to governance and transparency." But even as the media all but ignored the recommendation in light of the Comcast bid, there was no hiding the gloom in Orlando. Because of ISS's prominence, its independence, its conservative reputation, and its broad array of clients, the decision was a watershed for Roy and Gold, and a potentially devastating setback to Disney.

Although some Disney directors—Judith Estrin, in particular—seized on the language about separating the chairman and CEO to argue that the ISS verdict was more about the structure of corporate governance rather than Eisner personally, that seemed like grasping at straws. However the decision was construed, it was the first indication to Disney that Roy and Gold might have to be taken seriously.

Presentations to ISS and other shareholder advisory concerns are ordinarily closed to the public and the media, but many clients of the advisory firms like ISS participate via conference call, and in one of these sessions—to the Council of Institutional Investors—I am listening in.

After introductory remarks by Gold, Shamrock's Michael McConnell outlines the three major prongs of the campaign: Disney's poor financial performance, a loss of creative leadership, and board accountability. "We're looking for new leadership with the strategic vision to restore shareholder value," he says. "In other words, get rid of Michael Eisner."

"This company has had poor operating performance. We stand for a strong resumption of performance and growth. Creativity is a major issue. It surrounds the company, from the parks, to filmed entertainment, to animated art, to television product. Creativity is central to this company and needs to be restored. And there are serious issues regarding the board. There is not an effective board. We are looking for greater and increased accountability to shareholders. Executive compensation has always been an issue. There should be a clear linkage of pay and performance. There needs to be succession planning. We have to send a message to this board. That means voting no on Michael Eisner."

Questions ensue, including whether the Disney board's changes in corporate governance have had an impact. "They've paid lip service to corporate governance," Gene Krieger, a Shamrock executive, replies, "but if you look at their first real test on Monday, they failed. Michael Eisner rejected in less than five minutes a $50 billion offer. He summarily rejected it without consulting with any board member. This shows they haven't learned their lesson and that Michael Eisner in particular doesn't understand. The board found out when the news crossed the tape."

The Comcast bid has put Roy and Gold in an odd position, agreeing with Eisner and the Disney board that the offer is too low; at the same time agreeing with Comcast's argument that Disney needs new management. Gold elaborates: "The Comcast offer has been rejected; it ought to have been at that price. That is not the entire story. It validates our campaign. We have described the deterioration in the business, a steady decline over a seven-, eight-year period. This is the same as the Comcast briefing book. It's obvious to them, it's obvious to us, and it should be obvious to every shareholder. Comcast is further evidence of why there should be a no vote."

"How are you doing?" someone asks Gold.

"It's early," Gold replies. "We're getting a fair amount of traction. Lots of people are listening. The biggest validation was ISS. They're absolutely independent. It's the first time they've ever recommended a withhold vote on a Dow component." (Disney is one of the thirty stocks in the Dow Jones Industrial Average.)

A pension fund manager asks, "Other than getting rid of Michael Eisner, I don't see the strategic direction in your materials. I mean, they're nice words, but how would you take the company in a different direction? How would you execute?"

"Restoring creativity is the core business of this company," Gold replies. "Two hundred fifty executives, senior creative types have left, from films, television, parks, stuffed animals. . . . If you can restore creativity, you will get a much greater yield out of these assets. As for the future direction, we'd hire a CEO with strategic vision who understands the industry. We want to get the right person rather than preordain this. . . . We have in mind five to ten individuals who could run this company. It would be foolish to put these names on the table now. But we're not trying to be king makers—we want the board to have a real debate about who should run this company. Michael Eisner is arrogant. We don't want to fall into the same trap."

Roy steps in at this point. Though he still prefers to let others do the talking, he has overcome some of his aversion to public speaking as the campaign has progressed. His reticence coupled with the Disney name seem to lend a certain gravitas to his words when he does speak, and the room falls silent as he begins. "Thank you," he says. "I'm glad to talk about the creative part. We are a company whose roots are completely in the creative end of the world. We were a little studio that just made animated films. There was nothing there but creative people. I grew up in this atmosphere. The company needs to trust its creative employees. An obvious and egregious example of what's gone wrong is the Pixar relationship. Steve Jobs finally said, 'I can't deal with this man any more.' The party line is: The company was amazed. But in fact the relationship has been going sour the last six or seven years. . . .

It should never have gotten to the point where Steve Jobs says, 'I will not deal with this company as long as Michael Eisner is chief executive.'

"Another area," Roy continues, "is our parks. If you've been there in recent years, you will have noticed the lack of maintenance, the fewer number of characters on the streets. The cast members . . . have been pared back unmercifully. Their hours have been cut, benefits taken away. That gets reflected in their attitude toward the guests. . . . That's just a couple of examples of the way the company is being run. You start fixing this right away."

"How do you respond to the *Wall Street Journal* article?" someone asks, referring to an article headlined "Disney Dissidents Didn't Block Moves They Now Criticize."

Gold answers. "It's totally unfair. It is an attempt to demean us. This company has a history, when pressed about its performance, to call people names. Jeffrey Katzenberg was a 'midget.' Steve Jobs is a 'Shiite Muslim.' Now it's Stanley Gold and his 'client.' Yes, we were a party to some of the decisions," Gold concedes. "We tried to give management the benefit of the doubt. We didn't want to cause a ruckus in the boardroom. Fox Family is the best example. Roy and I voted on this based on management's projections. Three months into the deal, we asked, and they said they were behind. We said, 'Hold on, you failed to execute.' We tried to make them accountable. We said, 'Michael Eisner and Bob Iger should not get a bonus.' When you have this kind of mistake, there should be no bonus. Eisner got $5 million, Bob Iger $4 million. Yes, we voted for things, but we did it on management's projections, and when they failed, we tried to make them accountable. I'm proud of our approach."

After a detailed discussion of Disney's recent improved earnings—dismissed by Shamrock's Mike McConnell as "not sustainable given non-recurring events like *Nemo* and *Pirates,* the amortization of rights to sports events, as well as underinvestment in the theme parks"—Gold sums up:

"I'd like to make a final comment on corporate governance. The company acknowledged that in the near future, Michael Eisner will end up signing an acknowledgment that he violated the securities law and will enter into a cease-and-desist order. This is an enormously serious business when the CEO acknowledges violations of the securities laws. I go back to ISS—all roads lead back to Michael.*

"Who do you trust?" Gold asks. "They have failed to meet projections.

---

* In December 2004, without admitting or denying the allegations, Disney settled the SEC investigations and agreed to comply with the securities laws. Eisner was not required to acknowledge any personal responsibility.

They have failed on governance. They did not reform themselves when they got a bid. You can trust us. We will bring in management with a vision and a strategy who can operate these assets in a more efficient way."

On February 23, the campaign moved to a potentially pivotal battleground, the offices of Glass, Lewis, another influential shareholder advisory service. The importance to Disney was underscored by the delegation that attended: Eisner, Mitchell (by phone), Judith Estrin, Ray Watson (also by phone), and Tom Staggs, the CFO. Roy and Gold had addressed the firm and its clients the prior week, repeating many of the same elements of their earlier presentations.

Greg Taxin, Glass, Lewis's chief executive, led the questioning.*

After some preliminary discussion, Taxin asked why the board had chosen seventy-two as its mandatory retirement age, "which I note for the record is not a round number. So I guess I'm curious. I know, Senator Mitchell, you're 70 . . . Roy Disney at the time you adopted the 72 mandatory retirement age was 72. Why 72? Why not 70? Why not 75?"

Mitchell didn't really have an answer: "Now some argue that 70 is a better age, some 75 . . . 72 in light of our own evaluation and in light of the experience of other companies around the country seemed to make the most sense," he said.

Next, Taxin said he wanted to focus on Fox Family, a deal that Roy and Gold had criticized but also voted for as board members. "Was this their idea?" he asked.

After a long nonanswer from Judith Estrin, Eisner stepped in. "Fox Family is the last piece of beachfront property in the nationally distributed cable-basic universe and the company has been looking strategically at these kinds of things for years. The entire board was 100 percent unanimous in the acquisition of Fox Family. Certainly Mr. Gold was a giant advocate of it. . . . I wouldn't say that he was more or less enthusiastic than the management and other members of the board. . . . One of his closest friends [Haim Saban] was the seller of Fox Family, so we analyzed it. We looked at it. He was helpful in being a conduit between management and the seller and we together made an acquisition. . . ."

Taxin continued, "While we're on the topic of Fox Family, Mr. Staggs, maybe you can tell us. I've heard Mr. Eisner say that maybe he paid too much.

---

* While I wasn't listening to this confidential conference call, the session was recorded and I later obtained a transcript.

... The company has never taken a write-down of the goodwill associated with the Fox Family channel acquisition. Should you have? Might you in the future? Might this lead to a restatement of some past financial report?"

This, of course, was a question that took direct aim at one of Disney's most vulnerable points, especially given the valuation study that Staggs himself had commissioned.

"Well, I hate to state the obvious," Staggs answered, "but if the company believes it should take a write down, it would take a write down ... as Michael said, at least over time, we've got quite a valuable asset there."

Taxin turned to the Comcast bid. "Ms. Estrin, could you tell us when you, as a board member, first learned of the Comcast approach and then what the board did after learning?"

"I found out about it, I think, very soon after Michael got a call," she answered, presumably referring to Brian Roberts's call to Eisner on February 9.

Mitchell jumped in before Estrin could get very far in this potentially dangerous narrative. "Every member of the board was informed and made aware of the fact that a phone call might be made so that the call was not unexpected and all members were aware of, I guess, what I will call the interest. Mr. Eisner responded in accordance with the wishes of the board."

Eisner elaborated: "There had been some indirect vague conversations that led us to believe that this phone call could happen. Every board member was made aware of those conversations either by Senator Mitchell or myself. Because we were led ... had some sense they were going to come, we crafted the response before the telephone call was made. The response was vetted with three outside advisers. We discussed the response extensively and when I happened to be sitting at my desk when Mr. Roberts called and I put the response up on the computer and gave it word for word ... and the subject was immediately changed by him, and that was the end of the call."

It took Glass, Lewis only two days to issue its recommendation, and it was another rebuke to Eisner, as well as to George Mitchell. In unusually harsh language for a shareholder advisory service, its report stated that "The Disney board has been notoriously insular, famously gullible and blindly loyal to Mr. Eisner. ... Given the control Mr. Eisner is accustomed to, we are troubled that he still wields tremendous power over the operation of this board. ... Our concerns are substantial." As for Mitchell, the firm concluded, "We do not believe he is independent in the true spirit of independence" and questioned his naming John Bryson as head of the governance committee, when Bryson's wife was a senior executive of a Disney joint venture. Mitchell "should have known better," the firm scolded.

The revelation in the Glass, Lewis proceeding that Eisner had consulted with directors prior to the February 9 phone call from Roberts, and had been reading from a script, created a furor, both within the Comcast camp and among institutional shareholders of Disney. Eisner's reference to "indirect, vague conversations" all but confirmed that Mitchell had been talking to the intermediary, and that this was not a "complete fabrication," as Disney had publicly maintained. Comcast executives and advisers were now more convinced than ever that Mitchell had panicked and run for cover. Perhaps there had indeed been some misunderstandings, and Comcast had interpreted Mitchell's comments as more encouraging than he had intended, but they still believed the words had been spoken.

In any event, had such a possible Comcast bid been discussed with all the board members in advance of Roberts's phone call, as Mitchell maintained? Judith Estrin's answer in the Glass, Lewis presentation was certainly unpersuasive. As questions multiplied about what Disney's directors knew and when, Disney had to issue a press release. "The board had a process in place in how to respond regarding any communication regarding an overture and what the proper procedure was for handling it. That procedure was followed." Yet that statement left open the possibility that the "script" from which Eisner read was intended as a generalized response to vague, preliminary overtures, such as the one from Steve Case at AOL, and not a specific response crafted by the board to respond to a serious bid from Comcast. Fairly or not, the contretemps only reinforced the impression that Eisner had simply rejected the Comcast bid on his own initiative, and that Mitchell and the rest of the board had yet again fallen into line.

While the revelation seemed calculated to blunt Gold's criticism that Eisner had unilaterally rebuffed Roberts before consulting the Disney board, it deepened the mystery and begged the question of why the board would have told Eisner to reject a bid even before hearing a price or other terms of a proposed offer. As Roberts told *The New York Times,* "I purposefully raised the topic of a combination with Mr. Eisner in a way that I thought would lead to a discussion. How can it be in the best interest of Disney shareholders for him to not even talk to us?"

As the critical shareholder vote and Disney annual meeting neared, the campaign reached a fever pitch, with ads, a flurry of op-ed pieces in major newspapers followed by rebuttals, and television appearances—Gold on CNBC's "Kudlow & Cramer," Iger on CNBC, and Eisner in his preferred venue, CNN's "Larry King Live."

Among those watching the Larry King interview was Diane Disney

Miller and her husband, Ron. In response to a caller asking whether Walt Disney had really been frozen, Eisner said that no, Walt had been buried in an unmarked grave in a secret location. "His wishes were that it was unmarked, and not available to anybody to ever find out," he said. "But I went up there and talked my way into them showing me where he's buried."

Why would the grave be unmarked? King asked.

Walt "wanted his privacy forever," Eisner replied. "It's a beautiful little spot and nobody could ever find it, and I'm very proud that I talked myself into it."

Diane didn't know whether to laugh or cry. How could Eisner say this on national television? He knew perfectly well that Walt was not buried in an unmarked grave. Diane herself had told him that Walt had been cremated, after they had dinner all those years ago. There was a memorial in Forest Lawn cemetery containing Walt's and Lillian's ashes, and its location was no secret. There was no unmarked grave, and so of course Eisner couldn't have either discovered or visited it. Diane was really tired of other people, especially Eisner, trying to lay claim to Walt's legacy.

Diane was so upset that when James Bates, a *Los Angeles Times* reporter, left a message, she broke her long-standing public silence and returned the call. The reporter wasn't in, but Diane left a message. "As far as my cousin is concerned, Roy loves the company, but I think he's taken the wrong action here. I think he's put the company in play. As far as Michael goes, he's had a good run. It is time for him to go." Then she hung up.

When Bates returned her call, she elaborated, saying "New leadership is necessary. I think Michael Eisner did some great things for the company but there also are some not-so-great things," and she urged the board to move quickly to replace him. "Disney's Daughter: Eisner Must Go," was the headline in the *Los Angeles Times* on March 10, 2004.

As both Disney and Save Disney kept up their round-the-clock polling of shareholders, it became clear to both sides that the once unthinkable might happen: As many as 35 percent of Disney's shareholders might withhold their votes from Eisner. In an effort to blunt the shock value of any such result, Disney began floating to reporters the notion that as many as a third of the voters might vote against Eisner. Each day seemed to bring more bad news for the embattled Disney team.

On February 25, CalPERS announced that it would cast its votes with Roy and Gold and vote against Eisner, followed by state pension funds in Connecticut, Massachusetts, and New Jersey. Even New York, where Disney had done so much to help revitalize Times Square, and Florida, with its massive Disney presence, joined the fray, saying they would withhold support for Eisner. Mutual fund company T. Rowe Price, Disney's fourteenth largest shareholder, with 19 million shares, called for Eisner's ouster. Alan Hevesi, New York's comptroller and director of the state's retirement fund, which owned 8.7 million shares, issued a statement saying, "I call on Disney directors to separate the positions of chairman and chief executive and to replace Mr. Eisner as soon as possible."

Disney dismissed the state pension fund actions as headline grabbing by aspiring politicians motivated by personal political gain, and not the interests of Disney shareholders. But there was no denying the silence from Eisner supporters. Not one state government said it would vote for Eisner. Disney had mounted a campaign to generate letters of support for Eisner from prominent entertainment executives and other businessmen. It had yielded little. Marty Sklar, the head of Disney's Imagineers, wrote an op-ed piece calling Eisner "a great creative force and the ideal creative partner." Barry Diller, asked about Eisner on CNBC, said only that he was a "longtime friend and supporter" and that he thought Eisner would keep his job. General Electric's Jack Welch, also on CNBC, praised Eisner as "a creative genius." But otherwise the silence was deafening. Even Sid Bass, for so long Eisner's staunchest backer, remained silent.

On March 2, it fell to George Mitchell to make Disney's case in *The Wall Street Journal.* He argued that there was no immediate need to divide the posts of chairman and chief executive and stressed Disney's governance reforms. "The changes we have made have resulted from our listening. We listened to the concerns that have been expressed about the company and about all of corporate America. We heard the concerns that boards were too large; that they were not independent enough; had too little diversity and not enough expertise; that there was not enough turnover, that they were too insular. We listened—and we took action. Michael Eisner listened, too. He initiated many, and embraced all, of these changes—and encouraged their speedy implementation."

Two days before Disney's annual meeting in Philadelphia, Eisner spent the night in New York with Jane. The next day they were being driven to Philadelphia when Eisner got a call reporting that Disney had just heard from Fidelity, which controlled over 3 percent of Disney's shares. Disney had been counting on Fidelity's support—just days earlier Eisner had been assured he had it. Now he learned that Fidelity was casting its votes against him, voting "no" with Gold and Roy.

Eisner turned to Jane. "Everyone hates me," he said.

SEVENTEEN

March 2, 2004, is a clear, mild day in Philadelphia. Though Save Disney's rival meeting isn't scheduled to begin until 4:00 P.M., by 1:00 P.M. a line has formed on the sidewalk at the Loews Hotel, a nondescript modern building located around the corner from the Convention Center. By 3:30 hundreds of people are waiting. Many in the line are carrying anti-Eisner placards, and a few carry anti-Comcast signs. Nearby, the Christian Action Network hands out leaflets protesting "Gay Days" at the Disney theme parks as well as a video, "Gay Day at Disney Gone Wild." Five television satellite trucks crowd the narrow street.

Save Disney helped shareholders wanting to attend Disney's annual meeting find discounted airfares and hotel rooms, and an overflow crowd squeezes into the Loews Millennium ballroom festooned with "Save the Magic!" banners as a jazz band blares over the loudspeakers.

Tracy Lunquist, a thirty-four-year-old graduate student at the University of Illinois, has been a Disney shareholder since 1992, and would someday love to work at Disney. She's there with her friend Ian Mitchell of Philadelphia. They agree that Disney under Eisner has been in decline. They cite lapses at the theme parks, the exodus of high-level executives and creative people, the firing of animators, the cheap, straight-to-video sequels, and the falling-out with Pixar. Surprisingly well informed, they say they stay in touch through on-line Disney fan sites.

"That's totally Eisner," Lunquist says of the falling-out with Steve Jobs. "The guy gets rid of anyone who disagrees with him. But autocracy and creativity cannot coexist."

Mitchell nods in agreement. "People who buy stock in Disney don't do it just for the dividend check," Lunquist continues. "We want to be involved in the company."

Despite the antigay protesters across the street, Scott Ross and his domestic partner, Nathan Lee, have driven fifteen hours from Springfield, Missouri, to support Roy and Gold. Avid fans of the theme parks, they visit Disney World three times a year. "Over the last few years, the quality has gone downhill," Ross told *The New York Sun*. "They're more worried about profits than making sure you have a magical experience."

As the lights dim and the music swells, Gold takes the stage. He introduces members of the Disney family sitting in the front row: Roy, Patty, Abby, Tim, Susan, Roy P., and Andrea Van de Kamp, the former board member who has now openly thrown her support to Roy and Gold's effort to unseat Eisner. There is deafening applause as they stand and acknowledge the crowd.

After a nostalgic slide show of pictures from Disneyland, circa 1959, Shamrock executive Michael McConnell presents many of the themes and arguments honed during the presentations to the shareholder advisory services and institutional investors during the past two months.

Then Roy mounts the stage and moves to the podium. It's clear that to this audience, he is the embodiment of Disney, the values that transcend profit and loss and which have drawn them to Philadelphia. The audience jumps to its feet and gives him a prolonged ovation.

"There's a pretty long list of changes we'd all like to see," he tells the audience. "For instance, I think the short list would include management. We know that for sure. Improving the cleanliness, the maintenance, and the guests services in the parks, and that would include putting the smile back on the faces of both cast members and guests."

The audience breaks into applause. "Making better movies and television shows," he continues, "especially in feature animation. Fixing the ABC Network and dragging it out of its perennial fourth place. Being better corporate citizens of the country and the world, and to just plain being Disney again." There is more wild applause.

Shamrock executive Gene Krieger reads questions submitted by audience members to Gold, Roy, and McConnell. One of the first is about Pixar, and Roy responds, "We want the whole gang at Pixar back. They told us . . ." He pauses. "Forgive me for saying 'us.' I still forget I don't work there. But the night before last, I heard that all of them in the blink of an eye will come back when Michael Eisner is no longer at Disney."

Krieger reads another question. "If Eisner leaves, who should run it? Would you do it?"

"No," Gold replies. "We think there is a short list of five to ten people who could run it much better than Eisner."

"Are you pandering to the Christian Right? Are you tolerant to all?"

"No, and yes," Roy replies, eager to distance himself from some of the demonstrators outside. (Abby and Tim Disney were particularly upset by what they consider fringe groups trying to attach themselves to their father's cause.)

"We need to get stronger after tomorrow," Gold continues. "We need to keep the drumbeat current. . . ."

"Stay tuned," Roy injects. "We have thirty-one thousand registered names so far, but we need more. I used to say, if we had enough rifles, we could have this over tomorrow."

There is awkward laughter. Roy's daughter Abby visibly cringes at this gaffe. (Roy later says he meant the comment in jest, and regretted it as soon as the words were out of his mouth.)

"I think this is an unprecedented campaign in the history of American business," Gold says, trying to steer things back to a loftier plane.

Krieger reads another question: "What are your feelings about Comcast?"

"My absolute druthers would be for Disney to be a movie studio and theme parks with ancillary publishing and good merchandising things," Roy answers. "But I'm also practical enough to know there are other limbs—like ABC—that you don't just cut off. But if we run everything well, we'll be worth too much to entice other companies to take over."

There is more prolonged applause, and then the band breaks into Henry Mancini's "Moon River." Hundreds of people line up to get Roy Disney's autograph, including Lunquist and Mitchell. "It's not every day you get to shake the hand of a real Disney," Mitchell says. "Roy is so in touch with the company and what the people want out of this company. Now, I don't know if he was prepped, but he got it right. He knows us."

Afterward, Save Disney is host to a reception, with free hors d'oeuvres and soft drinks, beer, and wine. Roy mingles in the crowd, under a moving halo of television cameras, shaking hands and exchanging pleasantries. However shy by nature, he seems in his element among the Disney faithful. One of them is Michelle Kutch, a teacher in the Brandywine, Delaware, schools. She's seven months pregnant, and has a two-year-old. They've already visited Disney World twice and taken a Disney cruise. She drives a Volkswagen painted to look like Herbie in *The Love Bug.*

"Thank God Roy has come to our rescue," she says.

That night, the eve of the annual meeting, Eisner, Iger, and the Disney board gathered in the Four Seasons Hotel, a quiet refuge some distance from the Convention Center. The mood was grim. All the latest indications suggested that the vote was going to be worse than anyone had feared—far worse, even, than the 30 percent Disney had been quietly projecting to the media. The latest polling by Disney's proxy solicitors suggested the final result would be closer to 40 percent, the highest withhold vote against a chief executive ever recorded by a major American corporation.

Eisner maintains that he began with a dramatic gesture, offering to resign. "If you think this will go away, I'm happy to get off the stage," he said. There was a chorus of protests: Eisner couldn't leave because no one else could do the job, and it would leave Disney more vulnerable to the Comcast offer. A majority on the board felt that it had to find a way to both keep Eisner and placate what was clearly an angry group of shareholders.

Ten days earlier, takeover defense lawyer Martin Lipton had suggested splitting the positions of chairman and chief executive, as many shareholder advocates and both Gold and Roy had long recommended. The board had resisted, but now Lipton argued forcefully that the board had to do something to show it was responding to shareholders. To ignore the massive vote of protest might play into Comcast's strategy of portraying the directors as advocates of management rather than shareholders. Eisner hated the idea that he was giving in to shareholder pressure, or that he was being "stripped" of his title, but in principle, he said he didn't mind ceding the title of chairman as long as he remained CEO, with his authority undiminished. But that meant the chairman had to be someone he'd be comfortable with.

Ironically, separating the titles of chairman and chief executive gave Eisner enormous leverage over the board. Under his contract (drafted by Irwin Russell, Eisner's lawyer and until recently a board member) relieving Eisner of either the chairman or chief executive title constituted a breach of his contract, giving Eisner the right to leave within thirty days with all the benefits specified in his contract, which would cost Disney millions. Indeed, Russell was on hand to underscore this very point. Thus, if Eisner were relieved of his title on terms he didn't like, he could leave at once and force Disney to pay him an enormous sum.

Eisner's choice to succeed him as chairman was George Mitchell; he felt he was the only person on the board with the stature to quell public criticism, and he was someone who, over time, Eisner had come to trust, at least up to a point, notwithstanding the awkward matter of the Comcast negotiations. In the eyes of at least a few of the directors, however, Eisner's motives were more transparent: Eisner felt he could control him.

Hours had already elapsed, and now Mitchell expressed doubts about taking the job. He pointed out that he didn't really know the industry, and lacked experience as a businessman. He also didn't want to spend more time in California, away from his home on the East Coast. Finally, at midnight, Eisner reminded the directors that he had to give a major speech the next day. He joined Zenia Mucha to practice, and then went to his room. But at 1:00 A.M., he got a call asking him to return to the directors meeting. Nothing had been resolved, but Mitchell had agreed to consider becoming chairman overnight. In the meantime, they wanted to make sure that Eisner wasn't feeling hurt or rejected. Finally, at nearly 2:00 A.M., the directors disbursed.

The next morning, thousands of shareholders and an enormous press corps have converged on the Philadelphia Convention Center adjacent to the Marriott hotel in downtown Philadelphia. Costumed Disney characters drift through the vast lobby as "Whistle While You Work" is piped through loudspeakers. Outside, hundreds of protesters have lined up, carrying signs denouncing Comcast, sweatshops, and the out-sourcing of jobs to Asia.

The vast meeting room is packed by 10:00 A.M., when proceedings begin. There's electricity in the air, a palpable sense of anticipation, a feeling of history in the making. All the comments I hear around me suggest that this crowd is hostile toward Eisner, and smells blood. The shareholders are passionate about something far more profound than Disney's latest quarterly results. I can only wonder if this was what it felt like at the famous tennis court gathering of the bourgeoisie on the eve of the French Revolution.

There is a ripple of murmurs, even a few boos, as Eisner steps to the podium. "Good morning everybody. I'm Michael Eisner," he begins, his voice hoarse, perhaps because he stayed up so late the night before. "As it happens, this annual meeting is taking place at a time when the amount of vision is once again resulting in a dramatic, and we believe, a sustainable upswing in Disney's performance. . . . We now anticipate earnings gains from continuing operations in excess of thirty percent in fiscal 2004, and we have set a target of double-digit compounded growth in earnings through 2007 . . . and of course we are thrilled with a nearly sixty percent increase in our stock price since our last annual meeting."

Eisner acknowledges the "slow movement" of ABC prime time, and the collapse of the Pixar talks. That Sunday, *Finding Nemo* won the Oscar over Disney's *Brother Bear,* and "No one would have wanted to continue this relationship more than me," Eisner maintains. "But the economics of the ongoing relationship were not in the interest of our shareholders." Otherwise, he gave a glowing assessment of Disney's prospects. "I love this company. The board loves this company, and we are all passionate about the output from this company."

After brief remarks from retiring directors Tom Murphy and Ray Watson, Eisner announces that the board has reached an agreement to allow Gold and Roy to make fifteen-minute presentations. To a prolonged wave of applause that clearly signals the audience's sentiments, Gold comes to the podium. "Roy Disney and I have been on a mission," he says. "A mission not to promote ourselves but to save our company." After reciting a litany of board and management failures and compromises, he says, "This is the story Roy Disney and I have told as we have crisscrossed the country in the last thirty days talking to small and large shareholders alike . . . Let me be clear. No half measures, no excuses, no amount of spinning will be tolerated. Michael Eisner must leave now." Gold turns and says directly to Eisner: "You have compromised your soul and lost your integrity."

Sitting on stage, Eisner looks grim as Gold's barrage comes to an end. Eisner stares straight ahead, and looks like he is struggling to keep himself in check. There can't have been many chief executives subjected to such a withering tirade in front of thousands of shareholders.

Then, on the darkened stage, Roy suddenly appears at the podium, and many shareholders leap to their feet, applauding wildly. Once the applause subsides, Roy begins. "The Walt Disney Company is more than just a business. It's an authentic American icon, which is to say that over the years it's come to stand for something real and meaningful and worthwhile to millions of people of all ages and backgrounds around the world . . . Our mission has always been to be bringers of joy, to be framers of the good in each of us, to be teachers. To speak as Walt once put it, 'Not to children but to the child in each of us.' This is the core of what we have claimed to call Disney."

From the rapt attention of the crowd it's clear that this is what they have come to hear—not projections of compound earnings growth. "Creativity is a funny thing," Roy continues. "It's a living, breathing force with a life of its own and it tends to flower among individuals and in small groups." Disney must "resume our trajectory of creativity and financial success" by "trusting the talents and imaginations of its creative people—and I can't emphasize enough the word *trust*—and then by supporting them with the resources they require. We need to install a new management team. . . . Speaking as someone with the name of Disney, it is my firm belief that we are not a commodity. As long as we continue to believe in the power of creative ideas then our best years will still lie ahead."

There is thunderous applause.

Eisner comes to the podium. "Thank you, Stanley. Thank you, Roy. I enjoyed that. But I think I have to say the conclusions you've just heard are fundamentally wrong. . . . You have just heard rhetoric from our critics that frankly displaces reason."

Over the next two hours, Disney executives and division heads—Bob Iger, Tom Staggs, Dick Cook, Lloyd Braun, Susan Lyne, Anne Sweeney among them—give polished presentations lauding their operations and unveiling new products, like the much anticipated *Hidalgo* and *The Alamo* for the studio, *Home on the Range* in animation, and a Stephen King series, "Kingdom Hospital," as well as a return of "Super Millionaire" on ABC. But as the lunch hour comes and goes, the audience is clearly anxious to get to the climax, the results of the final shareholder vote.

Late that afternoon, after a few more questions from the audience, Eisner abruptly accepts a motion to adjourn the meeting, seeming to have forgotten that no tally has been announced. "I think it's about that time . . . the meeting is adjourned," he says.

Howls of protest arise from the room, and cries of "Vote! Vote!"

Eisner realizes his oversight. "I almost got away with that," he quips. "I've been informed that the inspector of elections is prepared . . ."

An inspector steps to the podium. "For item one, the election of directors," the inspector began, and then reads the exact vote tallies, all of them in the millions of shares.

There are more howls, since without a calculator, it's hard to know what percentage of the votes has been withheld. Ultimately, it's determined that 43 percent of the shareholders have withheld their votes from Eisner, and 24 percent from Mitchell. Even more devastating to Eisner, though not released to the public, 72.5 percent of Disney "cast members" voting through their 401(k) retirement plans, have voted "no" on Eisner. A remarkable 63.7 percent voted against Mitchell as well.

To a smattering of applause and murmurs, the crowd begins to disperse. The shareholders have just delivered a stunning repudiation of Eisner's leadership.

At the Four Seasons Hotel, the Disney board reconvened at nearly 5:00 P.M. By the time the vote was announced, it didn't come as a total shock. Word had circulated among board members that morning that the "no" vote would surpass 40 percent, worse than anyone had imagined. The sizable vote against Mitchell—larger, in fact, than the 22 percent withhold vote that had driven out AOL's Steve Case—was hardly grounds for reassurance.

Nonetheless, Eisner turned to Mitchell, saying again that he wanted him to assume the chairman's title. In the wake of the shareholder rebuke, Mitchell announced that he had pondered the matter and had decided that he didn't want the position. After all, the vote against him had been second only to that against Eisner himself. He'd already been criticized as being too closely identified with Eisner and beholden to him. As a Nobel laureate and esteemed former senator, he had his reputation to consider.

The discussion turned to two other potential candidates, Robert Matschullat, the chairman of Clorox, a relatively new board member, and former head of investment banking at Morgan Stanley; and Gary Wilson, the chairman of Northwest Airlines and former Disney chief financial officer. The board thought Wilson and Matschullat's financial skills would complement Eisner's creative instincts. But before either of these suggestions could gain any traction, Eisner brought the discussion to a halt. "Maybe I'll just trigger my out now," he said—in effect, threatening to quit and exercise his breach of contract provisions. He turned to Mitchell: "George, I really want you to do this."

At least some directors were stunned by what they considered Eisner's naked exercise of power. It was clear to them that Eisner wouldn't be comfortable with a business executive who might actually challenge him, and that he preferred the more malleable former politician.*

At this juncture, Eisner suggested that he and Mitchell leave the room for

---

* Eisner denied this, saying it was John Bryson who insisted on Mitchell's being chairman and that he never threatened to exercise his contract provision.

a private conversation. As they walked in the hall, Eisner put his arm around Mitchell and insisted that "You're the only guy I can work with. Anyone who can bring an end to six hundred years of fighting in Ireland can handle the Walt Disney board," flattering Mitchell even as he cajoled him into taking the position. "We need your common sense," he argued.

Just before 9:00 P.M., Disney issued a press release: The board of directors, "mindful of the shareholder vote today, announced that it is separating the positions of CEO and Chairman. Effective immediately, the Board created the position of Chairman of the Board. The Board has unanimously elected former Senator George Mitchell to serve in that non-executive position. While making this change in governance, the Board remains unanimous in its support of the Company's management team and of Michael Eisner, who will continue to serve as chief executive officer."

Despite the professed support for Eisner, there was no mistaking the board's action: Nearly twenty years into his reign, Michael Eisner had been deposed as Disney's chairman.

Though exhausted by the day's historic events, that night Eisner appeared on ABC's "Nightline" to defend himself against Roy and Gold, who vowed to press their campaign. It was galling, really, that the Disney-owned ABC Network would even devote a program to the Disney vote, and no doubt it was yet further retaliation by Ted Koppel, still angry about the David Letterman affair. Still, if he was going to have Roy and Gold on the show, Eisner was determined to have his say. Then Eisner joined Mitchell and the two flew in the Disney jet to New York, an opportunity for Eisner to further cement their new relationship.

The next morning Eisner awoke to page-one headlines: "Defied in Vote, Disney Leader Loses One Post" (New York Times); "Eisner Loses 43% of Vote; Rebuke by Shareholders Weakens CEOs Grip, May Spark Board Shift" (Wall Street Journal); "Eisner Under Fire: Disney's Eisner Loses Top Post, Stays as CEO" (Los Angeles Times).

A call from Martin Lipton helped cheer Eisner up. Lipton had watched him on "Nightline." "I'm getting calls," Lipton reported, "Jerry Speyer [the real estate developer Eisner had displaced from Disney World], others. You have no idea how good you were. I know what a day you had."

Several weeks later, on March 30, I meet Eisner at his office at the ABC building in New York. Disney has just had some good news, winning a lawsuit brought by the heirs of the Milne estate over the rights to Winnie the Pooh.

Eisner predicts the press, in its eagerness to write anything bad about him or Disney, will give Disney's "Pooh" victory short shrift.

The courtroom triumph is especially sweet for Eisner, who notes that it marks a defeat for attorney Bert Fields, who represented Katzenberg, represents Harvey Weinstein, and who, Eisner believes, has made a name for himself by harassing Disney.* Eisner observes that "Hollywood is a microcosm of the world. There's a group of ethical people, serious, eager to work. Then there's the underbelly, and the seedy part of that group, the people who supply the underbelly. There are the struggling runaways, the prostitutes—male and female—the dregs of the earth. The vultures. They take the low road. They may wear suits, be articulate . . ." He trails off.

While Eisner seems in good spirits, he is defensive about the shareholder vote, and eager to rebut impressions in the press that the board took the chairman's title from him. He insists that the board asked him to stay, and tells me how they summoned him from his room at 1:00 A.M. to make sure his feelings hadn't been hurt. "It was touching," he says, then continues. "I was not 'stripped,' quote unquote, of my title. I had already suggested this two years ago, and if it was up to me, we would have done it then. The board didn't want to. Ira Millstein was against it. My goal was to follow the Tom Murphy model, the Bill Gates model. [The board] would have made someone the CEO, and then I would have become the chief creative officer and chairman. Now, because of the 'situation,' that won't work.

"Anyway, I don't care about the title. Many CEOs have had thirty-five to forty percent withhold votes, and nothing happens. But it was my view—the board's view—that this should happen." (According to Institutional Investor Services, that is untrue. The vote against Eisner was the seventh-highest ever recorded, but the others were all against directors, none of whom was a chief executive. Patrick McGurn, executive vice president of ISS, said he knew of no other withhold votes against a CEO in the range Eisner claimed, saying withhold votes against sitting CEOs are "extremely rare.")

Eisner tells me that the board meeting itself was "very emotional. There are three reasons they want me to stay: One, they like me. I know what I'm doing. I've been unjustly criticized.

"Two, they detest Stanley and Roy. You have no idea. Beyond what you can imagine. They're liars. . . ." Eisner pauses. "They have said horrible things about the board. First they went after me, then the board.

---

* Eisner is incorrect that this ruling was a "defeat" for Fields. He and his firm withdrew from the case in June 2003, nine months before this ruling.

"Three, Comcast. I'm strong. I told Steve Case to go to hell. They didn't want to weaken the company vis-à-vis Comcast."

After some more conversation, and just before we leave for dinner, Eisner gets a pen and a piece of paper. "Disney is a French name, not Irish," he reminds me. "Now look at this." He writes "D'Isner," "Deez-nay," as the French would pronounce it, "is Eisner without the D." *

But even as Eisner was musing on his possible dynastic claim to the Disney throne, it was apparent to many that his grip was slipping. Roy and Gold vowed that they would continue their crusade to replace Eisner, and would mount a full-scale proxy fight over the next year, even though the effort would likely cost them an estimated $20 million. Despite their support for Eisner at the March annual meeting, at least some Disney directors recognized that splitting the office of chairman and chief executive had only bought some time. The size of the withhold vote and the ongoing threat of a proxy fight made the status quo untenable.

No one had more at stake than Disney president Bob Iger. Speaking at an analyst meeting soon after the shareholder vote, he said he'd received an email suggesting a new reality show: "The Successor." It would combine elements of "Survivor," "Who Wants to Be a Millionaire" and "The Apprentice" to "figure out who succeeds Michael Eisner." Iger's contract was due to expire in September 2005, and while Eisner has said Iger never threatened to resign, Iger also made it clear that there was no reason for him to stay unless he was officially designated by Eisner as his chosen successor.

At the same time, both at Eisner's behest and some board members, Iger tried to distance himself from the fate of the perennially struggling ABC network. Barring a dramatic turnaround, it was hard to imagine that Iger would be named to succeed Eisner as chief executive after Eisner had so publicly linked him to the failure to revive ABC. Iger had begun to distance himself from the network that winter, when he'd turned over responsibility for ap-

---

* Many people can recount similar anecdotes in which Eisner discusses the similarity between his name and that of Walt Disney's French ancestors. When I asked him about this, he said he meant the comment in jest. He told me that the similarity was brought to his attention in 1989 by a projectionist at the studio, who had even written out the names in Disney script. "He thought this was a celestial event!" Eisner told me. "He said, 'You're genetically attached to the company!' It was hysterical. But this is a joke. I do not think I'm genetically attached." For the record, Roy Disney notes that the ancestral family name is "d'Isigny," after the French village, which is not an anagram of Eisner.

proving the pilots to Braun and Lyne. But now, with ABC still in fourth place, more dramatic measures were called for.

At the investor conference, sponsored by Bear Stearns, Iger had pointedly failed to express any confidence in Lloyd Braun or Alex Wallau when asked about ABC management. Instead, he had reserved all of his praise for Susan Lyne. "We made a big change two years ago when we brought Susan Lyne in as president of ABC Entertainment. Our job right now is to support her, to give her both the time and the room to perform, and I think that's critical. I believe in Susan strongly, and I thinks she has the goods to turn it around."

During the last week of March 2004, Lloyd Braun flew to Hawaii, where J. J. Abrams was filming the pilot for "Lost." Rumors were circulating that Braun might be quitting. Braun knew Iger and Eisner hated "Lost." He was tired of being second-guessed and overruled. The success of "The Apprentice" on NBC had been the last straw. Two weeks earlier, he'd told Kevin Brockman, the head of media relations for ABC, that he didn't want any part of another ABC management reorganization. "I'm ready to leave this place if it's handled appropriately," he said, knowing that Brockman would convey the message up the ranks.

A few days later, on March 25, with Braun in Hawaii, Iger sent Susan Lyne an email asking her to meet with him. When she walked into his office early the next morning, he announced that "We're going to be making some changes around here." He said he was going to ask Anne Sweeney to become head of the network as well as the cable division. Alex Wallau would be moved to some other job.

"What about Lloyd?" Lyne asked.

"Lloyd wants out," Iger said. "I'm going to take him up on his offer."

Naturally, Lyne wondered where she fit in, though after Iger's strong public statement of support at the investor conference, she wasn't especially worried. "Everyone wants you to stay," Iger assured her. "Not just me. You can take Lloyd's direct reports." But not, evidently, his title. "The chairman title is ridiculous," Iger said. "What do you think of Mark Shapiro?"

Lyne was startled by this turn. Shapiro was a rising star at ESPN, the young executive responsible for the controversial series about the NFL, "Playmakers." "I like him," Lyne said. "He's a pistol. He'll need some time."

"I know," Iger said. "That's why he'll work under you."

Lyne expressed surprise, saying that she, like others at ABC, were under the impression that Iger had taken an instant dislike to Shapiro.

"That's not true," he replied. "True, Mark makes mistakes. He didn't handle Rush . . ." (referring to the incident where Rush Limbaugh was fired as an ESPN commentator after making racially insensitive remarks on the air).

"Do you want me to call him?" Lyne asked.

"No, let me talk to him," Iger said.

Iger did call Shapiro, who flew from ESPN headquarters in Connecticut to Los Angeles to meet with Iger and Eisner. They offered him the title of president of ABC, reporting to Lyne, adding that in six months, if it wasn't working well, they'd get rid of Lyne. But Shapiro resisted. "No offense," he said, "because I love Susan, but firing Lloyd and promoting Susan doesn't make any sense." He noted that without one executive who was clearly in charge, they were "just rearranging the deck chairs." He felt he had the energy and charisma to go up against Jeff Zucker at NBC and Les Moonves at CBS. "ABC needs a leader and needs to be inspired," he argued.

"He's right," Eisner suddenly said. "Susan can't do this. Let's sweep her out and give it to Mark."

Iger looked troubled. "We can't. The press will be terrible."

No decision was made, and Eisner warned Shapiro that if anything about their discussion leaked, all bets were off. The next day Shapiro met alone with Iger. Shapiro acknowledged his lack of network experience and relative youth, but noted that Iger, too, had been young and inexperienced when he became president of ABC. He argued the press would praise a bold move like putting a thirty-four-year-old star from ESPN atop the network.

When he left Los Angeles, Shapiro thought he'd be replacing Lyne. But in subsequent calls, Iger said he felt Shapiro needed a transition period, and kept urging him to accept a position reporting to Lyne. To Lyne Iger reported that negotiations weren't going well, and that Shapiro didn't want to report to her. She rejected the idea of another co-equal; she and Braun had made it work, but both agreed it should not be a two-person job.

Braun returned from Hawaii on Saturday to a flurry of press calls. *Variety, Hollywood Reporter,* the sports section of *USA Today* all had stories that Shapiro was moving to a high-level position at ABC. Eisner and Iger were furious about the leaks, and suspected that Shapiro himself, or, more likely, someone close to him, was the source. (Shapiro told Iger he had told no one but his wife, and pointed out that given Eisner's warning, it wasn't in his interest to leak anything.) But as the rumors continued, Braun realized it was only a matter of time before he was replaced, if not by Shapiro, then someone else. On Monday, he was in a car with Brockman en route to a table reading for a new series when Iger reached him by phone. Iger had finally decided to fire him. The last straw had been reports from Alex Wallau, other Disney executives as well as TV producers and directors in Hollywood that Braun was criticizing and undermining Lyne. Iger had concluded that ABC's management was "dysfunctional." (Braun denied speaking ill of Lyne.) "I didn't realize you were in town," Iger began. "I understand you've had some discussions, and we'd like to proceed and make some changes. You should have your lawyer call Alan Braverman" (Disney's general counsel).

That was it. Their long, contentious rivalry was over. Braun immediately abandoned the table read and called Lyne. "It's over," he said. He sounded relieved. "This will be good for you," he predicted. "They need you. I'm cutting my ties now. I'll be in tomorrow morning to speak to our people, but that's it. Right now I'm going to Dodger Stadium." Braun is an avid Dodger fan, and it was opening day of the baseball season.

The next morning Lyne met Braun in his office. She confessed that she'd known for a week that he was going to be replaced, and felt bad that she hadn't told him. She hoped he understood. She'd loved working with him. "I'm glad you told me," he said. "I know you're in a difficult situation and I'm not going to let this ruin what has been a great relationship."

When Lyne returned to her office, people were lining up with questions. "Are you staying?" "What's going to happen?" Lyne tried to reassure them. "I hope I will be here," she said. "I expect to be here. In the meantime, we have to make good pilots. Hunker down. Don't let them see us sweat."

That Thursday, Lyne had a meeting scheduled with Iger at five. At two, Eisner called. He'd just returned from a trip. "Come over right now," he said. "I've got an hour."

When she arrived, Eisner seemed energized by the crisis at ABC, almost as though he was enjoying it. "Steve [McPherson, head of Touchstone] is coming over at three," he said. "What do you think of him?"

"Really talented," she said. She expressed a few concerns, but concluded, "I'd keep him in a heartbeat."

Eisner started lecturing her about ABC. "We've got to get a hit!" he said. "We need someone like Mike Darnell at Fox." (Darnell was the programming chief responsible for the reality shows "American Idol 2" and "Joe Millionaire.")

"We can't do those shows on ABC," Lyne countered. "We couldn't even do 'Are You Hot?' "

"Yeah, but we need a killer," he continued.

"What about Mark Shapiro?" Lyne wondered. The mention of Shapiro prompted an outburst.

"Shapiro! He's dead. We're writing him off. He's thirty-four and he thinks he should run the place. He has all kinds of demands. I won't take his calls. We won't answer his emails. When I was offered ABC in 1974 I didn't even ask what I'd be paid! When do you want me? Bob did the same thing. He was on a plane in an hour when Tom Murphy offered him the job. There was no contract, no deal." This rankled with Lyne, since she herself still had no contract.

When Lyne met with Iger at five, he was furious to discover that Eisner had inserted himself ahead of him, before he could talk to Lyne. Now Eisner was meeting with McPherson. "Maybe he's offering him my job," Lyne speculated.

"That's not going to happen," Iger said. "There's no interest in Steve at the network." He assured her that she'd run prime time. Iger confirmed that it was over with Shapiro.

Lyne went back to work, confident her position was secure. The following Wednesday she had dinner with Anne Sweeney and briefed her on the pilot process and what needed to be done, on the assumption that Sweeney would be replacing Wallau as president of the network and Lyne would be in charge of programming. It was a busy week, and Lyne returned to New York on Thursday night.

On Monday she was back in California, and met again with Iger. He looked somber as he moved to a chair, and she sat down on the sofa. The chairman and chief executive of McDonald's, James Cantalupo, had just died of a heart attack at age sixty while at a convention in Orlando. "I had lunch with him two months ago," Iger said. "It puts things in perspective, doesn't it?" Lyne nodded in agreement.

"Well, this is hard for me because I like and respect you so much," Iger continued. "I know I told you you'd run prime time. We decided to go another way. It was clear you wouldn't report to anyone other than Anne. Steve said the same thing. So we had to make a choice. The consensus was that Steve should do it."

Lyne was speechless. She realized she was being fired.

"We want you to stay with the company," Iger assured her. "You can keep your salary, move back to New York, whatever works. We'll figure out a job."

"Bob, you're taking away my job. I'm not going to say anything definite, but that's not going to work." Lyne got up and walked to the elevator. She was late for a pilot screening. Suddenly she turned around and went back. "What do I say to my executives?" she asked.

"Nothing," Iger replied. He added that he, Sweeney, and McPherson would announce their new responsibilities to her staff the next day.

When she reached her car, Lyne realized she couldn't attend the screening and pretend nothing had happened. Instead she called her husband and her lawyer.

The next morning, her phone rang at 7:30 A.M. It was Eisner. He told her how sorry he was.

"I was blindsided, Michael. Bob told me a week ago I had his support," she said.

Eisner launched into a tirade about Iger. "ABC has destroyed Bob! Unless he fixes it, he will never be CEO. He can't even get another job in this town. Bob is under terrible pressure. He had to do something."

"But he was doing something," Lyne replied. "He was bringing Anne in to run the network."

"Anne wasn't enough of an announcement."

Later that day, Lyne found herself in the odd situation of consoling others over her own firing. McPherson called, clearly uncomfortable over having helped to engineer her departure. "I wish you nothing but success," she said.

Then Sweeney called. She was in tears. "I feel terrible."

"It's okay," Lyne assured her. "Steve is a smart guy. He'll be great."

"I don't know him at all," Sweeney said.

Iger himself called as Lyne was returning from the set of *Their Eyes Were Watching God,* a movie she'd commissioned for ABC starring Halle Berry and produced by Oprah Winfrey.

"I feel horrible," Iger said. "There aren't many people out here I'm close to. I considered you a friend, and I hope we can stay friends."

"I understand," she said. "But not now. Give it time. Right now I can't do it."

With turmoil swirling at ABC, Harvey Weinstein notified Eisner that the controversial Michael Moore film *Fahrenheit 9/11,* was now finished, and, as he had suggested a year earlier, he wanted Eisner to see it. In preview screenings, the film was "testing through the roof," as Weinstein put it. Eisner expressed surprise, given that he thought he and other Disney executives had made it perfectly clear a year earlier that neither Disney nor Miramax would distribute the film. For his part, Weinstein didn't see how Eisner or anyone else at Disney could be surprised given that the company had been paying invoices related to the film. Disney said it didn't look at the invoices, and that Weinstein hid *Fahrenheit* by keeping it off production reports. In any event,

Eisner declined the offer to see the movie. So Weinstein invited Bob Iger, Peter Murphy, even George Mitchell to a screening. All declined. Finally Disney dispatched Brad Epstein, a studio production vice president, who saw *Fahrenheit 9/11* on April 24.

Epstein told Weinstein that he liked the film, that he thought it was "great," according to Weinstein. But in his written report to Eisner, subsequently distributed to the Disney board, Epstein evidently criticized it. Eisner called Weinstein after the next board meeting. "The board is against this," Eisner said.

"Why?" Weinstein demanded.

"I don't want to be political," Eisner said. Weinstein thought this was rank hypocrisy, since Disney-owned stations broadcast conservative commentators Rush Limbaugh and Sean Hannity.

Furious, Weinstein called George Mitchell, all but begging him to see the film himself. Mitchell, after all, was a prominent Democrat; surely he would sympathize with a documentary critical of the Bush administration. But Mitchell refused. "It's a management decision," he said, not something the board should get involved in.

Weinstein had lawyer David Boies weigh in on the matter, also to no avail.

All the conditions for a public relations hurricane were now in place, and on May 5 *The New York Times* ran a page-one headline: "Disney Is Blocking Distribution of a Film That Criticizes Bush." In the ensuing media frenzy, Disney, and Eisner in particular, was cast as the censor caving into political pressure. Disney refused to reconsider. Spokeswoman Zenia Mucha had the thankless task of trying to refute the charges, stressing that Disney had told Weinstein a year earlier that Disney and Miramax would not distribute the film, and that Weinstein and Moore were free to find another distributor.

Adding to the furor, *Fahrenheit 9/11* won the Palme d'Or, the top prize, at the Cannes Film Festival later in May, and Weinstein had no trouble lining up distributors. By the time the film opened nationally in the United States on June 24, it was a cause célèbre. While noting that the film was unabashed propaganda, critics were generally positive. No doubt reflecting on Moore's stand against Disney as well as the quality of the film, A. O. Scott in *The New York Times* called Moore "a credit to the republic." Lines formed at big-city theaters on opening day, and box-office revenues quickly soared past $100 million, making it the highest-grossing documentary ever.

Made for $6 million, *Fahrenheit 9/11* ultimately grossed $220 million worldwide. After paying distribution fees of about $60 million and marketing and other costs of another $40 million, Miramax realized about $120 million in profit, which Disney has said it will donate to charity.

Though Eisner has characterized himself as the Weinsteins' biggest supporter inside Disney, noting that Dick Cook and other studio executives would have loved to get rid of them, this was too much even for Eisner. In a June conference call with analysts, he said that Miramax had only earned a profit in two of the previous five years, a claim that infuriated Harvey Weinstein. It was especially damaging to his efforts to raise capital on Wall Street to either buy Miramax back from Disney or to finance a new studio in the event he and Bob left Miramax and Disney. Weinstein charged that Eisner's figures were false; that for 2003, for example, Miramax's profits were actually $211 million, and that he and his brother wouldn't have earned a bonus in each of the five years if Miramax hadn't earned a profit.

But Disney was using generally accepted accounting practices, and Miramax was not. Miramax amortizes costs over a longer period; Disney allocates to Miramax a share of corporate overhead, among other differences. But haggling over year-to-year profit figures isn't really the issue. No one disputes that Miramax has, over time, produced valuable assets for Disney that will continue to generate substantial revenue. Notwithstanding his irascible temperament, Harvey Weinstein has displayed an eye for talent and both artistic and commercial instincts that are unrivaled in Hollywood.

By the summer, Eisner and the Weinsteins were at loggerheads. A last straw for Weinstein was Eisner's claim, reported in *The New York Times,* that Harvey Weinstein had hidden the financing of *Fahrenheit* from Disney, a claim Weinstein denounced as an "out-and-out lie." But with Miramax a wholly owned subsidiary of Disney, Eisner held all the cards. When the brothers wanted to raise capital and buy back Miramax from Disney, Eisner refused to take any proposal to the board. The brothers suggested splitting up, leaving Bob and his Dimension studio at Disney, freeing Harvey to go elsewhere. Disney offered Bob a contract that was so inadequate it was "insulting," Harvey maintains. Talks shifted from renewing their employment arrangement to severance terms. With their options dwindling, the Weinsteins watched the shareholder unrest and the Save Disney campaign with keen interest. Their relationship with Eisner was, for all practical purposes, over. Their only hope was that Eisner would have to leave before their contract ended in 2005. The question was, Who could hang on longer?

*   *   *

At its June 2004 meeting, the Disney board conducted a "management review" of all high-ranking Disney executives, and pressed Eisner on the issue of succession. Iger finally got his wish: In the wake of the upheaval at ABC, Eisner told the board that Iger was his chosen successor as CEO. In July, Eisner and Iger both appeared at Herb Allen's annual Sun Valley media conference. This year's appearance loomed large for Eisner, his first conference since the humiliating shareholder meeting the previous March. He also promised Iger that he would introduce him to this exclusive crowd for the first time as his heir apparent.

Eisner's talk drew a standing-room-only crowd. Afterward there were some questions from the audience. But as the session reached its end, and even before Eisner received a warm round of applause, Iger rose from his seat and stalked out of the room, obviously angry, prompting a buzz of speculation. Eisner had failed to even mention Iger, let alone introduce him as his designated successor. (Eisner later maintained that he assumed someone would ask him a question about succession, at which time he would have mentioned Iger. But no one did.)

At the shareholder meeting in March, Eisner had staked his reputation—and his future—on Disney's bottom line, and as the year unfolded, Disney remained on track to deliver the earnings growth that Eisner had promised. But much of the earnings came from DVD sales of *Finding Nemo* and *Pirates*, hits from 2003, as well as a recovering economy and higher attendance at the theme parks. At the feature film meeting I attended, Eisner had been right to worry about the summer of 2004.

Disney's performance at the box office in 2004 was nearly as abysmal as 2003's had been outstanding. The studio unveiled a string of critical and box-office flops. The much touted *Hidalgo, Alamo, Around the World in Eighty Days,* and most surprisingly, the latest Bruckheimer epic, *King Arthur,* each costing $100 million or more, opened to mostly devastating reviews and disappointing ticket sales (though *King Arthur* did better overseas). Even *The Woods,* now renamed *The Village,* Shyamalan's latest thriller, faded after a strong opening and tepid reviews. Although it eked out $100 million in domestic box office, it was no *Sixth Sense.* Another Bruckheimer film, *National Treasure,* performed well, but Disney didn't even have an "event" movie on its release schedule for the vital holiday season. The only sure thing seemed to be November's *The Incredibles,* but that, after all, was a Pixar project.

Disney's own major animated release, the two-dimensional *Home on the Range,* sank from view with hardly a trace, all but sealing the fate of Disney's traditional hand-drawn animation unit. The film was excoriated as "seldom funny" and the theme song as "corny, jokey," by *The New York Times*. Its watercolor backgrounds were inevitably compared unfavorably to the vivid images of *Finding Nemo*. The forgettable score by the celebrated composer of *Beauty and the Beast*, Alan Menken, only underscored once again the loss of Howard Ashman. It was especially galling that Katzenberg's *Shrek 2* proved to be the highest-grossing movie of the year, raking in $450 million in the United States alone by the end of summer, and that even *Shark Tale*, an animated effort from DreamWorks that suffered from comparison to *Nemo*, grossed over $150 million.

As the September board meeting approached, Eisner found himself thinking increasingly about his own future at Disney. As a result of the shareholder vote, his options had narrowed drastically. Except for a few die-hard Eisner loyalists on the board, Disney directors had decided not to extend Eisner's contract as CEO when it expired in September 2006. While none has acknowledged explicitly telling Eisner this, others have said it was implicit in their conversations leading up to the June board meeting, when Eisner named Iger as his chosen successor. Moreover, Eisner was the lightning rod for Stanley and Roy's campaign. As long as Eisner remained CEO, there remained the real chance that they would win the proxy fight the following year, and Eisner would be forced out even before the end of his contract.

So as Eisner's twentieth anniversary at Disney approached, he began drafting a letter to the Disney board resigning as chief executive, effective when his contract expired in 2006. He relied on Jane as his editor and showed it to no one at Disney. "Putting last things first, I plan to retire from my role as Chief Executive Officer of the Company upon the conclusion of the term of my employment agreement on September 30, 2006," he wrote. "Until then I shall continue to exert every effort to help the company achieve our goals, to assist the Board in selecting the new Chief Executive Officer, and to make the transition expeditious, efficient and smooth and easy."

Over the Labor Day weekend and during the following week, Eisner met or spoke with board members individually and discussed his plans. He showed copies of the letter to at least some of them. *The Wall Street Journal*'s Bruce Orwall had been hearing reports all summer that something was afoot with Eisner, and was already close to writing a story when he heard about some of these meetings. Faced with the imminent prospect of a story, Eisner gave Orwall a copy of his letter and an exclusive interview that Thursday. Eisner insisted that his decision had nothing to do with the shareholder vote, the loss of his chairman's title, Stanley and Roy's campaign, or any pressure from the board. It was "not asked for, not motivated by current circumstances at all," Eisner insisted. In a September 10 page-one scoop, Orwall wrote that "The decision signals the end of Mr. Eisner's two-decade stewardship of one of the world's best known brands."

But did it signal the end of Eisner's reign? Or was the resignation a clever ploy to derail Roy and Gold's proxy fight and buy time? Eisner's conversations with directors triggered a flurry of phone calls and conversations among them. Except for Judith Estrin and Leo O'Donovan, most agreed it was the latter, noting that Eisner's letter said nothing about remaining on the board or reclaiming his title of chairman. In Eisner's "master plan," as one director described it, Iger would assume the chief executive's title in 2006, Eisner would remain as chairman—and nothing much would really have changed.

Gold and Roy were certainly skeptical in a September 13 letter to board members. "While Mr. Eisner's announcement at first blush looks like a major change, it is in truth mere window dressing," they warned. "What he has really proposed is a scheme to arrogate the authority of the Board and maintain the status quo at the Company's expense . . . his 'succession plan' is for a company led by Michael Eisner and his obedient lieutenant, Bob Iger, to be handed over to . . . Michael Eisner and Bob Iger." They urged the board to hire a qualified search firm, and announce that Eisner would leave as soon as his successor was decided—no later than the 2005 annual meeting. If not, they would proceed with their proxy fight.

Not just Roy and Gold, but numerous experts in governance and executive recruitment complained that Eisner's two-year plan was seriously flawed, since no serious outside candidate for the chief executive job would come forward with Eisner planning to stay for two more years, and possibly longer as chairman. As the furor grew, Eisner gave an interview to *Fortune* magazine, which released the results just as the Disney board convened in Burbank for its crucial September meeting. In a critical exchange, the *Fortune* reporter asked Eisner if he wanted to remain on the board or be chairman after the end of his current contract. Eisner replied:

"I have not asked the board to stay on the board or be chairman after the end of my contract. My assumption is that I would not continue on the board or as chairman. I have a full business life ahead of me. Clearly I'm not the type to retire, particularly after I've heard all these lectures from medical experts about how an active mind is good for the body. But as far as continuing on the board or as chairman, it's just not in my mind at this time."

The answer was widely reported to mean that Eisner would not remain as a board member or as chairman.

The board gathered on Sunday evening, September 20, and continued through lunch on Tuesday. While several items were on the agenda, the critical discussion of succession took place on Monday afternoon. In a clear signal that Eisner's influence had waned, most of the discussion was held in executive session, with Eisner excluded. The critical issues were whether the board would hire a professional search firm and how long and in what capacity Eisner would stay at Disney. Hiring a search firm, as Roy and Gold clearly understood, was in itself a repudiation of Eisner's "master plan," since it shifted the power to influence the board from Eisner to professional outsiders. And it was a blow to Iger's chances. Had it wished to, the board could simply have designated Iger as Eisner's successor, as the General Electric board did with Jeffrey Immelt, Jack Welch's choice to succeed him.

Eisner was readmitted only at the end of the session. By then, it was clear that Eisner had lost his grip on the board. The board not only decided to hire a search firm, but also included in the press release a statement that the independent directors had concluded that Eisner would not remain as chairman after 2006. Eisner argued furiously that the language denying him the chairman's title be dropped from the release, and ultimately he succeeded.

The press release began: "The Board reaffirmed its strong support for Michael Eisner, Bob Iger, and the entire management team. . . . The Board took special note of the fact that today marks the 20th anniversary of Michael Eisner's service as Chief Executive Officer. The Board formally acknowledges Michael's recent decision regarding the CEO position, thanked him for his outstanding creative leadership, and looks forward to his continued leadership through the rest of his tenure."

At the same time, the statement made clear that a new era had begun. "The Board will engage in a thorough, careful, and reasoned process to select as the next CEO the best person for the company, its shareholders, employees, customers, and for the many millions of others who care so much about The Walt Disney Company. The Board is keenly aware of the special place our company holds in the hearts of people all over the world and the importance of its responsibility in choosing a CEO."

Despite the carefully worded praise for Eisner and the management team, the statement was the equivalent of the board's declaration of independence. In a press briefing after the meeting, to which I listened, Mitchell seemed to make explicit what Eisner hadn't wanted in the press release. In response to a question about whether Eisner would step down if a new CEO was appointed and if Eisner would remain as chariman, Mitchell said, "Michael has made his statement on that and we take him at his word. As far as the board is concerned, that's the end of it." When a questioner noted that Eisner's statement wasn't definite on those points, Mitchell referred to news accounts of the *Fortune* interview reporting that Eisner wouldn't stay as chairman. "I read several newspapers and there was nothing indefinite about it. It was definite as far as we were concerned."

Though the board's action stopped short of meeting Save Disney's demand that Eisner be out by the 2005 annual meeting—it promised a decision on a new chief executive by June 2005—it was almost everything that Roy and Gold had been asking for. After pondering the implications for a few days, on September 28, Roy and Gold declared a qualified victory. "In announcing that it will be retaining a qualified executive search firm to help select a new CEO . . . the Board displayed precisely the kind of leadership and independence which we and the vast number of shareholders who share our concerns had been requesting. . . . We are willing to take Chairman George Mitchell at his word that Mr. Eisner will step down as both CEO and a member of the Disney board as soon as his replacement is installed.

"As we have stated all along, our effort was never about Roy Disney and Stanley Gold. It was about the importance of shareholder democracy and need for change at the Disney Company. . . . To George Mitchell and the Board: we are most supportive of this encouraging beginning to what we trust will be the revitalization of the Walt Disney Company—once the happiest place on earth!"

Roy and Gold put their ambitious plans for a proxy fight on hold. At the same time, they pledged to remain vigilant, and to hold the board to its promises. In a letter to Save Disney supporters in October, Roy reminded them that "eight or nine months ago, I had been informed that I was no longer wanted or needed as a member of the Disney board, and with that, I had, along with Stanley Gold, resigned from that body. Michael Eisner probably thought we might make a little public fuss that would soon die away, that the board would obediently renew his contract into eternity, and life would go on as 'normal.'

"That is all quite different now. Eisner has 'decided' to end his imperial reign in some foreseeable future, as soon as a new CEO has been found and installed. . . . While we would all love to think of this as a victory, it is in fact only a step along the way, and there is still much to do, many things to watch over. Stay with us as we go forward and together we can give this tale the happy ending it deserves. No matter what . . . we'll be watching."

On September 29, 2004, less than a month after his resignation letter, I met with Eisner at his office at ABC headquarters in New York. He was in town for the Four-square media conference I'd attended the year before, as well as several other events. As I walk into his office he's standing behind his desk, talking on the phone. That morning I'd read a full-page ad in *The New York Times* touting the success of "Lost," which had debuted the previous week to glowing reviews and strong ratings. After so many years, it looked like ABC might have a hit. Simply as a pleasantry, I mention seeing the "Lost" ad.

To my surprise, Eisner seems annoyed. "That *New York Times* ad was a total waste of seventy-five or a hundred thousand dollars," he says angrily. "It's all about ego, impressing the so-called New York intelligentsia. Let me tell you, that ad isn't going to get one more viewer. Maybe if it had been in *USA Today* . . ." His voice trails off, but it turns out he is just warming to the subject. " 'Lost' is terrible," he says. "The pilot was two hours; it was broken into two one-hour episodes. Then the show goes off a cliff. There's no more plane crash! Who cares about these people on a desert island?"

Eisner's reaction baffles me. Why would Eisner attack his own show?

(Later, I made some inquiries, and only then did I learn that "Lost" was Lloyd Braun's project, and that both Eisner and Iger had disliked it. Braun, of course, had been fired. The following Sunday, "Desperate Housewives" debuted to even stronger ratings, and ABC beat both CBS and NBC during the first two weeks of the new season among young adults. "Housewives" was Susan Lyne's special project, which didn't stop *Variety* from fawning over Anne Sweeney and Steve McPherson, who "have shown what a difference regime change can make.")

I was there to discuss Eisner's resignation, not the new ABC season. Eisner says he drafted his letter on the company plane two weeks before submitting it and discussed it only with his wife and his lawyer, Irwin Russell. "I like the letter," he says. "I put twenty years of performance into two sentences. I like the ending." ("I'm going to Disneyland.") His main motivation, he says, was "Do the right thing." Eisner tells me he knew eight years before, when he signed a ten-year contract, that it would be his last at Disney. "I wanted to be young enough to have another career," he says.

Eisner says he realized he'd made the right decision at a dinner on Tuesday evening, September 7, where the featured speaker was Dr. Mehmet Oz, the head of the Columbia-Presbyterian Hospital cardiovascular surgery department. Dr. Oz spoke about the effects of an unhealthy lifestyle and stress on the body, which naturally brought back memories of Eisner's own heart surgery, not to mention thoughts of former president Bill Clinton, who just had a bypass operation at Columbia-Presbyterian. "This was a wake-up call to our mortality," Eisner explains. "It made me think about what's important and what's not important. I'll have done this job for twenty-two years when I step down." He reminds me that in twenty-eight years in the entertainment industry, he has taken only one week off.

Over the course of our interviews, Eisner has mentioned to me several times the need to reduce stress. But always, in the next breath, he says that work is what keeps him healthy. He does this again, telling me that his public relations adviser, Gershon Kekst, has just told him that the key to longevity is to keep working into one's nineties.

Finally I ask him why, if he was resigning as CEO and planning to leave Disney, he waited two weeks to indicate that he didn't want to remain as chairman or as a board member. "I didn't realize it would be an issue," he said. Then he adds, "Besides, I didn't say I didn't want to be chairman. Zenia has been saying that," indicating Zenia Mucha, who is sitting with us. "I don't want to be irrelevant. I'm not going to ask the board to be named chairman. I'm not going to beg for it. But the board might come to me. Then I'd have to consider it. Will I continue to play a creative role?" He ponders this for a moment. "That's up to Disney." (Later, when I check Eisner's quoted remarks in *Fortune* and other media, I see he's technically correct: all he has said is that he won't ask the board to name him chairman and doesn't "expect" to remain as a board member. He also said that Mitchell has assured him that the board will consider keeping him as chairman.)

"Anyway, talking about the future is counterproductive. I'm looking forward to the next two years. I'm going to be even more involved in the creative process." It dawns on me that for Eisner, this war is hardly over. Unlike the long-ago boxing match at Camp Keewaydin, he is still standing. No wonder Roy Disney is wary.

"I intend to create content forever," Eisner tells me. "Or at least for as long as I can."

EPILOGUE

No matter when or how Michael Eisner leaves Disney—even if he's carried out on his shield, as Stanley Gold predicted—nothing will erase his record of extraordinary achievement. There are the many animated hits destined to be classics; the extensive film library, which grew from 158 to 900 theatrical releases during Eisner's tenure; the 140 Academy Awards; the acquisition of ABC; the explosive growth of the cable channels, especially ESPN and the Disney channel; the Broadway shows and restored New Amsterdam Theatre; the acclaimed architecture at the theme parks and at Disney's Burbank headquarters. Despite Roy's quibbles about maintenance and cleanliness standards at Disneyland and Disney World, the strong and unique culture of the theme parks endures.

So does the Disney brand, even though Roy finds the notion of "branding" to be distasteful. Indeed, the Disney brand is so strong that it's often a constraint, despite Disney's efforts to develop independent brands under the Disney umbrella. Nor has Eisner been on a mission to impose traditional Disney values on the nation's culture. Disney during the Eisner years has tried to produce entertainment products that sell, and to do so has been willing to push the limits of the Disney brand. As Eisner put it in his film manifesto, "We have no obligation to make art. . . . We have no obligation to make a statement." Disney is as much a mirror of American culture as it is an influence on it.

Eisner can also boast a remarkable financial record. When Eisner arrived in 1984, Disney's operating income was $100 million; for 2004 it was projected to be $4.5 billion. Revenue was $1.6 billion in 1984; in 2004 it was a projected $30 billion. Adjusted for splits, the stock price was $1.33 in 1984;

twenty years later it was $25. And Disney's performance was strong in 2004, with cash flow hitting a record high. Eisner's own personal wealth has also soared; in 2003 he was ranked 385 in the list of *Forbes* magazine's 400 wealthiest Americans, with an estimated net worth of $630 million (in the same year, Roy was ranked 294, with an estimated net worth of $900 million. Eisner dropped from the list in 2004, while Roy climbed to 278 with an estimated worth of $1 billion). Eisner has earned his place among Hollywood's creative and business legends—Jack Warner, Louis B. Mayer, Cecil B. De-Mille.

But there's no denying that the seeds of Disney's creative and financial renaissance were nearly all planted in the first years of Eisner's tenure. Stanley Gold and Roy Disney are also correct that by nearly every financial measure, Disney's performance since 1995 has been weak. While Disney's stock price climbed to $28 in 2004, it was $42 as recently as 2000. And even Eisner's vaunted creativity—clearly the attribute that he himself holds most dear—seems to have been in eclipse. There have been some recent successes, such as *Pirates of the Caribbean,* but even there, Eisner criticized Johnny Depp's teeth and effeminate demeanor. The animation unit has been devastated and is a shadow of its former self, overshadowed by rivals Pixar and DreamWorks. The film studio has never again duplicated the string of hits during the early years under Eisner and Katzenberg. Eisner dismissed *Finding Nemo,* and Disney sold off most of the rights to *Sixth Sense.* Eisner criticized "Lost," ABC's first breakout hit in years. Although he insists on being judged only by what he has done, and not what he has failed to do, the hit projects he rejected, from "CSI" to *Lord of the Rings* and *Fahrenheit 9/11,* loom large.

But without benefit of hindsight, creative judgments are notoriously difficult both to make and to evaluate. There are far more objective and damaging measures of Eisner's performance. Beginning with the lavish, even reckless, overspending on Euro Disney, and continuing with the poorly planned and executed foray into the Internet, and perhaps worst of all, the acquisition of the Fox Family cable network—each of which is a more than $1 billion mistake—Eisner squandered Disney's assets. Even one blunder of that magnitude, let alone three, might have cost a chief executive his job at any public company that was acting in the interests of its shareholders and had any meaningful board oversight. This is even before considering the exit of Jeffrey Katzenberg, the failure to honor his contract, and the hiring and firing of Michael Ovitz, personnel and judgment errors which, in the cost to Disney and the vitriol and publicity they generated, are without parallel in American business history.

For all the lip service paid to shareholder value, Disney under Eisner was managed not for all of its shareholders, but primarily for three: Eisner himself, Sid Bass and his family interests, and, until their rupture, the Disney family represented by Roy and Stanley Gold. Nowhere was this more evident than in the makeup of the Disney board, which for most of Eisner's tenure was riddled with conflicts of interest. Board members were no doubt lulled into complacency by the extraordinary success of Eisner's early years. Still, Eisner controlled and manipulated the board by keeping members isolated, preferring to communicate one-on-one; selectively doling out information, access, and benefits, like tickets to the Super Bowl; and ruthlessly dispatching anyone who dared challenge him. The most striking example is Eisner's shameful treatment of Andrea Van de Kamp, a symbolic execution in which other board members sat passively by. Only an elementary school educator, Reveta Bowers, had the courage to speak out—and she, too, was already on her way out.

Eisner and other executives, especially Tom Staggs, deserve credit for not running seriously afoul of securities laws during a time of rampant corporate scandal. But Disney's decisions not to revalue the Family channel and seek a substantial tax benefit, and not to take this issue to the board, raise serious questions.

When did things start to go wrong? Almost everyone who has ever worked at Disney offers the same answer: the sudden and tragic death of Frank Wells in 1994, ten years into Eisner's reign. They argue that Wells was Eisner's check and balance, his rudder, his sounding board. Wells—and Wells alone—could question Eisner, disagree with him, get him to change his mind. When anyone had a problem with Eisner, from Katzenberg on down, they could "go to Frank" for redress. Wells was their ombudsman, their court of appeal. He made Disney executives feel valued and appreciated, leavening Eisner's sometimes harsh demands for ever harder work followed by scant praise.

There is no doubt a good deal of truth to these assessments. But they fail to explain the fact that Disney was already beginning to decline by the time of Wells's death. Wells hadn't succeeded in restraining Eisner in the building of Euro Disney. He had not been able to resolve the mounting crisis with Katzenberg. Wells's relationship with Eisner was fraying, suggested by Eisner's outbursts in front of Ovitz and his wife and Wells's own laments to Stanley Gold.

The answer seems more deeply rooted in Eisner's complex personality. Eisner is intelligent, charming, and funny. As his early years demonstrated, he has enormous creative skills and energy, and his management style in his early years at Disney, admittedly unorthodox and highly centralized, unleashed the same in others. Then, slowly but surely, as success mounted, Eisner's own identity fused with that of Disney itself. Many observers date this process to Eisner's insistence that he host "The Wonderful World of Disney" television program, just as Walt had done, and to claim the mantle of Walt Disney. It was a process reinforced by growing wealth and the trappings of power that, at Disney, a company deeply rooted in a culture of fantasy, actually do take on the aura of hereditary royalty. Eisner insists that his conjecture about his last name and the Disney name isn't meant to be taken seriously and, in his words, that "I'm not genetically attached" to Walt Disney. But why else would he repeat the comparison so often, if not to suggest that he is the rightful heir to the Disney legacy?

Perhaps this also helps explain Eisner's failures as a corporate manager. When Eisner lamented to me, as he did during our ride in his SUV, that it's unlikely there will be another entertainment or media chief executive like him, he may well be right. His management failures include an inability to delegate, a frequent mistrust of subordinates, impulsive and uncritical judgments, his pitting of one executive against another, his disrespect for any hierarchy of authority other than his own, his encouragement of a culture of spying and back-channeling, his frequent failure to acknowledge the achievements of others, and above all, his inability to groom a successor, notwithstanding his designation of Bob Iger as his heir apparent. Though Iger is praised by many as a hardworking and inherently decent person, Eisner placed him in many untenable positions, including ABC, where he had the responsibility but not final authority for the faltering network.

Iger could, of course, have quit, as did so many other Disney executives. There are many talented, creative, hard-working executives still at Disney. But the roster of Disney alumni either fired, forced to resign, or who left of their own initiative and who now occupy important posts elsewhere in corporate America is also unparalleled: Steve Burke, president of Comcast; Paul Pressler, chairman and chief executive of the Gap; Steve Bollenbach, chairman and chief executive of Hilton Hotels; Gary Wilson, chairman of Northwest Airlines; Peter Rummell, chairman and chief executive of St. Joseph; Judson Green, president and chief executive of NAVTEQ; Meg Whitman, chairman and chief executive of eBay; Richard Nanula, chief financial officer of Amgen; and Susan Lyne, chief executive of Martha Stewart Omnimedia.

In Hollywood, Joe Roth is chairman of Revolution Studios; Steve Bornstein is chief executive of the NFL Network; Bill Mechanic was chairman of

Twentieth Century Fox; Lloyd Braun is head of media and entertainment at Yahoo!; and Jeffrey Katzenberg is chairman and chief executive of Dream-Works Animation, which in October 2004 raised $812 million in a public stock offering. Disney both attracted and then disposed of an extraordinary group of senior executives—any one of whom might well have proven a worthy successor to Eisner. Indeed, the Disney board said it would consider former Disney executives in its quest for a new CEO.

The fusion of Eisner's identity with that of Disney—l'état, c'est moi—is hardly a rare phenomenon in either business or history. It has traditionally led to the downfall of nearly all absolute monarchies. When Eisner himself sometimes referred to the drama swirling around him as "Shakespearean," he might well have been describing the Bard's obsession with this very theme, in which a ruler disregards his subjects and answers only to the demands of his own ego.

A familiar tragic character in Shakespeare—Lear, Henry IV, Macbeth, Richard II, Richard III—is the monarch whose power is such that he bends the truth itself to suit his will. Perhaps that accounts in some part for what is clearly Eisner's most glaring defect, the one quality more than any other that has caused him to leave behind a trail of deeply embittered former colleagues: his dishonesty. Considering the importance Eisner places on honesty in others—dating at least to the childhood incident in which he believes his mother lied about his bedtime—it is extraordinary that Eisner himself has been so reckless with the truth, in ways both large and small, to a degree that suggests he is at times incapable of distinguishing one from the other. Far more than just a personality quirk, Eisner's tendency to distort, embellish, or forget the truth had direct and costly business consequences for Disney. More than any other single factor, what Steve Jobs and the Weinstein brothers considered Eisner's dishonesty accounts for the failure of the important Pixar and Miramax relationships. Katzenberg was so angry and bitter—and willing to sue—because he believed he was lied to and felt betrayed.

Like so many others emboldened by power, Eisner ultimately sealed his fate by overreaching. He lost a critical ally when Sid Bass, humbled by the post–September 11, 2001, collapse of technology stocks, divested his huge stake in Disney. And then Eisner turned against the one other check on his power, Roy Disney, embracing the effort to force Roy off the board. Eisner failed to recognize both the determination of Walt's long-underestimated nephew and the strength of a growing national movement of shareholder democracy activists, which led to Eisner's humiliating repudiation by 45 percent of Disney's shareholders. In the wake of the vote, even the Disney board had to face its responsibilities to shareholders, and not just to Eisner.

Perhaps most of all, Eisner underestimated the power of the Disney name. Eisner may have taken the place of Walt Disney before a weekly national television audience, but in the public imagination, there was only one Disney. Roy emerged as the guardian of Walt Disney's creative flame, the champion of the Disney faithful. "It's that Disney name!" Eisner exclaimed in exasperation to Diane Miller, seemingly oblivious to the fact that Diane herself is Walt's daughter and has proudly kept Disney as her middle name.

And so Eisner will go, perhaps on his own terms, perhaps not. A new era at Disney will begin. New generations of children and their parents will discover and be enchanted by *Snow White, Cinderella, The Little Mermaid,* and *Beauty and the Beast. The Lion King,* the musical, will be playing to packed houses. Glenn Close will still "adore fur" as Cruella De Vil, Johnny Depp will ride the high seas as Captain Jack Sparrow, and M. Night Shyamalan will find new twists to the supernatural. Visitors to Disney's theme parks will feel the gravitational pull of the moon as they head toward Mars and will soon come face-to-face with the Abominable Snowman of the Himalayas.

And somewhere—in Orlando, perhaps, or Anaheim, Paris, Tokyo, or Hong Kong—a small child will swallow his shyness and give Goofy a hug.

Afterword

I was at home with a bad cold on Tuesday morning, January 18, 2005, when the phone rang. *DisneyWar* was finished and on its way to the printer, or so I thought. It was Zenia Mucha at Disney, sounding much worse than I felt. She'd stayed up all night reading my manuscript. I didn't bother to ask where she'd gotten it, and never determined which of several drafts she had obtained. Simon & Schuster had kept the book under tight security, embargoing the contents until publication and circulating no review copies. To the best of my knowledge, only a handful of people inside Simon & Schuster had read it, and copies had been tightly controlled and accounted for. Still, I can't say I was all that surprised. I'd seen firsthand how information circulates in Hollywood, whether it was the latest hot screenplay or the Katzenberg manifesto that had so annoyed Eisner and was reprinted in *Variety*.

I braced myself for more reactions. I had always known the day would come when Eisner would read the book, even though this was somewhat sooner than I had expected. He had often quizzed me about it, asking if we'd still be speaking once it was published. I had remained noncommittal. I didn't know how he would react, and had long given up predicting reactions of people I'd written about. But I knew how sensitive Eisner could be, how angry he had often been over even minor perceived slights that appeared in the press. I also knew he could carry grudges for years, even decades.

The next evening Eisner called me. To my surprise, he seemed calm. He told me that Mucha was upset about the book, and she seemed to be his primary concern. This hardly seemed the Eisner I had come to know. Perhaps I'd underestimated his maturity. Then he called on Thursday morning. This time he seemed apoplectic. It turned out that the day before, he hadn't read any of the manuscript. Now he had read the introduction and the conclusion. He insisted on reading and commenting on the entire manuscript. This wasn't an opportunity anyone else had been given, but he was the central character, and since he already had it, I agreed. But the production schedule couldn't be delayed by much. I told him he had to give me his comments by the close of business Friday, which would give me the weekend for any additional research and corrections that might be warranted. The book was going to press Monday morning.

Beginning Friday afternoon and continuing with a few interruptions until late at night Eastern time, Eisner and I were on the phone as he paged through the manuscript, deciphering handwritten notes he'd made while reading, and adding additional comments. I have to hand it to him. At times he was predictably angry, both at me and others he perceived at having betrayed him; at times cajoling, trying to inject his interpretation or get me to delete material, and at times surprisingly good natured, even funny. Maybe it was just the late hour, but we both ended up laughing over a few passages. He called again on Monday morning, but I told him the book was out of my hands, and that the presses were rolling. Eisner vowed that he'd never speak to me again.

By coincidence, the accelerated publication of *DisneyWar* coincided with Disney's annual meeting on February 11, held in snowbound Minneapolis, a venue likely to discourage the kind of support Roy Disney and Stanley Gold had mustered the previous year in Philadelphia. This time the meeting was uneventful; Roy and Gold had suspended their campaign to oust Eisner now that he had pledged to resign, and were awaiting the results of the board's search for a successor.

In that regard, Chairman George Mitchell stated that the Disney board was committed to a process to find "the best possible person to decisively and creatively lead this company into its very promising future."

This supposedly wide-ranging search process exposed at least three factions within the board, with some directors wavering between one group or the other. There were the stalwart, pro-Eisner directors, with Judith Estrin the most vocal. They not only supported Iger, Eisner's choice to succeed him as chief executive, but wanted Eisner to reclaim the title of chairman, or at least stay on as a member of the board. Eisner naturally aligned himself with these directors, and even suggested that he might move into Walt's old office—the same office recently vacated by Roy. Another group wanted Iger as chief executive, but had become disillusioned with Eisner. Though increasingly skeptical of Eisner and his motives, they deemed the appointment of an outsider as chief executive to be too radical a step for Disney. The third group opposed both Eisner and Iger. These directors wanted a thorough search and felt Iger had been compromised by his fealty to Eisner. They were comfortable with the prospect of bringing in someone from the outside and were strongly opposed to Eisner remaining at Disney in any capacity.

To judge from the rhetoric about the "process," and given that Disney had hired a leading professional search firm, the camp opposed to both Eisner and Iger seemed to be in control. In reality, a majority of directors opposed any meaningful search outside the company. Some quietly discouraged leading candidates such as Peter Chernin at News Corp. and Les Moonves at Viacom by intimating that Iger had already secured a board majority. When the search firm did put out feelers, they were rebuffed, with some candidates indicating it was too risky to put their necks on the line for a job they were unlikely to get. In the end, only Meg Whitman, eBay's highly regarded CEO, and a former Disney executive, agreed to meet with the board, and she was recruited directly by board members, not the search firm. Both Iger and she were formally interviewed by the board, with Eisner present for part of the sessions.

Whitman performed brilliantly, in the view of at least some directors. But it didn't really matter. A majority had already concluded that Iger deserved the job, especially on the strength of the "Lost"- and "Desperate Housewives"-led turnaround at ABC. To turn to an outsider, even a Disney veteran like Whitman, was too radical a step. Even before a formal board vote, Whitman withdrew her candidacy, having been warned that she would go down to defeat.

Even as directors reached a consensus to support Iger, many on the board recognized that the Eisner era had to come to a definitive end. In return for supporting Iger, and making the board's decision unanimous, the anti-Eisner directors extracted a pledge from the others that his departure would be accelerated from September of 2006 to 2005, that he would not be permitted to regain the title of chairman, and would not be allowed to remain on the board when his term ended the following year. The decision, made in a session from which Eisner was excluded, came as a blow to Eisner, a repudiation of his twenty-year tenure at the head of the company. Any hopes he may have had that an Iger-led Disney would accommodate Eisner's outsized personality were dashed.

On March 13, Mitchell announced that "after a lengthy, thorough and professional search process, comparing both internal and external candidates against our criteria for CEO, I am pleased to announce the decision of the Walt Disney Board of Directors to select Robert Iger as the company's next chief executive officer. Bob is an experienced, talented and visionary leader." While Disney's continued insistence that the search process had been "thorough and exhaustive" strained credulity, the choice of Iger nonetheless came as a relief to many at Disney, ending a boardroom and executive suite drama that had drained energy and attention from more pressing concerns. At the same time, Eisner issued a statement that "Although I intend to remain as a Disney director until the annual meeting of 2006, I will not make a request of the Board to nominate me for an additional term nor will I seek the chairmanship of the company after the retirement of Senator Mitchell."

Eisner's long-standing fears about being a lame duck were soon realized.

The new Iger era began months before Eisner's planned departure. Iger dismantled the much-despised strategic planning department under Peter Murphy. The Miramax relationship was beyond salvation, and Disney's ties to the Weinstein brothers were severed. But Iger promptly resurrected talks with Steve Jobs about the future of the far more important Pixar relationship as well as a variety of joint initiatives between Disney and Apple. Perhaps most remarkably, Iger managed to bury the hatchet with Roy and Gold. In return for dropping a lawsuit that called the search process a "sham," a proceeding that threatened to once again drag Disney's boardroom politics into public view, Roy agreed to return to the company as director emeritus and as a consultant. When Hong Kong Disneyland opened on September 12, Roy and his son attended, as did Eisner in his last ceremonial appearance as Disney's chief executive. The "war" was over.

Iger consciously patterned the new era on the decentralized, genial model of Tom Murphy's at the old Cap Cities/ABC, not Eisner's idiosyncratic and often chaotic management style. After the steady drain of talent during Eisner's last decade, it was too soon to know if this could spawn the creative rebirth that Roy was so eager for. Both animation and live action had dismal years, with Disney having to announce a write-off for the film division in September of $250–300 million, much of it from over-valued Miramax assets, but also a reflection of the weak results Disney had endured at the box office, without a single bona fide hit. It hardly seemed possible that Disney's big summer movie—*Herbie: Fully Loaded*—was a remake of *The Love Bug*, the 1968 film derided by Gold when Roy quit the board back in 1977. Even *The Shaggy Dog* was due for a 2006 remake. Animation pinned its hopes on Disney's first fully computer-generated animated film, *Chicken Little*. Eisner had upset some of the animators by insisting that the chicken be a boy, rather than the girl of the original fable. The film opened on November 4, 2005, to some scathing reviews. "The studio's first fully computer-animated feature is a deep disappointment," the *Wall Street Journal* reported. "For those of us who grew up on the magical splendors of Disney animation, this magic-free film is heartbreaking." While Disney hailed the $40 million opening weekend, it was a far cry from Pixar's *The Incredibles* $70-plus million opening a year earlier. (J.P. Morgan estimated that Disney had spent $125 million on *Chicken Little* promotion and advertising alone.) More telling was Disney's announcement that it was delaying other animated films in the pipeline and further scaling back production.

The bright spot was the performance of ABC, which, on the continued strength of "Lost," "Desperate Housewives," and a newer hit, "Gray's Anatomy" (the last show developed by the Lloyd Braun/Susan Lyne regime), captured first place in the key eleven- to forty-nine-year-old demographic by mid-October, although CBS retained the overall ratings crown. The strong ratings came "just in the nick of time. Next week I couldn't take credit for it," Eisner told an audience at the Beverly Wilshire hotel the week before his exit, without any evident irony that Braun and Lyne had been fired.

Overall, Disney's financial results remained fairly strong during Eisner's last year, boosted by gains at the theme parks, the continued success of ESPN, and better ratings and advertising revenues at ABC. But a host of problems weighed on the stock price, including faltering DVD sales, the weak studio results, fears that theme park revenues were cyclical with little chance for continued double-digit gains, and the flight of advertising dollars from traditional media to the Internet. Disney shares on the day of Eisner's departure were just over $24, down from nearly $30 in February, just before Disney's annual meeting.

Eisner had often posited that entertainment is a cyclical business, and a bad season or two won't override Eisner's creative legacy. But the last word on his tenure as Disney's chief executive may well have come in a Delaware court case that revisited in exhaustive detail the hiring and firing of Michael Ovitz, surely the signature saga of Eisner's tumultuous final years at Disney.

The case was a suit that put Eisner, Ovitz, Roy, Gold, and other Disney directors in the unlikely roles of allies and co-defendants. The plaintiffs were Disney shareholders, whose lawyer, Steve Schulman, argued that Disney's executives and board had breached their duties to shareholders and should reimburse the company for the $140 million Ovitz payout plus interest and expenses. After wending its way through various Delaware courts, the case came to trial in October 2004. Eisner testified for several days and avidly followed the proceedings via closed-circuit television.

The eagerly awaited decision by Chancellor William B. Chandler III was issued on August 9, 2005. On the surface, it was a sweeping victory for Disney management and the Disney board, since the chancellor ruled that, however flawed the process and inattentive the board in hiring and firing Ovitz, the directors still hadn't breached their duty of acting in good faith. The opinion noted that Ovitz not only couldn't have been fired "for cause," as the plaintiffs' lawyers had argued, but noted that he had worked quite diligently in his capacity as Disney president, many of his ideas were sound, and the facts didn't support Eisner's frequent charges that he was dishonest, untrustworthy, and unethical.

In contrast to his relatively benign characterization of Ovitz, Chandler called Eisner the "long-time friend of Ovitz and the instigator and mastermind behind the machinations that resulted in Ovitz's hiring . . . Eisner is the most culpable of the defendants. He was pulling the strings; he knew what was going on. . . . By virtue of his Machiavellian (and imperial) nature as CEO, and his control over Ovitz's hiring in particular, Eisner is to a large extent responsible for the failings in process that infected and handicapped the board's decision-making abilities." After lambasting Eisner for "stacking" the board of directors with "friends and other acquaintances," "yes-men" with "sycophantic tendencies," he concluded that Eisner had "enthroned himself as the omnipotent and infallible monarch of his personal Magic Kingdom." Chandler noted that his conduct, though not in explicit violation of Delaware law, "does not comport with how fiduciaries of Delaware corporations are expected to act."

The Delaware chancellor's characterization of Eisner was scathing, especially considering the context, a judicial opinion that was otherwise a sober, restrained, and scholarly review of facts and law. It was particularly devastating because it was delivered by a neutral observer who had spent months studying the evidence. It couldn't be dismissed as the biased allegations of a disgruntled former employee, or a reckless journalist, or shareholder activists, or an embittered Disney family member.

With less than two months remaining in Eisner's tenure at Disney, the opinion effectively ended the possibility of any remaining role for Eisner at Disney. Having given up any chance of becoming chairman himself, he had been maneuvering among board members to secure the position for Judith Estrin, and many saw his efforts as a transparent attempt to maintain influence behind the scenes, since Estrin had emerged as his most consistent and loyal supporter on the board. Though the choice wouldn't be made until 2006, Chandler's opinion seemed likely to doom this effort as well.

Both in public and in conversations with other Disney executives, Eisner seemed his usual cheerful, optimistic self, oblivious to any blows to his reputation or to his diminished status at Disney or in Hollywood. If his long-held fears that his phone calls would no longer be returned were being realized, he gave no indication. Even directors angered by his earlier maneuvering to remain on the board or regain the chairmanship gave him credit for stepping aside gracefully and letting Iger take the spotlight.

Even Eisner's appearance at Hong Kong Disneyland attracted scant attention, and he continued to maintain a low profile. He declined to comment on his plans for the future. To some he mentioned starting an independent film production company, but he was also looking at investment possibilities on Broadway and exploring investments outside the entertainment industry. He was seen less often at the Team Disney headquarters. He said he wanted no farewell celebrations, and his last day was marked by an informal gathering of Disney employees in the studio commissary. Recent controversies went unmentioned, and he reminisced about his first day on the job in 1984, when he had spoken to Disney employees and confused "BVD" with an underwear company.

His final gesture as Disney's chief executive was, in characteristic Eisner fashion, an email to the company's 129,000 employees:

This company, which I so love, is poised for a tremendous future, with superb management at all levels, entrusted to the brilliant and steady chief executive officer, Bob Iger. I want to thank everybody for letting me share a piece of your lives for two decades.

While I leave Disney with less hair than I had when I arrived, I do know creative inquisitiveness never ages or tires. I feel as optimistic as I did on Oct. 1, 1984.

By the way, I have since learned that BVD stands for Buena Vista Distribution. Good luck, and go see Chicken Little.

Michael.

That same day, Eisner resigned his seat on the board, nearly six months before the end of his term. In a filing with the Securities and Exchange Commission, Disney disclosed that Eisner's tenure as chief executive had ended on October 1, 2005, and that he "no longer tenders any services" to Disney.

A Note on Sources

This book is based primarily on firsthand reporting consisting of hundreds of interviews and a review of many thousands of pages of documents. In part because Michael Eisner and Disney extended a degree of cooperation, and because I had become a familiar presence in and around the company by the time many of the critical events in this story took place, I had remarkable access to people on all sides of the conflict as many of the events were unfolding, including Eisner, Robert Iger, and Roy Disney and Stanley Gold.

With respect to Disney and its executives, I say a "degree" of cooperation, because their participation, helpful as it was, did not rise to a level that I would describe as cooperation, certainly not as compared to the enthusiastic and exhaustive cooperation shown by many other sources. Disney did give firsthand exposure to many of its businesses and allowed me to assume the role of a character at Walt Disney World. To my knowledge, Eisner didn't discourage anyone inside or outside the company from speaking to me. He introduced me to numerous executives and sometimes, in my presence, urged them to speak candidly. I spent many hours with Eisner, often in interviews in his offices both in New York and Burbank, on the phone, exchanging emails, observing him in meetings and other situations, riding with him in cars, and sharing meals. Most of the time Disney's head of corporate communications, Zenia Mucha, was also present. I have nothing but admiration for the effective, professional, and courteous reception extended me by Mucha and her staff at Disney, especially Paul Roeder and Anne Wolanski. Craig Dizern was an impeccable host at Disney World, and Walt himself would have been proud of Jonathan Frontado, who served as my guide.

Disney was of course free to decide to what degree it would share information with me. By the traditional, secretive standards of Disney (and most corporations, for that matter) it no doubt thought it was being extraordinarily open.

But I quickly realized that its willingness to cooperate was limited. My requests to spend time with Eisner at his homes in Aspen and Bel Air, or on the corporate jet, where I had hoped to have extensive and uninterrupted time for interviews, were declined or went unanswered. No such meetings took place. My repeated requests for copies of written communications—letters, memos, emails—many of which I knew existed, were denied. Eisner declined to discuss, or was willing to discuss only to a limited degree, many aspects of his career. When he did sometimes provide narrative accounts of events I had already heard described by others, there were major omissions and inaccuracies. Other company executives were often put in difficult positions by my questions, having to choose between speaking openly and saying something for which they feared retaliation. I quickly realized on which side of that divide most of them would fall.

Despite this lack of full-scale cooperation, I had the extraordinary advantage of access to a rich lode of material describing Eisner's actions, words, and state of mind throughout his career at Disney, as well as many other executives and board members. Has there ever been a chief executive who put more of his thoughts in writing than Eisner? I know of none. Though Eisner appears to have curtailed the practice in recent months and years, he is a natural—some might say compulsive—writer, in letters, handwritten notes, and especially in emails. Even then, I might never have had access to these communications had Eisner and Disney not embroiled themselves in prolonged and contentious litigation, first over Jeffrey Katzenberg's bonus and then over the hiring and firing of Michael Ovitz. Many of these written materials were introduced as evidence and read into the record at trial and in depositions.

My sources for much of the narrative describing Katzenberg's career at Disney and his relationship with Eisner are the transcripts of testimony and the exhibits in *Jeffrey Katzenberg vs. The Walt Disney Co.*, Case No. BC 147864, in the Superior Court of the State of California, Los Angeles. These include many of the notes taken by author Tony Schwartz, which played such an important role in the trial.

An even more voluminous record has been compiled in *In Re The Walt Disney Co. Derivative Litigation*, Consolidated Action No. 15452, which was pending in the Delaware Court of Chancery as this book went to press. Thanks to the rulings of Chancellor William B. Chandler III, whose opinions consistently recognized the high level of public interest in Disney's conduct, as well as the First Amendment guarantee of public access to court proceedings, I was able to review tens of thousands of pages of deposition testimony, trial testimony, and related exhibits, which exhaustively explored the hiring and firing of Ovitz as well as other events at Disney during the period. I have quoted extensively from these materials, as indicated in the text. Whatever the outcome of the case, credit belongs to Steven Schulman, the lead lawyer for the plaintiffs, and his colleagues at the firm of Milberg, Weiss, Bershad & Schulman, for diligently pursuing a case

against formidable odds that is likely to set new standards for corporate governance. Jennifer Hirsh, also of Milberg, Weiss, provided invaluable assistance in
helping me gain access to these materials.

I am also grateful to Martha Rainbolt, Andrea Sununu, and Cynthia Cornell,
members of the DePauw University Department of English, for their guidance
in comparing Eisner to characters in Shakespeare.

This book would not be what it is without the unstinting cooperation of
many people with firsthand knowledge of events at Disney over the past twenty
years. Some of these people are or were employed at Disney and spoke to me at
considerable risk to their careers, especially given Disney's reputation for vindic-
tiveness and litigiousness. Many of these people spoke on a not-for-attribution
basis; others were on the record. An advantage of using a narrative approach is
that none of these sources are identified. Nearly all the quotes taken directly
from my interviews and attributed to the speaker are those from Eisner. Otherwise, to identify some sources and not others would simply invite speculation,
by process of elimination, about who was or wasn't a source.

As part of the narrative, I have included passages of dialogue. Dialogue—
what words were said—is a fact like any other. It is not necessarily a quotation
from an interview with me and I would discourage readers from inferring that
one or both of the speakers is a direct source. Especially in today's world of instant communication, it is sometimes amazing how many people turn out to be
privy to what others may assume is a private conversation. Many of the conversations reported in this book either took place before an audience or became
known to a wide circle of people, often within minutes of their taking place.
Many of these conversations were the subjects of testimony. In a few cases other
people were listening in on speakerphones, extensions, or overheard conversations without one or both of the speakers' knowledge. Readers should bear in
mind that, given the vagaries of human memory, remembered dialogue is rarely
the same as actual recordings and transcripts. At the same time, it is no more nor
less accurate than many other recollections.

There is an extensive bibliography on the subject of the Walt Disney Company and its founders. Apart from the many travel guides to theme parks, uncritical fan and movie enthusiast publications, histories and picture books on
the theme parks and the animated classics, much of it is of dubious accuracy, to
judge from my reporting as well as comments from members of the Disney family and current and former employees. I have cited below only those works on
which I relied in some part. The biographies of Walt and Roy Disney by Bob
Thomas were consistently reliable and did not shy away from controversy, such
as the schism between the "Walt" and "Roy" sides of the Disney family and
within the company, even though they were authorized books, in that Disney
executives had prior approval of their content.

Among journalists covering Disney, a few stand out for the quality, reliability, and insightfulness of their work: Bruce Orwall and Richard Turner at *The Wall Street Journal;* Laura M. Holson and Bernard Weinraub at *The New York Times,* Claudia Eller and James Bates at the *Los Angeles Times,* Bryan Burrough in *Vanity Fair,* and Ken Auletta in *The New Yorker.*

BOOKS

Biskind, Peter. *Down and Dirty Pictures: Miramax, Sundance, and the Rise of Independent Film.* New York: Simon & Schuster, 2004.

Broggie, Michael. *Walt Disney's Railroad Story: The Small-Scale Fascination That Led to a Full-Scale Kingdom.* Pasadena, Calif.: Pentrex Media, 1998.

Dunlop, Beth. *Building a Dream: The Art of Disney Architecture.* New York: Harry N. Adams, 1996.

Eisner, Michael, with Tony Schwartz. *Work in Progress.* New York: Random House, 1998.

Imagineers (Group). *Walt Disney Imagineering: A Behind the Dreams Look at Making the Magic Real.* New York: Hyperion Books, 1996.

Manvell, Roger. *Art and Animation.* New York: Hastings House Publishers, 1980.

Masters, Kim. *The Keys to the Kingdom: How Michael Eisner Lost His Grip.* New York: HarperCollins, 2000.

Taylor, John. *Storming the Magic Kingdom: Wall Street, the Raiders, and the Battle for Disney.* New York: Knopf, 1987.

Thomas, Bob. *Walt Disney, an American Original.* New York: Simon & Schuster, 1976.

————. *Building a Company: Roy O. Disney and the Creation of an Entertainment Empire.* New York: Hyperion Books, 1998.

ARTICLES

Prologue

Orwall, Bruce, and Emily Nelson. "A Hidden Wall, Upheld by 80 Years of Culture, Shields Disney Kingdom: For Comcast or Any Suitor, Mastering Insular Ways Would Be Daunting Job; Walking in Mickey Mouse's Shoes." *Wall Street Journal,* February 16, 2004.

One

Cieply, Michael. "Hollywood Star: An Agent Dominates Film and TV Studios with Package Deals; Michael Ovitz Puts Together Clients of Creative Artists in Single High-Fee Unit; Huffled Voices of Protest." *Wall Street Journal,* December 19, 1986.

Harmetz, Aljean. "Disney Hopes Eisner Can Wake Sleeping Beauty." *New York Times,* October 17, 1984.

Hayes, Thomas C. "Disney's Chief Is Forced Out." *New York Times,* September 8, 1984.

Schwartz, Tony. "Hollywood's Hottest Stars." *New York Magazine,* July 30, 1984.
————. "Son of Hollywood's Hottest Stars: Behind the Quake at Paramount that Rocked the Business." *New York Magazine,* July 30, 1984.

Two
Frook, John Evan. "Disney Changes Its Toon." *Variety,* October 18, 1993.

Three
Ebert, Roger. " 'Down and Out' Is Authentic, Funny: Film Is Perfectly Cast." *Chicago Sun-Times,* January 31, 1986.
Harmetz, Aljean. "Looking Ahead." *New York Times,* December 20, 1987.
Kempley, Rita. "The 'Rabbit' That Roared; From Disney and Spielberg, a Charmer, More Fun Than a Barrel of Bunnies." *Washington Post,* June 22, 1988.
Knowlton, Christopher. "How Disney Keeps the Magic Going." *Fortune,* December 4, 1989.
Leerhsen, Charles. "How Disney Does It." *Newsweek,* April 3, 1989.
Masters, Kim. "Bunny Hop." *Premiere,* July 1988.

Four
Boyer, Peter J. "Katzenberg's Seven-Year Itch." *Vanity Fair,* November 1991.
Ebert, Roger. "Sweetly Innocent 'Woman' Glows with True Romance." *Chicago Sun-Times,* March 23, 1990.
Kerwin, Kathleen, and Antonio N. Fins. "Disney Is Looking Just a Little Fragilistic." *Business Week,* June 25, 1990.
Maslin, Janet. "Andersen's 'Mermaid,' by Way of Disney." *New York Times,* November 15, 1989.
————. " 'Beauty and the Beast': New Form and Content." *New York Times,* November 13, 1991.

Five
Crary, David. "Weather Is Cold, President Tepid, But Mickey's Welcome Warm." Associated Press, April 13, 1992.
Drozdiak, William. "Cheers, Jeers Greet Disney Debut in Europe." *Washington Post,* April 13, 1992.
Hopkins, Nic. "Euro Disney's New Studio Park Puts It in the Red." *The Times* (London), November 14, 2002.
Rose, Frank. "Can Disney Tame 42nd Street?" *Fortune,* June 24, 1996.

Six
"Disney Roars in Kingdom of Movie Merchandise Marketing: The Entertainment Giant Could Reap $800 Million in Pretax Profits Over Three Years from the Sale of 'Lion King'–related Items." Reuters, August 11, 1994.

Maslin, Janet. "The Hero Within the Child Within." *New York Times,* June 15, 1994.

Newton, Edmund, and James Bates. "Disney President Wells Killed in Copter Crash." *Los Angeles Times,* April 4, 1994.

Turner, Richard. "Jungle Fever: Disney, Using Cash and Claw, Stays King of Animated Movies." *Wall Street Journal,* May 16, 1994.

Weinraub, Bernard. "A Shock for Disney, but No Turmoil." *New York Times,* April 5, 1994.

Seven

Auletta, Ken. "The Human Factor." *New Yorker,* September 26, 1994.

Citron, Alan, and James Bates. "For Roy Disney, Legacy Is Everything." *Los Angeles Times,* August 26, 1994.

Eller, Claudia, and Alan Citron. "Angst at Disney's World." *Los Angeles Times,* July 24, 1994.

Reckard, E. Scott. "Eisner Illness Provokes New Debate on Disney Future." Associated Press, July 19, 1994.

Weinraub, Bernard. "Hollywood Sees Tension at Disney." *New York Times,* July 20, 1994.

———. "Katzenberg Leaving Post at Disney; Studio Head Is 2nd Top Executive Lost." *New York Times,* August 25, 1994.

Eight

Auletta, Ken. "Awesome." *New Yorker,* August 14, 1995.

De Moraes, Lisa. "Three Outs Strike Dis; Hightower in for Frank." *Hollywood Reporter,* March 13, 1995.

Fabrikant, Geraldine. "Walt Disney to Acquire ABC in $19 Billion Deal to Build a Giant for Entertainment." *New York Times,* August 1, 1995.

Harris, Kathryn. "The Loneliest Man in the Kingdom: Forget Walt, Michael Eisner, Disney's Hands-on Chairman, Is Shaping the Company in His Own Image." *Los Angeles Times Magazine,* March 26, 1995.

Hofmeister, Sallie, and Jane Hall. "Disney to Buy Cap Cities/ABC for $19 Billion." *Los Angeles Times,* August 1, 1995.

Huey, John. "Eisner Explains Everything." *Fortune,* April 17, 1995.

Landro, Laura, Elizabeth Jensen, and Thomas R. King, "Disney Creates a New Magic Kingdom." *Wall Street Journal,* August 1, 1995.

Powers, William F. "Eisner Says Disney Won't Back Down." *Washington Post,* June 14, 1994.

Spayd, Liz, and Paul Farhi. "Eisner Ended Disney Plan; Chairman Saw Park Fight Harming Company's Image." *Washington Post,* September 30, 1994.

Swoboda, Frank. "Disney Ends Negotiations to Buy NBC." *Washington Post,* September 27, 1994.

Weinraub, Bernard. "Katzenberg to Form Studio with Geffen and Spielberg." *New York Times*, October 12, 1994.
———. "Clouds Over Disneyland." *New York Times*, April 9, 1995.

Nine

Anson, Robert Sam. "Geffen Ungloved." *Los Angeles Times Magazine*, July 1995.

Ebert, Roger. "Brilliant Animation Makes 'Toy' a Feast for the Eyes." *Chicago Sun-Times*, November 22, 1995.

Groves, Martha, and James Flanigan. "Ovitz Ideal Pick for Global Giant." *Los Angeles Times*, August 15, 1995.

Guthrie, Julian. "Pixie Dust: Can Steve Jobs Take Another Bite Out of the Apple with 'Toy Story'?" *San Francisco Examiner*, November 12, 1995.

Snider, Burr. "The 'Toy Story' Story: How John Lasseter Came to Make the First 100-Percent Computer-Generated Theatrical Motion Picture." *Wired*, December 1995.

Ten

Burrough, Bryan, and Kim Masters. "The Mouse Trap." *Vanity Fair*, December 1996.

Eller, Claudia. "Rumor Mills Grinding over Ovitz Exit." *Los Angeles Times*, November 26, 1996.

———. "Awful Truth: Is Lying a Practiced Art in Hollywood?" *Los Angeles Times*, February 28, 1997.

Hirschberg, Lynn. "Jamie Tarses' Fall, as Scheduled." *New York Times Magazine*, July 13, 1997.

Nathan, Jean. "What China Would Bury in Moroccan Sand." *New York Times*, December 22, 1996.

Zoglin, Richard. "A Better Mousetrap? With Disney Ready to Rebuild Things, ABC Braces for Change and Lots of Trips to Space Mountain." *Time*, April 15, 1996.

Eleven

Bates, James, and Claudia Eller. "Ovitz to Leave Disney After Rocky Year as President." *Los Angeles Times*, December 13, 1996.

———. "Disney's Michael Eisner Is Alone Again, Naturally." *Los Angeles Times*, December 14, 1996.

Boehm, Mike. "A Rocky Road, Step by Step: Disney Hall Is Here, But It Wasn't Easy." *Los Angeles Times*, September 14, 2003.

Burrough, Bryan. "Ovitz Agonizes." *Vanity Fair*, August 2002.

Canby, Vincent. " 'The Lion King' Earns Its Roars of Approval." *New York Times*, November 23, 1997.

Eller, Claudia. "Disney's Spreading of Financial Risk Made 'Sense' Then." *Los Angeles Times*, August 31, 1999.

Gay, Verne. "Not Changing Channels; Embattled ABC Exec Tarses Staying Put." *Newsday* (New York), July 24, 1997.

Jenkins, Holman W., Jr. "Beavis and Butt-head Do the Disney Shareholders." *Wall Street Journal*, January 7, 1997.

Orwall, Bruce. "Disney Says Michael Ovitz Is Resigning as President; Decision Is Called Mutual; Move Rekindles Issue of a Successor to Eisner." *Wall Street Journal*, December 13, 1996.

Orwall, Bruce, and Joann S. Lublin. "Plutocracy: If a Company Prospers, Should Its Directors Behave by the Book?; Disney's Eisner Shoots Back at Critics Who Say Board Isn't Truly Independent." *Wall Street Journal*, February 24, 1997.

Rosenthal, A. M. "Hardtack for the Journey." *New York Times*, December 20, 1996.

Samuelson, Robert J. "What's $90 Million Between Friends?" *Washington Post*, December 25, 1996.

Weinraub, Bernard. "Down but Probably Not Out; Despite His Defeat in Disneyland, Ovitz Remains a Force to Reckon With." *New York Times*, December 14, 1996.

Twelve

Bates, James, and Claudia Eller. "Empire Builders." *Los Angeles Times Magazine*, March 26, 2000.

Bowman, Lisa. "Jailbait and Switch." ZDWire, April 1, 2000.

Brenner, Marie. "The Man Who Knew Too Much." *Vanity Fair*, May 1996.

Carter, Bill. "Olympic-Caliber Performance." *New York Times*, November 24, 1999.

———. "From Creator of 'C.S.I.,' Testimonials to Himself." *New York Times*, August 11, 2003.

De Moraes, Lisa. " 'Millionaire's' Clean Sweeps." *Washington Post*, November 17, 1999.

Dreher, Rod. "Very Good 'Sense': Word-of-Mouth Lifts Scary Film." *New York Post*, August 23, 1999.

Fabrikant, Geraldine. "Hey There! Hi There! It's a New Michael Eisner; Disney Leader Woos a Fretful Wall Street." *New York Times*, August 18, 1999.

Hansell, Saul. "Mouse Attack in Cyberspace." *New York Times*, December 13, 1998.

Harris, Kathryn. "Best of Bloomberg." *Chicago Sun-Times*, May 9, 1999.

Jenkins, Holman W., Jr. "Mouse Gets a Whiff of Waterloo." *Wall Street Journal*, May 19, 1999.

Jensen, Elizabeth, and Brian Lowry. "ABC Losing Key Television Personnel." *Los Angeles Times,* August 25, 1999.

Krantz, Michael. "Disney's Brain Drain: Some of Eisner's Top Executives Have Shipped Out, but the Company's Profit Machine Rolls On." *Time,* June 15, 1998.

Lowry, Brian. "Tarses Resigns as Head of ABC Entertainment." *Los Angeles Times,* August 29, 1999.

Morgenstern, Joe. "What? A Good Sequel? A Brilliant 'Toy Story 2' Proves It Can Happen." *Wall Street Journal,* November 26, 1999.

Orwall, Bruce. "Hostility Between Disney's Eisner and Katzenberg Explodes in Court." *Wall Street Journal,* May 5, 1999.

Rich, Frank. "Who Doesn't Want to Be a Millionaire." *New York Times,* November 20, 1999.

Thirteen

Carter, Bill. "Britons Revamp American TV." *New York Times,* July 18, 2000.

Eller, Claudia, and James Bates. "Disney, Pixar in Dispute Over Pact." *Los Angeles Times,* October 22, 2001.

Eller, Claudia, and Richard Natale. "Hit Status Elusive Target for 'Pearl Harbor'; Disney's Hopes for Its Own 'Titanic' Have Been Sunk." *Los Angeles Times,* June 17, 2001.

Gabler, Neal. "Win Now, or Lose Forever." *New York Times,* May 3, 2000.

Greppi, Michele. "Execs Spin the Positives as Key Nov. Sweep Ends." *Hollywood Reporter,* November 29, 2000.

Hansell, Saul. "America Online Agrees to Buy Time Warner for $165 Billion; Media Deal Is Richest Merger." *New York Times,* January 11, 2000.

Holden, Stephen. "Old Sorcery, New Tricks." *New York Times,* December 31, 1999.

James, Meg, and Sallie Hofmeister. "This Family Was Really Messed Up: Michael Eisner Saw a Gem When Disney Paid $5 Billion for a Kids Cable Channel." *Los Angeles Times,* June 15, 2004.

Rich, Frank. "The Best Years of Our Lives." *New York Times,* May 26, 2001.

Rosenberg, Howard. "The Day the World Shattered; a Junket That Will Live in Infamy." *Los Angeles Times,* May 25, 2001.

Welkos, Robert W. "Marshalling All of His Forces." *Los Angeles Times,* May 20, 2001.

Fourteen

Bates, James, and Claudia Eller. "Key Disney Board Members Are Putting Heat on the CEO to Act More Aggressively; Shares Are Lowest Since November 1994." *Los Angeles Times,* August 8, 2002.

Bates, James, and Richard Verrier. "Eisner Crimping His Own Style." *Los Angeles Times*, August 14, 2002.

Carter, Bill. "ABC's 'Millionaire' May Not Survive Beyond the Current Season." *New York Times*, November 29, 2001.

———. "Koppel Is the Odd Man Out as ABC Woos Letterman." *New York Times*, March 1, 2002.

———. "Networks Try to Sell Letterman on Conglomerate Muscle." *New York Times*, March 8, 2002.

———. "Letterman Will Remain in CBS Slot." *New York Times*, March 12, 2002.

Dolan, Kerry A. "Beyond Power Rangers: Billionaire Haim Saban Revels in the Sweet Deal He Got From Fox and Disney." *Forbes*, November 26, 2001.

Goodman, Tim. "Who Wants to Be a TV Programmer? ABC's Pompous Executives Put All Their Money on 'Millionaire' and Lost Big." *San Francisco Chronicle*, December 9, 2001.

Gunther, Marc, and Noshua Watson. "Has Eisner Lost the Disney Magic?" *Fortune*, January 7, 2002.

Hofmeister, Sallie, and Brian Lowry. "No Happy Ever After for ABC in Disney Saga." *Los Angeles Times*, March 31, 2002.

Holson, Laura M. "As Disney Loses Steam, Insider Loses Patience." *New York Times*, August 18, 2002.

Holson, Laura M., and Bill Carter. "Disney's Chief Seems Cool on a Hot Seat." *New York Times*, February 15, 2002.

Merzer, Martin, Lenny Savino, and Kevin Murphy. "Disney Sites, Sears Tower on Terrorists' Study Lists." *Miami Herald*, October 13, 2001.

Morgenson, Gretchen, and Riva D. Atlas. "Bass Family, in Need of Money, Forced to Sell 6.4% of Disney." *New York Times*, September 21, 2001.

Starr, Michael. " 'Millionaire' Doesn't Want Me: Regis." *New York Post*, November 30, 2001.

Fifteen

Auletta, Ken. "Beauty and the Beast." *New Yorker*, December 16, 2002.

Bianco, Robert. " 'Lost' Fits into ABC's Bad Year." *USA Today*, April 1, 2003.

Boedeker, Hal. "The Guy Who Saved ABC." *Orlando Sentinel*, January 15, 2003.

Drudge, Matt. "Mickey's Millions: Disney to Finance Michael Moore's New Bush-Bashing Documentary." Drudge Report, May 11, 2003.

Ebert, Roger. "Movie Turns 'Lizzie' into Britney Wannabe." *Chicago Sun-Times*, May 2, 2003.

———. "A Wild Ride: Johnny Depp Takes 'Pirates' Over the Top in Great Swashbuckling Tradition, but the Film Goes on Forever." *Chicago Sun-Times*, July 9, 2003.

Elder, Robert K. " 'Treasure for the Eyes, but Disney's Latest Gets Lost in Space." *Chicago Tribune*, November 27, 2002.

Flint, Joe. "Outside the Lines: ESPN's Risky New Game Plan." *Wall Street Journal*, October 24, 2003.

Gliatto, Tom, and Lorenzo Benet. "Wonderful Company." *People*, September 29, 2003.

Grover, Ronald. "Harvey on the Line: With Disney Breathing Down His Neck, Miramax's Weinstein Needs a Hit." *Business Week*, November 11, 2002.

Johnson, Reed, and Gina Piccalo. "Hollywood Has Fine Romance with Gehry's Sound Palace." *Los Angeles Times*, October 26, 2003.

Mitchell, Elvis. "Mascara as Black as a Jolly Roger." *New York Times*, July 9, 2003.

Nelson, Emily, and Bruce Orwall. "Change of Season: Desperate for a Hit, ABC Is Refocusing on Middle America." *Wall Street Journal*, September 13, 2002.

Orwall, Bruce. "A Dilemma for Duff and Disney; 'Lizzie's' Success, Teen Star's Goals Seem to Be on Opposite Tracks." *Wall Street Journal*, May 8, 2003.

Scott, A. O. " 'Treasure Island' Flies into Neurosis." *New York Times*, November 27, 2002.

Verrier, Richard, and James Bates. "Disney Board Endorses Steps to Turn Company Around." *Los Angeles Times*, September 25, 2002.

Verrier, Richard, and Claudia Eller. " 'Treasure Planet': A Disney Dud in the Making for a Long Time." *Los Angeles Times*, December 9, 2002.

Weiner, Allison Hope. "Lizzie Tizzy: Why Did Tween Star Hilary Duff Blow Off Disney's Lizzie McGuire?" *Entertainment Weekly*, June 13, 2003.

Sixteen

Bates, James. "Eisner Comment on Disney Grave Site Raises Questions." *Los Angeles Times*, March 9, 2004.

———. "Disney's Daughter: Eisner Must Go." *Los Angeles Times*, March 10, 2004.

Carter, Bill. "Eisner's Top-Down Style Hobbled ABC." *New York Times*, March 7, 2004.

Emshwiller, John R., and Joann S. Lublin. "The Battle for Disney: Ex-Senator Mitchell to Play Big Role in Disney Bid." *Wall Street Journal*, February 12, 2004.

Grant, Peter, and Bruce Orwall. "Disney, Struggling to Regain Glory, Gets $48.7 Billion Bid from Comcast." *Wall Street Journal*, February 12, 2004.

———. "Comcast's Secret Efforts to Win Over Board May Hurt Takeover Bid." *Wall Street Journal*, March 4, 2004.

Holson, Laura M. "2nd Member of Board Resigns at Disney." *New York Times*, December 2, 2003.

———. "Disney Board Adopts Rules That Affect Leadership." *New York Times*, January 7, 2004.

———. "Pixar Sees End to Its Disney Partnership." *New York Times*, January 30, 2004.

Holson, Laura M., and Andrew Ross Sorkin. "Valuing Disney: What Is a Mouse Worth?" *New York Times*, February 13, 2004.

King, Susan. "Poignant Salute to Ritter." *Los Angeles Times*, November 6, 2003.

Orwall, Bruce. "Roy Disney Quits Company Board and Calls on Eisner to Resign." *Wall Street Journal*, December 1, 2003.

————. "CalPERS to Withhold Voting for Eisner," *Wall Street Journal*, February 26, 2004.

Orwall, Bruce, and Joann S. Lublin. "Disney's Dissidents Didn't Block Moves They Now Criticize." *Wall Street Journal*, February 19, 2004.

Solomon, Deborah. "Reanimated." *New York Times Magazine*, February 22, 2004.

Stanley, Alessandra. "No Simple Rules for Dealing with Death." *New York Times*, November 5, 2003.

Seventeen

Carter, Bill. "Disney Is Said to Be Considering a Managerial Shake-up at ABC." *New York Times*, April 6, 2004.

Grant, Peter, and Bruce Orwall. "Dwarfed: Disney's Eisner Steps Down from Chairman Post After Protest Garners 43% of Voted Shares." *Wall Street Journal*, March 4, 2004.

Gunther, Marc. "Eisner's Last Act." *Fortune*, March 8, 2004.

Holson, Laura M. "Defied in Vote, Disney Leader Loses One Post." *New York Times*, March 4, 2004.

————. "Disney in Talks on Independence for a Weinstein." *New York Times*, August 10, 2004.

James, Meg. "ABC Network May Oust Top Programmer." *Los Angeles Times*, April 7, 2004.

Magill, Ken. "Disney Shareholders Rally to Attack CEO Eisner." *New York Sun*, March 3, 2004.

Mitchell, Elvis. "A Western with Watercolor Vistas and a Passel of Parody." *New York Times*, April 2, 2004.

Mnookin, Seth. "How Harvey Weinstein Survived His Midlife Crisis (for Now)." *New York*, October 11, 2004.

Orwall, Bruce. "Eisner's Critics Keep Up Pressure at Walt Disney." *Wall Street Journal*, March 10, 2004.

————. "End of the Ride: Disney's Eisner Will Quit in 2006 After Surviving Bruising Battles." *Wall Street Journal*, September 10, 2004.

Orwall, Bruce, and Joann S. Lublin. "Disney's Eisner Says He Plans to Stay as CEO." *Wall Street Journal*, March 5, 2004.

————. "The Job of No. 2 Just Got Harder for Disney's Iger." *Wall Street Journal*, March 11, 2004.

Orwall, Bruce, and Brian Steinberg. "Disney Meeting: New Adventures in Dissidentland." *Wall Street Journal*, March 3, 2004.

Rutenberg, Jim. "Disney Is Blocking Distribution of Film That Criticizes Bush." *New York Times,* May 5, 2004.

Scott, A. O. "Unruly Scorn Leaves Room for Restraint, but Not a Lot." *New York Times,* June 23, 2004.

Verrier, Richard, and James Bates. "Disney's Eisner Loses Top Post, Stays as CEO." *Los Angeles Times,* March 4, 2004.

Waxman, Sharon. "Miramax Principals Acquire Film That Disney Shunned." *New York Times,* May 29, 2004.

Acknowledgments

DisneyWar is my eighth book. In what seems to be an increasingly rare occurrence in the publishing world, I have had the same editor, Alice Mayhew, and the same agent, Amanda Urban, for all of them. Researching and writing this book was an enormous project, and I'm not sure it would have come to fruition if not for Alice's unwavering confidence that Disney would prove to be a compelling subject. She has the remarkable ability to provide encouragement and make demands at just the right moments. She holds her writers to the highest standards while always communicating that she has our interests at heart.

Amanda Urban was also a staunch advocate for this book, and intervened with excellent ideas at critical junctures. Her judgment and experience in book publishing are invaluable. And I consider myself fortunate that both my editor and agent are also friends.

Kelly Crow was my research assistant. I first met her as a student in my class at Columbia University's Graduate School of Journalism. After graduating, she worked at *The New York Times,* and when she contacted me to say she was considering exploring other opportunities, I leaped at the chance to enlist her in this endeavor. Kelly handled numerous interviews herself, traveled to California, and did an enormous amount of research in addition to fact-checking and proofreading. She has cheerfully worked long hours and proven herself to be a fine reporter. I will miss her good humor and enthusiasm.

As with previous books, my assistant, Julie Allen, helped manage the often chaotic process of dealing with many sources as well as countless others, always with good humor, discretion, and courtesy.

At Simon & Schuster, I owe special thanks to David Rosenthal, publisher, who has always been enthusiastic about the subject of this book, and who came up with the title; Carolyn Reidy, president of the adult publishing group; Roger Labrie, editor; Miriam Wenger; Victoria Meyer, executive director of publicity;

Rachel Nagler, publicist; and Jackie Seow, who designed the cover. Alexandra Truitt did the photo research.

At *The New Yorker,* John Bennet, my longtime editor, did his usual extraordinary work on the excerpt from this book, and Andy Young and Sasha Smith did the rigorous fact-checking. Editor David Remnick offered his support and enthusiasm, for which I'm grateful. So did Dorothy Wickenden. Lauren Porcaro provided additional research and assistance.

I am also grateful to my colleagues at *SmartMoney,* including Ed Finn and Fleming Meeks.

As before, much of the burden of writing this book has fallen on my family and friends. I don't see how it could have been written without their support and understanding. This is especially true of my parents in Quincy, Illinois, Ben and Mary Jane Stewart. In New York, I'm fortunate to live near my brother, Michael, his wife, Anna, and their children, Aidan and Cassie (born during the gestation of this book), and I'm also grateful to my sister, Jane Holden, and her family: John, her husband, and my nieces and nephew, Lindsey, Laura, Maggie, and Jack. And to my rapidly growing godchildren, Langley Grace Wallace and James Swartz, and to Kate McNamara. Richard and Daphne Weil offered their hospitality and treated me like family.

Among my friends, special thanks to Jill Abramson, Jane Berentson and Fred Bleakley, John Brecher and Dottie Gaiter, Jeannine Burky, James Cramer, Edward Flanagan, Joan Fuerstman, Jim Gaver, Joel Goldsmith, Marisa and John Koten, Monica Langley and Roger Wallace, Arthur Lubow, Bari Mort, Dave Nogaki, Gene Stone, and Neil Westreich.

This book is dedicated to Benjamin Weil, who bore the brunt of my absences, distractions, and complaints. I'm not sure I can repay him, but I intend to try.

INDEX

200
201
ABC

About the Author

JAMES B. STEWART is the author of *Heart of a Soldier*, the bestselling *Blind Eye* and *Blood Sport*, and the blockbuster *Den of Thieves*. A former Page-One editor at *The Wall Street Journal*, Stewart won a Pulitzer Prize in 1988 for his reporting on the stock market crash and insider trading. He is a regular contributor to *SmartMoney* and *The New Yorker*. He lives in New York.

ALSO BY

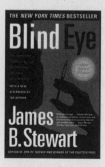

JAMES B. STEWART

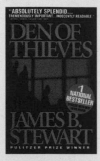

#1 National Bestseller

"Absolutely splendid ... tremendously important ...
indecently readable."

—*The New York Times*

In masterfully reported detail, this is the full story of the
insider-trading scandal that nearly destroyed Wall Street.
Pulitzer Prize winner Stewart shows for the first time
how four of the biggest names on Wall Street created the
biggest insider-trading ring in financial history until a team
of downtrodden detectives brought them to justice.

Stewart weaves all the facts into an unforgettable
narrative—a portrait of human nature, big business, and
crime of unparalleled proportions.

"A revealing, disturbing tale of
what can happen when greed runs
rampant."

—*The Seattle Times*

"Stewart takes the reader through the
maze of arcane Wall Street dealing as
if he were writing a detective story."

—*The Philadelphia Inquirer*

Follow the Story is the indispensable guide to writing
successful nonfiction books, articles, feature stories,
or memoirs. Stewart provides concrete directions
for conceiving, reporting, structuring, and writing
nonfiction—techniques that he has used in his own
successful books and stories. By using examples from
his own work, Stewart illustrates systematically a way of
thinking about and executing stories, a method that has
helped numerous reporters and Columbia University
students become better writers.

SIMON & SCHUSTER
PAPERBACKS
A VIACOM COMPANY

www.simonsays.com